The Rise and Fall of
the Political Press in Britain

Volume One:
The Nineteenth Century

STEPHEN KOSS

The Rise and Fall of the Political Press in Britain

Volume One:
THE NINETEENTH CENTURY

HAMISH HAMILTON

London

For Juliet and Richard

First published in Great Britain 1981
by Hamish Hamilton Ltd
Garden House 57–59 Long Acre London WC2E 9JZ

Copyright © 1981 by Stephen Koss

British Library Cataloguing in Publication Data

Koss, Stephen Edward
  The rise and fall of the political press
  in Britain.
  Vol. 1: The nineteenth century
  1. Press and politics – Great Britain
  – History
  I. Title
  320.941   PN5124.P6
  ISBN 0–241–10561–7

Photoset, printed and bound in Great Britain by
REDWOOD BURN LIMITED, Trowbridge & Esher

CONTENTS

Acknowledgments		vii
1	Prologue	1
2	'Within Proper Bounds'	30
3	Coming of Age	70
4	The Palmerstonian Ascendancy	121
5	Disraeli v. Gladstone	167
6	Conflicts of Interest	215
7	Conflicts of Principle	264
8	New Wine in Old Bottles	306
9	Fin de Siècle	356
10	Retrospect and Prospect	409
	Manuscript Sources	436
	Index	439

ILLUSTRATIONS

Between pages 184 and 185

1a Charles Dickens, editor of the newly hatched *Daily News*, among the strutting peacocks of Fleet Street. 1846.

1b The French Emperor, with *Le Moniteur* in his back pocket, dispenses bribes to the *Morning Post*. 1856.

2a Lord Derby and Disraeli try to avoid the impression that the *Standard* ('Mrs Harris') is in their pay. 1862

2b *The Times* and Sir Moses Montefiore, the philanthropist, celebrate their 100th birthdays. 1885

3 A Song of John Bright and the *Morning Star*. 1865

4 *The Times* scolds Lord Randolph Churchill for parliamentary misconduct. 1886

5 *Punch* cartoon of the General Election of 1880

6 *The Times* repents for its publication of the Pigott forgeries. 1889

7a 'Teaching the Young Idea'. 1889

7b Journalism in France – Journalism in England. (A Contrast). 1890

8a Robert Lowe, the leader-writing MP and Cabinet Minister. 1869

8b Alfred Austin, leader-writer for the *Standard*. 1896

ACKNOWLEDGMENTS

During a visit to the University of Texas, where I went to consult various manuscript collections, I presented a seminar paper on the subject of my research. A professor of journalism, taking a kindly interest in my project, afterwards asked what sort of a 'team' I had working with me. I explained that I was – in local parlance – a lone wolf, partly by choice (as I considered too many studies of the press to have been more assembled than written), and partly by circumstance. Upon reflection, I gratefully realize that I exaggerated.

This book, the first of a pair of volumes on the political history of the modern British press, has been a collaborative venture. It could not have been written without assistance and encouragement from many people. By electing me to a visiting fellowship, the warden and fellows of All Souls College afforded me a splendid sanctuary from normal academic routines. By awarding me a research grant, the National Endowment for the Humanities made possible a sabbatical year in England.

Archivists and librarians made available materials and delved for information. To name only some of them is a somewhat invidious task. Yet special mention is due to J. S. G. Simmons at All Souls, and to his assistants, Norma Aubertin-Potter and Barry Britton, who ministered to every need. Others, who responded with particular generosity, include A. S. Bell (National Library of Scotland), Geoffrey D. M. Block (Conservative Research Department), Mrs J. M. Chandler (United Oxford and Cambridge University Club), R. H. Harcourt Williams (Hatfield House), Gordon Phillips (*The Times* Archives), Angela Raspin (British Library of Political and Economic Science), and C. J. Wright (British Library). Vere, Lady Birdwood, guided me through the Russell Papers.

J. H. Burns helped me to trace and to date documents among the Bentham Papers. Queries arising from Disraeli's correspondence were deftly fielded by Donald M. Schurman, one of the principal investigators of the Disraeli Project, Queen's University, Kingston. Janet O. Minihan lent a hand with the Benjamin Moran diaries, Philip Ziegler with the Cust Papers, and Nancy Carpenter with George Wyndham's correspondence. Michael Howard allowed me access to the Esher Papers, then in his custody, Lord Blake to the papers of the 14th Earl of Derby, and Joseph O. Baylen and J. E. Mennell loaned me their microfilms of the Stead and Cook papers. A. P. Duncum shared his knowledge about the Rowntree Trust. S. E. Finer and Kenneth O. Morgan gave delightful companionship and lending privileges. Among those who helped me to wrestle with intransigent problems were Lucy Brown, John Cannon, Alan J. Lee, and Norman McCord. David Astor offered stimulating conversation and called my attention to Harold Macmillan's remarks at an *Observer* banquet on 7 December 1977, for which Kenneth Harris provided a transcript. Sir Christopher Chancellor and Lord Ardwick both supplied recollections and suggestions, and Donald Tyerman proved a valuable correspondent.

Chris Stevens checked additional references at the Newspaper Library in Colindale, where I myself had burrowed for many months. James Jaffe and Albion Urdank assisted my preliminary research in New York. My wife contributed her editorial expertise – and boundless patience – at every stage. Our children became adept at arranging notecards, compiling lists, and preparing an index. Christopher Sinclair-Stevenson, prince among publishers, gave unstinting support.

Material from the Royal Archives has been quoted with the gracious permission of Her Majesty The Queen. Others who gave permission to quote from documents to which they hold copyright, too numerous to list individually, have received my private thanks. In some cases, descendants were impossible to trace, and I ask any whom I failed to contact to accept my apologies.

Peter Clarke and Robert Webb put me further into their debt by subjecting the whole of the manuscript to rigorous scrutiny. John Stubbs, too, read the penultimate draft and offered incisive criticisms. Chapters or groups of chapters were read by Bernard Barber, Lord Blake, Roy Foster, Peter Marsh, A. J. P. Taylor, and William Thomas, some of whom disagreed with me and – more comfortingly – with one another. Each of them obliged me to sharpen my ideas and my prose. None, of course, is responsible for any errors of fact or judgment that may remain. All added immensely to the intellectual rewards of the exercise.

The reader is directed to the second part of Chapter One – a prologue to this two-volume study – for a discussion of aims and methodology. It remains to be said that spelling and punctuation in quotations follow the original sources, except where changes were required for purposes of intelligibility. I have also standardized references to newspapers, so that *The Times* appears uniformly as *The Times*, not as the *Times*, 'The Times', 'the Times', and countless other variations.

Stephen Koss

One

PROLOGUE

In the beginning was the Word and, in the fifteenth century, William Caxton set the English Word into print. Since that time, there have been newspapers of one sort or another, fulfilling some of the same functions, engendering many of the same controversies, and employing most of the same methods of enquiry and production. In the middle of the nineteenth century, however, a change occurred. Like most vital British institutions, political and social, the press assumed its modern form during the mid-Victorian age. The difference between the new press and its precursors was essentially one of emphasis and perception, no less significant for the fact that neither the hopes nor the fears it inspired have been effectively realized.

The repeal of the stamp duty in 1855, prefigured by the abolition of the tax on advertisements two years earlier and capped by the abolition of the tax on paper six years later, created a new forum for national debate by according newspapers a vastly enlarged readership and, consequently, an enhanced potential for political influence. As anticipated, there followed a rapid proliferation of metropolitan and provincial journals which, coupled with the strengthening of pre-existing ones, afforded opportunities for publicity which politicians of every persuasion, including those who most strenuously protested their indifference, were quick to recognize and to exploit. With scant pretence to objectivity, editors and proprietors vied to reciprocate this welcome attention and to justify it. Systematically and, for the most part, unabashedly, newspapers were used on an unprecedented scale to formulate party programmes, to implement political strategies, and to serve personal ambitions. This collaboration, pursued with varying enthusiasm and success, helped to determine alignments in Parliament, allegiances in the constituencies, and, to a decreasing extent as time wore on, general patterns of electoral behaviour.

Fitful but steady, this development drew its primary impetus from the concurrent growth of broadly based party organizations to which journalists, like politicians themselves, became affiliated for various motives of self-interest and ideological commitment. A parallel increase in literacy undoubtedly accelerated the process, but did not – as some commentators have claimed – initiate it. In this respect, the Education Act of 1870, however prominent as a

legislative landmark, contributed no more significantly to the rise of the political press than competition from newer media contributed to its eventual
decline, as we shall see. Technological advances in printing and distribution
likewise played a part, as did the introduction of the telegraph and the establishment of news agencies. These innovations merely facilitated a process
which had been long under way. Basically, as this two-volume study will
attempt to demonstrate, this was a political phenomenon, stimulating and
reflecting factors of political change.

During preceding centuries, newspapers were, at best, crude and transitory
weapons for partisan combat. As such, they were virtually indistinguishable
from other forms of political expression, among them the broadsheet, the
pamphlet, the ballad, and the theatre.[1] With the removal of what Richard
Cobden denounced as the 'taxes on knowledge', newspapers came into their
own as moulders of public opinion. In unequal proportions, they immediately
acquired a new respectability, along with a heightened self-consciousness and
a sophistication with regard to political tactics. Fired by a rhetoric of which
they were as much the beneficiaries as the disseminators, they ventured boldly
into the political fray, which was concentrated in and around Parliament.
Economic security, or at least an improved prospect for it, encouraged them.
Still more, they responded to moral imperatives, as they discerned them, and
to the responsibilities that were conferred upon them by consciences which
shaped their own.

Eager and seemingly equipped to exercise a decisive influence on the course
of national – and, by extension, international – affairs, these custodians of the
printed word arrogated to themselves the designation of the Fourth Estate,
thereby creating a myth that has outlasted the purposes for which it was initially intended.[2] Similarly, they referred to themselves as 'the Press', with a
capital letter (denied them in the present text) that denoted a formal, collective entity, analogous to Parliament itself. Their persuasiveness, no less than
the uncertainties that attended the evolution of popular democracy, ensured
that they were alternately courted and feared for the authority at their disposal
and, more vaguely, for the authority which they were imputed to command.
To the perpetual frustration of newspapermen and politicians alike, much of
that power was to prove more apparent than real. Nevertheless, it weighed
heavily in political calculations, if only because newspapermen were slow to
surrender their pretensions and politicians were slower still to spurn any possible source of support. Thus, the press has operated as an active force in the

---

[1] Raymond Williams has made this point in an essay, 'The press and popular culture: an historical perspective,' in G. Boyce, J. Curran, and P. Wingate, eds., *Newspaper History* (London,
1978), pp. 41–50; by ignoring these distinctions, G. A. Cranfield has vitiated his argument in *The
Press and Society from Caxton to Northcliffe* (London, 1978).

[2] See George Boyce, 'The Fourth Estate: the reappraisal of a concept,' in Boyce, Curran, and
Wingate, eds., *op.cit.*, pp. 19–40; it was Macaulay who, in 1828, popularized the designation,
which has been attributed to Hazlitt, among others.

history of British politics, although arguably in a more restricted sphere than popular impressions might allow. While its effects on public opinion can never be ascertained with any degree of precision, least of all after the concept of public opinion had widened, its effects on parties and their leaders were always important and occasionally profound.

Over the course of generations, the character of the press has simultaneously reflected and articulated attitudes within an expanding political society. Successive extensions of the franchise, each implying an attempt to accommodate new social forces, created new electoral conditions that, in turn, necessitated new responses on the part of politicians and a new orientation on the part of the press. Like other 'traditional' relationships within the political community, the partnership between politicians and their journalistic allies was always a complicated one, fraught with misapprehension and recrimination on both sides. Subjected to countervailing pressures, it underwent periodic adjustments before it ultimately came to an end. But its passing, no less than its inception, was a lengthy process, and part of a larger transformation which it documented in its columns.

By the middle of the twentieth century, newspapers had been divested either by choice or by circumstance of the political role in which they had been cast for the better part of a hundred years. To be sure, they usually continued to favour one party over another and to take partisan stands, particularly at the time of general elections. But they had abandoned and, in certain cases, repudiated the avowedly political objectives to which they had been dedicated through and beyond the second half of the nineteenth century. Such links as they may retain with party spokesmen and party agencies are informal, and they do not bestow their support without taking care to reassert their independence. Today, it is perhaps difficult to recall how intimately newspapers were once bound to political organizations or to factions and individuals within them, and how dutifully they had once served those interests, even to the detriment of their own commercial viability. Adjudicating in a recent case involving the National Front and the *South East London and Kentish Mercury*, the Press Council upheld the right of any newspaper 'to act as an instrument of propaganda for any cause it chooses' and 'to express its convictions and political views forcefully'.[1] One cannot imagine that right even coming into question in an earlier period.

For, during the Victorian heyday, partisanship was the dominant characteristic of newspapers, recognized not only as their right, but also as their obligation. Freedom of the press, which was then construed as the freedom to make a political choice, later came to be regarded as the freedom to resist political intrusion which, in any case, was already on the wane; here, as elsewhere, theory had caught up with practice and retroactively ratified it. Emancipated from state control in the 1850s, newspapers were gradually

[1] *The Times*, 23 February 1978.

emancipated from the political controls, diverse and sometimes imperceptible, that replaced it. Those interim arrangements, as they now appear, were
eventually superseded by the more amorphous, yet equally stringent,
restraints of the marketplace which prevail in our own day and which are
generally considered incompatible with political affiliation in any strict or
abiding sense. Bearing in mind that each successive phase in the history of the
modern press has been the product of a particular confluence of conditions
and expectations, one can trace a halting transition from official to popular
control. Or, from another perspective which must be rejected as too mechanis-
tic, there has been a shift by stages from the pre-industrial forms imposed by
governmental decree to the post-industrial specifications of a few profit-
seeking capitalists.[1] However conceived, it remains for the time being an open
question whether this trend has promoted an improvement in either journalistic standards or social values.

To reduce the argument to simple terms: newspapers, which formerly
derived an overriding purpose and a financial sustenance from their close political connections, have retreated from those connections and, especially,
from the mutual demands they entailed. No sooner had legislative trammels
been lifted from them than newspapers proudly affixed to themselves the
labels Tory, Whig, or Radical, which broke down into such sub-categories as
Peelite or Disraelian, Russellite or Palmerstonian, Cobdenite or Gladstonian.
As new lights appeared in the political firmament, party constellations
assumed new patterns and, accordingly, newspapers modified or exchanged
their loyalties. They continued to espouse men (most notably Lord Randolph
Churchill, Joseph Chamberlain, and David Lloyd George, who were disciples
of Lord Palmerston in the art of press manipulation) and movements (including Liberal Unionism, Irish Home Rule, Liberal Imperialism, Tariff Reform,
Socialism, or Empire Free Trade), always with the same techniques, if not
quite as obsessively. Increasingly reluctant to flaunt their political associations, all the more so when they were predicated on the subscription of party
or party-related funds, they sometimes resorted self-consciously to euphem-
isms – national or imperial, free trade or protectionist – that served much the
same purpose; or, at the lowest common denominator, they identified themselves at any given time as pro- or anti-ministerial. These badges, worn more
defensively, could not have deceived anyone who attentively perused their
columns, day by day, or week by week.

In retrospect, it is easy to see that these kaleidoscopic labels never fitted as
comfortably as contemporaries might have supposed, and had lost their significance even before they lost currency. Retained for a time out of pride or habit,

---

[1] Such abstractions are the staple of much recent work that subordinates empirical study to
ideological commitment. Stuart Holland grinds a sharply honed axe in 'Countervailing Press
Power,' in J. Curran, ed., *The British Press: a Manifesto* (London, 1978), pp. 94–123; Stanley Harrison, a blunt one in *Poor Men's Guardians* (London, 1974).

they ultimately became suspect and were disavowed. Contraction within the newspaper industry, a reversal of the nineteenth-century process, has had a dual effect: on the one hand, it has severely limited the opportunities for politicians, who may be so inclined, to recruit dependable press support; on the other, it has made surviving newspapers acutely aware of their vulnerability, and wary of entanglement. 'Practically all of our big papers take, broadly speaking, one political line – Conservative, Labour or Liberal – but not one of them would dream of taking orders from a party political office,' one Fleet Street veteran insisted in 1966.[1] That statement carries far greater conviction than the periodic disclaimers which nineteenth-century editors had felt compelled to issue. And, in the past crisis-ridden decade, that 'one political line' has tended to blur further, as signalled by *The Times*'s proclaiming itself (21 November 1970) 'a Liberal newspaper', wedded to a body of abstract principle that transcends party.

In large part, this assertion of newspaper sovereignty has been dictated by economic considerations and may therefore betoken greater weakness than strength. Making a virtue of necessity, editors and publishers have been forced to diversify their appeal in order to allow their properties a chance for survival in the face of mounting costs and fierce competition. In their bids for mass circulation and the advertising revenues that accrue from it, they have discovered political involvement to be an irrelevance or, worse, a distinct liability.

It was a self-fulfilling prophecy of the 'new journalism', born in the closing decades of Victoria's reign, that the newspaper-reading public, as it expanded, became proportionately less politically minded, and indeed impatient with the parliamentary transactions that had been the fixation of the older press. Furthermore, and perhaps more accurately, it was understood that a class of better-educated readers, although numerically less impressive, demanded greater objectivity in the coverage of political questions. A few newspapers aspired to bridge this gulf; most, however, were content to exploit it. In either instance, it came to be accepted as axiomatic that politics neither sold papers nor followed them. Richard Crossman, whose academic training had disposed him to presume otherwise, 'had an interesting talk with Mike Randall, the editor of the *Daily Mail*', over dinner on 9 March 1966:

> He was taking the line that the [approaching] election was a disaster for the newspaper industry because of its appalling cost and because people weren't interested in it. Every column you devote to it, he told me, reduces circulation and it is not going to warm up or be anything more than a titular election because the decision has already been taken by ordinary people.

Crossman, whose ministerial career was an interlude between stints in journalism,

[1] Sir Colin Coote, 'The Editor's Job,' in V. Brodzky, ed., *Fleet Street* (London, 1966), p. 13.

said in reply that I thought newspapers could still exert an enormous influence on campaigns. For example, if the Conservatives were to launch a strong anti-coloured-immigration and anti-trade-union line they might really start winning votes. That is the kind of difference papers can make. To this Randall replied that he couldn't possibly touch that kind of thing with a barge-pole unless, of course, he added, he were to have a directive from the proprietor.[1]

It would be tempting, but a mistake, to ascribe this transformation exclusively to the crass commercialism of a newer breed of press magnates who, after all, deserve credit for rescuing many properties from extinction. Obviously, they stand in contrast with their predecessors who, while not averse to financial gain, were often resigned to collecting moral dividends. On behalf of party causes, which many of them also served as MPs and in assorted other capacities, these men and women were prepared to sustain newspapers out of pocket in an attempt to guide opinion. Their investment in newspaper enterprises, encouraged by their party leaders, was an extension of their own political careers, sometimes a sublimation of them. But they could not discharge this duty indefinitely and, after incurring staggering losses without commensurate gratification, their capital was no longer readily available. Their successors were hard-headed businessmen, who began by maintaining that solvency was the prerequisite to influence, and who went on to abjure influence as the price to be paid for achieving solvency. Reproached by 'one of the most distinguished living journalists' for 'taking the wrong line', Lord Northcliffe's response was 'to call for his circulation ledgers and to show the favourable effect that his policy had had upon the sales of his journals'. Yet not even the legendary Northcliffe was appeased by mere commercial success: 'I see my way to getting large circulation, but how am I to get influence?' he asked of E. T. Cook. 'Tell me that.'[2] Those who followed in his wake were relatively less demanding and more candid. Lord Southwood, who directed the firm that published the *Daily Herald*, dissociated himself from its socialist message: 'Machines, ink and paper don't take sides. . . . My purpose is to keep the machines going.'[3] And Lord Thomson of Fleet, who counted *The Times* among his prize acquisitions, went so far as to dismiss 'editorial matter [as] being the stuff between the ads'.[4]

Despite the claims advanced by Northcliffe, and on his behalf, he was more the harbinger than the perpetrator of the revolution in proprietorial aims and ethics. Larger than life, he magnified trends which he cannot justly be said to

[1] Richard Crossman, *The Diaries of a Cabinet Minister*, I (London, 1975), p. 475.
[2] Quoted in A. M. Gollin, *The Observer and J. L. Garvin* (London, 1960), p. 2.
[3] Quoted in R. J. Minney, *Viscount Southwood* (London, 1954), p. 42.
[4] Quoted in R. Boston, 'Growing Pains,' in R. Boston, ed., *The Press We Deserve* (London, 1970), p. 11.

have precipitated. As we shall see, he followed the traditional path, hand in hand with political leaders, until it led to an impasse; even then, he continued to hanker after the alliances which he adamantly disowned, vainly attempting to resurrect them on his own idiosyncratic terms. His arrogance and scale of operations, coupled with the fact that he spanned the period, made him the obvious candidate for depiction 'as everything from the supreme newspaper-genius to the corruptor of English journalism'.[1] A. G. Gardiner, who condemned him as the latter, faulted Northcliffe ('with his eager interest in the moment, his passion for sensation, his indifference to ideas, and his dislike of abstract thought') for running his newspapers 'with the same material outlook as that with which a brewer runs a brewery'.[2] Yet Northcliffe had not created the taste for sensationalism to which he unashamedly catered in most of his papers; nor was he as immune from political influence as he liked to pretend. No single individual deserves either credit or blame for the developments to which he called attention. On the contrary, Northcliffe straddled the old and new journalisms, if only because his mercurial career straddled the nineteenth and twentieth centuries. While he anticipated many modern practices, he preserved other customs from the past. It would be as arbitrary to assign paramount responsibility to him, although he would not have demurred, as it would be to cite the death of Queen Victoria as a watershed in newspaper history.

There is no fixed point at which the transformation occurred or its ramifications were fully appreciated. In his presidential address to the Institute of Journalists, meeting at York on 18 August 1913, Robert Donald surveyed 'the changes which have taken place in the newspaper world during the last twenty years' and, on balance, saw greater reason for hope than for despair. Noting 'the growth of the corporate-owned press [which] ... has now become commercialized', he did not wish his audience to infer that old-style 'personal ownership was a combination of paternalism and philanthropy. The private owner', as he knew from his editorial experience at the *Daily Chronicle*, 'was a man who liked his profit and made it, but, as he had no responsibility towards shareholders, preferred less profit to compromise with principles.'[3] Five years later, when the *Daily Chronicle* and its principles were sold out from under him, Donald must have modified his opinion. Others, however, held tenaciously to a sentimental view of past arrangements. 'Newspapers in former days were owned and directed by men who were journalists and felt first their sense of service to the community and put profit-making as a secondary, though by no means negligible, consideration,' Arthur Mann wrote in 1941 to one of the principal proprietors of the *Yorkshire Post*, where his long editor-

[1] A. J. P. Taylor, 'The Chief,' in *Politics in Wartime* (London, 1964), p. 150.

[2] For Gardiner's views on Northcliffe, see 'From the Old Order to the New,' the *Graphic*, 4 October 1919; 'Two Journalists,' the *Nineteenth Century and After*, cxi (1932), 247–56; and, especially, *Prophets, Priests and Kings* (London, 1914 edn.), pp. 88–97.

[3] *The Times*, 19 August 1913.

ship had recently ended in acrimony. 'I was brought up, and continue to regard journalism in that light.'[1] His stand was admirable, but it was not securely grounded in historical fact.

The golden age of independent newspaper-owners and illustrious editors, to the extent that it had ever existed, evinced a growing awareness of commercial temptations and a corresponding divergence from official party lines. More demonstrably, however, the dissolutions and amalgamations of the twentieth century have accentuated those tendencies. The cost of launching a new journalistic enterprise became prohibitive, and that was only the initial investment; it required further reserves of capital to nurture it through its infancy, which was often prolonged. At first glance, it might appear more practical to acquire a flourishing property with a view to adapting its political character; but that, too, demanded massive resources along with infinite dexterity. J. L. Garvin instructed Kingsley Martin 'that the policies of a paper must change from time to time, but that it is wiser for an editor to proceed in curves rather than right angles',[2] which ran the risk of frightening away one clientele without attracting another. Consequently, as the structure of the press tightened, it admitted to fewer possibilities for the representation of all shades of political opinion, once considered natural and equitable. The Victorian ideal, as usual, died hard. As late as 1952, R. J. Cruikshank, then editor of the *News Chronicle*, lamented 'that if some new movement in politics developed it would not be able to start a national daily paper'.[3] Eight years later, with the sudden demise of his own newspaper, the field became still more sparse. Old creeds, let alone new ones, have had to manage without the benefit of a platform in Fleet Street.

'Human beings, after all, are not immortal; papers should not expect to be either,' Anthony Howard has bluntly argued.[4] Yet, in the struggle that has been waged within the British newspaper industry, it is not necessarily the fittest (by any standard) that have survived; and, more ominously, no reproductive capacity has been revealed. Admittedly, during the second half of the nineteenth century, there was haphazard over-expansion, much of it politically incited and abetted. In due course, there followed a process of attrition which politicians, among others, have proved powerless to arrest. The economic and social consequences, although significant, need not concern us here. In many ways, the effects on political thought and conduct have been more remarkable in that they were less predictable. As they dwindled in number, newspapers in Britain grew increasingly jealous of an integrity which, paradoxically, they might not choose to manifest. They kept greater distance from party organizations, and proved less susceptible to the directives and blandish-

---

[1] Mann to Sir Stanley Jackson, 17 January 1941 (copy), Mann Papers.
[2] Kingsley Martin, *Editor* (London, 1968), p. 36.
[3] Quoted in J. W. Robertson Scott, *The Life and Death of a Newspaper* (London, 1952), p. 1n.
[4] *The Times*, 22 July 1978.

ments of individual politicians. The evidence leaves no doubt, however, that these barriers were erected to afford protection to both sides. The partnership that had existed between politics and the press eventually broke down not only because newspapers declined to accept accreditation, but also because politicians found it inadvisable to extend it.

In the mid-Victorian decades, when political alignments were constantly shifting, each faction – and the more dynamic elements within those factions – considered it imperative to secure prominent, sympathetic, and reasonably accurate publicity for its views. By the same device, they hoped to see embarrassing items suppressed or, at any rate, treated with an obliging discretion. Then, as now, newspapers provided the cheapest, most effective, and most convenient outlet for information; moreover, with their extensive intelligence networks, rudimentary but reasonably efficient, they were strategically placed to alert their chiefs to the latest comings and goings at Paris, Vienna, or Cairo, Hawarden, Hughenden, or Hatfield.

For reasons of expediency, therefore, it was deemed mandatory for any political movement to have its own organ, or preferably several that might boom its slogans in unison. It was equally a matter of self-respect, for, without adequate journalistic backing, a party neither seemed to take itself seriously nor could it expect to be taken seriously by its rivals. As status symbols, joined to political agencies, newspapers augmented their own status; as an integral part of an elaborate system of party management, they were invested with a new vitality, and an implicit authority. Through the receptive columns of an expanding press, politicians communicated to the public, to foreign powers, and, in no small measure, to one another. As if by ventriloquism, they could float proposals or intimate intentions to which they were not yet ready to pledge themselves formally. John Thaddeus Delane built the reputation of *The Times* by elevating this procedure into the principle that 'the duty of the Press is to speak; of the statesman to be silent' (6 February 1852).

Like many of the masters of his craft, Delane mistook privilege for duty, and, not surprisingly, abused it. In any case, politicians of his era were more than willing to foster his illusion. They took advantage of a compliant press to inspire and sometimes to write anonymously articles that were calculated either to justify their own actions or to discredit an opponent, occasionally a Cabinet colleague. Many of them had served an apprenticeship in journalism before (as it was said of John Morley) they 'drifted into the resolution to quit the ambush of the editor's room and serve in the ranks on the open field of battle'.[1] Lord Salisbury coyly confessed that, in his youth (as Lord Robert Cecil), he had 'eke[d] out his means by writing for newspapers'; in 1895, T. H. S. Escott vividly recalled – and, perhaps to win a wager, got Salisbury to confirm – their association thirty years earlier, when Salisbury had 'lingered in

[1] H. W. Lucy, *Memories of Eight Parliaments* (London, 1908), p. 226.

the office' of the *Standard* in Shoe Lane.[1] Some contrived to dabble in both professions at the same time, ideally each to the benefit of the other. 'It is exactly because I hope to become a thoroughly useful political writer that I lean to Parliament,' Morley professed to Chamberlain.[2] Although he soon came to despair of this ideal as impracticable, he was more fortunate than George Brodrick, a former warden of Merton College, who perpetually hoped to forsake journalism for a political career that never dawned. Delane wrote consolingly to him: 'I humbly think that, until you obtain a seat, you exercise as large an influence as most private MPs by writing such good articles as you do on your own subjects.'[3] Robert Lowe had the best of both worlds by continuing to write leaders for *The Times* until 1868 'without allowing his promotion to the Treasury Bench to interrupt the connection'.[4] From his day onwards, the journalistic presence in Parliament became more noticeable in the chambers as well as the lobbies, occasionally reaching to ministerial altitudes. Provincial editors and proprietors, prominent citizens in their localities, were often elected to represent them at Westminster. Metropolitan journalists, already under direct tutelage, qualified as excellent candidates. But the traffic did not flow in one direction. Just as newspapermen infiltrated party ranks, parliamentary parties were reservoirs from which newspaper investment could be drawn. Theoretically, the two spheres remained separate: to all intents and purposes, however, they were concentric.

Those who gravitated from journalism to politics, and similarly those who were recruited to newspaper management through politics, were fascinated to the point of obsession by the tricks of the trade. It had long been understood that a successful journalist had to operate as something of a politician; it equally became assumed that political success depended on a mastery of the press. Kennedy Jones, who was Northcliffe's henchman before embarking on his own parliamentary career, allowed himself to

> dream that were I an Haroun-al-Raschid I would pass a decree that no man was competent to occupy an editorial chair until he had sat in the House of Commons for at least one Session, and that no man was eligible for a seat in the House of Commons unless he had filled an editorial chair for twelve months.[5]

By his presumption no less than by his connivance, Jones was himself living proof of the progressive convergence of interests between politics and the press. As a self-appointed nexus between Fleet Street and Downing Street, he

---

[1] Salisbury, quoted in Lady Gwendolen Cecil, *Life of Robert, Marquess of Salisbury,* I (London, 1921), 70; Escott to Salisbury, 6 and 10 June 1895, Salisbury Papers.

[2] Morley to Chamberlain, 3 January 1878, Chamberlain Papers.

[3] Delane to Brodrick, n.d., quoted in A. I. Dasent, *John Thaddeus Delane* (London, 1908), II, 296.

[4] G. P. Gooch, *Life of Lord Courtney* (London, 1920), p. 74.

[5] Kennedy Jones, *Fleet Street and Downing Street* (London, 1919), pp. 329–30.

both shared and helped to inculcate an exaggerated notion of the powers which newspapers were supposed to wield. His views, like his achievement, may be discounted, but not dismissed. If nothing else, his wishful thinking stands as a reminder that the fantasies of one generation could easily become the conventions of the next.

'Opinion now is supreme, and opinion speaks in print,' Disraeli declaimed provocatively in his novel *Coningsby*, published in 1844. 'The representation of the press', he asserted, 'is more complete than the representation of Parliament.' That was palpably not the case then, if indeed ever. But Disraeli, who had earlier failed where Kennedy Jones was later to succeed, eventually proved instrumental in glorifying the press to an extent that did credit to his imagination. A journalist to his fingertips, even after he had nominally retired from the profession, he lent verisimilitude to his fictional claims, making the preposterous seem prescient. In the course of events, he paved the way for the likes of Kennedy Jones by familiarizing the public with newspaper methods that suited his partisan objectives. Predictably, familiarity bred contempt. 'In the old days men had the rack,' Oscar Wilde complained in 1892.

> Now they had the press. That is an improvement, certainly. But still it is very bad, and wrong, and demoralising.... The Lords Temporal say nothing, the Lords Spiritual have nothing to say, and the House of Commons has nothing to say and says it. We are dominated by Journalism.[1]

It is noteworthy that Wilde made his rueful assessment four years before Alfred Harmsworth (later exalted as Lord Northcliffe), with the assistance of Kennedy Jones, founded the *Daily Mail*, which came to symbolize this phenomenon.

By then, of course, the pretensions of the press were boundless, and not without cause. Having singularly failed to serve as the vehicle for public enlightenment as was confidently anticipated by Cobden and John Bright, who had led the agitation to abolish 'the taxes on knowledge', the press was instead employed with diminishing scruple for sectional purposes. To get their way, as they usually did, politicians wheedled and cajoled, pleaded and harangued, promised preferential treatment and threatened retribution. Palmerston, incorrigible at the game, set the pace by plying newspapermen with advertising income, sinecures, and invitations to his wife's glittering soirées at Cambridge House. Disraeli, his own press misadventures behind him, dispensed flattery from his overflowing trowel. Lord John Russell and the 14th Earl of Derby, both more discreet, relied on intermediaries to 'nobble' the press. Gladstone, to the surprise of the editor of his diaries, demonstrated an 'awareness and use of the newspaper press ... much more acute than has

---

[1] Oscar Wilde, 'The Soul of Man Under Socialism' (1892), in *Collected Works*, X (Garden City, N.Y., 1923), 40–41.

hitherto been allowed'.[1] With lofty motives and meagre results, Cobden and Bright contributed their prestige and their supporters' money to equip Manchester Radicalism with a London voice. From all directions and at all levels, politicians joined in the scramble for press support. It was contagious.

The next generation of political leaders, notably less reluctant to bring outside pressures to bear on the decision-making process, contracted an assortment of interlocking alliances with editors, leader-writers, and proprietors, all of whom were expected to do their bidding. Without incurring financial liability, which was to be avoided except as a last resort, they strove to harness journalistic energies to their respective chariots. Joseph Chamberlain, like Bright before him, resented the lack of attention paid him by the 'so-called Liberal press', and ensured himself due prominence through an ever-widening circle of newspaper dependants, whom he consulted and otherwise cultivated. Those who eluded his grasp were often snatched by Lord Randolph Churchill, who resourcefully favoured more than one eager recipient with the same exclusive tip. Lord Rosebery had a stable of journalists whom he kept nearly as well groomed as his stable of racehorses. Lord Salisbury reworked leaders which Alfred Austin contributed to the *Standard*; through party functionaries, he kept close watch over newspaper transactions. A. J. Balfour and H. H. Asquith affected an indifference to the press, but consorted with select journalists and, behind the scenes, authorized schemes to prop up certain shaky properties on which they relied. Lloyd George proffered breakfasts in Downing Street (like Gladstone) and peerages (like Balfour); when all else failed, he was ruthless, as when he formed a syndicate in 1918 to purchase the *Daily Chronicle* and displace its intractable editor. 'The Press? What you can't square you squash, what you can't squash you square,' was said to be his motto. Stanley Baldwin constrained the press by rousing public indignation against it, Neville Chamberlain by deceiving it ('Quite simply, he told lies,' Geoffrey Dawson of *The Times* explained), and Winston Churchill by appealing to personal and patriotic loyalties. The methods were as various as the men themselves, and this list is by no means exhaustive.[2]

One should not take journalists and their employers too severely to task. No less than their mentors, they were the captives of vanity and ambition. As the confederates and accomplices of eminent statesmen, they were amply rewarded with confidences, with a social acceptability previously denied to men of their calling, and with an array of honours, including the poet laureateship for Austin, who surely did not merit it on literary grounds. Their professional status had risen dramatically since 1829, when Sir Walter Scott admonished John Lockhart, his son-in-law and future biographer: 'Your connection with

[1] H. C. G. Matthew, ed., *The Gladstone Diaries*, V (Oxford, 1978), xliv.
[2] Lloyd George and Dawson are quoted in James Margach's highly personal account of 'the war between Downing Street and the media, from Lloyd George to Callaghan,' *The Abuse of Power* (London, 1978).

any newspaper would be a disgrace and degradation. I would rather sell gin to poor people and poison them in that way.'[1] To be sure, there persisted an intellectual bias against journalists long after newspapers had begun to recruit talent from the universities, after publicists had been transmogrified into pundits, and after 'gentlemen of the press' had confirmed their gentlemanliness by obtaining election to the best London clubs. As A. D. Godley knew from firsthand experience, Oxford in the 1880s was inclined to take a dim view of those 'who sometimes wrote like *Genesis* and sometimes for the *Daily News*',[2] and the disdain was mutual. In 1881, E. T. Cook was interviewed for a position on the *Pall Mall Gazette* by Morley, a black sheep from Lincoln College, who

> asked me if I was an Oxford man. I said 'Yes'; and then he asked me whether I was a very confirmed one – whether, for instance, I was a Fellow of a College. When I said 'No', he said, 'Then there is still some hope for you.'[3]

Betraying his own snobbery, which he bequeathed to the Bloomsbury set, Leslie Stephen protested that J. R. Green, although he had written regularly and remuneratively for the press, was not a journalist, for 'by "journalism" is to be understood, I suppose, writing for pay upon matters of which you are ignorant'.[4] Understandably, such attitudes made journalists even more determined to assert their dignity and, as some saw it, their constitutional responsibilities.

According to Fleet Street lore, William Mudford (who edited Austin's leaders for the *Standard* after the Prime Minister had reworked them) refused to rise from the dinner table to receive 'a great statesman' who had had the temerity to call uninvited: 'Tell him I'm out!' Mudford reportedly bellowed from the next room when his butler brought the visitor's card to him.[5] Perhaps apocryphal, the incident anticipated Lord Northcliffe's strenuous insistence that Lord Midleton, who variously served in the Salisbury and Balfour administrations, had not granted the *Daily Mail* the favour of an interview, but *vice versa*. Although Mudford and Northcliffe, separated by a generation, were amenable to party influence, both resisted it after hours or when they considered it inimical to the better interests of the cause, which they were prepared to judge for themselves. That the *Standard* under Mudford qualified as 'the only distinctly and professedly Conservative journal among the morning newspapers of London' did not deter it from showing 'a certain independence with regard to its own party, and ... much fairness of mind in

---

[1] Quoted in Francis Williams, *Dangerous Estate* (London, 1957), p. 48.
[2] Quoted in Mrs W. L. Courtney, *The Making of an Editor* (London, 1930), p. 33.
[3] J. Saxon Mills, *Sir Edward Cook* (London, 1921), p. 38.
[4] Leslie Stephen, ed., *The Letters of John Richard Green* (London, 1901), p. 66. Stephen himself wrote for the *Pall Mall Gazette*.
[5] There are many versions of this story, the most authoritative being Mills, *Cook*, pp. 230–31.

relation to its opponents', the source of 'a standing quarrel between it and the leaders of successive Conservative governments'.[1] Northcliffe, too, constantly collided with party officials; and, because he bulked larger, the impact was all the greater. Nevertheless, at his most wayward, he remained – like Mudford – true to party principles as he defined them. 'If my newspapers can be of any service to whatever government may be in power, I am only too pleased,' he wrote from his desk at *The Times* during the constitutional crisis of 1911 to the Liberal chief whip, 'if without disloyalty to my own party.'[2] That codicil absolved him from treachery, and pinpointed him on the political spectrum.

Especially on the evening papers, which specialized more in views than news, there had always been editors who were known for their pride and who duly suffered for it. Frederick Greenwood, who preceded Morley at the *Pall Mall Gazette* in its first Tory incarnation, reckoned that he occupied 'a place of power, at least equal to half a dozen seats in Parliament'.[3] W. T. Stead, who sat in the same chair after Morley had refurbished it with Liberal upholstery, declared that he would not trade it for a seat in the Cabinet. 'The Press has become the Chamber of Initiative', superseding the Commons as the Commons has superseded the Lords, he trumpeted in 1886.

I am but a comparatively young journalist, but I have seen Cabinets upset, Ministers driven into retirement, laws repealed, great social reforms initiated, Bills transformed, estimates remodelled, programmes modified, Acts passed, generals nominated, governors appointed, armies sent hither and thither, war proclaimed and war averted, by the agency of newspapers.[4]

In old age, A. G. Gardiner looked back on his own tenure at the *Daily News* with a modesty born of frustration: 'Nothing like being an editor,' he admitted to a friend, 'for getting [a] swollen head – except getting on the Treasury bench which is equally fatal to one's sense of proportion.'[5]

As heads swelled, egos inevitably clashed. Editorial assumptions were difficult to reconcile with political exigencies. Greenwood nursed a grievance against Disraeli, who failed to acknowledge the services he had allegedly rendered in the acquisition of the Suez Canal shares. Stead, who arrived in Fleet Street with a fervent admiration for Gladstone, whom he had helped to raise an outcry against the Bulgarian Horrors, lost faith when his hero was ensconced for a second time in Downing Street. Gardiner, devoted to Lloyd George as an Edwardian social reformer, turned against him during the First World War with a fury that cost him his editorship. The examples may be multiplied, but in every case the journalist saw himself as carrying the sacred torch

[1] *Nation* (New York), 26 August 1880.
[2] Northcliffe to Alexander Murray, Master of Elibank, 12 August 1911, Elibank Papers.
[3] Robertson Scott, *Life and Death of a Newspaper*, p. 4.
[4] W. T. Stead, 'Government by Journalism,' *Contemporary Review*, xlix (1886), 664.
[5] Gardiner to Frank Swinnerton, 4 September 1936, Swinnerton Papers.

which the politician had ignominiously jettisoned.

Precariously, but effectively, the interdependence between politics and the press survived the nineteenth century. Yet, even before Kennedy Jones (as he outrageously boasted to Morley) had converted journalism from 'a profession' into 'a branch of commerce',[1] a change of tone and direction can be detected. The triangular relationship between editors, proprietors, and politicians, iso-sceles rather than equilateral, was disrupted by new forces. At the same time, old tensions were exacerbated. Proprietors, torn between their obligations to party and those to their faltering journals, shifted their priorities. Politicians came to resent servants who postured as masters, and whose allegiance was, in any case, problematical. Editors, on the whole, were the least adaptable, clinging to a nineteenth-century tradition that was found to be commercially unsound and politically dispensable. That is why the most celebrated among them met with dismissal and disillusionment.

H. W. Nevinson grimly contended that 'all the very best editors' of his life-time were 'deposed on account of their excellence', and he could count no fewer than seven for whom he had worked.[2] By 'excellence', Nevinson meant forcefulness, individualism, and fidelity to one's convictions. Put to the test, all of these virtues were revealed as editorial encumbrances. The men who em-bodied them, once esteemed as assets to their papers and their parties, were no longer tolerated at the helm. Garvin, who survived at the *Observer* on bor-rowed time, was the last of the species. During his marathon reign, he had set his stamp on that paper: every week, Harold Macmillan recalled, 'we read the *Observer*, not really for anything else in it, but to see what Garvin had written.... Everybody wanted to know what Garvin's views were.'[3] In 1942 (too late to qualify for a place on Nevinson's roster of editorial mortalities), Garvin's proprietor broke with him, significantly on political grounds, and he rounded off his career as a featured columnist for other newspapers with whose policies he did not necessarily agree. As a gadfly, whose opinions appeared under his own name, he was free to venture into areas of controversy where a modern editor would fear to tread.

In spite of his assertion that 'I never was a proper journalistic journalist',[4] Garvin exemplifies the major themes of this study. Born in 1868, when news-papers existed in profusion and were expected to toe one party line or another, he died in 1947, when newspapers were far fewer and their bonds with parties had been eroded. He was trained in the late-Victorian school, and carried its precepts through to the middle of the twentieth century, when not even his own brilliance could maintain them. After the usual stint in provincial journal-ism, he had come to the metropolis, which was the nerve-centre of the political

---

[1] Kennedy Jones, *Fleet Street and Downing Street*, p. 173.
[2] H. W. Nevinson, *Last Changes, Last Chances* (New York, 1929), p. 273.
[3] Speech by Harold Macmillan, 7 December 1977; I am grateful to David Astor for bringing this speech to my attention, and to Kenneth Harris for making available a transcript.
[4] Garvin to Stanley Morison, 29 June 1943, *Times* Archives.

press. There, through a number of successive and concurrent appointments, he championed the policies of the politicians to whom he attached himself. From 1908, he had his Sunday pulpit at the *Observer* which, from 1912 to 1915, he combined with the daily editorship of the *Pall Mall Gazette*, previously restored to the Conservative fold. But his prodigious energies were not exhausted by his standing in party councils. The years before and during the First World War saw his influence at a zenith. Thereafter, he grew more isolated, temperamentally and geographically (he withdrew to his home in Beaconsfield), from the men in power. The Second World War, which completed so many of the processes initiated by the First, brought his editorial career to an end.

During the 1914 –18 war, there had been a party truce. Instead of muzzling the political press, it had diverted it into new channels in which Garvin and others like him had flourished. Afterwards there had been a reaction, in large part reflecting the debility of the Liberal Party and its organs. During the next war, political disputation was suspended, if not quite to the extent that legend would have it. The post-war press knew better than to try to recover a political authority which it was in no position to sustain. Nor did post-war political leaders seek to revive those powers, which they recognized as not so much dormant as dead. Robin Barrington-Ward of *The Times* jotted in his diary on 24 June 1947 that he had had 'some talk with Attlee, but chiefly about the Crossword! Characteristic'.[1] True to form, Attlee projected a diffidence that masked a keen appreciation of political realities.

His successors, some with less grace and pangs of regret, have resigned themselves to a new relationship with newspapers. They might continue to recruit advisers from their staffs, and, through informal contacts, strive to obtain sympathetic publicity for themselves and their programmes. They might rant and rail – 'Why should we . . . allow ourselves to be scared by headlines in the capitalist Press?' Aneurin Bevan demanded to know. 'It is the most prostituted Press in the world, most of it owned by a gang of millionaires'[2] – or they might lodge protests with the Press Council. But they have accepted that any attempt to intervene directly in the internal affairs of newspapers would be futile and demeaning. While press criticism is never welcome, all but the most thin-skinned have learned to take it in their stride. After all, as public opinion polls have conclusively ascertained, newspapers do not sway massive numbers of votes. A party may as easily triumph in the face of a hostile press as it may go down to defeat with press opinion solidly behind it.

To the consternation of the redoubtable Lady Astor, who reminded her son that his grandfather had entered British journalism in order to propagate Tory views, the *Observer* proclaimed itself 'independent' in the General Election of 1945. Other newspapers followed suit, and those that resisted the trend were

[1] Barrington-Ward Papers.
[2] *The Times*, 17 May 1948.

doomed to perish. Consequently, independence from party, which had been sporadically claimed but never meaningfully realized, has become the norm among Britain's national newspapers. Because it would be too much to expect an abstract principle to apply consistently, let alone to universal satisfaction, certain Labour and Liberal spokesmen have habitually complained that they have suffered neglect and misrepresentation at the hands of a preponderantly Tory press; for that matter, certain Conservative politicians, representing minority views within their party, may have felt similarly slighted. One must differentiate, however, between the predispositions of newspapers, which cannot – and should not – be regulated in a free society, and the system of partisan controls that formerly obtained.

That difference, more comparative than absolute, may be illustrated by an incident in Harold Wilson's stormy relations with the press and other media. On 20 September 1974, in a speech at Portsmouth, he alluded to 'a smear campaign' being conducted by 'cohorts of distinguished journalists' who had 'a mandate to find anything, true or fabricated, to use against the Labour Party' in the coming election. The Press Council solicited and eventually, in April 1977, received the evidence on which Sir Harold (as he had since become) had based his charge, along with the incidental explanation that he had used 'distinguished' in an ironic sense. It ultimately rejected his complaint for reasons that bear scrutiny:

> There is no doubt that over most of this century the Labour movement has had less newspaper support than its right-wing opponents and that its beliefs and activities have been unfavourably reported by the majority of the press.
>
> Some national newspapers are still strongly partisan, with the *Daily Telegraph, Daily Mail* and *Daily Express* on the one side and the *Daily Mirror* on the other. The provincial press is more likely to be neutral or slightly to the right.
>
> We do not feel able to pronounce on whether there is political bias at work in drawing up the agenda for discussion and comment. This would require difficult value judgments to be made about politics and society, as well as about the press.
>
> Within the terms of the agenda actually drawn up, however, the evidence we have had does not suggest that in either the national or the regional press at present the balance against Labour is a strong one.[1]

Without shrinking from 'difficult value judgments ... about politics and society, as well as about the press', this study accepts those general conclusions, and proposes to support them by an analysis of broad historical

[1] *The Times*, 16 October 1978. There is much to be gleaned about Wilson's relations with the press from Crossman, *The Diaries of a Cabinet Minister*, especially II (London, 1976), 155, 229–30, 334, 350, 368, and 609; also see David Wood, 'The Reporting of Westminster Politics,' *The Times*, 6 February 1978.

patterns. That the majority of newspapers, by 'emphasising consensual and dominant values',[1] foster a conservative ideology is indisputable; that they also foster the electoral interests of the Conservative Party is more questionable. Moreover, support that is volunteered is a far cry from support that is commanded, although the distinction may not be sufficiently appreciated by those who lack the resources to secure either variety. Freedom from party control, as distinct from party commitment, is now so much taken for granted that it requires no reaffirmation. It extends to the major provincial dailies and even to the weekly journals of opinion, their explicit party preferences notwithstanding. The *Morning Star*, linked to the Communist Party, is the single exception that proves the rule.

Lord Beaverbrook, who created his press empire on the ruins of the old system, personified this drastic change for which he had acted as a catalyst. With as little respect for wilful editors as for domineering politicians, he rejoiced that the press was no longer beholden to elected officials for 'scraps of information', and argued 'that the two forces are infinitely better in separation – because they check each other when divided and are irresistible in union'.[2] While it would be fanciful to suggest that Beaverbrook's newspapers hesitated to take a partisan stand, they were too undisciplined and erratic to satisfy any formal criterion.

Admittedly, his actions often belied his pronouncements: in the course of running circles around his adversaries, he suffered from flights of giddiness. Never was he more adept or more mischievous than when he testified in 1948 before the Royal Commission on the Press. 'When you were more actively engaged in the conduct of the papers,' the chairman asked him, 'was your main purpose (a) the commercial success of the paper, (b) the support of a particular political Party, or (c) the support of special political views which happened to be near to your own heart?' Beaverbrook replied in a flash that he had used the *Daily Express* 'purely for the purpose of making propaganda' for a cause, namely Empire Free Trade, that 'we would always support any political party that took a favourable attitude to our views, and we attacked parties one after the other because they would not take favourably to our views'. If less than the whole truth, that was not quite a falsehood. The chairman proceeded to enquire whether Beaverbrook had 'formed any definite opinion on the question to what extent a paper with a great circulation like yours actually moulds the opinion of its readers'. With mock solemnity, the witness responded: 'I sometimes think that we have a tremendous influence, and then I get quite despondent about it.'[3]

Harold Macmillan had 'the extraordinary experience' of serving under

---

[1] The phrase is used by Graham Murdock and Peter Golding, 'The structure, ownership and control of the press, 1914–74,' in Boyce, Curran, and Wingate, eds., *Newspaper History*, p. 147.

[2] Beaverbrook, *Politicians and the Press* (London, 1925?), pp. 9–10.

[3] Cd. 7416, questions 8656–8662. 'I remember, but great men must be allowed their inconsistencies', Francis Williams has written, 'an occasion in his study at Cherkeley [*sic*] when he

Beaverbrook at the Ministry of Supply for nine months during the Second World War. 'He used to say to me,' Macmillan related, ' "Since I came into the Government I have nothing to do with my paper's character." Then he'd pick up the telephone and say "Put me on to [E.J.] Robertson" ', his general manager, 'and he'd tell him to do something.' On the one hand, Macmillan's recollection cautions us that newspapermen ought not to be taken strictly at their word, even when that word appears in print; on the other, it tellingly reminds us that politics and journalism were not mutually exclusive categories, however emphatically or eloquently Beaverbrook (or Delane or Stead or Garvin) might insist to the contrary.

'Those proprietors were great characters,' Macmillan continued. 'Fossilized now in a kind of past, but in their period they played a great role. They created the modern newspaper. With all their faults they created it.' As Macmillan knew, his was a highly contentious view: 'This state of affairs was much attacked – though it had some merits.' Northcliffe, Rothermere, and Beaverbrook, even 'in their period', which extended through the interwar years, aroused fierce resentment, not least among their hirelings. 'Journalism has been killed by newspaper owners,' Thomas Marlowe told H.A. Gwynne in 1932, a decade after Northcliffe's death and six years after Northcliffe's brother, Lord Rothermere, had dispensed with Marlowe's services at the *Daily Mail*, which he had edited for thirty years. Gwynne, at the time, was fighting 'a losing battle' to sustain the *Morning Post*, which merged with the *Daily Telegraph* five years later. 'Mass production of newspapers, directed to serve purposes not disclosed to their readers, nor even to their staffs, will doubtless continue for some time to come,' Marlowe declared. 'But the people pay less and less attention. Costly insurance schemes and money prizes, and other frantic efforts to keep up circulation figures, show what is happening. People want news and instruction, which they will get by radio development.'[1] His moroseness, like Macmillan's romanticism, was understandable. By bringing to life successive generations of fossils and the contexts in which they once flourished, this book will test empirically the validity of these and other hypotheses.

Macmillan offered his reminiscences on the evening of 7 December 1977 at a dinner in honour of David Astor and Lord Goodman who, with unconcealed relief, had relinquished control of the *Observer* to an American petroleum company, pledged to uphold its proud tradition of independence. How many of those present were aware how recently and under what circumstances that tradition had been established? More than an event in the history of a single newspaper, the occasion belatedly commemorated the end of a long chapter in

---

[Beaverbrook] told me the exact opposite. "Oh, how I hate propaganda," he said then.' Williams, *op.cit.*, p. 214.

[1] Marlowe to Gwynne, 20 May 1932, Gwynne Papers.

the history of the British political press. Who could have supposed, when the 'taxes on knowledge' were repealed and newspapers were no longer clients of the state, that they would eventually subsist as the appendages of multinational conglomerates? Cobden, one suspects, would have been surprised, but not dismayed.

*   *   *

The preceding discussion, surveying critical shifts in public attitudes and professional behaviour, rests on certain assumptions. These would be better specified than inferred.

Any attempt at synthesis, and especially one that aspires to reformulate and refine general notions, must begin with a consideration of the methods to be employed. That the present study undertakes to trace 'the rise and fall of the political press in Britain' is self-evident from its title. But what are the connotations of each of these elements? What characteristics are ascribed to them? What are the perimeters within which they will be approached, and from what perspective? What is the justification for concentrating attention on certain factors, inevitably at the expense of others? What kind of evidence will be brought to bear, and what kind of conclusions do they permit the author to draw? These questions are addressed at the outset so that the reader will appreciate not only the purpose of the endeavour, but also its accepted limitations.

'Rise', 'fall', 'political', and 'press' are fairly elementary terms. Nevertheless, all readily admit to rival definitions. For that matter, the designation 'British' – as opposed to 'English' – has been known to spark controversy. To some extent, each of these labels implies a value judgment, consciously made. None is satisfactory in every respect, and each will require further clarification and qualification in due course. It is believed, however, that the ensuing narrative will establish their relative weight and applicability. This explanation is therefore intended neither to deflect criticism nor to preclude investigation of areas that have been deemed tangential to the work at hand. Rather it is meant to suggest ways in which this contribution may fit into an emerging historical and historiographical framework.

The starting point may be most easily defended on both scores. To the contemporary mind, the events of the 1850s signalled a break with old forms and the beginning of a new era in the political conduct of the press. Those signals were frequently misread, but no matter: what men thought was, as always, decisive in determining their responses. There is the additional consideration, which looms justly large, that the period from 1780 to 1850 was spanned by Arthur Aspinall in his classic volume, *Politics and the Press*, published in 1949. Setting a standard which few have been able to meet, Aspinall effectively demonstrated that a distinct phase in newspaper history had culminated in the middle of the nineteenth century, when another phase began. In a sense he laid the foundations for this edifice, although he cannot, of course, be held responsible for its construction.

When did that succeeding phase end? Here, the line of demarcation is not so clear. Lacking a comparable set of legislative signposts, the historian is forced to chart his course by means of other indicators. And, as he moves into periods that fall within living memory, any choice becomes more obviously subjective. A logical case could be made for concluding in either 1939 or 1945, at the outbreak of war or at the election that followed it. Equally, one might fasten on the Royal Commission on the Press that sat through 1947–48, and reported in 1949. Instead, for considerations that transcend those of symmetry, this account – after making a halt for refuelling at the turn of the century – will ultimately extend through the General Election of 1951. By then, the effects of wartime and post-war experience were unmistakable, and their pre-war antecedents were more fully appreciated. Within the newspaper industry, new arrangements had been instituted, and political practice had altered to take them into account.

The geographical dimension, like the time factor, carries distinct implications. It will be argued that, given the structure of British political society as it evolved through these decades, the London press was tantamount to the national press. For better or worse, its voice was heard most audibly by policy-makers, congregated in the capital, and its resources were those to which they attached paramount significance. That Gladstone should have been moved to denounce the metropolitan journals as representing the prejudices of Clubland and not the sentiments of the nation at large was, paradoxically a backhanded tribute to their special status; his dismay when they attacked him and his jubilation when they were won to his side underscored their pre-eminence in his mind. Their circulations might be minuscule, but the number of persons who mattered, so to speak, was likewise proportionately small and London-orientated. (When Macmillan reflected that 'everybody wanted to know what Garvin's views were' in the early 1920s, he was speaking about a paper with an average weekly print of 175,000 copies.) Because this generalization does not hold to the same degree for every episode and period, reference will be made to various press personalities and enterprises in the outlying regions. With few exceptions, however, they will be seen as satellites that revolved around the metropolitan base, sometimes impinging on it, but usually reflecting its values. Wales and, still more, Ireland lie outside the orbit.

Although the second half of the nineteenth century witnessed an efflorescence of the provincial press, capable of exerting political authority in their respective localities, these properties tended increasingly to draw their directives, inspiration, incentives, and capital from London. 'It is true the London newspaper of standing is, as to time and place, more closely in touch with ministers and statesmen,' conceded Charles Cooper, who began in 1861 as a parliamentary reporter for the *Morning Star* in London before he eventually defied the law of journalistic gravity by heading north to take up the editorship of the *Scotsman* in Edinburgh. 'But,' he insisted out of a vested interest, 'the advantage is more seeming than real.' While Cooper may be counted among the dozen or so provincial editors whom politicians intermittently kept 'well informed as to matters that may be known', he revealingly recounted the story of another exile from London journalism 'whose practice was to write his leading article or articles at home the night before publication'. A messenger, sent to fetch his overdue copy, found him

> with a glass of brandy and water before him, and newspapers scattered about. There was no article written.
> 'What do you want?' asked the editor.
> 'The article for to-morrow.'
> 'Didn't I send it?'
> 'No; at least it has not come to the office.'
> 'Give me *The Times*.'
> *The Times* was found and handed to him, and with unsteady fingers he cut out one of its leading articles. This he stuck upon a sheet of paper, and then taking his pen wrote at the top, 'What does *The Times* mean by this?' Nothing more.
> In that form and with that introduction it appeared next morning as the editor's leading article.[1]

With greater sobriety, more legitimate purpose, and an assortment of cosmetic touches, extracts from the major London dailies and weeklies were replicated from one end of the country to the other, and throughout the empire. The press, a ravenous animal, has always fed on itself, not always with appropriate acknowledgment. One of the standard features of most London newspapers was a column devoted to other newspapers' verdicts on the topics of the day. The reader of any one paper thereby had access to a broad spectrum of editorial views, supportive or contradictory, presented without so much embellishment as 'What does *The Times* mean by this?' But the provincial press, more likely to expropriate political reports from its London rivals than to encapsulate them, borrowed more heavily than it could ever repay. Accepting this dependency, schemes were frequently propounded by which a 'core' publication – containing all the essentials including leading articles – would be produced in Fleet Street, then delivered to regional centres, where sheets containing local news and advertisements would be added; in each instance, the obstacles were technical, not ideological. In spirit as well as practice, then, metropolitan newspapers have been linked not only to the politicians, with whom they share an arena, but also to their siblings in the

---

[1] Charles Cooper, *An Editor's Retrospect* (London, 1896), pp. 69–70 and 9. For a systematic and sympathetic account of the provincial press, see Alan J. Lee, *The Origins of the Popular Press, 1855–1914* (London, 1976).

hinterlands, with whom they share intelligence and ingredients. In the United States, by contrast, a dispersal of power and influence has given issue to a wholly different model. 'We are often told that Britain is the one country in the world that has a national press,' a recent critic has tartly stated. 'But we haven't got a national press. What we have is local newspapers that are nationally distributed.'[1] That, certainly, is one way to look at things. Yet there is no gainsaying that London is an exceptional locality. In any event, far from being a relatively new phenomenon, the journalistic hegemony of London already prevailed in the mid-Victorian age, when politics and the railways operated on parallel lines.

The enclosed nature of the British press, one of the recurrent themes of this book, awaits explication and possibly emendation in the ensuing chapters. Meanwhile, we may proceed to broach more complex questions that relate to it. The focus here on the metropolitan press is juxtaposed with an emphasis on developments in and around Parliament. Indeed the very concept of a political press rests on a particular interpretation of political culture which, as a scheme of values, may be more easily intuited than reconstructed. Although the components of that culture were never static in relation either to each other or to the larger social organism, certain tendencies were continual. Chief among them was a tacit acceptance of Parliament as the supreme political and social institution of the realm. Even after it had ceased to qualify as 'the first club in Europe', it remained the apex of the governmental system. Needless to say, neither social nor political pursuits were confined to Westminster and its environs. But the constituencies were regarded as outposts in much the same way as the country houses, where statesmen retreated for the recesses, were regarded as annexes. It was in the shadow of the Palace of Westminster, within an insulated enclave bounded by Fleet Street and Park Lane, that matters of consequence were discussed and decided by individuals who may have profoundly disagreed on points of principle, but whose objectives and tactics were strikingly similar. Momentous events might inconveniently occur in distant places, but their impact was fully registered only when they were debated in Parliament and appraised by the leader-writers of the London press. 'The essence of the parliamentary idea . . . is a system of institutionalized persuasion, . . . and persuasion is achieved by language', according to George Watson, who has thoughtfully examined its ramifications in Victorian fiction. No less signally, newspapers exemplified the 'elective and deliberative process for which "parliamentary" seems the only name'.[2]

The 'unstamped' press of the early nineteenth century, although blatantly political, lacked the durability and accountability that was characteristic of the political press after 1850. By definition, its efforts were unco-ordinated, and its effectiveness was random. In these respects, those publications were more

[1] R. Boston, 'Growing Pains', p. 8.
[2] George Watson, *The English Ideology* (London, 1973), pp. 135–37.

akin to the press of today than to the press of the intervening period to which
this study is addressed. From the middle of the nineteenth century until well
into the twentieth, a discrete set of attitudes and conditions infused journalism
with a mission which, before it gradually dissipated, helped to shape British
political consciousness. Following a period of sharp social antagonisms and
political turbulence, there came 'a heroic age of universalist political
controversy', as A. H. Halsey has called it, which eventually gave way to a
situation in which 'alienation from the state apparatus' was a 'widespread
popular experience'.[1] Meanwhile, to a greater extent than ever before or
since, it was taken for granted that any constructive movement required a base
in Parliament and, for that purpose, control over newspapers with which to
recruit and mobilize support. The parliamentary heritage, revered by many
and respected by all save a few extremists, laid down guidelines for effective
propaganda. Those who trespassed beyond them were doomed to censure and
disrepute. The expansion of the press, both in terms of circulation and esteem,
was thus embedded in a matrix of common values. It was correlative with the
growth of centralized party organizations, employing sophisticated techniques
of electoral management. Through successive permutations, the political
press was as much the product of the mentality of the times as the key instrument for formulating that mentality.

Every newspaper carried an amount of political coverage and comment, for
the simple reason that politics made news. Yet not every newspaper deserves
to be classified under the heading of the political press. The difference cannot
be measured simply in terms of column inches: the *Daily Mail*, for example,
which made it a policy to subordinate political features to those adjudged to be
more fashionable, nonetheless qualifies; the *Daily Graphic* or *Financial
Times*, although they allocated proportionately more space to political affairs,
obviously do not. Some newspapers – like the *Morning Post*, the *Daily News*,
the *Westminster Gazette*, and *The Times* – consistently fell within the category.
Others – like the *Morning Advertiser*, the *Sunday Times*, and the *Evening
Standard* – qualified intermittently, depending on the predilections of their
editors and owners. It was essentially a question of self-definition, sometimes
subtly articulated or casually intimated. There was no doubt in politicians'
minds as to which were the political newspapers and what were the purposes to
which they might lend themselves. They knew, if the average reader did not,
that those papers that lavished page after page on verbatim accounts of parliamentary proceedings were not necessarily political in the practical, partisan
sense.

Sales figures provide only one index to the political value of a particular
newspaper, and not the salient one at that. Parenthetically, more often than
not those statistics prove unreliable. A better standard of measurement, notoriously more difficult to handle, is the direct influence which a journal might

[1] A. H. Halsey, *Change in British Society* (Oxford, 1978), pp. 79, 91.

possess by virtue of its eloquence, persistence, or liaisons. 'It is an error to measure utility by circulation,' Abraham Hayward, a Peelite publicist, instructed Sir John Young, a Peelite politician, in 1853:

Every one of the leading papers is read at all clubs and reading rooms. Its good articles or arguments are reprinted or reproduced in the provincial papers, or worked up anew in the shape of speeches, and always furnish topics for the friends of the party it advocates. It thus influences constituents, and constituents command votes.[1]

The political persuasion to which Hayward belonged, like the protective system in which he operated professionally, was soon to fade away, but his presumptions survived long thereafter.

There were numerous occasions when journalistic strictures reverberated in the smoking rooms of the clubs in Pall Mall, along the corridors of power in Whitehall and Westminster, and in the inner sanctum of the Cabinet; these will be documented. There were other occasions when newspapers were put to ulterior uses either to provoke or embarrass. Stead recalled

being confidentially approached by a permanent official who holds a high place in an important department. . . . He wanted me to write an article praising a certain Act connected with his department, against which some interested clamour was being raised. 'Why just now?' I asked. 'To stiffen the back of my chief,' he replied.

Stead complied with a 'rouser' in the *Pall Mall Gazette* and 'soon afterwards had the satisfaction of knowing that it had had the desired effect'.[2] So far as the evidence permits, such machinations will be chronicled. Lastly, and most obviously, political newspapers afforded channels of communication: by preaching to the converted, a service not to be underestimated, they fortified them in their resolve to wage the party fight; by preaching to the middle ground of vacillating opinion, they clarified issues and tried to win adherents and, incidentally, readers; by preaching to the enemy, on whom they could depend to scrutinize their arguments, they raised the pitch of political debate which, at decisive junctures, they also deflected.

The political press could not have expected to exercise any of these functions had not certain ideas been presumed. Most notably, the authority of the printed word was accepted as an article of faith. What men said might be ascribed to impetuosity or caprice, all the more when they said it from campaign hustings or in spontaneous response to 'posers' from the opposition benches. What they wrote or what they authorized others to write constituted part of the record, however ephemeral the opinions expressed. 'The pulpit has

[1] Hayward to Young, 14 September 1853, *Correspondence of Abraham Hayward* (ed. H. Carlisle; London, 1886), I, 189.
[2] W. T. Stead, 'Government by Journalism,' pp. 659–60.

some power; the platform is gaining in influence,' H. W. Massingham wrote in 1892. 'But, in regard to the minds it reaches daily, the press surpasses them both.'[1] With sermons, clergymen could appeal once a week to conscience; with speeches, politicians could appeal at irregular intervals; but only the press was equipped to reiterate its message day after day. Oratory, distrusted in some quarters as demagogy, incited fleeting passions; moreover, it gave licence to hyperbole, and the complexities of an issue were lost amid the heckling and applause. Journalism, being a step removed, had an air of authenticity. Theoretically, at any rate, it could present a cogent argument on which men could ruminate in an atmosphere of calm. It spoke to the intellect, not to the emotions. To an age that posited a rationality in the conduct of human affairs, that was important.

Those ideas, delusions perhaps, obtained only so long as opinion-making was the vocation and pastime of a community of individuals who accepted and in turn imposed certain forms of discipline. Not always scrupulous in matters of terminology, they gloried in the sanctity of language, which has since been abused and corrupted. One must remember the backgrounds from which they came and the enclosed preserves in which they operated. As Robert Blake has tellingly reminded us, when Sir Robert Peel promulgated his historic Tamworth Manifesto in 1834, it was specifically addressed to the 586 voters in his constituency, yet relatively well circulated 'given the highly restricted opportunities for practical publicity at that time'.[2] The Reform Acts of 1867 and 1884 significantly widened the scope of the political nation, but were slow to change the methods of practising politicians, much less the perceptions of practising journalists. They were slower still, as recent scholarship has demonstrated, to disturb the deferential habits of those admitted to the franchise. Generations passed before the repercussions were actually felt. Then, despite dogged attempts to reverse the trend, it was obvious that the nexus between politicians and newspapers could not be retained, at least not on the old footing. Created to facilitate 'practical publicity', the political press proved an impediment to it. Its fall, less ceremonious than its rise in the 1850s, was inevitable once politics became more comprehensive, politicians more remote, and political rhetoric less credible. 'Newspapers are continually mis-representing the state of public affairs,' Lloyd George fulminated on 22 August 1919. 'They suppress information regarding things that are well done and magnify mistakes which are inevitable in the conduct of life.'[3] Whom could he blame more than himself?

The political press will be approached from a perspective which, although limited, is not arbitrary. There exists, of course, a welter of subjects in newspaper history apart from the theme of political commitment, specifically

---

[1] H. W. Massingham, *The London Daily Press* (London, 1892), p. 9.
[2] Robert Blake, *The Conservative Party from Peel to Churchill* (London, 1970), p. 39.
[3] Lord Riddell, *Intimate Diary of the Peace Conference and After* (London, 1933), p. 111.

defined by party affiliation: technological and organizational adjustments, marketing and revenue structures, countervailing demands of labour and management, the possible discrepancy between private ownership and the public interest, and other competing challenges posed by social, legal, and economic pressures. And, to be sure, political change reveals only one of its infinite facets through an analysis of press involvement. Mindful of the vast adjacent areas that remain inadequately charted, and without precluding consideration of them, this study assumes the relatively modest task of investigating the points of intersection between politics and the press. It is hoped that, in the course of this reappraisal, light focused on a particular area will illuminate overlapping sectors.

That task is itself more daunting than it may initially appear. 'It is a commonplace of criticism to say that the history of the Newspaper Press of England has yet to be written,' Francis Hitchman remarked in the *Quarterly Review* as long ago as 1880. 'Times without number the work has been attempted, but it still remains unachieved.'[1] Ninety years later, Max Beloff observed that 'the documentation of journalists and publicists is ... very uneven, and only now beginning to be explored'.[2] Since that time, there have been increasing 'signs of an awakening interest in the history of the press',[3] usually resulting in biographies of prominent figures or collections of essays on policy-orientated themes. Whereas the earlier works tended to be written by repentant or recriminative journalists in their anecdotage, the newer ones overwhelmingly bear the imprint of social scientists, determined to apply specialized maxims to segmented fields of inquiry. That is hardly surprising given the obstacles, which are manifold and obvious. Conceptually as well as methodologically, the press is difficult to encompass. To deal with it in all its aspects would baffle the wits and exhaust the lifetime of the most assiduous student. Described as 'the greatest untapped source for the writing of recent British political history',[4] the press is equally indispensable as a source for its own history. Yet to read carefully every copy of every newspaper would be an unfeasible and probably a pointless exercise. At best, it might allow one to trace editorial attitudes, but not to account for the motives that informed them. Nevertheless, a good deal has been written about the press without consulting its contents, and that is surely unsatisfactory. How and where does one strike a balance?

Several problems, encountered in the course of research for this volume and its successor, deserve special mention insofar as they may help to explain the

---

[1] 'The Newspaper Press Directory and Advertiser's Guide' (review article), *Quarterly Review*, cl (1880), 498.

[2] Max Beloff, *Imperial Sunset*, I (New York, 1970), 52.

[3] Gordon Phillips, 'A national press archive,' in Boyce *et al.*, eds., *Newspaper History*, p. 341.

[4] Trevor Wilson, *The Downfall of the Liberal Party 1914–1935* (London, 1966), preface; for the contrary view, emphatically stated, see Andrew Jones, *The Politics of Reform 1884* (Cambridge, 1972), pp. 11–12.

procedures followed. In addition to published materials – newspaper histories and directories, official documents, monographs, memoirs, biographies, review articles, and the files of newspapers themselves – this work relies to the greatest extent possible on collections of correspondence, including memoranda and diaries. By bringing to bear these sources, it is possible to distil personal sentiments from public statements, and to delineate patterns of influence. For purposes of convenience, these collections may be separated into two groups, each with peculiar virtues and liabilities: the first consists of the records of newspapers and the private papers of individuals connected with them; the second,,of party records and the private papers of politicians who regularly trafficked with the press.

When newspapers shut down, amalgamated, or (with the laudable exception of *The Times*) relocated to new offices, their archives – assuming that they had maintained any – disappeared. The *Guardian* is another matter: its archives contain essentially the papers of C. P. Scott, its venerable editor. Other editors, who did not have Scott's devotion or longevity of tenure (or who did not like him own their papers), regarded their professional correspondence as their personal possession, and carried it away when they left the premises. As a result, those materials that survived were dispersed. They exist, if at all, in private hands or in public depositories scattered around the globe. Such collections have been traced and, when available, consulted.

Wartime bombing took a heavy toll in Fleet Street, but not so heavy, one imagines, as the systematic destruction of newspaper records, apart from libraries of cuttings, which were used for in-house reference. At every stage, journalists were dedicated to probe other people's transgressions while they shrouded their own in obscurity. That was as much an ethic as a defensive tactic. As T. H. S. Escott, then attached to the *World*, wrote 'strictly in confidence' to William Blackwood, the Edinburgh publisher, 'the secrets of the prison house should not be repeated outside the walls of the prison'.[1] That is not to suggest that newspapers wished to hide incriminating evidence either from one another or from the prying eyes of posterity, though one may infer that this was sometimes a motive. Rather, their usefulness depended on their maintaining the anonymity of their sources, who might otherwise hesitate to communicate freely and frankly. 'When I was Editor of *The Times*', G. E. Buckle informed the daughter of the 3rd Marquess of Salisbury, who was preparing her father's biography,

> my practice was to destroy my correspondence with public men as soon as the matter with which it dealt was over and done with. I did it on principle ... so that no subsequent publication of confidential documents, which might have the effect of weakening the belief of statesmen in the good faith of *The Times*, should be possible.

[1] Escott to Blackwood, 28 May 1877, Blackwood Papers.

He might have invoked the precedent of John Walter II, whose 'undertaking . . . that the public men of his day were safe with *The Times*' has been interpreted by the official historians of that paper to suggest 'that their correspondence was destroyed almost as a matter of principle'.[1]

Fortunately, not every editor (not even every editor of *The Times*) felt the same compunction. From editorial correspondence that does survive, one may piece together half the story. The other half may be reconstructed from the political side. Here, too, one may safely surmise that materials were lost or discarded. Party records, often subsumed among the papers of party leaders, may be found in greater amplitude for some periods than for others. Certain politicians kept careful and seemingly complete accounts of their dealings with the press; others, whose relationships are known to have been far more extensive and intimate, left only tantalizing fragments.

The characters of these statesmen, their business habits, and, not least, the nature of their interventions help to account for what was saved or destroyed. But, again, other explanations must be considered. Because the majority of newspaper people were relatively unknown, their letters were not always considered worthy of retention. Because many of their communications were perfunctory – confirmations of an interview or a note to call attention to a particular article – they might not have been retained at the time or, more likely, when these collections were subsequently put in order by descendants or biographers. There is the further factor that, as a rule, journalists were poor letter-writers: they poured their ideas directly into print and, except for a few like Garvin, rarely expounded them in private correspondence. Nevertheless, sufficient clues remain to warrant investigation.

Given the quantity and quality of the evidence (not all of it catalogued above), there is a temptation to proceed impressionistically from topic to topic, theme to theme. It has, however, been stoutly resisted. Instead consecutive chapters will build a chronological narrative. Events may best be evaluated in the sequence in which they unfolded, which was how they impressed themselves – largely through journalism – on the public mind. That mind was constantly changing, both in composition and outlook, and the political press changed with it. Obsessed with the affairs of the moment, it was grounded on accumulated custom and tradition. At one level, it was the most public of public institutions, available for as little as a halfpenny at every news-stand; at another level, yet to be plumbed, it was one of the most private and restrictive. What we may discover about the forces that operated behind the scenes should afford insights into the workings of the press and, more importantly, into the political process as it evolved.

---

[1] Buckle to Lady Gwendolen Cecil, 31 July 1932, *Times* Archives; *The History of The Times*, I (London, 1935), viii.

Two

'WITHIN PROPER BOUNDS'

'I never take up a Newspaper without finding something I should have deemed it a loss not to have seen; never without deriving from it instruction and amusement': in this respect, at least, Dr Johnson was not unique. Successive generations of his countrymen have shared his inclination to 'read all about it', with the result that the British public has been singularly addicted to newsprint. In recent decades, the number of newspapers has dwindled, but not the supply. Newer media have intruded to compete for attention, and the balance between instruction and amusement has markedly shifted. Nevertheless, the daily consumption of newspapers remains among the very highest in the world. It was estimated in 1977 that 72 per cent of the population read one or more morning papers, with 66 per cent reading a national one (some reading a regional one as well), and 34 per cent reading an evening journal. A survey, undertaken to ascertain readers' interests, found that most people depended on the press for 'news about what is going on in this part of the country', followed by 'news about what the Government is doing in Britain'. In fifth place, after 'news about football', respondents looked for 'news about political parties'.[1] A hundred or even fifty years earlier, the priorities would have been different, partly because the press itself collectively imposed other ones.

Dr Johnson, one suspects, would have given pride of place to 'news about political parties'. With no false modesty, he accepted praise for the 'impartiality' of the parliamentary reports he contributed to the *Gentleman's Magazine* from 1740 to 1743, but admitted that, in framing his dispatches, he 'took care that the Whig dogs shall not have the best of it'. In his professional as well as his personal attitudes, he was typical. In fact, his assessment of a news-

---

[1] *The Times*, 2 September 1977. James Curran has convincingly put the case that, despite the drop in aggregate newspaper circulation since the early 1950s, 'real consumption' – calculated on the basis of such factors as the percentage of newspaper readers among the adult population and the percentage of consumer expenditure on newspaper copies – had not decreased. 'The Impact of TV on the Audience for National Newspapers 1945–68,' in J. Tunstall, ed., *Media Sociology* (London, 1970), pp. 104–31; see also S. Høyer, S. Hadenius, and L. Weibull, *The Politics and Economics of the Press: A Developmental Perspective* (London, 1975), for some useful comparisons with American and Scandinavian models.

paper's political function holds surprisingly well throughout the lengthy period presently under surveillance, notwithstanding profound changes which he could not have prophesied: the press, as he saw it, 'affords sufficient information to elate vanity, and stiffen obstinacy, but too little to enlarge the mind into complete skill for comprehension'. To the nineteenth-century idealist, such a view would have smacked of an unconscionable cynicism; to the twentieth-century historian, however, it savours of logic. That may be taken to indicate one of several curious ways in which presumptions about journalism have come full circle from Dr Johnson's day to our own.

In spirit, if rarely in substance, eighteenth-century newspapers anticipated many of the procedures and predicaments of their successors. Writing in 1827, Henry Hallam stressed their vital contribution to constitutional development:

> The publication of regular Newspapers partly designed for the communication of intelligence, partly for the discussion of political topics, may be referred upon the whole to the reign of Anne, when they obtained great circulation, and became the accredited organs of different factions.

Addison's 'Mr Spectator', a specimen of that age, set out his credo: 'I never espoused any party with violence, and am resolved to observe a strict neutrality between the Whigs and Tories unless I shall be forced to declare myself by the hostilities of either side.' That, too, has a distinctly modern ring. Because 'hostilities' were the staple of late-Stuart politics, Addison's 'neutrality' – like Dr Johnson's flaunted 'impartiality' – was, at best, relative.

In the early years of the eighteenth century, journalistic partisanship was vehement and vituperative; that newspaper content was generally also bawdy and licentious was generally taken as a lesser affront. In 1712, Parliament retaliated by enacting a stamp duty on publications which, as if to add insult to injury, was bracketed with taxes on soap and assorted sundries. The rate was fixed at a penny per printed sheet, or a halfpenny for half a sheet or less, with a further levy of twelvepence for each advertisement. The stringency of the measure may be inferred from Swift's complaint 'that all Grub Street is ruined by the Stamp Act'. Although crippled, the press limped on. Subsequent legislation tightened and extended these controls, but never to the extent that victims of press abuse might have wished.

The official motives were clear enough, and essentially divorced from the budgetary considerations with which they were conveniently coupled. Better than in any public pronouncement, they were articulated in the pages of Tobias Smollett's novel, *The Expedition of Humphrey Clinker* (1771), where Matthew Bramble 'made acquaintance with a Mr Barton, a member of parliament . . . [and] a good sort of man, though most ridiculously warped in his political principles'. Bramble innocently remarked that a certain noble gentleman, whom Barton was 'bedaubing', had been 'characterised differently in one of the daily-papers', whereupon Barton railed against the sins of journalism:

> This spirit of defamation is a kind of heresy, that thrives under prosecution. The *liberty of the press* is a term of great efficacy; and like that of the *Protestant religion*, has often served the purposes of sedition.... Like every other privilege, it must be restrained within certain bounds; for if it is carried to a branch of law, religion, and charity, it becomes one of the greatest evils that ever annoyed the community.... To what purpose is our property secured, if our moral character is left defenceless? People thus baited, grow desperate; and the despair of being able to preserve one's character, untainted by such vermin, produces a total neglect of fame; so that one of the chief incitements to the practice of virtue is effectually destroyed.

Bramble was prompted to reconsider the stamp duty as 'wise and laudable', a judgment confirmed, later in his peregrination, by a conversation with 'an old weather-beaten Scotch lieutenant, called Lismahago', who

> said, he should always consider the liberty of the press as a national evil, while it enabled the vilest reptile to soil the lustre of the most shining merit, and furnished the most infamous incendiary with the means of disturbing the peace and destroying the good order of the community. He owned, however, that under due restrictions, it would be a valuable privilege; but affirmed, that at present there was no law in England sufficient to restrain it within proper bounds.

With less comic effect, ministers of state translated these sentiments into legislation. Lord North, whose antipathy to the press was well known and amply requited, raised the stamp duty to 1½ d. in 1776; the tax on advertisements, raised to two shillings in 1757, was increased by another sixpence in 1780. The publishers of newspapers and pamphlets were required to register with the authorities, and page sizes were regulated by graduated rates of taxation. Then, in 1789, the government of the younger Pitt added another halfpenny to the stamp and another sixpence to the advertisement duty, at the same time making it illegal to lend or hire out newspapers at a reduced charge. As intended, these imposts put the price of newspapers beyond the reach of potential readers and particularly those members of the urban artisan classes whose mounting enthusiasm for political news gave cause for disquiet. Combined with difficulties of production and distribution, statutory and judicial censorship – including prosecutions for seditious, criminal, and blasphemous libel – had an inhibiting effect. As Arthur Aspinall has enumerated:

> The backwardness of communications, the illiteracy of the population, Post Office restrictions, the hostile attitude of the governing class, Sabbataria-

nism and heavy taxation, were ... important factors which tended to limit the sale of English newspapers.[1]

All the same, as Post Office ledgers attest, the press continued to achieve a slow but steady growth. Though encumbered, it was not shackled. The notorious Wilkes affair proves as much. It was sparked in 1763 by the unsuccessful prosecution of the member for Aylesbury, whose allegedly 'seditious and treasonable paper, the *North Briton*', was an anti-ministerial riposte to the *Briton*, edited by Smollett, who had himself suffered imprisonment for libel. Quickly enveloped in a wider agitation, the case raised fundamental issues about press freedom that soon echoed from the perimeters of the English-speaking world. The struggle for American independence, interpreted as a reasoned attempt to recover the liberties of freeborn Englishmen, gave fresh impetus and new slogans. At home as in the colonies, the representation of opinion both in Parliament and in print was jointly called into question. The debate, vigorous and sometimes vociferous, portended a more far-reaching revolution than the one that immediately occurred.

Betraying some of the worst instincts of the period, the dispute also exercised some of the best minds, acutely aware of its wider implications. In the right hands, newspapers might promote enlightenment and thereby render citizens more fit to maintain truly representative institutions; in the wrong hands, however, they might be the handmaidens of venality and servility. Who was to determine the proper auspices, and what were to be the safeguards? On this ground, political loyalties jostled with philosophical arguments. Whig or Tory spokesmen might appreciate the claims of their own publicists for free expression, but staunchly resisted any extension of the principle to newspapers in the opposing camp. Within each political phalanx, there were those who deemed the press an unsuitable instrument for popular education, along with others who disclaimed popular education as an objective. Fear of the mob, intensified by the example of revolutionary France, compounded the difficulty. Newspapers were regarded as vehicles of turbulence, which came to be equated with Jacobinism. It was not coincidental that the stamp duty was increased in 1776, 1789, and again in 1797, when it was fixed at 3½ d. In each of those years, the old order was girding itself to resist pressures from outside and below.

While most of his contemporaries halted or retreated, Jeremy Bentham remained deeply concerned with the uses and abuses of press power. As always, his ideas, however idiosyncratic, help to define the challenge as it evolved. In the autumn of 1776, for example, he drafted a 'Memorial' on the subject of establishing a newspaper (or possibly '*two* papers, an every-other-day and a daily') which, in fact if not in name, would serve ministerial

[1] Arthur Aspinall, *Politics and the Press, 1780–1850* (London, 1949; repr. New York, 1974), p. 7; Robert K. Webb, *The British Working Class Reader* (London, 1955), pp. 32–35.

interests. According to this scheme, elaborated in detail, 'the great mischief that is done by the Incendiary Newspapers' could be counteracted by this proposed organ, boasting 'the advantages of early & authentic intelligence' at a price of 'less than *two pence-halfpenny*'. As he put the case with proto-Harmsworthian logic, 'it would appear to be a *hazardous* undertaking indeed, but not demonstrably a *losing* one', for 'the price of the Advertisements might be raised a trifle, on pretence of the advantage to be derived from so extensive a circulation as might be expected in consequence of the abatement' in the price per copy. To confound critics, whose charges were easily anticipated, the editor was directed to furnish 'conspicuous proof of impartiality' by a willingness 'to insert any antiministerial *letters* that might be offered as well as ministerial' ones. 'Letters', after all, 'appear upon the face of them to contain nothing more than the sentiments of some unknown and nameless writer.' Paragraphs, however, were quite another matter, in that they could be taken to represent 'the sentiments and assertions of the Manager who is a politician and a patriot by profession, whose words are oracles, and who preaches as it were *ex cathedra* to the gaping multitude'.

Except as a commentary on Bentham's thought at this time, the 'plan' he devised is less remarkable than the moral argument with which he sought to justify it. 'The business of conducting News-papers may be considered as a very important branch of national Education,' he insisted. For that reason, it required careful administration. 'It can not be taken *out* of *improper* hands: neither is it to be wished that it could be taken out of such as a Minister should think improper.' Nevertheless, 'for the benefit of the state', a minister 'should have it in his power . . . to put it into hands that he thinks proper'. While it was 'by no means to be wished' that a statesman should be in a position to suppress what 'to him seems evil', he should possess the means to set before the public what 'to him seems good'. Thereby men would be able to 'read & judge'.

Bentham's 'Memorial', and especially the practical and philosophical conditions with which it was hedged, typified the eighteenth-century intellectual outlook. The fundamental question was how to reconcile a growing faith in rationalism with a traditional concept of responsibility. The scheme he propounded in 1776 invites comparison with his later writings, published and private, marking a shift to theories of democratic control. In *The Liberty of the Press and Public Discussion* (1821), he extolled 'that liberty which, under the name of *the liberty of the Press*, operates as a check upon the conduct of the ruling few'; in his *Constitutional Code* (1830), 'Rule I' was 'maximise publicity'. Nowhere did he deal more systematically with the relationship between the press and parliamentary government than in his 'Prospectus of the *Universalist*', drawn up in February and March 1831. Yet another of those ingenious Benthamite blueprints that never proceeded further than the drawing-board, it affords some striking contrasts with the 'Memorial' he had produced fifty-five years earlier.

With greater specificity, including a name, this 'Prospectus of a Morning Daily Paper' was intended to secure 'the application . . . of . . . the all-ruling principle – the greatest happiness principle' of Utilitarianism by the agency of a journal that was to be 'Impartial; in so far as it can be so consistently with that principle'. Designed to appeal across class lines, the *Universalist* was further expected to strike a balance in its coverage between 'Tories and Whigs (using these as terms of distinction only not of reproach)'. Bentham was impressed by the high level of journalistic achievement on the Continent, where specialists wrote with an authority supposedly derived from their unimpeded access to sources.

In France, though the *production* of articles *on any given* subject in the field of politics is confided to an individual, yet the sentiments to be advocated are always the result of the *collected* opinions of the managers. Hence little is seen of that *capricious* shifting which is so frequently exhibited in England and which has destroyed confidence in all the newspapers of the day.

Ideally, not only 'Editorial articles' should 'possess this character'; in his model

a far greater liberty of discussion would be allowed to hostile opinion than has place in any existing newspaper. The strictest impartiality would be observed as to the insertion of well-written communications from men of all political opinions, and the proposed newspaper would become a register of the current notions of the day on all the great topics of public interest.

Consequently, he predicted,

Parliamentary Debates would become a subject of special attention; and [as] their influence as a means of creating a sound public opinion is eminently great, it would be an object of particular care to unravel and expose the fallacies one after another which might obtain in the Right Honourable and Honourable Houses. The paper would thus become a Mirror in which constituents might *study* 'the true effigies' of their representatives, and it would exercise far more than any of its rivals an habitual check on evil, and hold out a more constant encouragement to good on the part of such representatives.[1]

Adumbrating themes that were to be debated long beyond his lifetime, Bentham's 'Prospectus' of 1831 was more a repudiation than a reformulation of ideas expressed in his 'Memorial' of 1776. Despite the sophistication and subtlety with which he had couched his earlier proposals, he had stood closer to Smollett than to Wilkes, sharing Dr Johnson's determination to ensure 'that the Whig dogs shall not have the best of it'. By 1831, he was prepared to license hounds of any political breed, provided they ran in the right direction. The *Universalist* was conceived as the auxiliary to a programme, whereas its

[1] Bentham Papers, Box 149 (dated with the assistance of Professor J. H. Burns).

predecessor was, to all intents and purposes, devised as a mouthpiece for the administration. To comprehend the progression of his thought and the significance that attached to it, one must take account of the extent to which the form and status of the press had evolved over the intervening decades.

* * *

Had the first of Bentham's schemes been implemented, an eighteenth newspaper would have been added to the seventeen published in London in 1777: seven appearing daily and ten at various intervals through the week. The following year, they were joined by the first regularly published Sunday paper. In 1783, when Pitt formed his government, the number of London dailies had risen to nine; in 1795, the count was fourteen, with a corresponding increase in journals published once, twice, or three times weekly.

Yet, amid plenty, there was scarcity. By any reckoning, the individual and aggregate circulations were (again to quote Aspinall) 'ridiculously small' in 1783, when the average sale was one copy daily for every 300 inhabitants, or (to quote A. P. Wadsworth) 'astonishingly small' in 1794, when one publisher estimated that 'the average sale of London Morning Newspapers may be fairly taken at 1,500 per day'.[1] More significantly, at least for present purposes, the vast majority of these newspapers were largely or wholly devoted to advertisements and therefore might more appropriately be classified as advertising sheets. Then, as now, advertisements could impart useful information, but of a sort which cannot be dignified as 'news'. The press of the late eighteenth century was more akin to its forebears than to its heirs. That may be said not only of the disordered array of journals that perished before the turn of the century, but also of those few that negotiated the transition to the next.

Among the short-lived ventures of the 1790s, there were several that enjoyed the countenance – usually a euphemism for Treasury patronage – of the Pitt administration. With encouragement from Edmund Burke and 'under the immediate sanction of Mr Pitt', the *True Briton* and the *Sun* were launched simultaneously in 1792. Evidence of regular payments from secret service funds lends credence to William Cobbett's assertion that both were, 'in some sort, the property of the ministers. They were, at any rate, as absolutely at their command as the *Moniteur* is at the command of Bonaparte.' Cobbett, whose prickliness earned him the sobriquet 'Peter Porcupine', was well placed to judge: then a resolute Tory, he was himself the recipient of Treasury support to the tune of £3,000 for the *Porcupine*, a daily that began in 1800 and quickly folded. The *True Briton* and the *Sun* proved relatively better value: the former lingered until 1805, when its imprudent attacks on official policy

---

[1] Aspinall, p. 7; A. P. Wadsworth, *Newspaper Circulations, 1800–1954* (Manchester, 1955). p. 7.

had cost it circulation and its subsidy; the latter was offered for sale in 1819 by its debt-ridden management, and, refused by Lord Liverpool, spent the next half-century on the Whig or Liberal side.

In the form of advertisements, commissions, pamphlet orders, personal allowances, and direct bounties, the Pitt government endowed its press supporters on a Walpolean scale. Calculating on the basis of extant secret service accounts, which cannot be assumed to reveal the full extent of these transactions, Aspinall was able to conclude

> that the Government's expenditure on the Press during the early years of the French Revolution was not far short of £5,000 a year.... These sums were not extravagantly large, and they were very much less than the subsidies paid to Irish newspapers. It should, however, be remembered that the expense of conducting a newspaper was still generally moderate, and the capital employed small.

It should be further remembered, as Aspinall's exhaustive research makes clear, that the dispensation of public funds was a waning, although persistent, source of newspaper investment. Without traversing the same ground which he covered, one may concentrate on particular cases that illustrate the transition from official control (as sanctioned by Bentham's 'Memorial' of 1776) to selective partisanship (as prescribed by his 'Prospectus' of 1831).

In retrospect, certain trends may be discerned. Government stipends, bestowed and received without shame, constituted one among three major forms of sustenance for a burgeoning press. The others were commercial capital, usually collected by syndicates in the City, and subscriptions from politicians who stood either in opposition to the government or at its fringes. Eventually, when the practice of Treasury control was abandoned as impracticable and disreputable as well, independent commercial and political interests vied among themselves. Because they shared many of the same goals and methods, their rivalry was obscured by a common rhetoric that lost conviction during the course of the nineteenth century. Thereafter commercial interests predominated, subsuming government and opposition influences alike.

The catalogue that follows is far from comprehensive, but sufficient to point out the direction that the subsequent analysis will take. Some of the enterprises to be considered here were atypical in their durability, but typical in the problems they confronted. Tentatively and sometimes inadvertently, each signalled a break with past traditions and an acceptance of new incentives.

Unlike the *True Briton*, the *Sun*, and a plethora of periodicals that adhered to the same basic model, the properties with which we shall deal here were established with commercial objectives firmly in mind. Some went so far as to brandish this fact in their mastheads: the *Morning Chronicle*, leading the pack, was founded in 1769 as the *Morning Chronicle and London Advertiser*; the *Morning Post*, following three years later, appended the *Cheap Daily Advertiser* to its title; the *World*, set on its axis in 1787, was properly known through the better part of its inaugural year as the *World and Fashionable Advertiser*. In most instances, the purpose was less explicit, but equally manifest. Financed and directed by combinations of businessmen, a high proportion of whom were printers or booksellers, these newspapers were expected to return a profit, partly calculated in terms of the free advertising space they would afford to their proprietors' assorted wares. Representing a diversification of shareholdings on the part of relatively small entrepreneurs, who pooled their resources in the hope of greater pecuniary gain, they originated as adjuncts to publishing houses or other mercantile establishments. More often than not, however, they proved a drain on the resources of their backers. In this specific sense, they may be seen as a microcosm of the conglomerates that exist today.

With capital from no fewer than twenty individuals, William Woodfall began the *Morning Chronicle*. A member of a family connected with printing and publishing, he edited this paper, which he produced on his own presses. 'Memory Woodfall', as he was known by virtue of his legendary retentive powers, embraced Whig causes, yet insisted that the *Chronicle* 'was not set on foot so much to promote certain political principles, as to accomplish commercial ends'.[1] In both respects, it failed. Through one of its many proprietors, it was receiving infusions of Treasury money by 1788, the year before Woodfall and his partners sold the foundering property to James Perry, who headed another syndicate that ranged in membership from the 11th Duke of Norfolk to John Bellamy, the vintner and victualler to the House of Commons. Pitt, on his deathbed, was said to have craved a Bellamy pork pie; he could not have relished, however, the pungent Whig flavour of the *Morning Chronicle*. Hazlitt, always sparing with his praise, recorded that Perry 'held the office of Editor for nearly forty years; and he held firm to his party and his principles all that time, – a long term for political honesty and integrity to last!'[2] Until his death in 1821, the paper ranked pre-eminent among opposition journals and, by some estimates, among all journals including *The Times*. Challenged by the latter, its fortunes dipped during the 1820s; but it was restored to fiscal and political vitality under the proprietorship of Sir John Easthope in the years from 1834 to 1847. To that phase we shall return.

The Times, denounced by Perry as 'the overweening tyrant of Printing House Square', got started in 1771, when the first John Walter decided to expand his printing works on that site.[3] Readily characterized by the

[1] Aspinall, p. 69; James Grant, *The Newspaper Press*, I (London, 1871), 257; T. H. S. Escott, *Masters of English Journalism* (London, 1911), pp. 153–55.
[2] 'The Periodical Press,' *Edinburgh Review*, xxxviii (May 1823), 361.
[3] *The History of The Times*, I (London, 1935), introduction and chs. I-X, *passim*; Francis Williams, *Dangerous Estate* (London, 1957), pp. 71–73; Aspinall, pp. 74–78.

resentments it subsequently evoked – Hazlitt accused it of invariably allying itself 'on the side of the big battalions', and Carlyle fulminated against 'the emphatic, big-voiced, always influential, and often strongly unreasonable, *Times*' – the paper was, in fact, slow to rise to a position of authority. From the first, it distinguished itself by its full and prompt coverage of foreign news, on which the government no less than the public relied. Yet, as dictated by commercial calculations, its political line was initially independent and thus implicitly anti-ministerial. For reasons that appear to have been more opportunistic than ideological, a change of policy occurred during the Regency crisis of 1788. Pitt, anticipating a challenge from the Prince of Wales and his Whig entourage, was eager to consolidate his powers. Naturally, he looked to the press, bartering favours for support.

The previous year, having failed in his bid to secure the lucrative printing contract for the Stationery Office, Walter was appointed printer to the Customs Office. He was therefore, so to speak, already on the administration's payroll when Pitt's 'Press managers' approached him with an offer of 'contradiction and suppression fees', augmented by a modest retainer 'to support Measures of Government'. From then until 1802, as the official history of that newspaper cautiously concedes, these regular payments, 'or some part of them, assisted the revenues of *The Times*, at least when the income from advertisements, puffs and sales of copies was found insufficient'. In addition, for a decade after 1789, Walter was the recipient of an annual allowance of £300 'in reward for the politics' which his paper espoused. This arrangement failed to afford him legal immunity when, carried away by what he called his 'Zeal & Duty to the Sovereign & his Ministers', he published certain offensive paragraphs about the unfilial machinations of George III's sons. For this transgression, he was fined and sentenced to imprisonment at Newgate ('a receptacle for felons'), where he suffered nearly sixteen months of 'shameful Neglect'. He owed his eventual release not to his ministerial benefactors, but to an intervention on the part of the Prince of Wales, from whom he could have expected little mercy. Walter nevertheless continued as a willing pensioner of the Treasury, at whose instigation he consistently tarred Whiggism with a Jacobin brush. The connection ceased at the end of the century, ostensibly on the grounds that *The Times* had libelled the House of Commons, but more certainly because its support had become increasingly erratic. In any case, that support was not worth the affront it gave to the proprietors of competing journals.

During Walter's incarceration, and more formally after 1795, he delegated responsibility to his eldest son, William, who encountered his own difficulties first with Pitt and then with Lord Addington, Pitt's successor. In 1802, John Walter II succeeded his 'bookish' brother as chief proprietor. Ignoring his father's advice and the wishes of the minority shareholders, he nurtured *The Times* to the prejudice of other operations at Printing House Square, with the result that he gradually 'changed a dying news-sheet into a flourishing newspaper'. Although his tempered preference for the Addingtonites over the Pittites lost him the Customs Office account in 1805, his political instincts usually worked to the paper's advantage. In the unedifying squabble in 1820 over George IV's divorce, for example, *The Times* chivalrously defended the conjugal rights of Queen Caroline. 'I have no doubt W[alter] really thinks he is doing right,' reflected Henry Crabb Robinson, who served him as an editor of sorts, 'but he is not aware perhaps how much he is influenced in the line he is pursuing by finding that since the trial the sale of the paper has risen from 7 to more than 15,000.'[1] By then, as Walter had the effrontery to recall in a leading article (19 June 1819), he had long since cast the Addingtonites 'adrift', and had taken sides with Canning in the latter's wrangles with Lord Liverpool's government.

It proved neither easy nor efficacious for John Walter II to combine the obligations of the chief proprietorship with the daily routines of the managing editorship. The editors whom he and his father had employed, including Robinson and the ultra-Tory Dr John Stoddart, could be better described as principal writers. In 1817, three years after the installation of steam-powered presses, Thomas Barnes was designated editor. Within a short time, he was invested with full jurisdiction over the contents of the paper. A self-effacing individual, who had no stake in the company until shares were assigned to him in 1819 – when total assets were valued at approximately £45,000 – Barnes revelled in anonymity. 'Power he loved,' the official historians of *The Times* (themselves, true to his tradition, unidentified) wrote, 'but it was sweeter to him for its secrecy.' Under his stewardship, which ended with his death in 1841, *The Times* spoke with a resonance that secured its reputation as 'the Thunderer'. By stages, Walter reduced his holding. With the paper safely entrusted to Barnes, he was released to enjoy the pleasures of country life and, in due course, to embark on his own political career.

While *The Times* prospered by trailing the soiled petticoats of Queen Caroline, the *Morning Post* opposed her, and its offices were stormed by the vengeful London mob. Founded in 1772, that paper had not always shown such strong ministerial proclivities. Indeed its early politics, so far as it had any, were mildly Whig, and it had greeted the French Revolution with relative cordiality. That, however, was against the better judgment of the early proprietors, among whom there were at least two auctioneers, a printer, a horse-dealer, and a reprobate cleric. They conceived of the journal chiefly as an advertising forum, indiscriminately at the disposal not only of 'ladies of the town', but also of William Wilberforce, who launched his Abolition campaign with a paid announcement in its columns.

Divided in their own party loyalties, the owners had all the more reason to eschew political comment or, when that proved impossible, to curb it. The

[1] Quoted in Harold Herd, *March of Journalism* (London, 1952), pp. 132–33.

Rev Henry Bate, who is deduced to have followed John Bell as editor, was in turn unshipped in 1781, when he was sentenced to a year's imprisonment for having libelled the Duke of Richmond. Adding Dudley to his name, in honour of an uncle whose estate he inherited, he founded the *Morning Herald* in reprisal. Two years later, an active interest was acquired by John Benjafield who, lacking an uncle's bequest, received reimbursement from secret service funds. In spite of its Treasury connections, the paper remained equivocal in its allegiances, dealing out gratification and consternation to Whigs and Tories by turns. In 1786, Benjafield and Richard Tattersall, the horse-dealer, jointly negotiated an agreement with their fellow proprietors, who accepted an annual fee of £1,370 in return for a seven-year lease on the dilapidated property: Benjafield, a young military man of uncertain assets, took charge of editorial content; Tattersall saw to business affairs. This arrangement was disrupted in December 1788, when the *Morning Post* divulged intimate details about the Prince of Wales's private life and, when rebuked, threatened to divulge more. With little consideration for his erstwhile patrons at the Treasury, Benjafield was easily persuaded to transfer his half of the lease to Louis Weltje, *maître d'hôtel* at Carlton House, the Prince of Wales's headquarters. Weltje had proffered an extravagant sum, apparently with his royal master's connivance. For the next twenty years Benjafield was continually engaged in litigation to collect his profit and to clear his name of the improprieties that attached to this transaction.

Saddled with a new co-lessee, Tattersall was involved more deeply and directly in politics, from which he instinctively recoiled. The literary side of the paper was now superintended by John Taylor, identified by the official historian of the *Morning Post* as 'the nominee of the Prince of Wales ... when that inestimable person was flirting with Whig politicians'.[1] Yet despite Taylor's dutiful attacks on Warren Hastings and mocking references to 'Prince Pitt', he was no conventional Whig propagandist. 'If Taylor had any personal political opinions, they were rather orthodox than original', it has been argued, and his subsequent proprietorship of the *Sun*, 'a violent Tory paper', may be seen to support that view. Nevertheless, it is likely that Taylor's proclivities were observed with apprehension at Carlton House. According to his own bemused recollection, he had been editor for two years when, in 1790, the proprietor – 'a rude, vulgar upstart' who answers to Tattersall's description – dismissed him on the grounds 'that the paper was wholly confined to politics, and had none of those little *antidotes* which had before diverted the readers'.[2] Justified or not, the complaint was revealing. The leaseholders were primarily concerned with profits, not policies.

As the seven-year lease neared its expiration, the Whig chieftains weighed

[1] Wilfrid Hindle, *The Morning Post, 1772–1937* (London, 1937), p. 58; Aspinall, pp. 71–72, 274–80.
[2] John Taylor, *Records of My Life* (London, 1832), I, 270.

various alternatives by which they might perpetuate their control. The obvious scheme was for them to buy out several of the lesser shareholders. Detailed lists and balance sheets were drawn up, but to no purpose. In the event, Tattersall was relieved of his burden by Daniel Stuart, who purchased a predominant interest for a mere £600. By 1795, his ownership was complete. Boasting impeccable Whig credentials, Stuart was the brother of Peter Stuart, who maintained the *Oracle* with a subsidy from the Prince of Wales, and also the brother-in-law of Sir James Mackintosh, the eminent Whig theorist. Yet he, like so many representatives of his tradition, asserted his patriotism during these tumultuous years by affirming his fidelity to established institutions. Estranged from Charles James Fox and other former companions, he swam with the ministerial tide and carried the *Morning Post* in his wake. After eight years, he sold the paper for £25,000 having converted it 'from an irresponsible Whig sheet into a moderate and highly responsible Tory journal. In so doing, he had increased its value by more than 400 percent.' Like Samuel Taylor Coleridge, its most distinguished contributor, the *Morning Post* had come to repent of its earlier pro-French effusions and anti-Tory tirades. Although it still occasionally gibed at Pitt for the stamp duty he had levied, its sharpest barbs were directed at Fox and the opposition Whigs. By the turn of century, the paper had taken 'its accepted place ... in reaction's ranks', where it remained ensconced until its demise in 1937. The inveterate foe of reform movements and the intrepid champion of lost causes, most of which deserved to be lost, it combined political conservatism with social snobbery. Eventually dubbed 'the fawning *Post*' by *Punch*, it was derided by Cobden in 1839 as 'the journal of London idleness'.[1] As such, its West End readership was assured.

Other newspaper ventures of these decades conformed to the same general pattern, regardless of the auspices under which they began. To catalogue them all would be a wearisome and redundant process. Several, however, merit brief attention either because they qualify as variations on the theme or because they were to achieve further significance in a later period.

The founding of the *Morning Herald* in 1780 has already been mentioned. Born out of a quarrel between the Rev Henry Bate Dudley and the managers of the *Morning Post*, it survived until 1869, invariably taking a stand contrary to that of its parent publication, with which it competed for circulation and influence: through the 1790s, when the *Morning Post* tended to adhere to the Whigs, its offshoot was a client of the Treasury; afterwards, when the *Morning Post* discovered the virtues of Toryism, the *Morning Chronicle* embraced the principles of progress which, under successive proprietorships, became increasingly liberal. In its inception and its impetus, it resembled the less successful *New Times*, which Dr Stoddart started in 1817, when he and his tendentious Tory doctrines were evicted from Printing House Square. A latter-day Sacheverell, Stoddart was immortalized as 'Dr Slop' by Hazlitt, his brother-in-

---

[1] Quoted in John Morley, *The Life of Richard Cobden* (London, 1881), I, 155.

law, who portrayed him as 'no flincher, no trimmer', but 'a violent partisan, blind to the blots in his own cause; and, by this means, he often opens the eyes of others to them'.[1] His rigidity doomed him to frustration, and he had to be rescued from the brink of bankruptcy in 1826 by his political mentors, who fitted him out with a knighthood and dispatched him to a judicial post in Malta. Whereas the *New Times* failed to eclipse the 'old' *Times* (in 1821, midway through its existence, it sold 2,700 copies as compared to *The Times*'s average sale of 7,000), the dextrous *Morning Herald* outdistanced the *Morning Post* (selling more than double the latter's run of a thousand copies in 1801). Yet sales alone did not confer prestige. The management of the *Morning Herald* assiduously traced the anonymous principal writers of *The Times*, whom they enticed with 'offers of extra-liberal remuneration ... to quit Printing House Square and become co-workers in Shoe Lane'. James Grant knew several fellow journalists who succumbed to temptation, but 'while their articles had produced a marked effect when they appeared in *The Times*, they produced none whatever when published in the *Morning Herald*'. All the same, the *Herald* had proved that pique could pay.

Love paid less well, at least in the case of Captain Edward Topham, who sank a considerable amount of his private fortune into the begetting of the *World* in 1787. If the story is to be believed, Topham's intention was to applaud in the daily press the thespian graces of a lady friend, whose attractions were on public view in Drury Lane.[2] Treasury agents, for more dignified reasons, were soon helping to sustain the effort with annual payments of £600. Unfortunately, Topham found them more fickle than the actress. The founding of the *Sun* as an official administration organ in 1792 moved him to protest to Pitt that he had been 'ill-used'. To its new rival, the *World* forfeited not only revenue and authority, but also the services of its editor. His pleas unheeded, Topham abandoned his love-child two years later.

The *Observer* must be noted, perhaps less for what it was than for what it became. Set up in 1791 by members of the Bourne family, it appeared on Sundays in defiance of sabbatarian practice. Within three years, it could claim a weekly circulation of 2,000 copies and the promise of a satisfactory profit. Its operation, however, required greater resources than those available to the Bourne brothers, who juggled it among themselves before offering its assets to the government. W. H. Bourne, the eldest, considered that preferable to accepting a bid from a London syndicate that proposed to reconstitute the property as 'a tri-weekly democratic evening paper', whose policies would have been abhorrent. Without acceding to Bourne's request, the ministry apparently agreed to assist in keeping the *Observer* afloat and, in the bargain, steadfastly Tory. As evidence of a continuing 'close connexion with the

[1] 'The Periodical Press,' *Edinburgh Review*, xxxviii (May 1823), 365–67; *History of The Times*, I, 159–64; Aspinall, pp. 98–99; Grant, II, 36–37.

[2] Aspinall, 72–74; Stanley Morison, *John Bell* (Cambridge, 1930), p. 8.

Treasury', Aspinall has cited the fact that, in 1817, complimentary copies of the paper 'were extensively circulated in Ireland as well as in Great Britain'. Early in Victoria's reign, the *Observer* was the recipient of Whig funds and accordingly became 'a kind of accredited organ' of the Melbourne administration. But James Grant, himself 'connected with the *Observer*', insisted that its managers 'possessed so much tact' that they could obtain 'early and correct Government information' from whichever party was in power.[1]

The *Courier* was yet another product of the journalistic ferment during the years of the French Revolution.[2] Regarded as sympathetic to the catchwords of 1789 and indeed rumoured to owe its inspiration to Talleyrand, it was established in 1792 by a twenty-four member consortium. Six years later, suspicions of French influence seemed to be confirmed when this evening paper risked a libel action to denounce the mistreatment of enemy prisoners-of-war at Liverpool. Pilloried by the *Anti-Jacobin* as 'sedition's evening host', the *Courier* enjoyed a vast daily sale which sometimes exceeded 8,000 copies. 'Even *The Times* itself was for several years below the *Courier* in circulation,' Grant noted in disbelief. As late as 1801, when Pitt temporarily stepped aside, the *Courier* retained sufficient audacity to rejoice. Soon thereafter, it came under the control of Daniel Stuart, who had shown his mettle at the *Morning Post*. Immediately the paper became more muted in its pacifism and more susceptible to Treasury influence. When the Whigs entered office in 1806, the *Courier* greeted them with unpredictable restraint: 'The public is our party,' it averred on 1 February, 'and it is the most honourable one as well as the best paymaster.' Adept at satisfying the ravenous public appetite for war news, its circulation was unimpaired by these proprietorial configurations, and it could afford to profess such lofty sentiments. Nevertheless, its Tory affiliation was soon enough revealed.

Stuart divided his holding in the *Courier* with T. G. Street who, probably without his partner's knowledge, was in the steady employ of the Treasury. As Stuart himself wrote in self-exculpation, although 'I was abused in the papers as the conductor of the *Courier*, the merit ... wholly belonged to Mr Street', who brooked no interference. It was on Street's initiative that the paper repudiated its former loyalties with such vengeance: in a matter of weeks during the autumn of 1809, it had ceased to be 'Canning's *Courier*' (as Thomas Greville resentfully called it) and instead became the purveyor of 'outrageous abuse' that filled Canning with 'indignation and disgust'. In 1817, Street relinquished his editorial chair to William Mudford, then embarking on a long career in Tory journalism. As co-proprietor, however, he ensured that the paper would continue to dog Canning. He faded from the picture in the late 1820s, having survived his antagonist. By then the paper, once an adulator of Bonaparte,

[1] Grant, III (London, 1873?), 34; Aspinall, pp. 83–85.
[2] Grant, I, 346 ff.; Alexander Andrews, *The History of British Journalism* (London, 1859), II, 63–64, 77; Norman Gash, *Sir Robert Peel* (London, 1972), p. 5.

had found its new hero in the Duke of Wellington. With Mudford's appointment, Stuart had begun a gradual withdrawal which was complete by 1822. In the next decade, the paper changed its colours from a deep-dyed Toryism to a pale Whiggism, then back again as it staggered to extinction.

The *Globe* was another evening paper with an equally chequered history. Although it came to be considered 'primarily an organ of opinion rather than a commercial undertaking',[1] it was founded in 1803 as a trade journal for booksellers, who craved more prominent display for their advertisements. (The *British Press* made a simultaneous debut under the same management.) Put down by Fox Bourne as 'respectable but unimportant', the *Globe* slowly awakened to political controversy, which it approached warily and from a Whig perspective. Its partisan links were reinforced in 1823, when it merged with the *Traveller*, a similar, but more successful, enterprise. Owned by Colonel Robert Torrens and edited by Walter Coulson, a disciple of Bentham, the *Traveller* had been – and the combined *Globe and Traveller* became – a forum for the political economists. In the course of the next few years, Torrens added to his collection of periodicals the *Statesman*, the *True Briton*, the *Evening Chronicle*, the *Argus*, and, intellectually the most impressive, the *Athenaeum*. More vigorously and consistently than its stable-mates, however, the revivified *Globe* gave expression to advanced Whig views. In fact, those views were often so advanced that they nettled the party leaders who, in the 1830s, denied its editors the rewards to which they felt themselves entitled.

During Lord Grey's reform ministry of 1830–34, the *Globe* was more skilful than any other of the so-called ministerial papers in eluding the clutches of Lord Brougham who, as an old hand at journalism, assumed responsibility for press relations along with the more onerous duties of the lord chancellorship. Thereafter, it resisted dictation from Melbourne, who fumed at its insubordination. Unable to count on its unflinching support, he and his colleagues were drawn involuntarily into controversies which it manufactured. Late in 1835, for example, the *Globe* published a scathing review of Disraeli's *Vindication of the English Constitution*. The affronted author, thinly veiled as 'Runnymede', addressed a series of letters to Whig statesmen in *The Times*, causing (by his own estimation) 'a great sensation' by being 'the first individual who has silenced the press with its own weapons'. The embarrassment was greater to the politicians than to the paper. In the next decade, Lord John Russell and Lord Palmerston played 'at battledore and shuttlecock' with the *Globe*'s editorial policy, and Palmerston emerged as victor. Contrary to his persistent denials, he contributed directly to its columns and to the pockets of its editors. In 1866, the year after his death, the *Globe* passed to Tory hands.[2]

[1] H. A. Taylor, *Robert Donald* (London, 1934), pp. 199–200; H. R. Fox Bourne, *English Newspapers* (London, 1887), II, 27–29; Grant, II, 71–73; Aspinall, pp. 285, 316–17.

[2] Disraeli's letter to his sister is quoted in Lucy, *Memories of Eight Parliaments*, p. 92. Greville described the rivalry between Palmerston and Russell in his diary entry for 9 October 1840, *The Greville Memoirs* (eds. Lytton Strachey and Roger Fulford; London, 1938), IV, 313–14. *Also see*

That Brougham and his deputy, Sir Denis Le Marchant, could have presumed to direct the editorial policies of *The Times*, *Morning Chronicle*, *Globe*, *Sun*, and *Courier*, among lesser publications,[1] testifies *prima facie* to a resurgence in Whig journalism. But perhaps the phenomenon may be perceived more accurately as the persistence of ministerial journalism, which was then entering its terminal phase. The Tories, while clinging to office, had lost popular support and political momentum. By contrast, the Whigs had recovered their respectability and were building parliamentary strength, which could be expected to augment their resources for patronage. Consequently, it made commercial sense to clamber aboard their bandwagon. The self-serving attitude of *The Times* should come as no surprise: even when it had postured as being above party, it was seldom above government. 'It floats with the tide; it sails with the stream,' Hazlitt observed in 1823. Eight years later, Cobbett echoed Hazlitt's verdict and imputed the same characteristic to the *Courier*, 'the fast partisan of every successive minister'.[2] With varying degrees of effort and grace, other newspapers likewise prepared for the Whig revival and, when it came, to attune themselves to it. Those already pledged to the cause grew more assertive; those arrayed against it, pursuing outdated vendettas against Jacobinism or the Prince Regent, grew fewer and more quixotic.

Several attempts were made on behalf of an embattled Toryism to reverse this process. The *New Times*, stricken by Stoddart's departure, was resuscitated as the *Morning Journal*, tottering for another three years before it finally fell. In 1827, Charles Baldwin came to the rescue of Wellington and Sir Robert Peel by starting the *Standard*, an evening daily under the editorship of Stanley Lees Giffard. A wealthy publisher, Baldwin was the proprietor of the *St James's Chronicle*, which had prospered since 1761 as a thrice-weekly journal. In the long run, as we shall see, the *Standard* was to rank as a bulwark of Tory journalism; in the short run, however, its implacability on the vexing issue of Catholic emancipation elicited more censure than gratitude from the politicians whom it was intended to serve. Small wonder that, when he was again solicited four years later, Baldwin declined to subscribe the capital for a Tory morning newspaper.[3]

A less durable property, lasting a shade over six months, nevertheless qualifies for closer scrutiny at this point. John Murray, the respected publisher of the *Quarterly Review*, had less responsibly published pamphlets written by Disraeli in order to promote the South American mining companies in which

---

Blake, *Disraeli*, pp. 128–30; Morley, *Cobden*, I, 113; *History of The Times*, I, 438–40; and H. E. Maxwell, *Life and Letters of George William Frederick, Fourth Earl of Clarendon* (London, 1913), I, 213.

[1] Aspinall, p. 237.

[2] 'The Periodical Press,' *Edinburgh Review*, xxxviii (May 1823), 364; *State Trials*, n.s., ii, 810–11 (*Crown v. Cobbett*, 7–8 July 1831).

[3] Grant, II, 101 ff.; Andrews, II, 23–25; Aspinall, pp. 327–28, 335; Gash, *Sir Robert Peel*, pp. 93–94.

they had jointly invested. In 1825, he 'yielded' to his young associate's 'unrelenting excitement and importunity', and agreed to provide half the backing for a new morning paper based on 'sound Constitutional principles'.[1] Disraeli, who committed himself to raise half the remainder (and who defaulted), chose the *Representative* as its name. John Lockhart and, more tangentially, Sir Walter Scott were among those connected with this misguided venture which, after repeated delays, made its pitiable appearance on 25 January 1826. Its format was haphazard, its leaders 'tedious to a degree and intolerably long', and its attempts at humour more derisory than amusing. 'The economic depression no doubt made such a venture hopeless,' Robert Blake has reasoned, 'but it is unlikely that the *Representative* would have been a success even in more propitious circumstances.' Murray, who had aspired to 'put down *The Times*', instead buried £26,000 of his own money. Disraeli, his 'right hand' in stoking this 'new intellectual steam engine', tried his best to forget his part in the affair and to have others do the same. While he was technically correct when he later denied that he had edited the *Representative*, he was less than candid in shrugging off his complicity as a malicious falsehood, propounded by unscrupulous adversaries. Far from subduing his enthusiasm for newspaper exploits, his dismal experience taught him some useful lessons and, as a bonus, yielded grist for his novels. In *Coningsby*, he dipped his pen into vitriol to create the character of Rigby, recognizably modelled on John Wilson Croker, whose 'subterranean journalism' appeared in the *Quarterly Review*. On behalf of the party bosses who had 'bought' him, Rigby wrote 'slashing articles' which – according to Tadpole – 'whispered as the productions of one behind the scenes, and . . . were passed off as genuine coin, and took in great numbers of the lieges, especially in the country'.

Save for Disraeli's participation, the tribulations of the *Representative* would scarcely be worth recounting. Before 1836, when the stamp duty was reduced from fourpence to a penny, newspapers came and went, leaving only their proprietors to mourn them. Thereafter, until total repeal was achieved in 1855, the chances for survival remained slim. 'Hemmed in by high taxes and by the advertising weight and circulation of *The Times*, the newcomer to the daily newspaper field had a desperate fight,' stated A. P. Wadsworth. 'The names on the tombstones,' he reflected, 'remind one of the oddities of a country churchyard – *True Briton, Porcupine, Morning Star, Aurora, Day, British Statesman, Representative, Daily Politician, Constitutional*, and so on.'[2] Countless others lay more deeply interred.

The preceding survey, an exercise in selective exhumation, will serve to indicate the political tendencies of the pre-Victorian press. It was, first and

[1] There is a splendid account in Blake, *Disraeli*, pp. 27–43; further details may be gleaned from Lucy, *Memories of Eight Parliaments*, pp. 84–85; H. M. and M. Swartz, eds., *Disraeli's Reminiscences* (London, 1975), pp. 144–46; Grant, I, 370–72; and Fox Bourne, II, 20–22, where pains are taken to refute the 'absurd statement' that Disraeli had been involved.

[2] Wadsworth, p. 10.

foremost, subservient to ministerial interests. In a minority of cases, where newspapers were established either as avowed opposition organs or as strictly commercial media, the pressure of external events conspired with economic calculations to win them to the side of the 'King's friends', as the party of government traditionally styled itself.During the late 1820s and early '30s, newspapers occasionally tried to anticipate the royal preference, which had come to depend less on personal whim and proportionately more on electoral response. Constitutional procedure, if it may be so dignified, had been modified, but not yet as it applied to the conduct of the press, which was seen and saw itself as a prop to authority. 'The *Courier* had been a Treasury newspaper for more than a quarter of a century,' Aspinall had reminded us; 'it remained such by changing its politics when the Whigs returned to power in November 1830.' Having persisted in its ministerialism during the disjunctive transition from Wellington to Grey, the *Courier* effortlessly swung behind Melbourne four years later.[1]

Secondly, and no less strikingly, daily journalism was the journalism that counted politically, if only by dint of its opportunity for reiteration. As weekly periodicals, the *Observer, John Bull* (from 1820, a strident voice of unreconstructed Toryism), the *Sunday Times* (from 1822, a cautious advocate of tempered Whiggism), and the *Spectator* (introduced in 1828 and later a platform for philosophic radicalism) could never pretend to appreciable authority. Moreover, daily journalism was London-concentrated as well as London-orientated. Despite abortive attempts at Liverpool and Manchester, where 'country weeklies' had long flourished, it was not until 1847, when the *North British Mail* got started in Glasgow, that a successful daily appeared beyond the confines of the metropolis. Since the early eighteenth century, 'most large cities or country towns managed to support one or more' weeklies – 'printers' papers', as Wadsworth has described them – which, on the whole, presented little more than 'a scissors-and-paste epitome of the London papers, with a few local paragraphs' to identify their places of origin.[2] It was from these humble roots that provincial dailies eventually sprouted in profusion. For example, the *Manchester Guardian* (not to be confused with the Whig-sponsored *Guardian*, an evening paper that flickered briefly in 1817), began weekly publication in 1821, went bi-weekly in 1836, and developed into a daily in 1855. Cross-examined in the Manchester magistrate's court in 1839, Jeremiah Garnett, its co-owner and 'joint editor', stated his professional priorities:

Q.   What is your calling in life?
A.   I am a printer.
Q.   Anything else?
A.   I call myself a printer always.

[1] Aspinall, pp. 101, 242.
[2] Wadsworth, pp. 6, 12–15; David Ayerst, *Guardian* (London, 1971), chs. 1–9; Donald Read, *Press and People* (London, 1961), pp. 62–64.

Q. Anything else?

A. I am one of the editors of a newspaper.[1]

Although the early provincial papers recognized the importance of maintaining offices in London, a compliment which the metropolitan press did not reciprocate, their distance from the capital tended to inhibit their political performance and, at any rate, to attenuate their impact.

Thirdly, then as since, there was no direct correlation between a newspaper's political influence and its circulation figures. Nor did the presumption of influence necessarily denote its effectiveness. Arguably *The Times* was more highly prized by its Tory allies in the mid-1830s, when its sales were temporarily on a downgrade, than it had been in the 1790s, when the party was the recipient of virtually unanimous press support. Conversely the *Morning Chronicle* rendered less valuable assistance to the Whig cause in 1837, when its circulation surpassed that of *The Times*, than in 1820–21, when its sale was more modest and its attitude more deferential. And the *Morning Herald* could not have endeared itself to its parliamentary patrons in the 1820s when, within eight years, it quintupled its sales largely by substituting raucous accounts of criminal cases for coverage of Westminster proceedings.[2]

An implicit conflict of interest may be discerned between those who looked to the press for purposes of investment – 'as a mere mercantile speculation', as E. L. Bulwer-Lytton (later the 1st Baron Lytton) contemptuously put it[3] – and those who conceived of it as a political instrument. To a decreasing extent, official assumptions worked to obscure this incompatibility. From the perspective of successive administrations, Whig and Tory, it was neither mandatory nor logical for newspaper concerns to strive for massive profits, for the press was a public trust, and it could not bow to mammon without debasing its quality and betraying its assigned mission. It was considered unseemly, to say the least, that *The Times* should return a dividend of more than £17,000 in 1841 and nearly £30,000 four years later.[4] Newspapers were encouraged to be self-supporting, but not affluent, on the grounds that excess profitability posed an irresistible temptation to irresponsibility. The stamp duty and especially the tax on advertisements were clearly intended to protect the press against itself.

By sales alone, newspapers could be neither self-supporting nor affluent. The eighteenth-century state had therefore assumed an obligation, bequeathed to its nineteenth-century heirs, to supplement the incomes of deserving publications by means of subsidies, variously administered. As time

[1] Quoted in Ayerst, p. 67.

[2] Circulation statistics are drawn from Wadsworth, pp. 7–10; in the case of the *Morning Herald*, there is a discrepancy between his estimate and that (cited here) provided by Ivon Asquith in 'The structure, ownership and control of the press, 1780–1855,' in Boyce, *et al.*, eds., *Newspaper History*, p. 107.

[3] *England and the English* (London, 1833), II, 14.

[4] *History of The Times*, II (London, 1939), 21.

passed, however, these arrangements proved less satisfactory: editors and proprietors came to resent this enforced tutelage; operating expenses steadily rose; and, more to the point, the governing authorities had relatively less to offer by way of financial inducements. Except for the small-scale enterprises – most conspicuously the evening papers whose circulations 'did not advance with the increasing size of the London population'[1] – the daily press was able to attract merchant advertising which, although subject to taxation, was more lucrative (and less compromising) than the paid announcements doled out by government agents. Consonant with a new moral climate, officials were held accountable for the expenditure of public funds and their capacity for dispensing bribes and rewards was thereby significantly reduced, it not wholly eliminated. The administration could still show favouritism in the release of news; but here, too, there developed alternative channels for those who could afford them.

'Perhaps the most important aspect of the history of the press in this period,' one historian has ventured, 'is the decline in the ability of governments to control it.'[2] Prosecutions for libel – particularly criminal libel – fell into desuetude: they were increasingly difficult to implement and, more often than not, backfired. The situation was fraught with paradox. Officials, grudgingly resigned to the fact that they could not command universal or even unwavering support, coveted the endorsement of the better selling, more dynamic journals; yet it was precisely these publications, fortified by their commercial success, that were equipped to withstand official pressures and entreaties. Subsidies, having been revealed as inadequate, demeaned their recipients. Influence accrued to those newspapers that were known to pay their own way, and journalistic independence could be asserted most demonstrably by dissociation from administration policies. For newspaper men, eager to express their personal opinions and, more vaguely, the opinions of the general public, the change was advantageous. For politicians, educated to regard a subservient press as one of the perquisites of office, it came as a rude shock. Nevertheless, their obsession persisted. In the next generation, under new conditions, they devised less formal and more flexible techniques to mine the resources of the political press.

*   *   *

In all likelihood, this transformation in the outlook and methods of the daily newspapers would not have occurred so dramatically in the second quarter of the nineteenth century without stiff competition from two further categories of periodicals to which attention must now be directed. Like the incipient provincial journals, neither the popular Sunday papers nor the illicit

[1] Wadsworth, p. 11.
[2] Asquith, p. 111.

unstamped papers fit comfortably under the rubric of the political press. The former, although duly certified by the stamp (and priced accordingly at 8d. or 10d.), were unsanctified by their contents: despite the professions of moral earnestness that usually introduced them, they specialized in sporting news, lurid crime reports, theatrical criticism and spicy backstage gossip, dollops of light fiction, and political commentary that carried flippancy to the extreme of ribaldry.[1] The unstamped, being clandestine operations, were more consummately impudent and more self-consciously subversive: the makeshift vehicles of disaffection, they reared their hydra-like heads in defiance of the law, catering to a mass readership that lay beyond the pale of the political nation as it was then constituted.

By and large, the Sunday press was as outspokenly radical as the run of unstamped papers, but differed from them in the crucial respect that, by accepting the stamp, it had accommodated itself to the system. Actually produced late on Saturday in order to confound the sabbatarians, these publications nonetheless smacked of blasphemy. They were distributed on the London streets by hawkers, whose boisterous cries and sensational billboards were an outrage to the decency of the Lord's day. There was the further complaint that they distracted men and women from their religious obligations, drawing them from the churches to the public houses, where Sunday journals were extensively read. Such evil could not be contained. 'These papers are also most diffusely circulated, by means of stage coaches, throughout the country,' a Tory critic wrote in 1807.[2] For encouraging atheism and other vile habits, the Sunday press was castigated in Parliament, where futile attempts were made to suppress it. That outrage was itself testimony to the success of the phenomenon.

According to Aspinall, 'eighteen Sunday papers, with a sale of from 1,000 to about 12,000, were published in London in 1812'. Prominent among them was *Bell's Weekly Messenger*, which sold no fewer than 6,000 copies on any given Sunday in 1803, and more than 14,000 copies when it lavishly commemorated the occasion of Nelson's funeral in 1805; in the late 1830s and '40s, after the reduction of the stamp duty, its circulation hovered around 12,000. Founded by the same publisher, *Bell's Life in London* gave a more titillating performance and attracted a more sizeable audience. Preserving its baptismal name through successive proprietorships, it passed to James Perry, who ran it in tandem with the *Morning Chronicle*, and, when Perry died in 1821, to William Innell Clement, who also owned the *Observer* at that time. The last, while it did not scruple to illustrate its murder stories with gruesome woodcuts,

---

[1] These paragraphs are based on the following sources: G. A. Cranfield, *The Press and Society* (London, 1978), pp. 86–87, 110–12, 119; Raymond Williams, 'The Press and Popular Culture,' in Boyce, *et al.*, eds., *Newspaper History*, pp. 48–49; Grant, III, 64–66; Aspinall, pp. 13–16, 305; Wadsworth, pp. 11–13; Morison, *The English Newspaper* (London, 1932), p. 255.

[2] John Bowles, *A Dispassionate Enquiry into the best means of National Safety*, pp. 114–15, quoted in Aspinall, p. 14.

preserved a relative dignity. Consequently, it failed to share in the boom. The *Sunday Times*, less fixed in its editorial and typographical ways, rose to a weekly sale of 20,000 copies in the early 1840s, whereas the *Observer* never exceeded 5,000. More typical of the species were the *Weekly Chronicle*, which entered the Victorian age with a circulation above 50,000, and the *Weekly Dispatch*, which peaked at 60,000 in 1842. In the same year, *Lloyd's Weekly* burst on the scene with an initial sale of 30,000. Restricting its contents to fiction, interlarded with fabricated news reports, it claimed exemption from the stamp and sold for a penny. Before too many weeks, however, it trespassed into the realm of fact. The authorities, ever vigilant, clamped down; the stamp affixed, *Lloyd's Weekly* was forced to adjust its price, with the result that its circulation tumbled by nearly a third before it climbed to 107,000 at mid-century. The *News of the World*, born in 1843, soared directly to the same dizzy heights: 'though radical', Morison has explained, it 'did not intend to antagonise the opposite sentiment. It had to succeed upon the broadest possible basis, upon its low price, and upon its comprehensiveness.' And the *Weekly Times*, launched seven years later, kept pace with it.

All the while, the daily newspapers were desperately struggling to maintain circulations that fluctuated between 1,000 (the figure around which most of the evening ones clustered) and 8,000. With the single exception of *The Times*, they experienced no comparable spurt in sales after 1836. The success of the Sunday press was therefore all the more redoubtable. It was estimated that, in 1829, the aggregate Sunday sale averaged 110,000, nearly four times that of the seven morning journals. Between 1836 and 1855, when the stamp duty was computed at a lower rate, the gap widened. How is one to account for this disparity? Wadsworth has offered two explanations, both eminently logical. Heavy burdens of taxation 'had made newspapers dear, hence it was cheaper to buy a newspaper once a week, even if it were 8d. or 10d., than to pay 7d. a day'. Thus, a Sunday newspaper was regarded as an economical substitute for those who lacked the money – and most probably the leisure time as well – to avail themselves of daily journalism. 'The Sunday newspapers had also learned the circulation trick,' Wadsworth knowingly added. 'They were far from being mainly political and their attention to crime and sport anticipated later publications, and in sheer frankness excelled them.' Decades before the respectable daily press saw fit to borrow these trappings, its managers became aware of a lucrative market from which they were barred by social conventions, lingering judicial prohibitions, and, presumably, the disability of the stamp.

Increasingly viewed as a punitive device and as a check on the formation of a responsible public opinion, the stamp continued to rankle after 1836, when it was reduced from fourpence to a penny. Instead of making the impost more tolerable, this concession was taken to point up its fundamental illogic and to hold forth the promise of further redress. Curiously, it failed to produce benefits on the scale which had been widely anticipated. The savings were largely passed along to the consumer, who could now purchase most dailies at fivepence and many of the provincial weeklies at fourpence; but the net effect on daily sales tended to disappoint. The first year of the penny duty saw an increase of roughly 55 per cent in the sale of stamps to London papers (inclusive of Sundays and other weeklies), according to William Thomas. 'Though their readers were more numerous,' he has observed, 'newspapers remained something of a luxury.' Understandably, the vast majority of those who had been unable to afford a sevenpenny paper were no better able to afford a fivepenny one. For the multitudes, the Sunday press remained a relative bargain, as its spiralling circulation figures suggest. 'So long as this penny lasts,' Cobden warned in 1850, 'there can be no daily Press for the middle or working classes; who below the rank of a merchant or a wholesale dealer can afford to take in a daily paper at fivepence?'[1]

Although the 'proper bounds' were significantly loosened in 1836, the ranks of the political press did not expand accordingly. There were no major additions to the galaxy until 1846, when the *Daily News* was started under the editorship of Charles Dickens. Perhaps *The Times* had been right when it insisted (24 May 1834): 'It is not the stamp duty that forms the grand outlay of a newspaper,' but rather the expense of gathering intelligence and employing qualified writers to present it. Much to the dismay of Daniel O'Connell and other reformers who had aimed to break its 'monopoly', that paper gained in sales and stature after the stamp duty was reduced. While its rivals languished, it became indispensable to merchants and wholesale dealers, no less than to men of higher station. Admittedly, the agitation against the newspaper stamp derived considerable impetus from the hostility in some quarters to the overweening pretensions of Printing House Square. Yet the official historians of *The Times* betray symptoms of corporate paranoia when they contend that the campaign had 'been manipulated, if not originated, by a group of politicians and others jealous of its power'; and they simplify matters when they conclude that 'relief from the tax' was sought only 'by Whig believers in the diffusion of knowledge, and by Radical mystics who would redeem the world from all evils by the unrestricted circulation of the printed word'.[2]

The motives of the agitators were more complicated, if not necessarily more disinterested, and party labels work to obscure them. Initiated by petitioners at Manchester in 1830, the renewed campaign against the stamp duty, alternately calling for its abolition or reduction, was integral to the concurrent movement for parliamentary reform. It was not – and consequently cannot be – considered apart from it. As a tributary of that floodtide, it recruited many of the same spokesmen, whose agreement sometimes extended no further than

[1] William Thomas, *The Philosophic Radicals* (Oxford, 1979), pp. 334–35; Cobden's remark is quoted, among other places, in Kennedy Jones, *Fleet Street and Downing Street*, p. 89.
[2] *History of The Times*, I, 322 ff.

the belief that existing facilities for the representation of interests and the expression of opinion were wholly inadequate. From their perspective, Parliament and the stamped press functioned as the twin pillars of oligarchic power, impervious to the will of the people. To transform either was to transform both, along with the cankered system they jointly supported. In this context, newspapers had a practical as well as a symbolic importance. The case for an enlargement of the electorate had to be cogently put not only to the defenders of the old order, who were predictably reluctant to listen, but also to the unenfranchised masses, who required instruction and a strategy. No matter that many of the newspapers that groaned under the weight of the stamp were indifferent or even antagonistic to the cause of parliamentary reform: the supposition was that proper ventilation of the issue could not fail to hasten the march of progress. On both sides of the debate, then, it was common to see the stamp duty as an obstacle to constitutional change. Indeed, it appeared to some contemporaries that neither goal could be realized without the other, which opponents took as an injunction to resist both. In the event, the reformers had to be content to achieve each of their objectives by stages. The stamp duty was lowered four years after the Reform Act of 1832, and it was removed a dozen years before the more far-reaching Reform Act of 1867.

Galvanized by the struggle for suffrage reform, which reached crisis proportions in the early 1830s, the attack on the stamp duty was sustained by new currents of economic thought, which the Utilitarians helped to codify. The drift to free trade, culminating in the repeal of the Corn Laws in 1846, began tentatively and pragmatically in the 1820s. As it accelerated, restrictions on the press became increasingly anomalous. Impediments to knowledge were no more defensible, and arguably more deleterious, than those to trade and industry. The stamp duty perpetuated a monopoly which, like the pretensions of the landed aristocracy and the Church, militated against the diffusion of ideas and, more generally, the fulfilment of social needs. On these grounds, progressive Tories, no less than Whig ideologues and 'Radical mystics', were slowly persuaded that press controls were counter-productive. Accordingly, the inherited structure was dismantled, plank by plank. After 1825, page sizes were no longer stipulated by law and, to the special benefit of The Times, advertising supplements were afforded a discount rate. Eight years later, the tax on other advertisements was more than halved, and the one on pamphlets was abolished. The duty on almanacs was revoked in 1834. The reduction of the stamp duty could not be long delayed. Its survival in any form, along with the twopenny tax on advertisements that persisted until 1853 and the paper duty that lingered until 1861, was too clearly an affront to enlightened self-interest, as perceived across party lines by statesmen who gauged the temper of the age.

In a real sense, the removal of economic restraints on the press prefigured the second Reform Act as a 'leap in the dark'. Although Bentham proffered assurances that the free flow of newsprint would prove 'one of the best means of directing opinion – of quieting feverish movements',[1] each successive step was taken with considerable trepidation. Despite the rhetoric spouted in certain parliamentary and intellectual circles, one could not take for granted the compliance of a fully 'capitalist' press, much less the loyalty and educability of the 'subordinate classes', who were an unknown quantity.[2] There was no gainsaying, however, that the stamp duty and other purported safeguards had abjectly failed to serve as effective instruments of social control: instead of inculcating public virtues, they had provoked mounting resentment; and, instead of fostering respect for the dominant ideology, they had identified it with repression. It seemed to Bulwer-Lytton that, having 'made a long and fruitless experiment of the gibbet and the hulks', the time had come 'to consider' whether 'cheap Knowledge may not be a better political agent than costly Punishment'.[3] But that, too, was conceived as an experiment with attendant risks. By alternate routes of faith and desperation, his contemporaries arrived at the same conclusion.

These changes were effected in an atmosphere of political excitement, intensified by events at home and abroad. In 1830, when the July Revolution occurred in France and popular agitation for parliamentary reform was at high pitch, nearly thirteen million copies of stamped newspapers passed through the post. From all indications, the growth of the unstamped press was still more dramatic. Owing to its illegal status, its circulation figures – much less its influence – cannot be ascertained with precision. By 1836, however, these unstamped journals had collectively surpassed their stamped rivals on both counts.

Uncontrolled and daringly uncontrollable, the unstamped press erupted along the ravelled fringes of pre-Victorian journalism. Descended from the radical publications of the Regency period, which had been extinguished or driven underground, it was revived with a vengeance when the Reform Bill controversy flared beyond the circumscribed boundaries of the responsible political community. 'In 1830 and 1831,' as E. P. Thompson has vividly written, 'the black ensign of defiance was hoisted once again,'[4] this time to new heights, from which it fluttered as a challenge and a reproach. Cobbett and other veteran crusaders, stimulated by the emergent forces of working-class radicalism, reiterated and extended their earlier demands. Patricia Hollis has elucidated the cardinal issue:

---

[1] Bentham, *Principles of Penal Law* (circa 1802), pt. III, ch. xix, in *The Works of Jeremy Bentham*; (ed. J. Bowring; New York, 1962), I, 568.

[2] These terms are used – anachronistically – in Curran, 'The press as an agency of social control,' in Boyce, *et al.*, eds., *Newspaper History*, pp. 57 ff.

[3] *Parliamentary Debates*, 3rd ser., xiii, cols. 633–34 (14 June 1832).

[4] *The Making of the English Working Class* (London, 1964), p. 728.

The Government's task ... since the 1790s was to manage the legitimate press so that it might avoid direct collision with respectable opinion, and to eradicate the illegitimate press, in the name of public order.... The function of the fourpenny stamp was not simply to suppress cheap violently radical papers; not simply to suppress dangerous ideas, but to keep those ideas from the dangerous classes.[1]

While it was not yet conceded that such a task was futile, it had to be acknowledged that the government lacked adequate means to perform it.

Upon close inspection, the unstamped press was more heterogeneous than its reputation would suggest. Several hundred of these periodicals published and perished during these turbulent years. One of the most ingenious was *Berthold's Pocket Handkerchief*, printed (until it was prosecuted in 1831) on cotton instead of paper. Strictly speaking, all of them were seditious in that, by evading the stamp duty, they deliberately violated the law. Yet, except for the most notorious among them, they were not dedicated to purposes of subversion. Nor, for that matter, were they uniformly blasphemous. Richard Carlile's ventures were indeed aggressively atheistical; but the aptly titled *Slap at the Church* confined its invective to the abuses of the episcopacy, while the *Witness* and several others were pious to a fault. A good many of these irregular publications were ponderously didactic, and even more were innocuously humorous. Some retailed literary content, some the rinsings of police blotters, and some commercial or professional intelligence. To most of them, politics were an irrelevance. That held especially true for the various theatrical sheets, whose readers could be expected to take keener interest in wigs than Whigs.

Yet the 'great unstamped', as the most obstreperous of the genre have been celebrated, evinced a high degree of political consciousness, much of it unfocused. They may be further subdivided into two ideological categories or persuasions: those in the first, usually without truculence, propagated the views of such 'combinations' as the friendly societies, trade unions, the co-operative movement, and the Owenite socialists; those in the second, being more autonomously mutinous, levelled virulent tirades at the persons and privileges of the hereditary ruling class, often preaching doctrines that sanctioned the severing of the union with Ireland and the plundering of property. Although differences tended to blur when tensions were exacerbated, Hollis does well to remind us that 'all was not sweetness and light' within their ranks. Carlile's *Republican* or Henry Hetherington's *Poor Man's Guardian* and *Destructive* – to instance three among dozens – scorned the trade-union and Owenite organs as parochial and pusillanimous, and as the pawns of parliamentary radicalism. In turn, they and their ilk were condemned as fanatical by the less militant, who welcomed alliances with the middle-class reformers and, so far as discretion

[1] Patricia Hollis, *The Pauper Press* (Oxford, 1970), pp. 26, 147.

would allow, accordingly strove to emphasize their limited and essentially defensive objectives. This distinction was a good deal more obvious to the agitators than to the authorities, who recognized that 'the "great unstamped" was emphatically a working-class press'[1] and, as such, a provocation.

Still less clear, and hence more fiercely debated, was the capacity of the unstamped press to stir up the lower classes, whose grievances were real enough, but whose cohesiveness may be disputed. Some of the newer stamped journals, particularly the *Morning Advertiser* and the *Weekly Dispatch*, indulged in the same sort of vituperation; but their higher price and legal status served to render them more trustworthy. The penny newspaper constituted 'the principal resource of the working man', whose soul was not uplifted by the respectable press unless he frequented 'places of public resort' – pubs, coffee houses, mechanics' institutes, or reading rooms, often annexed to bookshops – or chanced to find his household purchases wrapped in its tattered pages.[2] At many of the same communal centres, the unstamped papers were also displayed and distributed. Did the working man buy them because he was predisposed to their incendiary doctrines or merely because they were the only newspapers within his budgetary reach? Having made his purchase, was he then inflamed by their fiery rhetoric and thereby recruited for what protagonists have depicted as the class or democratic struggle? That no one could be certain did not prevent contemporaries on both sides from leaping to conclusions.

A further point of contention, somewhat more germane to the overriding theme of this study, was the effect of the unstamped press on its stamped competitors. The common assumption was that these insurgent periodicals had siphoned readers and, more problematically, advertising revenues from their journalistic betters. This impression seemed to be confirmed by the general failure of the regular dailies to sustain their momentum after the passage of the Reform Act. Others countered with the argument that the unstamped had, more dangerously, tapped a new readership. According to this interpretation, the circulations of the stamped newspapers were not materially affected, much less afflicted, by the fourpenny tax. There could be no doubt, however, that the 'great unstamped', along with the improvised broadsheets that developed alongside them, had excluded their elders from a wider market, and indeed one in which their salutary influence was felt to be particularly needed.

Against the considered judgment of *The Times*, which counted a 'formidable minority' of MPs (including its principal proprietor, then the 'Liberal-Conservative' member for Berkshire) in its corner, the Melbourne government acted in 1836 to lower a battery of duties, including the newspaper

[1] Thompson, p. 728.
[2] Webb, pp. 32–35.

stamp.[1] Inclusive of passage through the post, the London dailies now sold at fivepence or sixpence. This 'moderate' concession fell short of the expectations of Lord Brougham who, goaded by Whig and Radical spokesmen, had campaigned for a total repeal. Nor did it satisfy the logic of Lord Lyndhurst, the former Tory Lord Chancellor, who asked his fellow peers: 'Why not abolish the duty entirely?'

Insufficient to rob *The Times* of its hegemony, as Brougham and others had intended, the reduction of the tax from fourpence to a penny nonetheless dealt a deathblow to the 'great unstamped'. In both respects, but especially the latter, the consequences were curious. Though faced with a steep rise in production costs and intensified legal harassment, the unstamped journals retained a relative commercial edge: the gap in retail price between themselves and the stamped papers had been narrowed, but not closed. To the poor, as Francis Place pointedly argued, the expenditure of an additional penny was no small matter. Economic factors, therefore, do not suffice to explain the subsidence of the unstamped press.

For the sake of principle, if no longer profit, the 'great unstamped' – as distinct from the apolitical miscellanies – might have been kept alive. In many cases, it was simply that expediency triumphed over ideology. Whereas it had been well worth the risk of prosecution to evade a fourpenny impost, it was easier to pay the penny and be done with it. To shut down, of course, was easiest of all. In part, these calculations reflected exhaustion after nearly a decade of frenetic activity, punctuated by intervals of imprisonment; in part, too, they reflected a fleeting sense of optimism. For reasons that virtually defy explication, 'working-class and middle-class radicals (who also sought to abolish the stamp, for educational ends) were closer allies than they were in 1830'[2] or, needless to say, than they would be in the 1840s, when their paths again diverged. Equally unpropitiated by the provisions of the 1832 Reform Act, the middle-class radicals boasted well-placed contacts and a formidable propaganda apparatus that extended through the provinces, where the reduction of the samp duty gave an immediate stimulus to newspaper expansion. In the London press, however, they were less well represented. Among pre-existing properties, the *Morning Chronicle* (acquired by Sir John Easthope in 1834) was receptive to their views, and neither the *Examiner* nor the weekly *Spectator* could be discounted. But their greatest hopes, along with their capital, were invested in the *Constitutional*, which made its first appearance on the morning that the penny stamp took effect and did not survive its natal year. Ably edited by Samuel Laman Blanchard, and employing such talents as Douglas Jerrold, William Makepeace Thackeray (who signed his contributions 'T. T.'), and Thornton Hunt, its patrons

---

[1] Andrews, II, ch. XIII; there is an instructive account in Joel Wiener, *The War of the Unstamped* (Ithaca, N.Y., 1969), ch. I.
[2] Hollis, p. ix.

included Place, Sir William Molesworth, Joseph Hume, and other 'reformers in the fullest meaning of the term'. Priced at 4½d., a halfpenny less than *The Times*, against which it vaingloriously competed, this 'firstfruit of the Penny Stamp' pledged its efforts to the removal of that 'badge of Ignorance in the form of a penny, ... the shortening of the duration of parliaments, and extension of the suffrage, and the vote by ballot'.[1]

A commercial failure, the *Constitutional* was emblematically significant. The widespread debate in 1836 over the purpose and responsibilities of the press had quickened the pulse of political journalism. The symptoms were more easily detected than diagnosed. Writing in July to his nephew, George Villiers (later the 4th Earl of Clarendon), Lord Morley noted the

> virulence ... exhibited by the newspaper writers. *The Times*, the *Morning Herald*, the *Morning Post* brawl on one side, and the *Chronicle, Spectator* and *Examiner* on the other, but without producing the slightest effect.[2]

His observation, if not his complacency, was shared by the King of the Belgians who, stung by attacks upon him, told Princess Victoria on 18 November:

> If all the Editors of the papers in the countries where liberty of the press exists were to be assembled, you should have a *crew* to which you would not confide a dog that you would value, still less your honour and reputation.[3]

Not even *The Times* was exempt from his strictures. Like the *Morning Herald*, it had transferred its loyalties from the Whigs at the advent of Melbourne's administration, and thereafter embarked on a course of Tory progressivism. Surely not by accident, Barnes's editorial policies mirrored the position of John Walter II in the parliamentary arena. An opponent of the Poor Law Amendment Act of 1834, which he regarded as vindictive in spirit, Walter declined to defend his seat at the 1837 election, expressing

> dissatisfaction with the present state of the House of Commons, as an assembly brought together for advancing the real interests of the people, or as a system of machinery through which any independent and disinterested man, unfettered and therefore unsupported by party, can hope for clear, fair, and impartial justice in his exertions for what he conceives to be the public good.[4]

[1] Wiener, p. 273; Fox Bourne, II, 96–100.
[2] Morley to Villiers, 24 July 1836, quoted in Maxwell, *Clarendon*, I, 122; Villiers, who apparently did not share his uncle's view, wrote to his brother Edward on 3 December 1837:

> The newspapers I take in are the *Chronicle* and *Times*; Hervey takes the *Globe* and *Standard*, and Otway (just as one would expect of a jackass like him) the *Morning Post, Age* and *Satyrist*.

Quoted in *ibid.*, I, 141.
[3] Quoted in *The Letters of Queen Victoria* (eds. A. C. Benson and R. B. Brett, 2nd Viscount Esher; London, 1907), I, 68.
[4] *Reading Mercury*, 8 July 1837, quoted in Norman Gash, *Politics in the Age of Peel* (London,

Could any radical, regardless of class background, have put the case more forcefully?

His anger cooled, Walter returned to the House as the Conservative MP for Nottingham, a Whig stronghold, in 1841. Reportedly, his candidacy had received valuable backing from local Chartists. By then, the radical alliance of the mid-'30s had been dissolved. Put to rout at the polls in 1837, that fragile union helped to draft the People's Charter the following year, but was torn asunder by the movement that took its name from that six-point manifesto. The Chartists established their own newspapers, all sedulously working-class (by affectation if not by birthright) and most condoning the resort to physical force. Pre-eminent among them was the *Northern Star*, which never outgrew its initial function as 'an organ of personal publicity' for the mercurial Feargus O'Connor.[1] Founded at Leeds in November 1837, it moved its office to London in 1844, when George Julian Harney succeeded to the editorship. A throwback to the 'battle of the great unstamped', in which Harney had served his apprenticeship, it inveighed against the 'reduction in stamps' for having 'made the rich man's paper cheaper, and the poor man's paper dearer'. That resentment notwithstanding, it paid the statutory duty and, at a price of 4½d., boasted weekly circulations that reached as high as 42,000. With few exceptions, other Chartist organs likewise grudgingly complied with the law and, with smaller circulations, sold at 6d. These weeklies had their chief impact in the industrial north, where Chartist discontent ran strong. There, Disraeli's 'two nations' were further demarcated by a bitter newspaper rivalry.

Struggling to assert their own credentials and their middle-class values of self-improvement, the fledgling journals of Manchester, Liverpool, Leeds, and Sheffield faced competition from the Chartist press on the one flank and from the London dailies on the other. With the help of the railways, W. H. Smith and lesser newsagents were able to supply the provincial cities with increasing quantities of the metropolitan morning papers which, before the introduction of the telegraph, travelled as quickly as the intelligence they contained. Nevertheless, the provincial weeklies and bi-weeklies were indispensable to their business communities and, essentially for this reason, continued to grow. As Smith himself described the situation in the north: 'Almost every one who now takes a London paper also sees a country paper.'[2]

Although the circulations of the major northern newspapers must 'seem exiguous by modern standards', such statistics are an unreliable index to their readership. Exchanged within families and among friends, copies were also avidly consulted in public newsrooms for the local comment and coverage that their London rivals could not provide. Paradoxically, given the devotion of

---

1953), p. 312; see also Gash, *Sir Robert Peel*, pp. 250, 297, and Bonham to Peel, 15 April 1841, Peel Papers, Add. MSS. 40, 429, fols. 199–200.

[1] Cranfield, pp. 194–95; Stanley Harrison, *Poor Men's Guardians* (London, 1974), ch. 6.

[2] Quoted in Read, p. 203; *also see* the excellent discussion in Ayerst, pp. 92–96.

their proprietors to principles of Free Trade, these publications developed under the protection of the stamp, advertisement, and paper duties that 'continued long enough to save [them] from the threat of suffocation by the London papers'. Like the popular Sunday press, the provincials offered their subscribers a week's journalism at a price far below that of six issues of *The Times* or *Morning Chronicle*. But they could not have it both ways. To the operatives of Cottonopolis, a Chartist weekly at 4½d. or even 6d. was considered better value than the *Manchester Guardian* at 9d., and it spoke more directly to their concerns. As conceded by the 'biographer' of the *Guardian*, 'it was not lack of desire but lack of purchasing power which made Manchester an unprofitable market for a daily newspaper' before 1855. By the time the stamp duty was removed, prosperity had returned and Chartism had fizzled.[1]

In the preceding decade, the provincial press was more robust intellectually than economically. Arguably the three most important properties were the *Manchester Guardian* and the *Leeds Mercury*, both with an approximate sale of 9,000 copies in 1845, followed by the *Sheffield Independent*, with an average circulation of roughly 3,000. Each represented a different shade of middle-class opinion, as appropriate to its social and geographical base. Yet certain influences were pervasive, making them prototypical. All were closely affiliated with the forces of religious dissent and active champions of parliamentary reform. Although their political pretensions were as often exaggerated as disparaged, they struck mutually beneficial alliances with local MPs, who shared their backgrounds, favoured them with articles and informal advice, and were vaguely amenable to their influence. The connection was most intimate at Leeds where, from 1834 to 1841 and again from 1859 to 1874, the Baines family combined the management of the *Mercury* with parliamentary representation of the constituency. At Westminster, the elder Edward Baines was governed by his conviction, enunciated in his journal on 12 December 1840, 'that influence of the press and public opinion will be substituted for the traditional influences of landlordism and feudalism'.

Free Trade, and specifically the abolition of agricultural protection, was the means towards this end. It appealed to middle-class reformers not only as an ethic, but also as a strategy after political reform had been rendered a dim prospect by the electoral returns of 1837. Their base of operations was Manchester, where the Anti-Corn Law Association was founded in 1838 and reconstituted the following year as the Anti-Corn Law League. Its driving forces were Cobden and Bright, who collected substantial funds from merchants and manufacturers naturally sympathetic to their cause. An *Anti-Corn Law Circular* was published and given free of charge to anyone who contributed £1 or more, but its costs (including the penny stamp) exceeded its usefulness. The need to rally press support was recognized. Bright, dismayed by the feebleness of the *Manchester Times* and the equivocations of the *Manchester Guardian*,

[1] Read, p. 201; Ayerst, p. 95; *also see* Wadsworth, pp. 12–18.

which insisted on maintaining its editorial sovereignty, was instrumental in launching the *Manchester Examiner* to fight for 'Free Trade without sham, mistake or compromise'. Cobden, who felt that the *Leeds Mercury* had let him down, was instructed by Villiers that the press was not 'a *self-acting* machine and wants as the Yankees would say an *Almighty* power of *grease* to set it going'. He professed his willingness to apply as much 'grease' as could be purchased for £500; this amount was allocated as an annual subvention to the *Sun* in return for its backing. With Cobden's promise that the League would defray 'one half of the charge', the *Morning Chronicle* commissioned a series of 'letters' that surveyed distress in the factory towns and farming districts from an anti-Tory, anti-Chartist slant. The League was further committed to buy for complimentary distribution '3,000 copies of eight weekly papers if those papers included an editorial warmly recommending the League fund to its readers'. And, more lastingly, the *Economist* was started in 1843 as an official League organ.[1]

The scale of this journalistic onslaught, quite apart from the League's other publishing and electoral activities, was monumental. 'Cobden had, at that time at any rate, supreme faith in the potency of this vast propagandis n,' John Morley explained. Or, as Cobden himself told one of his associates: 'When I address an audience, it is from a sense of duty and utility, from precisely the motive which impels me to write an article in the *League* newspaper, and with as little thought of personal *éclat*.'[2] G. M. Trevelyan said the same of Bright, whose literary output was prodigious: 'He wrote much for the League newspaper, and also for Miall's *Nonconformist* and many other Liberal papers,' finding time to engage in a quarrel over Church rates in 'his little Rochdale paper, *The Vicar's Lantern*'.[3] To these men, the League was a religious crusade against the sinfulness of the agricultural constitution and those who defended it in Parliament and the press. No argument could be left unanswered, no taunt ignored.

Whether the League was as effective as its adherents claimed is a moot point. Ultimate responsibility, as *The Times* bitterly recognized, rested with Sir Robert Peel, whose 'conversion' to Free Trade owed little, if anything, to League or Chartist pressures. On 4 December 1845, that paper startled its readers with 'exclusive information' – obtained from Lord Aberdeen – that Peel had decided to 'recommend an immediate consideration of the Corn Laws, preparatory to their total repeal'. The *Standard* and *Morning Herald*

---

[1] The preceding paragraphs are based largely on Norman McCord, *The Anti-Corn Law League* (London, 1958), particularly pp. 49–50, 65, 141, 181–82; Cobden's letter to McLaren (21 November 1842) and Villiers's letter to Cobden (9 November 1842) are quoted therein. Cobden's letters to John Black (7 September 1842) and Sir John Easthope (15 September 1842), respectively editor and proprietor of the *Morning Chronicle*, are among the Easthope Papers.
[2] Morley, *Cobden*, I, 291; and Cobden to George Combe, 29 December 1845, quoted in *ibid.*, I, 208.
[3] *The Life of John Bright* (London, 1913), p. 108n.

issued strenuous denials that rang false. John Thaddeus Delane, who had become editor of *The Times* four years earlier at the tender age of twenty-three, could not be denied his coup. 'Glorious news,' Bright rejoiced, while confusion reigned in government circles. The Whig newspapers responded with glee tinged with incredulity; the Tory papers sputtered with rage.

Assailed for his premature disclosure, Delane could plead that he had merely followed the dictates of responsible journalism, as they were coming to be interpreted. In precisely this spirit, a contributor to the 1846 edition of the *Newspaper Press Directory* declaimed that

> the press has now so great and so extensive an influence on public opinion
> ... that ... its conductors should be GENTLEMEN in the true sense of
> the word. They should be equally above corruption and intimidation; incapable of being warped by personal considerations from the broad path of truth and honour, and superior to all attempts at misrepresenting or mystifying public events.[1]

Yet there are indications that Delane's considerations were more complicated. Henry Reeve, who assisted him as chief leader-writer on foreign affairs and who was privy to Aberdeen's confidences, later reflected that the celebrated announcement might have been more 'skilfully expressed'.[2] Disputing Reeve's imputation, Sir Edward Cook speculated that Peel, through Aberdeen, was angling for *The Times*'s support. Evidence would suggest that, on the contrary, Delane had cunningly exploited Aberdeen's indiscretion.

Relations between Aberdeen at the Foreign Office and Delane and Reeve at Printing House Square had been sufficiently close to elicit protest from other journals, denied comparable advantages. Those between *The Times* and Peel had been less cordial and sometimes decidedly antagonistic. Although Delane occasionally addressed terse notes to the Prime Minister, to whom he forwarded 'intelligence' gathered by correspondents on the Continent, in India, and in Ireland, it was through Aberdeen that he approached Peel on 22 July 1843 on behalf of his brother, 'an officer in the Customs Department', who sought promotion.[3]

Peel's difficulties with John Walter II, who wished to exchange his hard-won seat at Nottingham for a more convenient and secure one at Windsor, added to the strains. As the 1841 Parliament wore on, 'the gap had widened' between the Conservative leadership and the proprietor of *The Times*, who 'could not

---

[1] Charles Mitchell, *Newspaper Press Directory* (London, 1846), p. 104.

[2] E. T. Cook, *Delane of 'The Times'* (London, 1916), pp. 20–29; *History of The Times*, II, 53–54, 108–10; Dasent, *Delane*, I, 52. For an interesting assessment of Reeve, see *Greville Memoirs* (1 September 1840), IV, 276–77.

[3] Delane's 'intelligence' reports are among the Peel Papers (cf. Add. MSS. 40, 588, fols. 76–77); his letter of 22 July 1843 to Aberdeen, who forwarded it to Peel, and Peel's directions to Sir Thomas Fremantle are likewise among the Peel Papers, Add. MSS. 40, 453, fol. 402, and 40, 476, fol. 211.

by any stretch of party discipline be considered still a follower of Peel'.[1] Walter had given hospitality at Bear Wood, his Berkshire estate, to a conclave of the Young Englanders, who took an anti-Peelite stand within the Conservative fold and enjoyed 'generous treatment' from The Times. Disraeli, prominent within this small band, impressed George Smythe by his 'great hold on Walter and The Times'.[2] With Delane, too, Disraeli established a rapport that lasted through the decades. A lady, who was present when they 'first met', described how the Young Englander had 'overwhelmed' the young editor 'with flattery. "Did you like it?"' she asked Delane afterwards. '"No," he replied; "but I like to think that Disraeli thought I was of sufficient importance to make it worth his while."'[3]

Over many years in office and especially in opposition, Peel's skin had toughened against attacks on himself. But in 1845, provoked by The Times's 'scandalous' abuse of Sir James Graham, his Home Secretary, he urged Aberdeen to contemplate 'the discontinuance of all communications from the Foreign Office'.[4] Throughout that year, the bitterness increased. 'The Times has gone into open opposition to the Government on all points except foreign policy: it is conducted with most spiteful ability, and made good use of, by Disraeli,' Richard Monckton Milnes wrote to a colleague on 26 June 1845, less than six months before Delane's bombshell.[5]

On the crucial question of the Corn Laws, The Times had taken no fixed position. In splendid isolation, it had delighted in 'dealing out blows at Protectionist and Free Trader alike from that loftiest moral vantage-ground of one who waits for the final leap of the cat'.[6] Even after the cat had leapt, Delane and his associates maintained a cynical detachment. Greville recorded in his diary on 16 February 1846 that the Liberals, to the extent that

> they support Peel, encourage and confirm the Tories in their indignation and resentment, and they abuse the Government quite as lustily, not for what they are doing now, but for all they have been saying and doing for the last four years. The whole of the press takes the same line, the Tory and Whig papers naturally; and The Times chuckles and sneers, and alternately attacks and ridicules Whigs, Protectionists, and Peelites.[7]

As the gadfly of Fleet Street, The Times functioned as an alter ego for Disraeli who, before he delivered a three-hour speech on 4 September 1848, 'sent word to Delane . . . in order that he might have one of his best reporters there'.[8]

[1] Gash, Politics in the Age of Peel, pp. 378 ff., and Peel, p. 387; Blake, Disraeli, p. 176.

[2] Smythe to Lord John Manners, 19 October 1842, quoted in Blake, Disraeli, p. 174.

[3] Sir Algernon West, Recollections (London, 1899), I, 244–45.

[4] History of The Times, II, 95, and, for background, 53–55.

[5] Monckton Milnes to C. J. McCarthy, 26 June 1845, quoted in T. W. Reid, The Life, Letters and Friendships of Richard Monckton Milnes, First Lord Houghton (London, 1891), I, 356.

[6] Trevelyan, Bright, p. 92.

[7] Greville Memoirs, V, 298.

[8] Ibid. (5 September 1848), VI, 105.

The Peelite rump of the Conservative Party, fortified by Whig and Radical votes, effected the repeal of the Corn Laws. With the abolition of the 'stomach taxes', as agricultural protection was known to its enemies, the 'taxes on knowledge' rose to priority on the agenda of reformers. In a letter to Bright on 16 November 1848, Cobden outlined a 'People's Budget' that 'would only leave about fifteen articles in the tariff paying customs duties', paper and advertisements definitely not among them.[1] The next year saw the formation of two organizations to realize his goals: the London Committee for Obtaining the Repeal of the Duty on Advertisements, established under the presidency of William Ewart, then MP for the Dumfries Burghs; and the Association for Promoting the Repeal of the Taxes on Knowledge, with Thomas Milner-Gibson, another Free Trader who sat for Manchester, at its helm. The latter soon absorbed the Newspaper Stamp Abolition Committee, created by the council of the People's Charter Union, and thus signalled the restoration of ties between middle-class and working-class radicalism.[2]

In anticipation of the impending onslaught, the unreconstructed London press looked helplessly to Disraeli, who by then had emerged as leader of the Tory opposition, to safeguard those vestiges of protectionism behind which they sheltered. Peter Borthwick, who had vacated his seat at Evesham and taken control of the *Morning Post*, importuned him: 'One word from you in the House will be esteemed a very great favor. The advertisement Duty and the 1d. stamp on papers we have no wish to destroy.'[3] Borthwick spoke not simply out of an antipathy to the principle of Free Trade, but in dread of any change that was likely to accord further advantage to *The Times*.

Rebuffed by Lord John Russell, who succeeded Peel in the premiership, Milner-Gibson and Ewart unsuccessfully moved repeated resolutions in the House, where they achieved nothing more substantial than the appointment in April 1851 of a select committee to examine the workings of the stamp duty. In its brief lifetime, the first Derby ministry proved no more accommodating. Then, in December 1852, Gladstone was appointed to the Exchequer in Lord Aberdeen's coalition government. Delane, who had gone 'down to Oxford' to vote for Gladstone in 1847, sternly remonstrated against the choice, but to no avail.[4] Named after William Ewart, his father's close friend, the new Chancellor carried the promise of redress.

Declaring that 'he should be delighted to see the day when the duty on newspapers might be removed', he doubted whether it had yet dawned.[5] But

[1] Quoted in Morley, *Cobden*, II, 34.
[2] Grant, II, 310–11; Fox Bourne, II, 210–11; C. Dobson Collet, 'How the Taxes on Knowledge Were Abolished,' in Justin McCarthy and Sir John Robinson, *The 'Daily News' Jubilee* (London, 1896), pp. 126–29.
[3] Borthwick to Disraeli, 15 April 1850, Hughenden Papers.
[4] Delane's diary entry of 21 July 1847, quoted in Dasent, *Delane*, I, 67; *Greville Memoirs* (24 and 28 December 1852), VI, 384–85.
[5] Quoted in Fox Bourne, II, 216.

the advertisement tax was a separate question. Disraeli, who had proposed nothing so rash in his own budget the previous year, now suggested that it might be expendable. Taking the cue, Milner-Gibson moved on 14 April 1853 'that the advertisement duty ought to be repealed'. He found himself surrounded by Tories in a crowded lobby, with a majority of 31 against the government. Bright, among their number, scoffed at the qualms of his fellow Radicals: 'Our men frightened when they heard Disraeli was going to vote with us! Afraid to carry their object, fearing to hurt a Government which refuses them this trifle!' The day after he had helped to inflict this humiliation, Bright talked 'plainly' to Sir Charles Wood, Gladstone's Cabinet colleague and a former Chancellor: 'We wished the press to be free from taxes,' he said, 'and no consideration of convenience to a Government would prevent our insisting upon it.'[1]

To appreciate Bright's impatience is not to deny the 'very stiff work' that Gladstone accomplished. A Peelite by precept as well as by conviction, he received deputations, pored over evidence, and consulted privately with Ewart, Milner-Gibson, Delane, and John D. Cook, editor of the *Morning Chronicle*. On the afternoon of 18 April, he 'spoke 4¾ hours in detailing the Financial measures; and my strength stood out well thank God'.[2] Cook congratulated him on his 'great and far-reaching scheme' that stipulated a timetable for the gradual elimination of the income tax along with the extinction or reduction of nearly 300 duties. Included was a compromise formula for an abatement of the tax on advertisement supplements. 'And,' Cook assured him,

> if you have not now the best and most cordial support of *The Times*, all I shall say is that you will have great cause to complain of its ingratitude, for you certainly put £40,000 a year into the pockets of its proprietors without improving, in any perceptible degree – so far as regards supplements – the financial position of any other journal.[3]

As Cook doubtless knew, it was not the gratitude of Printing House Square to which Gladstone aspired.

At a 'Cabinet dinner at Ld. Granville's' on 20 April, the advertisement duty figured as a major topic of discussion. Given the scope and complexity of the issues that confronted him, Gladstone could scarcely afford the attention he lavished on this particular item. On the 22nd, he saw 'Mr Gibson & Deputa-

[1] Bright's diary entries of 14 and 15 April 1853, quoted in Trevelyan, *Bright*, p. 212; for a comprehensive account of the 1853 budget, see J. B. Conacher, *The Aberdeen Coalition* (Cambridge, 1968), ch. 3.
[2] Entries of 14 and 18 April 1853, *Gladstone Diaries*, IV (eds. M. R. D. Foot and H. C. G. Matthew; Oxford, 1974), 516, 519.
[3] Cook to Gladstone, 19 April [1853], Gladstone Papers, Add. MSS. 43,374, fols. 239–40; Cook expressed his own misgivings about Gladstone's scheme on the 23rd (Add. MSS. 44,374, fol. 275).

tion (Advt. Duty)', and took notes on testimony delivered before the select committee on the stamp duty: 'Advertisement Duty bears most heavily on small circulations. . . . Mr Bright said this was not a question of £50,000 of tax but of the freedom of the press, wh. ought to be as free as the platform.'[1] Cook, kept apprised of his considerations, called on the 28th, and promptly 'stated your views as fully as I could do to several gentlemen connected with the management of the London Journals'; these 'proprietors and managers' had agreed

> to meet . . . and consider whether they can frame a letter, or memorial, that would convey to you clearly their opinions with reference to the stamp duty on supplements. . . . You may depend that I shall do what I can to keep them within the bounds of reason; but my own feelings and convictions are all with them, for I cannot but fear the operation of your plan.
>
> P.S. The great difficulty is that . . . it is impossible for the other London Journals to move in the matter, and to appeal to you, without having the appearance, at least, of attacking *The Times*.[2]

On the same day, Cobden broached the matter in debate, where he implored the Chancellor not to 'make two bites at a cherry'. Referring to rumours, which he refused to credit, that Gladstone, 'in proposing to remit the stamp upon supplements containing only advertisements, would be giving a boon to only one paper', he

> repeat [ed] that, in my opinion, the Government should have no connection with the press whatever. I hope, therefore, that if they adhere to their resolution, and deal with the advertisement duty at all, they will abolish it altogether.[3]

After midnight, Gladstone went home 'a good deal overset', and had to have 'recourse to [a] blue pill' to get to sleep.[4]

Deliberations continued through May and June. Within a divided Cabinet, Lord Granville, for one, could 'not see why an arrangement becomes more desirable from the fact that it obviates the advantages which *The Times* has obtained by fair means over other papers'.[5] That, of course, was standing the Free Trade argument on its head. At Cook's instigation, 'Proprietors and Representatives' of the *Morning Herald, Morning Post, Morning Advertiser, Morning Chronicle,* and *Daily News* petitioned the Chancellor against 'the

[1] *Gladstone Diaries* (22 April 1853), IV, 520; memorandum of 22 April 1853, Gladstone Papers, Add. MSS. 44,742, fol. 137.

[2] *Gladstone Diaries* (28 April 1853), IV, 521; Cook to Gladstone, 28 [obviously 29] April 1853, Gladstone Papers, Add. MSS. 44,380, fols. 135–36; Morley, *The Life of William Ewart Gladstone* (London, 1903), I, 462.

[3] Speech in the House of Commons, 28 April 1853, in *Speeches on Questions of Public Policy by Richard Cobden MP.* (eds. J. Bright and T. Rogers; London, 1870), II, 571–73.

[4] *Gladstone Diaries* (28 April 1853), IV, 522.

[5] Memorandum of 2 May 1853, Gladstone Papers, Add. MSS. 44,778, fols. 122 ff.

Remission of the Newspaper Stamp on Supplements', which would 'be to confer on *The Times* a monopoly of the worst description, to the serious injury of every other Morning Metropolitan Journal'.[1] A deluge of letters and memorials insisted that 'the entire abolition of the Advertisement Duty would be a greater boon to the trading and general public, and to the majority of the Newspaper Press, than the remission of the Duty on the Supplemental Stamp'.[2]

Doomed since the vote in mid-April, the advertisement tax died a slow death. On 1 July, Gladstone reworked his compromise, which was rejected by a small majority in a thin House. On the 20th, he wrote in his dairy with good humour and a hint of relief: 'H. of C. 12¼–3: we overthrew the Attornies & made a holocaust of the Advt. Duty.'[3] A proposal to reduce it by two-thirds, from 18d. to 6d., was amended by substituting a zero in the crucial clause. By this sleight-of-hand, the tax was consigned to oblivion. Those who fretted about the effect on the national debt were advised that the consequent increase of advertising would guarantee a greater yield on the surviving paper duty.

Such reasoning did not in the least appeal to the press reformers who, buoyed by their success, regrouped their forces and redoubled their efforts. In May 1854, Milner-Gibson introduced a motion 'so cleverly contrived' that it was carried without a division: justly observing that 'the laws in reference to the periodical press and newspaper stamp are ill defined and unequally enforced', it blandly concluded that 'the subject demands the early attention of parliament'.[4] Progress was interrupted by the fall of the Aberdeen coalition and its replacement by Lord Palmerston's first government, in which Sir George Cornewall Lewis held the chancellorship. Gladstone's successor, following in his footsteps, introduced a Bill that gave newspapers the option to pass through the post stamped or unstamped. The predictable argument that the public revenue would suffer was met by the calculation that at least half the loss would be recouped through postal charges. When it was pointed out that *The Times*, outweighing its rivals literally as well as figuratively, would secure a continued advantage, the Treasury imposed a four-ounce limit to the penny post. There were squeals of protest from Printing House Square, but Bright had the satisfaction of quoting *The Times* against itself on 'the absurdity of a tax which, as it is a tax on news, is a tax on knowledge, ... a tax on the progress of human affairs, and on the working of human institutions' (17 May 1854). For himself, he was 'quite satisfied, from years of attention to the

---

[1] Memorial [May 1853], Gladstone Papers, Add. MSS. 44,576, fol. 16.
[2] Resolution moved by W. P. Byles, founder of the *Bradford Observer*, 4 June 1853, Gladstone Papers, Add. MSS. 44,577, fol. 21; *also see* the petition from the Society of Arts, Manufactures and Commerce, 25 June 1853, *ibid.*, fol. 145.
[3] *Gladstone Diaries* (20 July 1853), IV, 543, with editors' note: 'Govt majority of 84, Hansard cxxix, 484.'
[4] Fox Bourne, II, 218–19.

subject, that there never was so large a measure involved in a small measure, so to speak, as is the case with regard to this proposition for making the press free'.[1] Unceremoniously, on 15 June 1855, the stamp duty was laid to rest alongside the advertisement tax.

The effects were immediate, but, before proceeding to assess them, it would be logical to pursue the question of the paper duty, the final remnant of the old system. It has been estimated that, by the late '50s, there were no fewer than 120 MPs who, as 'friends of an untaxed political journalism', were resolved to abolish this tax.[2] Gladstone, back at the Exchequer under Palmerston, complied with a suitable measure in 1860. Passed by the Commons, it was rejected by the Lords, whose assent to 'money Bills' had long been taken as perfunctory. Forcing a constitutional showdown, Gladstone incorporated the remission of the paper duty in his 1861 budget. He had called the bluff of the Upper House, and the tax on paper ended on 1 October.

'What had the abolition of *all* the taxes on newspapers done for political journalism? This is a question worthy of serious and interesting inquiry,' James Grant wrote in 1871.[3] By that time, major developments had already occurred, and further tendencies could be discerned. Yet, with the benefit of extended hindsight, their significance clarifies. Established facts, as they then seemed to journalists and politicians alike, admit to interpretations which they could not have attempted, much less anticipated. 'Who, then, shall appraise at their proper value the benefits derived from the abolition of the taxes on newspapers?' Grant asked. The ensuing chapters, accepting his challenge, might have offered him some surprises.

---

[1] *Parliamentary Debates*, 3rd ser., cxxxvii, cols. 810–11 (19 March 1855).

[2] Grant, II, 317–20; *Gladstone Diaries* (12 and 13 April 1861), VI (ed. H. C. G. Matthew; Oxford, 1978), 23–24; Lee, *The Origins of the Popular Press*, pp. 48–49.

[3] Grant, II, 319, 322.

Three

COMING OF AGE

The lifting of economic constraints brought an immediate and fundamental change in the structure of the British press. The broad outlines of that change, particularly as it affected political relationships, had been foreshadowed by reciprocal adjustments in the attitudes of politicians and journalists. This cumulative transformation was largely concentrated in the mid-Victorian decades when, as Asa Briggs has written, 'prosperity and security together encouraged a belief in the superiority of English representative institutions',[1] among which newspapers variously aspired to classification. Typical of the age, they defined 'representative' in contradictory ways, depending on material conditions and, still more, the elements of political instability to which they responded at any given moment.

Although the concept of a Fourth Estate had been a commonplace for generations, it was now invested with a new purpose by those who invoked it, self-consciously and often self-servingly. 'The prevalence or scarcity of Newspapers in a country affords an index to its social state,' Frederick Knight Hunt argued in 1850 in a two-volume work, *The Fourth Estate*, which cast an envious eye on developments in the United States and France. 'Where Journals are numerous', he reasoned, 'the people have power, intelligence, and wealth; where Journals are few, the many are in reality mere slaves.'[2] A dubious correlation, it was nevertheless widely posited by reformers of that day.

Dedicated 'to the Journalists of England and to their "Constant Readers"', Hunt's pioneering study was subtitled, with due humility, 'Contributions towards a History of Newspapers'. Like most others of its genre, then and since, it is more notable for its spirit than its substance. A compilation of apocryphal anecdotes and 'scattered' facts, it is discursive and generally unreliable. As a polemic, however, it retains considerable interest. One of the first in a spate of contemporary assessments, it both reflected and helped to stimulate further a concern with the responsibilities of the press, real or potential.

[1] *Victorian People* (London, 1954), pp. 16–17.
[2] Hunt, II, 292.

Despite its manifest deficiencies in methodology and analysis, it provided the semblance of historical justification for the legislation which its author, whose editorship of the *Daily News* was cut short by his death in 1854, did not live to celebrate.

In the third quarter of the nineteenth century, as never before, journalists' perceptions of their professional obligations were inseparable from their fulfilment of them. Especially in the 1850s, when so much was in a state of flux, newspapermen – traditionally a secretive and self-effacing breed – publicly scrutinized their own ethics, which were in a process of reformulation. Hunt's manifesto, bound in hard covers, dealt with themes that had figured with increasing prominence in pamphlets, lectures, and private correspondence. Explicitly a denunciation of official restrictions, which had worked to the detriment of the public interest, it was implicitly a challenge to the hegemony of *The Times*, which those restrictions were assumed to favour. Since its inception in 1846, the *Daily News* had waged in its daily columns the struggle its editor attempted to explain in historical perspective.

More than one might expect, the Goliath of Printing House Square was vulnerable to the missiles slung by the David of Bouverie Street. 'Once more, don't let the bullying of the *Daily News* annoy you,' Delane wrote from Vienna in 1851 to his assistant editor, G. W. Dasent. 'It is Reeve's battle; let him fight it.'[1]

Delane, to be sure, knew his man. In October 1855, after the repeal of the stamp duty had conferred a retrospective significance on Hunt's 'contributions', Henry Reeve replied, belatedly and anonymously, in the pages of the *Edinburgh Review*.[2] Conceding that 'the permanent effect of the abolition of the stamp on newspapers ... is yet too early to predict', he discounted the possibility of 'an entire revolution in the newspaper press' such as Hunt had anticipated. From his desk at *The Times*, which he was soon to leave, it appeared to him that the revolution had already quietly occurred:

> In no respect does the Journalism of the Present stand out more distinguished from the Journalism of the Past – and the Newspaper Press of England from that of every other land – than in its freedom from all impure and corrupt influences. All charges to the contrary we hold to be utterly without foundation.

Nor would Reeve have any truck with the assertions of 'Mr Milner Gibson and his associates', among whom he counted Hunt, that a cheap press would serve a greater diversity of political opinions:

> Whenever a newspaper is the established organ of a party, its circulation is limited and its existence precarious and costly. Journalism, therefore, is not

[1] Delane, to Dasent, 28 October 1851, quoted in Dasent, *Delane*, I, 118–19.
[2] *Edinburgh Review*, cii (1855), 470–98.

the instrument by which the various divisions of the ruling class express themselves: it is rather the instrument by means of which the aggregate intelligence of the nation criticises and controls them all. It is indeed the 'Fourth Estate' of the Realm: not merely the written counterpart and voice of the speaking 'Third'.

Had it not been for intervening events, it is unlikely that Reeve would have deigned to take formal notice of Hunt's pronouncements: published five years earlier, *The Fourth Estate* was reviewed jointly with two books that appeared as recently as 1855 and, unrelated to the subject of journalism, evoked only passing comment. But in the light of those events and the controversies that enveloped them, Reeve felt compelled to issue a rebuttal to his late adversary. At any rate, his defence had been well rehearsed.

During the early phase of Delane's editorship, Reeve had exercised virtual autonomy in the conduct of *The Times* with regard to foreign affairs, which impinged inordinately on domestic politics. Lord Palmerston, who (according to Greville) regarded him with 'especial abhorrence and dread', informed Prince Albert in August 1850 that he had at last made peace with Reeve, who admitted to 'have been making open and honourable (?!!) war upon him'.[1] That concordat was shortlived: by the end of 1851, *The Times* was again calling for Palmerston's removal from the Foreign Office, where he allegedly championed the cause of Bonapartist despotism.

The dismissal of Palmerston, for which *The Times* was assigned a measure of credit which it did not scruple to disclaim, led to the stopgap appointment of Lord Granville, described by his biographer as enjoying 'intimate personal relations' with Reeve. Within weeks, the practical value of those ties was put to the test.[2] On 17 January 1852, the new Foreign Secretary gently reproved Reeve for *The Times*'s continuing 'castigation' of the French régime. A correspondence ensued into which Lord Clarendon and, necessarily, Delane were drawn. When Parliament assembled on 3 February, the dispute was made public. Lord John Russell, whom (again to quote Greville) *The Times* had treated 'with indecent acrimony', made a restrained and oblique reference to the embarrassment caused in diplomatic circles by the indiscretions of certain newspapers. Lord Derby, addressing the other House, did not mince words. Consulted by Delane, John Walter agreed that 'some answer is certainly called for to so violent an attack. . . . A very good article might be written,' he supposed, 'pointing out the different functions of statesmen and

---

[1] Memorandum by Prince Albert, 8 August 1850, quoted in *Letters of Queen Victoria*, II, 314; *Greville Memoirs* (11 August 1850), VI, 253; *also see* Jasper Ridley, *Lord Palmerston* (London, 1970), p. 114.

[2] For this episode, see the following: Fitzmaurice, *Granville*, I, 68; Maxwell, *Clarendon*, I, 343; J. K. Laughton, *Henry Reeve* (London, 1898), I, 250 ff.; *Greville Memoirs* (2 March 1851), VI, 277; and *History of The Times*, II, ch. viii. A note in *The Times* archives, dated 6 February 1852, states that the 'leader on "Freedom of the Press"' was 'actually written by Lowe & Reeve'; various sources err in assigning responsibility to one or the other.

journalists'. The task, so defined, was entrusted to Reeve and Robert Lowe, who supplied a pair of leading articles (6 and 7 February) which came to be regarded as sacred texts:

> We do not interfere with the duties of statesmen; our vocation is, in one respect, inferior to theirs, for we are unable to wield the power or represent the collective dignity of the country; but in another point of view it is superior, for, unlike them, we are able to speak the whole truth without fear or favour.

In these articles, and during a second brush with Lord Derby two years later, Reeve enunciated the principles that he found lacking in Hunt's depiction of the Fourth Estate.

Before Hunt had 'sent his two volumes into the world', Alexander Andrews, another practising journalist, had begun to amass 'a collection of notes and particulars' for a similar project. It was Reeve's piece in the *Edinburgh Review*, 'calling for further details of newspaper history', that persuaded him to return to the materials which he 'had consigned . . . to oblivion' and 'to polish them up and see what we could make of them'. The result was another two-volume survey, *The History of British Journalism to 1855*, published in 1859. Disputing much of the evidence that Hunt had 'thrown together', Andrews did not escape some of the same pitfalls. Yet, with the hindsight denied to his predecessor, he could clearly discern 1855 as a watershed. Indebted to Reeve not only for a stimulus, but also for a vision of 'our free press – at once our censor and our champion', Andrews proceeded to assign to 'our public journals' the mission 'to educate and enlighten those classes whose political knowledge has been hitherto so little, and by consequence so dangerous'.[1]

More tellingly than he presumably realized, Andrews articulated a heightened awareness of the overlapping political and social functions of the press as they had evolved over the preceding decade. He was therefore able to accept as a challenge a situation that Hunt, nine years before, had been able to contemplate only as a Panglossian hope. In that respect, his delay proved fortunate. He owed his comprehension neither to superior intellect nor to greater familiarity with the techniques of journalistic management, but rather to the extent to which issues had since crystallized.

From the time that Andrews first conceived his project until the time he completed it, newspapers had grown tremendously in number, in circulation, and in stature. In Parliament as in print, the question of their accountability had been intensively – and sometimes fiercely – debated. Competing influences, each to a varying degree an amalgam of ideological and commercial interests, precluded any effective resolution of this problem. Meanwhile,

---

[1] Andrews, I, 2–3; II, 348.

through the interplay of those influences, politicians and publicists sought to achieve in practice the formula that eluded them in theory.

* * *

In *The Political Impact of Mass Media*,[1] Colin Seymour-Ure has systematically employed sociological precepts to distinguish between the cases of 'naturally developing' party systems (as found in Great Britain and the United States), and 'imposed ones' (such as those 'in many modernising régimes of Africa or in Eastern Europe after 1945'). According to the model he has constructed, in the first of these categories, *'politicians tend to be the clients of newspapers* ... [which] aid the transfer of allegiance from parent group to party and reflect the broadening of group appeal implicit in the party's launching'. His 'supposition', framed with sufficient sophistication to accommodate permutations, acknowledges that 'there are many "naturally based" parties throughout the world which are closely linked to newspapers'; nevertheless, 'compared with "imposed" parties, fewer of them are able to "command" their newspapers, particularly when the transfer of legitimacy is complete'. Although there are reasons to qualify Seymour-Ure's inference that, in the British context, 'the transfer was complete for the Conservative Party before 1914, and ... for the Labour Party ... not ... until perhaps as late as 1945', his major proposition is accepted here as axiomatic. With this framework in mind, the connections between the press and party associations in the nineteenth century acquire an added dimension and perhaps greater coherence.

The arrangements that took shape during the 1850s, establishing procedures that were to persist for the better part of a century, evolved in certain instances from pre-existing relationships. That was only to be expected, given that the careers of prominent statesmen – Palmerston, Russell, Gladstone, Derby, and Disraeli – spanned the period of transition, as did many of the editorships and proprietorships of their collaborators. The point to be made, however, is that the nature of these relationships changed, sometimes subtly and sometimes markedly, as alternative relationships presented themselves and as party alignments shifted.

As in other areas of public life, Lord Palmerston personified continuity in an atmosphere of change. His involvement with newspaper enterprises can be traced at least as far back as June 1834, when Joseph Parkes, an intermediary between the Benthamite theorists and the parliamentary Whig reformers, introduced him to John Easthope, 'a Co-adventurer with me in the *M[orning] C[hronicle]'*.[2] Weeks earlier, Easthope had acquired the *Chronicle* at the head

[1] (London, 1974), p. 196.
[2] Correspondence in the Easthope Papers is supplemented by items in the Broadlands Collection: Parkes to Palmerston, 7 June 1834 (PRE/A/2); Easthope to Palmerston, 7 June 1834 (CC/EA/2); Maberly to Palmerston, 4 July 1834 (PRE/A/3); Palmerston to Easthope (copy), 12 July 1838 (GC/EA/26/2); and Palmerston to Easthope, 18 September 1842 (GC/EA/33/1). *Also see*

of a syndicate that included two Scots businessmen, Simon Macgillivray ('who had made a fortune in Mexico') and James Duncan ('a noted publisher of Hebrew Bibles'). Along with Parkes, Nassau Senior and Francis Place were believed to have invested capital. The purchase price, initially rumoured to have been as high as £30,000, has been put at £16,500, a sum which Thomas Barnes of *The Times* considered more than three times the value of the dere-lect property. That Easthope, temporarily excluded from the House of Commons, was himself a successful financier led Barnes naturally to surmise that his object was to make the paper 'useful as a medium of Stock-Exchange speculation'. Sensitive to 'unfounded' accusations that *The Times* had engaged in similar malpractices, Barnes predicted that Easthope would soon 'find himself woefully mistaken' in his purpose. On all counts, it was Barnes who was 'woefully mistaken'.

When Easthope took control, the circulation of the *Morning Chronicle* was a mere 800 copies a day. Thereafter, it steadily rose above 9,000. John Black, a holdover from the previous ownership, retained the editorship until 1843, when he was replaced by Andrew Doyle, the foreign editor and Easthope's son-in-law. Meanwhile, the staff was revitalized by new talents and by contacts with Whig politicians and party managers. Lords Brougham, Althorp, and Durham were close acquaintances of Easthope, or Black, or both. But Lord Palmerston quickly eclipsed them.

The way having been paved by Parkes's introduction, Easthope promptly advised Palmerston of his intention to go 'to Paris and Brussels [*sic*] on Monday to engage Correspondents for the *Morning Chronicle*', and he solicit-ed 'some safe opinion . . . to aid me in selecting fit persons for the employ-ment'. One may assume that Palmerston approved the choice of Eyre Evans Crowe for the Paris assignment. Soon afterwards, Parkes's commendation was seconded by John Maberly, a Whig stalwart: 'My friend Mr Easthope whom *you know*, having bought the *Morning Chronicle* & being anxious to place that paper on the best footing possible with regard to foreign news', looked to Pal-merston 'in order to raise its influence, its circulation and its profits'. The order of priorities, as put by Maberly, was the reverse of that imputed by Barnes.

Apart from an interruption in 1834–35 during Peel's 'Hundred Days', the Foreign Office was Palmerston's fief from 1830 to 1841 and again from 1846 to 1851. In or out of office, he commanded 'slavish worship' (as it was aptly described by Charles Mackay, a former employee) from Easthope, who was rewarded with a baronetcy for himself and a flow of privileged communica-tions for his paper. But even 'slavish worship' required the ministration of fre-quent directives and occasional rebukes: whereas criticism 'in *The Times* or in

Maxwell, *Clarendon*, I, 213; Ridley, *Palmerston*, p. 287; *History of The Times*, I, 305–9; Charles Mackay, *Through the Long Day* (London, 1887), I, 268–69; and *Greville Memoirs* (28 March 1839), IV, 139–40, which provides a highly idiosyncratic and retrospective account.

any opposition Paper would be of little consequence', Palmerston explained to Easthope in 1838, 'when such attacks are published in a Paper, which like the *Chronicle* supports the Govt., the case is wholly different'. Palmerston thus prescribed the topics to be addressed and also those to be ignored. He was as grateful for the paper's tirades in 1840 against French designs in the eastern Mediterranean as he was for the paper's 'silence' two years later on the Ashburton Treaty with the United States, 'as *The Times* might have defended the Treaty if the *Chronicle* had begun by attacking it'.

Although Palmerston rose in Parliament to deny the allegation, articles in the *Morning Chronicle* were certainly written at his dictation and probably by his own hand. Not even Lord Melbourne, who headed the government in which Palmerston served from 1835 to 1841, could be sure. Betraying ineptitude as well as embarrassment, the Prime Minister told Queen Victoria that he had been a guest at Broadlands, the Foreign Secretary's country retreat, early in 1842, when an article to which she took exception appeared in the *Morning Chronicle*. Melbourne had 'talked it over with Lord Palmerston', and did 'not think that Palmerston wrote it, because there were in it errors, and those errors to Palmerston's disadvantage'. Rather, Melbourne deduced, 'it was written by Easthope under the impression that it conveyed Palmerston's notions and opinions'. A politician of an older school, Melbourne explained as best he could methods that he was neither disposed nor equipped to deploy:

> Your Majesty knows very well that Palmerston has long had much communication with the *Morning Chronicle* and much influence over it, and has made great use of it for the purpose of maintaining and defending his own policy. In this sort of matter there is much to be said upon both sides. A Minister has a great advantage in stating his own views to the public, and if Palmerston in the Syrian affair [of 1840] had not as devoted an assistant as the *Morning Chronicle*, he would hardly have been able to maintain his course or carry through his measures.

Without being censorious, Melbourne stated that it was his own

> policy to keep himself aloof from the public press and to hold it at arm's-length, and he considers it the best course, but it is subject to disadvantages. You are never in that case strongly supported by them, nor are the motives and reasons of your conduct given to the public with the force and distinctness which they might be.[1]

In the ensuing decades, Palmerston devised ways to exploit the advantages while minimizing the disadvantages.

His candour, though an affront to his senior colleagues, was all the more refreshing for the contrast it afforded. Increasingly, there were those who

[1] Melbourne to Queen Victoria, 17 January 1852, quoted in *Letters of Queen Victoria*, I, 470–71.

emulated Palmerston. Yet they could rarely match his zeal and never his zest. To the outrage of Lord John Russell, whose priggishness might be mistaken for rectitude, Palmerston played off the *Morning Chronicle* against the *Globe* (which Russell, too, supplied with intelligence). After 1848, when Easthope sold out to the Peelites, Palmerston struck alliances first with the *Morning Post* and eventually with *The Times*. By 1865, when he and Easthope died, their partnership had been long dissolved, but its spirit survived in the conventions of the next generation.

Politicians on the Conservative side, as their publicists perpetually complained, were relatively slow to learn the lessons taught by Palmerston. On 18 August 1841, poised to take office, Peel was addressed on the subject by C. Eastland Michele, who identified himself (thereby implying that identification was necessary) as 'the acting Proprietor & Conductor' of the *Morning Post*:

> I can honestly affirm that my sincere wish is to serve the cause of the Conservative party, and to avoid any mistake which might operate to its prejudice. I do not look merely to the profit of the Paper. I wish to make it as useful as I can to the great party which I conceive to have for its object the preservation of the fundamental institutions of the country, combined with an honest zeal for improvement in all matters where good sense, and the public convenience, appear to demand a change for the better.

Without asking Peel 'to shew any favour to the *Morning Post*', he urged him 'merely to consider whether something might not be done which would promote the efficiency of the Conservative press as a political engine'. In the interest of accuracy, no less than political expediency,

> very great advantage might be obtained, and very great disadvantage avoided, by the elevation of the character of the political press, and by making it a more legitimate, and more truth telling organ of statesmanship.... At present we get our information in all sorts of ways, and from all sorts of people ..., and so far as the convenience of our party is concerned, there is no one who takes the trouble to give us a word of guidance, or perhaps has sufficient confidence to do so. *We* do not lose by this, for we sell as many, or more papers than if we were more discreet, but the good cause is not served as it might be by the Press.

As circumstances required, Michele couched his recommendations in general and deferential terms:

> Considering the effect of journalism upon the Public mind, I venture to suggest that the heads of the Party ought to think it worth their while to direct this journalism in some degree themselves – that they should actually use it in addition to Parliamentary speaking for the purpose of guiding &

informing the Public upon points that it may not be convenient to speak upon in Parliament, or for which there may not be Parliamentary opportunities.[1]

Such appeals were fated to fall on deaf ears, for Peel was too unbending in his principles to stoop to the level of Palmerstonian demagoguery. His invariable response was to refer newspaper matters to Sir Thomas Fremantle, his patronage secretary. When Michele registered a protest that anti-ministerial journals had been favoured with intelligence withheld from the *Morning Post*, Peel blandly assured him that similar complaints 'were received by me from other parties connected with the public press, to whom you suppose undue preference to have been shown, within two or three days preceding the date of your letter'.[2]

The *Morning Post*, with Disraeli among its occasional contributors, had never reconciled itself to the currents of Peelite Conservatism. Nursing a 'deep anxiety' with regard to electoral reform (8 June 1832), it was also unflinchingly protectionist. In 1842, distressed by Peel's fiscal pragmatism, Michele raised a mortgage of £25,000 and bought out other shareholders less resolute than himself. It was a noble gesture, but a disastrous investment. Sinking further into debt, he turned to the Tory protectionists for assistance. 'If the hated name of "Peel the Traitor" is made to ring from side to side of the habitable globe,' he plaintively asked Lord George Bentinck in December 1847, 'what is to be the fate of "Michele the faithful"?' Professing 'the highest feelings of admiration', Lord George declared himself 'quite helpless to help you in any way', then died before the application could be renewed. Lord Henry Bentinck, whom Michele next approached, was equally discouraging: 'I am a borrower: not a lender.' With less logic and no more success, Michele threw himself on the mercy of the eldest Bentinck brother, the Duke of Portland, who had once sent him a Christmas gift of £50, but who remained a follower of Peel.[3]

Hard pressed by his creditor, T. B. Crompton, a Lancashire paper manufacturer, Michele enlisted Peter Borthwick to put the case for a protectionist organ to other Tory peers and MPs. Borthwick, if only by his negative qualities, was a suitable choice. As member for Evesham, he had irritated Peel by coquetting with the Young Englanders ('the party of malcontents, G. Smythe, D'Israeli & Co', Fremantle called them), by his requests for preferments and loans, and by his adherence to protectionism. In February 1845, on the basis of an erroneous report in the *Morning Post*, Borthwick had raised the question in Parliament whether Prince Albert was to be elevated to 'King Consort', presumably as a 'preliminary to a demand for

---

[1] Peel Papers, Add. MSS. 40,486, fols. 130–35.
[2] Peel to Michele, 2 January 1842, Peel Papers, Add. MSS. 40,499, fol. 19.
[3] Extracts from Michele's correspondence with the Bentincks, Borthwick, and others are included in Reginald Lucas, *Lord Glenesk and the 'Morning Post'* (London, 1910), pp. 28–34.

an increased grant'. Peel was obliged to issue a denial, and 'the Queen was much hurt at Mr Borthwick's most impertinent manner'.[1]

Borthwick's brief was to find a purchaser who would relieve Michele of his financial burden without divesting him of responsibility. During the months that he negotiated on Michele's behalf with Lord Malmesbury, Lord John Manners, and others, Borthwick fulfilled an aspiration of his youth – and probably augmented his insufficient income – by assuming joint managerial control of the paper. Portentously, he and Michele began to receive letters of appreciation and encouragement from Palmerston, then restored to office.

On 5 October 1849, Michele conceded defeat and tendered his resignation to Crompton, to whom the shares reverted. The details were communicated to Disraeli by a journalist '(after a fashion) attached to the establishment of the *Mng. Post* as a political writer', who felt compelled to 'exonerate myself':

> As soon as Parliament was up this year I went into Westmorland. On my return in the middle of September, I found that a revolution had taken place in *Morning Post* matters. Mr Michele's creditor, Mr Crompton, had come into full possession of the paper, and had appointed Mr Peter Borthwick ... as the manager. Mr Michele had found favour in the sight of Her Majesty's Government, and had been appointed Consul at St Petersburg ...; and with the exception of Mr Borthwick being in Mr Michele's place, the personnel of the establishment was unchanged.
>
> Not so, however – as it seems to me – the politics. I found that nothing against the present Ministers would be admitted. Free Trade might be attacked but not the government which upholds it. . . . I asked explanations of Mr Borthwick and I have been assured by him with all the emphasis which is compatible with great redundancy of words, that no change has taken place in the politics of the paper. I am also given to understand in a certain circumlocutory manner, that the Whigs in office are better Tories than the Tories out of office.[2]

It was soon apparent that, while the Tory chieftains had dithered, Palmerston had struck. His audacity was more astounding than the complicity of either Borthwick or Michele. 'Palmerston has sent the Editor of the *Morning Post*!! Mr Mitchell [*sic*], consul to St Petersburg,' Sidney Herbert told Gladstone on 29 October. 'It is said he was in possession of inconvenient information. Peter Borthwick succeeds him in the *Morning Post*!!!'[3] The Peelites'

[1] Borthwick's awkward relations with Peel are documented in the Peel Papers: Add. MSS. 40,476, fols. 266–67; 40,530, fols. 403–8; 40,560, fol. 77; 40,581, fols. 317–18; 40,600, fols. 390 ff. For the royal view, see Queen Victoria to Peel, 18 February 1845, quoted in *Letters of Queen Victoria*, II, 39–40. A more flattering portrait of Borthwick, written under family auspices, appears in Lucas, *Glenesk*, pp. 39 ff.

[2] W. Johnston to Disraeli, 23 October 1849, Hughenden Papers.

[3] Gladstone Papers, Add. MSS. 44,210, fol. 21. During 1854, Lord Clarendon received letters from 'C. Eastland de Michele, HM Consul at St Petersburg'. Peel Papers, Add. MSS. 40,032, fols. 371, 396.

incredulity was as nothing to the indignation of the Tories. 'As to the *M. Post* – we are sold,' Malmesbury lamented on 12 November to Lord Stanley:

> Last year when Aberdeen & Co's adhesion to us on the Navigation Laws wd. have brought you into office I sent for Michele to give him his cue. To my astonishment he sent me Peter Borthwick whom I knew to have been a paid spy of Palmerston's & I refused to have anything to say to him upon our affairs, extracting however from his vanity that *he* wrote the articles against Aberdeen,

with whom the Tories might then have combined. Neglecting to mention his own failure to intervene, Malmesbury spelt out the consequences:

> *Michele* is now appointed Consul at Petersburgh [*sic*] with £1200 a year & there is no doubt that it is for *past* services that P. has paid him, he P. very sensibly thinking that praise & silence respecting his Policy in the Opposition press was worth anything to him. Crompton is the Mortgagee upon the paper & I must find out what he will do. His only care is of course to get a good sale, & no doubt Michele told him that P. Borthwick would be the best man. Borthwick in his vanity said the other day that he had got Michele the appt. & that P. could refuse him nothing.[1]

In still higher dudgeon, Malmesbury wrote six days later to Disraeli:

> The most urgent advice I have to ask you is what is to be done about the *M. Post*. If I had not other excellent reasons to know that Mr Michele has been for some time betraying us, Palmerston's appt. of the said Michele to so lucrative a place proves that it is '*for value received*'. . . . The worst part of the case is that he has left P. Borthwick behind him, who I am told on excellent authority, has declared that he will write for Protectionism (the paper wd. stop if he did not) but that he can say nothing against *Palmerston* & *Clarendon* at any time. . . . You will see the mischievous spirit of the leading article in yesterday's (Saturday's) *Post* respecting yourself, [Sir John] Young, &c.
> . . . Now what are we to do? Should we not go to Crompton & shew him that the Party will forsake his paper if it is not in trustworthy managements, & shd. we not look for another Editor? [Robert] Knox told me some man connected with the *Chronicle* wished to manage the *Post*, & wd. invest £10,000 in it, & that he spoke to you about it last summer. I am sure that Crompton wd. be glad to have a partner in the lien on the paper. . . . Nothing can be more fatal to us than the present state of things, & it is clever of P. to have 'made our paper safe' but it must be shewn up if we do not get Borthwick out.[2]

---

[1] Malmesbury to Stanley, 12 November 1849, Derby Papers 144/1.
[2] Malmesbury to Disraeli, 18 November 1849, Hughenden Papers.

Disraeli agreed that 'the state of our Press is deplorable', as he had been saying for years, and he advised consultation with Knox, the editor of the *Morning Herald*, 'with whom I only some months ago had a casual conversation on the subject in the hall of the Carlton'.[1] Malmesbury got back to Stanley on the 25th: he reiterated his accusations (raising Michele's salary to £1,400) and his vow to oust Borthwick, 'as Dizzy Lonsdale Beresford &c are all aware of his character'.[2]

Borthwick, however, was not dislodged: able to obtain for himself the backing he had been unable to obtain for Michele, he met the payments on the mortgage which Crompton had threatened to foreclose. Nor was Borthwick weaned from his Palmerstonian allegiance, despite the overtures made to him by the Tories when they came to power in 1852; instead their acquiescence in Free Trade seemed to vindicate his judgment. Later that year, he died at the age of forty-six. His son Algernon (the future Lord Glenesk) took over the paper and its political enthusiasms. Eventually, in 1897, he purchased full control from W. J. Rideout, Crompton's heir.

'At first sight Palmerston seems a curious idol for the *Morning Post*,' conceded its official historian.[3] But first sight can be misleading. A chauvinist who moreover stoutly resisted any extension of parliamentary reform, this most English of statesmen answered to the specifications of this most English of newspapers, paradoxically founded and usually edited by Scotsmen. A Conservative in bygone decades, when the *Morning Post* had sniped at him from the left, Palmerston was always (like Canning, his mentor) perversely indifferent to the party labels that attached to him. James Grant, who had 'frequent conversations . . . in private' with him during the 1850s and '60s, was left with no 'doubt that he was Conservative in his heart, and that even the little Liberalism – for it never was much – that he professed was to be ascribed to expediency, not to any special affection for Liberalism as a creed'. It was not fanciful, then, for the *Morning Post* to eulogize its hero as 'the staunchest Conservative in the kingdom' (19 October 1865). T. H. S. Escott shrewdly discerned that under the Borthwicks, father and son, the paper 'had mirrored . . . the prejudices of the Conservative voters who kept a nominally Liberal premier, Palmerston, in office'. His ecclesiastical appointments may have offended their High Church sensibilities, but he amply compensated by his vigorous defence of British interests abroad. The Turkish ambassador did not exaggerate when he proclaimed that, on paramount questions of foreign policy, 'the *Post* is Borthwick and Borthwick is Palmerston'.

[1] Disraeli to Malmesbury, 21 November 1849, quoted in Malmesbury, *Memoirs of an Ex-Minister* (London, 1884), I, 254.
[2] Malmesbury to Stanley, 25 November 1849, Derby Papers 144/1.
[3] Hindle, *Morning Post*, p. 187. Other sources cited in this paragraph are: Gaunt, I, 415–16; Escott, *Masters*, pp. 188–89; Algernon Borthwick to Peter Borthwick, 21 June 1852 and Algernon Borthwick to his wife, n.d., quoted in Lucas, *Glenesk*, pp. 117, 241.

At mid-century, Palmerston was the envy of all his parliamentary rivals. Although the diminished resources of the *Morning Chronicle* had been lost to him, the *Morning Post* stuck to him through thick and thin. The *Globe* was in his corner and, it was said, in his pocket. Neither the *Daily News*, with its progressive leanings, nor the *Standard*, with its ultra-Tory ones, was immune to his appeal. And despite 'the well-known fact' (cited by Greville) that *The Times* 'was Aberdeen's paper',[1] it was veering in his direction; after 1855, when Delane's instincts had triumphed over Reeve's bias, it took its natural place in the Palmerstonian ranks.

The old-guard Tories suffered the greatest deprivation. Lord Malmesbury, whose responsibilities – assigned or assumed – ranged far beyond his formal duties as Opposition whip in the upper House, faulted Derby (as Stanley became in 1851) for an inability 'to realize the sudden growth and power of the Political Press, for which he has no partiality'.[2] His exasperation was understandable, but the indictment was less than fair. With so vigilant a lieutenant as Malmesbury, Derby was not obliged to develop an aptitude for newspaper 'nobbling'. His reticence dictated by an aristocratic sense of propriety, he deputized others to handle matters to which he was by no means oblivious.

'I believe that we are sufficiently near to a *new* Parliament to make it advisable to put forth some positive ... policy,' Malmesbury told his chief on 27 November 1850, amid a furore over papal action to restore the Roman Catholic episcopacy in Protestant England. '... We must give a cue to our newspapers who are all in the dark & afraid to write on anything but Wiseman', the new Cardinal Archbishop of Westminster, and the Pope. 'Pray let me know whether our papers may abuse the Inland Tax & Poor rates.'[3] Unable to pronounce on party policy, least of all on the emotive question of protection, the *Morning Herald* and the *Standard* regaled their readers with 'fabulous stories' (as Lady Clarendon dismissed them)[4] about intrigues and counter-intrigues among the Whig ministers.

The Ecclesiastical Titles Bill, Lord John Russell's heavy-handed reply to 'papal aggression', subjected his *modus vivendi* with the Peelites to intensified strain. Even so, the rift between them and the protectionists remained too wide to bridge. While attention focused on religious controversies, a constitutional crisis arose with lightning speed. On 20 February 1851, the government met defeat on a motion for franchise reform, and Russell promptly resigned. Delane, who dined at the Granvilles' that evening, broke the story in *The Times* where, predictably but prematurely, he plumped for a coalition under Aberdeen. After both Aberdeen and Stanley had failed to recruit requisite support, Russell resumed the premiership on borrowed time.

---

[1] *Greville Memoirs* (24 December 1852), VI, 388.
[2] Malmesbury, *Memoirs*, II, 73 (29 June 1857).
[3] Malmesbury to Stanley, 27 November 1850, Derby Papers 144/1.
[4] Lady Clarendon's journal, 7 February 1851, quoted in Maxwell, *Clarendon*, I, 323.

If nothing else, the episode was a test of strength. Although Stanley's bid had failed, chiefly because Gladstone declined his tempting invitation to lead the Commons, he had brought his party within reach of office. It was universally conceded that he and his colleagues would soon have their chance, if only because their opponents had come to realize that a Tory government would be the ultimate spur to Whig-Peelite union.[1]

Encouraged by the drift of events, Malmesbury redoubled his efforts. He did not have much to work with, however. The *Standard* vacillated, evincing an infuriating concern for the susceptibilities of Palmerston. The *Morning Herald*, pledged to safeguard the Reformation, was consumed by its bigotry; it ignored or, worse, garbled the dispatches sent to it. There was cause to fear that the *Morning Herald* might go the way of the *Morning Post*. Knox, its editor, acquainted Malmesbury with an offer of 'pecuniary assistance' from a Mr Powles – not improbably J. D. Powles, who had been involved with Disraeli on the *Representative* in 1825–26 – whose purpose was unclear. Malmesbury prevailed on Knox to delay, and sent Stanley copies of the correspondence,

> the meaning of which is that some persons have offered to support the *Herald* with money & articles, & Knox seems afraid that some conditions may be demanded respecting political questions, wh. it might not be desirable for our Party to accept.

Stanley commended Malmesbury's tact:

> It is not very easy to write civilly to a man that his paper is conducted with very little talent; and I admire the way in which you have managed to compliment the Editor, and smooth down any possible soreness he might feel.

Yet the fact remained that the *Morning Herald*, whatever its foibles or inadequacies, could not be spared. Malmesbury attempted to raise alternative capital from G. F. Young, a prospective Tory candidate. His application, he was 'sorry to inform' his leader, was rejected: Young 'stated that he had not a shilling, so that all hope of exercising an authoritative censorship over that foolish paper is at an end'.[2]

Early in 1852, improved party prospects made the vagaries of the *Morning Chronicle* all the more intolerable. On 16 January, Malmesbury wrote to keep Derby (as Stanley had since become) abreast of the problems:

> Last week Knox the Editor sent me an article written by Mr Philipps the

---

[1] J. B. Conacher, *The Peelites and the Party System, 1846–52* (Newton Abbot, 1972), pp. 75–82.
[2] Malmesbury to Knox, 19 August 1851 (copy), Malmesbury to Stanley, 19 August 1851, and Malmesbury to Derby (formerly Stanley), 4 December 1851, Derby Papers 144/1; Stanley to Malmesbury, 5 September 1851, quoted in Malmesbury, *Memoirs*, I, 286–87.

tendency of which went so completely to declare that you meant to throw over Protection immediately you came into office that he [Knox] would not print it without asking my advice. I gave it him plainly enough, & begged him not to publish anything which took your name in vain, etc. . . . This day's post brings me the inclosed letters – one from Knox, & one from Philipps, who is, as you will see, angry at having his first article stopped & declares he has *your* authority for writing to prove protective duties impossible. . . . In spite of Philipps' undaunted letter I have written to Knox to hold on to what I told him, & I send you his and Philipps' letters. If I have done wrong you will understand why I have taken this responsibility. . . . I know D'Israeli wants to throw over Protection. . . . It appears to me that the line our papers ought to take is, to say that what you can & will do, must depend on the power placed in your hands, & to wait for the events wh. apparently are working in our favour.[1]

Aware of the dissension that flared among the Whigs, Malmesbury saw no reason to alienate potential supporters in Parliament or the country by a precipitate announcement.

He did not have long to wait. In February, Palmerston evened the score with Russell, who had dismissed him from the Foreign Office, by toppling the government. The Queen sent for Derby, who formed an administration with Malmesbury as Foreign Secretary and Disraeli as Chancellor, a position first offered to Palmerston. Spurned by the Peelites, with the unremarkable exception of Lord Hardinge, the Conservatives lacked first-rate talent ('Who? Who?' the aged Duke of Wellington enquired loudly as the unfamiliar names of Cabinet members were recited in the Lords) and, more conspicuously, a majority.

While Derby allocated places in his 'Who? Who?' ministry, Disraeli had other, larger fish to fry, assuming – as he did – that he could catch them. He was 'in constant touch' with Delane, to whom he sent 'not less than four letters' within these 'forty-eight hours'. With the approach of a summer election, he worked to cultivate *The Times*. 'I shall be very curious indeed to see your manifesto and sincerely hope to be able to back it,' Delane assured him in June, when Disraeli proffered an advance copy. In the event, Delane proved antipathetic: *The Times* (16 and 17 July) put down Disraeli as an 'inimitable illusionist', whose policies consisted of 'sweet words and the vapour of some spiritual chloroform'. With varying degrees of reluctance, the Conservatives accompanied Disraeli in his retreat from the principle of protection. Nevertheless, when the votes were counted, they were still a minority. 'Our returns would have been several seats better', Disraeli fantasized, if *The Times* had 'not deserted'. But the greatest mischief had been perpetrated by the *Morning Herald*, from which the party was more entitled to expect compliance; lacking

[1] Malmesbury to Derby, 16 January 1852, Derby Papers 144/1.

the dexterity and possibly the ingenuity to adapt to ministerial contortions, it underscored the inconsistencies of Tory spokesmen. At the outset of the campaign, Algernon Borthwick was visited 'by a member of the Government' who confirmed that the party leaders were already 'dissatisfied with the *Herald*' and eager to restore ties with the *Morning Post*. 'The *Morning Herald* is not my organ, and I trust never will be', Disraeli told Delane soon after the new Parliament assembled; 'in fact, I never wish to see my name in its columns.'[1]

Normally ravenous for publicity, Disraeli would have been glad at this time to have his name disappear from the press altogether. On 15 November, a few days after he had written to Delane, he was obliged as leader of the House to pay a memorial tribute to Wellington, who had died during the recess. Unthinkingly ('he would never have been such a fool as to do it on purpose', Robert Blake has insisted),[2] his speech contained a passage that was strikingly reminiscent of Thiers's eulogy of Marshal St Cyr, delivered in 1829 and reprinted by the *Morning Chronicle* in 1848. The *Globe* gleefully published Thiers's text alongside the corresponding extracts from Disraeli's speech. By implication, the Chancellor's opportunism had extended to plagiarism.

Worse was to come. The government's fiscal policy, left studiously vague in the Queen's Speech on 4 November, awaited clarification in Disraeli's December budget. It was a tricky assignment and one to which Disraeli did not bring the best credentials. He had to reconcile conflicting interests in a way that would neither offend his supporters nor reunite his adversaries. The relative forbearance of the Commons contrasted sharply with the excitement in the press, where opinion converged against him. The *Morning Post* considered Palmerston more capable of meeting the challenge, which Granville took as a hint that Palmerston was now ready to try his hand. The *Morning Herald* and the *Standard* questioned the wisdom of Free Trade, the *Daily News* and the *Morning Chronicle* the sincerity of Disraeli's conversion to it. *The Times*, aside from occasional gibes, held its fire for the substance of Disraeli's proposals, presented in a five-hour speech on 3 December. The debate began a week later, and raged for four nights. Accepting the inevitability of defeat and the likelihood of a coalition thereafter, Disraeli rose on the final evening to defend himself, to taunt his critics, and to issue his famous dictum 'that England does not love Coalitions'. Unconvinced by his computations, especially after Gladstone had torn them to shreds, the House voted down the budget and turned out the government. Unconvinced by his constitutional argument, *The Times* retorted (22 December): 'Nothing suits the people to be governed and the measures to be passed so well as a good coalition.'

At last Delane had his wish. On the morning of the 19th, Aberdeen saw the

[1] Dasent, *Delane*, I, 133; Delane to Disraeli, 3 June 1852, Hughenden Papers; Algernon Borthwick to Peter Borthwick, 21 June 1852, quoted in Lucas, *Glenesk*, p. 117; Disraeli to Delane, 11 November 1852, quoted in Dasent, *Delane*, I, 148; Cook, *Delane of 'The Times'*, pp. 59–60.
[2] Blake, *Disraeli*, p. 335; *also see* Lady Clarendon's journal, 16 November 1852, quoted in Maxwell, *Clarendon*, I, 351.

Queen, and that evening he saw Delane. Separately, both commissioned him to bring together the Peelites and the Whigs in a second Ministry of All the Talents. In its leader the next morning, *The Times* lauded the supreme virtues of Aberdeen and tartly reminded Russell and his friends that the future of Liberalism did 'not rest solely with them'. Impatient to achieve inter-party co-operation, Delane rejected the tactics of gentle persuasion and instead attempted to browbeat the Whigs into submission. His daily strictures were calculated to convince the Russellite contingent (270 MPs by Russell's own count, as compared with 30 Peelites) that quality should take precedence over quantity. On Christmas day, *The Times* flaunted its highly placed contacts by accurately anticipating the full list of Cabinet appointments. Then, as if to add insult to injury, it gave a warmer welcome to the Peelite ministers than to their Whig associates. The Foreign Secretary, not yet officially confirmed, received no welcome at all:

> Lord John Russell has so little of the accomplishments specially required for his new office that we can only suppose he is keeping it for a successor, most probably Lord Clarendon, who otherwise will not have a seat in the Cabinet.

That *The Times* was correct in its surmise – Russell, continuing as leader of the House, ceded his portfolio to Clarendon the following February – confirmed that it had had access to inside sources. Clarendon, himself embarrassed, protested that *The Times*'s article 'was as offensive to the Whigs as possible and evidently intended to bring Lord John into contempt'. Far from facilitating amalgamation, it had unleashed 'anti-ministerial feeling' among Whigs, whose claims to office were not only denied, but also disparaged. Russell, he reported, was 'mortified and annoyed, because the friendship between Lord A. and Delane is, as he said, well known, and nobody will suppose that attacks on him would find their way into *The Times*, unless they were agreeable to Lord A.'[1]

Although the *Morning Post* and the *Globe* would have preferred Palmerston at the Foreign Office, his appointment to the Home Office assured the Aberdeen Coalition of their benevolence. The *Daily News* was placated, at least for the time being, by the inclusion of Sir William Molesworth as a representative of Radical views; with Delane to vouch for him, his place as First Commissioner of Works carried Cabinet rank. And, needless to say, the *Morning Chronicle* was exultant.

Since 1848, the *Chronicle* had been secure in Peelite hands.[2] Sir John Easthope, caught in the cross-fire between Russell and Palmerston and

---

[1] Clarendon to Reeve, 26 December 1852, quoted in Maxwell, *Clarendon*, I, 355; *also see* Conacher, *Aberdeen Coalition*, pp. 25–26.

[2] This account is based on the following: memorandum by Prince Albert, 6 July 1846, quoted in *Letters of Queen Victoria*, II, 102; *Greville Memoirs* (20 February 1848), VI, 17; Gash, *Peel*, pp. 637–38; *History of The Times*, II, appendix 2, 533–34; John Oldcastle [Wilfred Meynell], *Journals and Journalism* (London, 1880), pp. 83–84.

angered by the Whigs' 'subserviency to *The Times* and treason to him', saw no further reason to sustain his steady losses. The purchasers included Lord Lincoln, Sidney Herbert, and Edward Cardwell; and there were unconfirmed reports that Gladstone was among them. In disposing of the property, Easthope (according to Greville) 'tried to bargain for its continued support of Palmerston, which was flatly refused', as a leader on 10 May attested. W. F. A. Delane, father of the editor of *The Times*, was installed as manager, a position that conferred less authority than he had hoped to wield. J. D. Cook, Lincoln's protégé, became editor. And Abraham Hayward, who looked to Lincoln to set 'the proper tone', supervised the political content. Immediately, the paper took up so militant a stand against the Whigs that Peel confessed to disquiet; he did not object, however, to its attacks on the protectionists. After Peel's tragic death in 1850, the *Chronicle* was all the more determined to kindle the sacred flame. Aberdeen, too, found its devotion an impediment to his aims. The favouritism he showed *The Times*, emulated by his successive foreign secretaries, brought indignant protests. 'The *Chronicle* is the only morning paper that has uniformly supported the government', Hayward remonstrated to Sir John Young, the Chief Secretary for Ireland, on 14 September 1853, 'and *The Times* constantly turns against it on the chance of gaining any stray ray of popularity.'

Hayward, who interrupted a career as a literary essayist to assist Lincoln, a personal friend, personified the *Chronicle*'s plight. His loyalties were divided between the ministerial Peelites, who retained office on Whig sufferance, and the journalists, who were all too quick to detect signs of betrayal. That is not to imply that all members of the *Chronicle* staff were ardent Peelites. In his quest for talent, Cook invited W. V. Harcourt, then a Cambridge undergraduate, to submit 'articles now and then according as I had the opportunities'. Harcourt, who 'did not fancy selling myself to their views altogether', joined the paper as a leader-writer in 1849, when he was twenty-one years old. His pugnacity, for which he was later notorious in Parliament, was already evident in his articles for the *Chronicle*. 'What has come over Harcourt?' Hayward asked the 5th Duke of Newcastle (as Lincoln had been retitled) on 19 December 1853. 'His language about the government seems borrowed from the *Herald* or the *Standard*. Cook, too, was getting too bellicose,' Hayward added. 'He is a good fellow, and always open to reason, but rather apt to be swayed by men like Harcourt, who . . . is rather too fond of strong language and uncompromising steps.'[1]

The *Morning Chronicle*, as Fox Bourne recalled it, 'was a serviceable, if a costly, engine for the leading of the Peelites from the Conservatism from

---

[1] Hayward, *Correspondence*, I, 189, 200; A. G. Gardiner, *The Life of Sir William Harcourt* (London, 1923), I, 51–52; and Conacher, *Aberdeen Coalition*, pp. 132–33, for an account of Hayward's grievances against Aberdeen and Russell.

which they started to the Liberalism in which most of them found rest'.[1] It could not have served such a purpose without generating tensions, and Hayward had borne the brunt of them. Like him, Cook had given valuable support through the paper and behind the scenes. His relations were exceptionally close with Gladstone, to whom he had appealed for 'guides to the path I ought to adopt, and . . . lights to enable me to follow it with advantage'.[2] Their correspondence and confabulations, enumerated in Gladstone's diaries, reveal Cook's usefulness as a publicist, adviser, and emissary.

Yet, by 1854, the proprietors of the *Morning Chronicle*, along with its dwindling readership, had obviously wearied of it. Writing to Young on 30 May, Hayward strenuously denied 'a prevalent report that the *Chronicle* has been sold'.[3] As he must have suspected, the rumours were not wholly without substance. That autumn, the paper passed to the ownership of William Glover, a serjeant-at-law, who was said to have extracted the promise that his capital would be returned with interest over a three-year period if Peelite principles were respected. Hayward, literally a hostage to fortune, stayed on, participating on an increasingly occasional and tenuous basis; but the link had been effectively severed. Anxious to turn a quick profit, Glover angled for a subsidy from Louis Napoleon and, when that expedient failed, sold out to J. M. Levy, whose *Daily Telegraph* swallowed the *Chronicle* in 1862. Gladstone, hoping to stave off Levy and the inevitable, had proposed a scheme in 1855 whereby Goldwin Smith would assume political direction, while financial responsibility would quietly rest with Sir Arthur Elton, a poet with parliamentary ambitions, who was to be MP for Bath from 1857 to 1859. Smith, however, 'earnestly' counselled Gladstone 'not to allow your name . . . to be connected in any way with the transaction' which, he warned, seemed 'questionable in principle and likely to lead to unsatisfactory results'.[4]

While Gladstone was attempting his salvage operation, Cook transferred his editorial services elsewhere, taking with him Harcourt, Smith, and other exiles from the *Chronicle*. To Sidney Herbert, whom he met in October, he outlined plans for 'a weekly review without news but with reviews of all the stirring subjects'.[5] As the *Saturday Review*, the journal made its début in November. Over the next dozen years, Cook's team of regular contributors

[1] *English Newspapers*, II, 156.

[2] Cook to Gladstone [1852], Gladstone Papers, Add. MSS. 44,373, fol. 126; for examples of the 'guides' and 'lights' Gladstone furnished, see Cook's letters among the Gladstone Papers, especially Add, MSS. 44,372, fols. 126, 137, and 306.

[3] Hayward, *Correspondence*, I, 221.

[4] Smith to Gladstone, 25 July 1855, Gladstone Papers, Add. MSS. 44,303, fol. 89. *The Gladstone Diaries* (ed. H. C. G. Matthew) record letters to Elton on 14, 18, and 21 July, and 2 August, in addition to meetings with Smith on 14 July and with Elton on 31 July. V (Oxford, 1978), 64–68. Smith had written to Gladstone on 2 and 6 May about his 'idea . . . to set up *a new joint stock newspaper*'. Gladstone Papers, Add. MSS. 44,303, fols. 77 ff., 84.

[5] Herbert to Gladstone, 7 October 1855, Gladstone Papers, Add. MSS. 44,210, fols. 210–12; *also see* M. M. Bevington, *The Saturday Review, 1855–1868* (New York, 1941).

expanded to include Lord Robert Cecil (later 3rd Marquess of Salisbury), Fitz-james Stephen, Henry Maine, Walter Bagehot, and John Morley. The money for the venture was subscribed by Alexander Beresford Hope, a prosperous Tory MP and brother-in-law to Cecil, with whom he shared an antipathy towards Disraeli. His beneficence and sophistication afforded Cook considerable latitude. The founding of the *Saturday Review*, contemporaneous with the overhaul of the *Spectator* by Hutton and Townsend, indeed 'marked most decisively the advent of a new era' in literary culture.[1] In the history of the political press, it figures less prominently as a postcript to the story of the *Morning Chronicle*.

In strictly political terms, weekly journalism was more significantly enlivened by the appearance on 7 May 1853 of the maiden number of the *Press*, Disraeli's second excursion into proprietorship. Lord Stanley, more attentive to newspaper affairs than was his father, Lord Derby, agreed that something needed to be done to raise the level and circulation of the Tory papers. Various schemes had been mooted, including an improbable liaison with G. W. M. Reynolds, who approached Disraeli in October 1850, six months after he had successfully launched *Reynolds's Newspaper*: 'Although having no sympathy with your political opinions of the present day,' Reynolds admitted, 'I am a great admirer of your writings, and have read *Sybil* more than once. Before I had a newspaper of my own I was Literary and Foreign Editor of the *Weekly Dispatch* for some years.'[2] Disraeli did well to resist the temptation: *Reynolds's*, marked by an unsettled Radicalism that did not stop short of republicanism, was an inappropriate vehicle for his self-styled Tory progressivism.

The *Press*, on the contrary, was a full-fledged Disraelian production: he raised the capital from among his friends; he hand-picked the contributors (who included Stanley, George Smythe, and Bulwer-Lytton); and, although he tried to throw his readers off the scent by deriding the prolixity and 'Yankee ... rhetoric' of his own speeches, many of the polemics flowed from his pen. 'D's ardour, great from the first, rose higher and higher as the plan assumed definite form,' Stanley wrote in his diary. 'He talked of a circulation of from 10,000 to 15,000: of driving all other weekly journals out of the field: even of shaking the power of *The Times*.'[3] At its peak, the circulation of the *Press* was reckoned at about 3,000, and the only quavers it caused were on the part of the Tory hierarchy. An irritant to Derby, who had dissuaded the Duke of Northumberland from subscribing capital, it was also a standing invitation to ridicule. 'If the Disraelites are to find their way through the desert of Opposition

---

[1] John Gross, *The Rise and Fall of the Man of Letters* (London, 1969), p. 63.

[2] Reynolds to Disraeli, 23 October 1850, Hughenden Papers; for a depiction of *Reynolds's News*, see Fox Bourne, III, 96–989.

[3] Stanley's diary. 14 March 1853, in *Disraeli, Derby and the Conservative Party* (ed J. Vincent; Hassocks, Sussex, 1978), p. 102. The following July, Stanley recalled (*ibid.*, p. 109) that 'the party supplied about £2,500' for the *Press*; 'the same amount was subscribed by Disraeli himself. . . . I declined to give money, but wrote in every number, not on personal subjects.'

by the columns of cloud of the *Press*, we wish them good deliverance,' mocked
the *Globe* on 20 October 1855. Scanning 'this day's number . . . which is lying
before us', the editors of that Palmerstonian paper summed up 'the Disraelite
policy' on the Crimean War as one of 'hunting with the hounds, and holding with
the hare'. Truth to tell, the *Press* did equivocate, bringing to mind the Fleet
Street formula:

> If you preach war, JOHN BULL will throw you down, and call you mad. If
> you preach peace, JOHN will approve, but he will think you poor-spirited.
> But if you preach *Peace* AND *War*, JOHN will praise you, buy you, and dub
> you his organ.

Disraeli, who assiduously attended the meetings of the managerial committee
during this period, could not have put it more sardonically himself. The *Press*
mirrored his own inability to decide where, if at all, to stand firm.

Its editor was Samuel Lucas, who regarded the new journal as 'our literary
crusade'. Promising to 'be as brief as possible', he wrote Disraeli an eight-page
letter on 5 July 1853 to acquaint him (assuredly not 'in a spirit of complaint')
with assorted problems of finance, production, and personnel:

> We have obtained the *nucleus* of a great success. I don't mean as a specula-
> tion but as an instrument to affect opinion (for I doubt whether we shall ever
> do much more than meet our expenses and I am certain that from a party
> point of view we ought to be content if we do as much). . . .

Yet there existed serious difficulties, for the most part inherent in the structure. 'We are expected to produce an *Organ* which shall adequately represent
a great party . . . by a variety of superior original matter of a kind which
cannot be obtained from hack writers.' Unlike the *Spectator* where, under a
'systematised plan, . . . one mind initiates and comprehends and directs everything', the *Press* suffered from a diffusion of control. Its contributors, being
public men unused to the ways of journalism, tended to ignore deadlines,
exceed word limits, or resist editorial injunctions. 'In some instances as you
know I have had subjects declined and cast upon myself in the last resort. On
the other hand I have simultaneously received three articles upon one
question.' Political considerations compounded his burdens and detracted
from his authority:

> In conducting *this organ of a party* I have often to satisfy the requirements of
> various members of the party who have a stake in the enterprise . . . or I
> have to explain to each respectively the impediments which prevent his
> views being carried out. . . . I am to a considerable extent the confidant of
> individual complaints and representations arising out of the disorganisation
> of our party.

It was precisely in this respect that Lucas had been encouraged to believe that he could render

> more service even than any of us have contemplated. . . . The reorganisation of the party should be in some way connected with the *Press*. . . . The *Press* offers facilities for acquiring information and knowledge of men and their views. . . . Indirectly it acts by bringing a few keen energetic men into the habit of working together – induces mutual reliance and a knowledge of each other's capacities – supplies a *nucleus*. It becomes in fact a sort of *outpost* of party from which we can discern and act upon the enemy.[1]

Having written (by Stanley's tabulation) ten of the first eleven leading articles that ran in the *Press*, Disraeli could not have been impressed by Lucas's claims of overwork. Nor did he require an editor to lecture him on party strategy. Small wonder, therefore, that Lucas soon departed for *The Times*, where his talents were employed to better advantage as a reviewer. David T. Coulton replaced him, and the columns of the *Press* did not record or reflect the change. Disraeli's flagrant efforts at self-promotion, typified by his dominance of the *Press*, told against him. 'I can see that many believe Disraeli would like to place himself at the head of the Conservative party, to the exclusion of Lord Derby,' Malmesbury wrote on 26 April 1856. 'These suspicions are strengthened by the tone of his paper, the *Press*, which avoids ever mentioning the name of Lord Derby, or of anyone except Disraeli himself, whom it praises in the most fulsome manner.' Derby's resentment, long suppressed, was brought into the open on 4 March 1857 when, in a speech in the Lords, he 'denied the correctness of a paragraph in the *Press*' that reported a recent party conclave: 'it was a gross misrepresentation – that words were put into his mouth which he had never used and that he was even made to say the exact contrary to what he really said.' Malmesbury, who described the scene, gloated that 'Disraeli will not like this, for the *Press* is conducted by him, and is his organ, always putting him forward and ignoring Lord Derby.' In fact, according to Mrs Disraeli, the *Press* had 'ceased to be under his control' since the previous winter, although he continued as a proprietor.[2] In 1858, when he returned to the Exchequer in Derby's second administration, Disraeli was only too happy to dispose entirely of his holding, which had probably done him more harm than good.

The *Press* limped along without him. That he was no longer in the market,

[1] Lucas to Disraeli, 17 April and 5 July 1853, Hughenden Papers. For discussions of the *Press*, see *Greville Memoirs* (22 June 1853), VI, 429; Blake, *Disraeli*, pp. 352–53; and Escott, *Masters*, pp. 205–6. Lucas's description of editorial arrangements at the *Spectator* were confirmed by Thornton Hunt to his father on 30 October 1845, in a letter preserved among the Peel Papers, Add. MSS. 40,579, fol. 360.

[2] Malmesbury, *Memoirs*, II, 45, 63; Mrs Disraeli to Mrs Willyams, 18 March 1856, quoted in G. E. Buckle, *The Life of Benjamin Disraeli*, IV (New York, 1916), 30–31; *also see* Robert Stewart, *The Foundation of the Conservative Party* (London, 1978), pp. 291–92.

so to speak, discouraged neither newspapermen from offering their wares nor
him from showing interest. James Birch, for example, obliged him in August
1858 with

> a copy of the *Sunday Times* – a journal which very lately was adverse to the
> present Government and the party which supports it – though now as you
> may see – tolerably favourable to both – a change which I trust I have
> slightly assisted in producing.
>
> While struggling with great difficulties and endeavouring to get out of
> troubled waters in which I am unfortunately still immersed, your appreci-
> ation has cheered me and flattered me.[1]

Declaring its 'principles' as 'Liberal-Conservative' in the 1860 edition of the
Newspaper Press Directory (where they were labelled 'Conservative' only in
1882), the *Sunday Times* denounced the Whigs as 'conceited and supercilious,
though there is not one among them whom history does not enable us to trace
to a low origin', and it averred that 'Lord Derby and his colleagues act upon
totally different principles, and are willing to take up with merit, wherever it
can be found' (8 August 1858). Celebrating Disraeli over Bright as an electoral
reformer, it portrayed him 'not as a reactionary or stationary statesman, . . .
but as the friend of progress and the advancement of the working classes' (10
July and 18 September 1859). Here was support worth having, and cheap at
the price.

*   *   *

Tutored in the traditional school of political journalism, Disraeli adapted
with Palmerstonian alacrity to the requirements of new institutions that
evolved during the pivotal decade of the 1850s. Apart from the paper duty,
which survived until 1861, the 'taxes on knowledge' were repealed, with the
result that the press expanded, quantitatively and qualitatively, to encompass
new sectional interests. As Alan J. Lee has comprehensively stated: 'Whether
commercial or ideological, a matter of profits or of national education, the
need was recognised for a multiplication of readers and of newspapers.'[2]

More plentiful and more cheaply priced, respectable newspapers penetra-
ted into social and geographical regions from which they were previously
excluded. 'The best part of the Press (*The Times*, for instance) seldom finds its
way to the cottages and reading-rooms of the lower classes,' Greville had
observed with dismay in 1848. Cobden confirmed his impression on a visit, two
years later, to Midhurst, 'a Sussex hill-side village': 'The only newspapers
which enter the parish are two copies of *Bell's Weekly Messenger*, a sound old

---

[1] Birch to Disraeli, 8 August 1858, Hughenden Papers. Birch was presumably the same journalist who had been involved in disreputable dealings with the *Dublin World* (see Aspinall, pp. 375–
78); although his letter to Disraeli appears to have been dated '1859', its contents indicate that it
was written soon after Parliament was prorogued on 2 August 1858.
[2] Lee. *Origins of the Popular Press*, p. 54.

Tory Protectionist much patronized by drowsy farmers.' C. D. Collet, a vigorous propagandist for the unstamping of the press, weakened his case somewhat by conceding in 1851 that 'many persons in the country ... are utterly unable to understand a London paper'.[1] He did not mean to imply that the provincial public was uncultivated, much less illiterate, but rather that the metropolitan journals – despite their 'national' pretensions – were unduly parochial in their focus. If so – and Gladstone, for one, later concurred that the London papers habitually catered to 'the opinions of the Clubs rather than the opinion of the great nation'[2] – These newspapers, stamped or unstamped, would have been unintelligible and possibly offensive to the multitudes.

Although the growth of the press after 1855 was especially pronounced in the provincial centres and among the less affluent classes, it would be a simplification to interpret the phenomenon exclusively in those terms. That growth was also manifest in Clubland, the refuge of the governing élite. The accounts of the United University Club show an expenditure on English newspapers of £207. 3s. 4d. in 1852 (when *The Times* and other quality dailies sold at 5d.), £255. 9s. 8d. in 1856 (when *The Times* sold at 4d. and the *Daily Telegraph* and *Morning Star* at a penny), and £231. 13s. in 1866 (when *The Times* sold at 3d., its price until 1913, and its chief competitors at either 2d. or a penny). These figures, incidentally, exclude the substantial amounts spent on newspapers bought by the club for resale to members. For the Oxford and Cambridge Club, the earliest committee minutes are for the second half of 1861, when the appropriation for newspapers was £134. 8s. Throughout the ensuing decade, as newspaper prices continued to drop (the *Standard*, the *Daily News*, and the *Globe* to a penny; the *Daily Chronicle* and the *Echo* to a halfpenny), annual totals stayed fixed at approximately £300. In other words, the reduction of prices allowed both of these clubs to purchase considerably more copies of a growing profusion of papers. From this fragmentary evidence,[3] one may deduce that part of the dramatic increase in overall consumption, arguably the most politically significant part, occurred among the privileged orders, whose appetite for newspapers became an addiction.

'The effect of the repeal of the stamp and paper duties,' in the considered judgment of John Vincent, 'was to raise to first position a quite new class of newspaper, democratic but not Radical, cheap but respectable, interested more in politics as it affected circulation, less in being the oracle of aristocratic factions and politicians.'[4] In essence, this rings true; in detail, it is open to dispute. Though a new class – or category – of newspapers certainly did appear, it was neither the immediate nor the exclusive effect of legislation in

[1] *Greville Memoirs* (21 July 1848), VI, 92; Cobden to Henry Ashworth, 7 October 1850, quoted in Morley, *Cobden*, II, 4; Collet's testimony is quoted in Lee, p. 73.

[2] Quoted in *The Times*, 4 September 1871.

[3] The records of the United University and Oxford and Cambridge Clubs were consulted at the library of the United Oxford and Cambridge University Club, London.

[4] *The Formation of the Liberal Party, 1857–1868* (London, 1966), pp. 58–59.

1855 and 1861. In format, content, and – above all else – the values it aimed to inculcate, 'the cheap press [did] not differ greatly from the dear press that preceded it', at least not for the better part of a generation, declared Frederick Moy Thomas, a Fleet Street veteran.[1] Furthermore, 'politics as it affected circulation' remained associated in many minds with 'being the oracle of aristocratic factions and politicians', themselves often inseparable. There can be no quibbling, however, with Vincent's general conclusion:

> The main developments in the London press between 1855 and 1870 were the attrition of the eighteenth-century aristocratic prints, the conquest of the popular market by two papers representing the orthodox Parliamentary parties, and the capture of the Radical press by militant Gladstonians.[2]

In each instance, the process had tentatively begun before 1855, but took impetus from the events of that *annus mirabilis*. And, in each instance, a pattern was firmly established by 1870.

Of all the London newspapers, the *Morning Post* had most actively perpetuated the traditions of the eighteenth-century aristocratic prints. Only gradually and by necessity did it divest itself of these primordial features. In 1864, after the paper had conformed to a nineteenth-century model, Algernon Borthwick and his dining companions hatched the *Owl* as an outlet for their pent-up levity.[3] Improvised as a prank, it saw print at irregular intervals, when it amused high society by its quips and quiddities. Among its progenitors were Evelyn Ashley, son of the 7th Earl of Shaftesbury, Lord Wharncliffe and his brother, James Stuart-Wortley, and Sir Henry Drummond Wolff. Five years after its inaugural flight, 'the pestilential bird', as Wharncliffe called it, fluttered no more. 'It was clear . . . that the game was played out,' he explained, and he might have said the same for the genre. That was in July 1869, five months before the deadline set by Vincent.

The other developments to which Vincent alludes require more extensive explication. The *Owl* was an atavism, whereas the *Daily News* was a harbinger. It made its first appearance on 21 January 1846, ten years after the stamp tax had been lowered from 4d. to a penny and nearly a decade before this surcharge was entirely abolished. The editor was the illustrious Charles Dickens who, with the massive sum of £100,000 reportedly at his disposal, raided other newspaper offices for his staff. Among his acquisitions was John Forster (his future biographer) from the *Examiner*, Eyre Evans Crowe from the *Morning Chronicle*, and Robert Russell from *The Times*. Russell was deputized to recruit his cousin, William Howard Russell (who was to achieve fame as a war correspondent for *The Times*), but the *Chronicle* outbid the

---

[1] Quoted in Sir John Robinson, *Fifty Years of Fleet Street* (London, 1904), pp. 216–17.
[2] Vincent, *Formation*, p. 61.
[3] Lucas, *Glenesk*, pp. 195–96, 217–18; Dasent, *Delane*, II, 116–17.

Daily News by two guineas, and William Howard 'was ready to fight for the side which paid me the highest salary'. Dickens, whose own salary was put at £2,000, entrusted the management of the paper to his father, whose performance lent credence to the legend that the elder Dickens was the prototype for Mr Micawber. Something of a family affair, the *Daily News* appointed as its music critic George Hogarth, Dickens's father-in-law. More to his credit, the editor also hired Frederick Knight Hunt and W. H. Wills as sub-editors, William Weir as financial writer, and a string of top-notch parliamentary reporters.

The financial resources came from the printing firm of Bradbury and Evans, with notable assistance from Sir Joseph Paxton (better remembered as the architect for the Crystal Palace than as a Liberal MP), Sir Joshua Walmsley (a Free Trader from Liverpool who founded the National Reform Association and was an MP from 1849 to 1857), and Sir William Jackson (another progressive MP, who had made his fortune in railway construction). Bradbury, in old age, estimated his company's total loss at £200,000, and 'could not bear to pass the office and see the name painted up outside it'. And Jackson told Charles Mackay, 'with a rueful countenance and a groan, that he had thrown away seven thousand pounds on the speculation. "Yes," he said, "seven thousand pounds in real *golden* sovereigns!"'[1]

Shoddily produced – Robert Russell heard 'reports of a Saturnalia among the printers' – the first number of the *Daily News* was an eight-page sheet that contained the statutory postulation of its editorial creed:

> The principles advocated by the *Daily News* will be principles of progress and improvement, of education, civil and religious liberty, and equal legislation – principles such as its conductors believe the advancing spirit of the time requires, the condition of the country demands, and justice, reason, and experience legitimately sanction.

The leader that morning was written neither by Dickens, who was never 'much of a politician in the partisan sense', nor by Crowe, whose Palmerstonian leanings disqualified him for this particular task, but instead by William Johnson Fox, a paid evangelist for the Anti-Corn Law League and afterwards MP for Oldham. That this assignment had to be farmed out was symbolic of the incongruity between the paper's political commitments and its editor's literary predilections.

Before the first accounts were in, Dickens had abruptly withdrawn from the editorship. He had lasted twenty-six days and seventeen issues, and looked

[1] This discussion is based on the following: J. B. Atkins, *Life of Sir William Howard Russell* (London, 1911), I, 55–56, 58; Robinson, *Fifty Years*, pp. 139–41; Mackay, *Through the Long Day*, I, 342–43; Escott, *Masters*, pp. 212–13; Fox Bourne, II, 148–51; Grant, II, 79–83; Justin McCarthy and Sir John Robinson, *The 'Daily News' Jubilee* (London, 1896), pp. 13–16; T. P. O'Connor, *Memoirs of an Old Parliamentarian* (London, 1929), I, 51; and H. W. Massingham, *The London Daily Press* (London, 1892), pp. 42–43.

back on the experience as a 'brief mistake'. His father departed with him, leaving business affairs to the more capable hands of Charles Wentworth Dilke (grandfather and namesake of the Liberal politician), who tried to raise the circulation by halving the price to 2½d.; as a penny of that amount was consumed by the stamp, it proved necessary to revert by stages to the original fivepenny price. All the same, Dilke had shown enterprise. Under his management, which terminated with his retirement in April 1849, the *Daily News* (as his grandson wrote) 'became the forerunner of [the] cheap press' that was to flourish after 1855.

Forster succeeded to the editorship, at first informally. He, in turn, gave way to Frederick Knight Hunt, during whose relatively brief tenure the paper came into its own. It was Hunt who launched the journalistic career of Harriet Martineau who, in the years between 1852 and 1866, contributed some 1,600 articles, many of them diatribes against 'that rotten oracle', *The Times*. When Hunt died in 1854, Weir replaced him. When Weir died in 1858, Thomas Walker was promoted from assistant editor, and John Robinson became managing editor. Walker retired in 1869, when Gladstone pensioned him off with the editorship of the *London Gazette*. T. P. O'Connor described him as 'a very brilliant and very cynical and rather saturnine figure', but a devoted Gladstonian nonetheless. By that time (again, the terminal date of Vincent's study), the *Daily News* was an incontrovertible success. At a penny, it sold 150,000 copies a day. Yet commercial considerations, while impossible to ignore, always yielded to ideological ones. On that score, the paper could take justifiable pride. H. W. Massingham, who was to become its parliamentary correspondent early in the next century, described in 1892 how the *Daily News* had both assisted and reflected

> the rise of the middle classes, and especially the Nonconformist bodies, to political power, with their triple watchwords of free commerce, Parliamentary reform, and civil and religious freedom; abroad it has preached the doctrine of nationalities, at home that of the realisation of the political side of democracy, and withal it has represented and represents the voice of official and organised Liberalism.

Following the lead of the *Daily News*, the *Morning Advertiser* – the accredited organ of the Licensed Victuallers' Association – adopted a tone of greater moral earnestness. For two decades, from mid-century until 1870, it was edited by James Grant who, disclaiming 'the purpose of magnifying myself', professed to have 'conducted that journal on thoroughly Independent as well as thoroughly Liberal principles'.[1] The repeal of the stamp duty, a quarter of the way through Grant's editorship, affected the paper's profits, but scarcely its attitudes. Its mission, as promulgated by its religious editor, was nothing less than 'to Enlighten, to Civilise, and to Morally Transform the World'.

[1] Grant, II, 63; *also see* Vincent, *Formation*, p. 61.

The abolition of the stamp had its most direct repercussions in the northern conurbations, where weekly and bi-weekly journals – such as the *Manchester Guardian*, the *Liverpool Post*, and the *Scotsman* in Edinburgh – converted to daily publication, and other papers sprang into existence. In the metropolitan press, there was a delayed reaction. Colonel A. B. Sleigh, anticipating parliamentary action, had been incubating plans for the *Daily Telegraph and Courier*, which he brought out on 29 June. Its four pages, with a larger typeface and a livelier design, implied a break with the past that was more apparent than real. The proprietor's motives were, in fact, a throwback to the eighteenth century: he was carrying on a feud with the Duke of Cambridge, whom he hoped to discredit through his columns. With a selling price of 2d. and advertising receipts on the first day of 7/10d., the paper quickly exhausted Sleigh's modest assets. In July, he switched to a new printer, J. M. Levy, to whom he pledged his shares as collateral. Levy, who already had a stake in the *Sunday Times*, soon took over the property which, with an abridged masthead, appeared on 16 September as London's first penny paper. Within a few days he could boast: 'The Circulation of the *Daily Telegraph* EXCEEDS THAT OF ANY LONDON MORNING NEWSPAPER, with the exception of *The Times*. More than that, the Circulation of the *Daily Telegraph* is greater than any FOUR MORNING Newspapers all put together.'[1]

Unlike the *Daily News*, with its rapid turnover at the helm, the *Daily Telegraph* had only six editors (some not officially designated as such) in the course of its first hundred years. All of them worked in the shadow of Levy and his descendants or, after 1927, members of the Berry family. The first was Thornton Hunt, son of the great Radical journalist, Leigh Hunt. He is guardedly described in the *Dictionary of National Biography* as having 'practically edited' the paper. Clustered around him were Edwin Arnold (whom Edward Levy-Lawson, Levy's Anglicized son, subsequently acknowledged as 'the head of my staff'), Edward Dicey, J. M. LeSage (after 1863), and the irrepressible G. A. Sala, who produced 'two leaders of fifteen hundred words each, every day save Saturday'. As a rule, Sala did not tackle political topics, which he left to 'two members of the gifted family of St John': J. A. St John and his son Horace. Bayle St John, another son, was the *Telegraph*'s correspondent in Paris.

Twenty-two years old when his father acquired the *Daily Telegraph*, Edward Levy-Lawson (created a baronet in 1892 and the 1st Baron Burnham in 1903) had already served as drama critic for the *Sunday Times*. His father saw to it that he knew every facet of newspaper production, and – even during Levy's lifetime – he was expected to exercise ultimate authority. W. L. Courtney, who came down from Oxford in 1890 to undertake a second career in

---

[1] Lord Burnham, *Peterborough Court* (London, 1955), chs. I–II, and p. 161; *History of The Times*, II, 294–97; G. A. Sala, *Life and Adventures* (London, 1895), I, 394–97; Massingham, *London Daily Press*, pp. 98–99.

journalism, watched his chief 'at his best', working over a leader 'line by line, word by word, making erasions here, adding a sentence there, deleting, strengthening, building up – and all the time explaining why he did this or that and what object he was aiming at'. There were not many nineteenth-century proprietors so assiduous as Levy-Lawson; nor, for that matter, were there many professional journalists so obsequious as Courtney.

'The paper', Courtney recalled from his earlier days as a reader, 'was for some time consistently Liberal, and Gladstone himself was at one time a prime favourite at Peterborough Court', where the editorial offices were located. That, by the time of Courtney's arrival, was ancient history. Massingham confirmed that the *Telegraph* had 'started on the lines of tolerably advanced Liberalism', from which it diverged in the late 1870s, when Gladstone embarked on his crusade against the 'unspeakable Turk'. At least in part, its early loyalty to Gladstone was predicated on mutual economic assumptions. As a printer as well as a newspaper owner, Levy was anxious to secure the remission of the paper duty. During the second Derby administration, he and Sala led a deputation to Downing Street, where the Prime Minister (as Sala pungently recounted) 'looked on them as Jupiter Hostis might be expected to look on an assembly of black beetles'. Gladstone, by contrast, was responsive to their grievance. As Chancellor of the Exchequer in the next government, he won their gratitude by sponsoring legislation that trimmed the *Telegraph*'s expenses by £12,000 in 1861, when its daily sale was certified at close to 142,000 copies.

By his 1861 budget, which qualifies as a constitutional no less than a financial feat, Gladstone cemented his relationship with the *Daily Telegraph*. On 15 April, he presented his statement to the House: 'The figures rather made my head ache.' The debate on the paper duty, resumed after an adjournment, culminated on 30 May ('One of the greatest nights on the whole of my recollection'), when Gladstone 'spoke 1 hour' and carried repeal by a majority of fifteen. Among his callers on 11 June was 'Mr Levy (Ed. *Daily Telegraph*)', who doubtless proffered congratulations. But his most intimate contact at the *Telegraph* was Thornton Hunt, whom he thereafter saw regularly. Hunt, who replaced J. D. Cook as Gladstone's journalistic amanuensis, was particularly helpful during the prolonged controversy over franchise reform. From the middle of 1865 through 1867, Gladstone's diary entries are punctuated by references to correspondence or, usually, meetings with 'Mr Thornton Hunt' (or 'Th. Hunt'). There were weeks when they communicated daily and, in one instance (15 January 1866), twice in a single day.[1]

To the popular *Daily Telegraph*, Gladstone was appropriately 'The People's

---

[1] *Gladstone Diaries*, VI (Oxford, 1978), especially 25, 36, 39, 408–11. For a Conservative view, see Malmesbury, *Memoirs*, II, 252 (31 May and 2 June 1861); for a Radical view, see Trevelyan, *Bright*, pp. 289–95; and for the royal view, see Queen Victoria to the King of the Belgians, 22 May 1860, in *Letters of Queen Victoria*, III, 509–10.

William'. To the pious and pedagogic *Daily News*, he was invariably 'Mr Gladstone', even after his death. It would be wrong to regard this distinction as simply a matter of literary style, and still more wrong to impute to it a difference in degree of deference. 'The *Telegraph* served the Liberalism of convention, the *Daily News* the Liberalism of conviction,' Vincent has persuasively argued, 'but both regarded themselves and their readers as at one with the Parliamentary Liberal Party. Both papers,' he further asserts, 'marked great steps forward in the conquest of previously unattached or hostile areas of opinion by Parliamentary party.'[1] In order to measure those steps and to trace the direction they took, one must return to the tangled events to which the political press responded.

*   *   *

No one was more attentive to developments in the political press, or more alert to its every nuance, than were the preceptors of the Manchester School. Their agitation against the Corn Laws had left Cobden and Bright deeply, if perhaps mistakenly, convinced of the efficacy of newspaper propaganda. It had also left them the legacy of two journals: the *Manchester Examiner* (a daily from 1855) and the weekly *Economist*. Neither commanded adequate resources to wage new and intensified battles against privilege, the *Examiner* because Manchester was too remote from the centre of power, and the *Economist* because it had been uprooted and moved to London, where it proved susceptible to 'the atmosphere of the clubs and political cliques'.[2] There was an obvious contradiction here, and one which the Manchester Radicals never resolved.

Despite his personal involvement and his friends' investment, Bright's attitude towards the provincial press was strikingly ambivalent: on the one hand, he celebrated its intrinsic virtues; on the other, he wished it to replicate the functions and features of the London papers. 'I don't think the *Examiner* up to the mark,' he wrote dolefully in February 1850 to George Wilson, who shared the proprietorship with Henry Rawson; 'its leaders are often too long & the subjects are not sufficiently to the time – they should ... explain questions which are being discussed in Parlt.'[3] Without stinting his efforts to promote the *Manchester Examiner*, which had absorbed the *Manchester Times* in 1848, he – like Cobden – looked hopefully to changes in metropolitan journalism. The weekly *Examiner*, edited by Albany Fonblanque, was no relation to Bright's Manchester paper, but was in many ways a kindred spirit. To some

---

[1] Vincent, *Formation*, p. 61.

[2] Cobden to Bright, 24 October 1846, quoted in Morley, *Cobden*, II, 11–12.

[3] Bright to Wilson, 13 February 1850, Wilson Papers. 'I should fill every paper with debates in the House of Commons', Bright once declared; 'I would have no editorial leading article, but would leave the readers to form their own conclusion from what they read for themselves.' Quoted in A. Kinnear, 'Parliamentary Reporting,' *Contemporary Review*, lxxxvii (1905), 370.

extent, so was the *Spectator*, with a smaller weekly distribution. But it was the
Daily News that bore the greatest promise for middle-class Radicals. Pledged
to the twin ideals of peace and progress, it encouraged Bright and Cobden to
believe that even the London daily press was not beyond redemption.

Not surprisingly, that belief was soon dispelled. 'I fear our support of the
Daily News has done little good – it is evidently sinking into a mere organ of
Whiggism,' Bright told Wilson in July.

> First Palmerston secured it – & now I think I perceive its tone less & less
> earnest in all matters on which we take an interest. *The Times* had a better
> *toned* article on the County franchise the other day than the *Daily News* – &
> its *friendly* feeling to *me* is manifested in its cold & miserable article on
> capital punishment on Saturday, in which it studiously avoided any allusion
> to my speech, which was in truth the only speech of any length or force in the
> debate. I told Mr Crowe that *The Times* would beat them even in the Liberal
> field, & I believe it will before long. . . . The Lords have mangled the Irish
> franchise Bill – the only important Bill of the Session, & the *Daily News*
> advises the Govt. to accept it as it is![1]

Thereafter, Bright's complaints came fast and furious, with Cobden
expressing identical sentiments in letters to the Rev Henry Richard, then
secretary of the Peace Society and later a Radical MP. On 2 December 1850,
he called Richard's attention to a recent article in the *Daily News* so
Palmerstonian in spirit that it 'made me rub my eyes and look again at the
heading of the page to see if it could really be that paper'. Echoing Bright, he
concluded that the *Daily News*

> has more power to injure us than has *The Times*, because it is supposed to be
> honestly with us. It must be repudiated and exposed by the Peace
> Party. . . . For my own part I consider the *Daily News* henceforth utterly
> untrustworthy. You may substitute *The Times* for it in your office again with
> my full consent whenever you please. . . . Will the time ever come when an
> *honest* daily paper will pay?

An advocate of non-intervention in Continental embroilments, Cobden
decried the *Daily News* as 'a mere instrument in the hands of the Foreign
Minister'. Writing to Richard on 19 September 1851, he contrasted the
editorial views of the 'London *Examiner*', which had 'shown a courageous
adherence to its convictions', with those of 'the dastardly *Daily News*. By the
way, *entre nous*', he disclosed, a representative of the *Daily News* had
approached him,

> soliciting my co-operation, and offering to make the *D.N.* the organ of the

[1] Bright to Wilson, 15 July 1850, Wilson Papers; on newspaper rivalries in Manchester before
1855, see Ayerst, *Guardian*, pp. 99–102.

Progressive Party. In reply I told him that I ceased to take in the *D.N.* more than six months ago, and that for the last month I had not seen a copy of it, *and I told the reason why. . . .* I suppose by his writing to me that the paper is not doing well – how could it?[1]

Cobden and his associates were heartened by Palmerston's removal from the Foreign Office at the end of 1851, but could have taken little consolation from the foreign policies pursued by his successors. The perennial Eastern Question, after a period of mounting tensions, erupted into a war between the Russian and Ottoman Empires into which the British and French were inexorably drawn. The diplomatic origins of the conflict were obscure, to say the least; but the British public, wildly Russophobic, awaited any pretext, and found one in the destruction of the Turkish fleet at Sinope in November 1853. The western powers broke off relations with Russia in February and declared war in March. Cobden had seen the crisis coming. 'I have watched naturally the tone of the press upon the late (as I think monstrous) proposal to increase our armaments. It is decidedly against us,' he informed Joseph Sturge in March 1852. 'I do not speak of the dailies', whose militarism was a foregone conclusion,

> but of the weekly papers; and I do not allude to such papers as the *Examiner* or *Spectator*, but to the *Weekly Dispatch*, read by artisans and small shopkeepers, and the *Illustrated Weekly News*, a thorough middle-class print. By these and such as these I have been denounced and put out of the pale of practical statesmanship for opposing an increase of armaments. . . . To change the press, we must change public opinion.[2]

After the outbreak of hostilities in the Crimea, he must have had second thoughts about Palmerston, whose rhetoric had been inflammatory, but who was far better equipped to restrain popular passions than were Aberdeen, Russell, and Clarendon.

Palmerston had fortuitously left the Aberdeen coalition before the news from Sinope. Until his resignation from the Home Office, where he had felt misplaced, his behaviour was 'very reserved'; but, as Greville recorded, 'his wife as usual talks à qui veut l'entendre of the misconduct of the whole affair, and affirms that, if P. had the management of it, all would have been settled long ago'. Lord Aberdeen demonstrated none of Palmerston's decisiveness. On the evening of 4 October 1853, he sent for Delane, whom he told 'that he was resolved to be no party to a war with Russia on such grounds as the present, and he was prepared to resign rather than incur such responsibility'. On the 15th, he stiffly advised Delane that 'there is not the least truth in the report of a land force being sent to the East', and he could not resist adding

---

[1] Cobden to Richard, 2 December 1850 and 19 September 1851, quoted in J. A. Hobson, *Richard Cobden: International Man* (London, 1918?), pp. 70–71, 78.
[2] Cobden to Sturge, 11 March 1852, quoted in Morley, *Cobden*, II, 114.

'that *The Times* this morning contains an article as *practically warlike* as any that has appeared'.[1]

The Times was not the only sabre-rattler: after the Sinope incident, even the *Morning Chronicle* and the *Manchester Guardian* took up the cry. But *The Times*, regarded abroad as a semi-official organ, gave particular distress to the beleaguered ministry. Harcourt, who was to write for it in the 1860s as 'Historicus', debated this point with Lord Clarendon:

> The impression that everything which *The Times* may say on the Eastern question is directly inspired by the Government & represents their sentiments is due to the fact that it is made the *exclusive* vehicle for the information communicated to the public by the Government. It is not unnaturally argued . . . that there cannot be any material difference of view between the Cabinet & *The Times*. . . . I cannot help feeling very strongly that the enormous influence of *The Times* instead of really supporting the Govt. as it would do if it took a straightforward course is really encumbering it with a weight of odium & suspicion which does it infinite mischief.

Clarendon thought Harcourt 'quite right in saying that *The Times* does harm to the Govt.', but otherwise gave no ground. 'After the bitter opposition or lukewarm support it has given to various important measures I can't understand why it shd. be considered the organ of the Govt.', he replied.

> One leading art. generally is at variance with the other & both cannot represent the opinions of the Govt. The ways of *The Times* are inscrutable but as its circulation is enormous & its influence abroad is very great a Govt. must take its support on the terms it chooses to put it.
>
> You however much overrate the amt. of information supplied to *The Times* & I can give you no better proof . . . than the fact that not long ago I was shewn a letter from Delane complaining in bitter terms that from *no* Govt. had *The Times* been so ill treated as by the present Govt. with respect to information.[2]

However cogent Clarendon's defence, there was no gainsaying that the members of the government, himself included, were 'now popularly judged' – as Abraham Hayward wrote the same month to Sir John Young – 'not by their own acts and despatches, but by the vacillating tone and occasionally unprincipled articles of *The Times*'.[3]

Bright could not have expected any better from either the government or *The Times*, but the national temper came as a profound shock to him. 'All that

[1] *Greville Memoirs* (6 and 7 October 1853), VI, 453; Aberdeen to Delane, 15 October 1853, quoted in Dasent, *Delane*, I, 163.

[2] Harcourt to Clarendon, 10 October 1853, Clarendon Papers, Clar. dep.c. 103, fols. 105 ff.; Clarendon to Harcourt, 13 October 1853, Harcourt Papers. Delane's disputes with Aberdeen are chronicled in *The Greville Memoirs* (10 and 22 December 1853), VI, 466–67, 475–76.

[3] 11 October 1853, in Hayward, *Correspondence*, I, 194.

is passing around us only shows how fearfully unsound our people are on war and intervention, and how necessary it is to teach them by a free press, and other means,' he told Cobden on 24 December. What struck him as particularly ironic was a newspaper assault on Prince Albert, whose plea for moderation was attacked as an unconstitutional interference in public affairs and, more ludicrously, as an attempt to protect his Germanic interests.[1] The *Daily News* and the *Morning Advertiser* (the latter running 'five or six articles on the same day') led the pack, but the *Standard* and *Morning Herald* matched their virulence. Queen Victoria, as much appalled as was Bright by 'the credulity of the people', begged for assistance from Aberdeen, who assured her that the clamour was 'not sanctioned by the most respectable portion of the Press'. Delane 'offered (if it was thought desirable) to take up the cudgels in defence of the Court', but Aberdeen reflected to Sir James Graham that, with the intervention of *The Times* '*as my organ*, the discussion might assume a more inconvenient character'. Instead, it was left to the *Morning Chronicle* to mollify the Queen by 'an admirable article' on 16 January: 'Has Lord Aberdeen any idea who could have written it?' she asked. The Prime Minister gave the credit to Gladstone, 'although he would not wish it to be known', and welcomed 'a very sensible letter' in the same day's *Standard*. As he had promised, the matter was properly aired when Parliament assembled. By then, the attacks had run their course, and the newspaper-reading public was diverted by the imminence of war.

The Royal Address on 31 January provided a fitting occasion for Aberdeen in one House and Russell in the other to vindicate Prince Albert. Impatient to ascertain the government's other plans, newspapers vied to obtain a copy of the speech. Previously, Greville recalled, 'great bother' had been caused when 'one of the Derbyites' had breached confidentiality to satisfy the curiosity of the *Morning Herald*. This time, 'Aberdeen refused to give it even to *The Times*, and of course to any other paper', and he sternly instructed Palmerston 'not to send it to the *Morning Post* (which is notoriously his paper)'. To his irritation, the document was published not only in *The Times*, but also in the *Morning Advertiser*. Delane might have procured the text from any number of sources: he told Greville 'that he had no less than three offers of it'.[2] But Grant's source remained a mystery.

A minor episode amid momentous events, it was nonetheless significant as a commentary on the mutual accommodations between politicians and journalists. As the ship of state sailed headlong into the Crimean gale, it sprang leaks on every side. Some of these disclosures, one may presume, were innocent enough: on 14 February, J. D. Cook thanked Gladstone for an

[1] Bright to Cobden, 24 December 1853, quoted in Trevelyan, *Bright*, p. 229; *Greville Memoirs* (15 and 16 January 1854), VII, 4–7; Dasent, *Delane*, I, 168; Queen Victoria to Aberdeen, 16 January 1854, and Aberdeen to Queen Victoria, 17 January 1854, quoted in *Letters of Queen Victoria*, III, 8–10; Conacher, *Aberdeen Coalition*, pp. 269–73.

[2] *Greville Memoirs* (2 February 1854), VII, 12–13.

unspecified 'idea' which Goldwin Smith developed in the *Morning Chronicle*: 'I took great care to guard against the possibility of its being even conjectured that the suggestion originated with you.' Far more seriously, Cabinet deliberations on foreign policy, including the precise terms of the ultimatum to Russia, appeared in *The Times* on 28 February. Aberdeen was furious. 'At a time when I was protesting in the House of Lords against revealing the intentions of the Government, our most secret decisions are made public!' he exploded to Clarendon. 'It can only be from the Foreign Office that the information was obtained.... I hope you will exert yourself to correct this evil which has become a scandal not to be endured.' Clarendon appreciated the embarrassment, but refused to accept responsibility:

> The newspapers are among the many curses of one's official existence & I never was more disgusted than in reading the art. in *The Times* this morng. but I am at a loss to imagine why you say that it can only be from the F.O. that this informn. is obtained unless you suppose that I furnished it.... I met Delane in Westr. Hall as I was going to the H. of Lds. this eveng. and asked him where he got the information; he wd. not tell me but he promised that the subject shd. not be adverted to again.

Russell, playing the awkward role of peacemaker in a war Cabinet, urged Aberdeen to decree 'that no communications should be made to the press not authorized by you, as the head of the Government'. Meanwhile, he implored: 'Let bygones be bygones, but let the future be honourable to our station and character.' That was more easily said than done. A fortnight later, a private banquet was held at the Reform Club as a send-off to Sir Charles Napier, incidentally Delane's principal informant, who had been appointed to command the Baltic fleet. Palmerston took the chair, and Molesworth and Graham participated in the boisterous festivities. Referring to Napier's boast that, 'when he goes to the Baltic he will declare war', Graham provocatively affirmed that 'I as First Lord of the Admiralty give him free consent to do so'. Bright ('Excited and not well') described 'the discreditable speeches' in his journal on 9 March, and condemned them in the Commons four days later. By then, a full account, replete with Graham's indiscretion, had appeared in *The Times*. Once again, Bright found an unaccustomed ally in the Queen, who considered 'dinners of that description ... very bad taste', and who 'entirely' agreed with Russell's 'observation respecting the information obtained by *The Times* which she thinks he and the Cabinet ought positively not to tolerate any longer'.[1]

Bright, in a letter 'unknown to any one but myself', poured out his grief to

---

[1] Cook to Gladstone, 14 February 1854, Gladstone Papers, Add. MSS. 44,377, fol. 231; Aberdeen's exchanges with Clarendon and Russell, along with Russell's correspondence with the Queen, are published in *History of The Times*, II, appendix 2, 561–62; Bright's diary, 9 and 13 March 1854, quoted in Trevelyan, *Bright*, pp. 233–34.

the Prime Minister. Although he neither solicited nor expected a reply, he was invited on 22 March to Argyll House, where Aberdeen 'expressed his fear that hostilities with Russia were now unavoidable'. The conversation led inevitably to the incendiary and unscrupulous conduct of 'the Newspaper Press'. Bright

> pointed out how much it is in the hands of individuals and cliques, referred to the *Morning Post*, Palmerston's paper, and its abuse of Lord Aberdeen, and urged that the repeal of the Stamp was the only mode of improving the character of the English Press.

On the 24th, he pursued his lonely mission by appealing to John Walter, the proprietor of *The Times*, 'to seize any chance of preserving or making peace'. When he 'remarked upon *The Times* being brow-beaten into a support of the war', Walter matter-of-factly responded that 'when the country would go for war, it was not worth while to oppose it, hurting themselves and doing no good'. That, to Bright, betokened an abdication of moral responsibility.[1]

What *The Times* did not dare to say in print, its editor did not hesitate to admit privately. In April, Delane discussed the war with Bright: 'His opinion as to its non-necessity agrees precisely with mine.' The more Cobden studied *The Times*, the more he was convinced of its culpability in having failed to warn 'the English people half plainly enough' of the consequences. As if to repent, the paper commissioned a series of dispatches from William Howard Russell, who vividly recounted the sufferings of the troops and the deficiencies of their commanders. Transmitted by telegraph, Russell's 'Gallipoli letters' turned a mood of euphoria into one of disillusionment: 'the official people have confined themselves to deprecating "premature judgments", but the public has sided with you completely,' Delane told his controversial war correspondent on 20 July. A few weeks later, he boarded a French steamer at Marseilles to visit the Crimea. Upon his return in October, he communicated his impressions to the Cabinet through the Duke of Newcastle. It was already clear to him, if not yet to the optimistic politicians, that the long and costly siege of Sebastopol would drag on through the coming winter. Finding the government impervious to his advice, he stepped up his campaign in *The Times*, where (on 3 November) Bright published his 'letter to Absalom Watkin', a reproach to those who had recklessly pushed the country into war. But it was Russell, by his daily accounts of hardship and bungling, who gnawed most deeply at the national conscience. Molesworth, his philosophic radicalism a dim memory, sought to restrain him by imposing censorship. Greville, too, was annoyed: '*The Times* (as usual) has been thundering away about reinforcements, and urging the despatch of Troops that do not exist and cannot be created in a moment,' he wrote in his journal on 26 November. 'I had a great battle with Delane the other day about it.' A month later, *The Times* was thundering away not only for new reinforcements, but also for new leadership:

[1] Bright's diary, 22 and 24 March 1854, quoted in Trevelyan, *Bright*, pp. 232–33.

'we have really shown no more skill or artifice in the siege of Sebastopol than our ancestors would have done 2,000 years ago' (26 December). Four days later, it ended the year by opening its columns to a flood of letters from military men, who testified to 'the almost total disorganization of our army in the Crimea and its awful jeopardy, not from the Russians, but from an enemy nearer home – its own utter mismanagement'.[1]

The Times's shift of attitude towards the Aberdeen coalition was gradual and never total. As late as 26 November, when his colleagues were under heavy fire, Gladstone was obliged to concede that 'the Government have received from *The Times* valuable support in giving effect to their views of financial policy under critical circumstances'.[2] No support was forthcoming from Printing House Square, however, when Parliament reassembled in January and J. A. Roebuck moved for a select committee to enquire into the prosecution of the war. Lord John Russell resigned in anticipation of the government's humiliation in the Commons; Lord Aberdeen in the wake of it. It was Roebuck who precipitated the crisis. But, as the Duke of Newcastle said upon making the acquaintance of *The Times*'s correspondent: 'It was you who turned out the Government, Mr Russell.'[3] The advent of Palmerston to the premiership did not appease *The Times*, which persisted (as Greville disapprovingly noted on 24 May) in its 'furious opposition'. It took the better part of a year, and the departure of Reeve from the editorial staff, before Delane and Palmerston came to admire each other. Until then, it was said to be Palmerston's habit to throw his copy of *The Times* into the fire. His opinion of the paper rose as it adapted to his views.

In one crucial respect, though, Palmerston proved no friend of *The Times*. His administration, while acting on Roebuck's successful motion, yielded to demands for a repeal of the stamp duty. *The Times* may have alienated many of its former friends, but it had failed to reconcile Cobden, who could not forget 'how greatly it is responsible for an expedition which every rational man now in his heart condemns', and who was all the more determined to 'impair the force of its war advocacy in future'. Nor could the pacifists forgive the *Daily News*, the *Manchester Guardian*, and the *Leeds Mercury* for having left them in the lurch. Writing to Henry Richard on 10 January 1855, Cobden prophesied that 'the stamp will come off this spring. Could not a cheap daily paper be started to advocate the doctrine of the "Manchester School" . . . – peace, non-intervention, economy, etc?' He reasoned that 'after the present war there will be a reaction which will give a good opening for such a paper. In fact it is a great unoccupied field in London, the only one connected with the Press not occupied'. In successive letters to Richard, he did not ignore

[1] Bright's diary [April 1854], quoted in Trevelyan, *Bright*, p. 233; Cobden to Richard, 8 June 1854, quoted in Hobson, *Cobden*, p. 111; Delane to Russell, 20 July 1854, quoted in Atkins, *Russell*, I, 146; Dasent, *Delane*, I, 196; *Greville Memoirs* (26 November 1854), VII, 78.

[2] Gladstone to Delane, 28 November 1854, quoted in Dasent, *Delane*, I, 202.

[3] Quoted in Atkins, *Russell*, I, 200.

financial considerations: 'I feel convinced that it would prove a good mercantile speculation if the business part of the undertaking were well managed,' hastening to add that 'I would trust nobody who set up a paper on merely mercantile principles to oppose the current passions and prejudices even for a day.' If a suitable scheme could be floated, 'Bright and I would not hesitate to take it in hand'. Admittedly, 'our paper must have a country circulation', but its example would 'promote the establishment of good papers in other places besides London'. In short, what he envisioned was the first link in an eventual chain.[1]

Bright had reasons of his own to foster the plan. 'The London papers are hostile to me,' he told George Wilson on 27 February, after his parliamentary speech on press reform had gone virtually unreported. A few weeks later, it gave him inestimable pleasure to relate that Gladstone's introduction of a Bill to repeal the stamp duty had set *The Times* 'howling, & splashing about like a harpooned whale'. He praised Wilson for an 'admirable' article in the *Manchester Examiner* (14 March) that combined support for Gladstone's measure with a denunciation of *The Times*'s 'most arrant and unblushing piece of selfish egotism and audacity that ever raised its head in defence of a public wrong'. But the voice of the *Manchester Examiner* did not carry to London, where parliamentary and public debate on the issue continued through the month. 'The old papers are furious against free trade in newspapers, & I almost tremble for the result,' Cobden wrote to Joseph Sturge on the 20th. 'The stamp will I expect certainly come off,' he declared with greater confidence on the 29th, '& there will be many new ventures . . . & I hope we shall have one of the Manchester School amongst the rest.'[2]

As usual, Cobden and Bright worked as a team: the former provided the inspiration and many of the contacts; the latter the impetus. Both were disposed to move cautiously. 'The new Newspaper Law will come into force in a few weeks (if the Lords do not throw it out),' Cobden reminded Sturge in mid-May. Then, and not before, constructive action could be taken. 'A person in whose talents I should have confidence, but who has no *feeling* in our direction', had recently submitted to him 'a plan for a daily penny paper which he says would only require a capital of £5,000'. Cobden, who knew that talents were no substitute for *feeling*, was not interested.[3]

Months passed before anything happened. Finally, on the morning of 4 August, Sturge, Cobden, Richard, and John Bell came to Bright's London 'lodgings to talk the matter over'. A campaigner against such evils as the slave trade, the Corn Laws, and drink, Sturge made it known that he had journeyed from Birmingham specifically 'at Richard Cobden's request'. He volunteered

[1] Cobden to Richard, 10 January, 15 July, and 5 August 1855, quoted in Hobson, *Cobden*, pp. 120–23, 126–27.

[2] Bright to Wilson, 27 February 1855, Wilson Papers; Cobden to Sturge, 20 and 29 March 1855, Sturge Papers, Add. MSS. 43,722, fols. 53–54.

[3] Cobden to Sturge, 1 and 15 May 1855, Sturge Papers, Add. MSS. 43,722, fols. 59–61.

to 'raise some money – perhaps £2,000 or more – but the question', as Bright phrased it, was

> how can security be given that the paper shall be *permanently honest*? The temptation to 'trim' is so great . . . especially in London, where all sorts of attempts are made on the virtue of public writers, & generally with complete success.

To guard against temptation, Bright proposed the appointment of 'arbitrators', who would be 'empowered, in some way, to control the course of the paper as to politics, so that we may not be sold as the *Daily News* sold us'. Three weeks after their meeting, he recapitulated the deliberations for Sturge:

> The daily Paper it is proposed to start in London is intended to support generally the views which Cobden & I have advocated in & out of Parliament. It will of course be thoroughly liberal in its politics, will write as occasion offers in favour of parliamentary reform – of religious equality . . . & generally . . . of just & humane conduct in Government. It will oppose the present war, & will support the policy of non-intervention in the affairs & quarrels of Continental Europe.

As one businessman to another, Bright minuted that financial responsibility was 'to be entrusted to Geo. Wilson & myself', with payments

> to be advanced to the Paper in the name of Geo. Wilson, with I undertaking to make such arrangements with the proprietors as shall secure to him, along with Cobden and myself, as much certainty as is attainable with regard to the principles on which the paper shall be conducted.

In conclusion, as one Quaker to another, Bright told Sturge that 'if thy friends could raise £2,000' – a figure which 'some of the subscribers think . . . shd. at least be £3,000' – he believed 'the rest of the capital could be obtained in Manchester'. These projections, which seemed to him 'liberal & accurate', were based on 'the experience in the management' of the *Manchester Examiner*, a penny daily since 18 June, before repeal had officially taken effect.[1]

Bright did not forsake the *Manchester Examiner*, and applauded Wilson's decision to bring it out every morning at a reduced price. Yet its sale, like that of other local journals, was circumscribed by problems of distribution. On a July visit to his native Rochdale, Bright took stock of the newspaper competition: 'I find the *Guardian* at 2d. goes down badly on the line from Yorkshire & at this Station,' he informed Wilson, and he could not imagine how that paper (which, in his boyhood, he had read aloud to his father) 'can live at 2d. against you at 1d. unless political economy be all nonsense'. (To comply with the immutable laws of political economy, the *Guardian* dropped to a penny in

---

[1] Bright to Wilson, 4 August 1855, and Sturge to Wilson, 6 August 1855, Wilson Papers; Bright to Sturge, 23 August 1855, Sturge Papers, Add. MSS. 43,723, fols. 41 ff.

October 1857.) Bright 'heard also that the *Leeds Mercury* will find great difficulty with its 3 papers in a week for 7d.'. (It became a daily in 1861.) On a stop-
over at Wakefield, he learned that 'they sell the *Telegraph* largely, & the
Examiner also', but the vendor whom he queried replied 'the *Telegraph* most',
as the *Examiner* did not arrive 'always in time & in sufficient quantity'.[1] All
the same, there was cause for satisfaction. Gladstone was 'glad to hear' from
Wilson, who was to be one of his chief patrons in Manchester a decade later,
'of the circulation and consequent influence of a print which opposes itself to
the favourite ideas of the moment with respect to the existing war'. As the
statesman who had abolished 'the compulsory Stamp', he considered that his
action could not have been 'more opportune than at a time when so large a
proportion of the previously existing newspapers were employed in making
mischief on that great & absorbing subject'. His 'warm interest' was its own
reward.[2]

Colonel Sleigh's *Daily Telegraph* was a summer novelty. By September, it
was 'begging everywhere for money', and Bright was aware of proposals 'to
make it a *penny* paper', London's first. 'Under its present managers I think it
cannot live,' he diagnosed on the 12th. Five days later, it was revivified under
Levy's ownership. Cobden, sending Richard a copy for perusal, saw the cruel
irony: 'The paper which offered itself to the Peace Party "for a consideration"
has now been changed to a penny paper, and has gone right over to the War
Party.' Bright, more embittered ('alas for all human expectations!'),
reproached Cobden – and, in effect, himself – for all the hopes they had invested in 'the Cheap Press'. The penny *Telegraph*, he recounted, 'in its desperate
effort not to die, . . . has become as violent for war as the *Advertiser* or the
Daily News'.[3]

Pre-empted by the *Telegraph*, the Cobdenites could not claim the
distinction of having launched the first metropolitan daily to sell for a penny.
Disappointed, they were galvanized by the set-back. 'There is nothing settled
yet about the Newspaper,' Bright wrote on 14 September to Cobden. The
delay was due to a number of factors: unsuccessful negotiations for the
purchase of American machinery, 'which is evidently far superior to anything
here'; prospects (dangled by Sir Arthur Elton) that the *Morning Chronicle*
might be bought from Serjeant Glover or the *Daily Telegraph* from Colonel
Sleigh or Levy; the 'rather lukewarm' response among Bright's 'friends in
Manchester', owing to 'the state of trade & of the money market'; Sturge's
objections to certain proposed editorial appointments; and Cobden's qualms

[1] Bright to Wilson, 7 and 9 July 1855, Wilson Papers. Similar problems afflicted the *Scotsman*,
whose management recognized in 1865 'the unpleasant fact' that circulation was 'mainly confined
to Edinburgh and its immediate neighbourhood'. Cooper, *An Editor's Retrospect*, pp. 166–67.
[2] Gladstone to Wilson, 4 October 1855, Wilson Papers.
[3] Bright to Wilson, 12 September 1855, Wilson Papers; Cobden to Richard, 18 September
1855, quoted in Hobson, *Cobden*, p. 129; Bright to Cobden, 21 September 1855, Bright Papers,
Add. MSS. 43, 384, fol. 12.

about managerial structure. Caught between the demands of his Manchester
investors and the irreconcilable stipulations of Sturge and Cobden, Bright
threatened on 14 December 'to wash my hands of the whole affair'. But a
compromise was reached whereby W. T. Haly, despite misgivings about his
peace views, 'would manage & direct the Editorial department', but would not
be permitted to hold shares 'so that the proprietary may be free from the
difficulty which always arises when Editors are proprietors'.[1] Richard,
engaged as principal leader-writer, acted as general overseer. Members of
Bright's family subscribed capital; but, at least in the first instance, Bright
himself did not. Cobden could truthfully maintain that he 'never had a shilling
of money in it',[2] although he was said to have contributed a gift of £250. As the
Morning Star, the organ of the peace party began publication on 17 March
1856. The *Saturday Review* (22 March) cordially welcomed its appearance,
free 'alike from the vulgarity of the *Daily News* and the imbecility of the
Morning Herald'.

To what extent was the *Morning Star* a sounding-board for the two
politicians whose names were most closely identified with it? Cobden,
bypassing Haly, kept up a steady correspondence with Richard. 'I can often
give you rapid hints for an article without any trouble to myself if I know that
my own language is not necessarily to be printed,' he stated on 25 July 1856,
adding with characteristic modesty that 'when writing *for the Press* I am beset
with a fastidiousness that almost paralyses my fingers'. Three days later, he
forwarded an item for Richard to 'put ... into your own language'; he had
'purposely written ... on both sides' of the given issue 'to compel you to
rewrite it'.[3] Inevitably, Richard's language sometimes failed to do justice to
Cobden's hints, but Cobden preferred to maintain their respective
autonomies.

Bright was less reticent, though by no means so actively involved as was

[1] Bright to Cobden, 14 September 1855, Bright Papers, Add. MSS. 43,384, fol. 11; Cobden to
Richard, 29 September 1855, quoted in Hobson, *Cobden*, pp. 129–30; Bright to Cobden, 3
October 1855, Bright Papers, Add. MSS. 43,384, fol. 16; Sturge to Richard, 9 November 1855,
Richard Papers; Bright to Sturge, 26 October and 22 December 1855, Sturge Papers, Add. MSS.
43,723, fols. 49–50, 59 ff. Regarding schemes to take over the *Morning Chronicle* or *Daily Tele-*
graph, see Elton to John Hamilton, 25 November 1855 (copy), and Elton to Wilson, 2 January
1856, Wilson Papers; and Bright to Cobden, 11 January 1856, Bright Papers, Add. MSS. 43,384,
fol. 49.

[2] Cobden to T. B. Potter, 4 January 1864, quoted in Vincent, *Formation*, p. 61. A list of original
shareholders (n.d.) is to be found among the Bright Papers, Add. MSS. 43,392, fol. 183. In
November 1856, when it was found necessary 'to increase the capital' of the *Morning Star* (see
Sturge to Richard, [23] November 1856, Richard Papers), Bright overcame his reluctance 'to run
newspaper risks' and agreed to take shares that 'should really entitle me to 1/5th of the paper' on
the understanding 'that the reference to Cobden & myself remains in force, & that management
will remain with Rawson & [Wilson] as heretofore' (Bright to Wilson, 6 November 1856). It is not
clear whether his colleagues saw fit to accept his terms. In any case, Cobden's principles were
inviolate, and his £250 was presumably part of a 'testimonial' to Richard, who could not afford to
purchase shares on his own account (Sturge to Wilson, 25 July 1857, Wilson Papers).

[3] Cobden to Richard, 25 and 28 July 1856, quoted in Hobson, *Cobden*, pp. 141, 163.

widely assumed. On one occasion, he contributed a long leading article that received 'due prominence' and, the next day, a rejoinder from a Tory journal that began: 'The Great Tribune has laid aside his pen and some miserable hireling of the *Morning Star* has taken it up.' Sir Edward Russell, relating the anecdote, recalled how Bright had appeared 'at the *Morning Star* office that afternoon, and with a placid, good-natured smile, said, "I don't think leader-writing can be my forte"'. Unlike Cobden, Bright came by frequently to chat about parliamentary affairs, Irish disturbances, Mill's philosophy, or Milton's poetry. There was one night when he forgot to discharge his cabman, who sat waiting in the Strand for three hours. In the procession of *Morning Star* editors, Haly gave way to John Hamilton, who was followed by Samuel Lucas (not to be confused with the erstwhile editor of the *Press*, he was Bright's brother-in-law), Justin McCarthy, and ultimately John Morley. 'I am afraid,' McCarthy confessed, 'that we younger men ... made Bright seem responsible for many a policy of attack which our combative pens originated in the columns of the *Morning Star*.'[1] Held accountable for views that often clashed with his own, Bright ended his connection in 1868, before taking office in Gladstone's first ministry. It was not completely coincidental that the paper folded the following autumn.

*　　　*　　　*

The sort of inconveniences that Bright and Cobden suffered as a result of their affiliation with the *Morning Star*, more usually over matters of synchronization than of substance, were similar to those encountered by other politicians who trafficked with the press: the Peelites had their troubles with the *Morning Chronicle*; the Derbyites with the *Standard* and the *Morning Herald*; Disraeli with the *Press*; and Palmerston with the *Morning Post* and the *Globe*. All of them were slighted and bruised by *The Times*. Newspapers were unreliable servants that unpredictably showed too much devotion or too little, unable to judge which was appropriate until the damage was done. All the same, it was better to receive their support than to be denied it. The plight of Lord John Russell was proof of that.

Through his more sociable Whig colleagues, Russell had repeatedly tried – and failed – to temper Delane's animosity. *The Times*'s growing intimacy with Palmerston intensified his distress. In 1855, Russell had humbled himself by accepting the colonial secretaryship under Palmerston, and his subordination rankled. Playing upon it, *The Times* began by attacking the government as a whole, then (after the Peelite exodus) levelled its charges more selectively at its Russellite component. 'Things may improve but at present they don't look well,' Clarendon wrote from the Foreign Office on 26 February, '& the

---

[1] Russell, *That Reminds Me* (London, 1899), p. 84; McCarthy, *Reminiscences* (London, 1899), I, 81–82, 86.

hostility of *The Times* is as unabated as its influence unfortunately is.' The next month, Russell protested from Vienna that an account of his peace negotiations there 'should be given in a garbled form in *The Times*, even tho' accompanied by only a moderate sneer against myself'. Not for the first time, Clarendon was rebuked for the apparent fact 'that the For. Off. is in communication with *The Times*. I wish you would stop such things in future.'[1]

In July, Delane's suspicions were confirmed that Russell, instead of demanding punitive terms, was 'giving up all that is asked'.[2] Under a barrage of criticism, Lord John was forced to resign. 'I need not say that I am disgusted with the violence & injustice of the Press, & of the Clubs against you,' the Duke of Argyll wrote in condolence. Lord Fortescue, another of the Old Whigs, deplored how 'the rascally *Times* laboured not without effect to prejudice the Public against you'. Clarendon likewise referred to 'the rascally motives of *The Times*'. 'As one cannot horsewhip Delane & Co., the best way is to go on never minding them,' he feebly advised. Russell, letting slip his mask of disdainful unconcern, was not so sure 'that the "rascally motives" of *The Times* ought not to attract our attention'. More important than its insults to him, it had helped to subvert his peace mission. And, in reconstructing the government, Palmerston kowtowed to the mandarins of Printing House Square: Thomas Phinn, 'a jackal of that paper', was appointed to a secretaryship at the Admiralty; Molesworth, 'an intimate friend of the Editor', was elevated to the Colonial Office; and Robert Lowe, 'a constant contributor', was made vice-president of the Board of Trade and a privy councillor to boot. 'The whole official fry were in hot water on account of *The Times*, & thought it best to forswear me who had made the fortunes of most of them,' Russell fumed. 'These are not matters of indifference in the govt. of an Empire.... If England is ever to be England again, this tyranny of *The Times* must be cut off.'[3]

Lowe's preferment was particularly galling. A leader-writer for *The Times* since 1851, he had doubled as MP for Kidderminster since 1852. His appointment to office obliged him to defend his seat in a by-election on 14 August, and *The Times* promoted his candidacy. On the day before polling, Lowe's electoral address – in which, 'at some length', he identified 'the Government of Lord Palmerston' with the policy of 'a vigorous war, carried on until we can obtain an honourable and a lasting peace' – was extensively reported. Delane, celebrating Lowe's safe return, admitted that he had been

[1] Clarendon to Russell, 26 February 1855, Russell Papers PRO 30/22/12B/163 ff.; Russell to Clarendon, 20 March 1855 (copy), Russell Papers PRO 30/22/12C/214–15.
[2] Delane to Dasent [13 January 1855], *Times* Archives.
[3] Argyll to Russell [July 1855], Russell Papers PRO 30/22/12E/110–13; Fortescue to Russell, 20 July 1855, and Clarendon to Russell, 22 July 1855, are reprinted from the Russell Papers in *History of The Times*, II, appendix 2, 555–56; Russell to Clarendon, August (n.d.) 1855 (copy), Russell Papers PRO 30/22/12F/26–28.

very anxious for Lowe as at first the contest looked dangerous & it would have been so disgusting to be blocked out of a promising career by a few drunke[n] carpet weavers. I must say he bears his new honours meekly and on the Sunday before going to Osborne he wrote the summary of the Session.[1]

Lowe's article (14 August), betraying no sign of the haste with which it was prepared, was a good deal more censorious than his electoral address, published the day before: it described

a Session in which there have been displayed much talent, but little discretion; much zeal, but little firmness; in which many have fallen and few have risen; which has seen one Government [Aberdeen's] overthrown and another [Palmerston's] modified; and which leaves the prospects for peace, we fear, more remote than it found them.

There was no disputing Lord Goderich's conclusion that Lowe had 'certainly played his cards well for *his* purposes. How far that has been a high one I will not pronounce.' Lord Brougham, never reluctant to pronounce, told Russell that Lowe, 'an able but an unsafe man, ... conveys to Mr Delane (unfaithfully it is said) a report of every conversation he hears in the H. of Commons or in Clubs'. The solution, he proposed, was to strip newspapermen of their anonymity by requiring them to sign their articles.[2] That was a subject others were to take up in the next decade.

The Times, its circulation unchecked by the repeal of the stamp duty and boosted by the war, gave offence on every side. 'I wd. rather be honoured, like Lord John, by their abuse,' Lord Enfield wrote to the Duke of Bedford, Russell's brother, 'than disgraced like 3 of his colleagues, by propitiating Mr Delane, with dinners, & society for which he is not adapted.' Sidney Herbert thought it likely that 'the army will lynch' Russell after his 'most scandalous' allegations on 26 September. 'The *Daily News* letter is written in a juster & a fairer spirit,' he told Gladstone. Clarendon, too, was 'really in despair at the doings of *The Times*. Three pitched battles gained would not repair the mischief done by Mr Russell and the articles upon his letters.' Bright found the paper 'more than usually savage and insulting with me', and the Queen took umbrage at the aspersions cast on the Prussian Crown Prince, her prospective son-in-law. Greville observed the situation with abject despondency. '*The Times* is very powerful,' he acknowledged to Reeve, who had just left its employment,

& it has got a great hold upon the public mind, & when once this sort of power is established, it is difficult to undermine it, but the whole tone of the

---

[1] Delane to Dasent, 18 August [1855], *Times* Archives.
[2] Goderich to A. H. Layard, 25 August 1855, quoted in *History of The Times*, II, appendix 2, 555; Brougham to Russell, 21 August 1855, quoted in *Later Correspondence of Lord John Russell* (ed. G. P. Gooch; London, 1925), II, 213.

paper is so bad, its writing is so deteriorated, and the disgust and indignation it excites are so vehement and so general that I can not help thinking it would have a fall, if there was but any other paper better deserving of attention & patronage, but really the extreme mediocrity, or the coarse vulgarity of all the other morning papers still leave *The Times* in undisputed possession of its ascendancy.[1]

There were glimmers of hope, most of them illusory. Bright noted on 14 September that 'the *Globe* has written somewhat as if to prepare for peace', and the *Press* condemned the senseless prolongation of the war, raising speculation that Disraeli might join with Gladstone and other Peelites in a new political combination.[2] The *Morning Herald* derided the idea on behalf of official Conservatism, while the *Globe* (16 and 27 October) staunchly defended Palmerston's statesmanship against 'the hebdomadal organ of the Disraelite section of the promised, or threatened, Coalition'. The *Morning Advertiser* (6 and 7 November) warned that the danger came not from Bright or Cobden, who had isolated themselves, but from those who 'surrounded' the Prime Minister and 'who are secretly doing all they can to undermine his position . . .', because they have purposes of their own to serve'. *The Times*, which (as Palmerston told the Queen on 19 October) had recently 'in some Degree changed its Tone', emphasized the peril to the government, the war effort, and a victorious peace. Lord Stanley, in a private 'memorandum on public affairs', confirmed these suspicions of Disraelian intrigue: 'In a word, as D. had written up the war in the *Press* during the summer of 1853 in order to turn out Aberdeen, so he now prepared to write it down, in order to turn out Palmerston.' But Edward ('Bear') Ellice, a Whig elder statesman, was justly sceptical. 'A Gladstone-d'Israeli party is impossible,' he well knew.[3]

Had Gladstone been so inclined, he could have taken under his wing a journal to compete with – or possibly to complement – Disraeli's *Press*. In late October, he was addressed in confidence by George Thompson (possibly the former member for Tower Hamlets) and John Hamilton (a future editor of the *Morning Star*), who advised him that the *Empire*, established in London two years previously to advocate 'the Christian principles of Peace', needed £10,000 to continue. Various 'subscriptions have already been promised', they

[1] Enfield to Bedford, 17 August 1855 (copy), Russell Papers PRO 30/22/12F/51–54; Herbert to Gladstone, 27 September 1855, Gladstone Papers, Add. MSS. 44,210, fol. 207; Bright to Cobden, 8 October 1855, quoted in Trevelyan, *Bright*, pp. 249–50; Clarendon to Reeve, 3 October 1855, quoted in Maxwell, *Clarendon*, II, 100–101; *Greville Memoirs* (7 October 1855), VII, 163–64; Greville to Reeve, 19 October 1855, Greville-Reeve Correspondence, Add. MSS. 41,185, fols. 266–67.

[2] Bright to Cobden, 14 September 1855, Bright Papers, Add. MSS. 43,384, fol. 11; Bright to Cobden, 8 October 1855, quoted in Trevelyan, *Bright*, pp. 249–50.

[3] Palmerston to Queen Victoria, 19 October 1855, quoted in *History of The Times*, II, appendix 2, 556; Ellice to Aberdeen, 20 October [1855], Aberdeen Papers, Add. MSS. 43,200, fol. 155; Stanley's memorandum dated 'November 1855', in *Disraeli, Derby and the Conservative Party*, p. 135.

told him, including a token pledge of £10 from Henry Richard. Gladstone replied on the 26th

> by frankly stating to you that I have never at any time thought it compatible with the exigencies & duties of my more immediate sphere of action to contract that kind of responsibility for the conduct of any newspaper wh. is implicitly a pecuniary loan or contribution for its support.

With the *Morning Chronicle* probably in mind, he was compelled

> to add that there are newspapers in existence wh. perhaps wd. have a prior claim upon me were I to depart from my rule but I feel myself prevented by the strongest reasons from abandoning it. . . .

Yet his scruples did not deter him from appreciating either the *Press*, 'which is now admirably written in its articles on the War', or the 'most able & interesting paper' in the second number of the *Saturday Review*, which he traced to the anonymous pen of Sidney Herbert.[1]

Russell, unlike Gladstone, was bound by no self-denying ordinance. Unlike Disraeli and Palmerston, however, he lacked agility. Gilbert Elliot, the Dean of Bristol and his cousin by marriage, acted in his interest to procure the press support that was deemed necessary to restore Russell to favour, if not directly to power. The Dean, despite his social credentials, was poorly suited for the job. Joseph Parkes, who took charge of electoral organization, thought him 'a perfect Ignoramus on the subject of the London Press; a Goose on a Common'. Elliot's henchman was W. W. Clarke, a writer for the *Examiner*, who was more astute, but even less authoritative. Spurred on by the impending appearance of the *Morning Star* under the editorship of Haly, allegedly 'a desperate Tory Radical whose hatred of the Whigs is intense', Clarke turned to the *Daily News* which, as Herbert and others noted, was giving evidence of a slight shift in its editorial position.[2]

Clarke's original strategy was to acquire the holding of Sir Joshua Walmsley who, he discovered, 'cannot be bought out; he won't sell, but he gives no trouble'. Next on his agenda came a 'most promising' interview with two of the other proprietors, 'Allcard and old Smith', both 'sensible shrewd men of business' who could see 'advantages from the connexion' he proposed. (Allcard was William Allcard, who had stood at Warrington in 1847; 'old Smith' was

---

[1] Thompson and Hamilton to Gladstone, n.d., and a copy of Gladstone's reply of 26 October 1855 are in the Gladstone Papers, Add. MSS. 44,384, fols. 206–7. For Gladstone's responses to the *Press* and the *Saturday Review*, see Gladstone to Herbert, 20 November 1855, and Herbert to Gladstone, 25 November 1855, Gladstone Papers, Add. MSS. 44,210, fols. 218–21. Abraham Hayward, too, was encouraged to see the *Press* 'stronger for peace', but heard conflicting reports of Disraeli's 'complicity or agreement with the articles'. Hayward to Gladstone, 12 and 16 January [1856], Gladstone Papers, Add. MSS. 44,207, fols. 28, 32.

[2] Parkes to Ellice, 10 January 1856, Ellice Papers. For Clarke's jealousy of 'the Manchester People', see Clarke to Elliot, 16 November 1855 and [March 1856], Russell Papers PRO 30/22/12G/80–82, 30/22/13B/275.

almost certainly John Benjamin Smith, MP for Stockport, though one cannot
rule out the possibility that he was John Abel Smith, MP for Chichester.) Yet,
as Clarke soon realized, the advantages they saw were different from the ones
he anticipated:

> We want better principles, a higher tone, greater constancy, better writing.
> What they chiefly aim at is above all getting authentic information, &
> forming good relations with official people. The one is consequently no suf-
> ficient substitute for the other. . . . How far they will admit to controul [*sic*]
> in return for this sort of relation is of course a question; but I suspect that
> they have no serious attachment to any of their present contributors & that
> if we could only give them reputation, we might have a good deal of our own
> way – at least as an experiment. Still I repeat this at best wd. be a feeble sub-
> stitute for your higher & better scheme.

Capital would still be required, and Russell himself had none to spare. Lord
Panmure offered assistance, and Clarke urged the Dean to collect offerings
from Ellice, the Duke of Bedford, and Lord Minto. 'If the Magnates will
unite,' he predicted, 'the Minor Stars will shine brightly enough.'[1]

While Clarke haggled, Russell waxed impatient. 'Even the *Morning Post*
repeats the story of my coalition with Bright, Disraeli, & Gladstone,' he wrote
to Elliot on 27 October. 'I wish you would have it again contradicted if Mr
Clarke will be so good as to do it, both in the *Globe & Daily News*.' Taking
care to utter no 'unkind word of Bright . . . nor of Gladstone either', Clarke
complied. But the incident showed how much the press preyed on Russell's
nerves. After dinner on the 30th, Clarke retired to the smoking room at the
Reform Club, 'where the conversation turned on Lord J . . . & against the
treatment he had received from *The Times*'. A week later, *The Times* was 'at it
again': the death of Sir William Molesworth had created a vacancy in the
Cabinet, and *The Times* (6 November) protested the selection of 'anyone
whom continental Europe could in the least identify with the opinions of Lord
John Russell, Mr Bright, or Mr Gladstone'. Clarke also called the Dean's
attention to the *Morning Advertiser*'s absurd suggestion that Russell 'has
lately "been as busy as a bee intriguing against Lord P."', and, under the pseudonym of 'Veritas', he published a letter on the 7th that set the record
straight.[2] Significantly, he did not write to *The Times* as well.

Improved prospects for a diplomatic settlement revived Russell's spirits and
his newspaper ambitions. 'The *Daily News* is & probably will be too much
against peace on any condition short of the subjugation of Russia,' he said,
logically enough. 'I am for supporting the Ministry, who seem to me to carry
on the war very well, & will I hope not refuse a fair opportunity of making an

[1] Clarke to Elliot, 25, 26, 27, and 29 October 1855, Russell Papers PRO 30/22/12F/241 ff.

[2] Russell to Elliot, 27 October 1855, and Clarke to Elliot, 29 and 30 October and 6 November
1855, Russell Papers PRO 30/22/12F/248–49, 255–66, and 30/22/12G/44.

honourable peace.' Thus, there existed a gulf between the *Daily News*'s position and his own. Matters would be different, he assumed, 'if a man like Ellice had a control of the paper'. He therefore instructed the Dean on 12 November to consult Ellice who, as a former whip, was the Whig equivalent of Lord Malmesbury: 'If he approves of the plan, he can raise the money more easily than any one.' Clarke endorsed the idea, and nominated Joseph Parkes as an intermediary. But Parkes was perplexed by Russell's vagueness on certain points. 'Am I to understand from Lord J's letter that he declines to give even his personal views or to have any conn. direct or indirect with the Paper?' he asked the Dean. 'If so, that to my mind wd. be a great drawback.'[1]

Thereafter, events followed a familiar course as expectations succumbed to realities. Parkes, contacted by Clarke, gamely said that 'the Party ought . . . to buy both *D.N. & Chronicle*, & raise at least £30,000 for the purpose'. All it would require would be 'old Ellice's recommendation'. Clarke ascertained that the purchase of the *Morning Chronicle* 'could only be made on terms that were out of the question', namely that Peelite tenets would be upheld, and that 'the leading proprietors' of the *Daily News* were 'willing (tho' not very desirous) to part with its command'. Meanwhile, Parkes was in touch with Ellice, who raised hopes one day only to dash them the next. Agreeing that Russell might 'rehabilitate himself in popular esteem & that a well conducted Journal might assist him', he made clear that he regarded Palmerston 'as his party leader just now'. That posed no problem for Clarke, who relayed assurances through Parkes that

> in desiring to secure a daily paper, there is . . . no sectional object. Its just duty would be to support Lord Palmerston's Cabinet as the best possible representation of the Liberal Party now practicable. . . . But its main objects would of course be of a higher & more permanent kind. At present there is no Journal associated with the leading minds of Parliament. . . . Those who agree in [the] suggestion seek nothing else for Lord John than what they would for Lord Grey, or . . . Cobden, Bright or Gladstone, & less for their sakes than those of the Country.

Ellice remained in every sense 'bearish'. On 15 December, he scrawled a memorandum to Parkes, who received it on the 22nd, transcribed it on the 27th, and sent it to the Dean of Bristol on 4 January. Deciphered and interpreted by Parkes, Ellice's basic points were as follows:

> that *he declines the initiative* – that he concurs in the value, if not the necessity, of the Establishment of a Journal to represent more truly and forcibly the *old* Liberal party . . . – that he thinks you and some of your . . . Correspondents partly mistake Causes for Effects, and *vice versa* – that he by no

---

[1] Russell to Elliot, 12 November 1855, and Clarke to Elliot, 12 and 15 November 1855, Russell Papers PRO 30/22/12G/67–69.

means has such a horror or fear of any part of our present Press as you and some of your friends have – that he thinks the present temporary macadamization of Parties not the most propitious moment for your project ... – that, before the Establishment of any such Journal as you propose, the Liberals ... must be in accord on limited, defined, practical and practicable objects – That, notwithstanding, he thinks you ought to be prepared to 'come together' and to arrange for such an Organ.

Parkes knew that the document would be 'rather a "bitter pill"', although its arguments struck him as 'able and sagacious'. Greville, who got hold of another copy of Ellice's 'strictly confidential' memorandum, likewise found 'a good deal of truth in what he says'. But Russell was unconvinced, and furthermore angry that Ellice had tagged him as 'the chief Promoter of the Journal Scheme'. He told the Dean of Bristol on 4 January: 'Ellice's paper seems to me false in facts, & inconclusive in result. What remains to be done? The plan of getting together contributions from the leading men of property among the Whigs must, I think, be given up,' he ruefully conceded. 'If a new Editor could be found for the *Daily News*, I would willingly communicate with him, when I go to London.'[1] That, for Russell, was a bold step; but for the sake of Whig journalism, it was not bold enough.

Parkes's attitude towards 'the Very Reverend the Dean of Bristol' was distinctly irreverent. He trusted that he and Ellice had 'given the Priest a new Revelation. He will make a good Bishop, but a d-mn-d bad Journalist'. Nor, between themselves, were Parkes and Ellice any more respectful of Russell, the petulant patrician. Early in 1856, Parkes was pleased to hear from Clarke that the proposal to acquire a London daily 'has died a natural death, as certain from the beginning'. Instead Russell would make do with a casual and circuitous arrangement with the *Daily News*. Citing ecclesiastical questions, Clarke told the Dean:

> I think we have abundant evidence that the *D.N.* is open to your view.... We have a 'Willing Editor' & the true policy is I think to use him ... without any pre-arrangement. He will pull us up short enough when he thinks us wrong whether there is a previous understanding or not; & it is I think better in yr. situation that he shd. only suspect that you occasionally inspire me than to [be] completely aware of the fact.

Clarke's miscalculation was obvious as early as 15 January, when the *Daily News* derided Russell's speech at Gloucester on labour conditions as 'scarcely one degree above twaddle'. In reply to Clarke's 'remonstrance', Smith pro-

[1] Clarke to Elliot, 15 and 26 November and 3 December 1855, Russell to Elliot, 19 November 1855 and 4 January 1856 (copy), Clarke to Parkes, 7 December 1855, Parkes to Elliot, 27 December 1855 (sent 4 January 1856), Russell Papers PRO 30/22/12G/74–75, 91, 118 ff., 144–45, 159–60, 237 ff., and 30/22/13A/21–24; memorandum by Ellice, 15 December 1855, Ellice Papers; *Greville Memoirs* (4 January 1856), VII, 188.

fessed 'how much personally he desires [a] good relationship'. Unfortunately, he subsequently complained to Clarke, 'he has only his own imagination to guide him'. Denying 'any wish to receive a subvention or pecuniary assistance', Smith (as Clarke recounted to the Dean) 'asks for the name of a gentleman competent to assume in our opinion the duties of acting, if not of nominal Editor'. Taking up one of Ellice's recommendations, Clarke nominated Alexander Russel, who had raised the circulation of the penny *Scotsman* from 3,400 to 6,000 copies a day; but Russel preferred the bracing climate of Edinburgh. Other candidates were also canvassed, including Alexander Knox of *The Times*. 'I confess I am puzzled,' Clarke told the Dean. 'Writers we can readily get – an Editor is a very different thing.' For want of anything better, Clarke accepted 'as a temporary arrangement' Smith's offer to prepare a letter to William Weir, 'telling him how he wished the paper conducted & authorising him to receive comms. &c &c from me'. Smith submitted a draft of these guidelines to Clarke, who invited comments from the Dean. It came with private assurances that, 'if a really fit man were found, he [would] quickly supersede Mr Weir in name as well as in reality', thereby providing 'an efficient dependable Editor at hand'.[1] In the event, Weir remained until his death in 1858.

These long and embarrassing efforts accomplished little, if indeed anything. Through Clarke, Russell was asked to state his views on education and the repeal of the abjuration oath, but the *Daily News* would surely have solicited his opinion in any case. When the *Morning Chronicle* maliciously stated that Russell was to go abroad for 'one or two years', he did not care whether it was the *Daily News* or the *Globe* that issued a contradiction. Parkes inferred that Clarke contributed an occasional article to the columns of the *Daily News*: 'I wish they would let him write oftener, but the Paper has a bad Editor.'[2] The subject on that occasion, dear to Ellice's heart, was the Canadian fur trade, and not any aspect of party politics.

In the aftermath of the general election of 1857, a stunning triumph for Palmerston, Clarke received an unexpected visit from Smith, who announced 'that at long last he & Mr Allcard had got rid of Sir J. Walmsley', presenting renewed opportunities to transform the directorship of the *Daily News*. Clarke, who had 'not lately communicated with Weir' – 'it wd. have been dishonourable for me to have told him anything that I knew' – was 'as ready as ever' to conclude a pact with the paper. That success again eluded him was evident from Russell's scornful disapprobation of *Daily News* policies. 'I am not of opinion that much good can be derived from the *D.N.* in its present hands,' he wrote to the Dean on 20 March 1858, when it ran a leading article

[1] Parkes to Ellice, 6 and 10 January 1856, Ellice Papers; Clarke to Elliot, 16, 24, 26, 28, and 30 January 1856 and 'Tuesday' [1856], Russell Papers PRO 30/22/13A/153, 214–15, 217–18, 234–38, 240–45, and 30/22/13B/290; Cooper, *An Editor's Retrospect*, pp. 166–67.

[2] Clarke to Russell, 23 February 1856, and Russell to Elliot, 11 August 1856, Russell Papers PRO 30/22/13A/263 and 30/22/13B/176; Parkes to Ellice, 4 September 1857, Ellice Papers.

on nationalist movements in Italy and Hungary, 'implying that we may be forced to join the democrats all over Europe'. For a time, he ceased to read the paper that espoused such deplorable doctrines; but he returned to it early in 1859, 'tho' its language about the aristocracy is in the lowest stile [*sic*] of vulgarity'.[1]

Like the age in which it developed, the political press was marked by tendencies towards democracy and vulgarity. Cobden and Bright adapted to them instinctively, Disraeli impudently, Gladstone with thoughtful apprehension, and Palmerston with rollicking duplicity. Russell, however, could not adapt at all, and his failure reflected the limitations of Whig traditionalism as much as his personal traits. Unable to appreciate the methods of parliamentary and electoral management that Parkes and others were then beginning to improvise, he and his confederates deluded themselves that politics and the press could be manipulated by remote control. The Dean of Bristol, a quaint survival from pre-1855 days, illustrated and exemplified the incompetence of Whiggism in an era that witnessed the growth of party organization and, consequently, an increased dependence on newspaper facilities.

[1] Clarke to Elliot, 'Thursday' and 'Friday' [1857], Russell to Elliot, 20 March 1858 (copy) and 10 January 1859 (copy), Russell Papers PRO 30/22/13C/22–24, 30/22/13E/281 and 30/22/13G/9.

Four

THE PALMERSTONIAN ASCENDANCY

In the dozen years between the abolition of the newspaper tax and the passage of the second Reform Act, the Victorian press took shape. The most demonstrable change occurred in the provinces, previously a journalistic wasteland, where cheap morning and evening papers sprouted at a quickening pace. In 1864, their aggregate daily circulation was put at 438,000, far surpassing the 248,000 copies published in London. Between 1855 and 1870, as many as seventy-eight new provincial dailies had appeared, mostly in areas of population density that coincided with the major parliamentary boroughs. The mortality rate among them was predictably high: fifty-nine survived to welcome the 1870 Education Act to which they looked for an expanded readership. But, on the whole, the initial 'crop of cheap dailies was . . . a sturdy one'.[1]

Whether their editorial authority matched their commercial resources is quite another matter. Tending to reflect the diffused radical sentiments of middle-class Nonconformity, they had an influence still more circumscribed than their distribution. With few exceptions, they aspired merely to complement and not to displace the London journals from which they habitually took their cue on questions of public policy. Not until well into the 1870s did the more enterprising of these properties, employing the electric telegraph and establishing Fleet Street facilities, emerge from the shadow of their metropolitan rivals, and then only for a relatively brief time. The 1890s brought a further revolution in newspaper management, popularly associated with the image of Harmsworth, that cast them back into the shade.

In political as distinct from social terms, the phenomenon of the provincial press was more apparent than real. An American observer, writing in 1880, acknowledged its capacity for local service and literary distinction, but responded 'sceptically and with much reservation' to claims of its relative superiority: 'In a great part of their contents the leading provincial newspapers are simply detachments of London in the provinces,' he argued, citing the 'fact that what is most valuable and interesting in the provincial papers is simply an

[1] Lee, *Origins*, pp. 67–68; Vincent, *Formation*, pp. 58–59.

infusion of London life'.[1] Although provincial journalists would have been loath to admit as much, his impression was essentially valid.

While there is no denying that 'the growth of the provincial press after 1855 gave a tremendous boost to local politics'[2] (as evidenced by the *Manchester Guardian*'s pitched battle against Bright's candidacy in 1857) or that there developed a strong 'connection between local Liberal politicans and the new local press'[3] (as exemplified by the Baineses at Leeds), the channels of influence constantly flowed in a single direction, at least at the higher levels. And those were – and to a surprising extent have remained – the levels which were considered to count. 'There is no immutable law which requires national newspapers any longer to be printed in London,' declared Albert Booth, the Secretary of State for Employment, in a Commons debate on 18 May 1978, when Fleet Street operations were disrupted by industrial disputes.[4] There had never been such a law, of course. Yet, like other clauses in Britain's unwritten constitution, such a law has invariably applied.

It has long been standard practice for journalists to prepare obituary notices in advance. Abraham Hayward cannot therefore be blamed for prematurely pronouncing a death sentence on a system that was to outlive him. Scarred by his experience at the *Morning Chronicle*, which he had struggled in vain to keep in Peelite hands, he travelled the length of the kingdom at the end of 1855. With unconcealed satisfaction, he reported to Gladstone that already 'the cheap newspapers have gained enormously on the London press' throughout Scotland and the 'far north' of England:

> Within a given radius round Aberdeen, for example, you get all the most interesting news 24 hours before the arrival of a London paper & so in proportion round Edinburgh, Glasgow, Newcastle &c &c. I myself actually ceased taking in a London paper whilst I was in Scotland.[5]

The remainder of his letter, however, pointed to the opposite conclusion: back in the capital, he promptly returned to his obsession with the workings of the *Morning Post*, the *Saturday Review*, the *Press* ('which only tells half the truth'), and *The Times*. In short, from the periphery it often appeared as though the London press were expendable; but at the nerve-centre it was difficult to doubt its continued hegemony. Cobden keenly appreciated the situation: 'The *country Press*, which to a considerable extent follows the lead of *The Times*, is really to be pitied,' he wrote in June 1856.[6]

So long as the metropolitan papers were fed, cultivated, and, in certain

---

[1] 'English Provincial Journalism,' *Nation* (New York), 28 October 1880.
[2] H. J. Hanham, *Elections and Party Management* (London, 1959), p. 109; Ayerst, *Guardian*, pp. 126–27.
[3] Vincent, *Formation*, pp. 64–65.
[4] *Parliamentary Debates* (Commons), cmil, col. 805.
[5] Hayward to Gladstone, 2 January [1856], Gladstone Papers, Add. MSS. 44, 207, fols. 17 ff.
[6] Cobden to Richard, 17 June 1856, quoted in Hobson, *Cobden*, p. 156.

cases, financed by party chiefs and their organizers, the provincial dailies were fated to function as satellites. Individual MPs could not afford to ignore journalistic activity in their constituencies and sometimes attempted, with greater success as the century wore on, to interest party chiefs as well. Nevertheless, overriding importance automatically attached to the views promulgated along Fleet Street. While not necessarily more accurate or less prejudiced, these were weighted by the authorities whom they were known or presumed to represent. Failing support from one or more London organs, politicians who held or coveted power strove at least to gain their attention. The endorsement of a paper in Bradford or Basingstoke might help them to get elected, but only recognition from a London paper conferred national stature. Calculation, fortified by conceit, decreed that parliamentary leaders should be equipped with instruments for spreading light or, alternatively, for whistling in the dark. Newspapers, in turn, depended upon political affiliations, which grew increasingly formalized, to augment their own stature.

Again, Cobden unhappily testified to the process. The *Morning Star,* which he had helped to launch in 1856, showed somewhat unexpectedly 'that there was no demand for a paper unconnected with an official party' and that parliamentary factions lacking significant press connections were doomed to frustration. Much money was lost (according to one reckoning, a sum in excess of £80,000) and many illusions were shattered before its absorption by the *Daily News* in 1868. Determined 'that the *Star* should not appear the organ of a sect', Cobden went so far as to propose to its editor 'a bargain ... not to let my name appear in your leaders (unless to find fault with me) for two years'.[1] That, however, was the least of its self-inflicted disabilities.

Consonant with the mentality of its patrons, the *Morning Star* was conceived and conducted as a London outpost of Manchester radicalism. From the start, Bright was disappointed by its editorial performance, which he deemed inferior to that of the *Manchester Examiner*: 'I have only seen two *tolerable* Leaders in it yet,' he complained to Cobden on 31 March 1856; 'generally they are loose in style – inaccurate, & shewing no literary ability – it must beat Col Sleigh's *Telegraph* before it measures itself with *The Times*!' Cobden agreed, and called Henry Richard's attention to two 'symptoms' of the paper's distress: 'a tendency to systematically quote from the *Press*', which was 'Disraeli's organ, a sneerall ... without a heart, plan, sympathy, or conviction'; and an unfortunate 'proneness to praise and champion Gladstone', whose 'conscience has not yet taken him in our direction'.[2]

By contrast, the proprietorship was less critical of the paper's contents than of its 'scale of expenditure'. Henry Rawson and George Wilson jointly pressed

[1] Cobden to Samuel Lucas, 17 October 1856, quoted in Morley, *Cobden*, II, 385.
[2] Bright to Cobden, 31 March 1856, Bright Papers, Add. MSS. 43, 384, fols. 59–60; Cobden to Richard, 27 January 1857, quoted in Hobson, *Cobden,* pp. 200–2; Bright to Wilson, 27 March 1856, Wilson Papers.

this point, urging reductions in staff and salaries. The result was dissension in the London office, which could not be controlled by the absentee management in Manchester or the secondary shareholders in Birmingham. 'I don't believe the best man of business in the world, in *Manchester,* can carry on a daily paper in *London* in competition with others who live on the spot,' Cobden told Joseph Sturge. 'The worst of leaving a concern without any supreme head,' he concluded after a subsequent interview with Rawson, 'is that every body gets out of his proper place.'[1]

Charles Cooper, who began as a parliamentary correspondent for the *Morning Star* in 1861 and became its sub-editor before moving on to the *Scotsman,* noted that its 'peculiar' proprietorial arrangements militated against effective 'editorial supervision'. With a 'reporting staff . . . not more than half the size of that of *The Times,* and . . . smaller than that of any other paper', the *Star* over-extended itself to provide reports of proceedings in the House of Commons (while virtually ignoring the House of Lords) that 'were often as long as those of *The Times,* and were almost invariably longer than those of its other contemporaries'.[2] Obviously the proportions were wrong, but they were dictated by the priorities of Cobden and especially Bright. An evening edition, intended to increase revenue, instead compounded difficulties. Although Cobden could 'see no limit to its sale',[3] it fared no better, and Bright's scheme for a weekly was consequently shelved.

Cobden saw the problem as one of insufficient capital.[4] Mistaking the cause, he nonetheless correctly discerned the effect. 'Between ourselves,' he wrote to Sturge on 30 August 1856,

> I consider the circulation to be a dead failure *in London.* . . . It seems for the month of August to have averaged about 17,000 daily viz – 13,000 morning & 4,000 evening. From this 10 per ct must be deducted for returns, leaving net sale 15,300. The *morning paper* has less than 12,000 net circulation, & of this a considerable portion goes to the Country. So that we have really a poor hold on the metropolis. . . . Not only the advertisements, but the pol-

[1] Cobden to Sturge, 5 June and 5 July 1856, Sturge Papers, Add. MSS. 43,722, fols. 120–21; Rawson and Wilson to Cobden, 9 May 1856 (copy), Cobden Papers, Add. MSS. 43,663, fol. 186. For general accounts of the *Morning Star*'s proprietorial and financial difficulties, see Cooper, *An Editor's Retrospect,* pp. 110 ff.; [J. F. Hitchman], 'The Newspaper Press,' *Quarterly Review,* cl (1880), 504; Edwin Hodder, *Life of Samuel Morley* (London, 1887), pp. 243–45; and Justin McCarthy, *Reminiscences,* I, ch. ix.

[2] Cooper, *An Editor's Retrospect,* pp. 82–83, 100, 110; Cooper to Rosebery, 17 November 1884, Rosebery Papers.

[3] Cobden to Sturge, 19 March 1856, Sturge Papers, Add. MSS. 43,722, fol. 111.

[4] The following discussion is based on Cobden to Sturge, 30 August 1856, Sturge Papers, Add. MSS. 43,722, fols. 154 ff.; Bright to Wilson, 21 October 1856, Wilson Papers; Cobden to Sturge, 26 December 1856, Sturge Papers, Add. MSS. 43,722, fol. 196, Cobden to Richard, 20 December 1856 and 'Wednesday' [1857], quoted in Hobson, *Cobden,* pp.231–32; Sturge to Richard, 7 July 1856, Richard Papers; Hamilton to Wilson, 2 August 1856, and Cobden to Wilson, 30 May 1857, Wilson Papers.

itical influence of the paper depends altogether on its circulation, & I consider that for a penny paper the sale is insignificant.

Bright offered the same assessment to George Wilson in October. From the
experience of the preceding seven months, it was 'evident that something not
yet tried, or perhaps discovered, is needed for the London circulation', which
carried paramount importance. But the formula eluded him, and he was left to
'hope the opening of the next Session & great attention to *debates* may give the
Paper a move onward'. That indeed was wishful thinking.

'In all our consultations, 50,000 was the circulation aimed at,' Cobden gloomily reminded Sturge at year's end. 'It is not much more thàn 1/4th that for *both
papers* . . . , quite a failure as compared with our expectations.' More quickly
than Bright, he accepted the need for typographical and structural alterations.
'Let the essay style be avoided', he urged Richard, to whom he commended
the communication of news 'in a compendious form'. Richard, deputized as
the proprietors' 'representative in London', was in a weak position to implement policy: 'Cobden & I and others who know the state of things look almost
solely to thee to keep matters from getting very wrong though we know thou
hast no authority,' Sturge told Richard, his friend and future biographer; and
John Hamilton lodged a stiff protest when Richard invaded his editorial room
and usurped 'rank, title, and dignity'. Cobden could not have eased tensions
by dealing exclusively through Richard and by 'remarking' to him (as he
recounted to Wilson)

> that I thought the *Star* was *tame* in its tone, & gave one the impression that it
> was cowed. I don't know what the circulation may be, but I don't think its
> influence will be very revolutionary or dangerous to a ministry unless there
> is a little more spice in its writing. To my judgment the only way to make a
> London penny paper a power in the world of journalism is to take the
> *Herald, Tribune* &c of New York as the models. I don't mean of course in
> politics or in every respect of style – but in the mode of covering news & of
> *condensing* their comments.

A generation later, showing exactly the same instincts, Stead and Harmsworth
were to qualify as Cobdenites.

His experience with the *Morning Star* failed to shake Cobden in his belief
that '*the cheap daily press will do more than any other human agency to form
the public opinion of this Country*'. Nor did it dissuade him from encouraging
Sturge to attempt similar experiments, particularly in the West Riding of
Yorkshire, where he regarded the *Leeds Mercury* as a traitor to the pacifist
ideal. 'The House of Commons was not so much to blame as the people for the
last war,' he asserted. 'It was the *press* as Lord Aberdeen told me that forced
him into the war. It is by the press that the public must be taught to abstain
from future wars.' Alone, if necessary, the *Star* had to keep 'manfully to its

colours' at a time when the *Daily News* was applauding Napoleonic exploits in Italy, the *Examiner* ('the worst and most barefaced offender') was condoning the Opium War on the China coast, and newspapers of all other persuasions had joined in the cry for revenge against the sepoy mutineers in India. Small wonder that the *Star* earned a reputation as 'a thoroughly anti-British paper': even Bright was aware that its 'tone of complaint & asperity' had 'interfered with its circulation, without doing any good to the good cause'.[1]

Despite its ostensible want of patriotism, the paper was 'paying its expenses' by the summer of 1857 and, as Bright was pleased to inform Cobden in September, selling 'as many as they can conveniently print'. Plans were made to acquire new machinery and more capacious premises in the Strand. A new editor was likewise required, although 'it is extremely difficult to meet with one capable & honest & holding the views of the promoters of the *Star*'. Samuel Lucas, Bright's brother-in-law, was selected. Unlike his two unsatisfactory predecessors, he was made an 'active managing partner' with a financial interest in the concern. Thereafter, Richard faded out of the picture: on 13 June 1859, Charles Sturge confirmed that he 'had ceased to write for the *Star*'.[2]

Each of these improvements meant that further capital had to be raised if the *Star* was not to lag too far behind in the race. In addition to its other rivals, it competed against the *Standard,* which James Johnstone purchased in 1857 and converted from a fourpenny evening paper into a twopenny morning one, eight pages in size; soon afterwards, on 4 February 1858, it halved its price without sacrificing either size or quality. Bright surmised that 'the *Standard*, double size at a penny, ... must be losing far more than £100 per week, & therefore can hardly last long in its present state'. He expected that, like the *Daily Telegraph* in 1856, it would soon be forced to revert to four pages. Instead the *Telegraph,* having since installed presses of the latest design, met the challenge by going to eight pages in May. Its average circulation rose to 30,000, and that of the *Standard* was not much less.

If the threat to *The Times* (as conceded by its official historians) 'was bound to be serious', how much more so was it to the *Star*? By August, Bright had reluctantly come to the conclusion that the *Star* would be enlarged 'before Xmas', possibly at the same time as the founding of 'a Weekly Paper at 2d' to help offset losses. Within weeks, he had revised his timetable: 'Owing to the competition of the *Standard & Telegraph,* it will be necessary to increase the size of the paper before Parlt. meets,' he notified Joseph Sturge, '& it is intended also to bring out a first-rate popular weekly paper at 2d.' The Sturge brothers, Joseph and Charles, were wealthy Birmingham Quakers who

[1] Cobden to Sturge, 31 October, [25 November], and 15 December 1856, Sturge Papers, Add. MSS. 43,722, fols. 165, 178, 192; Bright to Sturge, 8 January 1858, Sturge Papers, Add. MSS. 43,723, fols. 87 ff; Grant, I, 378.

[2] Bright to Cobden, 19 September 1857 and 9 April 1868, Bright Papers, Add. MSS. 43,384, fols. 111, 126–27; Charles Sturge to Richard, 13 June 1859, Richard Papers.

contributed generously 'to create a really useful newspaper establishment' at Bright's behest. For their investment, they were content with his assurances that 'only *The Times* has a greater political influence of all the London Journals' and that the *Star* was 'every month . . . increasing its circulation & its influence'. In just 'another year', Bright perennially promised, they would 'see it all that its friends hope for'.[1]

That promise was not fulfilled. Nor was Bright's hope of starting a radical weekly. By way of compensation, a merger was effected with the *Dial* in 1860. Edited by Peter Bayne, it had been started by the Rev Dr David Thomas, a Congregational minister, whose ambition was to develop it into 'a righteous daily newspaper. . . , permeated with the spirit of religion'. Having nearly exhausted its funds, which were said to have been prodigious, the *Dial* soldiered on as a weekly. Two years after the *Morning Star* had taken over Ernest Jones's *People's Charter* at the paltry price of pledging two columns a week for Chartist news, its directors negotiated a more complicated agreement with 'the *Dial* people', as Bright called them. 'There is no surrender of principle & no change *of course* in any particular, conceded or demanded,' he insisted to Cobden. Under the joint company, the holding was evenly divided, with 'Lucas to be continued as managing proprietor for 7 years, & Rawson to superintend the finance'. Through this amalgamation, the *Dial* acquired a stake in daily journalism and the *Star* a vicarious presence in the weekly market. Each side was relieved of a measure of financial anxiety, and neither any longer had reason to fear the prospect of competition from the other. Bright, betraying a degree of disrespect towards his new partners, explained that the union would 'prevent the establishment of a compromising & useless paper under the original *Dial* scheme', elaborated in an 1857 prospectus.[2]

The *Star* proprietorship obviously had the better of the deal. Its capital siphoned away, the *Dial* was allowed to wither. The *Morning Star*, enlivened by the contributions of Edmund Yates and Justin McCarthy, showed some resilience in the early '60s; but the *Evening Star* was hard hit first by Johnstone's decision to publish a penny *Evening Standard* in 1860, then by the début of the *Pall Mall Gazette* in 1865. Never higher than 15,000, the combined net circulations of the two *Stars* had fallen to 5,000 in 1868, when the directors transferred their 'interests', accompanied by their 'public principles and aims', to the *Daily News*, recently lowered in price from threepence to a penny. The *Evening Star* was immediately extinguished. In the belief that 'the publication of an evening newspaper was found inconsistent with the arrangements called for by the extending circulation of the *Daily News*', it was soon followed into ob-

---

[1] Bright to Sturge, 14 February, 23 August, and 21 September 1858, and 3 May 1859, Sturge Papers, Add. MSS. 43,723, fols. 91, 111, 114, 134–35; *History of The Times*, II, 298–99.
[2] Cooper, *An Editor's Retrospect*, p. 149; Bright to Cobden, 10 October 1860, Bright Papers, Add. MSS. 43,384, fol. 227.

livion by the *Express*, which the *Daily News* had run unprofitably since 1855 as its evening companion. The *Morning Star* flickered until 13 October 1869. Its final leader, ascribed to the pen of John Morley, adduced that 'there is no longer any sufficient reason for dividing the newspaper forces of the Liberal party'. That was an ironic epitaph for a journal that had begun, fourteen years before, by eschewing the party fold.[1]

By then, Bright was launched on his ministerial career, and Cobden was dead. In his last years, Cobden had been increasingly preoccupied with the ways of the press, its wasted potential for moral instruction, and its alleged disregard for fact. '*There is far more corruption going on in connection with the public Press than in any other walk of political life,*' he insisted to Henry Richard in 1857; newspapers had been liberated from official controls only to succumb to hidden influences. He was not alone in his apprehension. 'What is behind the Press is now a very grave, not to say terrible, question,' Goldwin Smith professed a few years later. Everywhere evident, this evil seemed to be epitomized in the conduct of *The Times*.

While Lord John Russell and others privately bristled, Cobden prepared 'to meet that journal with a bold front, and neither to give nor to take quarter'. Dominant and domineering, *The Times* provoked him by its sneering references to Bright and himself, and, still more, by the cloak of corporate anonymity behind which it shielded its operations. Even the identity of its editor, though well known in political society, was by convention never acknowledged in print. Regarding this 'strict incognito' as incompatible with the interests of democracy, Cobden vowed to unmask 'the Doge of Printing House Square' and, in the process, to reveal 'the illicit secret intercourse' between that newspaper and government officials. 'I believe that Delane & Co have had a far larger share of government patronage than an average couple of Cabinet Ministers,' he told Thorold Rogers in 1863. Bright, arguably for selfish reasons, concurred: 'I think *The Times*' men are lost to all moral sense,' he wrote to Cobden, '& would sell you, or me, or any body else, & their own souls apparently, for any personal & present object of low ambition.'[2]

Although Cobden feigned indifference ('*The Times* never enters my house, except by accident'), his correspondence told against him: 'I never see the Cockney papers except *The Times*,' he casually mentioned to Richard in 1856; and, two years later, he disclosed to Rogers that 'the thunder of *The Times* fails to arouse me from my political apathy'. In any case, he was certain to see copies of the offending journal at the clubs he frequented or at Westminster.

---

[1] F. W. Hirst, *Early Life and Letters of John Morley* (London, 1927), I, 154–57; Fox Bourne, II, 271–72.

[2] Cobden to Richard, 17 June 1857, quoted in Hobson, *Cobden*, p. 219; Cobden to Rogers, 11 December 1863, Rogers Papers; Bright to Cobden, 8 October 1862, Bright Papers, Add. MSS. 43,384, fol 306. The quotation from Smith appears in Wilson Harris, *The Daily Press* (London, 1943; 4th ed., 1946), p. 52.

From numerous platforms and in letters to an array of editors, most of whom declined to publish them, he attacked Delane by name for playing 'a game (I purposely use the word) ... of secrecy to the public and servility to the Government' in order to obtain 'corrupt advantages'. Articles in the *Morning Star,* written either at his instigation or on his behalf (one, on 7 February 1861, was signed 'Amicus Cobden, sed Magis Amicus Veritas'), accused *The Times* of engaging in stock-jobbery, place-hunting, character assassination, and systematic misrepresentation. Riding in Rotten Row with the 2nd Duke of Wellington, Delane contrasted 'the conduct of *The Times* to that of the *Morning Star*', and 'said that *The Times* does not lend itself to attacks on individuals of a calumnious kind'.[1]

Rooted in an antagonism that can be traced to the stormy events of 1846, the controversy festered for over a decade before it flared into the open in February 1861. Apart from renewed criticisms of himself and Bright, Cobden had further reason to resent *The Times*. The 'lies' propounded by the 'immoral gang' in Printing House Square threatened the 'good understanding ... between France & England' which he had secured by means of a commercial treaty; he enlisted the assistance of the *Illustrated London News* (in which Edward Watkin, the railway promoter and future MP, had 'a voice in the control') to help 'refute' them. Without false modesty, he saw his treaty as 'the cornerstone' of Gladstonian fiscal policy, which *The Times* plotted to discredit so as 'to prevent the paper duty from being abolished and thus being itself swallowed by the cheap Press'.[2] Although such a link was admittedly hypothetical, it was no secret that Delane was using his influence with Lord Palmerston to delay the remission of the excise on paper, the last vestige of newspaper protectionism. 'If Gladstone consents,' Bright warned, 'I shall have no particle of faith in him on any matter whatsoever.'[3] But Gladstone held firm and, contrary to all expectation, *The Times* gained enormously from the reform which, in its 'baseness', it had tried to obstruct: its circulation, which had hovered around 50,000 since the incursion of the *Standard,* rose to 65,000 at the end of 1861, its price having dropped to 3d. on 1 October; its sale on 16 December, when it reported the death of Prince Albert, soared to 89,000. Abroad, as at home, its strength was redoubtable. On a visit that year to the United States, William Howard Russell was introduced to President Lincoln, who extended 'his hand in a very friendly manner', and said: 'The London *Times* is one of the greatest powers in the world; in fact, I don't know anything which has more power, except perhaps the Mississippi.'[4]

[1] Cobden to Richard, 1 December 1856, quoted in Hobson, *Cobden,* p. 181; Cobden to Rogers, 4 October 1858, Rogers Papers; Wellington to Delane, 14 August 1859, *Times* Archives.
[2] Cobden to Watkin, 18 October and 3 November 1860, Watkin Papers, M/219/3/6–7; Cobden to Richard, 13 November 1860, quoted in Hobson, *Cobden,* pp. 266–67.
[3] Bright to Cobden, 20 May 1860 and 28 March 1861, Bright Papers, Add. MSS. 43,384, fols. 199, 251; *also see* Robinson, *Fifty Years,* p. 110.
[4] *History of The Times,* II, 299; Dasent, *Delane,* II, 64; Atkins, *Russell,* II, 14.

Circulation, as always, contributed to power, but was itself insufficient. Delane's relationship with Palmerston, far more intimate than his earlier relationship with Aberdeen, was the key factor. Since 1857, Palmerston had been the grateful recipient of Delane's 'handsome and powerful support', which he reciprocated by hospitality at Cambridge House in town and Broadlands in the country. From the time of Palmerston's ascent to the premiership, he became 'Delane's principal mentor', a source of inspiration and encouragement: 'The Editor gave him firm support in matters both great and small. Palmerston could think and do no wrong, almost.'[1] Symbolically, it was not until 11 January 1861 that Palmerston first addressed his ally as 'My dear Delane'.[2] The ripening of their friendship made the Olympian pronouncements of *The Times* all the more offensive to Radical susceptibilities.

As the organ of Cobdenite disaffection, the *Morning Star* was too censorious for most tastes. Joseph Parkes found the *Telegraph* 'much better written', and was not dismayed to hear that 'the "Kept Press", the *Star*, has ... suffered in circulation from its blaggardism [sic] & ultra nonsense'.[3] Its persistent gibes at *The Times,* purportedly undertaken in self-defence, redounded to its discredit. They died down after the early months of 1861, only to revive in December 1863, when a *Times* leader gratuitously likened Bright's proposals for land redistribution to the larceny of Robin Hood. Cobden stood ready to resume his crusade, which gave issue to a heated exchange of letters. Neither he nor Delane emerged unscathed from the fray, on which *The History of The Times* has delivered the definitive verdict: 'Although the facts were with Cobden, he spoilt his case by seizing the opportunity to make an intemperate attack upon anonymous journalism and patronage.' Even Morley, his sympathetic biographer and an advocate of signed articles, admitted that Cobden had 'put himself in the wrong' by going too far. Like other critics of the press, then and since, Cobden overstated the problem without proposing any practical remedy. The popular press, whose interests he presumed to defend, sided overwhelmingly against him, and he was left to rely on the *Star* and the Rochdale *Observer,* Bright's home town organ, to publish his diatribes. The Duke of Wellington resented Cobden's 'insolence' and, less predictably, Parkes thought 'that his mind certainly had been off its balance'. It was altogether an unedifying climax to a proud career.[4]

Yet Cobden would not have pursued his vendetta had he not been convinced that, 'as a rule, grown-up men, in these busy times, read little else but newspapers'. What appalled him was that so disproportionately large a

---

[1] Palmerston to Delane, 4 March 1857, quoted in *History of The Times,* II, 323, where it is correctly dated from internal evidence; this description of the relationship appears in *ibid.*, pp. 333–34.

[2] *Times* Archives.

[3] Parkes to Ellice, 29 August 1860, Ellice Papers.

[4] Dasent, *Delane,* II, 84–93 (including Wellington to Delane, n.d.); Morley, *Cobden,* II, 420–39; *History of The Times,* II, 335–36 (including Parkes to Delane, 3 April 1865).

segment of the national readership was attracted to *The Times,* which was likely to be taken as gospel. His inveterate distrust of 'the Palmerston imposture' made it impossible for him to credit that *The Times* followed rather than led public opinion, much less that its managers were motivated by anything other than personal ambition. Just as he had once rebuked 'Jemmy' Wilson for having used the editorship of the *Economist* as 'the stepping-stone to Office', he decried the denizens of Printing House Square who enjoyed the emoluments of appointments to the civil and colonial service. William Hargreaves, his associate, dwelled on these 'coincidences' in a pamphlet that demanded a second printing:

> Talk to any one of those habitués of the Clubs, who are interested in busying themselves in such matters, and he will tell you, as the current opinion of the circles in which he moves, that, during the last few years, Government patronage to the value of many thousands a year has been bestowed upon the writers for *The Times* and their connexions.[1]

In a speech at Birmingham on 26 January 1864, Bright likewise alluded to Clubland gossip, and contemplated the elevation of John Walter to the peerage 'as a compensation for the services offered to the present Prime Minister of England'. His harshest words, however, were reserved for 'the Editor of *The Times*', who had been 'domesticated in the houses of Cabinet Ministers and members of high families in London', where he had 'learnt ... to fetch and carry for Cambridge-house', Palmerston's London residence.

Delane's predilection for fashionable company was no secret. 'I have, as the *Post* will say, "returned to London after a turn of visits" – having been to Chevening, Tedmouth, Broadlands and Hatfield,' he informed John Blackwood a year later. 'I have shot many pheasants & drunk much claret.'[2] But these amusements were no index to the politics of his paper: for better or worse, he was often capable of biting the gloved hand that fed him. On 28 January, the day after *The Times* had given a full report of Bright's Birmingham speech, it replied to his imputations:

> It matters little to anyone except himself in what society the Editor of this journal moves, or where he spends the hours of relaxation, which Mr Bright devotes to the Smoking Room of the House of Commons or the Billiard Room of the Reform Club. It will be time enough to accuse any gentleman interested in *The Times* of seeking for a peerage when it can be shown that he has ever striven to put himself in a position beyond that which naturally

---

[1] *Revelations from Printing House Square. Is the Anonymous System a Security for the Purity and Independence of the Press? A Question for The Times Newspaper* (London, 1864), p. 19. On 27 April 1857, Delane 'intruded on' Clarendon to ask a favour on behalf of his younger brother, Captain George Delane of the Indian Army, who wished to be transferred for financial reasons to 'some less expensive place than Calcutta'. Clarendon Papers, MS Clar. dep.c.80, fol. 166.

[2] Delane to Blackwood, 20 January 1865, Blackwood Papers.

belongs to him, when he can be shown to have sought any favour at the hands of the Government, or when the public is ready to assume, as Mr Bright does, that a connexion with the Press is a virtual disqualification for any office or any honour for which a person might otherwise be fit.

Bright was bested, and deserved it. By personalizing the issues, he had trivialized them. The question of anonymous journalism was too important to be debated at this level. It was bound up in conflicting value judgments concerning professional responsibility and personal integrity, public interest and private enterprise. Sidney Herbert, 'taking the balance of the two sides', had tentatively concluded that 'the weight and influence of the newspapers would be increased if anonymous writing were diminished where it is for the public good that it should be diminished'.[1] Bright and Cobden were able to avoid his ambiguity with a doctrinaire demand for abolition, essentially more authoritarian than democratic.

For all his talk of 'confidence in the future of a Press now for the first time for a century and a half really free' and enjoying 'perfect freedom to all the world to publish their opinions either anonymously or with their signatures as they please', Cobden proved more respectful in theory than in practice. Adulation of Palmerston, for which he took the newspapers to account, had inspired him with second thoughts on the rectitude of the press and the gullibility of the electorate. 'Is it not time to open fire upon some of those papers which support Palmerston and call on them to explain the *public* grounds on which they do so?' he asked Richard on 7 March 1857. Finding himself in rare agreement with Disraeli, he had 'not the least doubt that Palmerston has . . . *made greater use of that means of creating an artificial public opinion than any Minister since the time of Bolingbroke'*. The pliancy of *The Times, Morning Post,* and *Globe* (which 'gets all its news from the Treasury', W. W. Clarke told the Dean of Bristol) went without saying. But Cobden also detected the cloven foot of Palmerston in the foreign dispatches of the *Daily News,* the weekly *Leader,* and the *Morning Advertiser,* even occasionally in the columns of the *Morning Star.* On the subject of diplomatic wrangles with America, he was furious to 'see such papers as the *Dispatch* and *Sun* howling to the same tune as the *Post* and *Times'.*[2]

There was no consolation to be taken from the fact that politicians of other persuasions shared his distress. The Duke of Newcastle ventilated Peelite grievances against the press in a speech at Sheffield on 5 September 1856 to which Delane had Alexander Knox reply in 'a moderately civil article' that ascribed the Duke's misfortune to 'the intrigues of his colleagues', principally Lord John Russell. Inured to abuse from that camp, Russell and his followers studied the papers in the hope of gleaning some complimentary comment.

[1] Speech at the Warminster Athenaeum, 28 October 1858, *The Times*, 29 October 1858.
[2] Cobden to Richard, 17 and 18 June 1858, 7 March and 22 April 1857, quoted in Hobson, *Cobden,* pp. 157, 202, 213; Clarke to Elliot, 7 July [1856], Russell Papers, PRO 30/22/13B/285–86.

Parkes drew Clarke's attention to a piece in the *Saturday Review* which 'tho' partially kind is nevertheless bitter', and a more favourable one in the *Leader*, 'an odd quarter for backing of Lord John'. Inclined to be more tolerant towards Cabinet ministers who trafficked with the press, Parkes saw no harm provided 'they agree together as to their communications, which may be . . . equally useful to the Paper, the public, & themselves'; the possibility for 'evil' could only arise through 'communication, not with one, but with several papers, of the discordant, or separate views, of different members of the same Cabinet'. It is doubtful, however, that he would have sanctioned the conduct of Lord Clarendon, who supplied Delane with confidential information on the state of Anglo-American affairs, imploring him '*pray* don't announce it for Derby wd. be sure to interpellate me about preferring *The Times* to the H. of Lds. as a medium of communn. to the public'.[1]

Although Russell managed to survive 'an attempt to extinguish me, . . . set on foot by a cabal, & supported by *The Times*', his contempt for Palmerston could not be contained. 'I will not dispute any more with you about Palmerston', he wrote on 23 January 1858 to Ellice, who pleaded with him to forget old quarrels for the sake of Whig unity. 'But Palmerston was popular with the mob & *The Times*, & therefore I was thrown over!' In a matter of weeks, Palmerston was overthrown, too. Greville recorded in his diary on 28 January: 'As the day approaches for the re-assembling of Parliament there is an increasing impression that this Government is very likely not to get through the session.' *The Times*, 'always ready to assist in the discomfiture of a losing party', was 'showing unmistakeable symptoms of its own doubts if the Government is any longer worth supporting'. The previous day, Delane had told him 'he thought they would not remain long in office, and that it is time they should go, and he ridiculed the idea of its not being practicable to form another Government'.[2] Derby and Disraeli were eager for a turn, although conscious of their numerical weakness in the Commons, and a spell in opposition might enable Palmerston to rid himself of the Russellite incubus. *The Times* was neither surprised nor disturbed when Palmerston resigned on 20 February, as indeed it had urged. A leader, said to have been written by Delane himself, extolled the accomplishments of the late administration and accepted its successor as a necessary stopgap.

Disraeli, angling for more substantive support, attempted to restore himself to Delane's good graces by keeping him abreast of ministerial assignments. Repaying Delane for his 'generous support of me in 1852', he divulged the

[1] Delane to Dasent [6 September 1856], and Clarendon to Delane, 15 June [1856], *Times Archives*; Parkes to Clarke, 30 November 1856, Russell Papers, PRO 30/22/13B/245; *The Times*, 8 September 1856.

[2] Russell to Ellice, 7 April 1857 and 23 January 1858, Ellice Papers; *Greville Memoirs* (28 January 1858), VII, 334. Ellice himself was on cordial terms with Russell's enemies. 'Tell Delane & Lowe they will find a chop, if they have time to come from the House,' he instructed Parkes on 2 February 1858. Ellice Papers.

process of Cabinet making in what he admitted to be 'about as imprudent a letter as was ever written'. *The Times,* knowing that Derby had made an offer to Gladstone but not that Gladstone had declined, mistakenly tipped him for the Exchequer. With Disraeli's assistance, it was quick to correct this error and to publish an accurate roster. Confident that he had restored the 'old spirit of camaraderie' between himself and Delane, which had existed only fleetingly, Disraeli advised Derby 'that *The Times* has decided to support you. So much for public opinion'. And he quoted Delane as saying that 'we "shall do much better without Gladstone"'. His embarrassment must have been acute when, on 23 and 24 February, *The Times* denounced the formation of the Derby government as a 'suicidal act', branded the list of Cabinet appointments 'a penitential sheet', and mocked Derby himself for accepting the premiership on the sufferance of Milner-Gibson and other Radicals. By May, Disraeli was again attacking *The Times* as 'the drawing-room organ of Whiggism'. Among his colleagues, Lord Malmesbury received praise for his handling of foreign policy and Lord Stanley for instituting 'measures of improvement and utility' in the government of India. But, for the time being, Disraeli's indiscretions reaped no reward.[1]

Their experience in office pointed up to the Conservative leaders a deficiency of which several of them had long been mindful. If Palmerston's monopoly on newspaper opinion was to be broken, the initiative would have to come neither from the Cobdenites nor Russell's old Whigs, who had shown themselves equally ineffectual, but from the Conservative side. Before 1857, that party had had few resources at its disposal. Disraeli's fling with the *Press* was an attempt to redress the balance, but that journal was too much a maverick and, besides, only a weekly. The metropolitan Tory dailies were few and pitiably weak. Stanley, indicating his interest in Indian reform, 'tried to open an attack in the *Herald*' on the East India Company directorate in 1853: 'The editor refused, being friends to them.' Early the following year, he broached with Robert Knox, the editor of the *Herald,* 'the subject of a cheap weekly journal to circulate among working men, but found his ideas of what such a journal ought to be widely different from mine'. Furthermore, Knox 'thought the stamp duty would be an obstacle'.[2] In 1855, that obstacle was removed, but still the Conservatives were slow to take the field.

The spring of 1857 saw a burst of Conservative activity. Knox, overcoming his earlier qualms, proposed 'a chit-chat' with John Blackwood, the Edinburgh publisher, whose guidance he sought for his 'project (no longer a mere project I believe) of starting three newspapers in combination'. Although his grand design came to nothing, it was a straw in the wind. The *Herald* had be-

[1] Disraeli to Delane, 22 February 1858, quoted in *History of The Times*, II, 328; Disraeli to Derby, 22 February 1858, quoted in Buckle, *Disraeli,* IV, 117–18; *also see* Blake. *Disraeli,* pp. 380–81, and Cook, *Delane,* pp. 112–14.

[2] Stanley's diary, 21 May 1853 and 6 February 1854, *Disraeli, Derby and the Conservative Party,* pp. 107, 119.

longed for two years to Edward Baldwin, whose son Charles was proprietor of the *Standard*. Confronted with bankruptcy, the Baldwins sold both properties to James Johnstone, who reportedly paid £16,500 for the package. The *Herald* continued to sell at fourpence after the *Standard*'s rapid transformation into a morning paper, priced first at twopence and then at a penny. Economically run in tandem, they provided basically the same news coverage, but different leaders, and came to be known by readers of *Punch* as 'Mrs Gamp and Mrs Harris'. In time, they were joined in Johnstone's stable by a cheap *Evening Standard* and a pricey *Evening Herald*.[1]

On 29 June 1857, the *Herald* made its first appearance under its new management. Lord Malmesbury thoroughly approved of its format, which 'seems well arranged, with plenty of fashionable news to amuse the ladies'. No less gratifying was the request he had received from a *Herald* representative, 'Mr Hamilton', for an interview 'to arrange as to the line which was to be taken'. In all probability, 'Mr Hamilton' was Captain Thomas Hamber, in whom Johnstone invested complete editorial control over his multiple ventures. Like most of Johnstone's decisions, his choice of Hamber was an unconventional one that paid off. Previously an official at an insolvency court, where he had met Johnstone and perhaps where Johnstone had learned of the Baldwins' plight, Hamber was a 'gentleman's son' who had been an undergraduate at Oriel with G. J. Goschen. His acquaintance with French political society elicited rumours that he, like Borthwick of the *Morning Post,* was in the pay of Napoleon III. Beyond any doubt, however, his loyalties were not to Bonaparte's empire, but to Johnstone's, which lasted longer. Disraeli, recognizing a kindred spirit, quickly warmed to him, and he was soon 'admiringly pointed to by the wirepullers and minor scribes of the party as a model Conservative editor of the most brilliant and chivalrous type'. Until the early '70s, when Johnstone, in a fit of jealousy, summarily relieved him of his command, Hamber infused Conservative journalism with a new vitality.[2]

It was Hamber who decided whether a particular feature would be better appreciated by the 'penny public' of the *Standard* or by the 'quality' readership of the *Herald*. His instinct was unerring. The eight-page *Standard,* affording the greater scope for innovation, experimented with serialized fiction and intensive scrutiny of City transactions. Proclaiming (4 February 1858) its 'politics' to be 'those of the age – enlightened amelioration and progress', its 'staunch Protestantism, without narrow sectarian bigotry or polemical zeal', was a retreat from the 'No-Popery' extremism of its past. 'Bound to no party', it nevertheless faithfully represented, as H. W. Massingham said, Conservatism's 'severer and more businesslike or perhaps I should say *bourgeois*

[1] Knox to Blackwood, 30 May 1857, Blackwood Papers; Grant, II, 111; H. D. Jordan, 'Daily and Weekly Press of England in 1861,' *South Atlantic Quarterly,* xxviii (1929), 308.
[2] Malmesbury, *Memoirs,* II, 73; Escott, *Masters of English Journalism*, pp. 197–200. Delane had mistakenly informed Dasent (23? June 1857) 'that our Ex-City [editor] Evans is to edit the new *Standard'*. *Times* Archives.

element, always more or less allied with political opportunism'.[1]

Yet the 'thoroughly independent' creed to which the *Standard* swore fidelity on 29 June 1857 was no sham. On the same morning (11 August 1857) that it castigated Russell for 'a sort of fatal facility, a happy knack of blundering', it spared tender words for Bright: 'There are many points in which we cannot agree with him; yet we can freely and fully admire his honesty, fearlessness, and independence of spirit.' After Lord Derby formed his minority government, the *Standard* gave him measured support and opened its correspondence columns to those who defended him against *The Times*'s imputations (5 July 1858) that he had sullied Tory honour in quest of 'the dream of Mr Disraeli's life – Tory Government on Radical principles': 'The Premier's conduct' was described by 'A Conservative' as

> thoroughly praiseworthy, and this constitutes the true cause of *The Times*'s strictures. Disappointment sours the heart and dulls the brain. Let *The Times* emancipate itself from fetters which must be irksome, and abandon the disappointed clique who have become tangled in their own meshes: such conduct will be worthy of its high position. [12 July 1858]

Unlike the *Morning Star,* the *Standard* preferred to avoid open warfare with its mighty rival and to allow others to take up cudgels in letters to the editor. Thus, 'R.M.' was allotted a full column on 30 June 1858 (when the leading articles attended to such bland topics as the pollution of the Thames and the reform of the Scottish universities) to decry 'the mendacity of *The Times*' which, with 'its Whig followers in the press', agitated against the growth of cheap newspapers:

> Are Conservatives really sincere, honestly attached to their convictions? Then they ought to aim at extending their views, at publishing forth what they conceive to be the truth as far and as widely as possible. But there is only one way to do this, and that is, by encouraging on all occasions and by every means, their own press. . . . Let them communicate to it, if to any; let them send advertisements to it, if to any. In fine, let our assistance and patronage be devoted to the support of our own papers.

The sentiments were those of Johnstone and Hamber, but prudence dictated that 'R.M.' should express them.

Prudence may also have reflected a certain ambivalence in the *Standard*'s counsels. Among its leader-writers was Lord Robert Cecil (later 3rd Marquess of Salisbury), who incurred parental disapproval not so much by his calling as by his enmity towards Disraeli: 'I have never concealed my opinion that his influence with Lord Derby in the management of the party has been preju-

[1] Massingham, *London Daily Press,* p. 75. On 29 June 1857, its first day of twopenny sale, the *Standard* declared its 'political principles' to be 'thoroughly independent, devoted to the great interests of the public good, and wholly untrammelled by party'.

dicial,' he told his father in 1859. The next year, as member for Stamford, he opposed the Bill to abolish the paper duty: 'Could it be maintained that a person of education could learn anything from a penny paper?'[1] Deeply ingrained among Disraeli's antagonists, who misprized cheap journalism, this orthodoxy hamstrung the Conservative press: by lowering its price to become competitive, a journal was held to forfeit respectability.

In 1860, a commentator in the *New Quarterly Review* differentiated between the 'high-priced' *Herald,* 'the only morning organ of Conservatism', and the *Standard,* 'a happy notion' that deserved 'every support and consideration from the Conservatives', but one that was, strictly speaking, *with* them and not *of* them. George H. Townsend, possibly the author of this anonymous review, wrote on the subject to Lord Malmesbury, whom he understood to have 'consented to act on a Committee appointed for the purpose of taking into consideration the present condition and prospects of the Conservative Press of the Metropolis'. Under previous owners, he argued, the *Morning Herald* had declined because it was 'fearfully mismanaged', not because it had adhered to Conservative doctrines: 'The result [would] have been precisely the same with any Whig, Liberal or Radical Newspaper conducted in a similar manner.' Disputing received opinion 'that it was absolutely impossible for a Conservative Newspaper to obtain a large circulation, especially amongst the working classes', Townsend pointed to the success of the *Standard*. Yet that paper had been overtaken by the *Daily Telegraph,* boasting 'superior quality' and better 'facilities for production'. He was 'prepared to prove that without the slightest change of any kind . . . in the tone of its politics, . . . the *Standard* might be at this moment circulating from fifty to sixty thousand Copies daily'. Put simply, supply had not kept pace with demand.

> The best mode of securing the proper extension of the Conservative press of the Metropolis and of thereby giving the Conservative cause an impetus that shall be felt throughout the United Kingdom is by forming a *Joint Stock Company in which Conservatives dwelling in town and country shall be invited to take shares.* . . . Many Conservatives are impressed with the necessity that exists for the establishment of new organs and would readily support such a project. They desire to possess influential exponents of those great principles which all sections of the Conservative party hold in common.[2]

Townsend's scheme was too ambitious even for Disraeli, to whom Malmesbury forwarded it. It had been only 'with the utmost difficulty' that Disraeli had 'prevented the *Press*', when he withdrew from it in 1857, from falling into

[1] Cecil to Salisbury, 25 July 1859, in Cecil, *Salisbury,* I, 85–86; *Parliamentary Debates,* 3rd ser., clvii, col. 389 (12 March 1860).

[2] Townsend to Malmesbury, 16 February 1860, Hughenden Papers; 'Conservative Journalism,' *New Quarterly Review,* ix (1860), 388. A. J. Lee thinks that the author of this anonymous article was not Townsend, but 'probably Haydon', editor of the *New Quarterly* (Lee, *Origins,* p. 149).

the clutches of 'that lot of mysterious capitalists' – can he have meant John-stone? – 'who are buying up all the Tory papers'. Having eluded one syndicate, he had no wish to create another, over which he could expect to exercise no direct control. Better than Townsend, he perceived the divisions that persisted among those who espoused the 'great principles' of Conservatism. Better than Derby, he likewise perceived the necessity to nurture the party press. For him to take the initiative would have been to give substance to the suspicions, entertained by Cecil and others, against him. Yet for him to decline was to perpetuate the vacuum. Lord Stanley testified to the dilemma by recounting two conversations on 29 January 1861. The first was with Hamber, 'an intelligent and moderate man', who had 'called, wishing to know ... something of the policy of the party', and whom Stanley 'could tell ... little, for in truth there is no policy at this moment, except that of keeping quiet and supporting ministers'. The second was with Disraeli, who had been at Court, where he 'made some allusion to the strength of the Conservative party' in a candid discussion with Prince Albert: '"What is the use of that," said the P[rince], "the country is governed by newspapers, and you have not got a newspaper."'[1] To Disraeli, of all men, that must have rankled, and all the more because, to all intents and purposes, it was true.

*   *   *

'An English statesman in the present day lives by following public opinion,' Walter Bagehot wrote in 1860; 'he may profess to guide it a little; he may hope to modify it in detail; he may help to exaggerate and to develop it; but he hardly hopes for more.'[2] That was true enough, but truer of some than of others. Of Lord Palmerston, it was hardly true at all.

'You may with truth say to who likes to hear you,' Palmerston answered a reproach from Lord Napier,

> that I do not write or dictate articles of the *Morning Post* and that I am not responsible for them. The Editors speak their own opinions, and it is in consequence of their own opinions that they give a general support to Her Majesty's Government.[3]

A master of diplomacy, he struck this pose less to disarm his assorted critics, who easily saw through his disguises, than to salve the *amour-propre* of his

[1] Disraeli to Sir John Pakington, 6 October 1857, quoted in Buckle, *Disraeli*, IV, 100; Stanley's diary, 29 January 1861, *Disraeli, Derby*, pp. 165, 168.

[2] Mr Gladstone' (1860), reprinted in *Bagehot's Historical Essays* (ed. N. St John Stevas; Garden City, N.Y., Anchor edn.; 1965), p.260.

[3] Palmerston to Napier, 25 May 1857 (letterbook copy), Palmerston Papers, Add. MSS. 48,580, fol. 198. Malmesbury had his doubts: 'The *Morning Post* has received orders from the French Emperor to attack me in every possible occasion,' he wrote on 26 January 1859. 'Mr Borthwick, the editor, saw him at Paris, and got his orders from himself. This paper is also Lord Palmerston's, so the connection between them is clear.' Malmesbury, *Memoirs*, II, 150–51.

journalistic confederates, who did not wish it to be assumed that they were taken for granted. 'Independence is the first condition of influence,' declared the *Post* on its centenary (2 November 1872), 'and a Journal to be listened to must speak in its own name alone.' Palmerston was more than happy for that paper to speak in its own name, knowing as he did that its sentiments were attuned to his own.

He treated the *Globe,* another favourite of the Whig country-house set, in the same spirit. The oldest of the surviving metropolitan evening papers, it was successively edited by W. T. McCullagh Torrens (who resigned to pursue a full-time parliamentary career), Gibbon Merle, and George Hooper. 'Look at the *Globe,* my dear fellow, this evening,' Palmerston was reported to have instructed those who importuned him for information about ministerial deliberations. To the extent that it suited his purpose, such information appeared there. In 1866, the year after his death, the *Globe* shifted to the Conservative side. In a real sense, it was Palmerston who had kept it going as a Whig property, and it could more easily reconcile itself to Conservatism than to Russell's leadership.[1]

In the case of *The Times,* Palmerston trod more cautiously. 'I quite concur in the reasoning of your article today about the Functions of a free Press,' he assured Delane on 6 December 1858,

> but I would suggest for your Consideration whether it might not be good to slacken *The Times* fire against the Emperor of the French. . . . Of course I do not mean to suggest the Cessation of Criticism, but might not just Criticism be equally effectual with less . . . personal asperity of Tone [?][2]

More than any of his counterparts, Delane was at liberty either to accept or reject Palmerston's injunctions. Fortified by the unequivocal support of his proprietor, the massive circulation of his paper, and his own station in political society, he might – if he was so disposed – defy Palmerston, who could have little recourse against him. The temptation was obvious during the Derbyite interregnum, when Palmerston languished in opposition.

Derby, seeking to strengthen his tenuous grip on office, tried again in May 1858 to recruit Gladstone, who gave serious thought before replying that he saw no 'prospect of public advantage . . . from my entering your government single-handed'. That Gladstone was prepared to serve under Derby in a full-scale coalition remained distinctly possible. That Bright and the Radicals might support an administration that excluded Palmerston was not wholly improbable. Delane, contemplating 'the party result of the smash', which he took to be imminent, requested Robert Lowe 'to write a very careful & moderate article'; at the same time, he asked Thomas Chenery 'to notice

---

[1] 'The Evening Newspapers,' *Nation* (New York), 7 October 1880; Massingham, *London Daily Press,* pp. 168–69.
[2] Palmerston to Delane, misdated 5 December 1856, *Times* Archives.

Bright's speech about Palmerston's treatment of his party'. Deploring Bright's 'total renunciation of our Imperial pretensions and policy in India' (22 May), *The Times* proclaimed itself against any disruptive change in party alignments:

> It was assumed that if Lord John Russell and Lord Palmerston could only be brought to unite, the destruction of the Derby Government was certain. Well, the dreaded conjunction has taken place, and the Derby Government is at least as strong as before. . . . It is now only too evident that the present organisation of the Liberal Party is too weak to withstand the small but united phalanx of the Tories, backed by the threat of dissolution. . . . Everyone must see how little chance a Liberal Government would have of remaining in power if it must rely for support on an assembly so clever in finding reasons for deserting it. [24 May]

Derby, 'eminently an opposition leader' and inferior to both Russell and Palmerston in 'those more solid if less brilliant qualities . . . which are indispensable in a Prime Minister' (20 May), triumphed by default. For *The Times* to have helped, however grudgingly, to sustain him was a sign that its Palmerstonian ardour had cooled. Even more significant was that it bestowed equal praise on him and Russell. In November, Delane ventured that Ralph Bernal Osborne, then MP for Dover, might 'safely recant your allegiance' to Palmerston (in whose honour Bernal Osborne had taken the chair at a Reform Club banquet in 1850) and Clarendon: 'No star shines very bright above the horizon but these two seem to have hopelessly set. Your old leader. Lord John, is well and *fat*.'[1]

Often described as a barometer of public opinion, *The Times* proved itself a fair-weather friend. Out of favour, Clarendon 'was rather amused' to see it berating 'the Lords & Dukes for not sallying forth to have a tilt with John Bright' at the close of 1858. On the question of Italian unification, which loomed large through that winter and spring, *The Times* considered Clarendon's pro-French stand only slightly less noxious than Bright's dogmatic non-interventionism. Malmesbury's pragmatism was more to its liking. By the same token, Derby's government earned its respect by promulgating modest proposals for franchise reform, a cause to which Palmerston was singularly unresponsive. 'They appear to have thought it adviseable to bespeak the good word of *The Times,* and accordingly they sent Delane a copy of their Bill,' Greville wrote on 27 February 1859. 'This morning the heads of it appear in *The Times* with an approving article.' Other newspapers, requiring no such tutelage, accorded a warm reception to the measure introduced by Disraeli. 'I send you the *Chronicle,* and you shall have some more papers to-morrow, to give you some idea of Dizzy's great success

[1] Gladstone to Derby, 26 May 1858, quoted in Morley, *Gladstone,* I, 580; *Gladstone Diaries*, V, 299–300; Delane to Dasent, [21 May 1858], and Delane to Bernal Osborne, 25 November 1858 (copy), *Times* Archives.

last night,' Disraeli's wife proudly told a friend on 1 March. 'Even the *Daily News,* our enemy's paper, ... acknowledge his power.' That power was insufficient, however, to secure the passage of the Bill, which the Radicals dismissed as a joke and the ultra-Tories feared as a subversion of the constitution.[1]

Deprived of a parliamentary victory, Disraeli could take solace from the encomiums he garnered. E. W. Searle had been present at Slough the previous May and had heard his 'celebrated speech' attacking *The Times.* Then newly installed as 'sole proprietor of the *Sunday Times* Newspaper', Searle had 'had the honour of being introduced ... after the proceedings were over'. He now reminded Disraeli that, 'in the few minutes conversation I had with you', he had promised 'my most strenuous support' to the Derby ministry so long as 'it conceded the just demands of the people, on the one hand, and resisted demagogue pressure from without, on the other'. Satisfied by Disraeli's reformist effort, which the *Sunday Times* had endorsed, Searle stepped forward 'unhesitatingly' to

claim my reward. Do not start. I want neither money, nor honour, nor patronage of any kind, but simply your opinion of how I have performed what *I* consider to be a sacred duty to my country, and if the course that I have pursued has met with your approval.

Disraeli gratified his petitioner with vague compliments ('I am pleased with your labours, and I honour your motives'), only to have these phrases thrown back five years later, when Searle solicited more tangible benefits.[2]

To an even greater extent than the suffrage controversy, pushed into the background, Italian affairs clarified the issues of the day. 'A genuine line of division, instead of the spurious line chosen by the manipulators of parliamentary reform in 1858, helped to determine the composition of government and oppositon,' Asa Briggs has explained. 'It was not on a domestic issue at all, but on the unification of Italy that the parties regrouped.'[3] As usual, newspapers recorded the process and, in various ways, served as catalysts.

Spurred on by France, Sardinia mounted a challenge to Austrian sovereignty in Italy. Although Malmesbury furtively tried to avert war through mediation, he and his colleagues conveyed an impression of sympathy for the claims of Austrian legitimacy. Gladstone, whose conscience had been wakened by a visit to Naples in 1851, was drawn to the Sardinian side by the eloquence of Cavour, whom he met at Turin in March 1859. Palmerston, for more mundane reasons, moved in the same direction: eager to resume a bold

[1] Clarendon to Russell, 29 December 1858, Russell Papers, PRO 30/22/13F/235; *Greville Memoirs* (27 February 1859), VII, 398; Mrs Disraeli to Mrs Brydges Willyams, 1 March 1859, quoted in Buckle, *Disraeli,* IV, 203. For a general account of the 1859 franchise Bill, see Stewart, *Foundation of the Conservative Party,* pp. 353–58.
[2] Searle to Disraeli, 20 March 1859 and 19 April 1864, Hughenden Papers.
[3] Briggs, *Age of Improvement* (London, 1959), p. 424.

foreign policy and cooperation with France, he embraced Italian liberation with a passion that (according to Gladstone) 'overrates the strength of the Revolutionary party in Italy'. And Russell, no stranger to the complexities of the Italian question, was not prepared to be outbid. The Radicals joined in condemning the Derby government less because they suspected it of abetting Austrian oppression than because they doubted its capacity to maintain British neutrality.[1]

Upon the rejection of its Reform Bill in March, the government requested a dissolution. Disraeli expected to capture as many as 40 seats in the ensuing election, which lasted through late April and early May. In the event, the Conservatives added 30 members to their parliamentary ranks. The opposition had lost ground, but gained cohesion. Derby retained office until 10 June, when his government was defeated by 13 votes on a no-confidence motion. The Queen sent for Granville before she bowed to the inevitability of a Palmerston premiership, which was to last six years. Its advent may be charted in the columns of the political press.

The Italian question dominated the 1859 campaign, and the newspapers played it for all it was worth. The *Globe* did not exaggerate when it declared on 19 April that 'debate' on this topic 'brings out something more', namely the principles and strategies of the competing factions. 'Lord Palmerston's view of the complications in Europe stands in perfect contrast to that of Mr Disraeli and Lord Malmesbury,' it averred, 'and it will certainly be more widely shared by the people of this country.' Scorning the 'sham reformers of the Tory party', the *Globe* asked rhetorically on 5 May: 'What are the politics of the Government? It is impossible to tell.'

The *Morning Herald*, described by the *Globe* on 23 April as taking 'what may be surmised to be a semi-official view of the actual situation', had no difficulty in discerning or defending the Derbyite position. Much as the *Globe* dealt more tenderly with Derby than with Disraeli and Malmesbury, the *Herald* exempted Palmerston from its tirades, which were levelled at Russell ('the veteran Marplot') and Bright. In fact, it went to great lengths to emphasize the affinity between Palmerstonian and Conservative diplomacy. Its Foreign Office connections enabled it to issue an 'authoritative denial' on 2 May 'to the false statments of *The Times* newspaper, respecting an alliance, offensive and defensive, between France and Russia'. Those statements, it maintained, 'may be regarded as nothing more than a disgraceful calumny intended to influence the electors', who fortunately had not been fooled. 'In the history of British journalism no parellel will be found to the flagrant and unjustifiable course pursued by *The Times* during the past week.' To substantiate its charge the *Herald* published, along with detailed contradictions, 'the principal

---

[1] *Gladstone Diaries* (3 and 4 March 1859), V, 377, and 'Copy Memorandum on Italian Affairs,' 30 June 1859, Gladstone Papers, Add. MSS. 44,748, fol. 93; *also see* A. J. P. Taylor, *The Struggle for Mastery in Europe* (Oxford, 1954), pp. 108–13.

calumnies' which *The Times* had 'invented with a view of damaging the Ministry. . . . The conduct of the organ to which we refer is opposed to ordinary notions of right and wrong,' it concluded. 'It is calculated to bring England, as well as English journalism, into discredit, and has already inflicted a heavy blow on industry and commerce.'

The political convulsions of the spring invited newspapers to intensify their attacks on each other and, *ipso facto,* on each other's heroes. From points that were diametrically opposed, the *Morning Herald* and the *Morning Star* sniped at *The Times.* The *Herald* desisted after 18 May, when it approvingly noted that 'the Palmerstonian organs, and even the foremost of them', had tempered their criticism of the Conservative leadership. The *Star,* however, had all the more reason to keep up its barrage. Finding it 'NOT possible to imagine that Lord Palmerston and his friends' sincerely intended to topple the Derby régime, it did not hesitate on 9 May to 'judge from the inspired articles which appear in Tory newspapers' that 'the Government do not seem to have abandoned all hope of an alliance between Lord Palmerston and themselves'. Far from being dismayed at this prospect, the *Star* was relieved:

> Not more desirous are we that Moloch should take up his permanent abode in the desert of Sahara, than that Palmerston should for the remainder of his days cast in his lot with the Tory party.

With greater remorse, the *Daily News* (16 May) also detected 'the rapid ripening of the seeds of compromise in the attempt to form a Derby-Palmerston administration'. The *Morning Post* encouraged these rumours, and thereby helped to keep open Palmerston's options, by its studied politeness towards Derby. Its tone changed abruptly on 17 May, when it began to fault him for want of authority and direction. On that day, too, the *Globe* saw fit to deny categorically any collaboration between Palmerston and Derby:

> To suppose that Lord Palmerston would abdicate the position he holds before England and before Europe, to associate himself with a number of condemned politicians awaiting the execution of the sentence passed on them, is certainly not very flattering to his understanding.

Still, the suspicion lingered. On the 22nd, the *Observer* announced that Palmerston had received and declined 'with becoming dignity' an invitation to coalesce with Derby. The next morning, the *Herald* dismissed this 'monstrous libel' as a fabrication on the part of 'the Sunday organ of the Opposition', a journal that 'is more virulent, and pays even less regard to truth and decency, than its daily contemporaries'. Reversing its editorial policy, the *Herald* now turned with a vengeance against 'le grand Palmerston', whose 'seventy-six years . . . have brought neither physical weakness nor matured wisdom'. No longer was it convenient to stress the elements of mutual agreement in foreign affairs:

> Lord Derby and his colleagues are pledged to observe a strict neutrality, and to maintain peace at home, though war rages around. Lord Palmerston thinks that England is bound to lend a hand in remodelling Italy, and for this purpose would send English armies and English fleets against kindred nations, who never have injured us, and whose policy has ever been to cultivate friendly relations with the English Government and people. If, therefore, as the *Observer* states, the advent of Lord Palmerston to power is certain, the public may prepare for a long and expensive war, for increased taxation, and declining commerce.

Although it carried little conviction, the appeal to Radical opinion was obvious.

From the dissolution of Parliament in March until the resignation of the Derby government in June, no one could predict with certainty who would combine with whom and on whose terms. Under these exceptional circumstances, the press was scanned for clues, many of which appeared between the lines. Newspaper reports, more easily disowned than platform utterances, were used by the politicians to test the reactions of their followers and opponents, sometimes to goad or mislead them. From a survey of leading articles, day by day, it is possible to draw a number of conclusions: that Palmerston was naturally inclined towards Derby, whose commitments to Disraeli and Malmesbury blocked the way to rapprochement; that Russell was more pushed than pulled in Palmerston's direction; that the Conservatives, denied a majority at the polls, preferred Palmerston to either Russell or Gladstone as a bulwark against upheaval; that Gladstone was torn between a genuine respect for Derby and the courage of his own Peelite convictions, which brought him into league with Russell; and, finally, that Bright and the Radicals were thoroughly bemused.

Writing to Gladstone on 7 May, Abraham Hayward 'thought I observed a disinclination' on the part of Palmerston 'to turn out the Government on Reform – which, of course, would give Lord J. R. the advantage'. By his estimate, '*The Times* understates & the *Herald* overstates the Liberal hopes' for the new Parliament: 'They will eventually be about 25 or 26.'[1] The Liberal label was, as yet, difficult to affix. An amalgam of 'old' and Palmerstonian Whigs, Peelites (who had recently taken to calling themselves liberal conservatives), and Radicals, the party derived a corporate identity from its opposition to Conservative rule. But some were willing to go further than others to displace Derby. In the crucial division on 10 June, Palmerston voted for the fatal amendment, Gladstone against it.

On 19 May, the Derbyite *Sun* catalogued – and so hoped to widen – the

[1] Hayward to Gladstone, 7 May [1859], Gladstone Papers, Add. MSS. 44,207, fols. 95–96.

divisions among these strange bedfellows: 'Lord Palmerston with *his* followers', who abhorred reform movements; 'Lord John Russell with *his* select supporters, the Whigs of the old school . . . looking to Woburn Abbey as to the fane of the political Delphos'; and Bright, who demanded 'a measure of reform so sweeping that the more timorous opponents of his bold scheme look forward, as to its inevitable consequence, to the eventual triumph of Democratic over Monarchial institutions'. Some of them advocated the introduction of the ballot, some deplored it. Some were pro-war, some were for peace at any price. What chance did they have against the Conservatives, 'an organised and united party, who have the additional advantage of being *in*'?

The answer gradually unfolded. Five days later, the *Daily News* allayed 'considerable anxiety' among its readers by trumpeting that Russell and Palmerston had reached an accord 'on the two all-important subjects of Parliamentary Reform and Foreign Policy'. The *Morning Star* had also heard 'it rumoured that a better understanding is likely . . . than has hitherto existed,' and expressed

> hope that it is founded upon concession on the question of Parliamentary Reform on the part of Lord Palmerston rather than upon any giving-up by Lord John Russell of the plan to which he has already publicly given his adhesion.

By contrast, the Conservative papers suspected a Palmerstonian sell-out that would bring a sweeping Reform Bill, replete with the ballot. The *Globe* could neither have convinced them nor conciliated the Radicals by its retort on the 25th:

> We are authorised to state, – for there can be no question on the point, and our authority is obvious, . . . that there is no intention whatever on the part of the accredited Liberal leaders to render 'the various institutions of the country' more democratic. . . . We may be tolerably certain . . . from past experience, that the ballot will not form any one of the clauses in the Bill which is putatively and prophetically ascribed to Lord John Russell.

Determined to wrap Russell in a Palmerstonian mantle, the *Globe* defended him that day and the next against taunts that he was 'left without a party'; on the contrary, it riposted, he 'will be found acting, on the fit occasion, as the agent of that same Liberal party of which Lord Palmerston is for the present the leader'. Far more vigorously, it disputed assertions in the *Morning Herald* and the *Standard* ('the penny-satellite of Shoe-lane, which is *Herald* in all but its leading articles') that 'Lord Palmerston's very name is a war-cry over the whole Continent'. It was well to remember 'that the only two wars which have occurred between leading States in Europe since Lord Palmerston first engaged in the conduct of foreign affairs, have taken place at periods when he was *not* conducting them'.

Aware of Russell's notoriously thin skin, which it had bruised often enough, the *Globe* guardedly recognized Palmerston as 'for the present the leader' of the Liberal forces. The *Morning Post* followed suit on the 30th:

Lord Palmerston is leader of the opposition: he has been acknowledged such by Lord John Russell, and Parliamentary image points to him as the person to be sent for when Lord Derby resigns. . . . . But there is always a chance of events taking an unusual turn, and circumstances are possible which might give the first place to Lord John Russell. In that case it is not to be doubted that, if his services are required, Lord Palmerston, who has so willingly assisted in so many Administrations – the unanimity of whom in seeking his help is the highest tribute to his public usefulness – would again place himself at the disposal of his friend.

In reality, nothing had been conceded, but Russell was permitted to save face. Perhaps, too, the Peelites and Radicals would be mollified. Through his newspaper associates, Palmerston had made a gesture that implicated, but did not bind him.

On 2 June, *The Times* intruded on the Whig honeymoon by cautioning Palmerston and Russell not to evict the Derby government prematurely. The *Morning Post* scoffed at this 'appeal' as one 'altogether to the inferior motives – to the love of the advantages of office as distinct from its duties'. The *Daily News* waxed more indignant, mocking *The Times*'s leader of the previous day as

a perfect prose idyll of serene sentiments, disinterested friendship, and good advice. Having suddenly conceived a tender concern for the Liberal party, it finds that a continuance on the Opposition benches would be highly beneficial to its interests. . . . Why, asks our contemporary with the candour and simplicity of *Joseph Surface,* should these noble lords and estimable gentlemen seek to abandon hastily such a brilliant, dignified, and useful position? The champion of Austria has overdone its part as 'Guide, philosopher, and friend' of the Liberal party. . . . Why, after having more than once done its best to eject it from power, has our contemporary conceived such a tender regard for the Derby ministry? . . . A common sympathy with despotism covers a multitude of sins. And, though scarcely a single member of the present Government enjoys the confidence and respect either of the country or the journal in question . . . , still its Austrian sympathies, its obvious leanings towards the Pope and the Emperor . . . , atone for all other defects, and secure for it a support it could not have enjoyed on its own merits.

Thus, by patronizingly advising not to oppose, *The Times* galvanized the opposition. The political press has its negative as well as its positive effects.

It waited for Parliament to convene to see what action would be taken. On 4

June, the *Morning Star* reported 'that a circular has been generally addressed to the members of the Liberal party in the House of Commons', who were summoned to a meeting in Willis's Rooms, King Street, on Monday afternoon, the 6th. Among the many signatories to this invitation were Palmerston, Russell, Sidney Herbert, Ellice, and Milner-Gibson. For its part, the *Star* welcomed the occasion, and all the more because it could

> perceive from the tone of Conservative journalism ... that the Government places its chief reliance, not upon any declaration of opinion which it may be ready to make, but upon the divisions that are supposed to exist among the Liberal party.

The *Star* did not deny that the Independent Liberals, for whom it spoke, had had their differences with the Whigs; 'and more than that', save for 'certain concessions on the part of the Whig leaders, the Independent Liberals would even lend their aid to uphold the present Government'. But, in the belief that satisfactory assurances were forthcoming, the *Star* stood 'ready to give . . . its cordial, generous, and ungrudging support'.

The historic conclave on the 6th sealed the fate of the second Derby government. 'A few days will show the results of this meeting,' the *Morning Post* boasted the next day, 'the fusion of every section of the Liberal Party, the accession to power of a strong Government, and the utter discomfiture of an Administration which has never carried a single measure.' Defeated on the 10th by a vote of 323 to 310, Derby and Disraeli delayed a full week before they announced to their respective houses 'their termination of office with a becoming modesty and manliness of spirit quite refreshing'. That, at any rate, was how the *Sun* fulsomely depicted it on the 18th. Having drained its cup of praise, that paper had few kind words for 'the Ministry of the factions' which Palmerston had 'at last patched up': with sixteen members, 'it is a little Parliament in itself'.

The *Daily News*, among others, amply compensated. It hailed the formation of the Palmerston government, in which Russell returned to the Foreign Office and Gladstone to the Exchequer. On 24 May, the *Daily News* had described itself as 'pursuing a perfectly independent course', in that 'we do not profess to be in the confidence of either of those eminent and distinguished men', Palmerston or Russell. A month later, it could no longer make such a statement. On Russell's behalf, Clarke made contact in mid-June with Thomas Walker, its editor, who

> assures me he has full power over the Daily N—, that he is resolved it should give the new Govt. a fair trial – not hesitating or critical but full & generous, that he will insist on discipline for its writers, & that their disappointments if any shall not influence him.[1]

[1] Clarke to Elliot, 'Thursday' [16 June 1859], Russell Papers, PRO 30/22/13G/ 256 ff.

Not surprisingly, therefore, it was Russell, 'the standard-bearer of Parliamentary Reform', whom the *Daily News* celebrated on 14 June:

> He has ... shown an entire forgetfulness of self by refraining from the exaction of what everybody must acknowledge him entitled to. ... By the course he has thus pursued Lord John Russell has given another proof of that true elevation of mind and genuine public spirit which have so long made him the acknowledged head of the Liberal Party.

By going to the Foreign Office, the *News* continued the next day,

> Lord John has gallantly and generously thrown himself into the breach and saved the country from the disappointment and mortification which at one moment seemed awaiting it.

Much as Palmerston depended on the *Globe* and *Morning Post* to say the things that tact (if not modesty) forbade him from saying, Russell relied more informally on the *Daily News*.

When the dust finally settled, it was possible to evaluate the performance of the political press. By its disclosures and still more by its intimations, it had signposted and set the pace for Liberal unification. Through the newspapers on which they relied, political leaders were able to take soundings, make threats, dangle concessions, and ultimately define their positions. Given the ephemeral nature of daily journalism, they could score points, then safely retreat from them. Preserving their dignity, they stood above the fray while their battles – ostensibly waged against rival journals – were fought for them. The outcome of the meeting at Willis's Rooms was a foregone conclusion. When opposition MPs gathered there on 6 June, they already knew from what they had read precisely what to expect. All that remained was to put a proper gloss on it. Here, too, their respective newspapers did not fail them.

Liberalism's solidarity, barely sufficient to dislodge Derby's minority government, did not extend to its newspaper properties, which continued to keep a watchful eye on each other. That, of course, was their business, but also their mandate. The following year, a Conservative critic categorized 'the liberal organs' as 'Whig, Radical, or Republican', significantly investing the sub-species with capital letters. All the same, he thought it an 'absolute necessity' that his own party should redress the balance:

> If Lord Palmerston has not exaggerated the importance of the press, in putting it in competition with the steam engine and the electric telegraph, it is high time for the Conservatives to look into the present condition of journalism ... and to ask whether the moment has not yet arrived to improve and develop those organs which, in trying and difficult times, have the courage to maintain consitutional principles.

To Ellice, it seemed 'the old story – the same complaint of all parties. The only remedy', he jested, was 'the same for a bad kitchen': improve the bill of fare. 'Nobody likes to have unpalatable & unwholesome food crammed down their throats – & especially by Tories.'[1] From experience, he should have known that too many cooks could spoil the party broth.

* * *

Back in the wilderness, the Conservatives had more time and renewed determination to attend to their press requirements: as in 1880, 1906, and 1945, adversity was the mother of inquiry. This time, paradoxically, an improved showing at the polls provided the incentive: 'The Conservative feeling in the country must indeed be deeprooted', it was reasoned, if, 'despite an excess of two hundred newspapers in favour of liberalism', the electors 'could return to the present Parliament three hundred members to support the government of Lord Derby'. It is all too 'easy' to ascribe this discrepancy, as did the anonymous critic of 'Conservative Journalism' in the *New Quarterly Review,* to the belief among 'speculators' that profit was assured 'by the advocacy of extreme principles in politics'.[2] In any case, such a belief was not easily dispelled.

In the early 1860s, cheap Conservative dailies were started in Nottingham, Birmingham, Liverpool, Manchester, Exeter, and Bristol. The most durable among them was the *Yorkshire Post and Leeds Intelligencer,* launched in July 1866. The map of provincial journalism was also dotted by Conservative penny and a few halfpenny evening papers, eventually followed by party weeklies. Dependent on the services of the Central Press Agency, established in 1863, these publications tended to resemble one another not only in their contents, but also in their financial distress. Outside the southern counties and isolated bastions elsewhere, the Conservative press did not flourish in provincial soil. Matters improved somewhat in the next decade, when Disraeli and his organizers took the problem in hand. Even then, however, its deficiencies were glaring. The *Globe,* flying Tory colours, warned on 12 January 1874 that 'the provincial and suburban press might do well to look to its doings or its days may be numbered in favour of a vicious centralisation'. A hollow threat, to be sure, it was distinctly a cry of exasperation. Through the century and beyond, the provinces remained predominantly Liberal terrain, for whatever that was worth.[3]

In London, the Conservative breakthrough was slower to occur. Party chiefs had to tidy up their press affairs before they were ready to embark on new ventures. The weekly journals offered them a shaky base. These included the *Press* which, in its post-Disraelian afterlife, passed from one owner to

[1] 'Conservative Journalism,' *New Quarterly Review,* ix (1860), 385; Ellice to Parkes, 16 October [1860], Ellice Papers.
[2] 'Conservative Journalism' *New Quarterly Review,* ix (1860), 385–87.
[3] Lee, *Origins,* pp. 151–53.

another – Charles Newdegate, the ultra-Protestant MP, among them – until it
gave up the ghost and merged with the *St James's Chronicle* in 1866. Having
long since outlived its usefulness, it 'subsided by degrees to the level of mediocrity'.[1]

The birth of the *Press* in 1853 had been an affront to *John Bull,* the self-
styled 'old-established weekly organ of the Conservative party', which by then
had given 'steady and faithful support . . . for upwards of thirty years'. Successive proprietors appealed in vain to the party agents for loans or subven-
tions. One such applicant was K. H. Cornish, who bitterly told his story to
Disraeli in 1859:

> your friend Mr Coleridge Kennard having informed me, some ten days ago,
> that the Party, though they would have pleasure . . . in working up the *John
> Bull* should I succeed in obtaining it, was unwilling to contribute towards
> purchasing the paper. I determined on endeavouring to raise the requisite
> funds from my own private and personal resources. . . .
>
> I had hoped to have rendered the *John Bull* a nucleus for erecting a Con-
> servative structure which might rival the great monument of John Walter's
> genius & writing enterprise . . . , but as I have been played fast and loose
> for nearly two years by the Conservative Party, though I refused several
> handsome offers from their antagonists (one of £1000 a year), I may fairly
> be excused if I work on my own convictions, regardless of all party men or
> party measures.

Cornish did not stay long and, the next year, Disraeli had an opportunity to
make amends. C. G. Prowett, identifying himself as 'editor & proprietor' of
John Bull, published in its pages yet another diagnosis of 'the reasons which
always *tend* to make the Conservative press less efficient than that on the other
side'. Confident 'that this tendency may be counteracted' by an expenditure of
party effort and funds, he suggested to Disraeli that some 'gentlemen connected with the party in Parliament should . . . take a proprietary interest' in *John
Bull,* which offered the 'peculiar advantage' of having 'not the reputation of
being fostered with direct pecuniary aid from the leaders of the Conservative
party – a reputation which seriously weakens the influence of other Conservative journals'. Neither logic nor commercial sense commended the proposition, which was evidently rejected. Yet Disraeli was a magnet for proposals
of this type. Another suppliant was Frank Fowler, who requested a loan of £50
to meet expenses on the *Weekly Mail,* since 1858 'the only cheap London
Weekly *Conservative* Paper'. Lord Stanley, who had dipped into his pocket to
aid Tory journals from time to time, took a more realistic view: 'Heard that a
new weekly paper is talked of, Disraeli much interested in its success, Lytton

---

[1] The judgment is that of T. E. Kebbel in *Lord Beaconsfield and Other Tory Memories* (New
York, 1907), p. 28. According to Escott (*Masters,* p. 243), 'the fact' that Newdegate also owned
the *St James's Chronicle* 'was a secret shared by its proprietor with his printer'.

also concerned in it, Sir H[enry Drummond] Wolff the chief promoter,' he jotted in his diary on 8 November 1862: 'I doubt the experiment being tried, after the failure of the *Press,* and still more doubt of its success if it be tried.'[1]

As a genre, quality weeklies were temporarily out of fashion, regardless of their politics. On 30 June 1860, the *Leader* ended a decade's run. Edited by George Henry Lewes, its staff included such luminaries as Marian Evans (George Eliot), Herbert Spencer, and, at the close, John Morley. The *Saturday Analyst* absorbed the *Leader,* only to perish five months later. The *London Review,* launched with a dinner at the Reform Club, made its début as a threepenny weekly on 7 July 1860. 'After six months of worry and discomfort', Charles Mackay (who had been brought from the *Illustrated London News*) laid down his 'editorial sceptre', which was taken up by 'an unliterary aristocrat who ruled by right of his banking account'. The *London Review* eventually folded in 1869, a year after a shake-up at the *Saturday Review*. The field of weekly journalism was littered with the remains of these and other casualties. Of the monthlies, the *Conservative Magazine* surely held the distinction for being the shortest lived. G. A. Sala, 'utterly unable to explain' its partisan title, financed it with the proceeds of the 'Christmas burlesque' he had written for performance at the Gaiety Theatre, and its inaugural number in 1870 was also its last.[2]

Catering to an expanding market, the metropolitan dailies posed an irresistible temptation to party strategists. Although the *Morning Herald* could not deny that credit for 'the abolition of the newspaper stamp duty belonged to a very different school of politicians from ourselves', it had 'every reason to be satisfied with the result'. On 9 May 1859, it exulted at its own success and especially that of its sister paper, the *Standard*: with the substitution of new machinery, 'which will print from 16,000 to 20,000 copies per hour', it would be henceforth possible 'to meet the demands of the public' and fully to compete with Whig and Radical 'opponents in the dissemination of their political opinions'.

Circulation tailed off after the election campaign, and Johnstone soon realized that, in making these costly improvements, he had overreached himself. The situation came to the attention of Disraeli, who was advised on 16 February 1860 'that the proprietor would be satisfied if the Conservative Party would purchase 1000 copies of the *Morning Herald* a day'. The *Standard* could be trusted to fend for itself. 'It may be true that this would put money into Mr Johnstone's pocket, but it is certain that some of the money would go to

---

[1] Memorandum of 12 July 1853, quoted in Stewart, *Foundation,* p. 291; Cornish to Disraeli [6 September 1859], Prowett to Disraeli [17 October 1860], and Fowler to Disraeli, 27 July 1860, Hughenden Papers; James Birch (on 4 November 1862) and Prowett (on 24 December 1864) made further attempts to obtain Disraeli's support. Stanley's diary is quoted in *Disraeli, Derby,* p. 192.

[2] Hirst, *Morley,* I, 40–41; Gooch, *Courtney,* 62–63; Lucy, *Memories of Eight Parliaments,* pp. 109–10; Ralph Straus, *Sala* (London, 1942), pp. 165–67; G. A. Sala, *Life and Adventures* (London, 1895), I, 266.

increase the salaries of the gentlemen who form the editorial staff.' There were to be no strings attached to such assistance, as 'the Proprietor would strongly object to any plan which robbed him of the political direction of the paper'. Nevertheless, Disraeli's informant supposed, 'this may be arrived at, if the proper kind of influence is brought to bear upon him in the proper way'.[1]

In spite of these limitations, or possibly because of them, Disraeli was prepared to comply. In return for unspecified support, which may well have exceeded the initial request, he was sent on 30 March 1862 the balance sheets for the '*Morning Herald & Standard* Newspapers . . . during Mr Johnstone's Proprietorship . . . from the 1st of May 1857 to 31st December 1861'. Transmitted by Hamber, who found it 'a very unpleasant duty', they showed a 'Total Loss' of some £31,500. An expenditure of £17,500 was included as 'Interest of Capital brought in by Mr Johnstone and for his services as Financial & General Manager estimated at £3500 pr Ann', but a 'Note' confirmed that 'during the whole of the period that Mr Johnstone has been the Proprietor of the above Newspapers . . . he *has not in any way drawn one farthing from the Concern*'.[2]

With Disraeli's encouragement, Hamber addressed himself to 'the question of retrenchment in each paper by turns'. At the same time, he promised leading articles to back Disraeli's call for retrenchment in public spending.[3] '"Bloated armaments" is a homely phrase, but voting money and wasting money are prosaic,' the *Herald* wrote to specification on 28 May 1862:

> Mr Disraeli had therefore no choice than to call spades spades. He wanted Parliament to know what was going on, and it was necessary he should speak plainly. . . . So many evidences exist of downright jobbery, downright defiance, and unsophisticated blundering, both in the dockyards and out of them, both on the coast and off the coast, and in Whitehall and out of it, that it . . . can hardly be said that Mr Disraeli has misnamed the armaments on which the treasure of the country is unwisely wasted.

Three days later, after the wind-up of a tempestuous parliamentary debate on the nation's finances, the *Herald* celebrated the display of Conservative unity and declared that 'the country . . . will again have to thank Lord Derby and Mr Disraeli for its rescue from the ruin and disgrace into which it was fast drifting'.

Hamber's task was not always so easy, as Disraeli himself could be caught off guard. On the evening of 3 June 1862, for example, Spencer Walpole threw the parliamentary party into confusion by moving an anti-taxation amendment, which Lord Palmerston cleverly chose to regard as a vote of confidence.

---

[1] H. W. Carr to Disraeli, 16 February 1860, Hughenden Papers.

[2] Hamber to Disraeli, 30 March 1862, with 'Statement . . . taken from the Books of the Establishment,' Hughenden Papers.

[3] Hamber to Disraeli, 27 May 1862, Hughenden Papers.

Unwilling to risk a dissolution, the party leaders prevailed on Walpole to back down, but Tory credibility had been impaired. 'What could the Opposition do but submit? What could the house do?' the *Herald* asked on the 5th:

> The Minister took both at an unworthy advantage. The threat of regarding Mr Walpole's amendment as one of want of confidence was a most unwarrantable stratagem, and one which could only be met by a quiet submission.

For its own part, the *Herald* expressed

> serious regret . . . that Mr Walpole's amendment did not go to a division. Its success would have been unquestionable; and the worst inconvenience, even a change of Ministry or a dissolution of Parliament, would be preferable to a compromise of principle by the House of Commons.

That, of course, was after the fact. And even then, as Hamber confessed to Disraeli, he had written 'with some difficulty' and a 'degree of self restraint'. Trusting to his own instinct, he had tried to articulate 'moderately . . . what I believe will generally be the opinion respecting the withdrawal of Mr Walpole's amendment. My present intention', he stated,

> is to proceed in the same track in both papers, still holding on retrenchment as the principle of the party. The character of the papers for consistency and self-respect almost requires this; but I should be sorry to act in any manner contrary to your views.[1]

He could depend on Disraeli to restrain him from going too far wrong.

In fact, there were times when the Disraelian bridle was felt to pinch. 'A little demonstration of independence does the *Standard* much good, and I venture to think, is not without its influence upon the parties who provoke it,' Hamber remonstrated on 27 October 1862. 'You will be pleased to hear', he added by way of mitigation, 'that our circulation is increasing almost daily. We published last week a greater number than we had ever issued – and this at a dull season of the year.' Having made his point, Hamber was content to accede to Disraeli's frequent directives for leading articles. On 3 November, *The Times* deprecated Disraeli's proposals, enunciated in a speech at High Wycombe, for an extension of Church control over education and an enlargement of the episcopacy. 'I will answer *The Times* immediately,' Hamber wrote to Disraeli the next day. 'I should have done so before but I had a great influx of subjects & few available hands.'[2] Accordingly, the *Standard*'s leader on the 5th

> supplied the key with which to unlock all those hostile attacks of *The Times* upon the Church of England and Mr Disraeli. The fact is . . . that the

---

[1] Hamber to Disraeli, 4 June 1862, Hughenden Papers.
[2] Hamber to Disraeli, 27 October and 4 November 1862, Hughenden Papers.

Church's allies are not to be found among the present occupants of Downing-street, and we would add that it would be equally in vain to look for them in Printing-house-square.

Hamber ingratiated himself with Disraeli at the cost of alienating Johnstone, who could not have been pleased by the famous *Punch* cartoon (3 May 1862) in which Derby and Disraeli, out for a stroll, were shown with 'Mrs Harris' at their heels: 'For goodness sake give her a penny', Derby said. 'People will think that she belongs to us.' According to Massingham, who put the date at 'about 1862', Johnstone's 'mortgage was paid off with some suddenness', and the *Standard*, 'without of course qualifying its attachment to Conservatism, was no longer a virtually subsidised organ'. In all probability, the change was not effected until 1863 at the earliest, and had been made possible by the *Standard*'s popularity as a champion of the southern cause in the American civil war. Accounts differ whether Johnstone thereafter came to resent Hamber for deferring too much or too little to party headquarters in Parliament Street. But, as the decade wore on, that resentment was plain enough. 'Captain Hamber permitted his very noticeable personality to be felt and seen to a degree inexpedient for the newspaper under our anonymous system,' recalled T. H. S. Escott, who wrote leaders for him. Johnstone sent his solicitor to give notice to Hamber, whom he replaced with his own son and namesake. To compensate for the lack of political experience at the helm, the paper employed the services of J. E. (later Sir John) Gorst, the party agent. This cumbersome arrangement lasted only a year before it broke down over a disagreement between father and son. The proprietor then appointed W. H. Mudford, whose father had edited the *Courier* and who had himself attained distinction as the *Standard*'s correspondent in Jamaica during the troubles of 1867. Mudford soon got rid of Gorst, whose criticisms in 1874 of Conservative colonial policy undermined his position. When Johnstone died in 1878, Mudford inherited the editorship 'in perpetuity' along with a fixed share of the company's profits.[1] Disraeli, then Prime Minister, had lost his grip on the *Standard*.

Even when that grip had seemed secure, Disraeli was shopping for supplementary press support. To have won the *Daily Telegraph* to his side, where it was to be found after 1877, would have been a sensational coup. James Birch, an Irish journalist with a rascally past, claimed to have worked to that end. Writing again to Disraeli in 1852, he described how he had 'aided in starting

[1] Massingham, *London Daily Press,* pp. 74–80; Kebbel, *Lord Beaconsfield,* pp. 230–32; Alfred Austin, *Autobiography* (London, 1911), II, 106 ff.; Escott, *Platform, Press, Politics and Play* (London, 1895), pp. 235–37, 250–51, and *Masters of English Journalism,* pp. 197–202. Escott's memory was more reliable for personalities than for dates: in this earlier volume, he recalled Hamber's dismissal as having occurred 'in the autumn of, I think, 1873'; in the later one, on an 'October morning in 1870'. From the Hughenden and Salisbury Papers, the year appears to have been 1871. The 'very curious but still painful story' of the altercation between the Johnstones, father and son, was told to Corry by Burton Blyth, 30 December 1876, Hughenden Papers.

the *Daily Telegraph* in this metropolis and published in it such articles as met with the approval of such patriotic and honest Conservatives as the Right Honble Joseph Napier'. In particular, he had told its vast readership 'that it would be for *the interest of the country* that Lord Derby and you should be called to power'. Consequently, Birch alleged, 'the Palmerston party intrigued and succeeded in obliging me to secede from a journal that it is well known I had spent toil and time to establish', and the columns of the *Telegraph* were now 'abounding in abuse of you, and condemn[ation] of your public conduct'.[1]

Birch's testimony, impossible to corroborate, may be suspect: he was, after all, seeking Disraeli's benediction for a proposed press venture. Yet it cannot be said that he exaggerated Palmerston's sway in Fleet Street. *The Times,* having done its best to retard, if not to prevent, Palmerston's second premiership, quickly adjusted to the fact of its existence. Pretending that its earlier sentiments had been more anti-French than pro-Austrian, it declared on 12 April 1861: 'What we must all desire is that Lord Palmerston and Lord John Russell should be able to convince foreign powers that in no quarter is there any antipathy to the Italian cause.' Apart from its attitude towards Prussia, which was more Palmerstonian than that of the Prime Minister, the paper's views on foreign policy were identical with those of the government. On domestic issues, including Gladstone's remission of the paper duty, Delane and Palmerston saw eye to eye. 'They were not only political associates, but personal friends,' Sir Edward Cook reminds us. In 1861, Palmerston showed solicitous concern for Delane's failing eyesight, going so far as to offer him 'daylight work' as permanent under-secretary at the War Office.[2]

Delane, obviously flattered, declined the post, which 'would have the look of a job for me and a bribe for the Press'. He was more interested in appointments for other people. In 1860, *The Times* reported that Sir James Hudson was to be transferred to the embassy at St Petersburg in order to create a vacancy at Naples for Henry Elliot, another of Russell's Minto clan. The nomination, as announced in 'a low blackguard article' on 25 November, smacked of nepotism. 'When will *The Times* be satisfied to leave Ld John & me alone?' Elliot whined. Sensitivity to press criticism being a family trait, he was again incensed three years later, when similar insinuations cropped up in the *Daily News*. But *The Times* gave him greatest offence. Palmerston assured him on 9 September 1863 'that DeLane [*sic*] was now aware that Hudson's resignation had been entirely voluntary', but still *The Times* refused to publish documents that would have cleared his name and Russell's. From other papers, Russell obtained better value, now that he was Palmerston's lieutenant. Benjamin Moran, an American diplomat in London (and a recent shareholder in the *Spectator*), was relieved at the Anglo-American settlement of the 1862 *Trent*

---

[1] Birch to Disraeli, 27 May 1862, Hughenden Papers.
[2] Cook, *Delane*, pp. 129, 155–56; Dasent, *Delane*, II, 26–27.

Dispute, 'received everywhere but at *The Times* office with unfeigned joy'. The Russellite version of diplomatic negotiations published in the *Morning Post* was 'quite correct in the main and shews that the *Morning Post* does not always get its facts from Palmerston'.[1]

Usually, however, Delane's lobbying was more constructive and less subtle. Though unable to procure the Indian viceroyalty for his nominee, whom Palmerston considered 'not quite strong enough for the place', he successfully promoted the claims of Lord Monck for the Canadian governor-generalship. Lord Torrington owed his appointment at Court to Delane: '*but for you* I should not have been here,' he wrote from Windsor on 23 December 1860, 'and I like to feel that so it is.' On 24 July 1861, Palmerston wrote to 'My dear Delane' to reveal – and, in certain cases, to justify – his allocation of Cabinet portfolios: 'You yourself recommended Sir Robert Peel for Ireland so I need say nothing about him.' If further proof was required, Lady Peel told Delane that she was 'well aware to what extent we are endebted to you for the brilliant opening to what I hope may prove a prosperous political career'. Delane would have been all the more pleased had he been able to hasten the advance of Robert Lowe to Cabinet rank; but, as Lowe himself realized, the push was premature.[2]

The Times was not the only newspaper that Palmerston favoured with his custom. He kept up close contact with the *Morning Post* and the *Globe,* and extended his courtesies to the *Daily Telegraph,* which billed itself from January 1860 as 'espous[ing] the principles and measures of Lord Palmerston'. When Thornton Hunt went to Dublin in 1861 to cover Irish affairs for the *Telegraph,* he carried with him an introduction to Lord Carlisle, the viceroy, to whom Palmerston commended Hunt as 'an intelligent man ... who is not insensible to civility and attention from his superiors in Rank & Condition'. Hunt's devotion was promptly won by Gladstone, who treated him without condescension, and whom he vigorously supported 'in the paper duties affair' against Palmerston's equivocations. To strengthen Gladstone's hand, then and later, he was prepared to do battle with Palmerston's press cohorts. '*The Times* today hazards an intimation that 2d. is to come off the Income Tax,' Hunt advised the Chancellor on 21 February 1863. 'This is quite contrary to what we understood to be the prospect. But we hesitate to counteract the statement without having some trustworthy reason for knowing that the writer is mistaken.' Gladstone presumably clarified matters when he saw Hunt on 2 March. Editor of the *Telegraph* in all but name, Hunt was more politically active behind the scenes than in print, owing to the character of his paper and

[1] Elliot to [?], 25 November and 24 December 1860 (extract copies), Russell Papers, PRO 30/22/14B/11–12; Elliot to George Elliot, 25 August 1863 and Thomas Walker to George Elliot, 9 September 1863, Russell Papers, PRO 30/22/14F/189–90, 219; Moran's diary, 9, 15, and 16 January 1862.

[2] Cook, *Delane,* pp. 157–58; Palmerston to Delane, 24 July 1861, Lady Peel to Delane, 24 July 1861, and Lowe to Delane, 22 June 1861, *Times* Archives.

the dispostion of his proprietor. 'Politics are fearfully dull and it is not good forcing them when there is a superabundance of social matter *immediately* calling for attention,' Edward Levy instructed him on one occasion.[1]

The Conservative journals lay beyond Palmerston's reach, although they were by no means immune to his appeal. Arguably, the most significant resistance he encountered came from the *Daily News,* the *Morning Star,* and the Sunday *Observer,* all sympathetic to the north in its war to extirpate slavery from American soil, and all more or less dedicated to parliamentary reform. Yet differences of tone and emphasis kept them apart. Bright wrote to Cobden in 1862 that 'except when in London I rarely see' (significantly, he struck out 'never') the *Daily News:* 'It has written admirably on the American question, & the letters of Goldwin Smith are remarkable,' he conceded. His own paper, the *Morning Star,* realized a modest profit that year and the next, notwithstanding the unpopularity of its American views. Palmerston shrugged off these 'democratic' organs so long as he was convinced that they spoke neither for the mass electorate nor for any of the major politicians on whom he depended to sustain him in office. Yet he reacted sharply on 15 May 1864, when the *Observer* construed Gladstone's speech on the extension of the borough franchise as a plea for universal suffrage. As much afflicted by gout as by Gladstone's recalcitrance, Palmerston directed his secretary to

Send for Behan of the *Observer* and say I much wish he would not write such articles as his leading one today calculated to rouse agitation which upon every account it is most desirable not to excite. He should be made aware that Mr Gladstone Spoke for himself alone, and not by any means as the organ of the Government and he and Mr Behan must surely be aware that Mr Gladstone's Speech has produced an unfavourable Impression upon a large Section of the Liberal Party.[2]

Newspaper criticism was bad, Cabinet dissension was worse, and the two together were intolerable, especially with the approach of a general election.

As that prospect drew imminent, 'the great paucity of newspapers in the Conservative Interest' came to be felt more acutely. Robert J. Cooper, the son of a former Tory MP for Gloucester, broached the subject with Disraeli, appending to his letter a list of six journals 'Of Conservative Tendency' and twelve 'Of Whig & Destructive Tendency'. To say the least, Cooper's

[1] *Mitchell's Press Directory,* January 1860, where the *Daily Telegraph* previously appeared as 'neutral, bound to no party'; Palmerston to Carlisle, 27 February 1861 (letterbook copy), Palmerston Papers, Add. MSS. 48,582, fol. 45; Hunt to Gladstone, 2 August 1861, and 21 February 1863, Gladstone Papers, Add. MSS. 44,397, fols. 3–4, and 44,400, fol. 65; *Gladstone Diaries,* VI, 185; Levy to Hunt, 25 September 1862, Hunt Papers.

[2] Bright to Cobden, 6 September 1862, Bright Papers, Add. MSS. 43, 384, fol. 304; 'Report of the London Press Co., Ltd. for the *Star* and the *Dial* Newspapers,' 18 November 1863, Wilson Papers; Palmerston to Barrington, 15 May 1864, quoted in Ridley, *Palmerston,* p. 565. The portion of Gladstone's speech that caused 'some sensation' (*Gladstone Diaries,* VI, 275) is found in *Parliamentary Debates,* 3rd ser., clxxv, col. 324 (11 May 1864).

classifications were impressionistic: he included certain Church publications, but ignored Nonconformist and provincial ones alike; and he had doubts about the *Standard,* which 'will sometimes refuse articles sent by me containing the true principles of Conservativism'. Nevertheless, he proposed to submit his hypothesis to an empirical test: 'if we look over the Drawing or Library Table of any of the Clubs in London we shall find that three fourths of the Journals there' are antagonistic to the Tory cause.[1]

The criterion was not merely symbolic. The gentlemen's clubs, all conveniently situated within walking distance of the Palace of Westminster, were homes from home for public persons: MPs, peers, diplomats, senior civil servants, and select journalists. As well as meals and accommodation they provided a conducive atmosphere for conversation and for the transaction of informal business. Party meetings, including banquets to commemorate the launching of new publications, were often held in these premises.

Before 1868, these institutions were relatively few, and the ones with explicit party affiliations were still fewer. The avowedly Conservative clubs were the Carlton (with 800 members 'plus peers and MPs'), the Conservative Club (with 1,500 members), and the Junior Carlton, founded in 1864 (with 2,100 members). Apart from certain Peelites who strayed into the Carlton out of habit, Liberals congregated at Brooks's (with 575 Whiggish members) or the Reform, a less exclusive establishment (with 1,400 members). In the period between the second and third Reform Acts, the geographical and social perimeters of Clubland rapidly expanded. The City Carlton (with 1,000 members) opened its doors in 1868, the St Stephen's (with 1,500 members) in 1870, the City Liberal (with 1,150 members) in 1874, the Devonshire (with 1,500 members) in 1875, the Beaconsfield (with 900 members) in 1882, the Constitutional (with 4,054 members) in 1883, and both the City Conservative and the City Constitutional (each with 1,500 members) in 1884. Thereafter, the pace slackened. It was not uncommon for individuals to hold multiple memberships. Many of them also joined the provincial clubs and dining societies that flourished after 1867. In addition, with the appropriate social credentials, professional backgrounds, or educational qualifications, they might obtain election to such non-political clubs as White's, the Travellers', the United Service, the Athenaeum, the Oxford and Cambridge, the United University, and the New University.[2]

We cannot, of course, scan the club tables as Cooper enjoined Disraeli to do. And regrettably, as previously noted, the records do not survive that would enable us to compile anything that would remotely resemble a comprehensive catalogue of the newspapers that were read at the various clubs, many of them since merged or demolished. The best that can be done is to cull

---

[1] Cooper to Disraeli, 17 April 1865, Hughenden Papers.
[2] Membership figures for 1868 and 1885, along with a discussion, appear in Hanham, *Elections,* pp. 99–105.

entries from the minute-books of a few clubs.

At the Reform, a newspaper committee reported to the general committee. Its function was sufficiently important for instructions to be issued to the librarian in 1864 'to prepare Lists of the Periodicals and Reviews taken in by the Club and ... that ... said Lists be posted up in the usual places ... for the information of the Members'. Those lists, which would have been invaluable, have proved impossible to trace.[1] Instead we have only scattered references among the general committee minutes: 6 June 1862, one additional copy of the *Telegraph*, one additional copy of the *Star*, and one copy less of the *Daily News*; 17 October 1862, three additional copies each of *The Times* and the *Globe*; 20 February 1863, four additional copies of the *Globe*; 11 March 1864, two additional copies of the *Daily News*; and 1 May 1864, 'in reply to a requisition signed by 9 members, the *Dublin Express* added to other Irish Newspapers'. With due allowance for the fragmentary nature of the evidence, one may discern a pattern of increasing consumption that was appropriate for a Palmerstonian stronghold, where Delane belonged.

Whether the impetus was political or financial, the general committee of the New University Club decided on 11 August 1864 to discontinue 'until further notice' two copies of *The Times*, two of the *Globe*, two of the *Saturday Review*, and one each of *Bell's Life*, the *Observer*, and *Puck*. A third edition of the *Sun* was to be substituted for the first edition, presumably to satisfy the demand for late sporting news. On 21 February 1865, a fortnight after its first issue, the *Pall Mall Gazette* was included among the 'papers and magazines ordered to be taken in'. Meanwhile, the general committee of the United University Club took the following actions:

16 November 1865: 'Another *Sun, Express & Evening Standard* to be taken in. The *Sun* and *Standard* are to be placed in the Drawing Room and the *Express* in the Coffee Room.'
26 October 1865: 'Two more Copies of the *Pall Mall Gazette* to be taken in and one Copy of the *Globe* to be discontinued.'
2 November 1865: '... It is ordered that two Copies of the *Express* be added to the List of Newspapers, and one Copy of the *Globe* reduced.'
15 February 1866: 'Two second editions of the *Pall Mall Gazette* and a *Sunday Gazette* to be ordered.'

Aptly christened, the *Pall Mall Gazette* catered expressly to a Clubland clientele. Its features, high middle-brow, were easily digested after a hearty lunch or at teatime. Its eight-page format, loosely set, was not daunting. Its price, 2d., was not prohibitive. George Smith, the wealthy publisher who is

---

[1] Minutes of the Reform Club general committee, 11 March 1864, and library committee, 14 April 1864. Again in 1879, the librarian was requested 'to undertake a revision of the whole Newspaper Supply to the Club'; the minutes record the librarian's agreement, but do not contain the list as stipulated (14 February 1879).

better known as the founder of the *Dictionary of National Biography*, endowed the project, and Frederick Greenwood was its editor. Greenwood had served on the *Cornhill Magazine* under Thackeray, who had impressed on him the necessity for a paper 'written by gentlemen for gentlemen'. Although his personal politics were 'Sceptical Tory', those of his journal were initially indeterminate. T. E. Kebbel, from whom Greenwood sought advice and occasional reviews, looked upon the *Pall Mall Gazette* as 'Liberal', insofar as it was anything; and H. R. Fox Bourne classified it as 'Liberal in the Palmerstonian sense'. Leslie Stephen, a regular contributor, saw its mission to be essentially cultural: 'to fight *The Times* and endeavour to supply a cultivated British audience with first-class literature and high principles at the low rate of twopence'. In line with these objectives, the *Pall Mall* refashioned itself as a twelve-page morning paper in 1870, only to switch back within the year. Its partisanship then grew more pronounced. Fiercely anti-Gladstonian and jingoistic, it accurately reflected club opinion.[1]

The *Pall Mall Gazette* was in its infancy at the time of the 1865 elections. Where it feared to tread, its older competitors rushed in. But all the journalistic sound and fury could not disguise either the scarcity of major issues or the apathetic mood of the nation. It was reasonably assumed that Palmerston, aged eighty, was confronting the electorate for the last time. On the whole, newspapers did him prouder than they did themselves.

*   *   *

'We are drifting rapidly along, and we are now within eight or ten weeks of a general election,' the *Morning Advertiser* solemnly noted on 3 May 1865,

> ... and yet, on the greatest question of all, the position of the Liberal Party is eminently unsatisfactory. A general declaration of a willingness to support Reform may be drawn from any candidate, Whig or Tory; but what is such a vague, unmeaning profession worth?

Looking beyond Palmerston, the *Advertiser* brushed aside Russell ('If he really means once more to propose a bill, he owes it to himself and to the country to tell us something of its outlines'), and pinned its hopes on Gladstone, who supported Edward Baines's annual motions to enlarge the borough franchise. The *Morning Star*, too, trusted to Gladstone, who supposedly 'had been converted by Mr Bright as Sir Robert Peel was converted by Mr Cobden'.

Yet Gladstone was not a free agent. Obliged to consider the predicament of his Cabinet colleagues and the sentiments of his Oxford constituents, he declined to make franchise reform a plank in his election platform. The *Adver-*

---

[1] Kebbel, *Lord Beaconsfield*, pp. 220–21; Fox Bourne, II, 273–74; *History of The Times*, III, 92.

tiser, eight days after it had extolled him, thought him no better than the rest. By 11 May, the government had 'strangely managed ... to place itself in a position to deserve and receive the derision of every newspaper in London', with the 'single exception' of 'the polite and easily pleased *Morning Post*, ... regarded by some as a member of Lord Palmerston's own establishment'. The result, it prophesied, 'is likely to be disastrous', for the Liberals' 'political paralysis ... may give us a Tory House of Commons and a Tory Government, which it will take years to over throw'. The beneficiary, it warned on the 23rd, would be Disraeli, whose 'intrinsic weakness is ... that no man knows what he believes, or feels any certainty that he really believes anything'.

Weeks passed, and still the administration held to a collective silence. On 12 June, the *Daily Telegraph* put up a brave front:

> Some of our contemporaries express surprise that ... the leaders of the Liberal party have not been more anxious to put forth some such manifesto as that issued by Mr Disraeli to the electors of Bucks. But the accomplished gentleman who conducts the Tory party in their long wanderings through the Desert of Opposition feels very naturally that if *he* did not invent a policy for his party none would exist.

Against Disraeli's 'policy of parade', the Liberals could point to a 'programme' that 'really consists in events which speak for themselves, and in dry statistical facts the romance of which is not apparent at first sight', though not without 'a unity and grandeur of its own'. In ranking order, the *Telegraph* enumerated the 'cardinal point[s] of the Liberal creed': retrenchment in public expenditure, 'the firm maintenance of Peace', 'the steady continuance of the extension of free trade', 'a practical extension of the franchise', a reformulation of Irish policy, and 'the final disposition of the income tax'. Ten days later, although firm in its own commitment, the *Telegraph* had lost patience with 'leaders ... stiff of limb, or not in their full armour'. Calling for 'a blast upon the trumpets, and ... a tuck upon the drums', it tried to rouse the party from its torpor. Paying tribute to 'the venerable Premier' and to Russell's 'splendid merits', it lavished particular praise on Gladstone, who was fighting hard – and, in the event, unsuccessfully – to hold his seat at Oxford. On 21 June, the day before the paper truculently urged his return ('if Oxford ... should show that she has no sympathy for the principles that now form the basis of our national life, she will expose herself to a peril of no ordinary magnitude'), Gladstone saw Thornton Hunt, with whom he communicated frequently during the campaign.[1]

Closer to its doorstep, there were two London boroughs in which the *Telegraph* took special interest. Each, in its way, revealed something about the dis-

---

[1] *Gladstone Diaries* (21, 22, and 24 June, 1, 5, 11, and 27 July 1865), VI, 364, 366–68, and 373. The *Morning Star*'s commendation of Gladstone is quoted in Richard Masheder, *Dissent and Democracy* (London, 1864), p. 249.

pensation of press patronage. At Lambeth, Thomas Hughes, the Christian socialist, stood as the Liberal candidate, and the *Telegraph* backed him ardently. The reason was somewhat curious. James Macdonell, a twenty-four-year-old Aberdonian, had recently arrived from Newcastle, where he had worked on the *Northern Daily Telegraph*. A letter of introduction from H. Gilzean Reid, the northern newspaper magnate, secured him employment as 'confidential helper' to Edward Levy. To repay Reid's kindness, Macdonell promised to do all he could to 'assist Mr Hughes, through the *Daily Telegraph*, in his contest for Lambeth'. His hand may be detected in the laudatory references to Hughes that appeared almost daily, including the stiff denial on 29 June that Hughes had withdrawn from the race. On 12 July, the paper rejoiced that Lambeth had returned 'two Liberal members . . . by ringing majorities at the head of the poll'. By giving Hughes second place, 'so near the very top', the electors had 'asserted the principle of "men and not money". . . . The artisans of the district knew him for their friend, and worked for him heart and soul'.[1]

Across the river at Westminster, the line of battle was less clearly drawn. W. H. Smith, the bookseller and newsagent, was known to Levy as a 'personal friend' and a Liberal. Indeed, Levy had once pressed Palmerston to consider Smith's qualities. When the two friends next met, Smith announced plans to contest Westminster. 'Delighted to hear it,' Levy responded. 'Rely on me to do all in my power for you.' Smith thereupon revealed that he had been adopted in the Conservative interest. 'Whew! that alters matters,' replied Levy. 'Then, rely upon it, I'll do all I fairly can to keep you out!'[2]

Smith's opponents at Westminster were John Stuart Mill, the Liberal progressive, and R. W. Grosvenor, the Whig scion. The *Telegraph* plumped for the former, and treated the latter with courteous restraint. Quick to consign Smith to 'the category of political nobodies' (6 May), it tartly observed on 6 July that his election address was

> so liberal in its tone that it ought to have been dated from the Reform Club. . . . Yet this gentleman is accounted a champion of Conservative principles, simply because he is opposed to two candidates of advanced Liberal views.

To the *Morning Advertiser,* however, Smith was eminently satisfactory. On 24 June, it predicted his 'return by a large majority', and argued that 'his Conservatism is of so Liberal a complexion that it is quite as good as most of the Whig class of politicians'. Disillusioned with party labels, the *Advertiser* found Smith preferable to either 'so poor a Whig representative as Captain Grosvenor, or so crotchety and impracticable a member as Mr John Stuart

---

[1] W. Roberston Nicoll, *James Macdonell* (London, 1897), pp. 119, 124; *Daily Telegraph*, 30 May, 13, 20, and 29 June, and 13 July 1865.
[2] Sir Herbert Maxwell, *Life of the Right Honourable William Henry Smith, MP* (Edinburgh and London, 2nd edn., 1894), pp. 71–72.

Mill', whose 'irreligion' was a further disqualification (26 and 30 June, 3 July). The *Globe* conceded on 7 July that Smith 'looks formidable, but he is the very mildest type of Conservative we know'; all the same, it was 'glad to see the committees of the Liberal candidates, Captain Grosvenor and Mr Mill, at length working harmoniously to secure their joint success'. On 11 July, Westminster went to the polls, and Gladstone voted early for Grosvenor and Mill, the victors. 'The election of Mr Smith . . . would have been a serious party defeat,' the *Daily News* declared the next day; 'but the return of Mr Mill with Captain Grosvenor is much more than a great party victory', being also a rebuke to Mill's 'Pharisaical assailants'. In 1868, after boundary changes and three years of assiduous constituency work, Smith was able at last to displace Mill.

Gladstone had to contend with his own 'Pharisaical assailants' at Oxford, where polling (prolonged by postal voting) began on the 13th. The *Daily News,* agreeing with the *Telegraph* that his 'career as a statesman will certainly not be arrested' if he lost his university seat, refused to 'waste time in vain reflections on the folly of the bigots at Oxford' (17 and 18 July). The *Morning Post,* 'in one word' on the 17th, asserted that 'Mr Gladstone's ejection from Oxford would discredit the claims of intelligence to the franchise'. The following afternoon, the *Globe* had 'no doubt that Oxford has ostracised Mr Gladstone, and whether the act is more dishonourable to the constituency or the candidate we shall leave others to decide'. Its own decision was made clear in a spate of leading articles that contrasted Gladstone's eloquence with Disraeli's ineptitude. The pro-Disraelian *Morning Herald* was pleased to think that Gladstone's 'most ambitious hopes have received an almost insuperable check' at Oxford: expecting that he would now embrace 'that Radical programme with which he has hitherto coquetted', it proclaimed on the 19th that as representative 'for a Radical constituency he will be at once sincere and harmless'. The *Morning Herald,* however, was nearer the mark: it took a perverse delight in Gladstone's

> dismissal . . . by the University of Oxford. . . . Hence he can hardly avoid . . . becoming one of the most resolute and foremost champions of the Liberal cause. . . . Mr Gladstone will from this hour be regarded by the country as the Coming Man,

it wrote on the 20th, the day that he was hastily returned 'unmuzzled' for South Lancashire. What had begun as a struggle between Disraeli and Palmerston (with Derby and Russell shunted to the sidelines) ended as a duel between Disraeli and Gladstone.

In the early stages of the campaign, it was tempting for candidates of nearly every stamp to clamber aboard the Palmerstonian bandwagon. The *Globe* (1 July) deplored the 'unscrupulous use . . . being made of Lord Palmerston's name' by politicians who would combine against him at the first opportunity, but the *Morning Post* considered it only natural, given that 'Lord Palmerston was trusted and honoured on both sides of the Speaker's chair'. The *Post* (7 July) poured scorn on 'the pompous insincerty of [Disraeli's] inflated phrases', so different from 'the modest common sense of the Premier'; and the *Morning Herald* (17 July) retaliated that Palmerston's 'habitual caution and reserve, disguised under an affection of levity and carelessness', was 'wearisome', and no match for Disraeli's 'calm, truthful, and dignified' appeal. The dividing issue between parties seemed to be one of forensic style.

But Bright, for one, would not abide by these rules. In a speech at Birmingham, he accused the Palmerston administration of having defaulted on 'its solemn pledges' to deliver parliamentary reform. The *Globe* (3 July) expressed disgust with Bright's 'unfortunate characteristics', and the *Herald* (17 July) thought him 'as frank, as extravagant, and as untruthful as ever'. The angriest retort came from the *Morning Post* of the 15th:

> Mr Bright may say what he pleases, but it will appear hereafter that, instead of betraying any cause, her Majesty's Ministers have essentially promoted the same cause which Mr Bright himself is, if not betraying, prejudicing and, as it may turn out, again postponing.

Yet the *Morning Advertiser,* confessing to 'a feeling of mingled disappointment and indignation' with Palmerston's record (6 July), shared Bright's frustration to the extent that it looked to Disraeli (15 July) to bring forward a reform measure.

Long before the final polls were declared, it was clear that the Conservatives had lost ground since 1859. They refused to concede that they were beaten, however. On 14 July, the *Herald* rejected as 'ridiculously incorrect' *The Times*'s calculation that the government had picked up six borough seats: if they had not propounded a 'deliberate falsehood', the 'conductors' at Printing House Square were alleged to have shown 'the grossest inattention to their duties'. (The aspersion must have amused Delane, who was described that day as unable to attend to literary matters: 'The Elections absorb all his time & will do so till the end of next week.') 'Practically,' the *Herald* was still insisting on the 24th, '. . . Conservatism has never been so strong in the House of Commons since the dissolution of the Parliament of 1841.' (Gladstone, the same day, counted '26 seats gained'.) 'The Liberals may say that we are defeated if they please,' the *Herald* allowed on the 25th; 'we know they have won nothing but embarrassments', by which it meant an increased complement of Radicals. As Bright wrote in disbelief on the 27th: 'The elections are over, and nobody has been able to discover the great Tory reaction.'[1]

The way that the Conservatives cloaked their reverse was not half so galling

---

[1] Mowbray Morris to Samuel Lucas, 14 July 1865 (letterbook copy), *Times* Archives; *Gladstone Diaries*, VI, 372; Bright to Charles Villiers, 27 July 1865, quoted in Trevelyan, *Bright*, p. 343.

to Bright as the way that the Palmerstonians flaunted their success. On the 25th, the *Morning Post* accepted the Liberal majority as a national vote of confidence:

> Liberalism is not Democracy, and the Parliament which is now being returned with its large Liberal majority will, there is no doubt, look to the preservation of the institutions of the country with a vigilance no less keen than if it was composed exclusively of gentlemen who write Conservative after their names.

Hardly a reassurance to Bright, it implied a willingness (as Disraeli appreciated) 'to form an anti-revolutionary party on a broad basis'[1] as a means to safeguard property and to resist pressure for reform. With skilful negotiation, such a 'reconstruction' might have brought together not only Tories and Palmerstonian Whigs, but also anti-reformist Liberals like Lowe, who carried weight with Delane. The object would have been to deprive Russell of the succession, for which he had long waited, and to isolate Gladstone and his newly acquired Radical friends.

'There is no disguising the fact, that the central figure in the general election has been Mr Gladstone,' the *Daily News* stated on 26 July, amid rumours of impending coalition. 'It is instinctively perceived on all sides that he is to be the pivot upon whose position the movements of majorities and minorities will turn.' The paper rejected with contempt the idea that Gladstone's 'highest political ambition should be to deserve the empty and evanescent popularity of the last Whig Premier', and it further

> regretted that Lord Palmerston does not teach his personal followers a little better taste and tact at a time when Tory journals, with sufficient plausibility, are eagerly consoling the party for its defeat by the assurance that the Liberal majority in the new Parliament will split into fragments when a chief who is a Liberal by party designation only has ceased to conciliate the trimmers and deserters who fill its ranks.

Nevertheless, the rumours continued. Sparked by fears of Palmerston's duplicity, they were soon fed by evidence of his debility.

'The only political news is in reality personal,' Delane wrote to John Blackwood on 22 September:

> Both leaders are in a bad way. Palmerston is undoubtedly failing. His family declare that he is as well as ever, that he is completely restored &c. But I saw him the other day and was painfully struck by his altered look and by the absence of that animation and keen interest in all subjects. . . . He was also

---

[1] Disraeli to Derby, 6 August 1865, Derby Papers. For a pungent analysis, see Maurice Cowling, *Disraeli, Gladstone and Revolution* (Cambridge, 1967), pp. 82–83.

... palpably shrunk – did not half fill his clothes and seemed slipping off his chair.

That can't last long. But Derby is very little better.[1]

On 19 October, *The Times* reported Palmerston's death with a nine-column obituary prepared by Delane himself: 'There never was a statesman who more truly represented England than Lord Palmerston.' In death as in life, Palmerston served *The Times,* which attained a record sale that day of over 76,000 copies.

[1] Delane to Blackwood, 22 September 1865, Blackwood Papers; *History of The Times,* II, 354.

Five

DISRAELI v. GLADSTONE

The inconclusive outcome of the 1865 elections, soon followed by the death of Lord Palmerston, plunged parliamentary politics deeper and deeper into disarray. Had Palmerston survived, he might yet have imposed order, possibly through the mechanism of the anti-reform alliance at which his press supporters had broadly hinted. His removal, however, put an abrupt end to any notions of maintaining, let alone institutionalizing, a system of inter-party compromise. The tacit arrangements that he had superintended for the better part of a quarter-century were broken up. The forces of polarization, which he had so long held firmly in check, were suddenly released. In the scramble to pick up the pieces, newspapers acquired even greater significance.

Whether they had lost a mentor or an adversary, the metropolitan journals were obliged to accommodate themselves to a change of circumstances. Some managed more gracefully than others. For Delane, Palmerston's death was a personal grief as well as 'a journalistic problem of the utmost seriousness': his 'most valuable source vanished'. That Russell, aged seventy-five and a peer, should exercise his right of reversion was a foregone conclusion, but nevertheless an unpalatable prospect to *The Times*. His seniority, it wrote on 23 October, was 'no recommendation . . . for the post of Premier, but quite the contrary'. The next day, Abraham Hayward described to Delane the 'outcry' against this attack, confirming that it had made 'the waverers begin to doubt the duration of the ministry. People say, of course, that Lowe is the writer . . . which I much doubt.'[1] On that score, Hayward was mistaken.

Robert Lowe, a leader-writer for *The Times* since the middle of the century, had emerged in Parliament as a trenchant opponent of franchise reform. He suspected Russell of being a stalking horse for Gladstone, whom he detested, and Gladstone of being a stalking horse for Bright, whom he detested more. Delane had tried without success to obtain for Lowe a Cabinet appointment in 1861 and 1863. Disappointed by Palmerston, Lowe would not have condescended to take office under Russell. 'I would not enter in a government I

[1] Hayward to Delane, 24 October [1865], *Times* Archives; *History of The Times*, II, 393–94.

approved, much less in such a concern as this,' he sniffily told Delane on 30 October, two days after *The Times* had expressed its 'regret that ... the representative of the narrowest school of Whiggism' had formed an administration in which the vital 'departments ... have been placed in the hands of Peers'. Dasent, who was deputizing for Delane, had asked Lowe 'to write on John' – as he referred to the new Prime Minister – 'a propos of some reflexions I had permitted myself in a former article', and Lowe was delighted to comply: 'I never could resist the temptation of pitching into him and I think we of the ribald press don't owe him much quarter.'[1]

For Lowe to sacrifice his own ministerial ambitions was one thing; for him to compromise *The Times* was something quite different. Lord Torrington reported gossip at Court 'that the difficulties for the reformation of the Govt. were very great', and that '*The Times* articles ... had their full weight' as a contributing factor. He noted that 'information was given to the *Globe*', but withheld from *The Times*. The following February, the paper was denied an advance copy of the Queen's Speech, although one was evidently supplied to the *Daily Telegraph*. Delane kept his composure. 'I never knew the paper in a better position,' he wrote to Dasent from Dublin on 2 November: 'it has a freedom of action which is always most enviable.' His proprietor, 'Griff' Walter, was not so sure. 'Don't let B[ob] L[owe] ride his Anti-Reform hobby too hard – for reform we must have of some sort,' he admonished Dasent. Accordingly, when Delane returned from his Irish holiday on 23 November, he gave instructions that Lowe was no longer to make *The Times* a vehicle for his instransigent views. Other subjects, too, had to be put off limits: 'Bob Lowe wrote such an article upon Bright. It made my hair stand on end, and I have had to alter it almost beyond recognition,' Delane subsequently informed Dasent. The editor's apparent inability to assert control gave rise to rumours that, in exchange for a peerage, Walter was prepared to sack him. Although Walter laughed at these 'pleasing stories', his 'funk' puzzled and worried Delane.[2]

The Times muted its aversion to reform, while remaining hostile to a government that was 'merely the Palmerston Ministry without Lord Palmerston' to keep it in bounds. In a vain attempt to temper its prejudices, Edward Cardwell, the colonial secretary, assured Lord Torrington that 'no one was more anxious to do justice to Palmerston's memory than Gladstone'. Cardwell 'lamented the line taken by *The Times*', and 'complained ... that the Press in general had not done justice to the whole Cabinet'. That was no understatement. Although various newspapers befriended specific ministers – *The Times* showing a tender regard for Lord Clarendon at the Foreign Office and the Duke of Somerset at the Admiralty – the government as a whole found little

---

[1] Lowe to Delane, 30 October 1865, *Times* Archives.
[2] Torrington to Delane, 1 November 1865, *Times* Archives; *History of The Times*, II, 397; Delane to Dasent [2 November 1865], *Times* Archives; Dasent, *Delane*, II, 159–60.

favour. Divided in their response to anticipated reform legislation, the papers were more united in their bloodthirsty reaction to an uprising in Jamaica. '*The Times, Telegraph, Post & Herald* support & applaud the murder as they always support every evil thing done by Englishmen abroad, and as they supported Jeff Davis & his Brethren in America,' Bright wrote to Thorold Rogers. 'What a fearful evil there is in a Press under the control of evil men, & how difficult it is to counteract it.'[1]

Elected in July 1865, the new Parliament was not called into session until 6 February 1866. In the intervening months, the government attended to Jamaican affairs and slowly drafted its reform proposals. Delay inevitably increased apprehensions on both sides. 'Every day we have to chronicle fresh testimony to the growing earnestness of the public on the subject of Reform,' declared the *Daily Telegraph* on 4 January 1866; it found less to fear from the Tories, whose 'honest opposition' could be directly met, than from Liberal 'trimmers', whose 'only endeavour ... is to delay the march by plausible pretences'. Should the government '"shelve" Reform – we use another favourite phrase of the trimmers – it will stand self-convicted of having ... deluded a trusting people'. Much would depend not only on Russell and Gladstone, both 'pledged to Reform', but also on Bright, whose recent speeches gave welcome evidence 'that he is no longer the mouthpiece of a sect, but the spokesman of a people'. Had Bright backed the Reform League agitation, he would have played into the hands of those who cowered in what he called the Cave of Adullam. Instead, he behaved with notable restraint, and urged Justin McCarthy, then editor of the *Morning Star*, to do the same. 'I would suggest that you should not insert any letters or paragraphs criticising the Queen', he wrote on 19 January. 'It is no use making enemies; and the Court is not averse to the Reform cause.' Otherwise, he thought 'the paper is looking well, and the writing is *good*'.[2]

A week before Parliament met, Hayward gratified Gladstone with a report that 'the Cave has split already'. Lord Elcho, estranged from Lowe, had circulated 'the prospectus of a new paper he and Lord Grosvenor are about to set up'. This was the *Day*, its publication postponed for fourteen months, probably because its sponsors persisted in the hope of winning over *The Times*. 'Delane and Lord Russell seem to have quarrelled,' Lord Stanley noted in his diary on 4 February, 'and Lord R. gives whatever information he has to a new journal called the *Sunday Gazette*, which is in his interest.' The mutual antipathy between Delane and Russell was widely known. 'I am aware that Mr Delane was very angry that I did not ask to kiss his hand instead of the Queen's when I was appointed to succeed Palmerston,' Russell told Clarendon. No enthusiast for reform, Delane was prepared to believe that 'the

[1] Torrington to Delane [9 November 1865], *Times* Archives; Bright to Rogers, 23 November 1865, Rogers Papers.
[2] Bright to McCarthy, 19 January 1866, quoted in McCarthy, *Reminiscences*, I, 95–96.

subject was disinterred only to meet the personal exigencies of Lord John, and he may carry it, if he can'. Against his better judgment, he saw 'a chance for a third party' in which Lowe (who had 'enormously improved his position') and other Liberal dissidents might combine with Stanley and the Tory moderates.[1]

Discretion forbade him from promulgating such views in print. So, more decisively, did the instincts of John Walter, whom he was obliged to consult 'as to the line to be taken by the paper'. Although editorial policy impressed Walter as 'equally reasonable & prudent', he was disposed to 'add a word or two of additional caution'. Admittedly, both literally and figuratively, Russell was too small to fill Palmerston's shoes. 'At the same time,' Walter counselled from Paris on 28 February,

> I don't see how the Tories could be allowed to claim their innings under existing circumstances. They are numerically weaker than they were in the last Parliament; and though the Liberal party is merely a piece of patchwork, it would be a proof of disgraceful weakness on their part were they to give up the game without a vigorous effort to play it out. They have excellent materials, & only want a good leader. Gladstone of course is the stumbling block. He might succeed – though I doubt it – but he is ambitious enough to be able to make success almost impossible for any one else. . . . On the other side, I believe that, with all his faults, Lord Stanley is the most likely man to succeed in forming an administration, if the Tories came in; & if they should renew their attempts at a Reform Bill, which I wd. hardly advise them to do, he would be the most likely man to frame a good one.[2]

It was fundamentally Walter's position that prevailed.

On the very day Walter wrote, *The Times* committed one of its worst gaffes. Only four weeks into the new session, it proclaimed it 'idle to disguise the fact that the course of Government since the meeting of Parliament has been such as to excite the gravest anxiety among the friends of a Liberal Administration'. Along with this somewhat premature assessment, it related the startling news that Russell, unable to contend with a 'Cabinet . . . divided against itself', was said to have 'begged permission to resign' and 'recommended her Majesty to send for the Duke of Somerset'. The *Daily Telegraph* handily refuted these assertions and ventured an explanation for them. 'For many weeks past,' it stated on 1 March,

> *The Times* has directly and indirectly, by open attack and covert insinuation, by ridicule and innuendo, no less than by argument and ratiocination,

---

[1] Hayward to Gladstone, 31 January 1866, Gladstone Papers, Add. MSS. 44,207, fol. 102; Stanley's diary, 4 February 1866, in *Disraeli, Derby*, p. 245; Russell to Clarendon, 26 April 1866, quoted in Maxwell, *Clarendon*, II, 313–14; Delane to Bernal Osborne [February (?) 1866], quoted in Dasent, *Delane*, II, 166.

[2] Walter to Delane, 28 February 1866, *Times* Archives.

opposed the Government scheme of Reform. . . . By giving a rude shake to so delicate an organisation and so complicated a fabric as a Cabinet, *The Times* hopes to create that want of harmony of which it speaks as already in existence.

Shown to have trespassed beyond the 'well-understood limits within which the influence of the newspaper press of England is happily uncontrolled', *The Times* henceforth had to mind its step.

On 12 March, Gladstone, as leader of the House of Commons, unveiled the government's reform scheme, which was more studiously circumscribed than the Bill Russell had introduced in 1860. Delane, who listened from the gallery, thought the 'speech very laboured, and not by any means one of his best'. (He could not have known that Gladstone was suffering 'with a stuffed head'.) Dutifully defended by Bright, the measure was condemned as stinting by more militant Radicals and as dangerous by more timorous Whigs and Adullamites. *The Times* damned it with faint praise as the best that could be expected from such auspices. Yet gradually Delane swung round. Impressed by 'so many Reform meetings' (the reports crowded out literary reviews from the pages of *The Times*), he advised Dasent: 'Pray don't let anybody write any Toryism.' The government, he had concluded by the end of March, 'is quite safe to carry the Second Reading of this Bill and though our position is good as far as it goes we ought not to go beyond it'. As he predicted, the Bill passed its second reading, but by a narrow margin of five votes. The *Daily Telegraph*, reiterating 'that we feel no misgivings as to the ultimate passing into law of the present Reform Bill', recognized Gladstone as 'the inspiring and animating genius' of an administration that 'has a right to ask of the people patient and trusting moderation' (7 and 17 March).[1]

Despite Gladstone's misgivings the government coupled franchise reform with a redistribution Bill. The *Telegraph* (17 and 20 March) deplored this concession to the enemy ('As drowning men cling to a straw, so do the followers of Mr Disraeli to the point') and demanded 'settling the question of the suffrage before approaching that of redistributing the seats'. *The Times*, said to have fastened on redistribution 'in its ill-temper and despair', was mollified by a measure 'so just in principle, that we ask with wonder why it was not introduced before' (8 May). The dual package proceeded to the committee stage, where it suffered severe mutilation. Defeated by nine votes on a backbench motion to tamper with the provisions for the borough franchise, the government decided on 19 June to resign. Gladstone and Russell would have preferred to dissolve. *The Times*, thinking either course too drastic, put the case that 'the fate of the Ministry ought to be completely dissevered from the fate of the Reform Bill'. In the early hours of the 19th, Delane returned from the

---

[1] Delane's diary [12 March 1866], quoted in Dasent, *Delane*, II, 167; *Gladstone Diaries*, VI, 424; Delane to Dasent [30 March 1866], *Times* Archives.

crucial debate to address a personal entreaty to Clarendon:

> I hope ... that you will not think it necessary to ... break up a Ministry
> which has endured for seven years in great honour, and which still possesses
> a large and well-affected majority, on account of a paltry defeat on an
> amendment to a clause in Committee proposed by one of your ordinary sup-
> porters. It would be a most undignified end, and would go far to justify all
> that was said last autumn when Lord Russell assumed the Premiership.

Clarendon, too tactful to remind Delane that *The Times* had supported neither
the formation of the Liberal ministry in 1859 nor Russell's succession the previous October, replied that this 'humiliation will deprive the Govt. of anything
like substantial power'. Disregarding Delane's advice as well as a royal
appeal, the Russell government (as *The Times* put it on the 20th) threw 'itself
over a precipice' and the country into outstretched Tory hands.[1]

Exactly as Lord Derby had found in 1859, the backing of *The Times* came
too grudgingly and too late to serve its intended purpose. Walter was
absolutely correct when he identified Gladstone as 'the stumbling block'. The
Daily News, the *Morning Star*, and other organs of advanced Liberalism
already looked to him as the leader-elect. The *Daily Telegraph*, taking stock of
his 'lofty attributes', had defended his 1866 budget, which '*The Times*, with an
ingenuity which is perfectly intelligible, if not natural, has ... contrived to
misapprehend' (2 and 19 February 1866). Lord Granville, looking back on the
failures of the late government and possibly ahead to future challenges, told
Delane that 'immense use and advantage' might be gained if 'you and
Gladstone had more personal communication'; after all, he reasoned on 30
March 1867,

> for the director of such an important organ of public opinion as *The Times* it
> cannot be otherwise than an advantage to know the mind of one who in
> every position is sure to exercise so great an influence on public affairs.

Not without a hint of irony, Granville later wrote to Delane, when the reform
crisis was nearing its climax: 'You have carried *all* Gladstone's proposals,
excepting the one conservative restriction.'[2]

It was not, as the official historians of *The Times* have suggested, that 'Gladstone did not get, because he did not seek, any such advantage': the barriers
were not all on his side. Far from resisting the press, he prized his contacts with
Thornton Hunt, who secured him not only praise in the *Telegraph*, but also,
and more importantly, a flow of vital intelligence. 'I called to-day simply to *tell*
you something,' Hunt left word for him on 27 July 1866. Before Gladstone's
arrival at the House at eleven o'clock the previous evening, Hunt had detected

---

[1] Delane to Clarendon, 19 June 1866, quoted in Dasent, *Delane*, II, 169; Clarendon to Delane,
19 June 1866, *Times* Archives; *Gladstone Diaries*, VI, 444–47 (19–26 June 1866).
[2] Granville to Delane, 30 March and [June] 1866, *Times* Archives.

'a decided feeling among the Liberal Members . . . of regret at the absence' of party leaders during the debate on the proposed Reform League demonstrations in Hyde Park. 'Do not be offended with me,' he implored,

> or suspect me of 'meddling'. I had nothing to ask, nothing to 'suggest'; my purpose was absolutely limited to letting you *know* what I believed to be the state of feeling both within & without the House; & that purpose ends the very moment you have read these words.

Gladstone could not have expected such humility from Delane, who would have written a leader, not a letter. Although Gladstone took it on himself to expose as a forgery a letter in the *Globe* that linked him to the Reform League, he relied on Hunt to contradict the story in the *Standard* and elsewhere that he had had an interview with the Pope on behalf of the Kingdom of Italy.[1]

The Conservatives, whom Clarendon had described to Delane as '*wild for office*', had their chance when Russell resigned. Lowe, with the editorial columns of *The Times* at his disposal, worked feverishly to create 'a strong Constitutional party' that would bring together Tories and Adullamites. The attempt failed, possibly because he demanded too high a price: a Whig statesman at the helm. 'I take it Derby will make a pure Tory Government and so lose all chance of breaking up the Whig party,' he wrote ruefully to Delane on 28 June. 'I wanted him to try Granville, Clarendon or Somerset . . . but Dizzy is all for pure Tories.' Clarendon, who in fact received a bid from Derby, was the subject of a laudatory article in *The Times* that morning. He was grateful 'not simply because it was eulogistic, but because it stated with such remarkable preciseness the objects at wh. I have aimed in our foreign policy & the spirit in wh. I have attempted to carry out those objects'.[2]

For a third and final time, Lord Derby took office as head of a minority government. Even before his Cabinet was formed, *The Times* accurately designated its foreign secretary. 'I see Lord Stanley is announced as your successor,' Russell grumbled to Clarendon,

> and that Lord Derby has done that which I would not do, namely, submitted his appointments to Mr Delane before submitting them to the Queen. This is a new constitution of itself, and one much to be deprecated.[3]

Although Russell exaggerated in this instance, he did not overestimate the lengths to which Derby would go to cultivate *The Times*, now reconciled to the inevitability of reform. The *Telegraph*, 'in recording the conversion' on 24

---

[1] *History of The Times*, II, 406; Hunt to Gladstone, 27 July 1866, Gladstone Papers, Add. MSS. 44,411, fols. 127–28; *Gladstone Diaries*, VI, 454–55 (27 and 30 July 1866); Brand to Hunt, 10 November 1866, Hunt Papers.

[2] *The Journals of Lady Knightley of Fawsley* (ed. J. Cartwright; London, 1915), p. 230 (3 May 1872); *History of The Times*, II, 404; Lowe to Delane, 28 June 1866, and Clarendon to Delane, 28 June 1866, *Times* Archives.

[3] Russell to Clarendon, 27 June 1866, quoted in Maxwell, *Clarendon*, II, 230.

January 1867, piously reflected: 'There is more joy ... over one sinner who repents, than over ninety and nine just men who never went astray.'

In early February 1867, the Prime Minister invited Delane to his private residence in St James's Square for a preview of the Conservative reform resolutions. Afterwards, he tossed 'a crumb of comfort' to Disraeli, whose game he was playing with greater relish than skill:

> ... I have had a most satisfactory interview with Delane. He is cordially with us, and will do all in his power to carry us through. He listened most attentively to the whole of our programme, and pronounced oracularly, 'I think it will do.'

Either Derby had misheard his guest, or vice versa. On 13 February, after these general resolutions on reform had been laid before Parliament, *The Times* dismissed them as 'vague and unsubstantial', as indeed they appeared to a majority of MPs. Having been 'the repository of a secret heavy to bear', Delane unburdened himself to William Blackwood:

> I objected when they [the resolutions] were read to me that they were far too vague but was led to understand that they were but *cadres* which Disraeli would fill up in his speech. Imagine my disgust then & that I believe of his colleagues, & the disappointment of the whole House when after a three hour speech, he sat down without having told us anything at all. I never saw the House so indignant and so justly angry.

The government had no choice but to scuttle its resolutions. During question time on the 14th, Disraeli pledged to introduce a Reform Bill, which he duly delivered on 18 March. More sweeping than the unfortunate Liberal Bill of the previous year, it was amended over the ensuing five months to overhaul completely the electoral structure.[1]

The temptation must be resisted here to catalogue the intra-party manoeuvres and extra-parliamentary pressures, the philosophical arguments, and the appeals to expediency, that contributed in varying degree to the passage of the second Reform Act. Suffice it to say that the Conservative leadership, to the stupefaction and sometimes the consternation of its own rank and file, effectively disproved the *Morning Star*'s assumption (8 October 1866) that the reform 'question is the sole property of Liberals'. It hardly mattered to Disraeli, who piloted the measure with supreme exuberance, that the finished product bore scant resemblance to the government's original proposals and less to traditional party doctrines. He had scored a dazzling success: 'our great success', Delane greedily hailed it. What Derby took with trepidation as 'a leap in the dark' was, in Disraeli's case, a feat of political acrobatics.

---

[1] Talbot (Derby's secretary) to Delane, 7 February 1867, quoted in *History of The Times*, II, 405; Derby to Disraeli [February 1867], quoted in Buckle, *Disraeli*, IV, 492; Delane to Blackwood, 18 February [1867], Blackwood Papers.

Once the Reform Act was safely lodged in the statute book, Derby's most pressing concern was his gout. 'I expect great and startling changes in the Govmt. before Valentine's Day,' Delane confided to Blackwood on 30 January 1868. 'Derby is said to be too ill to meet Parliament and there will be a fierce struggle for the first place between Stanley & Dizzy.' It seemed that 'the only way to obviate a break up' would be to install some 'mediocrity . . . over both'. Derby eventually resigned on 25 February, and the Queen sent promptly for Disraeli, whom *The Times* accepted with mixed feelings. Overlooking its pointed reference to the 'apparently unmitigated distrust of the party' of their new leader (26 February), Disraeli wrote from Osborne on the 28th to remind Delane of their 'conversation at Lord Cairns'', which he claimed to have 'decided me' to appoint Ward Hunt to the Exchequer: 'Your clear, & sagacious judgment came to my aid opportunely – wh. shd. teach both of us the advantage of dining out.' That, to be sure, was a lesson neither of them had to learn.[1]

During the eight months that Disraeli clung to power, he received no appreciable assistance from *The Times*. The tenor of the paper became cautiously Liberal, as evinced by support for Gladstone's schemes for 'economical reform' and Irish disestablishment. Lowe severed his connection in 1868. 'I fear I am growing old and lazy,' he unconvincingly told Delane, who had hardly overworked him of late. The assignments Lowe coveted had gone instead to Leonard Courtney or William Stebbing, and it was symbolic that Delane tried to recruit James Bryce, a strong Liberal, as Lowe's replacement. Courtney had joined the staff at Printing House Square in 1864, but his strong 'Cobdenite' views had, for a time, limited the uses to which his talents could be put; from the summer of 1865, he was writing more than twenty leaders a month, including most of those on reform questions. It fell to Stebbing, however, to 'lament' that Disraeli's election address 'contains many promises to resist the policy of others, but no signs of any policy for the great Conservative party itself' (6 October 1868).[2]

By then, Disraeli had given up on *The Times*, and the rejection was mutual. G. G. Glyn, the Liberal chief whip, canvassed 'some of the Press people' in April 1868 to ascertain 'the line they are inclined to take' on the Irish Church issue. 'I think the *Post* & the *D. News* will go quite right,' he reported to Gladstone:

> The *Telegraph* I really cannot make out at all but I think it will not dare to break with you. With Delane I have had no direct intercourse but I think he will not back Disraeli, & that he feels the end is coming rapidly.

---

[1] Delane to Blackwood, 30 January [1868], Blackwood Papers; Disraeli to Delane, 28 February 1868, quoted in Dasent, *Delane*, II, 222.

[2] Lowe to Delane [1868], quoted in Dasent, *Delane*, II, 223; Gooch, *Courtney*, pp. 82–86; list of leaders written for *The Times*, Courtney Papers.

Disraeli himself was in no hurry. In August, anticipating a general election 'a quarter year away', he professed to Derby that he 'would not be surprised if the result might astonish, yet, the Bob Lowes, Higgins, Delanes, and all that class of Pall Mall journal intellect'. His hopes were dashed at the polls in October. On 4 December, the day after Gladstone kissed hands at Windsor, Disraeli denounced 'the malignant *Times*'.[1]

Delane's rebuff was as irksome to Disraeli as the ingratitude of the newly enfranchised working classes. Gladstone embarked on his first premiership with a solid parliamentary majority and with the blessing of *The Times*. He was 'most attentive' to Delane, with whom he dined at the Granvilles' on 6 December, and whom he thereafter permitted to call on him in his 'little room' at the Commons. Delane welcomed these gestures and, still more, Gladstone's Cabinet appointments: Clarendon and Granville, two old friends, returned respectively to the Foreign Office and the Colonial Office; and Lowe was made Chancellor of the Exchequer. Professing himself 'no worshipper of Gladstone's', Delane was reasonably satisfied with his conduct of domestic affairs; with regard to diplomacy, he came to think him 'parochial'. But those differences lay ahead. Without showing *The Times* any favouritism, Gladstone accorded it due respect. In 1870, when the Prime Minister (at Lowe's instigation) offered Dasent a post on the Civil Service Commission, it was on grounds of 'the public interest' and without any whiff of Palmerstonianism.[2]

That is not to suggest that Gladstone self-righteously avoided dealings with the press. He was willing, usually through Glyn, to provide Delane – and other editors – with 'information as soon as any is ripe'. By the same token, the *Telegraph*'s Gladstonian connections did not inhibit its proprietor from seeking confidential tips from Montagu Corry, Disraeli's private secretary.[3] How else was authentic news to be obtained?

Yet Gladstone rigidly held back from any closer involvement. The controllers of the Liberal press, unlike their Conservative counterparts, knew better than to solicit pecuniary assistance. The exception that proves the rule was a request from the owner of the *Chronicle*, a weekly that made its first appearance on 30 March 1867. His capital 'exhausted', he 'appealed' to Glyn 'in a delicate manner for aid upon party grounds'. In referring the matter to Gladstone on 10 February 1868, Glyn recalled that his predecessor, H. B. W. Brand, 'was always against all such subsidies'; moreover, Brand and Gladstone had agreed 'that under ordinary circumstances a weekly paper is not of much use to a party'. Nevertheless, Glyn told Gladstone, 'if you think this case

[1] Glyn to Gladstone, 14 April 1868, Gladstone Papers, Add. MSS. 44,347, fols. 113 ff.; Disraeli to Derby, 23 August 1868, quoted in Buckle, *Disraeli*, V, 86 (Higgins was M. J. Higgins, who often wrote as 'Jacob Omnium'); Disraeli to Grey, 4 December 1868, quoted in *ibid*.

[2] Delane's diary [6 December 1868], quoted in Dasent, *Delane*, II, 229; *History of The Times*, II, 411–14, 497.

[3] Gladstone to Delane, 3 December 1868, *Times* Archives; Levy to Corry, 14 August [1868], Hughenden Papers.

exceptional, I will do what I can' to raise the £1,500 that was 'needed to carry it over the Session' and into its second year, 'but I have no party funds!!'[1] Gladstone's reply may be inferred from the fact that the *Chronicle* discontinued publication on 15 February.

*   *   *

Had the *Chronicle* served the Conservative cause, its impoverished proprietor would have stood a better chance of procuring official support. At the very least, his request would not have been taken as anomalous. Disraeli was constantly importuned by journalists for assistance, financial and otherwise. That, in itself, was an indication of his susceptibility, which owed as much to his own background as to the distressed state of the Tory press.

The demands upon him were various and often direct: E. A. Fitzroy, having purchased *John Bull* 'without asking the party for a farthing', felt entitled to 'cordial support and sympathy' in the form of 'suggestions from Mr Disraeli'; Richard Lee, having bought 'the copyright of the *Court Circular* for the purpose of . . . devoting it to the Conservative cause and the interests of the Church', was 'desirous of securing the support of the Conservative party for the undertaking'; the Rev J. E. Cox, editor of *Bell's Weekly Messenger*, sent a proof of his leading article to Disraeli, whom he vowed 'to support . . . to the utmost extent of his ability & power, as he has already earnestly endeavored to do'.[2] These examples can be easily multiplied. Always couched in the most deferential terms, and often written in the third person, they tended to imply far more than they specified.

Reluctantly, the Conservatives conceded to their opponents a dominance in the provincial press. Without discounting the value of such properties, they recognized that they had not had much luck with them. 'As the political organ of the Conservative party in Leeds', where the Liberal *Mercury* held sway, the *Intelligencer* had 'consistently adhered to the principles it professed', and, in the opinion of Christopher Kemplay, its owner-editor, had 'not ineffectually discharged its functions in this respect'. But the *Intelligencer* ceased publication on 30 June 1866, and, two days later, the *Yorkshire Post* rose from its ashes. The new journal lost no time in putting the case for its existence:

> When we consider that the population of two such counties as Lancashire and Yorkshire, to say nothing of the north of England in general, now draws its political opinions quite as much from the Press of Manchester, Liverpool and Leeds, as from the Press of London, we shall understand at once the

[1] Glyn to Gladstone, 10 February [1868], Gladstone Papers, Add. MSS. 44,397, fol. 99; *also see* A. F. Thompson, 'Gladstone's Whips and the General Election of 1868,' *English Historical Review*, lxiii (1948), 198.
[2] Fitzroy to Disraeli, 10 October 1865, Lee to Disraeli, 14 November 1865, Cox to Disraeli, 1 November 1867, Hughenden Papers.

whole extent of the power which, for good or evil, may be wielded by provincial journalists. [2 July 1866]

Under the circumstances, this effort at self-glorification may be forgiven. The party chiefs in London, who took it in their stride, shared the hope that the *Leeds Mercury* might be 'outfought' on its home ground.[1] They were pleased to entrust that task, like others elsewhere, to wealthy followers in the locality, and busied themselves with more urgent business in the metropolis.

For sentimental as well as practical reasons, the Tories were less concerned with journalistic developments in Leeds than with the fate of the *Press*. In an abortive attempt to keep it afloat, Malmesbury entertained proposals from D. T. Coulton, the editor, and Sir Philip Rose. 'I suppose we might get money for this one,' he minuted to Derby, 'but £20,000 is hopeless & we must do our best with the *Herald* & [the *St James's*] *Chronicle* for the next 2 months.'[2]

The eventuality that Malmesbury contemplated was, almost certainly, the acquisition of the *Globe*. Bereft of Palmerston's guidance, that evening paper foundered badly during the period of Russell's premiership. In July 1866, Henry Cecil Raikes determined to capture it for the Conservative side. A writer for the *Herald* and the *Standard*, Raikes had money and parliamentary ambitions: he was elected at Chester in 1868. His designs were encouraged by Markham Spofforth, Rose's successor as party agent, who assured him that 'the possession of the *Globe* newspaper by the Conservative party, if unknown to the public, would be of material advantage'. It was not clear, even to Raikes, whether this possession was to be *de facto* or *de jure*, but he persevered. 'Do you ever see the new *Globe* which I bought for the party,' he asked his mother on 6 November 1866. 'It is the best paper going.'[3]

In fact, the transaction was a good deal more complicated than Raikes made out. When it became known that the *Globe* was on the market, a bid was tendered by Michael Bass, the brewer and Liberal MP for Derby. Thereupon, Sir Stafford Northcote and George Cubitt formed a Tory syndicate to which Raikes subscribed. With its cumulative resources, which must have included party funds, it was able to top Bass's offer. The actual proprietorship was vested in Charles Westcomb, who contributed £5,000 of his own money. He had owned the *Exeter Gazette* for the past six years, and his son was owner of the *Edinburgh Evening Courant*. In a printed circular dated 20 October 1866, Westcomb announced that he had 'recently purchased the *Globe*, an old established London Evening Paper', which would halve its price to 2d. on 1 November. Northcote introduced him to Corry the following February: 'He is, as you probably know, the proprietor of the *Globe*.' There can be no doubt, then, of

---

[1] Leaders in the *Leeds Intelligencer* (30 June 1866) and the *Yorkshire Post* (2 July 1866), quoted in M. A. Gibb *et al.*, *The Yorkshire Post, Two Centuries* (Leeds, 1954), pp. 27–28, 31, 34.
[2] Malmesbury to Derby, 'Wed'[nesday 1866], Derby Papers.
[3] Spofforth to Raikes, n.d., and Raikes to his mother, 6 November 1866, quoted in Henry St John Raikes, *Henry Cecil Raikes* (London, 1898), p. 57.

Westcomb's responsibility, which was well enough known to his creditors, if not to posterity.[1]

On 30 May 1868, Westcomb wrote to acquaint Corry with his efforts to raise a further £9,000: 'It would be in my opinion a very dangerous circumstance for our party to be compelled to sell the *Globe* at the present time.' Nine days later, he threw in his hand, having 'failed to obtain any aid except £500 on condition that I carry on the paper and . . . bear all responsibility and loss until after the General Election'. He had already 'written to Mr Spofforth with a view to effect a sale to some one interested in our party', and had suggested two alternatives: he might 'sell absolutely the plant and goodwill at £5,000', which would allow him to recoup his initial investment and settle his debts, leaving him with a loss of £6,000; or he might 'sell half of the *Globe* for £2,500 and give my services as Editor gratuitously' with a twelve-month option to a potential buyer. 'It appears to me very unfortunate that so small a sum cannot be advanced for so great an object,' he concluded:

> The *Globe* is now making marked progress, and it would be fatal to the interests of our party to transfer it back to our opponents, but I am not to blame. I have risked my own money. I have borrowed from my friends, am working hard daily to save expense and just as one might expect to reap fruit I am brought up by the inability or unwillingness of a great party to advance me £1,000 until Feby. next. . . .
>
> Just at this time it will have a most prejudicial effect for the opposition press to be crowing over the failure of the *Globe* so soon after the disaster of the *Day*.[2]

Before proceeding to the further troubles of the *Globe*, it would be instructive to examine the disaster to which Westcomb alluded.

First mooted in January 1866, when an Adullamite secession threatened to rend the Liberal Party, the *Day* appeared belatedly in March 1867. By then, the Conservatives were in office, and the movement for a 'Constitutional' party had lost impetus. Lord Elcho, resolved to put the clock back to 1832, could not have been expected to notice. 'Grosvenor and some of us are striving to fight the battle of the Constitution,' he trumpeted to Lord Spencer on 16 January 1867. 'An organ of the Press is said, and we believe rightly said, to be essential to this purpose.' The enterprise was as forlorn as its objective.

Disraeli regarded Lord Grosvenor (successively 3rd Marquess and 1st Duke

---

[1] 'The Evening Newspapers,' *Nation* (New York), 7 October 1880; [James B. Atlay], '"The Globe" Centenary,' the *Globe*, 1 January 1903; circular of 20 October 1866, and Westcomb to Blackwood, 29 June 1867, Blackwood Papers; Northcote to Corry, 18 February 1867, Hughenden Papers. Garbled accounts of this transaction are presented by Kebbel (who 'wrote for the *Globe* for a short time, but I cannot recollect much about it'), *Lord Beaconsfield*, p. 229; Massingham, *London Daily Press*, pp. 168–69; Fox Bourne, II, 275; Simonis, *Street of Ink*, p. 149; and Lee, *Origins*, p. 150.

[2] Westcomb to Corry, 30 May and 8 June 1868, Hughenden Papers.

of Westminster) as the key figure. 'Grosvenor has established a newspaper –
the *Day* – and has engaged Kebbel, an Oxford man, well acquainted with the
press, but a fine writer, and a scholar, for editor,' Disraeli told Derby on 14
March, five days before the first issue. His insertion of 'but' conveyed a hint of
inverted snobbery: T. E. Kebbel, a steadfast Tory, was acquainted not only
with the Press, but also with the *Press*, for which he had written; more
recently, he had helped to set up the *Yorkshire Post*, refusing its editorship to
serve as its London correspondent. 'Grosvenor and Elcho were with Kebbel
to-day, giving him his final instructions,' Disraeli continued. The editor, 'for
his general government', had asked the proprietors 'to let him know what they
really thought would be the result' of the parliamentary session. According to
Disraeli, 'Grosvenor said that if our [the ministry's] policy was what he
understood it to be, ... they had ascertained that they could pull the
Government through, *provided our men went straight*'. Disraeli, as we know,
did not go 'straight', and the *Day* was left in the lurch. It saw print for the last
time on 4 May, and, when the company was dissolved in September, the
investors – among them R. H. Hutton, who had subscribed £6,000 – received
9¼ d. in the pound on their shares.[1]

Nominally 'Constitutionalist', the *Day* was sufficiently dependent on Tory
talent and money to count as a loss to that party. It seemed likely that the
Globe would go the same way. It survived Westcomb's departure by strengthening its links with the electoral managers at the Carlton Club and won a
measure of credit in the 1868 elections for the Conservatives' impressive
showing in London constituencies. Early in 1869, Marwood Tucker entered
into a partnership with Cubitt and Sir William Hart Dyke, the Tory whip, by
which he agreed 'to carry on the paper until the end of this year, and to pay all
current expenses up to that time, on receipt of certain sums from them'. On 26
November, he gave 'reasonable notice' to Disraeli of his intention to withdraw
on 31 December:

> Since April last we have succeeded in nearly trebling the circulation, and as
> a natural consequence, in raising the value of the advertisements – but we
> have, I regret to say, as yet failed in making the paper pay its way, and there
> is still a large weekly loss.

Dyke confirmed to Corry that Tucker, 'who has been working at it for nine
months without receiving a half-penny, strikes work on December 31 unless
some definite arrangement is arrived at in which case he will remain as editor'.
At the same time, Dyke proposed to relinquish his own holding for reasons of
health. He was confident that, with a bit of encouragement from 'the heads of
the party', a company might be formed to take control. 'I wish much to shew

[1] Elcho to Spencer, 16 January 1867, quoted in Lee, *Origins*, p. 150; Kebbel, *Lord Beaconsfield*, pp. 225–26; Disraeli to Derby, 14 March 1868, quoted in Buckle, *Disraeli*, IV, 518; *Newspaper Press*, September 1868.

you the list of Subscribers,' he told Corry; 'it will give you some idea of the effect it will have on the party (at this time) if the *Globe* comes suddenly to an end.'[1]

Members of the *Globe* staff were disconsolate. Dr J. Mortimer Granville, identifying himself as the author of some articles on the Irish Church that Disraeli had once commended, heard 'rumours at the Clubs and elsewhere that the paper is to stop at the end of the year'. He made so bold as to write to Disraeli on 9 December, expressing his conviction 'that the undertaking has never for a day been conducted on commercial principles: the principles upon which other journals are made to succeed'. A specialist in applied psychology, he volunteered to try his hand. The same day, Tucker called on Dyke, and 'could scarcely believe that nothing had as yet been done'. He wrote indignantly to Corry:

> It is useless to shut your eyes . . . to the fact that if Mr Disraeli cares himself to show an active interest in the matter (I do not mean by giving money) it is almost certain that arrangements could even now be made for carrying it on: but that unless *he does so* the affair is perfectly hopeless. . . . If it is my own connection with the *Globe* that is distasteful to Mr Disraeli, & you will only say so, I am perfectly ready to assist in the transfer of its management in future to somebody else: but let me impress upon you that under no editor can a paper go on without money, and that nothing but Mr Disraeli's *personal influence* will induce the party generally to find the necessary funds.[2]

Tucker had evidently run foul of Disraeli, who was unmoved by Cubitt's assurances that the editor was 'a gentleman and you may thoroughly trust him'. On the contrary, Tucker's gentility – he was a son-in-law of Beresford Hope and thus a member of the Cecil clan – cast doubts on his trustworthiness. Early in 1870, Granville replaced him. He was joined (probably in 1871) by Captain George Armstrong, secretary of the Westminster Conservative Association, who tended to the business affairs in which he had a stake. In the summer of 1874, Armstrong took over as proprietor and editor. 'It is now *finally decided* that I leave the *Globe*,' Granville told Corry on 11 July. 'The paper has I am informed become the property of Captain Armstrong and I am principally engaged in preparing for his personal assumption of the direct control.' Unable to procure Corry's assistance in obtaining another post, Granville applied to Delane for 'work of *any* kind': he had retired from the editorship of the *Globe*, he explained,

because the proprietorship changed and the present owner edits it himself.

[1] Tucker to Disraeli, 26 November 1869, and Dyke to Corry, two undated letters [December (?) 1869], Hughenden Papers.
[2] Granville to Disraeli, 9 December 1869, and Tucker to Corry, 9 December 1869, Hughenden Papers.

You will readily understand that having taken a position of control and responsibility on a Tory paper I am now practically cut off from writing for journals not of the same way of thinking.

His predicament was a further commentary on the precarious state of the Tory press.[1]

Despite its debility, the *Globe* weathered these storms. As Cubitt had anticipated, 'the alteration of the price & arrangements of the *Pall Mall Gazette*' in 1870 worked to the *Globe*'s advantage by removing, if only temporarily, its most formidable evening competitor. The Tory revival of the early '70s was probably still more decisive in effecting its rescue. W. T. Madge, who assisted Armstrong until 1907 and was himself proprietor from 1912 to 1914, appended his 'opinion as to the future of the *Globe*' to a financial statement dated 27 October 1875:

I have never taken a too sanguine view of our position & have contended that as an evening paper & as a purely speculative concern the *Globe* will hardly ever become a great success ...; yet I must confess I am agreeably surprised at the steady progress made towards making it at least self-supporting.

Calculating a 'total loss somewhat over £4,000' for the fifteen months under Armstrong's ownership, he nevertheless could not 'help saying it would be a great & suicidal blunder to drop or even sell the concern'.[2]

More resilient than either Tucker or Granville, Captain 'Tom' Hamber had a better claim to party patronage. Ejected from his chair at the *Standard*, he was compensated by an invitation to Hughenden. 'I thank you sincerely for your kind appreciation of whatever support I have been able to give,' he replied to Disraeli. 'More powerful, I fear, it might have been. It could not have been, I know, more truthful; nor, I may add, more considerately recompensed.' Hamber next devoted his energies to the *Conservative*, a weekly that Escott quaintly described to William Blackwood as 'a wealthy man's organ, ... fairly progressive in its features'. It ran from October 1872 until December 1873. After it was launched, and before it capsized, Hamber informed Disraeli that he had another 'newspaper enterprise of some magnitude on hand, with reference to which I should like very much to ask your advice on one or two points'. This was the *Hour*, a new morning paper, which made its first appearance on 24 March 1873. Escott, who left the *Standard* to resume collaboration with Hamber ('with whom I have had a close connection of five years'

[1] Cubitt to Disraeli, 11 January [1870], Hughenden Papers (dated from internal evidence); 'The Evening Newspapers,' *Nation* (New York), 7 October 1880; Granville to Corry, 11 July 1874, Hughenden Papers; Granville to Delane, 1 December 1874, *Times* Archives. On 25 March 1876, Granville thanked Disraeli for 'help, wholly unexpected', during 'my enforced idleness' (Hughenden Papers).
[2] Cubitt to Disraeli, 11 January [1870], Hughenden Papers; Madge to Armstrong, 27 October 1875, Hambleden Papers; obituary of Madge, *The Times*, 31 January 1927.

standing'), apprised Blackwood of its progress: 'The paper has made a good start, is being generally taken up, & will, I doubt not, prove in the long run a success' (29 March 1873); 'The success of the *Hour*, I am glad to say, is no longer problematical' (6 May 1873). His optimism quickly dissipated. 'Ostensibly... Evangelical Protestantism's organ', owing to the largesse of a Presbyterian clergyman, the *Hour* made little headway against the *Standard*, since 1869 relieved of the encumbrance of the *Morning Herald*.[1]

The 'insolvency' of D. M. Evans, a former colleague on the *Standard* and a principal subscriber, was a setback to the *Hour*: 'He deceived both Hamber & myself as to the amt. of capital he had to support it,' Escott complained to Blackwood on 9 January 1874. Finding the remaining 'capital ... insufficient to the enormous outlay incidental to the conduct of a London daily paper', Hamber was 'compelled to look about for new resources'. To this end, he wrote on 18 May 1874 to beg Disraeli's 'support of the proposal I have to submit to you': a 'well known banker' had offered 'a sufficient sum ... provided the hint be given to him from good quarters that the work ... will be well regarded by the heads of the party'. A message from Disraeli, 'however indirectly given', would surely do the trick: 'Am I asking too much in soliciting that word?' Either Disraeli declined to grant this 'personal favour' or Hamber had misjudged its effect; the former was more probable. On 17 September 1875, Hamber announced despondently to Lord Salisbury that

> the *Hour* has failed. It has not sufficient capital; it is in the wrong hands. Even if it survives occasional crises, it can never be of service to the party or a credit to London journalism under its present régime. I find myself, having given up the best of my life to Conservative journalism, powerless as to the future yet full of power & will to work. ...

And, the following August, Disraeli reportedly 'heard with a pang that the *Hour* was no more'.[2]

Down, but not out, Hamber surfaced in 1877 as editor of the *Morning Advertiser*, which had conveniently changed its politics. Five years later, his journalistic career ended, where it had begun, in the bankruptcy courts. On 25 July 1882, he informed Salisbury (who responded with a cheque for £100) of his 'great distress ... : to-day I have been arrested and am in custody' of the sheriffs. Thereafter, he disappeared, a broken man. In 1890, Mudford, his successor at the *Standard*, was asked by Salisbury for information about the son of 'the late' Captain Hamber. 'He was alive six weeks ago, & I have not

[1] Hamber to Disraeli, 30 October 1870 and 7 February 1873, Hughenden Papers; Escott to Blackwood, 30 December 1872, 24 February, 15 and 29 March, and 6 May 1873, Blackwood Papers; Escott, *Press, Platform,* p. 252; E[scott], 'Politics and the Press,' *Fraser's Magazine*, n.s. xii (1875), 43.

[2] Escott to Blackwood, 9 January 1874, Blackwood Papers; Hamber to Disraeli, 18 May 1874, Hughenden Papers; Hamber to Salisbury, 17 September 1875, Salisbury Papers; Escott, *Masters*, p. 204.

heard of his death,' Mudford replied. 'I do not know anything of the son. . . . I knew a good deal of the father, twenty years ago, but your enquiry does not refer to him. I will just add, I am glad it does not.'[1]

These dislocations, personal and professional, were a source of perpetual anxiety to younger Conservatives, who wanted to appeal more effectively to an enlarged electorate. With Gorst in the chair, the National Union of Conservative and Constitutional Associations held its first conference on 12 November 1867. Among the aims it promulgated was 'to increase and multiply the influence of the Conservative Press throughout the United Kingdom'. In a vigorous debate, one delegate 'advocated the claims of . . . the *British Lion* . . . the only weekly paper properly and thoroughly representing our views'. A motion to assist that journal was moved and seconded, but withdrawn on the grounds that it was 'scarcely politic' for the conference to be 'pinning their faith to any particular paper'. Needless to say, it would have been a humiliation to acknowledge a reliance on so obscure a publication. The proceedings reflected the dichotomy in Conservatism's approach to the press. At the constituency level, there was an obsession with 'the pernicious doctrines which such papers as *Lloyd's* and *Reynold's* spread on Saturday nights through the length & breadth of the land'; in the higher echelons, as Gorst's political advisership to the *Standard* was soon to demonstrate, there was greater concern for the views that filtered through the smoke-filled clubrooms along Pall Mall.[2]

The secretary of the Reform Club, 'stating that the supply of Newspapers had gone on steadily increasing for the past two years', appointed a subcommittee on 3 May 1867 'to enquire into the whole matter of Newspaper supply'. The club's minute-books record the fluctuations in the market. 'Upon request', two additional copies of the *Daily News* were ordered on 1 December 1865, 'making in all 6 copies taken daily, . . . an adequate supply' in the opinion of the general committee. In 1866, two copies of the *Sunday Gazette* ('a new weekly paper to appear on the 7 inst.') were ordered on 5 January. In 1867, four copies of the *Day* were taken in from 22 March 'until further notice', and two copies of the *Chronicle* ('a newly issued weekly') were added on 12 April; neither lasted long. The *Pall Mall Gazette* was especially popular: from 7 February 1868, 'two extra copies' were acquired 'for the use of the Upper Library' during the parliamentary session; and, from 1 January 1870, four copies of its 'new issue' were 'taken in each day', with the supply of the '*Sun* evening paper reduced to 2 copies daily'. As elsewhere, the *Pall Mall Gazette* did not find favour in its reincarnation as a morning newspaper: on 4 February, it was decided that 'the daily supply . . . be reduced to 10 copies,

---

[1] Hamber to Salisbury, 25 July 1882, Salisbury Papers; Hamber to Stebbing, 30 December 1877, *Times* Collection (University of Texas); Mudford to Salisbury [21 February 1890], Salisbury Papers.
[2] National Union minutes, 12 November 1867.

Charles Dickens, editor of the newly hatched *Daily News*, among the strutting peacocks of Fleet Street. – *Mephistopheles*, 1 January 1846

The French Emperor, with *Le Moniteur* in his back pocket, dispenses bribes to the *Morning Post*. The *Standard* and the *Morning Herald* wait their turns. – *Punch*, 15 February 1856

A TORY PARTY! (SAVE THE MARK.)

Mrs. Harris (a struggling Newsvendor). "STANERD! STANERD! ONLY A PENNY! PLEASE SUPPORT AN OLD 'OOMAN, DEAR GENTS!"
D–rby (to Dizzy). "FOR GOODNESS SAKE GIVE HER A PENNY, AND TELL THE OLD GOOSE WE DON'T WANT HER CACKLE—PEOPLE WILL THINK SHE BELONGS TO US—JUST OPPOSITE THE CLUB TOO!"

Lord Derby and Disraeli try to avoid the impression that the *Standard* ('Mrs Harris')
is in their pay. – *Punch*, 3 May 1862

The *Times* and Sir
Moses Montefiore,
the philanthropist,
celebrate their 100th
birthdays. Sir Moses
died seven months
later. – *Punch*,
10 January 1885

TWO CENTENARIANS.

SIR MOSES MONTEFIORE CONGRATULATES THE *TIMES* ON REACHING
ITS 100TH YEAR.

A WORD WITH JOHN BRIGHT.

To the Tune of " John Brown."

Since a penny I can spend, for the *Star*
      I'll quickly send,
'Tis the paper that reports your speeches best,
      JOHN BRIGHT:
There doubtless I shall find a reflex of your mind,
Which from jar and jangle never seems to rest, JOHN
      BRIGHT.
Tho' of war you disapprove, a wordy war you love,
And oft in this your prowess you have shown, JOHN
      BRIGHT;
But it sorrows me to see that, 'spite of good advice
      from me,
The country you most fight with is your own, JOHN
      BRIGHT.

Some faults we may have got : we've shortcomings, who has not ?
      Are your Yankee clients all from failing free, JOHN BRIGHT ?
But JOHN BULL upon the whole is a very worthy soul, '
      And I wish the world were all as good as he, JOHN BRIGHT.
Let others vent their spite, and vow we ne'er act right :
      There are many our prosperity offends, JOHN BRIGHT :
We may safely trust our foes our errors to expose,
      And we need no ill-judged censure from our friends, JOHN BRIGHT.

I hate as much as you the silly boastful crew,
      Who vaunt our very vices to the skies, JOHN BRIGHT :
But they who snarl and sneer when from error we are clear,
      Such critics I most heartily despise, JOHN BRIGHT.
I hate the bunkum trick of rowdy rhetoric,
      That blackens with a breath the whitest acts, JOHN BRIGHT :
And I hate the carping tongue, that twists right into wrong,
      And from wisest deeds maliciously detracts, JOHN BRIGHT.

So prithee mend your ways, nor old England so dispraise,
      Of unpatriotic rancour clear your breast, JOHN BRIGHT :
While in comfort here you live, to JOHN BULL some credit give,
      'Tis an evil bird that fouleth its own nest, JOHN BRIGHT.
If Yankeeland you love all other lands above,
      Why not hasten to that Eden o'er the sea, JOHN BRIGHT ?
Prithee go and fraternise with the people you so prize,
      Who may value you more highly than do we, JOHN BRIGHT.

A Song of John Bright and the *Morning Star*. – *Punch*, 8 April 1865

A TIMES-LY CAUTION.

Dr. Times (with affectionate severity). NOW, MY DEAR MASTER RANDOLPH, REMEMBER THAT THE ERRORS OF YOUR PAST CAREER HAVE BEEN NEITHER FEW NOR SMALL. DO NOT LET ME HEAR OF YOUR REPEATING THEM. BE CAREFUL TO AVOID ANYTHING LIKE LEVITY, ILL-TEMPER, OR ANY FORM OF INDISCRETION : AND I TRUST YOU WILL DO YOUR BEST TO RISE TO THE LEVEL OF YOUR NEW POSITION AS CAPTAIN OF THE LOWER SCHOOL, FROM WHICH I HOPE I SHALL NOT HAVE TO SEND YOU DOWN FOR BAD CONDUCT. NOW, GO !"

The Times scolds Lord Randolph Churchill for parliamentary misconduct. – *Punch,*
28 August 1886

TACKING—"READY ABOUT!"

The General Election of 1880: the *Daily News* (upper right) takes an 'advanced Radical tack'; *The Times* in the foreground tips ominously; and the *Standard* and the *Daily Telegraph* (upper left) steer a smooth Tory course. – *Punch*, 17 April 1880

PENANCE!

"HIS HONOUR ROOTED IN DISHONOUR STOOD,
AND FAITH UNFAITHFUL MADE HIM FALSELY TRUE."—TENNYSON.

The Times repents for its publication of the Pigott forgeries. – *Punch*, 9 March 1889

"TEACHING THE YOUNG IDEA."

Shade of Jack Sheppard to Shade of Dick Turpin. "THEY SAY IT'S US AS UPSET THE YOUNGSTERS; BUT, BLESS THEIR SIMPLE 'ARTS, WE AIN'T IN IT NOWADAYS WITH THE PAPERS THAT ARE BOUGHT AND READ BY EVERYONE EVERYWHERE!"

– Punch, 26 January 1889

– Punch, 4 October 1890

JOURNALISM IN FRANCE.   JOURNALISM IN ENGLAND.
(A CONTRAST.)

Robert Lowe, the
leader-writing MP and
Cabinet Minister.
'An enemy to democracy,
yet a professor of liberal
principles, which tend to
democracy; the combination
will one day make him
Prime Minister of England.'
– *Vanity Fair*, 27 February
1869 (Mansell Collection)

Alfred Austin, leader-
writer for the *Standard*,
whom Lord Salisbury
appointed Poet Laureate
'because he wanted it
so much'. – *Punch*,
10 October 1896

THE POET-LAUREATE ON TURKEY.

[" You are not alone in the opinion you appear to entertain that it is in-
cumbent on me, by virtue of the office I have the honour to fill, not to remain altogether silent when the entire nation is palpitating with wrath at
atrocious massacres that have occurred in Armenia," &c., &c.—*Mr. A.
Austin's letter to a correspondent, quoted by the Westminster Gazette.*]

and that six additional copies of the *Echo* and two additional copies of the *Globe* be taken instead'. The premium put on club readership was illustrated by the case of the *Farmer's Newspaper*, 'regularly forwarded ... gratis' to the Oxford and Cambridge Club, yet never displayed on the table in the morning room. After an investigation, the secretary reported on 21 June 1867 that the hall porter, on his own initiative, had destroyed all unsolicited journals. It is unlikely that the *British Lion* would have been allowed to cross the threshold.

About this time, the *Saturday Review* underwent a change of ownership and editorship. Although, true to its word, it never 'ranged itself under the banner of some one or other of the rival politicians who are struggling for power and place' (12 June 1858), it was a voice of moderate Conservatism. Early in 1866, it lost the esteemed services of Lord Cranborne (previously Lord Robert Cecil and later 3rd Marquess of Salisbury), who was finding politics a full-time job. His brother-in-law, Beresford Hope, came to the same conclusion: after two unsuccessful candidacies, he was returned for Stoke in 1865 and for Cambridge University in 1868. Proprietor of the *Review* since its birth in 1855, he had come to find it 'a great bore' and was dissatisfied with the 'abnormal' editorial methods of J. D. Cook, who made it a rule to employ 'the Liberals to write on the matters where they were most Conservative, and the Conservatives on topics which they could treat liberally'. Cook's death in August 1868 ended the old order.[1]

Beresford Hope, if he could be classified as such, was not the only member of the journalistic fraternity who stood for Parliament in the general election of 1868. John Jaffray, editor of the *Birmingham Daily Post*, was a candidate in East Staffordshire. W. H. Russell contested Chelsea as 'a Conservative on independent principles', much to the mystification of Delane, who asked him: 'Do you really mean to go to the poll? Or are you making a diversion for some Tory swell?' *The Times* was disposed to take more seriously the fight of John Walter, branded 'unsound' for his support of Disraeli's foreign policy, to hold his Berkshire seat: 'though market day', there were 'scarcely 50 present' to hear the address of Walter's Tory opponent (13 July); but Walter's own address 'was received with loud and continued cheering' in a hall 'filled by a most respectable and attentive auditory' (26 September). Delane also promoted Godfrey Lushington at Abingdon. 'He seems proud of having written for us – so perhaps it will be well to encourage him a bit,' he suggested to Dasent, who boosted Lushington (14 November) as 'one who deserved the highest praise any political man could have – that of being "the working man's friend"'. There were numerous other candidates who were connected in various capacities with the newspaper world. For the time being, Leonard

[1] Cook to Cranborne, 8 January 1866, Salisbury Papers; Bevington, *Saturday Review*, p. 35; Charles Pearson, *Memorials* (ed. W. Stebbing; London, 1900), p. 89.

Courtney was not among them, though he contemplated standing at St Ives as 'an Independent Liberal'.[1]

Yet, as Wemyss Reid knew from firsthand experience in the reporters' gallery, where he doubled as the representative of the *Leeds Mercury* and the *Morning Star*, 'a gulf that was regarded as impassable divided the members of the Press from the members of the House'. Long after politics had come to be recognized as a respectable as well as a serious pursuit, those who plied the trade of political journalism could not scrape the mire of Grub Street from their boots. Even on the political left, where the distinction between intellectuals and publicists tended to blur (Morley, Courtney, and Frank Hill of the *Daily News* hobnobbed with Mill), a bias persisted against working, as opposed to thinking, journalists. It required an amendment of Reform Club statutes in 1877 to admit provincial and Scottish editors to membership. That Rosebery should offer to propose him under these provisions was, Cooper said, 'for me and for the *Scotsman* a great honour'. Mudford, typically, was more haughty. No sooner had he joined the Carlton in 1879 than he threatened to resign because Rowland Winn, a member of the government who had seconded his nomination, publicly attacked the *Standard*.[2]

It was all very well for Anthony Trollope to proclaim in the editorial introduction to the first number of *Saint Paul's* (October 1867) that 'he and his friends who will work with him intend to be political, – thinking that of all the studies to which men and women can attach themselves, that of politics is the first and finest'. These noble sentiments were qualified by Edward Dicey in the third number of that monthly journal:

> It is no exaggeration to say that many journalists who have produced articles which have been talked about day after day, and week after week, for many a long year, are less known to the general public than the second-rate actors at a minor theatre.

And, he might have added, they were often considered as no more socially acceptable. Trollope, as the creator of the unsavoury Quintus Slide, editor of the *People's Banner*, did little to improve the popular image of the profession.

The prevailing system of anonymous journalism was cited alternately as the cause and consequence of this disrepute. Writing with self-conscious anonymity in *Saint Paul's* five months later, Leslie Stephen whiggishly predicted that

> if journalism continues to progress in influence and dignity as it has done for the last few generations, it will shake off the traditionary stigma which clings

---

[1] Atkins, *Russell*, II, 151–52; Delane to Dasent, 25 September [1868], *Times* Archives; Courtney to his father, 6 July [1868], Courtney Papers.

[2] Reid, *Memoirs* (London, 1905), p. 123; L. Fagan, *The Reform Club* (London, 1887), p. 112; Mudford to Corry, 17 April 1879, Hughenden Papers; *Sheffield Daily Telegraph*, 16 April 1879; Cooper to Rosebery, 4 February 1881, Rosebery Papers. Secretary of the Carlton Club to the author, 19 August 1977.

to it. If it should rise in public estimation, there would no longer be the same innocent excuse for anonymous writing.

Morley, as befitting a Radical, put the case more bluntly in the *Fortnightly Review*: 'The immense predominance of helpless men' in Parliament 'will throw an ever-increasing power into the hands of journalists', who functioned namelessly and therefore without accountability.

The more stupid and incapable the man, the greater his reliance on the press; the less his power of forming an opinion for himself, the greater his obligation to those who will form an opinion for him. . . . We shall be governed by leading articles. . . . Every editor in London will be a minister without portfolio.

More than a recapitulation of Cobden's earlier arguments against *The Times*, the debate affirmed the growing influence that journalists – and specifically London journalists – were presumed to wield. To Morley, there was nothing innocent about these procedures. Not without justification, Lord Lytton urged him to bring his 'naturally robust practicableness and strong civic sense' to the parliamentary arena: 'The publicist who never condescends to be a politician is in danger of becoming a *doctrinaire*.' Conversely, a politician who held aloof from the press was increasingly in danger of becoming an anachronism.[1]

*   *   *

Liberalism's resounding victory in the 1868 elections, bringing Gladstone to power with a ministry that contained such disparate talents as Lowe and Bright ('the two most important members of the Administration in the House of Commons', tartly commented the *Pall Mall Gazette* on 9 December, and 'neither . . . likely to prove a sure stay'), gave a fillip to Liberal journalism. New properties were established, and pre-existing ones were refurbished. In Parliament as in the press, this buoyancy was not long to last. But, while it did, the spirit was intoxicating.

In its 'own humble opinion', the *Pall Mall Gazette* (9 December) thought the new government 'as well proportioned and as strong' as any Gladstone might have assembled. It took pleasure in noting 'symptoms of discontent . . . in several of the Radical journals' with the number of key portfolios that went to elderly Whig noblemen. The *Standard* had no complaint on that score, but quibbled that the right people had been put in the wrong places: 'The Cabinet Mr Gladstone has formed gives little promise of a long and vigorous life,' it mistakenly observed on the 12th, 'but the Cabinet which his Radical advisers

[1] *Saint Paul's*, i (October 1867), 4, and (December 1867), 315; ii (May 1868), 230; 'Old Parties and New Policy,' *Fortnightly Review*, n.s. iv (September 1868), 327. Contributors to *Saint Paul's* are identified in the *Wellesley Index to Victorian Periodicals* (ed. W. Houghton; Toronto, 1979), III, 365–67. Lytton to Morley, July 1873, in *Personal and Literary Letters of Robert, First Earl of Lytton* (ed. Lady B. Balfour; London, 1906), I, 308.

wanted him to form would certainly have broken up in a very few months.' The *Pall Mall Gazette* accepted Lord Clarendon's return to the Foreign Office as 'simply inevitable'; the *Spectator* put it down as a mistake. The *Morning Post* deplored the inclusion of Bright (which the *Morning Star* celebrated and *The Times* accepted in good grace), taking solace (as did the *Pall Mall Gazette*) in the appointment to the War Office of Cardwell, whom the *Spectator* dismissed as 'out of his element'. The *Daily News*, sharing the *Standard*'s regret that no position was found for W. E. Forster, who became vice-president for education in 1870, took particular satisfaction in the selection of Lord Spencer as Irish viceroy. It was clearly impossible for the Prime Minister to satisfy all those who aspired to office, let alone the conflicting claims lodged on their behalf.

On 8 December 1868, the day before the new Cabinet was sworn in, the *Echo* was hawked on London streets by brigades of boys in specially designed uniforms. Their odd tunics were quickly replaced by sensible caps, but the problem of distribution remained. W. H. Smith, who had opened his railway stalls to the *Day*, closed them to the *Echo*, the first halfpenny evening journal; and, until halfpenny stamps were issued in 1870, the post was prohibitive.

'We sought to make a newspaper, smaller, but for its size, as novel as any in existence,' recalled Arthur Arnold, its first editor. He had stationed 'a trusty friend' in Catherine Street, off the Strand, to test the reaction of the crowd on the first day of sale. 'It a'int 'arf as big as the *Telegraph*,' a disgruntled customer was overheard to remark. On 12 January 1869, the four-page *Echo* doubled its size, and began to flourish.

Arnold, later knighted for his services as chairman of the London County Council, was editor for seven years. As manager, Horace Voules was the intermediary between him and the proprietary firm of Cassell, Petter, and Galpin, whose publications already included several inexpensive literary weeklies and monthlies. Cheap in price, the *Echo* was highly regarded for its cultural content. It was also distinguished by its 'independent Liberal' principles, so described by James Grant, who knew 'no phrase that would designate them more fitly.... A liberal vein pervades the political views of the *Echo*', he explained in 1871; 'but its thorough independence often leads it to assume attitudes of antagonism to the present Liberal Government, as it would induce it to extend occasional support to a Tory Administration, were such in existence.' On Irish issues, for example, the paper stood 'somewhat in advance' of the Gladstonian position. It did not endear itself to either set of whips by making it a practice to obtain and publish division lists 'whenever there were important proceedings in the House of Commons'. From Charles Villiers, an old friend, Arnold obtained 'gossip concerning the "governing classes" which was of utmost value', and, on one occasion, an advance copy of the Queen's Speech. From Lord Granville, he collected 'hints' on foreign policy. But his most profound debt was to Mill, to whose stepdaughter he wrote a touching letter of condolence in 1873:

It is not more than a year or two since I told Mr Mill that when I was a child I thought he ought to be King of England & that if I had changed my mind, in manhood, it was only because I had ceased to believe in absolute and individual government.[1]

Known to Gladstone as the author of a book on the Lancashire 'cotton famine', Arnold was invited to stand at Huntingdon in an 1873 by-election in order to deny the Tory candidate an unopposed return. Beaten by a smaller margin than expected, he won praise from Gladstone for 'a brave effort'. In the 1880 Parliament, he sat for Salford. By then, his editorial career had ended. He resigned in 1875, when his proprietors sold out to 'Baron' Albert Grant, the financier and former Tory MP. Gladstone was among those who expressed regret:

The Liberal Press of London is (in my opinion) by no means so redundant in healthy principle or vigorous action as to be able to dispense even tolerably with the aid of a newspaper so widely circulated and so honourably and ably conducted as the *Echo*.

Grant, whose fortunes waxed and waned, gave up within a year, and the *Echo* returned to the Liberal fold under the control of J. Passmore Edwards, whom Massingham billed as 'undoubtedly one of the kings of modern newspaper enterprise'.[2]

Proud that Gladstone had chosen the *Echo* as his medium for a reply to a point of literary criticism in *The Times*, Edwards launched a fund in 1878 to present the leading Liberal, then retired as Liberal leader, with an ornamental axe to commemorate his sixty-ninth birthday. When Gladstone was ill, the *Echo* reported – with a pair of exclamation marks to denote incredulity – that two Tory opponents had called to enquire about his health. Entrusting editorial control to Howard Evans, Edwards pursued his own political ambitions. Defeated at Truro in 1868, he was elected at Salisbury in 1880. Two years later, he sold two-thirds of his shareholding in the *Echo* to a syndicate headed by Andrew Carnegie and Samuel Storey, the Liberal MP for Sunderland. According to Fleet Street gossip, he 'pretended he was making a large profit out of the little paper – £40,000 was the price he got'. Differences arose 'over matters of opinion and methods of management', and Edwards, who had not found Parliament 'such a fruitful field for usefulness as I expected', vacated his seat in 1882, and (probably in 1885) repurchased 'full command' of the *Echo*

[1] Grant, II, 122–23; 'The Founding of the *Echo*' (recollections of Sir Arthur Arnold and Horace Voules, *Echo*, 8 December 1898; Arnold to Helen Taylor, 18 May 1873, Mill-Taylor Collection VIII/114.

[2] *Gladstone Diaries*, VI, 292 (26 July 1864) and 386 (23 September 1865); Gladstone to Arnold [1875], quoted in the *Echo*, 8 December 1898; Massingham, *London Daily Press*, pp. 188–89; J. Passmore Edwards, *A Few Footprints* (London, 1906), pp. 38–42.

for £5,000 above the amount he had been paid for it. Evans, 'a Nonconformist of a singularly energetic type', returned to the editorial office that Aaron Watson had briefly tenanted. For the next dozen years, the paper thrived under the restored régime of Edwards, who wrote a high proportion of its articles. Respect for Gladstone did not deter it from endorsing Radical social programmes, from castigating his intervention in Egypt, or from embracing the Unionist cause in Ireland.[1]

The weekly *Examiner*, more directly pervaded by a spirit of Millite independence, led an equally chequered career. Albany Fonblanque, after a hapless attempt to renovate the property, sold it in 1867 to William Torrens McCullagh, who preferred to be known as McCullagh Torrens. By either name, he did not do the paper much good. Apart from lowering the price from sixpence to threepence, he 'did not change the shape or plan', with the result (according to Fox Bourne) that 'in his hands the *Examiner* lost all that was left of its old character and influence'. Late in 1870, when 'the paper had sunk to its lowest ebb, ... the copyright was bought by a too sanguine Radical, who hoped that, with the scanty means at his disposal, he might be able to restore it'. Modesty forbade Fox Bourne from identifying this individual as himself. On 7 January 1871, the *Examiner* reverted to the 'shape in which it appeared before 1838', vowing fidelity to 'time-honoured principles and traditions' that had not lost their power to render 'much useful service to the cause of progress'.[2]

With Mill, Swinburne, and Mrs Millicent Fawcett among its contributors, the *Examiner* gained immeasurably in esteem, but insufficiently in revenue. A circular of 1873 assessed its accomplishments and difficulties over the preceding three years:

> The *Examiner* passed into new hands in January 1871, and since that time its conductors have endeavored in pursuance of the tradition and practice of its early proprietors, to make it a thoroughly independent organ of Radical opinion in political, social, and theological questions.... The circulation ... has been considerably increased and its influence has increased in a yet higher ratio.

Additional funding was required for the expansion of facilities, publicity, and, possibly, a series of commissioned pamphlets. 'The present time appears to be especially opportune for making this effort', as the approaching elections could be expected to stimulate 'more energetic discussion ... of the political and other questions with which the *Examiner* concerns itself'.[3]

---

[1] Edwards to Gladstone, 19 December 1878, Gladstone Papers, Add. MSS. 44,458, fols. 239–40; 'The Evening Newspapers,' *Nation* (New York), 9 October 1880; Robert Wilson to Escott, 26 September 1882, Escott Papers. The *Echo* was still in their possession on 5 November 1884, when Carnegie commended it to Storey as 'highly creditable, one *must* read it'. (Copy; Carnegie Papers.)
[2] Fox Bourne, II, 288–91; Grant, III, 52–53.
[3] Circular signed by Edward Dallons [October] 1873, Mill-Taylor Collection IV/93–94.

On 5 May 1873, Fox Bourne thanked Mill for his articles, and reflected: 'I do not know whether the paper is worth assisting in any other way.' Noting that Helen Taylor, Mill's stepdaughter, had 'recurred the other day to her former plan of starting a paper', he wondered whether she might consider 'the *Examiner* worth taking up in lieu of this'. Beset by financial worries, Fox Bourne professed 'that I should very much prefer it passing to her hands than any others as that would ensure its being carried on in the way I want, and very much better than I could do it'. The next day, Mill died, and the *Examiner* filled a double number on 17 May with memorial tributes to him.[1]

Fox Bourne did not find it easy to deal with Miss Taylor. Hoping not to 'seem impertinent' by intruding on her grief, he waited until July before 'reminding you of a letter you were good enough to write to me from Avignon, with reference to the possibility of your taking some interest in the *Examiner*'. Her mother's daughter, she strenuously objected when he quoted in a circular, 'sent to a few friends of the paper', a commendation from her late stepfather. In fact, that document did not exaggerate the concern shown by Mill, who had 'pressed' Morley and Frederic Harrison to lend assistance. Harrison proposed that Admiral F. A. Maxse should give £10,000 – ten times the amount he had offered – to assume custody and install Morley as editor. But Morley demurred, knowing full well that anything he could do 'won't be enough to make the paper a *power*; and if it is not a power, why waste money in supporting a puling journal like that?'[2]

After further exchanges, Fox Bourne wrote on 21 November 1873 to acquaint Miss Taylor with 'a new circumstance': P. A. Taylor, a Liberal MP for Leicester and no relation to her, 'was willing to buy the paper', and negotiations were in progress. Within weeks, the sale was concluded. Too late, Helen Taylor had second thoughts. 'I agree with you in regretting very much the fate of the *Examiner*,' Professor J. E. Cairnes told her on 13 December.

> Though I have a very great respect and regard for Mr P. Taylor, I do not think he is a man in whose hands a newspaper is likely to prosper. I thought the opening number showed a great want of strength. From what I hear, I fear Mr Fox Bourne is a great loser by the whole business. His case is I think a very distressing one.

Before long, the *Examiner* again changed hands. Fox Bourne's testimony that the new owner was Lord Rosebery is impossible to corroborate and, in many ways, implausible. Yet there is no disputing his verdict that the journal 'was

[1] Fox Bourne to Mill, 5 May 1873, Mill-Taylor Collection II/621 ff.
[2] Fox Bourne to Helen Taylor, 23 July, 8 and 23 October 1873, Mill-Taylor Collection IV/87–92; Morley to Harrison, and Harrison to Morley [April (?) 1873], quoted in Hirst, *Morley*, pp. 242–43, 253.

allowed to die ingloriously in 1880'. Four years later, with Michael Davitt, Helen Taylor started the *Democrat*.[1]

At the same time that John Morley brushed aside the *Examiner*, he referred respectfully to the *Bee-Hive*. That weekly, a veteran of the trade-unionist campaigns of the 1860s, was acquired in 1869 by Samuel Morley, the Liberal philanthropist and MP. Engels was aghast that 'the only working-class paper which existed could be bought up by a bourgeois', a hosier, to be precise. The logic of events, however, was to foster Lib-Lab consensus. George Potter stayed on as editor under the supervision of the Rev Henry Solly, a Unitarian who promoted the working men's institute movement. On 19 February 1870, the new *Bee-Hive* professed its intention 'to render essential service to Working Men Candidates, and other Liberal Candidates for Parliament, by articles in its columns and by fully reporting their speeches on working-class topics'. Far from a repudiation of working-class ideals, let alone a betrayal of working-class interests, this proclamation signalled the convergence beneath the proverbial Liberal umbrella, of middle-class 'ultra' Radicalism (as endowed and personified by Samuel Morley) and fledgling trade unionism.[2]

Samuel Morley also played a part in revitalizing the *Daily News*, its voice having grown muffled and indistinct. On 8 June 1868, the paper slashed its price to a penny, which increased both its popularity and its operating deficit. Soon thereafter, a new company was formed to ensure an adequate supply of capital. 'The proprietors ... , a small syndicate which never exceeded ten men, were a mixed body, hardly any two of whom had anything in common,' recalled Sir John Robinson, who managed the enterprise. Among the charter members, three were dominant: Arnold Morley, Samuel's son and a future Liberal chief whip; Henry Oppenheim, a financier 'with politics of no very decided kind'; and Henry Labouchere, a flamboyant Radical recently displaced from the Commons. Thomas Walker, whose health was failing, vacated the editorship in October: Gladstone rewarded him with a berth on the *London Gazette*. Edward Dicey filled in until 1870, when Frank Hill formally succeeded. Presently, the circulation gained from the paper's outstanding coverage of the Franco-Prussian war: in a single week, the daily sale was said to have trebled from 50,000 to 150,000 copies. The dispatches of Archibald Forbes won great admiration, though perhaps not as much popular attention as the sensational letters penned by Labouchere, a 'besieged resident' in Paris during the conflict. Mowbray Morris, the manager of *The Times*, could not 'help feeling that the *Daily News* has beaten us on several important occasions,

---

[1] Fox Bourne to Helen Taylor, 21 November 1873, and Cairnes to Helen Taylor, 13 December 1873, Mill-Taylor Collection IV/ 95–96, 112–14; Fox Bourne, II, 291.

[2] Stephen Coltham, 'The *Bee-Hive* newspaper: its origins and early struggles,' in A. Briggs and J. Saville, eds., *Essays in Labour History*, I (London, 1960), 174–204; Engels to Marx, 30 July 1869, quoted in Harrison, *Poor Men's Guardians*, pp. 145–46; *also see* Hanham, *Elections and Party Management*, ch. 15.

both in speed & quality. Altogether,' he admitted to Walter, 'I fear we have not done well in this war.'[1]

Labouchere had occasionally contributed pieces to the *Daily News* before he purchased Henry Rawson's quarter share of the proprietorship for an estimated £14,000. He sold out in 1892 for a sum that has been put as high as £92,000, and no lower than '£62,000 or thereabouts'. Less remuneratively, he speculated in theatrical property and other newspaper investments. After a stint as financial editor of the weekly *World*, he started his own weekly, *Truth*, in 1876. Especially after his return to Parliament in 1880, he was 'strangely uninterested . . . in the affairs of the paper which he was supposed by the public to direct'; instead he delegated responsibility to successive editors, including Horace Voules and R. A. Bennett, who pointed up this irony. 'I have not seen the par[agraph] in *Truth* to which you allude,' Labouchere candidly replied late in the century to Moberly Bell of *The Times*, 'for I very seldom look through proofs that are not of my own writing.' Nor, he added, had he seen a particular item in the *Daily News*, 'as I seldom look at the paper, which seems to me to be conducted on the lines of a provincial weekly journal edited by a Nonconformist & a committee of elders'.[2]

To the readers of *Truth*, Labouchere offered an explanation for the severance of his ties with the *Daily News*:

> On Mr Gladstone's retirement, the party, or rather a majority of the officialdom of the party became tainted with Birmingham imperialism. My convictions did not allow me to be connected with a newspaper which supported a clique of intriguers that had captured the Liberal ship, and that accepted blindly these intriguers as the representatives of Liberalism in regard to our foreign policy.

It would be a mistake to accept this version literally, still more to infer that the *Daily News* had given unwavering support to Gladstone. Under no such delusion, Gladstone wrote stiffly to the editor on 14 May 1870:

> Having been accustomed in former years to look to the *Daily News* for accuracy & justice, I once (and it is the only instance of such an appeal during my life) appealed to it when I thought the Editor had fallen into an injurious error concerning me, and I received a most liberal reparation.

That morning, he insisted, the paper had misrepresented his views on the pol-

---

[1] Robinson, *Fifty Years*, p. 375; Robinson and McCarthy, *The 'Daily News' Jubilee* (London, 1896), pp. 61, 78–79, 93–94; Walker to Gladstone, 4 October 1869, Gladstone Papers, Add. MSS. 44,422, fol. 114; A. Thorold, *Life of Labouchere* (London, 1913), p. 87; Morris to Walter, 24 September 1870, *Times* Archives. Morris came to be less impressed by the *Daily News*'s reports from Paris: 'The *D.N.* publishes something purporting to be from inside the city', he wrote to W. H. Russell during the days of the Commune; 'on a careful examination of the article, I am convinced it is a fraud. At any rate, we could have written every word of it here, in P. H. Sqr.' (*Times* Archives.)

[2] R. A. Bennett, 'Mr Labouchere as a Journalist' and statement by Lionel Robinson, quoted in Thorold, *Labouchere*, 88–89, 444 ff.; Labouchere to Bell, 24 November [n.d.], *Times* Archives.

itical disabilities of women, and he sought to counteract this mischief by providing facts 'intended for suggestion, and not for controversy'. Three years
later, Professor Cairnes availed himself of the columns of the *Daily News* to
denounce Gladstone's Irish University Education Bill. For 'a journal which
might have been expected to deal favourably with any proposal made by the
Government' to level criticism, however 'courteous and cautious', was considered 'decidedly damaging'. As Gladstone's first premiership neared its end,
the attacks intensified. A leading article on 7 January 1874 defended Sir
Charles Dilke, the Radical MP and incidentally one of the paper's 'special correspondents', for views 'conscientiously formed and unreservedly expressed'
with regard to the government's performance in general and its civil list in particular:

> It is important that Ministers should be pretty freely criticised from within
> their own party; for the criticism which proceeds on a basis of common prin-
> ciples is alone worth having. But this criticism should not run, as it some-
> times seems in danger of doing, into needless antagonism.

For its own part, the *Daily News* neither forgot nor forgave W. E. Forster's
Education Act, with its provisions for clerical instruction and the public
funding of Church schools. On 28 January, when Forster confronted the voters
at Bradford (he came armed with '15,000 copies' of a *Times* article 'in his
favour'), the *Daily News* continued to 'disagree as strongly as ever' with the
1870 legislation. Gladstone did not hesitate to identify 'the more popular class
of independent liberals who have been represented by the *Daily News*' as 'one
main cause of the weakness of the government, though they (generally) and
their organ have rallied to us too late during the election'. To say that the *Daily
News* rallied was nearly as hyperbolic as to hold it accountable for the Liberal
rout. 'There can be little doubt that Mr Gladstone's Administration is practically at an end,' the paper soberly declared on 7 February, when most of the
returns were in. The electorate's

> mistake is possibly in some degree the consequence of other mistakes. . . .
> We will not go through the painful and ungracious task of reciting those
> errors now. We did not shrink from the melancholy duty, to use Mr Lowe's
> phrase, of pointing them out as they occurred, to the great indignation of
> some hangers-on of people in power who think that it is the part of a friend
> to flatter, and of an enemy to tell the truth.

That sounded more like an admonition than a recantation.[1]

[1] *Truth*, n.d., quoted in Thorold, *Labouchere*, p. 88n.; Gladstone to the Editor of the *Daily
News*, 14 May 1870 (copy), Gladstone Papers, Add. MSS. 44,426, fol. 216; Robinson and
McCarthy, *The 'Daily News' Jubilee*, pp. 102–103; Gladstone to Robertson Gladstone, 6 February
1874, quoted in Morley, *Gladstone*, II, 495; letter of introduction, Dilke Papers, Add. MSS.
43,898, fol. 1; Hayward to Gladstone, 11 February [1874], Gladstone Papers, Add. MSS. 44,207,
fol. 149.

On the whole, Gladstone could expect more sympathetic treatment from *The Times*. 'While our prosperity continues at the flood', Walter gloomily 'prepared for an ebb', which was staved off until the '80s. It may be inferred that his presentiment spurred *The Times* to an accommodation with progressive causes. H. A. Woodham, who had left the bustle of Printing House Square for the academic calm of Cambridge, was astounded by Goldwin Smith's depiction of *The Times* as a faltering, reactionary force. 'Why, it could hardly need telling that the paper is far more Radical now than 20 years since, & that the dividends have more than doubled,' he wrote to Delane in 1868. 'Look at my articles on Bright in 1850, & at yours now.' What he failed to appreciate was that Bright, too, had changed in the intervening decades.[1]

Propitiated by the announcement of Gladstone's Cabinet appointments, privately conveyed beforehand, Delane made a genuine effort to co-operate with the Liberals. To be sure, cordial relations were as much in his interest as in theirs. With older Whigs, like Lords Clarendon and Granville, and younger ones, like Lord Rosebery, he was on intimate terms. Sir William Harcourt, who still occasionally wrote as 'Historicus', was another link to the ministerial side: Delane affectionately addressed him as 'My dear Mr Solicitor', and indulged him by reporting his speeches at length. The policies that *The Times* considered most laudable were precisely those to which the *Daily News* took exception. The 1870 Education Act, for example, was justly hailed as a landmark. And, after hearing Gladstone promulgate his measure to create an Irish university, Delane permitted his enthusiasm to overwhelm his tactical sense: 'This is a Bill made to pass,' he remarked to Cardinal Manning, who momentarily shared his misperception. During the Franco-Prussian war, the official ban on British press correspondents at combatant headquarters moved Delane to commission 'a smart attack upon the Ministry', published on 21 July 1870. 'They are indeed a set of clerks excellent for Parliamentary purposes or the business of administration, but quite incapable of the courage required in such emergencies as these,' he wrote privately to Dasent, 'sorry to have to speak thus of friends'. All the same, he gave instructions to restrain Courtney, who tended 'to be violently anti-Ministerial' over the government's timorous response to the conflict and its diplomatic settlement. The subsequent decision to submit the *Alabama* claims to arbitration, although unpopular, was welcomed as a far-seeing concession to Anglo-American friendship. But the 1871 budget, imposing a tax on matches and thereby a hardship on the poor, incurred *The Times*'s censure, notwithstanding Lowe's presence at the Exchequer.[2]

[1] Walter to Delane, 4 July 1868, and Woodham to Delane [1868], *Times* Archives.

[2] Morley, *Gladstone*, II, 439; Cook, *Delane*, pp. 236–37; Delane to Dasent [17 July 1870] and 9 November [1870], *Times* Archives. For Harcourt's lingering connection with *The Times*, see Delane to Harcourt [January 1874], Harcourt Papers; Harcourt to Delane, 27 December 1875 (with regard to Harcourt's speech published on 31 December), and Harcourt to Stebbing, 8 March 1876 (with regard to an 'Historicus' letter), *Times* Collection (Texas).

The defeat of the Irish University Bill on its second reading was a blow that might have been mortal had Disraeli been prepared to form a minority administration. Opposed for different reasons by Nonconformists, Radical secularists, and the Irish hierarchy, the 'Bill made to pass' was rejected by three votes in the early hours of 12 March 1873. By then, even *The Times* had come to recognize its imperfections. The *Pall Mall Gazette* expected Gladstone either to dissolve or resign, and hoped for the latter. The *Daily Telegraph* advocated a dissolution, admittedly the more drastic course, but one that would allow the Liberals to put their case to the country. The *Daily News* sorrowfully, and the *Morning Post* and the *Standard* jubilantly, all agreed that Disraeli's turn had come. Yet Disraeli himself was not so sure. To the surprise of the *Telegraph*, the irritation of the *Standard*, and the relief of *The Times*, he decided that the moment for a second coming was not ripe. 'It is all up. Disraeli has respectfully declined. It is really a great triumph for us,' Delane told Stebbing (probably on the afternoon of 17 March, after 'a most curious interview with Disraeli', who had just been to see the Queen). 'But of course,' Delane conceded, 'all the honour & glory belong to our sleepless partner.'

In no small measure, *The Times* had paved the way for Disraeli's *nolo episcopari* by dwelling on the attendant risks: it was logical that he should not 'accept office until the verdict of the country shall have given him a majority sufficient to carry him into power and to maintain him in possession of it', the paper stated on 13 March; in its opinion, prematurely delivered on the 15th, 'Mr Disraeli has acted wisely and well in asking Her Majesty's permission to decline office'. To Delane, who knew Disraeli's mind perhaps better than he had known it himself, Disraeli sent a cryptic message on the 31st:

> If I could have caught you alone yesterday, I would have taken the liberty of thanking you for the support which you gave me during a recent incident. It was vigorous, generous and invaluable: & pardon me if I have the weakness to value it as a proof of personal friendship, as well as of public duty.

He felt no gratitude, however, for the *Standard*. Falsely assured by Gorst that the party chiefs were willing and indeed eager to take up the burden, that paper demanded inquisitorially

> to know ... why Mr Disraeli refused to form an Administration. As it is most distinctly denied – as we expected – that he was bound by any pledge to malcontent followers, and as he is a consummate parliamentary tactician, we presume that he had excellent reasons for his refusal, which are not apparent to the world. To many Liberals, and to most Conservatives, it appears as if a great chance has been thrown away. [18 March]

The embarrassment caused by the *Standard* was no worse than the one it suffered.[1]

[1] Delane to Stebbing, '2.30 p.m.' [17 (?) March 1873], *Times* Collection (Texas); Delane's

The crisis ended, as the *Pall Mall Gazette* 'supposed it would . . . , by the return of Mr Gladstone to office' (18 March). The *Standard* resumed its tirades against the Liberals' 'imbecile domestic administration' and 'craven foreign policy' (21 March). Its rage, partly directed at the Tory leadership, was as predictable as the *Telegraph*'s insistence that 'the store of Liberalism . . . is not yet spent, and we do not despair of seeing fresh legislative triumphs won during the ensuing term' (18 March).

Alas, there was no life after death. Apart from its Judicature Act, the restored ministry attempted little and accomplished less during the period of its ectoplasmic existence. On 24 January 1874, Gladstone applied for a dissolution. Not even his promise to abolish the income tax could obtain him a majority in the elections that followed. 'The constituencies, both town and country, appear to be running a-muck against their old beliefs,' the *Telegraph* reported on 9 February; 'an epidemic of Toryism has smitten the voters, vainly vaccinated by the Ballot.' During the campaign, Delane did his best for Gladstone, who acknowledged his assistance on 5 February: 'I was really ashamed to give you trouble yesterday but I am thankful for your notice of today. The reports of my speeches, so far as I have examined them, appear to me to be excellent.' Delane also complimented Bagehot as a sort of constitutional adviser. 'I have always thought that in 1868 nothing became Disraeli in office "like the leaving of it" & I hope Gladstone will not cling on,' he wrote on the night of the 10th to Abraham Hayward, a conduit to the Prime Minister. Appreciating that Gladstone was 'bound to wait until the Elections are over,' Delane counselled that 'then he should resign – so that Disraeli may prepare his Speech, select his Ministry & be ready to take his place when Parliament meets'. Gladstone, never one to depart in haste, did not budge until the 16th, when Delane wrote in his diary: 'The Government on the point of going out, but Gladstone clinging to the last moment. He determined at last to resign, and we announced it, though with some misgivings.' The leading article in the next morning's *Times*, written by the editor himself, proclaimed 'that no man ever made a more conscientious use than Mr Gladstone of great authority'; nevertheless, his 'feeling of personal ascendancy and of popularity with the masses, . . . inspired him . . . with a confidence which not infrequently misled him'. The judgment was no more severe than that of Radical journals, which observed the same tendency. 'Mr Gladstone aspires to be the Lord Paramount of Liberalism,' the *Examiner* had complained on 3 June 1871. Imbued with a spirit of individualism, the Liberal Party did not readily submit to Gladstonian discipline. The political press, as much by its provocations as its inducements, helped to force it into the mould.[1]

---

diary, 17 March 1873, quoted in Cook, *Delane*, p. 241; Disraeli to Delane, 31 March 1873, *Times* Archives; *also see* E. J. Feuchtwanger, *Disraeli, Democracy and the Tory Party* (Oxford, 1968), pp. 13–15.

[1] Delane's diary, 16 February 1874, quoted in Cook, *Delane*, p. 243; Gladstone to Delane, 5

*   *   *

In March 1874, Disraeli won the laurels which, the previous year, would have been entwined in nettles. During the six years of his second premiership, newspapers strengthened their party affiliations, often renegotiating them. Preponderantly Liberal when Disraeli took office, the metropolitan press was preponderantly Tory when he left it. The result of a constant interplay between influences and events, this transformation had the further result of making journalists more assertive and politicians more attentive to them.

Trollope, in *The Prime Minister* (1875–76), held a mirror to political society. His title character, the Duke of Omnium, typified the change of attitude:

> In his old happy days two papers a day, one in the morning and the other before dinner, sufficed to tell him all that he wanted to know. Now he felt it necessary to see almost every rag that was published. And he would skim through them all till he found the lines in which he himself was maligned, and then, with sore heart and irritated nerves, would pause over every contumelious word.

In life as in fiction, politicians showed an increasingly acute sensitivity to newspaper criticism, however much they might discount the impact or belittle the source. Charles Villiers could more easily accept the fact of his exclusion from Gladstone's 1868 Cabinet than the *Pall Mall Gazette*'s suggestion that his 'mismanagement of the Poor Law Board' was the reason. 'What the *Pall Mall* says to-night is the direct converse of the truth,' he told Delane on 9 December 1868. 'I don't suppose the *Pall Mall* really has any influence as I hear every day, people say it has become a *bore*, & that it is no longer amusing.' Nevertheless, the imputation rankled. Men whose stars were rising tended to be even more thin-skinned than those whom they passed along the way. Frank Hill, the editor of the *Daily News*, was *persona non grata* to Forster, who reserved his courtesies for Reid of the *Leeds Mercury* and Escott of the *Standard*, the latter confessing to a 'slack' Toryism. Joseph Chamberlain, then the ambitious mayor of Birmingham, sparred with Hill in the pages of the *Fortnightly Review*. When H. W. Lucy, 'a struggling journalist', went to Birmingham to cover a royal visit, he approached Chamberlain, who 'asked me how I could suppose a representative of the *Daily News* had any claim on him for personal assistance'. No longer left to inference, the terms of trade were bluntly specified.[1]

February 1874, *Times* Collection (Texas); Delane to Hayward, 'Tuesday night' [10 February 1874], enclosed in Hayward to Gladstone, 11 February [1874], Gladstone Papers, Add. MSS. 44,207, fols. 149 ff.

[1] Villiers to Delane [9 December 1868], *Times* Archives; Reid, *Memoirs*, pp. 195–96; Escott, *Press, Platform*, p. 59; Lucy, *Memories*, pp. 171–72.

For the Conservatives, willing and able to pay the price, it was a buyers' market. Their success, owing little to the creation of new properties, was primarily due to shifts among older ones. The *Globe* turned Tory in 1866, as did the *Echo*, briefly, in 1875. The *Morning Advertiser* gravitated in the same direction. Still nominally Liberal, though no longer vociferously Radical, it furtively opened its columns to Disraeli. On 9 December 1869, the editor sent him proof copies of three letters which were to be published: 'I shall take care that the note at the end appears as my note, not yours.' Aggrieved by Gladstone's 1872 Licensing Act, this 'Recognized Organ of the Licensed Victuallers' spurned its erstwhile Liberal allies. Though Fox Bourne doubtless exaggerated when he described it as 'nearly the most powerful journal in England' during the 1874 elections (much as Sir Robert Ensor overestimated the electoral effect of the publicans' revolt), the paper rejected Liberalism on the grounds of its subservience to the temperance movement. Almost imperceptibly, the *Morning Advertiser* drifted into the Tory camp. 'There is no apparent or probable likelihood of this Paper changing its politics, such as they have been these four years past,' Alfred B. Richards assured Disraeli's secretary in 1875. 'The "governing body" annually appointed for business and charitable purposes has never, since my appointment, shown any desire to interfere with my political conduct of the Paper.'[1]

The *Morning Post* arrived at the same destination by a flight of imagination. Accustomed to hero-worshipping Palmerston, it substituted Disraeli, and pretended not to notice the difference. At first glance an unlikely object for the paper's adulation, Disraeli was sufficiently flexible to overcome the disabilities of his ethnic and social background. The *Morning Post*, an opponent of reform in 1832 and so long as Palmerston had lived, endorsed Disraeli's 1867 proposals, calculating that 'the larger such a measure is made, the greater is the probability of its possessing the character of finality' (16 July 1867). But it was Disraeli's shimmering rhetoric about Britain's imperial mission that made him heir to Palmerston's mantle; that, and the fact that he employed Algernon Borthwick as a diplomatic agent in 1876. Borthwick, who had inherited control from his father, relinquished editorial chores to William Hardman in 1872, but retained 'the powers of direction' until his death in 1908. His successor was to have been his son Oliver, whose death at the age of thirty-two preceded his own, and his daughter Lilias, Lady Bathurst, ultimately replaced him. Despite rumours (vehemently denied by his biographer) that he considered standing for Parliament as a Liberal in 1874, and despite various Liberal family connections (including Lord Carlingford and Sir William Harcourt), Borthwick was an ardent Disraelian. It was not because they doubted his com-

[1] James Banks (?) to Disraeli, 9 December 1869, Hughenden Papers (the items in question were presumably those signed by 'Fabricus'); Fox Bourne, II, 327; Ensor, *England, 1870–1914* (Oxford, 1936), pp. 21–22; Hanham, *Elections and Party Management*, pp. 222–24; Richards to Corry, 4 February 1875, Hughenden Papers.

pliance, but rather because they feared it might 'entirely send the *Standard* into opposition', that Corry and his 'Chief' – who became the Earl of Beaconsfield in August 1876 – did not put the *Morning Post* to more extensive use. As it was, they could rely on it to defend the government's 'Palmerstonian' foreign and colonial policies. 'Please read my leader tomorrow – Monday – a justification of Lord B's speech – which so many people attack,' Borthwick wrote to Corry on 26 November 1876. It began: 'Peace is the one object of her Majesty's Government. Peace, on the foundation of public law and treaty rights.' In 1880, Borthwick was the first newspaper owner *per se* to be knighted. Salisbury made him a baronet seven years later and, in 1895, a peer.[1]

The *Daily Telegraph* followed in the wake of the *Morning Post*. Until this time, Arnold Bennett's grandfather, a Staffordshire draper who 'hated Gladstone' and 'worshipped "Dizzy"', read the *Standard*, [and] looked on the *Daily Telegraph* as subversive' (*Daily Express*, 6 June 1928). The transition 'from its radical beginnings to a steady conservatism' was hardly dictated by the simple formula, invoked by Lord Burnham, that 'as the proprietors got more firmly in the saddle their natural conservatism began to influence the paper'.[2] On the contrary, the instincts of J. M. and Edward Levy had been pugnaciously Radical. Likewise, the supplanting of Thornton Hunt by Edwin Arnold, Arthur's brother, was more effect than cause. How, then, did the paper that venerated Gladstone as 'the People's William' wend its way to the Conservative side?

Ridiculing Disraeli as a 'man of disgraceful jibes and sneering sophisms', the *Telegraph* had considered it a privilege to be at Gladstone's beck and call. Not only did it faithfully defend him from the onslaughts of the Tory opposition, but it also took his part against Dilke and other 'wild Radicals' (3 and 7 January 1874). As much by what it suppressed as what it printed, it worked to counteract the backstairs activity of certain Cabinet ministers. Lord Granville, the foreign secretary, was notorious for leaking information to Delane, whom he primed in 1871 to announce the appointment of Northcote to the American Commission, 'but as even Gladstone does not yet know the fact, don't put it in your official corner'. On 15 January 1874, Edward Levy saw to it that an injudicious 'passage was properly omitted' from the published version of a Foreign Office dispatch. 'I fancy Lord Granville's tendencies are towards *The Times*: so are Disraeli's,' he observed to Gladstone. 'It will be interesting to watch the actions of the paper under both influences.' The tug-of-war for the political backing of the *Telegraph* was to be no less interesting.[3]

---

[1] Corry to Borthwick, 22 November 1874 ('not sent') and Borthwick to Corry, 26 November [1876], Hughenden Papers; Lucas, *Glenesk*, pp. 246–50; Hindle, *Morning Post*, pp. 220–23, 228–29; George W. Smalley, *Anglo-American Memories* (London, 1911), pp. 294 ff.

[2] Burnham, *Peterborough Court*, p. 16.

[3] Granville to Delane, 13 February 1871, *Times* Archives; Levy to Gladstone, 15 January 1874, Gladstone Papers, Add. MSS. 44,442, fols. 55–56.

In the election campaign of 1874, the *Telegraph* put Gladstone above party, enjoining fractious Liberals to close ranks behind him. The appeal was unavailing, raising serious questions about the efficacy of a mass-circulation journal. Escott, citing the *Telegraph* as 'the only instance on record of a penny paper that has completely enjoyed the confidence of its party, and that has been exclusively furnished with official "tips"', doubted whether its 'championship' had in fact 'rendered Mr Gladstone the slightest practical assistance'. By 1875, the same thoughts had begun to occur to Levy himself. Perplexed by Gladstone's continued inaccessibility, he weakened in his resistance to Disraeli. While he declined to oblige Corry by contradicting an item in *The Times*, he intimated a willingness to build new bridges: 'Though I have not seen you for a long time,' he replied on 28 January 1875,

I always think of you as one of my best friends. Therefore I am unhappy when I cannot do as you bid me. But I am unable to print stale *Times* paragraphs. I do not complain because your respected Chief sends *every* item of political information to an esteemed contemporary. My regard for his judgment is very profound, and he cannot, probably, be wrong on such a subject. I, however, owe a great debt to an immense constituency, and I should be pronounced a defaulter if I did not at least try to be original.[1]

It was not that the *Telegraph* deserted Gladstone, but rather that Gladstone deserted the *Telegraph*, first by his ambiguous withdrawal and, finally, by his abdication of the Liberal leadership in January 1875. Refusing to accept the decision as irrevocable, Levy did his best to coax his hero back into the arena. Thanking him for a volume of essays on Free Trade ('They are very interesting, and are quite worthy of notice'), he told Gladstone on 16 July 1875 that he had 'listened with much pleasure to your speech last night; it really placed the matter in the true light before the public'. Yet Gladstone did not rise to the bait. His self-denying ordinance left the *Telegraph* no choice but to follow its own lights. For that, it earned Gladstone's reproaches. 'I fear you and I are diverging rather widely,' he wrote to Lawson (as Edward Levy had recently become by deed-poll) the following November, when the paper supported the government's purchase of the Suez Canal shares, 'but you have probably at least the advantage of having 999 of every thousand on your side.' Lawson hastened to defend himself and, if possible, to mend the rift:

Let me say that on most questions of political principle nothing could make me doubt my own judgment so much as to find yours in disagreement with

[1] E[scott], 'Politics and the Press,' *Fraser's Magazine*, n.s. xii (1875), 43; Levy to Corry, 28 January 1875, Hughenden Papers. (Lord Burnham mistakenly assumed Corry to be Gladstone's 'confidential secretary'. *Peterborough Court*, p. 20.)

it. But the more sincerely I can declare this, the more I hope to impress you with the necessity for not pronouncing against the cause which the Government has adopted with regard to the Suez Canal. . . . Here is an occasion absolutely unique, where maxims too rigid might betray the best Liberal into an unprofitable alienation from the spirit of his country.

Gladstone, however, was better placed to resist the public clamour than was the *Daily Telegraph*, which Disraeli mocked as the *Delirium Tremens*.[1]

Despite Gladstone's impulsive visit to the *Telegraph* office in Peterborough Court on a Sunday morning in 1876, after he had worshipped at the Temple nearby, the break came that summer. Roused to protest against the massacre of Bulgarian Christians by the 'unspeakable Turk', he clashed with Lawson, who tried at first to paper over the cracks. 'There is no subject that can keep us wide apart,' Lawson insisted on 11 September. 'We may differ on points of detail: but we have always had – and probably shall always have – the same ends in view.' And again on 9 October: 'There has never been any difference between us on the broad ground of humanity: we may have differed on questions of political detail.' To Gladstone, however, the Balkan crisis was no mere point of detail, political or otherwise. The threat of British intervention on the Turkish side in the ensuing Russo–Turkish war showed that he was not mistaken. Lawson, sharing Disraeli's Russophobic bellicosity, welcomed the prospect. 'I am in a big fight and I know how to use my guns,' he boasted on 17 May 1877 to Corry, to whom he volunteered his services as a trouble-shooter. 'The country will defend its interests. But these interests must have champions with courage in their hearts and bold and national utterances on their lips.' A month later, acknowledging to Gladstone that their ways had finally parted, Lawson trusted that 'your great breadth of mind – your genius – your generosity will, I am sure, always yield in my favour the belief – denied to me by the smaller men on your side – that I am moved solely by conscientious conviction'. Gladstone, too, was pained, and all the more when the *Telegraph* reported on 27 August that he had intrigued to stir up the Greeks against Turkey. Professing himself 'very unwilling to come out, in a polemical way as it needs must be more or less, in relation to you and yours', he demanded and received an apology.[2]

The 'smaller men', as Lawson called them, were bitterly resentful. Goldwin

---

[1] Levy to Gladstone, 16 July 1875, Gladstone Papers, Add. MSS. 44,447, fol. 299; Gladstone to Lawson, November [n.d.] 1875, quoted in Burnham, *Peterborough Court*, p. 20; Lawson to Gladstone, 29 November 1875, Gladstone Papers, Add. MSS. 44,448, fol. 257; Disraeli to Lady Bradford, 26 April 1876, quoted in Buckle, *Disraeli*, V, 475.

[2] Lawson to Gladstone, 11 September 1876, Gladstone Papers, Add. MSS. 44,451, fol. 166; Lawson to Gladstone, 9 October 1876, Gladstone Papers, Add. MSS. 44,452, fol. 45: Lawson to Corry, 17 November 1877, Hughenden Papers; Lawson to Gladstone, 20 June 1877, Gladstone Papers, Add. MSS. 44,454, fols. 207–208; Gladstone to Lawson, 14 September 1877 (copy), Gladstone Papers, Add. MSS. 44,445, fol. 51.

Smith called Gladstone's attention 'to the vast increase in the circulation of the *Telegraph* since it has turned Turk'. (Its daily sale rose from 191,000 in 1871 to over 242,000 in 1877.) 'It seems to me a terrible indication of the public mind,' declared Smith, who had heard, 'on the authority of [W. H.] Smith & Co., that the circulation of the *Daily News* has declined, though, Heaven knows, there is nothing in it that need shock any moderate Turcophile'. Labouchere, as part owner of the *Daily News*, therefore had double cause to impugn the motives of Lawson, against whom he waged a venomous campaign in the pages of *Truth*. In rhyme and prose, Lawson was mocked as an apostate from his religious as well as his political faith, who had betrayed his principles to safeguard his Turkish investments and possibly to obtain a baronetcy. A suit for libel was thrown out of court, leaving the dispute to be settled on the doorstep of the Beefsteak Club, where Lawson and Labouchere traded punches. If nothing else, the incident bore out Gladstone's impression that 'London is the great focus of mischief: through money, rowdyism, & the *Daily Telegraph*'.[1]

Having cut loose from its Gladstonian moorings, the *Telegraph* – to use its own vocabulary – became 'imperial'. Dedicated to the interests of 'the Empire at large' (14 March 1876), the paper came to accept as its 'duty' the 'support of the Imperial Government' (11 January 1878). It claimed to have pursued this course since the summer of 1876 'without heeding party ties or any dictates except those of sincere patriotism' (14 January 1878), and took umbrage at the Duke of Argyll's 'absurd and unwarrantable statement … that the *Daily Telegraph* is "a Conservative organ"' (18 January 1878). Nevertheless, to all intents and purposes, that was what it had become.

The realignment of the *Telegraph* was a severe setback to the Liberals. The giant of Fleet Street, it addressed the multitudes beyond the perimeters of Clubland. Gladstone told W. T. Stead, then the young editor of the *Northern Echo* at Darlington, that nine-tenths of the 'horrible letters' he received during the autumn of 1877 came from 'abusive correspondents' in the London area, a high proportion of whom quoted strictures from the *Telegraph*. The *Daily Chronicle*, pitched at the same class of readership, was no substitute. Acquired in 1876 by Edward Lloyd, who immodestly bestowed his name on a popular penny weekly, this halfpenny morning journal had previously circulated locally as the *Clerkenwell News*. As late as 1880, according to an objective source, 'its transformation into a general political paper is not yet, perhaps, complete'. Still essentially an advertising medium, the *Chronicle* gave short shrift to foreign news, and did not cater to more sophisticated tastes. E. A. Freeman, the historian, tried it 'for a while' after growing 'disgusted with the folly & half-heartedness of [the] *Daily News*', but found 'that it did not do'.

---

[1] Smith to Gladstone, 4 July 1877, Gladstone Papers, Add. MSS. 44,303, fol. 206; circulation statistics from Wadsworth, p. 20; Burnham, *Peterborough Court*, pp. 21–24; Gladstone to Bryce, 6 October 1877, Bryce Papers.

Like him, the Liberal leaders had a distressingly limited choice.[1]

That they retained a numerical superiority among provincial newspapers, which Gladstone considered 'far more true to the National sentiment', was cold comfort to Liberal strategists. Yet the costs of establishing new metropolitan dailies were huge, and the risks considerable. Lloyd paid £30,000 for the *Chronicle*, and an additional £150,000 to refurbish it, all to what political effect? Bright would have been 'very glad to see a good Paper started' in the summer of 1875, either a morning rival to the *Globe* or an evening one 'to compete with the *Pall Mall*, the most vicious opponent of the late Govt.'. He encouraged Thorold Rogers to explore the possibilities, although he himself would not participate. 'If I were as rich as some of my friends,' Bright told Rogers, 'I would not have suffered the *Star* to fail – or to want a successor – but I cannot afford to join in newspaper experiments. I have been in two of them, & have burned my fingers.' No longer confident of the ability of a cheap press to regenerate the masses, Bright left it 'for business people to determine' whether Rogers's projected journal should sell for twopence or a penny, but thought it might 'be made a better & more pleasant Paper to read if the higher price is adopted'. Similarly, Joseph Chamberlain would have 'very much' liked 'to see a Radical Daily' started; but, he cautioned an admirer in 1876, 'the time has not come yet. The middle class are daily getting more Conservative,' he noted, '& the working class hardly indulge in Dailies or get beyond *Reynolds & Lloyds*'. Clearly, along with the *Daily Telegraph*, many Liberal illusions had slipped away.[2]

The Conservatives, by contrast, enjoyed – literally – an embarrassment of riches. Their greatest problem was to ensure that, in stooping to collect one parcel, they did not accidentally drop another. The ranks of the metropolitan Tory press were swelled in the '70s by the appearance of new journals and the reorientation of older ones. Jealous of each other and, above all, of *The Times*, they required careful handling. Disraeli, on his own and through Corry, was usually adept at manipulating the press. In different ways, so were Salisbury, Northcote, Gorst, and W. H. Smith. But their improvisations, lacking co-ordination, were sometimes counter-productive.

The *Standard*, with the *Evening Standard* in tow, was the most prosperous and self-reliant of the lot. During the interregnum between the Hamber and Mudford editorships, Gorst took responsibility for its political direction. In that capacity and especially as principal party agent, he antagonized Disraeli, who retaliated by making oblique references in his speeches to the *Standard*'s 'consequential airs'. Disraeli also found reason to 'regret the inveterate

[1] Shannon, *Gladstone and the Bulgarian Agitation 1876* (London, 1963), p. 153; Estelle Stead, *My Father* (London, 1918?), pp. 79–80; Freeman to Stead, 'Xmas Day' 1879, Stead Papers; 'The Daily News – The Daily Chronicle,' *Nation* (New York), 30 September 1880.

[2] Gladstone to Hill, 6 April 1877 (copy), Gladstone Papers, Add. MSS. 44,454, fol. 24; Bright to Rogers, 28 August 1875, Rogers Papers; Chamberlain to W. H. Duignan, 7 October 1876, Chamberlain Papers.

manner in wh. Ld. Salisbury ... inspires the *Standard*'. Until Salisbury reluctantly accepted office from Disraeli in 1874, he was feared as a potential insurgent. Significantly, Hamber did not dare to promote the New Social Movement – a peculiar attempt to link Conservatism with 'the wage-receiving portion of the community' (as the *Standard* euphemistically wrote on 16 October 1871) – until he had first obtained a seal of approval from Salisbury as well as Disraeli.[1]

The New Social Movement, though a non-starter, was symptomatic of a restlessness on the part of Conservatives, who were anxious to present a new, more dynamic image. Although Disraeli had coined the slogans of Tory democracy, Salisbury appeared more disposed to give them substance. To the extent that a movement actually existed, it was fanned by the press. Captain George Armstrong, then business manager of the *Globe*, sent a cutting from the *Telegraph* to W. H. Smith, whom he served as constituency agent: 'I think you will be astonished. The Conservative Working Man is no longer a myth,' he wrote in an accompanying letter on 18 April 1871. Soliciting funds to assist working-class Tory organizers, he warned that 'it would be a dreadful "come down" after the leading articles in the different papers if their efforts collapsed'. On 8 September, the *Globe* posed the telling question: 'Have Conservatives a Programme?' The *Standard*, emboldened by directives from Disraeli and Salisbury, concurred that it was 'the natural function of Conservatives to take the lead' in matters of social welfare (14 October 1871). Nothing came of a scheme to convert the *Sun* into an instrument to promote a symbiotic union between classes. Nor did the Tory hierarchy see fit to utilize the *Bee-Hive* as a liaison with trade unionists, who were said to have lost patience with the Liberals. But Smith and Northcote, among others, understood both the need to associate the party with working-class aspirations and the vital contribution that could be made by newspapers.[2]

Northcote, notwithstanding his ostensible indifference ('Fancy a Cabinet Minister who gets his *Times* by post at 7 p.m.,' Delane remarked disbelievingly of him in 1875), was keenly interested in the press as an extension of electoral organization. In 1869, he had encouraged attempts to launch a Conservative weekly in North Devon. Five years later, shortly before he became Chancellor of the Exchequer, he 'gratified' Major Charles Keith-Falconer, the first secretary of the Conservative Central Office, by expressing warm approval for 'our little paper the *Sun*'. Not to be confused with the old

[1] E[scott], 'Politics and the Press,' *Fraser's Magazine*, n.s. xii (1875), 44; Chilston, *W. H. Smith*, pp. 59 ff.; Disraeli to Derby, 25 January 1871, quoted in Buckle, *Disraeli*, V, 132; Hamber to Disraeli, 11 October 1871, Hughenden Papers; Hamber to Salisbury, 11 October 1871, Salisbury Papers. Interestingly, Salisbury did not accept office in 1874 until he was prodded by *The Times, Daily News, Spectator*, and the *Pall Mall Gazette*. Salisbury to his wife, 10 and 13 February 1874, quoted in Cecil, *Salisbury*, II (London, 1921), pp. 44–45.
[2] Armstrong to Smith, 18 April 1871, Hambleden Papers; *also see* Paul Smith, *Disraelian Conservatism and Social Reform* (London, 1967), pp. 149–55.

evening *Sun*, much less the *Sun* that T. P. O'Connor started in 1893, this avowed party organ sprang in October 1873 from the *Town and Country News-paper*, itself begun three months earlier. Its proprietor, Alexander Mackie, had intended to go further and to co-operate with Keith-Falconer in bringing the *Sun*, the *Weekly Dispatch*, and the Central Press Agency 'under one man-agement', which, Keith-Falconer promised Disraeli, would 'form the basis of a sound commercial undertaking, irrespective of its great political value'. The *Dispatch* eluded their grasp; but – as the delegates to the National Union con-ference heard on 1 July 1874 – the *Sun* 'was published under the auspices of some prominent members of the party in and out of Parliament' with the special 'object of disseminating Conservative principles among the rural popu-lation, and the inhabitants of such small towns as do not possess a Conserva-tive Organ of their own'. To assist the enterprise, the National Union 'undertook to subscribe for copies of the paper, which were supplied for a con-siderable period to each of the affiliated Associations'. During the 1874 cam-paign, 'an extra enlarged edition of the paper . . . was published daily' for delivery 'to the headquarters of the local Conservatives in each contested elec-tion, together with supplies of placards, posters, and pamphlets'. This had been necessary, Keith-Falconer explained to Northcote, because 'since the death of the *Conservative* there is no Conservative weekly paper emanating from London with the exception of the *Sunday Times* and *Bell's Weekly Mess-enger*, the former of which is chiefly devoted to sporting & the latter to agricul-tural intelligence'. His further ambition was 'to issue a penny weekly edition of the *Sun* consisting of 24 pages which will be conducted in the same spirit as the present daily paper'. To ensure wide distribution, he proposed to offer 'such advantages to local printers . . . that by a trifling additional cost & the addition of 4 pages of local matter & politics any small town in the Kingdom may have a weekly Conservative paper of its own'; the only stipulation was to be 'that the title of the *Sun* be retained prefixing the name of the town in which the local matter is printed'. The Conservatives' victory at the polls was taken to imply that this degree of centralization was unnecessary, and Keith-Falconer's de-parture from the Central Office left no one to press for it.[1]

After an initial spurt of activity, including the establishment in 1872 of the *Marlow Chronicle and Wycombe Times* in Disraeli's own neighbourhood, the provincial Conservative press stagnated. Alan J. Lee has tabulated that nineteen of the twenty-six self-designated 'Conservative' or 'Constitutional' newspaper companies founded between 1870 and 1890 dated from after 1880. Yet George Webster adamantly denied to Gorst, who had personal reasons for dissatisfaction, that the party lacked country properties of sufficient

---

[1] Delane to Stebbing [15 October 1875], *Times* Collection (Texas); Mark Rolle to Northcote, August [n.d.] 1869, Iddesleigh Papers, Add. MSS. 50,038, fols. 36–37; Keith-Falconer to Disraeli, 31 October and 3 November 1873, Hughenden Papers; National Union minutes, 1 July 1874; Keith-Falconer to Northcote, 19 January 1874, Iddesleigh Papers, Add. MSS. 50,039, fols. 137 ff.

quantity or quality. 'On the contrary,' he insisted, the problem was 'the *gross neglect and positive ill-treatment of the Conservative press by the Conservative party themselves*'. His own paper, the *Advertiser* at King's Lynn, was 'Conservative because *we* are Conservative,' he said. 'If we cared for our private interests in preference to our principles, we feel convinced that we might soon double its circulation and largely increase its commercial value.' In Scotland, Conservative setbacks went hand in hand with the distress of the Tory press. Frederick Wicks of the *Glasgow News*, though he welcomed party efforts to convey 'important items of news' to 'the Conservative press exclusively' (he referred to the *Editor's Handysheet*, issued by the Conservative Newspaper Union with 'the sanction of the Whips'), told Corry of his plight: it was hard enough to compete against the Liberal *Scotsman* at Edinburgh, 'but unfortunately the London *Standard* persists in feeding our strongest Liberal opponent in Glasgow', the *Glasgow Herald*, whose correspondent gained admission to the gallery at Westminster by courtesy of the *Globe*. W. R. Lawson of the *Edinburgh Courant* felt still more directly menaced. 'It is not exaggerating to say that the influence of *The Times* in England is inferior to that of the *Scotsman* in this Whig ridden country,' he wrote to Corry. 'In addition to unlimited means', the *Scotsman* allegedly possessed 'peculiar facilities for getting London news', including 'an alliance with the *Daily Telegraph* and use of the *Morning Post* proofs'. George Thomson held shares in the *Courant*, though 'there is no dividend, nor is there likely ever to be'. He and his associates were 'however very unwilling that the newspaper should not be able to go on, as it is useful, especially in the matter of elections'. The Duke of Buccleuch contributed £2,500 to the *Glasgow News* on the same understanding. Save for such philanthrophy, many Conservative journals would have perished. Meeting at Manchester on 25 October 1876, the tenth annual conference of the National Union unanimously carried a resolution that 'urged the importance of strengthening the local Conservative Press'.[1]

From the vantage point of London, the perspective was altogether different. Queen Victoria might lecture Disraeli on 'the importance of securing some newspaper as an organ for the Government' (she thought the *Globe* 'badly written' and *John Bull* 'so ultra and extreme in its religious views as to prevent' her 'from taking it in . . . the last 3 years'), but the Prime Minister and his colleagues gloried in a superabundance of metropolitan press support. Edmund Yates of the *World* begged for 'scraps of official news', and took his place in a queue that included Delane. 'I hope you will maintain the wholesome practice of not anticipating the Queen's Message in tomorrow's newspapers,' the

---

[1] F. G. Baylis to Disraeli, 20 September 1872, George Webster to Gorst, 25 April 1874 (copy?), Frederick Wicks to Corry, 10 September 1874 and 16 June 1879, W. R. Lawson to Corry, 14 February 1876, George Thomson to Corry, 27 February [1876?], A. Macolie to Corry, 19 October 1876, Hughenden Papers; National Union minutes, 25 October 1876; Lee, *Origins*, p. 152.

editor of *The Times* wrote sanctiminiously to Disraeli on the eve of the 1875 session; 'but if there is to be a *communiqué*, pray do not exclude me from the benefit of it.'[1]

During his second premiership, Disraeli consummated his long flirtation with *The Times*. He and Delane, having grown old together, developed a sensitivity to each other's requirements. A tacit understanding evolved between them. *The Times* accepted Disraeli as 'completely master of the situation' (14 January 1874), and recognized his 'security of tenure which is derived from the absence of an adverse claim' (13 August 1875). In return, Disraeli, 'much to the mortification of the "Conservative press"' – as Escott put it – arranged 'to supply the authorities of Printing House Square with a priority of special intelligence'. His long-standing hope of 'making Delane my confidant' was at last, after a fashion, fulfilled. That did not deter the paper from criticizing aspects of government policy. '*The Times* may scold; it may rave and rant; but it will not daunt me,' Disraeli blustered to Lady Bradford on 10 August 1875, after the publication of a leading article which he presumed to have been 'written by Lowe'. But on crucial issues, including the Suez Canal purchase which Delane had advocated in Palmerston's day, *The Times* showered him with plaudits. 'There is an almost universal chorus of applause today at the bold step which Dizzy took yesterday,' Delane wrote to Walter on 26 November 1875. His only regret was that Thomas Chenery, in his leading article that morning, 'had been rather too cold' about the government's *coup*. 'It is, however, a fault which is easy to amend,' he thought. 'For myself, I can't help again rejoicing that we have a minister who, if occasion arose, would seize the Spanish frigates or burn the Danish fleet.' The *Morning Post* was therefore not the only journal that regarded Disraeli as Palmerston *redivivus*.[2]

Delane's task was made easier by the debility of the Liberal opposition. Gladstone, as much out of obstinacy as fatigue, neither relinquished nor exercised authority after the voters had turned him out of office. His front-bench colleagues were hamstrung and divided. 'The truth is none of them dare go near G. & nothing has been done,' Harcourt informed Hill, the editor of the *Daily News*. 'In the meantime G. still sulks & says he will not lead. . . . The disorganisation is complete. There is no whip no office *no nothing*. . . . You will be safe in saying there is nothing decided nothing arranged nothing proposed.' By the beginning of 1875, the situation had become intolerable. On 14 January, Delane pleaded for the revival of an effective opposition, which he did not commit himself to support: 'Let Mr Gladstone definitely retire and there will be lamentation; but the broken ranks would close together.' Delane knew that a meeting of former Liberal ministers was to be held that day. And

[1] Queen Victoria to Disraeli, 17 March 1876, quoted in Buckle, *Disraeli*, V, 468; Yates to Corry, 4 August 1874, and Delane to Disraeli, 4 February [1875], Hughenden Papers.

[2] E[scott], 'Politics and the Press,' *Fraser's Magazine*, n.s. xii (1875), 42; Cook, *Delane*, p. 247; Disraeli to Lady Bradford, 9 and 10 August 1875, quoted in Buckle, *Disraeli*, V, 392–93; Delane to Walter, 26 November 1875, *Times* Archives.

Gladstone, yearning for his freedom, knew equally well that this 'article . . . is undisguisedly aimed at getting rid of me'. Harcourt, who did not attend the conclave 'though I knew it was to be held', kept Hill closely informed of developments: 'Do nothing till you hear further from me.' Whiggishly inclined, he preferred Lord Hartington for the succession. 'Some newspapers speak of Forster, who had much cultivated the friendship of newspaper men,' Bright wrote to Gladstone on the 17th, 'but I do not think the plan will answer.' Neither did Edward Levy, still among the party faithful. 'The leadership question is settling itself and will end in the selection of Lord Hartington,' he assured Gladstone five days later. 'The *Daily News* turned upon me severely for hinting this at the very earliest date: but was speedily forced to come round to my view.' The *Examiner*, however, found it difficult to accept a Whig aristocrat at the helm. 'The Liberal Party has fallen on bad times,' it declared on the 23rd, hoping that 'its members may learn the value of Liberal principles from experience of the folly and danger of deserting them'.[1]

The last had not been heard of Gladstone. Released from the trammels of party leadership, he was more inclined than ever (as *The Times* had picturesquely written on 14 January) to 'appear comet-like at unknown periods and in unknown orbits'. In the summer of 1876, revelations of Turkish atrocities stung him into action. Disraeli, too, read the accounts that first appeared in the *Daily News*. Knowing that paper to be 'the real Opposition journal', he presumed that its accounts were, 'to a great extent, inventions', calculated 'to create a cry against the Government'. Their veracity was soon confirmed by reports in *The Times*, but still Disraeli remained sceptical and, worse, cynical. Delane, whose failing health had kept him away from his desk for much of the year, returned to take part in his last crusade. Trusting his own sources more than the deceptive statements that issued from the Foreign Office, he gave qualified support to the 'pilgrimage of passion' on which Gladstone embarked. At 'an interesting little party at Granville's' in late August, Gladstone 'had a long talk with Delane. We, he and I, are much of one mind in thinking the Turks must go out of Bulgaria, though retaining a titular supremacy if they like.' Delane, as R. T. Shannon has pointed out in his definitive study of the episode, 'was never an active advocate . . . in the same sense as Stead of the *Northern Echo* or Frank Hill of the *Daily News* or even C. P. Scott of the *Manchester Guardian*'; but, if only tentative and temporary, 'the sympathetic commitment of the most powerful daily paper was an asset of immense utility for the agitation'.[2]

[1] Harcourt to Hill [1874] and [14 January 1875], Harcourt Papers; Gladstone to his wife, 14 January 1875, quoted in Morley, *Gladstone*, II, 504; Bright to Gladstone, 17 January 1875, Gladstone Papers, Add. MSS. 44,113, fol. 99; Levy to Gladstone, 22 January 1875, Gladstone Papers, Add. MSS. 44,446, fol. 108.

[2] Disraeli to Lady Bradford, 13 July 1876, quoted in Buckle, *Disraeli*, VI, 43; Gladstone to his wife, 28 August 1876, quoted in Morley, *Gladstone*, II, 552; Shannon, *Gladstone and the Bulgarian Agitation*, p. 56. Delane's directives to Stebbing (one mistakenly addressed to 'My dear

Stead, whose proprietor was conveniently on holiday in Switzerland, put Darlington and himself on the journalistic map. Professionals like Wemyss Reid already 'admired his splendid enthusiasm and his engaging frankness', without ignoring the streak of fanaticism that often carried him to excess. A devout Nonconformist and a sturdy Radical, Stead was, above all else, an editor, which meant to him 'to think, write and speak for . . . thousands. . . . It is the position of a Viceroy. . . . God calls . . . and now points . . . to *the only true throne in England, the Editor's chair, and offers me the real sceptre'.* The Bulgarian agitation made Stead's reputation and enlarged his ego by allowing him, in his own estimation, to be 'more useful, more powerful than half-a-dozen ordinary M.P.s'. His *Northern Echo*, by no means the only provincial paper that took up the cause, was the one that carried it furthest. Freeman, commending it as the 'best paper in Europe', posted copies to friends in Russia and Montenegro. Gladstone extolled it as a shining example, and urged the *Daily News* to draw from its columns. Stead, with his intense evangelical impulse ('I felt the clear call of God's voice: "Arouse the nation or be damned"'), was quintessentially a provincial product. Not surprisingly, however, the provinces could not contain him, and he went to London in 1880 to assist John Morley, whom he eventually replaced, on the reconstructed *Pall Mall Gazette*. 'In every career capacity and character gravitate towards London,' explained a commentator in the New York *Nation*. 'Journalism is no exception to the rule.'[1]

Frank Hill, an editor of quieter brilliance, was Gladstone's metropolitan mainstay. 'In the matter of the Bulgarian outrages,' Gladstone wrote to him on 1 September 1876, 'you have led the people of England; and I am about to walk as best I can in your steps, by an immediate publication, in which I shall hope to pay the *Daily News* a just acknowledgment.' The publication to which he referred was a pamphlet, *The Bulgarian Horrors and the Question of the East*, which sold 40,000 copies within the next few days. His call for the removal of the Turks from Bulgaria, 'bag and baggage', reiterated in a series of public meetings, was too much for Delane, who drew back. 'To rouse the country against the Ministry without being prepared, if necessary, to accept the task and place of the Ministry would be unworthy of a serious politician,' *The Times* rebuked Gladstone on 26 September. At the time, Delane was a guest at Dunrobin Castle, where the Prince of Wales was also staying. He had left Stebbing in charge, and the leaders on the Eastern Question were assigned to James Macdonell, who 'was enthusiastically on Mr Gladstone's side'.

Courtney'), 21 and 25 February 1876, show Stebbing to have been in charge during Delane's absence. *Times* Collection (Texas).

[1] Reid, *Memoirs*, p. 310; Stead's journal of 16 April 1871 and 1876, quoted in J. O. Baylen, 'The "New Journalism" in Late Victorian Britain,' *Australian Journal of Politics and History*, xviii (1972), p. 368; Freeman to Liddon, 31 March 1877, quoted in Shannon, p. 71n.; Gladstone to Hill, 6 April 1877 (copy), Gladstone Papers, Add. MSS. 44,454, fol. 24; 'English Journalism,' *Nation* (New York), 22 July 1880.

From Dunrobin, Delane telegraphed instructions that Macdonell 'was to be shunted to safer subjects' and that editorial policy was to be reversed. On 5 October, when Delane returned to London, he struck Abraham Hayward as being 'very philo-Turk, no doubt misled by the uniform tone of the gay & fashionable world'. Hayward 'shook him a little', or so he claimed, with the result that *The Times*'s leader on the 6th was 'milder than I anticipated'. Henceforth, however, Delane's supicions of Russia prevailed over his reprobation of Turkey.[1]

The *Pall Mall Gazette*, not yet redeemed, was the fiercest of Gladstone's· Fleet Street opponents. Stead deduced from its 'hard swearing' that it was 'evidently hard hit', but that was wishful thinking. Gladstone, considering its 'language & conduct . . . nothing less than shameful', publicly conceded that it was 'by far the cleverest of all the journals that have been used to support the foreign policy of the Ministry in the metropolis'. In letters to Stead, who was later denied permission to publish them, Gladstone distinguished between the motives of his assailants: 'Though I do not think the man of the *Pall Mall* lies for an object, . . . I really cannot but guess that the *Morning Post* is paid' by the Turks, who 'perfectly understand the importance of working through the Press'.[2]

The embattled Tories, on the other hand, prized any and all assistance. 'One really needs encouragement just now,' Lord Derby, the foreign secretary, admitted to his chief on 1 October 1876. 'But we are fairly well supported in the press, which I suspect is a better test than provincial meetings.' He counted the '*Pall Mall, Telegraph, Post*, and *Standard* – for; *Times* uncertain and trimming; only *D. News* and *Echo* against us'. (His list tallied with one drawn up in January 1878 by the Queen, who thought that 'the *Daily Telegraph, Pall Mall* and *Post* are very strong in the right sense'.) Greenwood, the editor of the *Pall Mall*, protected his integrity by keeping a distance: he declined an invitation to dine at the home of W. H. Smith, leaving the First Lord of the Admiralty 'free to ask another'. Yet he prodded Delane by providing him with 'matter wh. must be new & interesting to many readers of *The Times*', namely a detailed account (published on 16 November 1876) of the 'deliberate butchery' perpetrated by Russian troops in Turkestan. If the Turks could not be condoned, at least the Russians could be condemned.[3]

[1] Gladstone to Hill, 1 September 1876, Gladstone Papers, Add. MSS. 44,451, fol. 102; Nicoll, *Macdonell*, p. 294; Hayward to Gladstone, 6 October [1876], Gladstone Papers, Add. MSS. 44,207, fol. 160.

[2] Stead to Gladstone, 30 September 1876, Gladstone Papers, Add. MSS. 44,303, fol. 239; Gladstone to Hill, 30 October 1876, Gladstone Papers, Add. MSS. 44,452, fols. 93–94; speech of 25 November 1879, Gladstone, *Midlothian Speeches* (reprinted, Leicester, 1971), p. 35; Herbert Gladstone to Stead, 22 December 1908, Stead Papers, citing portions to be omitted from Gladstone's correspondence of 1876–77.

[3] Derby to Beaconsfield, 1 October 1876, quoted in Buckle, *Disraeli*, VI, 76; Queen Victoria to Beaconsfield, 10 January 1878, quoted in *ibid.*, 217; Greenwood to Smith, 25 January 1879, Hambleden Papers; Greenwood to Delane, 14 November 1876, *Times* Collection (Texas).

Newspapers insinuated themselves into the ministerial divergences that soon surfaced. In February 1878, Lord Carnarvon made good his threat to resign from the Colonial Office. Disraeli was glad to be rid of 'little Carnarvon, who feeds the Radical press, [and] is always spared'. Salisbury, at the India Office, also came under heavy fire from 'the infernal newspapers, who dog our footsteps pretending to belong to us and howling for blood'. At least in public, however, he feigned indifference: 'my acquaintance with the newspapers is not so great that I can say whether the *Morning Post* abuses me or not,' he told the House of Lords; 'but if it likes to abuse me, I hope it will continue to do so.' In April, Salisbury went to the Foreign Office to replace Derby. The *Pall Mall Gazette* had denounced Derby as 'the peacemen's pawn' (12 February), and the *Morning Post* greeted the news of his departure with the taunt that 'Mr Gladstone has no longer a seat in the Cabinet' (29 March). The *Daily Telegraph*, with the zeal of a convert, was likewise more aggressively Tory than the Tory leadership. Salisbury was appalled by its 'indiscretion' in publishing the terms of the Anglo-Turkish convention before Parliament heard them on 8 July. The *Globe* was guilty of the same breach of etiquette, for which Marwood Tucker disclaimed responsibility: 'my only connection with that paper is a naturally warm interest in what was formerly my child (so to speak)', he answered Corry, who had taken him to task. By nipping at the heels of the government they supported, newspapers exacerbated tensions within its ranks.[1]

Of the major newspapers, only the *Daily News* kept up the Bulgarian agitation. Gladstone, able to 'apprehend that a London journal cannot give more than a limited space for this purpose', proposed that Samuel Morley should finance 'some special & temporary means' to publicize the Eastern Question. But Hill was moved to 'doubt whether a special organ of Eastern information and politics would gain the ear of the public' or, for that matter, carry conviction. Consequently, as Gladstone solemnly affirmed to Hill in April 1877, the *Daily News* was forced to 'stand alone among the Morning Journals of London in sustaining the views which I think we both believe to be those of the nation'. For a time, this belief seemed wholly delusive. When the Prime Minister returned to rapturous acclaim from the 1878 Berlin Congress, the paper could only 'remark that the absurd misuse of the word "Imperial" is becoming of late an intolerable nuisance' (23 July). But the mood had subsided by December 1879, when 'the People's William' celebrated his seventieth birthday and became 'the Grand Old Man'. Gladstone could not 'refrain from offering ... thanks' for Hill's 'eulogies, which a severer justice would have led you to limit or withhold'. He was 'particularly' grateful for 'the

[1] Disraeli to Lady Bradford, 26 April 1876, quoted in Buckle, *Disraeli*, V, 475; *Parliamentary Debates*, 3rd ser., ccxxxvii, col. 53 (17 January 1878); Salisbury's memorandum of 15 December 1877, and Salisbury to Cross, 12 July 1878, quoted in Cecil, *Salisbury*, II, 164, 294–95; Tucker to Corry, 17 July 1878, Hughenden Papers.

singular tact' with which the *Daily News* had referred to his awkward

position in the Liberal party. After what has been said I need hardly assure you that it is my *single* desire to render loyal service to that party, while I remain in Parliament, as a follower of Lord Granville and Lord Hartington.

It was already obvious that Gladstone, by his recent Midlothian campaign, had thrown Granville and Hartington into the shade, opening the way to his resumption of the leadership. In those eloquent speeches, he had made ingenious use of newspaper comment. On 5 December, for example, he had' issued an indictment of the government's Balkan entanglements: 'I would not venture to quote a statement such as I am going to read from the *Daily News*, or the *Echo*, or the *Scotsman*,' he told his audience at Glasgow, 'but I am going to quote it from where I am safe in my source. I am going to quote it from the *Standard* and *The Times*.'[1]

Invigorated by the scent of battle, Gladstone had set out on the road that was to take him thrice more to the premiership. Disraeli, five years his senior, was worn down by the weight of official burdens; even social engagements were a strain, though he realized it was 'necessary to show oneself, or else the *Daily News* says I am dead, or dying, wh. is the same'. Delane was wearier still. Having spent thrity-six of his sixty years as editor of *The Times*, he was driven by illness to retire in November 1877. He left his calling card at Downing Street on the 7th, the day before his farewell visit to Printing House Square. Two years later, he died. John Walter arranged to appoint Chenery to the vacancy, which various members of the staff had expected either Courtney or Stebbing to fill. 'He seems to me to be equal to anything,' Delane said of Chenery, who had served an apprenticeship of twenty years. The new editor's qualifications, including fluency in Arabic, failed to impress the Prime Minister. 'But is he versed in social diplomacy like Mr Delane?' he demanded to know.[2]

The least known among *The Times*'s editors, Chenery lasted six years, until his death in 1884. During his tenure, the circulation fell by twenty-five per cent. Chenery's Liberal sympathies were evinced at the outset. 'Two better articles than the first and third of yesterday I should not wish to read,'

[1] Gladstone to Hill, 18 October 1876, and Hill to Gladstone, 19 October 1876, Gladstone Papers, Add. MSS. 44,452, fols. 49, 57; Gladstone to Hill, 6 April 1877 (copy), Gladstone Papers, Add. MSS. 44,454, fol. 24; Gladstone to Hill, 29 December 1879, Gladstone Papers, Add. MSS. 44,461, fol. 303; speech of 5 December 1879, Gladstone, *Midlothian Speeches*, pp. 190–91. A decade later, Gladstone learned that Thomas Walker, whom he had appointed to the editorship of the *London Gazette*, returned to the *Daily News* 'when the Turkish outrages in Bulgaria first became known ... to take entire charge of that subject'. Walker to Gladstone, 10 November 1888, Gladstone Papers, Add. MSS. 44,505, fols. 112–13.

[2] Disraeli to Anne, Lady Chesterfield, 14 July 1877, quoted in Buckle, *Disraeli*, VI, 169; Henry Wace to Stebbing, 31 December 1877, *Times* Collection (Texas); Gooch, *Courtney*, p. 94; Corry to Disraeli, 7 November 1877, Hughenden Papers; E. H. Yates, *Recollections and Experiences* (London, 1884), II, 139; Escott, *Masters*, p. 183.

Gladstone told Lord Granville on 5 January 1878. Soon, however, the editor bowed to his proprietor's increasingly militant Toryism. 'I am writing as usual for the Paper,' Stebbing informed Delane in December 1878. 'But it has grown so Ministerial an organ that I cannot touch subjects of party character.' Hayward, discerning a swing in popular opinion towards Liberalism, reproached Chenery for 'missing a golden opportunity in not taking the tide upon the turn. But', Hayward explained to Gladstone, Chenery 'is in complete subjection to Walter who is playing for a peerage' and 'now dictates . . . policy and is, I hear, constantly at the office'. More than an idle rumour, Walter's ennoblement was his for the asking. 'Certainly nothing could happen more injurious to *The Times* under present circumstances than your acceptance of a Title,' J. C. MacDonald, the manager of the paper, frankly advised him. 'At any time it would be doubtful practice for you to receive such honours – but just now the universal feeling would condemn it.' Meanwhile, Corry contrived to placate Chenery, who politely thanked him on 1 February 1879 'for the information regarding the re opening of the Session, and also for your kind offer to communicate similar matters to me from time to time'. All the same, the phlegmatic editor was waiting for his chance, which came in the spring of 1880, when the reaction against 'Beaconsfieldism' – as Gladstone branded it in his Midlothian speeches – was running strong. 'Hayward will tell you what I learn from other sources,' Lord Acton wrote to Gladstone's daughter Mary, 'that Chenery really wishes to bring *The Times* round.' While Chenery was quietly at work, Stead arrived on the London scene. Before long, his name was to be a byword among millions who had never heard of Chenery.[1]

[1] 'English Journalism,' *Nation* (New York), 29 July 1880; Gladstone to Granville, 5 January 1878, Granville Papers PRO 30/29/29; Stebbing to Delane, December [n.d.] 1878, quoted in *History of The Times*, II, 521; Hayward to Gladstone, 15 and 29 September [1878], Gladstone Papers, Add. MSS. 44,207, fols. 168–70; MacDonald to Walter, 26 August 1878, *Times* Archives; Chenery to Corry, 1 February 1879, Hughenden Papers; Acton to Mary Gladstone, 23 May 1880, *Letters of Lord Acton to Mary Gladstone* (ed. H. Paul; London, 1904), p. 13.

Six

CONFLICTS OF INTEREST

Contrary to the impression that newspapermen sedulously strove to foster –
partly for reasons of self-esteem – the press in the final quarter of the nineteenth century did not so much lead as follow political opinion, itself increasingly volatile. As far as conscience and circumstance would allow, editorial
policies tended to swing with the pendulum; powerless to arrest, let alone
reverse, it, they struggled to keep pace. Occasionally, as the *Daily Telegraph*
and the *Northern Echo* demonstrated in markedly different contexts, journals
might even draw impetus from the ebb and flow of popular sentiment. Nevertheless, the relationship between politics and the press altered significantly
with the further lessening of external restraints and the rise of countervailing
forces. Once chiefly used to communicate ministerial views to the nation (as it
was then narrowly defined), newspapers now began to function less predictably as the agencies through which mass enthusiasms were conveyed to parliamentary leaders.

More readily sensed than understood, fundamental changes had occurred
by 1880. During his second premiership, Disraeli was hounded and ultimately
defeated by the passions aroused by his imperialist policies. Fanned by the
press, they first surged out of control and eventually turned vindictive. Gladstone, braving stern disapproval from the Queen and *The Times*, undertook
his Midlothian campaign, which bypassed Fleet Street and catapulted him
back into office. David Lloyd George later 'recalled tramping the fourteen
miles to Portmadoc and back to get a London newspaper with a full report of
one of Mr Gladstone's speeches', which his uncle proceeded to read aloud to
the community.[1] Thus, Gladstone proved it possible to stir the country
without stirring the press; and Disraeli, after stirring the press, was rejected
by the country. Although neither discredited nor spurned, newspaper alliances were henceforth concluded with greater mutual wariness. Having too
often bitten the hand that fed it, the press could no longer be regarded as
a tame animal. At the same time, politicians came to realize, sometimes

---

[1] Frank Owen, *Tempestuous Journey* (London, 1954), p. 32. Significantly, Lloyd George did
not rely on either the Welsh or English provincial press.

grudgingly that press opinon and public opinon were not necessarily synony-mous.

Fourteen years after Edward Dicey had anonymously lamented the obscu-rity that shrouded – and, in effect, incapacitated – members of the Fourth Estate, John Morley penned his editorial 'Valedictory' in the *Fortnightly Review*. 'The names of all important journalists are now becoming to be as publicly known as the names of important members of parliament,' he exulted, confident that this arrangement made for a healthier state of affairs. 'England is still a long way from the point at which French journalism has arrived in this matter.... But there is a distinctly nearer approach ... than there was twenty years ago.'[1]

Here, as in other respects, the general election of 1880 qualifies as a watershed. 'The entrance of so large a number of journalists to the House of Commons is a striking proof of the growing influence of the press, which is one of the most important training schools of modern politicians,' wrote an unsigned contributor (actually J. A. Hardcastle, the veteran Liberal MP) in the *Edinburgh Review*. By his count, the contingent had doubled in size to fourteen.[2] That, by most standards, was an exceedingly cautious estimate. Along with those who warranted the appellation, there were numerous MPs who scribbled for newspapers in order to augment their incomes and possibly to enhance their stature (as Lowe, Salisbury, and Harcourt had done, and Courtney was doing). Not a few backbenchers were self-styled journalists for want of any better designation. Still others, defying classification, were variously involved with the financial management of particular properties.

The striking thing was that, far from being a stigma, a career in journalism was accepted as 'a stepping-stone to higher things'. So describing it, Wilfred Meynell (who took the pseudonym of 'John Oldcastle') attempted to compile a list of newspapermen in the 1880 Parliament: Passmore Edwards of the *Echo* sat for Salisbury, and Arthur Arnold, formerly editor of his paper, for Salford; Joseph Cowen, proprietor of the *Newcastle Chronicle*, shared the representation of that city with Ashton Dilke, proprietor of the *Weekly Dispatch*; Courtney and Walter were connected with *The Times* in much the same capacities as were Justin McCarthy and Labouchere with the *Daily News*; and Charles Bradlaugh, returned with Labouchere at Northampton, was tagged as a journalist for having 'projected the *National Reformer*'. Like McCarthy, T. P. O'Connor was one of a phalanx of Irish scribes who arrived at Westminster. English constituencies elected the owners of *Punch*, the *Saturday Review*, and such provincial papers as the *Western Daily News*. In addition, Meynell cited the unsuccessful candidacies of Algernon Borthwick of the *Morning Post*, Thomas Gibson Bowles of *Vanity Fair*, Alfred Austin,

[1] *Fortnightly Review*, n.s. xxxii (1882), 516.
[2] [J. A. Hardcastle], 'The New Parliament,' *Edinburgh Review*, cli (1880), 547–64.

who wrote leaders for the *Standard*, and Morley, who was soon to take command at the *Pall Mall Gazette*.[1]

Admittedly, it is never easy to affix occupational labels to politicians, who – especially before the introduction of payment for members in 1911 – led double or triple professional lives. Because Meynell's criteria were subjective, his roster was far from comprehensive. For reasons best known to himself, he included Labouchere, but neither Arnold Morley (who was elected for Nottingham) nor Samuel Morley (who continued to sit for Bristol); and he evidently considered J. J. Colman more a mustard manufacturer than a newspaper magnate. As several of his examples had severed their press connections, his choice was all the more arbitrary. Yet, if the exercise was not done well, it remains remarkable that it should have been done at all. However ineptly, Meynell pointed up a tendency that was to be especially pronounced whenever the Liberals obtained a majority. In the 1906 Parliament, for example, it has been reckoned that journalists constituted the third largest occupational component.[2] Again, the figures lack precision, but the implication is clear.

There was no correlation, of course, between journalistic distinction and parliamentary authority. More often than not, one detracted from the other. Nor was there as much cross-fertilization between the two spheres as Radical ideologues had been inclined to believe. Morley, inspired by French models, had expressed to Chamberlain the view that experience in journalism and Parliament would richly complement each other. After three defeats, he entered 'the profitless beer-garden at Westminster' in 1883, and promptly conceded to T. H. Huxley: 'I used to think that I could perhaps improve politics; so far it looks as if politics had rather *dis*improved me.' The previous year, he had lightened his load by relinquishing the editorship of the *Fortnightly Review*. Months after his election, he was forced to give up the *Pall Mall Gazette* as well. 'His withdrawal . . . will be good for him, though he may miss the assistance it gave. But it bled him too constantly,' wrote his friend George Meredith, who heard that Morley 'is impressed for committee work, and that is fatiguing enough in itself'. Throughout his long political career, Morley was continually to reproach himself for having betrayed his true calling.[3]

Besides prompting a heightened awareness of the role of publicists in public life, the 1880 elections challenged many of the traditional assumptions about

[1] John Oldcastle [W. Meynell], *Journals and Journalism*, pp. 61–64. Leonard Courtney described how Ashton Dilke, Sir Charles's brother, had tried to buy the *Examiner*, then 'reverted to the notion of starting a journal first hand', before he finally acquired the *Weekly Dispatch*. Courtney to Stebbing, 10 November 1878, *Times* Collection (Texas).

[2] J. A. Thomas, *The House of Commons, 1906–1911* (Cardiff, 1958), pp. 22–23; Lee, *Origins*, pp. 198–99 and table 32.

[3] Morley to Chamberlain, 3 January 1878, Chamberlain Papers; Morley to William Rathbone, 19 August 1878, Rathbone Papers; Morley to Huxley, 22 January 1883, Huxley Papers; Meredith to F. A. Maxse, 1 May 1883, *Letters of George Meredith* (ed. W. M. Meredith; London, 1912), II, 340.

the effects of journalism on electoral behaviour. An essayist in the *Quarterly Review* (actually Francis Hitchman, who wrote for such Tory papers as the *Manchester Courier* and later the *Standard*) was convinced 'beyond question that the press of this country, and especially of the capital, is chiefly in the hands of Liberals, whose open-handedness, enthusiasm, and keen business habits, give them an immense ascendancy'. With a logic that would have astonished Gladstone, Hitchman computed that there were thirteen morning and five evening dailies published in London:

> Six of the thirteen morning journals may at once be struck out from the list, as exercising no influence on politics. . . . The remaining papers are all political, and are all more or less Liberal, with few exceptions. . . . The Conservative party are formally represented in London by one evening paper and informally by another, and partially by two published in the morning, whilst of all the weekly organs of opinion there are but two which can fairly be described as even tolerant of Conservative principles.

The discrepancy, from which Hitchman drew encouragement, was that 'the total number of votes cast for Liberal representatives at the late General Election exceeded those given for their Conservative opponents by no more than 200,000', making it 'obvious that Conservative electors must to a great extent obtain their political information from Liberal sources'. In that case, Conservatives might redress the balance with a modest degree of effort, which Hitchman called upon them to expend.[1] Yet he undercut his own argument. If, as he maintained, Conservative voters had indeed resisted the influence of an overwhelmingly Liberal press, might not Liberal voters equally withstand the appeal of a revitalized Tory journalism?

The underlying question was whether newspapers had a direct impact on the electorate, or whether they merely fortified commitments. No one then – or since – could be certain. 'The newspapers said that the people's minds would not be changed by anything said in election speeches or addresses',[2] and the same presumably held true for leading articles. Even so, some journals were adjudged to carry more weight than others. The circulation of *The Times* was restricted to a relatively small segment of the enfranchised population, but the paper was inestimably valued for its rapport with what it called (27 October 1879) the 'great mass of uncommitted opinion at the centre'. By contrast, the Liberal *Daily News* preached largely to the converted. So did the *Globe*, the *Morning Post*, and the *Standard*, and it was disingenuous of Hitchman to suggest that any of them was less than firmly loyal to the Conservative cause. The *Daily Telegraph* was the newest and biggest gun in the Tory armoury, although it let slip a hint of backsliding on 3 April 1880, when it found itself on

---

[1] [F. Hitchman], 'The Newspaper Press Directory and Advertiser's Guide,' *Quarterly Review*, cl (1880), 535, 537; *also see* [H. S. Northcote], 'Conservative Reorganisation,' *Blackwood's Magazine*, cxxvii (1880), 804–10.

[2] Trevor Lloyd, *The General Election of 1880* (Oxford, 1968), pp. 27–28.

the losing side. The *Daily Chronicle* and the *Echo*, both attached to the Liberal camp, were politically exiguous. Unlike them, the *Pall Mall Gazette* aggressively fought the election under the Conservative banner.

However much or little newspapers may have swayed voters' preferences, their political affiliations continued to command politicians' attention. Denied the benefit of hindsight, contemporaries habitually ignored the trends that historians have clearly perceived, and concentrated instead on developments that have come to be dismissed as chimerical. Thus Hardcastle and Meynell interpreted the influx of journalists into Parliament as a sign of influence rather than thwarted ambition or general social restlessness; and Hitchman abjectly failed to discriminate between quantitative and qualitative support. According to no less an authority than Stanley Morison, 'it became obvious' during the 1880s 'that the evening papers had taken the lead in London journalism'. Obvious to whom? Certainly not to Chamberlain, who divulged information to Escott and gave explicit instructions: 'Take care the evening papers do not get it first. They are the least important.'[1]

Obsessively concerned with the press, Chamberlain serves admirably as a touchstone. In 1874, he interrupted his Birmingham mayoralty to stand at Sheffield, where his candidacy was stymied by the hostility of the *Sheffield Daily Telegraph*, in Garvin's expert opinion 'at that time under Christopher Leng, perhaps the cleverest Conservative organ in the country'. Two years later, he was safely returned for Birmingham in a by-election. Through the National Education League and other pressure groups, he had already established ties with Stead at Darlington, and had incurred the enmity of Wemyss Reid at Leeds. These relations were supremely important to him. 'Somebody sent me the *Scotsman* whose article is not very gracious,' he wrote as a parliamentary novice. 'I am afraid I am out of favour with the Editor.' From J. C. Bunce and William Harris, editor and chief leader-writer of the *Birmingham Daily Post*, he could invariably expect better treatment. 'I wish to heaven I had a few of you fellows in London and in the House,' he told Bunce, his trusty ally, early in 1877. 'I am sure that we could do great things but at present there is not a soul I can depend on except Dilke. . . . If you have the chance, say a good word for him some day.' Before long, Chamberlain had extended his journalistic contacts into a veritable network that included Morley and Escott (with whom he invited Bunce to dine in 1881). As Kennedy Jones recalled in 1919: 'Thirty years ago there was no public man of the front rank so accessible to journalists as "Joe", a diminutive, always used in Birmingham, that in itself spoke volumes for his popularity with pressmen.' Bunce was the linchpin of his constituency machine. 'By the way, are all the London policemen correspondents of the *Daily Post*?' Chamberlain enquired flatteringly of its editor on 3 December 1881:

---

[1] Morison, *The English Newspaper* (Cambridge, 1932), p. 276; Chamberlain to Escott, 16 November 1883, Escott Papers.

On Thursday I met Gladstone in St James's Park and walked slowly with him across the Park to his garden door talking all the way without noticing anyone on the road except a policeman. Next morning the *Daily Post* informs its reader that I had a long interview with the Prime Minister. How on earth did you get the information?

Usually, he knew precisely how the *Daily Post* obtained its information: he supplied it.[1]

Chamberlain need not have worried about Dilke, member for Chelsea since 1868, who looked after himself. 'I am going to speak to-night about ten,' Dilke notified Frank Hill of the *Daily News* on Friday, 13 April 1877. It was not superstition, but the complexity of the Eastern Question, that made him nervous. 'It would be of great use to me if I could have at 9.30 any news that was later than the Evening Papers', and, for that purpose, he proposed to send a messenger to the office in Bouverie Street at nine o'clock. 'For the information of your leader writer I may tell you what is likely to happen to-night,' he offered in return. The following morning, Dilke's speech was duly reported and the first leader fastened upon it. On numerous other occasions, Dilke and Hill traded intelligence, and Dilke came to the defence of the *Daily News* when it was 'bitterly attacked by the *Pall Mall & Globe* for telling lies about the no. of sick in Cyprus'; ascertaining that its statistics were correct, he wrote to seven London papers, but a governmental *mot d'ordre* prevented the publication of his letters. Charles Cooper of the *Scotsman* demurred at Dilke's promotion to Cabinet rank: 'He has too much conceit and too close connection with the Bashi Bazouks of the newspapers.'[2]

For Leonard Courtney, who followed Dilke to Westminster, Chamberlain did not show the same tender regard. 'I expect Courtney (of *The Times*) will make his maiden speech,' he wrote to Bunce on 16 February 1877. 'He is no good from our point of view and though he calls himself a Radical he has voted on the two chief divisions of the session against us.' That night, as Courtney recounted to his sister, he spoke 'in a very thin house' on the subject of treaty obligations to Turkey. 'The *Daily News* refers to the speech in its leader,' he proudly noted the next day (in its words, Courtney had delivered 'a very effective piece of argument'); but *The Times*, apart from a brief quotation in its parliamentary report, took no notice. Doubtless because his line on foreign policy ran counter to its editorial views, Courtney was denied any support from the paper for which he continued to write. Disregard, however, was better than misconstruction. 'The report in *The Times* was absurdly bad of my speech,

---

[1] Garvin, *Chamberlain*, I, 165; Chamberlain to Stead, 29 December 1877 (copy), and Chamberlain to Bunce, 27 November 1876, 16 February 1877, 29 October and 3 December 1881, Chamberlain Papers; Jones, *Fleet Street and Downing Street*, p. 94.

[2] Dilke to Hill, 13 April 1877 and [16 August 1878], Dilke Papers, Add. MSS. 43,898, fols. 10, 19; Cooper to Rosebery, 16 July 1882, Rosebery Papers, Vol. 10,010, fol. 122.

being in many parts unintelligible,' he complained a year later to his sister, whom he urged to compare it with the text in the *Daily Telegraph*. And Henry Fawcett, the postmaster-general, wrote to him in 1883 'regretting *The Times* did not print what I said about Reform which pleased him very much'.[1] The influence conferred on an MP by a journalistic career was, again, more apparent than real.

The Radicals, divided among themselves, were not the only ones to play, and occasionally to lose, at the game. Perhaps they played for bigger stakes, for it was Chamberlain's design to renovate Liberalism with the organizational techniques he had perfected at Birmingham. Press support was indispensable to him. But many of his press supporters were irresistibly attracted to Gladstone, whom Morley tried 'to stir ... up to write for the *F[ortnightly] R[eview]*, ... the only magazine in which he does not write – the voluminous animal'. And Escott sent Gladstone copies of the *World*, 'a journal for the political management of which & for the authorship of whose political articles I am responsible'. Temporarily estranged from Toryism, Escott apologized to Gladstone for the intrusion:

> I am only anxious to acquaint you with the fact that my sympathies, worthless as they may be, are very strongly against the present Administration, & I hope, therefore, to employ such opportunities as I command in a manner which you may I trust approve.

Significantly, he did not address himself to Lord Hartington, the official leader of the Liberal Party, whom he ridiculed as 'Half-Hartington' in his number of 18 December 1878. To the Radicals, including reformed Tory Radicals like Escott, Hartington was a mere stopgap. Yet Hartington could not afford to dismiss the *World*, whose criticisms – Escott heard from a former Liberal minister – provoked him to speak out against the Afghan war. Edited by Edmund Yates, the endearing victim of his own incurable profligacy, the journal 'appeals mainly to what is called *society*', Escott confirmed, 'though we never drop below 22,000 a week'. On 27 March 1879, the general committee of the United University Club considered a request for further copies of the *World* and *Truth* to be taken in. These periodicals were gadflies, but they could sting.[2]

So, too, could *Vanity Fair*, better remembered for its pictorial than its political content. (Delane was one of the few notables who refused to sit for its portraitist). Sir Stafford Northcote wrestled with the question as to whether

[1] Chamberlain to Bunce, 16 February 1877, Chamberlain Papers; Courtney to his sister Margaret, 17 February 1877 and 9 February 1878, and Courtney to Kate Potter, 9 February 1883, Courtney Papers.
[2] Morley to Chamberlain, 30 September 1878, Chamberlain Papers; Escott to Gladstone, 18 and 24 December 1878, Gladstone Papers, Add. MSS. 44,458, fols. 235, 254–55; Escott to Blackwood, 5 June 1879, Blackwood Papers; general committee minutes, United University Club, 27 March 1879.

that paper had committed a breach of privilege by a disclosure in 1879. 'There is no doubt that the licence in which some of the Newspapers indulge is becoming a serious evil,' he acknowledged to the Speaker; 'but great caution is necessary in any proceeding that brings the House of Commons (or either House) into direct collision with the Press.' Northcote belonged to an administration that was beholden to journalists for their indiscretions. Frederick Greenwood, who claimed credit for having told Disraeli that the Khedive's Suez Canal shares were on the market – he got his tip from Henry Oppenheim, part-owner of the *Daily News* – was a valuable informant. From his 'unimpeachable sources' at the *Pall Mall Gazette*, he communicated reports about French official opinion, Balkan disputes, and developments in the Middle East. His 'suggestions' for the relief of distress in northern industrial districts were 'respectfully submitted to Lord Beaconsfield' on 20 December 1878. 'They are intended to meet a most serious difficulty, wh. without some remedy, is likely to prove (in the hands of the Opposition) a political danger.' Gladstone, keenly aware of the problem, asked Hill:

> Would it not be desirable, on grounds much wider and deeper than those of party, that some authoritative voice should without delay summon the Government and the country to look at home, and deal wisely and in time with the sufferings of the English poor? To allow Lord Beaconsfield to say the first word on the subject, and to relinquish to the Government the position of leading opinion and action, would be to give it an advantage which may help to secure it a further term of power, and opportunity of mischief.

Both sides, then, employed a double standard. While deploring the transgressions of the press, they were always ready to turn them to their own advantage.[1]

                    *   *   *

Gladstone's correspondence with Hill gave proof that *The Times* did not exaggerate when it declared on 12 February 1880 that 'every consideration has for some time been subordinated by the Opposition to the one object of turning the Ministry out of office'. Yet, the paper wrote sardonically, for all the invective that Liberals had spewed at 'this incompetent and untrustworthy government', the Conservatives began the new session firmly in control. By comparison, 'as an organized body the Opposition seems almost to have abandoned its functions'. For the sake of the two-party system, the fulcrum of con-

[1] Northcote to Sir Robert Peel, 21 April 1879 (copy?), Iddesleigh Papers, Add. MSS. 50,040, fol. 153; Greenwood to Beaconsfield, 20 December 1878, 24 February and 23 May 1879, Hughenden Papers; Gladstone to Hill, 24 December 1878, and other dates, Gladstone Papers, Add. MSS. 44,458, fols. 256 ff.

stitutional balance, this situation was deemed most unfortunate.

Such sentiments were 'highly approved of' by the Queen, who instructed her private secretary to ascertain 'the authorship' of this leading article. Unable to provide the information, Montagu Corry put the question to Chenery, who declined to satisfy the royal curiosity. It may have been true, as the editor insisted, that 'the articles, and the ideas and opinions they convey, are in all cases originated by me, and are in a very real sense my own production'; in fact, this particular piece was the handiwork of Dr Henry Wace. It was often difficult during these hectic months to tell who was representing whom and on what authority. Lord Hartington played host at Chatsworth to Henry Reeve, the editor of the *Edinburgh Review*, whom he furnished with guidelines for an exegesis of the Liberal programme. Entitled 'Plain Whig Principles' (which itself was a red flag to the Radicals), it appeared in the January number. Hartington, less than happy with the product, hoped that his inspiration would go undetected.[1]

The waters were further muddied when, in the inquests that inevitably followed polling, newspapers were blamed for letting down their friends and giving comfort to the enemy. It would be a mistake to accept these retrospective judgments at face value. 'The Conservatives had expressed considerable satisfaction at the way the London daily press had supported their foreign policy', which they played as their trump card. 'After the election, . . . their gratitude for this support diminished a little unreasonably,' Trevor Lloyd has written. Robert Blake has concurred: 'The pro-Government press was wildly optimistic, such papers as the *Daily Telegraph,* the *Standard*, and the *Morning Post* taking victory for granted,' as did Disraeli and the party managers. 'Even the cautious *Times* wept crocodile tears about the damage . . . likely to result from another Liberal defeat.'[2] Hitchman and other Tory apologists might wail that the newspapers had failed to deliver the goods. In fact, they had done their best to make bricks from the straws at which they clutched.

Similarly, it suited Liberal politicians to berate their own press for having betrayed doubts which they themselves had shared. Afterwards, it was fashionable for Hardman to ascribe the party's landslide victory to 'the staunch and consistent conduct of the country Liberal press. . . . They kept the light of political truth burning brightly while it was obscured or extinguished in the metropolis'. The leading proponents of this view were Wemyss Reid ('Public opinion . . . no longer finds its exclusive or even its most authoritative organs in the London press'), Charles Cooper, and others who had a vested interest in asserting the superiority of provincial journalism. Asked by Morley (a London editor), 'shortly after the general election', how

[1] F. I. Edwards to Corry, 12 February 1880, and Chenery to Corry, 18 February 1880, Hughenden Papers; 'Plain Whig Principles,' *Edinburgh Review*, cli (1880), 257–80; Hartington to Granville, 19 January 1880, Granville Papers, PRO 30/29/27.
[2] Lloyd, *General Election*, p. 99; Blake, *Disraeli*, p. 710.

he could have been so confident that the Gladstonians would win, Cooper replied

> that I had diligently read the provincial papers – the papers of Manchester, Leeds, Sheffield, Birmingham, Bristol, and others – and their tone, and the reports of proceedings which they gave, had convinced me that the London papers were wrong in their anticipations.

A few years later, Cooper reminded Lord Rosebery that the *Scotsman* and

> Scotland stood by Mr Gladstone at the last election when London newspapers were declaring that he had lost all hold of the country. This fact . . . ought to prevent him or anybody else from paying attention to what the London papers say. . . . Their opposition . . . is a compliment.

The myth does not stand up to scrutiny. Without denying the devotion of the *Scotsman*, the *Leeds Mercury*, and the *Manchester Guardian*, Lloyd has determined that 'few provincial papers had predicted a great Liberal triumph'. On the whole, they were scarcely more sanguine than the metropolitan Liberal press, and 'observed the same conventions'. The New York *Nation* put the point with Yankee bluntness: 'The fact is that this vital difference of opinion between London and provincial journals is little more than a fantasy of Mr Gladstone's own mind.'[1]

Moreover, it should be noted, the two *obiter dicta* cancelled out each other. To the extent that the London journals denied vigorous support to the Liberals, they refuted Hitchman's hypothesis. To the extent that they stinted their efforts on behalf of the Tories, they disproved the equally categoric assertions of the provincialists. Contemporary critics obviously could not have it both ways. From the evidence, one may conclude that they were not justified in having it either way.

While the Liberal press could not help reflecting the confusion within that party, it worked earnestly to mend the rifts. Well into the campaign, it remained unclear whether sectional interests had overcome their disillusionment and mutual antipathies. Hartington's titular leadership offered modest inducement. 'There is nothing at all to be ashamed of in the fact that it should be necessary on the eve of a General Election to preach the old lesson of union,' the *Daily News* candidly stated on 10 March 1880.

> A Liberal cannot expect to have as his representative in Parliament a member whose opinions are in all respects identical with his own. . . . When questions of grave moment are of issue he does not deserve the name

---

[1] [Hardcastle], 'The New Parliament,' *Edinburgh Review*, cli (1880), 554; Reid, 'Public Opinion and Its Leaders,' *Fortnightly Review*, n.s. xxviii (1880), 243–44; Cooper, *An Editor's Retrospect*, pp. 65–66; Cooper to Rosebery, 16 March 1883, Rosebery Papers, Vol. 10,010, fol. 162; Lloyd, *General Election*, pp. 32–33, 110; 'English Journalism', *Nation* (New York), 22 July 1880.

of Liberal if he withholds his support from a candidate on the ground that he is or is not pledged to this or that crotchet or fad.

Liberal factionalism, as well as the uncertainty that surrounded Gladstone's intentions, inhibited the performance of the party's press. Any clear-cut pronouncement on domestic legislation was likely to alienate one or another segment of Liberal opinion. The *Daily Telegraph* recognized this predicament. 'It could only be by a coalition of Birmingham Radicals and Home Rulers with Whigs and Liberals, that Lord Hartington could make a Government which would endure for a week,' it insisted on 11 March. Two days later, it predicted that 'intelligent Liberal electors', following the *Telegraph*'s example, would prefer 'candidates who ... are Englishmen first, and partisans afterwards', namely Disraelian patriots.

It is impossible to say with any degree of certainty whether these editorial psephologists seriously believed their own projections, or merely devised them in the hope of producing a desired effect. According to the *Morning Post* (22 March), for example, the Conservatives could count on picking up seven seats in the London boroughs and Middlesex; when the dust settled, they had lost three. For that matter, its proprietor failed to capture Evesham, despite the 'perfect Borthwick worship' that survived in his father's old constituency, and his agent's assurances that 'the only question is the size of the majority'. Repeated often enough, these estimates of impending Tory victory erased any doubts in the minds of those who spouted them. It was no idle boast for Borthwick to tell his wife that the Prime Minister 'looked to him especially'.[1]

That the *Globe* was antagonistic to Liberalism did not deter Herbert Gladstone from advertising his Middlesex candidacy in its pages on 2 April. Patronage of this sort, unthinkable in an earlier age, was not reasonably expected to affect editorial endorsements. Defeated in Middlesex, as was his brother William Henry in East Worcestershire, Gladstone's youngest son was promptly adopted at Leeds, where he had to tread more carefully. An electoral hornets' nest, the Leeds Liberal Association was torn between the supporters of Edward Baines and Radical enthusiasts for temperance and disestablishment, who neither forgave nor forgot Baines's defence of the 1870 Education Act. W. E. Gladstone was originally chosen as a compromise candidate; although he permitted his name to go forward successfully, he decided to cast his lot with Midlothian, where he stood simultaneously. Herbert Gladstone inherited the succession. As editor of the *Mercury*, which the Baineses had owned since the beginning of the century, Reid confessed that he was 'naturally anxious that Mr Baines should, if possible, have been selected' to contest the seat, which had been Baines family property for forty years until 1874. Nevertheless, warning the new Liberal candidate to beware of intra-

---

[1] Borthwick to his wife, undated letters [February and March 1880?], quoted in Lucas, *Glenesk*, pp. 273–74.

party strife, he expressed 'the desire of all of us here to unite heartily in supporting you'.[1]

By May, when Gladstone *fils* arrived at Westminster as member for Leeds, Gladstone *père* was again Liberal leader and, for a second time, Prime Minister. The process had been a complicated one in which the press had played a notable part. On 6 April, the *Daily News* reported that Gladstone had won Midlothian by a majority of 211 votes: 'If Mr Gladstone is willing to resume the leadership of the Liberal party, and the headship of a Liberal Government, no one, we imagine, would for a moment dispute his paramount title.' Not only was it necessary to persuade Gladstone to accept the consequences of his dramatic re-emergence, but also and more trickily Hartington had to be made to step aside gracefully. With the assistance of other Liberal papers, the *Daily News* took up the challenge. 'What is needed is not Mr Gladstone's name in a list of Ministers, or his bodily presence at occasional meetings of the Cabinet,' it argued on the 19th,

> but his influence and authority in the shaping and conduct of public business, his faculties of constructive legislation, and his experience and skill as an administrator. We do not want a mere modicum or residue of these things, but we want them to their fullest extent. It is only as Prime Minister that he can place all his resources at the disposal of the country.

And the next day: 'Other statesmen would be serviceable, Mr Gladstone is indispensable.' Hill adhered to this position even at the risk of causing disruption among front-bench Liberals. T. P. O'Connor recalled that

> when Harcourt, with his usual somewhat provocative self-confidence, proclaimed to Hill that he knew several men who would refuse to serve under Gladstone, Hill drily replied that the noughts might revolt against the figure one, but could not get on without it – which was a humorous but true description of the situation.[2]

Like Harcourt, the Queen, and *The Times*, the *Daily Telegraph* favoured a Hartington premiership, and thereby probably did as much as the *Daily News* to make up Gladstone's mind. On 22 April, Gladstone had an interview with Hartington, who had returned from Windsor, where the Queen 'indicated to him her confidence in his moderation'. It struck Gladstone as a curious coincidence that this was precisely 'the phrase under which he [Hartington] is daily commended in the *Daily Telegraph*, at this moment I think, Beaconsfield's personal organ and the recipient of his inspirations'. There was later some dispute – 'a barren controversy', Morley called it – as to whether Hartington attempted to assemble a ministry. But he quickly realized that he could not

[1] Lloyd, *General Election*, p. 92; Reid to Herbert Gladstone, 7 April 1880, Viscount Gladstone Papers, Add. MSS. 46,041, fol. 1.
[2] O'Connor, *Memoirs*, I, 51.

succeed without Gladstone, whose logical place was at the helm. The next day, after consulting the Queen, Hartington and Granville conveyed to Gladstone an invitation to appear at Windsor at 6.30 that evening. The purpose was clear. 'Receiving this intimation', Gladstone read to his callers 'an extract from an article in the *Daily News* of yesterday', in which it was stated that, if Gladstone

> accepts the task of forming and the duty of presiding over a liberal administration, it will be because Lord Granville and Lord Hartington, with characteristic patriotism, have themselves been among the first to feel and the most eager to urge Mr Gladstone's return to the post to which he has been summoned.

With their assent, Gladstone accepted the commission. 'Possibly enough,' the *Telegraph* consoled itself on the 23rd,

> after embodying in his Cabinet the principles of the victory which he has mainly helped to gain, and conducting the various sections of the majority through the simpler and easier stages of the first two or three Sessions, he may, if quiet times be in store, accept the dignified calm offered to veteran statesmanship in the Upper Chamber, and leave to younger politicians – who now stand aside in homage to his over-mastering claims – the burden and heat of the day.

How little the *Telegraph* knew the man! *The Times* showed a more generous spirit. Abraham Hayward, 'after being told the state of things' by the new premier, 'went off in the middle of the night' to see Chenery, 'an intimate friend of mine', and the leader on the 24th 'was the result'. It greeted with relief 'the natural solution of the crisis', and conceded that Gladstone 'has legitimately won his present position'. Tired, but elated, Hayward counted it 'a great point to secure *The Times*' at this critical moment.[1]

When the tumult died down, there were the usual recriminations. The *Kentish Mercury* was accused by the *West Kent Courier* (24 April) of having hoarded Conservative advertising without meeting its obligations to the party, which fared none the worse. In Scotland, where the Tories were dealt a 'rude shock', Frederick Wicks of the *Glasgow News* received 'letters from all parts declaring that notwithstanding the vigour of the *News* the persistent misrepresentations of the Radical press have been too much for the canvassers'. He brought this 'matter of commanding interest' to the attention of Lord Beaconsfield:

> The *News* ... does not reach the lower classes of voters who are taught chiefly by two Radical papers circulating between them 350,000; and two others circulating 80,000 besides 65 local radical weeklies. Twenty one indif-

---

[1] Gladstone's memoranda of 22 and 23 April 1880, quoted in Morley, *Gladstone*, II, 622, 624–25; Hayward, *Correspondence*, II, 315.

ferent Conservative weekly papers contest with this enormous mass of Radical literature.

Wicks wrote not to complain, but to advance a proposal: 'if I am provided with £4,000 a year for three years . . ., I cd. plant a strong weekly Conservative paper in every county in Scotland'. Already he had 'laid my plan before Lord Borthwick', whose knighthood he mistook for a peerage, 'who has undertaken to move in the matter'. All he asked of Beaconsfield was some 'means of expressing your desire in a way that will excite his zeal'. For whatever reason, the project was stillborn. Elsewhere, the Liberals encountered similar problems. Hartley Aspden described his early career on the *Warrington and Mid-Cheshire Examiner*, 'a Liberal weekly journal' owned by the Toulmin brothers, George and John, whose undertakings included the *Preston Guardian*, the *Blackburn Times*, and (from 1886) the *Lancashire Evening Post*. In the 1880 election, 'Warrington put a Liberal at the head of its poll for the first time in its electoral history', wrote Aspden (who ignored Peter Rylands's freak success in 1868), 'and much of this triumph was ascribed to the *Warrington Examiner*'. Yet this 'achievement' went unrewarded: 'The Liberal party had promised to support the *Examiner*, but their promises were like the proverbial pie-crust.' Perhaps Aspden and his employers were envious of the nearby *Macclesfield Chronicle*, which was discovered to have received substantial payments from Liberal agents, who neglected to declare them as election expenses.[1]

Six days after his return to the premiership, Gladstone had his first occasion to meet Frederick Greenwood, who wrote to him that evening, 'within forty eight hours of retirement from my own small region of power'. In the wake of the Conservative defeat, Greenwood was informed that the *Pall Mall Gazette* was changing ownership and, consequently, its political complexion. Under the circumstances, it was understandable that he should have been somewhat maudlin:

> My paper (I originated it, & have carried it on uncontrolled through its fifteen years of existence) – has since the elections been sold into the hands of a thorough going party-man of advanced Liberal views, & is henceforth to be no erratic independent but to be printed as a supporter of your government. If, sir, you care about such matters at all, you will not in the natural order of things regret that. But when I remember that you have more than once gone out of your way to speak generously of certain good qualities wh. you found in the paper, & since in its fiercest opposition to your policies never a line appeared to cast a doubt on their profound sincerity & their exalted motive, I venture to hope that you will not be altogether pleased

---

[1] Wicks to Beaconsfield, 5 May 1880, Hughenden Papers; Aspden, *Fifty Years a Journalist* (London, 1930), pp. 9–10; *Parliamentary Papers* (1881), Cd. 2853, xliii (pp. 11, 20), and minutes of evidences, qq. 1560–64.

that (for a time at any rate) the *Pall Mall Gazette* is to be virtually extinguished. The men who wrote its politics with me all resign with me.

Apart from the size of his parliamentary majority, Gladstone had had no better news. The *Pall Mall Gazette* was no longer to be 'an atheistical Tory organ', as Goldwin Smith had called it. In this Liberal government, unlike the last, John Bright did not have to contend with the 'raving lunacy of the *Pall Mall*'.[1]

According to Bungay, the proprietor of Thackeray's imaginary newspaper from which the *Pall Mall Gazette* derived its name: 'Our governor thinks the people don't mind a straw about these newspaper rows.' Here, however, was one that excited sufficient interest to find mention in the correspondence and diaries of numerous contemporaries, and to carry into the columns of rival newspapers. Greenwood, Thackeray's protégé on the *Cornhill*, was esteemed as a literary stylist and a recruiter of talent (much of it from the *Saturday Review*, and all of it handsomely remunerated), no less than as a political pundit. Lord Houghton, who was well placed to know, testified that Greenwood had 'many friends in political and social life' who would bitterly resent his displacement. The Conservative chieftains would certainly miss his astringent commentaries. 'Whenever I read Greenwood,' Disraeli was reported to have said, 'I feel myself in the grip of a statesman.' On topics of foreign policy, Disraeli's opponents must sometimes have felt themselves in the grip of a champion wrestler.[2]

George Smith, Thackeray's publisher, had owned the *Pall Mall Gazette* since the first issue, which sold fewer than 3,900 copies. He began in partnership with H. S. King, who withdrew early on. In theory, if decreasingly in practice, the paper was non-partisan. Smith was a Liberal sympathizer, as was Greenwood when their collaboration started. But, like Lawson of the *Telegraph*, Greenwood broke with Gladstone over the Bulgarian question (J. A. Froude suspected from his editorial vehemence that he 'must have Turkish securities'), and he thereafter espoused doctrines of Tory imperialism. His claim to be a 'philosophic radical' was easily seen through. Smith could not have been pleased when Sir Henry Maine, back from India in the late '70s, innocently asked whether the paper had been sold to the Conservatives. Smith's daughter rarely heard her father discuss politics, but had the impression that he was 'somewhat disappointed by Greenwood', who seemed 'politically ungenerous', particularly towards Gladstone.[3]

By the spring of 1880, Smith had had enough. Although the paper was then

[1] Greenwood to Gladstone, 29 April 1880, Gladstone Papers, Add. MSS. 44,463, fols. 264–65; J. W. Robertson Scott, *The Story of the Pall Mall Gazette* (Oxford, 1950), pp. 189, 235–36.
[2] Houghton to Henry Bright, 3 May 1880, quoted in Reid, *Monckton Milnes*, II, 387–88; Escott, *Masters*, p. 248; Grant, II, 116–17.
[3] Robertson Scott, *Pall Mall Gazette*, pp. 127, 139, 235–36; Robertson Scott, *The Life and Death of a Newspaper* (London, 1952), pp. 274–75; Hirst, *Morley*, II, 90; Escott, *Masters*, p. 253.

presumed to be self-supporting, the historians of *The Times* maintained on undisclosed authority that Smith 'had lost £25,000 for the good of Greenwood's cause', of which he did not approve, 'when ... the Liberals were returned and [he] saw vanish his chances of making the Conservative *Pall Mall Gazette* pay'. In any case, he had more lucrative business interests outside publishing, and seized the occasion to transfer the holding to Henry Yates Thompson, who had become his son-in-law two years previously. It was a sort of belated wedding present. The son of a Liverpool banker, the new proprietor was educated at Harrow and Trintity College, Cambridge. He was an accomplished classicist, the director of a railway company, and a discriminating bibliophile. In 1865, the year of the *Pall Mall*'s birth, Yates Thompson returned from a world tour to stand alongside Gladstone in South Lancashire. His defeat was sweetened by Gladstone's expression of hope that

> at some early period a gentleman of so much ability and of so high a character, anxious to devote his life to the service of his country, ... will find an easy and secure way, and an honourable way, into parliament.

Unable to obtain election elsewhere, he served as private secretary to Lord Spencer, when the 'Red Earl' (whose nickname derived from the hue of his beard) was Viceroy of Ireland. At Dublin Castle, he won a reputation for 'imperturbable courage and self-possession'.[1]

On 28 April 1880, the day before Greenwood met Gladstone, Leslie Stephen recounted the saga to a transatlantic friend:

> The *Pall Mall Gazette* has been the incarnation of Greenwood and, as you know, the most thorough-going of Jingo newspapers. A transformation is to take place, probably next Monday, in virtue of which the *P.M.G.* will appear as a Liberal organ. I am a good deal amused by the catastrophe, which will shock many virtuous old Tories, to whom the *P.M.G.* appeared as a kind of Abdiel. I fancy also that the experiment will be a very ticklish one, as it must clearly involve the loss of a great many of the old audience.

It remained to be seen how Yates Thompson would cope with this gift. He was a man 'whose worst flatterers', according to Stead, who was decidedly not among them, 'never claimed for him the pen of a ready writer'. J. Saxon Mills, who subsequently joined the staff, surmised that he 'managed to carry on' during this transitional period by dipping into 'the accumulation of manuscript left in the pigeon-holes by Mr Greenwood'. A perusal of the paper lends credence to this view. It was rumoured that Yates Thompson tried to entice C. P. Scott to London from the *Manchester Guardian*. Instead John Morley took charge, apparently on an informal basis at first. 'Things are very contrary,' he

[1] *History of The Times*, III (London, 1947), 92; *Daily News*, 24 July 1865; D. Chapman-Huston, *The Lost Historian: A Memoir of Sir Sidney Low* (London, 1936), p. 47; Mills, *Cook*, p. 47.

wrote to Chamberlain on 10 May, a full week after he purportedly had been 'installed' as editor. 'Such strong pressure was brought upon me about the *P.M.G.* that to-day at four o'clock I agreed to become editor-in-chief. God only knows what will come of it.' Morley spent the next night under Rosebery's roof at Mentmore, where it was arranged for him to meet Gladstone.[1]

On 1 May, the *Pall Mall Gazette* contained a terse and cryptic announcement that Greenwood 'will not be responsible for any political opinions in its pages after today'. On the 2nd, it felt 'bound to say how much the *Pall Mall Gazette* has owed to his untiring assiduity and unflinching independence'. Furious to see himself praised for the very qualities that had told against him, Greenwood gave his version in the next day's *Standard*:

> I was invited to remain editor of the *Pall Mall* on condition of parting with my principles, of bidding good-bye to all the men who had done so much in helping me to raise the paper to its high and honourable place in journalism, and of setting about making the paper a turncoat to please Mr Thompson and the new Government.

Smith, reluctant 'to enter upon a newspaper controversy with Mr Greenwood', replied on the 4th 'that many of the statements in Mr Greenwood's letter are inaccurate or based upon misapprehension'. He left it to his son-in-law 'emphatically to contradict' Greenwood's assertion 'that the *Pall Mall* will henceforward be a Ministerial Journal'.

Morley, who drew an annual salary of £2,000, nominated as his deputy W. T. Stead, who was being paid £400 a year at the *Northern Echo*. Yates Thompson, Morley promised, 'would be very acquiescent, on the whole, if he saw the thing alive and moving. He is not a very high-minded man but he is good-natured and very energetic.' Morley himself was eager 'to have someone with whom I can discuss every day the line of the paper. My official friends are too busy, and besides my notion is that we should inspire them rather than they us.' Stead received the invitation on his thirty-first birthday, and 'replied saying I hated London, it was the grave of all earnestness, but that it was the centre of power and . . . I would not feel justified in refusing'. The proprietor suggested an interview on Sunday, but Stead (who was 'in some doubt as to Morley's irreligion') evasively declined, 'chiefly because I would have felt wicked going to discuss a business engagement' on the Lord's Day. Before accepting, he consulted prominent Liberals: W. E. Forster, now Irish secretary, recommended that he 'should be editor of the *Daily Chronicle* instead of second to Morley'; but Sir James Stansfeld, the veteran statesman, urged him on. Morley, in turn, solicited – and rejected – advice from Wemyss Reid,

---

[1] Stephen to Charles Eliot Norton, 28 April 1880, quoted in Hirst, *Morley*, II, 91; Mills, *Cook*, pp. 47–48; Robertson Scott, *Life and Death*, pp. 57, 72; Morley to Chamberlain, 10 May 1880, quoted in Garvin, *Chamberlain*, I, 307n.

who warned that Stead 'would need to be watched closely, as he is a man of
such extreme views and of such daring originality . . . that . . . he might at any
moment seriously commit the newspaper with which he was connected'. Stead
had professional affairs to tidy up in Darlington before he could take up his
London duties. 'You will know that my new lieutenant has arrived,' Morley
wrote to his sister on 12 October. 'He is a queer child of nature, but a nice and
good fellow, and he will, moreover, be most useful.' His work at the office
'much lightened', Morley had been free to dine the previous evening with
Chamberlain and Bright.[1]

Morley and Stead made an odd, but effective combination: the first, 'a
queer child of nature', was a self-anointed servant of God; the second, a biographer of Rousseau, was notorious for having spelt 'god' in print with a small 'g'
(it was said that he reserved the capital letter for 'Gladstone'). Temperamentally, they were poles apart. Yet they politely tolerated, if they did not always
share, each other's enthusiasms, and they often arrived at the same conclusions from different perspectives. As a rationalist who trusted in science,
Morley faulted Stead for 'setting ignorance to instruct ignorance'. As a popularizer, Stead thought that Morley lacked

> nimbleness of mind. . . . He was deficient in the range of his sympathies.
> No power on earth could command Mr Morley's interest in three-fourths of
> the matter that fills the papers. He is in intellect an aristocrat. . . . To him a
> newspaper was simply a pulpit from which he could preach, and, as a
> preacher, like all of us who are absorbed in our own ideas, he was apt at
> times to be a little monotonous.

Stead, addressing himself to a wider and more heterogeneous congregation,
was inclined not so much to preach as to harangue. His prose, less fastidious
than Morley's, was tinged with purple. Certainly he proved the more innovative as a journalist: in time, he emulated American typography and interviewing techniques, and did not eschew sensationalism which, as he explained, was
'justifiable up to the point that it is necessary to arrest the eye of the public and
compel them to admit the necessity of action'. But, at least in the early '80s,
this distinction between the two men was neither evident nor applicable. 'The
Pall Mall of Friday is infinitely too stiff and crammed with politics,' Morley
complained to Stead on 6 August 1881. 'Only on the hardest compunction
should there be a word of politics after pages 5 or 6.' Perhaps a case can be
made that Morley was the grandfather of the 'new journalism'.[2]

Leaving the *Pall Mall Gazette* as a ship 'without captain and crew' (in Mills's

---

[1] Morley to Stead, 14 August 1880, Stead Papers; Morley to his sister Grace, 12 October 1880,
quoted in Hirst, *Morley*, II, 98; Stead's diary, 8 August 1880, Stead Papers; Reid, *Memoirs*,
p. 317.
[2] Morley's conversation with Stead, quoted in Mills, *Cook*, p. 49; Stead's view of Morley,
quoted in Hirst, *Morley*, II, 96; Stead, 'Government by Journalism,' *Contemporary Review*, xlix
(1886), 671; Morley to Stead, 6 August 1881, quoted in Robertson Scott, *Life and Death*, p. 67.

words), Greenwood immediately announced plans for the *St James's Gazette, an Evening Review and Record of News*. Writing to his friends at *Blackwood's Magazine*, to whom he looked for advertisements, he anticipated 'a paper wh. I hope to make worthy of your commendation & support. It will be produced under pressure of great difficulty of the mechanical kind,' he revealed, 'but yet I venture to promise that it will be a good paper from the beginning.' Money was apparently no problem. Greenwood found a ready benefactor in H. Hucks Gibbs (later Lord Aldenham), a City merchant who had been a governor of the Bank of England and who was to have a parliamentary fling in 1891–92. Lord Acton understood that Greenwood had collected '£110,000 for his newspaper, besides general offers of indefinite sums – enough to start it four or five times over'. Greenwood was optimistic; but 'the most sanguine man of all', he wrote to his daughter, was Henry Vizetelly, the publisher, 'who tells me he expects that we shall sell 20,000 copies of No. 1' which appeared on 31 May.[1]

With the same eight-page format, the same twopenny price, the same sedate tone, and the same 'cultivated British audience' in mind, the *St James's* considered itself the rightful *Gazette*. Its band of contributors, 'smoked out of our ancient quarters' in Northumberland Street by Liberal usurpers, was portrayed on the first day of publication as having 'gathered together again, to fall to work in the old spirit and in very much the old accustomed ways'. Sir James Fitzjames Stephen, Sir Henry Maine, W. E. Henley, and H. D. Traill were among those who followed 'the merry Greenwood' (as Henley paraphrased Ruskin's line about making 'merry in the good greenwood'). The romance, however, was more Arthurian than Ruskinian. Traill, who incidentally wrote verse of 'extraordinary cleverness', was singled out by Escott as 'the chief pillar' of the paper. 'I need not tell you,' Escott nevertheless told William Blackwood, that Traill 'is as good a Tory as you are yourself, & he has done more for the cause of Toryism with his pen, than any writer now living, in the daily press.' In 1882, Traill transferred to the *Telegraph*; from 1889 to 1891, he edited the *Observer*, and he concluded his career as editor of *Literature*, founded in 1897. To David Hannay, whose father James had graced the old *Pall Mall*, Greenwood denied a report in the *World* 'that Mr Traill had left the *St James's* voluntarily. . . . He left at my desire – not his – for reasons wh. have nothing whatever to do with the paper.' Likewise Fitzjames Stephen, to his brother's relief, 'ceased to contribute when the paper was about three years old'.[2]

Greenwood, progressively less merry, filled these vacancies with old-timers

[1] Mills, *Cook*, p. 47; Greenwood to *Blackwood's Magazine* ('Gentlemen'), 22 May [1880], Blackwood Papers; Acton to Mary Gladstone, 23 May 1880, *Letters of Lord Acton*, p. 13; Greenwood to his daughter, 28 May 1880, quoted in Robertson Scott, *Pall Mall Gazette*, p. 345.

[2] Robertson Scott, *Pall Mall Gazette*, p. 259; Escott to Blackwood, 12 August 1881, Blackwood Papers; Greenwood to Hannay, 26 October [1882?], Hannay Papers; obituary of Traill, *The Times*, 22 February 1900.

like T. E. Kebbel or newcomers like J. M. Barrie and Sidney Low. 'The *St James's* had a position of its own in those days,' recalled Low, Greenwood's right-hand man and eventual successor. 'Its circulation was what would now be called contemptibly small; but its influence was out of all proportion to the number of copies sold.' Yet Massingham objectively discerned that the paper 'had some conspicuous defects. It did not appeal to the general body, even of Conservative opinion; it was rigidly non-sensational, and it too steadily subordinated news to opinion.' Too explicitly for its own good, another critic reflected in its fifth month of publication, Greenwood's *St James's* was 'simply' Greenwood's *Pall Mall* 'in somewhat different form and with a new name, with an exaggeration of its antipathy to Mr Gladstone and its dread of what it calls the latter-day Radicals'. As a supplier of bespoke goods, the *St James's* grew marginally more successful, but paradoxically also more expendable. 'The paper is addressed to the cultured and critical, who probably do not take it in, but read it at their Clubs, & are ·a class whose tastes & feelings are Conservative,' deduced Lord Cranbrook. 'It may be an advantage to give them a line but they will not cease to support the Party from want of even so good a journal as the *St James*.'[1]

Owing to their natal circumstances, the new *Pall Mall* and the slightly newer *St James's* were direct competitors. Their modest circulations fluctuated in relation to each other. When one recklessly reduced its price to a penny in 1882, the other recklessly followed suit. On 20 May 1880, a member of the United University Club called the attention of the general committee to the advent of the *St James's*, 'a new evening paper', and asked 'for copies of it to be supplied'. At first, 'the Committee deferred ordering any copies until the publication of the paper'; but, on 3 June, 'it was ordered that 6 copies of the *St James's Gazette* be taken in and that 6 copies of the *Pall Mall Gazette* be discontinued'. A week later, there was 'further consideration of the manner in which the *Pall Mall* & *St James's Gazettes* were appropriated' on the premises, and 'an alteration was made in the number of copies of the *Pall Mall* & *St James's Gazette* taken in by the Club' on 13 January 1881. The same month, a member complained that 'the number of *Pall Mall Gazettes*' was insufficient. But the paper's contentious views on Irish and foreign policy made it anathema to most readers in Clubland, and Stead's 'Maiden Tribute of Modern Babylon' (6 July 1885), a lurid exposé of the white slave traffic, was the last straw. At the United University, all copies were cancelled: on 23 July, 'a letter was read' to the committee 'asking that the *Pall Mall Gazette* be restored to the list of newspapers; it was resolved that the *Pall Mall Gazette* be taken in', presumably in limited quantity. Showing greater tolerance, but equal concern, the Oxford and Cambridge University Club moved, after an unusual debate

[1] Low, quoted in Chapman-Huston, *Lost Historian*, p. 63; Massingham, *London Daily Press*, pp. 162–63; 'The Evening Newspapers,' *Nation* (New York), 7 October 1880; Escott, *Masters*, pp. 254–55; Cranbrook to Smith, 20 December 1882, Hambleden Papers.

on 1 January 1886, 'that no alteration be made in the number of copies of the *Pall Mall Gazette* taken in'.

Within three years of his appointment, Morley had tried Yates Thompson's generosity and his own patience. 'Thompson's régime will not last,' Stead prematurely concluded in 1883. He expected that Andrew Carnegie and Samuel Storey would annex the *Pall Mall* to their provincial empire, and that Carnegie, out of deference to Chamberlain, would appoint Escott as editor. 'Escott, however, gets tipsy after dinner and disgusts Carnegie,' he consoled himself. In the event, Carnegie and Storey bought the *Echo*, and Stead succeeded Morley at the *Pall Mall*, which Yates Thompson retained until 1892. The *St James's* ran aground even sooner. On 7 November 1881, Greenwood recited his 'melancholy story' to W. H. Smith:

> There is an imminent probability that the *St James's Gazette* will come to a stop. The calculation was that in due time handsome expenditure upon a good article would meet the usual return; & so the paper has been worked upon a rather costly scale. The reward has not followed. Though the circulation of the paper has not been bad (much exceeding that of the *Pall Mall*) & though it keeps up steadily, it ought to have been better. . . . The upshot is that the proprietary has got discouraged, & doesn't care to bear the loss altogether any longer.

Greenwood, without moneyed contacts of his own ('Mr Yates Thompson has the advantage of me there'), asked Smith to 'point to any means of assistance'. But the immediate crisis passed, and Gibbs held on until 1888. Meanwhile Labouchere informed Escott, who had taken Morley's place at the *Fortnightly Review*, that Greenwood ('a clever ass') was 'not getting on very well with the finders of money for the *St James*'. Labouchere advised Escott not to 'compromise yourself too much in your Art[icle]s in the *F.R.* as a Conservative, for we mean to have you one of these days a Liberal Journalist. I was only talking about this a few days ago to some Members of the Cabinet.' To Chamberlain, whom he knew to be Labouchere's principal Cabinet confidant, Escott confirmed that the prize in question was the editorship of the *Daily News*. 'It was of course indirectly & allusively put. Meanwhile "I know nothing" & am well content to let matters take their course & bide my time.'[1]

Had Escott been tapped to follow Morley at the *Pall Mall* or Hill at the *Daily News*, his allegiance might have been secured for Liberalism; indeed, as he told Chamberlain, he was prepared to serve up 'Radicalism as hot as it can be made'. Disappointed, he gravitated back to the Conservative fold.

[1] Stead's memorandum [1883], quoted in Robertson Scott, *Life and Death*, p. 123; Greenwood to Smith, 7 November 1881, Hambleden Papers; Labouchere to Escott, 'Tuesday' [1882], Escott Papers; Escott to Chamberlain, 12 December 1882 and 6 February 1883, Chamberlain Papers. Chamberlain subsequently dangled the prospect that Escott, who had recently begun to write a weekly column for *Lloyd's Newspaper*, might take over the editorship of the *Daily Chronicle*, which was 'in the gift of Lloyd'. Chamberlain to Escott, 31 July 1884, Escott Papers.

Notwithstanding his pledge to conduct the *Fortnightly* 'on a broader and less partisan basis', he indicated to Lord Carnarvon 'that it will wear a moderate Conservative complexion such as will connect it with the friends of the Constitution and distinguish it from its old Jacobin and revolutionary tendencies'. His four-year tenure was marked by 'an incursion of Conservative contributors', bearing out Trollope's prognosis that Escott was 'a man of opinions far too settled to admit of eclectic principles'. Nevertheless, in political as distinct from literary terms, eclecticism was Escott's dominant characteristic. Continuing to regard his friendship with Chamberlain 'as the great event of my life ... & I can honestly say the one point round which all my interests centre', he was simultaneously drawn to Lord Randolph Churchill and the country-house rebels of the Fourth Party. Not alone in perceiving an affinity between Chamberlain and Churchill, Escott enhanced his professional status by being all things to all men. That Lord Stanhope could endorse his 'principle' that the *Fortnightly* should not be run 'as a mere political review, ... especially as so many people know little and care less of what is going-on in the political world', did not preclude Lord Carnarvon from agreeing that 'the time has perhaps come when party organisation whether in politics or in literature has become one necessary element in English public life'. Under his own name, anonymously, or pseudonymously, Escott wrote for a wide range of periodicals. His connection with the *World* allayed fears 'that Yates was turning Jingo' on the part of Chamberlain, who was provided with opportunities to inspire articles. His editorship of *Home News*, which circulated primarily in India, was probably responsible for his introduction to Churchill. His direction of the *Fortnightly Review* afforded a forum for both Chamberlain and Churchill, who were consulted about topics and contributors. Mudford, who employed Escott as a leader-writer on the *Standard*, chided him for his multiple loyalties ('Why on earth you should get yourself into a disagreeable position ... for the sake of Ld. Randolph is really a mystery to me') and, still more, for his schizophrenic existence:

> The excessively voluble and singularly inaccurate person who masquerades of a morning as a Conservative journalist, and then appears once a month as the editor of an ultra-Radical review, also contrives – unless we are much mistaken – to figure, by way of variety, as a Ministerial apologist in the pages of the *World*.

There was no denying that Escott walked a tightrope, and a knotted one at that.[1]

---

[1] Mrs W. L. Courtney, *The Making of An Editor* (London, 1930), pp. 133–35; Escott to Chamberlain, 8 November 1883, Chamberlain Papers; Stanhope to Escott, 5 April 1883, Carnarvon to Escott, 24 August 1883, Chamberlain to Escott, 22 April 1880, and Mudford to Escott [1884?], Escott Papers. According to Antonio Gallenga, the Italian correspondent for *The Times*, Chenery regarded Escott as 'the writer in the *World* of all the cruel articles and paragraphs that are incessantly cutting him to the heart'. Gallenga to Escott, 28 October and 1 November 1882, Escott Papers.

But so did Mudford himself, after a fashion. It implies no contradiction to say that, although steadfastly Conservative, he was also doggedly independent. The *Standard*, in Garvin's estimation 'the great Conservative journal of that time', responded tepidly to Disraeli's 1880 election manifesto, in which it detected 'too much sonorousness for the fastidious ear'. Reviewing that campaign, Reid reflected that, 'strange to say, the *Standard*, the avowed organ of Conservatism, was the fairest and most moderate' of the ministerial journals. Gladstone, whom he met soon afterwards, shared his opinion:

> he paid a great compliment to the *Standard*, saying that it was a newspaper he always liked to read because he always found it to be fair and honest. 'When I read a bad leader in the *Standard*,' he said, 'I say to myself, Mr Mudford must be taking a holiday.'

Needless to say, these words, 'duly reported' to Mudford, afforded him 'intense pleasure'. But he did not allow them to influence his judgment.[1]

From his house in Kensington, Mudford was constantly 'in telephonic communication' with the *Standard* office in Shoe Lane, and – as Massingham wrote – 'his vigilant eye allows no important detail associated either with the editorship or the management to escape him'. His privacy was sacrosanct, as was his dignity. On 19 February 1880, when any other editor would have gone on bended knee to a lesser government official, Mudford replied to Lord Salisbury:

> The Editor of the *Standard* asks permission to return the enclosed telegram (just received from his assistant manager) which has been addressed to the *Standard* by Lord Salisbury's House Steward.
>
> The Editor of the *Standard* may, perhaps, be allowed to add that he is not much in the habit of receiving telegraphic instructions from House Stewards: not even when they are in the Household of the Secretary of State for Foreign Affairs.

Small wonder that Kebbel, despite the length of his employment on the *Standard*, 'never got to be on terms of very close intimacy with Mr Mudford'. All the same, Kebbel was convinced that 'he was a kind-hearted – nay, a warm-hearted man – in reality, though his manner was often cold and a trifle constrained, arising, I often thought, from nervousness rather than from any want of real sympathy'. Escott may have thought the same, as Mudford's undated (and sometimes illegible) rebukes were not without a glint of irony. 'I think you had better rest a day or two,' the editor prescribed on one occasion. 'Your Friday's leader was hardly up to yr. mark, & the one last night must fall under the same (not unfriendly) criticism.' Or, more accusingly: 'you're too much of a Radical . . . to write my political leaders. I love the H. of Lords – you loathe

[1] Garvin, *Chamberlain*, I, 278; Reid, 'Public Opinion and Its Leaders,' *Fortnightly Review*, n.s. xxviii (1880), 236; Reid, *Memoirs*, p. 299.

it.' When the subject warranted, Mudford farmed out leader-writing assignments to experts beyond the staff. But his best-known political contributor was
Alfred Austin, through whom Lord Salisbury – his house steward having
failed – tried to shape the editorial views of the *Standard*.[1]

Along with these rearrangements within and between newspapers, the early
1880s saw adjustments in the supply of news, domestic and foreign. Since the
'60s, most London dailies and the more prominent provincial papers as well
had depended increasingly on the overseas facilities of Reuters, which had
expanded from a financial service. The resources of that agency, far greater
than those of any single paper, were strained by the obligation to cover far-
flung imperial ventures: in 1884, for the first time, Reuters failed to pay a dividend to its shareholders. Its clients balked when the company proposed higher
subscription rates, but all but *The Times* resigned themselves to a settlement
whereby a surcharge was to be imposed 'in time of war or prolonged political
disturbance'. *The Times*, seeking to lessen, if not necessarily to terminate, its
costly reliance on Reuters, patronized other agencies, some of which it helped
to improvise into existence. But Reuters was never supplanted and indeed not
seriously challenged until the closing years of the century, when the leading
London papers negotiated bilateral news-exchange agreements with their
Continental counterparts.[2]

Concurrently, there developed new methods for the collection of news at
Westminster. 'Lobby Correspondents began to evolve as a distinct kind of
journalist early in the 1880s,' Colin Seymour-Ure has observed. '"Evolve"
seems the right word because the process was gradual – certainly until the start
of the Lobby list in 1885,' when representatives of the press were accredited by
the Speaker to patrol the corridors of power. Before then, their status had
been undefined and occasionally disputed. The doyen of lobby men was Henry
Lucy of the *Daily News*, better known to readers of *Punch* as 'Toby, MP', who
wove into his celebrated parliamentary sketches the threads of conversation
he overheard during his long hours at the House. Other London papers, most
notably *The Times*, preferred to rely on editorial connections. Again to quote
Seymour-Ure: 'The need for a Lobby Correspondent, one might say, was in
inverse ratio to the quality of an editor's contacts.' The provincial papers,
usually denied direct access to political leaders and lobby facilities, obtained
their information second- or third-hand. In 1880, for example, Reid introduced Herbert Gladstone, the newly elected member for Leeds, to the
London correspondent of the *Mercury*: 'Generally speaking, I may say, his

---

[1] Massingham, *London Daily Press*, pp. 84–85; Mudford to Salisbury [19 February 1880], Salisbury Papers; Kebbel, *Lord Beaconsfield*, p. 237; Mudford to Escott, undated letters, Escott
Papers.
[2] Graham Storey, *Reuters' Century* (London, 1951), p. 106; Oliver Boyd-Barrett, 'Market
control and whoesale news: the case of Reuters,' and Michael Palmer, 'The British press and international news, 1851–99: of agencies and newspapers,' in Boyce, *et al.*, eds., *Newspaper History*,
pp. 192–219.

functions . . . are confined to keeping us abreast of the London newspapers in political intelligence.' And Cooper found it 'very hard' to bear that the *Scotsman* in 1882 received only a partial and garbled summary of ministerial directives, which were given *in toto* to the London papers, including the *Standard*, which handed them on to the *Glasgow Herald* and the *Dundee Advertiser*.[1]

The institution of the Lobby list was one of many signs that journalists were becoming more self-assertive. On 14 May 1880, a meeting was 'specially called' of the general committee of the Reform Club to consider 'paragraphs' in the *Echo*, the *Scotsman*, and the *Standard* that 'made public' certain private proceedings. The chairman was 'requested to communicate on this subject with the Editors & Proprietors of such Newspapers who are Members of the Club'. Everywhere, newspapermen were on the prowl, and the politicians encouraged them. Edward Russell, who had given Lucy his start on the *Liverpool Daily Post*, wrote to Gladstone on 7 June 1880 to request 'five minutes of your precious time' to discuss 'a matter of business which I should wish personally to submit to you'. Invited to breakfast on the 17th, he ensured himself a warm welcome with a leading article on the 11th in praise of Gladstonian fiscal policy. Frank Hill continued to receive hints from Dilke, who was undersecretary for foreign affairs in the Liberal government, taking care not to jeopardize his special relationship with Gladstone. 'Letters addressed simply to the Editor of the *Daily News* are liable to be opened by the sub-editor or the business manager,' he instructed the Prime Minister. 'In case of communications which are in any sense confidential and which ought not to be seen by others than the editor, it might be best to address them to me by name.' Gladstone did even better: he addressed the editor as 'My dear sir' until 5 October 1880, when at last he wrote 'Dear Mr Hill'. Forster, whose radicalism had long since paled, kept up contacts with Reid, Mudford, and (it was believed) Chenery of *The Times*. Herbert Gladstone eventually superseded him as Reid's mentor. Rosebery, who entered the Cabinet in March 1885, lodged his confidence in the *Scotsman*, with an occasional aside to its rival, the *Glasgow Herald*; Chamberlain, who became president of the Board of Trade in 1880, undermined Forster's influence with the *Standard* by cultivating Escott. Disclosures of Cabinet business in the *Standard* brought recriminations against Chamberlain, who took them in his stride. 'I think we had better not meet for some little time,' he told Escott on 20 November 1880:

> Some cad or another has taken the trouble to inform certain people that we are close friends & to insinuate that the shrewd guesses of the *Standard* are the result of our intimacy.
>
> The best – & only – complete answer I can make to such statements is . . .

[1] Seymour-Ure, *The Press, Politics and the Public* (London, 1968), pp. 198–99; Reid to Herbert Gladstone, 18 May 1880, Viscount Gladstone Papers, Add. MSS. 46,041, fol. 3; Cooper to Rosebery, 9 February 1882, Rosebery Papers, Vol. 10,010, fols. 89–90; *also see* Jeremy Tunstall, *The Westminster Lobby Correspondent* (London, 1970).

that I have not seen you for some time – & I believe that this is necessary though more disagreeable to me than it can be to you.

Eight days later, however, Chamberlain invited Escott to 'run down' to Birmingham over the weekend. There, he could consort with whom he pleased.[1]

In his electoral stronghold, Chamberlain commanded firm support from Bunce, whom he thanked on 9 July 1880 for an 'admirable article in the *Daily Post*. I wish to goodness we could get similar articles in some of the London papers,' he declared, 'but it is lamentable to see how little grip and force they exhibit.' The single exception was 'the *Pall Mall* under Morley's management', which he considered 'the only reliable organ of the Liberal party at the present time'. Chamberlain and Dilke were good friends of Morley's: the three musketeers dined together after two of them were sworn in as ministers, and Morley 'saw their first red boxes brought in'. Besides congenial company, his ministerial comrades provided Morley with guidance and other useful favours. 'I should be very grateful if you would tell one of those brutal Cerberuses at the door of the H. of C. to let me pass tomorrow,' Morley wrote to Dilke. 'It will save me quarter of an hour's chafing and fuming at the indignities put upon the spiritual power by the d——d temporal.'[2]

The *Pall Mall Gazette* lent strong support to the 'courageous and effective Land Bill' (8 January 1881) that the government introduced to alleviate agrarian distress in Ireland, but balked at the countervailing policy of applying coercion to quell Irish disorders. Chamberlain conceded that 'the line of the *Pall Mall* is an awfully difficult one – more difficult than mine because more uncertain'; and, unlike Morley, he did not have to wrestle with a Millite conscience. The paper trusted to the instincts of the administration, if not to the specific measures promulgated and executed by Forster as Irish chief secretary. On 25 January, the day after Forster had unveiled his coercion scheme, the *Pall Mall* put aside its 'doubts' as to 'the efficiency of coercion for its own objects', and catalogued the approving responses that morning in *The Times*, the *Daily News*, the *Standard*, the *Daily Telegraph*, the *Morning Post*, the *Scotsman*, the *Daily Chronicle*, the *Newcastle Chronicle*, and the *Manchester Guardian*:

> The Government have not entered lightly on the task they have in hand, and it is certain they will not abandon it lightly. We trust, for the credit of the Liberal Party, that they will be deserted by none of their supporters.

In spite of these strictures, the *Pall Mall* itself soon deserted, recognizing Forster's policy to be pointless and retrograde. On 3 April, Morley pleaded for

---

[1] Russell to Gladstone, 7, 9, and 11 June 1880, Gladstone Papers, Add. MSS. 46,464, fols. 214, 223, 227; Hill to Gladstone, 28 September 1880, Gladstone Papers, Add. MSS. 44,466, fol. 118; Chamberlain to Escott, 20 and 28 November 1880, Escott Papers.

[2] Chamberlain to Bunce, 9 July 1880, Chamberlain Papers; Garvin, *Chamberlain*, I, 307; Morley to Dilke, 13 June 1882, Dilke Papers, Add. MSS. 43,895, fol. 156.

'A New Policy for Ireland', to be symbolized by the release from gaol of Parnell and other political detainees. Nothing less than 'a thorough overhauling of the administrative machinery of Dublin Castle' was required, along with the removal of Forster, whose 'name has become inseparably associated with a policy that is odious in Ireland'. These arguments were reiterated the next day, whereupon Forster was impelled to write to the Prime Minister: 'You may have seen an article in yesterday's *Pall Mall Gazette* urging my dismissal or resignation. . . . The *Pall Mall* is right in one thing – this is no time for personal considerations'. Contrary to the impression that Chamberlain had unleashed these 'thunderbolts', as he called them, he contemplated that, 'unless I am much mistaken, the immediate result has been to establish a kind of reaction in favour of Forster', whom Gladstone sustained. Thus Morley's victory was all the greater the following week, when Parnell was released (Chamberlain heard the news from Bunce), and Forster formally tendered his resignation. 'A fortnight later', Morley 'heard in the lobbies that Forster was out. . . . Harcourt said to Chamberlain: "Your mischievous friend, J. M., has done this."'[1]

The Times, dismayed by the government's volte-face, scorned the proposition that 'concession will accomplish what coercion has failed to achieve', namely the pacification of Ireland. Above all else, it deplored the breaking of the continuity of English politics by irresolute Liberals who shirked the 'imperative duty of the Queen's Ministers' (5 and 8 May 1882). The *Pall Mall* applauded the return of the 'Red Earl' Spencer to replace the colourless Lord Cowper as Irish viceroy, but could not contain its disbelief at the choice of Lord Frederick Cavendish to replace Forster:

> He is not to be Chief Secretary, but Chief Clerk. . . . He has unquestionable merits of his own, and very abundantly. . . . But the advantage to which he perhaps owes his appointment is that he is not likely to increase the disquiet with which the new policy is regarded in some quarters. If Mr Chamberlain or Sir Charles Dilke, Mr Lefevre or Mr Shaw, had been appointed, it would have been unmistakable that the Government were about to take up their new maxims of Irish policy in good earnest. [5 May 1882]

Algernon West, formerly Gladstone's private secretary, recalled that he met Morley and Yates Thompson 'on my way home . . . and told them how utterly wrong they were in their estimate of the man'. Cavendish never had the opportunity to prove himself. On 8 May, the *Pall Mall Gazette* and other papers reported that, with his under-secretary, he had been assassinated in Phoenix Park, Dublin.[2]

---

[1] Chamberlain to Morley, 30 December 1881 and 12 April 1882, Chamberlain Papers; Chamberlain to Bunce, 10 April 1882, quoted in Garvin, *Chamberlain*, I, 348; Forster to Gladstone, 4 April 1882, quoted in Reid, *Life of the Right Hon. W. E. Forster* (London, 1888), II, 411–12; Morley, *Recollections* (London, 1917), I, 175–77.

[2] West, *Recollections* (London, 1899), II, 150.

The Irish problems of 1881–82 complicated Liberal politicians' relations with the press and, in no small measure, presaged the split in party and journalistic ranks over Home Rule in 1886. Controversies, seemingly laid to rest in Parliament, continued to simmer among newspapers. The *Manchester Guardian*, unlike *The Times*, saw fit to dissociate Parnell from acts of Fenian terrorism (8 May); that its Irish articles were written by W. T. Arnold, Forster's nephew, did not inhibit the paper from advocating conciliation. Cooper of the *Scotsman*, who was later to side with the Unionists, was 'not inclined to believe in Mr Parnell. He will sell his country, sell his friends, sell the government, and sell himself,' Cooper told Lord Rosebery. 'By all means let the govt. get what they can from Parnell, but they ought not to trust him further than you can throw him.' Reid of the *Leeds Mercury* nursed the same suspicions. An ardent admirer of Forster for over a decade, he put his paper in an acutely embarrassing position. 'If you have time & opportunity to look at the *Leeds Mercury*,' Frederick Baines, its owner, wrote sniffily to Herbert Gladstone in October 1881, 'you will have observed the deep interest with which your friends hereabout follow the course of events in Ireland & the satisfaction' taken in Forster's retaliative proposals. The following spring, when Forster resigned under duress, the *Mercury* announced plans for a banquet in his honour. Herbert Gladstone shuddered at the prospect: 'The mere fact,' he instantly recognized, ' . . . should be laid hold of by many as constituting a protest against the Government.' He appealed to James Kitson (later Lord Airedale), the patriarch of the Leeds Liberal Association and the president-elect of the National Liberal Federation, to intervene. 'I confess I cannot understand the line taken by the *Mercury* and some assertions I have seen in its leaders lately are absolutely without foundation,' he wrote to Kitson, who agreed that 'Reid seems to have gone wrong altogether on Chamberlain & Forster'. In the general committee of the association, Kitson blocked 'two resolutions . . . which censured the *Leeds Mercury*', only to incur the paper's Forsterite wrath. ('So much for my consideration of the *Leeds Mercury*,' he concluded.) Reid insisted to Gladstone that the *Mercury* was merely defending Forster 'against attacks that (as you know) have been shamefully unfair and even untruthful in the columns of papers like the *Pall Mall Gazette* and in other organs of the Birmingham party'. But Gladstone, at the same time that he furnished Kitson with a letter to show to Baines, patiently explained to Reid:

> Your personal feeling for Mr Forster and your strong belief in his motives . . . does you harm & has I think led you to justify his later actions in a way which seems to me to carry with it the condemnation of the Government. This may have been your intention – you have of course every right to differ from the Govt.

His editorial sovereignty upheld, Reid was somewhat mollified. Kitson was confident that 'the criticism has done good. I think there will not be so many digs at Chamberlain' in the *Mercury*, 'though of course Reid has more of the devil in him and is sure to have a hit at me & others when he has a chance.' Forster went abroad after his resignation, and did not come to Leeds until October 1883, when he presided at the annual dinner of the Liberal Club. By then, he was a spent force. He lived long enough to dissent from Gladstone's Home Rule formula in letters to the *Daily News* and the *Standard* (23 December 1885). Three years later, Reid faithfully memorialized him in a two-volume biography that made no reference to the misbegotten banquet.[1]

*   *   *

In the spring of 1880, the Conservatives set up a standing committee under the chairmanship of W. H. Smith to investigate the causes of their shattering defeat. On its recommendation, J. E. Gorst was reinstated as party agent with expanded powers over finance and constituency organization. The following February, he reported to Lord Beaconsfield on his diverse responsibilities. His 'ordinary work' included

Publications: Pamphlets, etc. issued. Important speeches reprinted.
Press: Weekly publication, the *Editor's Handysheet*, issued to Conservative provincial press. Political telegrams sent from lobby to several provincial papers.

In addition, his 'special work since August 1880' included 'Much time taken up by persons who want to start newspapers'.[2] Ironically, many of these individuals were reacting against the behaviour of the *Standard*, which Gorst had formerly regulated.

It was the ultimate tribute to Mudford's agility that, without damaging the *Standard*'s reputation, he should have given offence so widely. He infuriated Liberal editors by divulging information which they either had not known or were pledged to keep secret. He disconcerted Liberal Cabinet ministers by flaunting an awareness of their most confidential decisions. And he antagonized his fellow Conservatives as much by his ideological waywardness as by his physical elusiveness.

'You will certainly read in the *Standard* tomorrow an account of the conclusions arrived at by the Cabinet today and of the character of their delibera-

[1] Ayerst, *Guardian*, pp. 210–12; Cooper to Rosebery, 30 May 1882, Rosebery Papers, Vol. 10,010, fols. 107–108; Reid to Herbert Gladstone, 27 May and 2 June 1882, Viscount Gladstone Papers, Add. MSS. 46,041, fols. 12, 21 ff., 83; F. Baines to Herbert Gladstone, 29 October 1881, Viscount Gladstone Papers, Add. MSS. 46,049, fol. 56; Herbert Gladstone to Kitson, 16 May 1882 (copy), and Kitson to Herbert Gladstone, 22 and 25 May, and 6 June 1882, Viscount Gladstone Papers, Add. MSS. 46,027, fols. 74 ff., 81–84, 86.

[2] E. J. Feuchtwanger, 'J. E. Gorst and the Central Organisation of the Conservative Party,' *Bulletin of the Institute of Historical Research*, xxxii (1959), 205–206; *also see* Feuchtwanger, *Disraeli, Democracy and the Tory Party*, pp. 143 ff.

tions,' Frank Hill (correctly) warned Arthur Godley, Gladstone's private secretary, on 19 November 1880. 'By virtue of what understanding, and through what subterranean channels, it may be derived, I will not speculate,' he went on. 'The information is used to discredit the Government, by exaggerating divergence of opinion, and to play into the hands of a certain section of it, which does not really profit.' His indignation as a Liberal was intensified by his frustration as a journalist:

> In the meantime, the reserve practised towards the *Daily News* seriously impairs its power of helping the Government. . . . In the present condition of the London press, the readers of the *Daily News* are those to whom it is essentially important that the actions and intentions of the Government should be explained. The other newspapers chiefly address open enemies or lukewarm friends.

Whereas Hill scrupulously declined to speculate on the *Standard*'s source, others did not hesitate to brand Chamberlain as the culprit. Admitting that 'Chamberlain has been often . . . indiscreet', Lord Acton was reluctant to infer from the circumstantial evidence that he had 'prompted the *Standard*' with regard to the government's Irish strategy in February 1881. Young Reginald Brett (later Lord Esher and already a busybody) was less reticent. He recounted in his diary how Lord Hartington, taken unawares by the Speaker's order to remove Irish obstructionists from the House, 'went at once to Mr Gladstone', who 'pulled from his pocket a letter describing what the Speaker was about to do. "I could not read this at the Cabinet"', Gladstone informed Hartington, '"unless I wished it to appear in the *Standard* tomorrow morning." Lately the Cabinet discussions have been reported in that newspaper,' Brett recorded, 'owing, it is said, to the indiscretion of Chamberlain.'[1]

As a new and dynamic force, who did not suffer fools or Whigs gladly, Chamberlain was a prime suspect. His identification with 'caucus' techniques of electoral organization, imported from America, implied his disrespect for gentlemanly conventions, as did the orchid that garishly adorned his lapel. There can be no doubt that he enjoyed Escott's adulation, and that Escott, who required little encouragement, was able to glean information from their casual conversations. Like Bunce and Morley, Escott was also a supplier of news: 'Of the *Standard* & many other matters I shall have much to tell you when I reach your hospitable roof on Saturday,' he promised Chamberlain on 27 October 1881. Chronology might therefore suggest that Chamberlain was responsible for inspiring the *Standard* to proclaim on 1 November that Gladstone was preparing to resign the chancellorship, a post he held in tandem with the premiership. On the contrary, Chamberlain was to upbraid Escott:

---

[1] Hill to Godley, 19 November 1880, Gladstone Papers, Add. MSS. 44,467, fols. 20–21; Brett's diary, 5 February 1881 (typescript copy), Esher Papers.

I do not think there is the least truth in the *Standard* report – & I doubt the wisdom of publishing such rumours as *information*.

If Mudford does not take care he will get a sort of *Figaro* reputation which I don't think will be for the advantage of a serious English journal. However it is his business & not mine – and he knows best what suits his interests.

(In fact, Gladstone did not relinquish the Exchequer to H. C. E. Childers until December 1882.) When the *Standard* condemned the 'political morality' of the administration on 12 November, Escott hastened to assure Chamberlain that he was not the author, 'and I may take this opportunity of saying that I should never be asked in the *Standard* office to write anything of the sort'. Without belittling its mutual usefulness, Chamberlain's link with Escott did not secure him obedience or even reliable support from Mudford, who – as Lord Salisbury discovered from his dealings with Austin – did not take dictation from his leader-writers.[1]

Of greater psychological than practical value, Chamberlain's association with Escott was sufficient to nettle his Liberal colleagues and to galvanize his Tory opponents, who anxiously saw the *Standard* slipping from them. 'You have on several occasions spoken to me about starting a Conservative Weekly for the Working Classes & as you know I have never been particularly sanguine as to it success,' Armstrong of the *Globe* reminded W. H. Smith on 30 April 1881. Now, however, he had second thoughts. The *Globe* was to move the next day to larger quarters across the Strand, and Armstrong proposed 'for the consideration of yourself and the leaders of the Party' that the old 'premises & plant' might be acquired 'to make the venture at very little expense'. He had given first refusal to Ellis Ashmead Bartlett, the Brooklyn-born member for the Eye division of Suffolk, who brought his brother, William Burdett-Coutts (husband of the banking heiress, Baroness Burdett-Coutts) to inspect the facilities; but Ashmead Bartlett had 'confessed to being unable to produce the requisite cash'. His offer successively refused by Smith, Cubitt, and Lord Percy, Armstrong soon made other use of the site. 'It seems a pity, after so much talk on the subject, that nothing can be done to supply what every body admits is a great want,' he mused.

Not one to put party above commerce, Armstrong heard a 'rumour . . . that a Conservative *halfpenny* evening paper is contemplated'. In the event that such a proposal came before him, Smith was politely asked to stress the costs

---

[1] Escott to Chamberlain, 27 October and 12 November 1881, Chamberlain Papers; Chamberlain to Escott, 2 November 1881, Escott Papers. In 1884, the *Standard* got hold of the government's draft scheme for electoral redistribution. 'Who is the traitor?' Chamberlain asked Dilke, whom the *Globe* and *Evening News* summarily indicted. Dilke confirmed Chamberlain's suspicions that there had been 'a theft in the Printing Office', where one of the printers first offered the document to the *Daily Telegraph*. Lawson acknowledged to Gladstone that the offer was made, but refused. Chamberlain to Dilke, 9 October 1884, and Dilke to Chamberlain, 10 and 11 October 1884, quoted in Garvin, *Chamberlain*, I, 483–84; Lawson to Gladstone, 14 October 1884, Gladstone Papers, Add. MSS. 44,487, fol. 292.

and the unlikelihood of success. 'For my part', Armstrong vowed, 'I need hardly say, I shall oppose it to the utmost, as under any circumstance it could not fail in some degree to injure the *Globe*.' The rumour became actuality on 26 July 1881 in the form of the *Evening News*. Its proprietor was Coleridge Kennard, Tory MP for Salisbury from 1882 to 1885, who sank £100,000 of his own banking fortune into the property before his heirs sold out to Harmsworth in 1894. Lord Salisbury (though not Armstrong) was presumably 'pleased to hear that the circulation of the *Evening News* frequently exceeds 50,000 per diem', and did not discourage Kennard's aspiration 'to take a modest part in the deliberations of the party over the developments of organisation'. Less welcome was Kennard's request in July 1883 for 'some passing assistance so as to allow me a little breathing time' to meet his creditors. His embarrassment resembled that of Ashmead Bartlett, who began publishing *England*, his 'weekly newspaper for all classes', in March 1881. It survived until May 1898, leaving him impoverished. In November 1883, Smith was among those invited to subscribe to the 'new company which is being formed to develop *England*'. He declined, describing Ashmead Bartlett's application as 'the third I have received within a very short period suggesting that aid in the shape of working capital should be found for the London press'. In extenuation, Smith cited 'a very strong feeling that assistance given to one paper is injurious to another'. When Smith subsequently offered a 'donation' towards expenses, Ashmead Bartlett returned his cheque with the explanation that he had asked for co-operation, not charity. '*England* has I believe three or four times the circulation of any other cheap weekly Conservative paper in London,' he reminded Smith; 'and it is the Lower Middle & Working Classes that have the voting power.' Although he craved official patronage, Ashmead Bartlett would not be patronized. Adding the *Primrose Chronicle* to its masthead, *England* probably obtained some support from the Primrose League.[1]

Like Gorst, Smith had 'much time taken up by persons who want to start newspapers' or who, having started them, ran into difficulty. His petitioners included Latimer Neville, the master of Magdalene College, Cambridge, who hoped to collect £10,000 to launch 'a cheap weekly Newspaper, conducted on Church principles. . . . The politics . . . should be conservative and constitutional.' Sir Stafford Northcote was said to be closely involved. Greenwood, as we have seen, importuned Smith on behalf of the *St James's Gazette* and, when that seemed a lost cause, on behalf of himself. In mid-August 1881, he broached the possibility that, with assistance from party coffers, a new morning journal might be established to display his talents. Smith was neither as enthusiastic nor as quick to respond as Greenwood had hoped. 'Everybody

---

[1] Armstrong to Smith, 30 April 1881 and 'Sunday' [May 1881], Hambleden Papers; Kennard to Salisbury, 17 September and 25 November 1882, and 13 July 1883, Salisbury Papers; Ashmead Bartlett to Smith, 1 November 1883, and 10 March [1884?], and Smith to Ashmead Bartlett, 1 November 1883 (copy), Hambleden Papers.

has gone away and it is not a matter on which one is disposed to write,' Smith replied after a week, professing that he had been unsure 'whether you wished to move at once or whether your idea was simply to get a scheme into shape for more deliberate consideration in the Autumn'. Informed by Greenwood that time was of the essence, Smith dawdled and equivocated. His letter of 26 August merits extensive quotation not only because it clarified his position, but also because it amplified – and partly contradicted – the sentiments he expressed to Ashmead Bartlett:

A new morning paper should certainly have a capital of £100,000 at its back if the proprietors would avoid the risk of losing all they may have embarked in the venture. I told you the Party as such, and the leaders of the Party have literally no funds at all at their command, but successful papers must be the properties of individuals and managed by a Dictator. I do not regret myself that the Party has not started a paper and cannot do so. A Cabinet of all the talents would certainly fail in such a task, and they should really be free from any responsibility for anything that may appear in print, but I have no doubt many people would be glad to join your friends if you and they see their way to start a popular, a complete and an attractive morning Paper.

I should wish you success most heartily for I believe it would be most useful in the times which are coming; & I can do so without wishing harm to any of the other papers which are in existence, for a new good paper finds a circulation without, in the majority of cases, taking to a sensible extent either the circulation or the advertisements from other successful papers. The appetite for news and political criticism appears to increase by what it feeds on.

Greenwood was enough of a realist to know that 'it was hardly to be expected that you should have any success' in extracting funds from frontbench Conservatives. 'Of course it would have been well if we could have seen our way soon', he agreed,

for next session is likely to be a very important one indeed from the party contest point of view; & it takes four or five months to set up new machinery. However the matter must pass for the time. You are right, I am quite sure, in thinking that it is not for the party, as an organisation, to start or subsidize newspapers. That I certainly should not like to have anything to do with. It should be done, as you say, by a partnership of individuals, as a private enterprise. But a large sum is wanted – not less than £100,000 as you say: for my part, I think £120,000 with the advantages we already possess in premises, plant, & reputation, would do well. And my notion in troubling you was that amongst your friends (we can't look for help from anybody on the Liberal side) you might find a few who . . . are rich enough to join in a venture that seems more pressing every day.

To Greenwood, whose purpose may have prompted him to exaggerate, it seemed that

> in all questions moderate men are fast losing ground in the press. The defection of the *Standard*, on every occasion when its loyalty would be of the least value, may now be counted on for certain. . . . There is now hardly a single news-sheet of importance in the three Kingdoms in opposition to Radicalism: & of course Conservatives & moderate men of all kinds, observing that, must be grievously discouraged.

Kennard, the proprietor of the *Evening News*, was similarly unimpressed with the doctrines of mercantilism to which Smith strictly adhered. At the request of Lord Salisbury, he investigated the 'very abrupt dismissal' of John Ralph from the editorship of the *Yorkshire Post*, and uncovered 'a series of details' that confirmed his 'fundamental objections to the management of a newspaper by means of a joint stock company'. Party management seemed to him to be far more dependable.[1]

The outlook was less bleak in October 1881, when the National Union met at Newcastle for its fifteenth annual conference. The council was 'glad to learn' of an imminent 'addition to the weekly Conservative Press', and was optimistic that it 'will go far to break down the almost complete monopoly of the popular Sunday press, at present enjoyed by the Radical Party'. Unable to dispose of the *Globe*'s former premises in the Strand, Armstrong launched the *People* expressly as an antidote to *Lloyd's Weekly News*. Its first issue was on the 16th, in time to celebrate the arrest of Parnell. Joseph Hatton was its editor, and W. T. Madge its managing director. For six years, it waged 'an uphill fight', until it made its mark by Madge's graphic accounts of the 'Jack the Ripper' murders. Lord Percy, who chaired the Newcastle proceedings, did not anticipate such fame for the *People*. He did, however, hearten the assembled delegates with an announcement that the *Sunday Times* had formally 'adopted Conservative principles. . . . We have, as you all know, the very important weekly paper called *England*, which is doing good work,' he impartially added. 'There is, I am sure, plenty of Conservative feeling in the country to support all these papers, and I trust they will be generally supported by our party.' Such pious platitudes meant nothing to Ashmead Bartlett, who continued to struggle against adversity. He harboured a fierce resentment against Smith, who 'was instrumental in having a rival started to my paper, which has done no good & cost its supporters much money. It would have been far better', he complained to Northcote in January 1883, 'had he treated me with confidence & tried to make *England* by friendly counsel what in his opinion it

[1] Neville to Smith, 21 July and 27 September 1881, Hambleden Papers; Smith to Greenwood, 26 August 1881 (copy), and Greenwood to Smith, 27 August 1881, Hambleden Papers; Kennard to Salisbury, 30 March 1882, Salisbury Papers.

should have been.' The more plentiful the journals that supported the Tories, the more feverish was the competition among them. A colleague on the *Standard* 'amused' Escott, who was on holiday abroad, with an account of 'the battle Royal' between their paper and the *Daily Telegraph*, each inflating its circulation figures to claim the distinction of outselling the other: 'There is just a trace of vulgarity in all this self-puffery.'[1]

During the summer of 1881, Alfred Austin sowed the seeds for a higher-toned Conservative monthly ('an organ of opinion, sentiment, & taste'), which germinated in 1883 as the *National Review*. He sought Lord Salisbury's support, not necessarily of a financial kind (though that would not have been unwelcome). After an exceedingly long gestation, Lord Carnarvon laid before R. A. Cross, Home Secretary in the previous Conservative administration, Austin's 'scheme . . . for the formation of a Club & the publication of a monthly magazine on thorough and Conservative principles'. Carnarvon was 'not generally very sanguine as to these attempts: but there is more in this than is usually to be expected', namely the creation of a club, which 'is to be the nursery . . . of the magazine'. Christened the 'Cecil' after Salisbury, it existed 'in the eighteenth rather than the nineteenth century signification of the term', and included among its charter members Lords Carnarvon, Barrington, and Lytton, along with such MPs as Balfour, Edward Stanhope, and Raikes, who 'always liked to consider himself its unofficial godfather'. (Mention has been made of Raikes's connection with the *Globe*; he was also credited with the appearance of the *Banner*, unfurled in 1883 'to support the Constitutional party in the State'. Stanhope, able to count on a contribution of £1,000 from Salisbury, purchased control of the *Farmer* and the *Mark Lane Express*, which circulated among the landed classes, and he entrusted their political direction to the Conservative Central Office.) In October 1882, the Cecil Clubmen issued a circular designating Austin and W. J. Courthope as joint editors of the *National Review*. 'I talked it over a gt. deal with Northcote,' Carnarvon told Cross, '& he is disposed to be hopeful.' On 27 October, Carnarvon presided at a meeting at the Junior Carlton, where publication was fixed for 1 March 1883. To Salisbury, from whom he solicited an article for the inaugural number, Austin delivered periodic progress reports: by 23 December 1882, '800 subscriptions' had been entered, making it likely that 'the subscriptions will exceed the thousand considered necessary' to get started; but, after six months of publication, Austin thought it 'would perhaps be most correct to say that success has not been reached, but would seem to [be] attainable, under favourable conditions'. The average monthly sale then stood at 'about 1,300 copies. . . . The contributors are paid, but the editors give their services gratuitously. This they are very happy to do.' One was apparently happier than

---

[1] National Union minutes, 11 October 1881; Simonis, *Street of Ink*, pp. 148–51; obituary of Madge, *The Times*, 31 January 1927; Ashmead Bartlett to Northcote, 8 January 1883, Iddesleigh Papers, Add. MSS. 50,041, fol. 128; Robert Wilson to Escott, 26 September 1882, Escott Papers.

the other, for Courthope bowed out in 1887, leaving Austin in sole command.[1]

Far from betokening renewed vitality on the part of the Conservative opposition, this frenetic activity offered a tacit commentary on the disruptions that followed Beaconsfield's death in April 1881. The leadership was parcelled out to Salisbury in the Lords and Northcote in the Commons, neither of whom was readily identifiable as a champion of Tory Democracy. Churchill, whose left-wing position was analogous to Chamberlain's on the Liberal side, unremittingly defied 'the old gang'. The Fourth Party, which clustered around him in the House, may have been able to invoke Disraelian precedents, but its techniques (and a good deal of its rhetoric) were distinctly Chamberlainite. Specifically, Churchill wielded the National Union as a blunt instrument against his party superiors in much the same way as Chamberlain utilized the National Liberal Federation. Perhaps the greatest similarity lay in their recourse to newspaper alliances, some of which overlapped.

Through Escott (who published 'a personal and political monograph' on him in 1895), Churchill had access to the *World*, the *Fortnightly Review*, and, more restrictedly, the *Standard*. He inspired – and, as Chamberlain studiously phrased it, was 'believed to be an occasional contributor' to – *Vanity Fair*. Morley, impressed by his support for franchise reform and a comprehensive Irish policy, was not immune to his appeal. And Lucy of the *Daily News* (who edited his speeches in 1885) wrote to him 'in true friendship'. To one extent or another, the Conservative journals divided between those that swore fealty to the official leadership (in Kennard's case, quite literally: 'I will pray your Lordship to give no thought to any response to this, but simply to accept my unswerving fidelity to you as my revered leader,' he told Salisbury) and those that worked with Churchill – or were worked by him – to challenge it.[2]

Borthwick of the *Morning Post*, according to his biographer, 'hesitated to give his unqualified allegiance to Lord Salisbury', and instead 'was quick to perceive the weight which was rapidly attaching to the rising personality' of Churchill, whose speeches were quoted verbatim from the early months of 1881. That was to put it mildly. What was less obvious, and partly untrue, was 'that Borthwick had a great respect for Sir Stafford Northcote, and that Lord Randolph most decidedly did not'. Neither had much regard for 'the goat', as Northcote was nicknamed, although Churchill remained on amicable terms with him. Churchill did not hesitate to brandish his connection with the *Morning Post*. 'The rumour is that Gladstone is to be made Earl of Oxford,' he alerted Northcote in November 1881; 'I suggested to Borthwick to draw a

[1] Austin to Salisbury, 28 August 1881, 23 December 1882, and 8 September 1883, Salisbury Papers; Carnarvon to Cross, 4 September and 16 October 1882, Cross Papers; Raikes, *Raikes*, pp. 193–95; memorandum by Stanhope, 25 November 1882, and Stanhope to Salisbury, 4 December 1882, Salisbury Papers; Salisbury to Stanhope, 6 December 1882, Stanhope Papers.

[2] Lucy to Churchill, 18 May 1884, Churchill Papers; Kennard to Salisbury, 11 August 1882, Salisbury Papers; *Parliamentary Debates*, 3rd ser., cclxxvi, col. 801 (23 February 1883).

historical parallel between Harley and Gladstone.' Able to appreciate a prank at Gladstone's expense, Northcote lost his sense of humour when he became the butt. On 9 March 1883, he took Churchill to task for 'the appearance of a kind of *communiqué* in the morning papers yesterday', threatening that the Fourth Party might field its own candidates at the next election. Churchill, 'declin[ing] to be responsible for the gossip of the Lobby which may find its way into the daily or weekly Press', countered:

> There would be less danger of 'marking out a separate party within the general body of the Conservatives' if you would use your influence with some of your late colleagues so as to induce them to abstain from holding my friends and myself up to ridicule and dislike by their speeches in the country, or covertly, by inspiring that portion of the daily Press which is notoriously under the influence of the Front Opposition Bench.

The war of words, spoken and printed, thereafter intensified, without so much as a truce on Christmas Day 1883, when Churchill hit back at the

> section of the Conservative Party, rather respectable than numerous, ... who ... always sacrifice the interests of their party to the pleasure of gaining a passing cheer from *The Times* Newspaper for their judicial impartiality.

Having tried – and failed – to enlist Chenery's support, he really had no right to complain.[1]

Rowland Winn, the Tory chief whip, comforted Northcote with assurances that the Fourth Party was a waning force in Parliament and the press. 'The *Morning Post* has a strong leader this morning against Randolph,' he noted on 3 April 1883.

> It is only a very short time since they opened their columns to him freely, a proceeding I hope Borthwick will not repeat. I think the *Morning Post* is losing ground. I judge by the advertisements falling off which is apparent.

His confidence was misplaced. Within weeks, Borthwick was arranging for Churchill to meet Ismail, the deposed Khedive of Egypt, who 'no doubt has pocketsful of information such as you desire'. In fact, Borthwick was more truculent than his present hero, whom he goaded on. 'It is no use to refer to the long past when the warfare of Parties was conducted on long forgotten principles,' he contended.

> Today we have to confront not only a different state of things but a more

[1] Lucas, *Glenesk*, pp. 284, 293–95; Churchill to Northcote, 4 November 1881, Iddesleigh Papers, Add. MSS. 50,021, fol. 67; Northcote to Churchill, 9 March 1883, and Churchill to Northcote [March 1883], quoted in H. Gorst, *The Fourth Party* (London, 1906), pp. 219–21; Churchill to Northcote [25 December] 1883, Iddesleigh Papers, Add. MSS. 50,021, fol. 95. Thanking Churchill for 'the indication of your views', Chenery would accept 'what is called a "signed article" to be published in *The Times*', but evidently not an anonymous piece. Chenery to Churchill, 7 December 1882 and 1 January 1884, Churchill Papers.

educated Public Opinion which all demand a swift decision and a strong
control. We are tending to Democracy & Democracy demands Empire.

In the summer of 1884, Borthwick declined to attend a conclave of Tory newspapermen under the auspices of the Central Conservative Association, and
afterwards to meet Salisbury and Northcote. Usually interpreted as a show of
editorial independence, his gesture was more probably an avowal of Churchillian heterodoxy.[1]

Such recalcitrance would have come more naturally to the *Standard*, which
prided itself on its indiscipline. While Escott and Austin tugged in opposite
directions, Mudford steered a middle course, admiring Churchill's spirit
without sanctioning his strategy. The balance tipped in the spring of 1884,
when Churchill, as chairman of the powerful organization committee of the
National Union, made public his acrimonious exchanges with Salisbury,
whom he accused of issuing 'vague, foggy, and utterly intangible suggestions'
for the overhaul of party machinery. On 5 May, the *Standard* came down with
a thud against Churchill, who was seen to have trespassed beyond the bounds
of propriety. 'Every sensitive man must feel that Conservativism may in a
wholesome sense be Democratic, without becoming Demagogic,' it reasoned;
'and it is with the idea of making its doctrines intelligible and acceptable to the
masses that, in his happiest moods and most effective efforts, Lord Randolph
Churchill labours.' But 'the prevailing anarchy' in the House could not be tolerated. If Churchill persisted in his unruliness, 'he must be taken at his word,
and treated as an independent member, whose ideas do not accord and whose
tactics conflict with those of the Conservative Opposition'. The *Standard* took
the liberty 'to remind ... the member for Woodstock ... that he is not yet
enough of a personage to stand alone'. Its reprobation was ostensibly directed,
however, at the Tory chiefs, who 'must either resign their authority or make it
effectively felt. They must no longer allow those to lead who disdain to follow.'

This denunciation of Churchill created a sensation. 'The *Standard* this
morning throws over Randolph Churchill and tells him the Conservative Party
don't want him,' wrote Lewis ('Loulou') Harcourt, the Home Secretary's pre-
cocious son. 'All this I hear is in consequence of R.C. as Chairman of the Conservative Union having got his committee to agree to a letter accusing
Salisbury of falsehood!' Escott 'ascertained' that Salisbury and Stanhope,
possibly with the connivance of Carnarvon and other 'gentry', had 'completely
nobbled Mudford & the *Standard*. A. Austin is the venal scribe of the gang,' he
disclosed to Churchill, on whose behalf he vowed to take vengeance: 'I know

---

[1] Winn to Northcote, 3 April 1883, Iddesleigh Papers, Add. MSS. 50,041, fol. 158; Borthwick
to Churchill [June 1883] and 29 December 1883, Churchill Papers; Hindle, *Morning Post*, p. 218;
Lucas, *Glenesk*, pp. 304–306. In 1882, the year before he helped Churchill to found the Primrose
League, Borthwick was adopted as Tory candidate at Chelsea. He did not contest the seat until
1885, but his Churchillian brand of Conservatism won plaudits from the *World* (12 December
1883).

exactly how to meet this combination, & it will give me peculiar pleasure to attack them at every turn.' Churchill himself was philosophical. 'No doubt the squabble now raging in the Tory Party is eminently adapted to the interpretation of little men & little minds,' he replied to Escott. 'However I trust greatly to your skill & ability & power to extricate the great principles which are undoubtedly involved from the grasp of these political brigands.' Under the circumstances, there was not much Escott could do. He provided Churchill with a forum in the September number of the *Fortnightly*, but took the precaution of sending a proof to Downing Street, where a member of Gladstone's secretariat 'glanced at the article which appears to be characteristic of the writer. His ignorance, his grotesque and exaggerated style, his self importance, show themselves on every page.' Truth to tell, Churchill did not have many friends in high places.[1]

In anticipation of the National Union meetings at Sheffield, Austin ('the venal scribe') extended an olive branch. Writing 'solely under my own inspiration & without communication or conference with anybody', he appealed to Churchill to use his 'great talents & great opportunities' to counteract the 'popular agitation' against the House of Lords: 'We are attacked; we must attack in turn & you are the person to lead the attack.' Churchill was not to be side-tracked. In any case, he was in no position to oblige. Audaciously, he resigned his chairmanship, and submitted to re-election on a vote of confidence. During his 'temporary absence' on 23 July, Gorst presided, and the debate centred on the party's neglect of the press. Delegate after delegate attested to this deficiency, with the implication that 'the recognised heads and officials' of the party were to blame. A resolution to direct the reconstituted council 'to appoint a committee to obtain the necessary information' was carried unanimously. Its conclusions could not have pleased Salisbury, who had wearied of the subject. Described by the *Spectator* as a 'foe of the people', he grimly remarked: 'The only restraint I should like to impose on the liberty of the press would be to make political abstractions penal.' Churchill, triumphantly returned to the executive of the National Union, seems also to have had his fill of the newspapers. On 5 January 1885, he drafted – but did not send – a letter in which he

> noticed with the utmost unconcern the malignant slanders constantly insinuated against me by the *Standard* & *St James's Gazette*, the morning & evening metropolitan organs of the Conservative Party. Whether the persistent repetition of these insinuations is to be attributed to encouragement given by persons in authority, I am not aware.

[1] L. V. Harcourt's diary, 5 May 1884, Viscount Harcourt Papers; Escott to Churchill, 5 May 1884, Churchill Papers; Churchill to Escott, 5 May 1884, Escott Papers; Horace Seymour to Escott, 27 August 1884, Escott Papers.

Clearly, he had his suspicions. And clearly, too, he was more deeply wounded than he was prepared to admit.[1]

* * *

Newspapers had come to be regarded with condescension and often with contempt by those who were best placed to evaluate their performance. 'It is a great assistance to us to know what the feeling of the constituencies is from those who have been in contact with them,' Salisbury wrote in 1883 to Edward Hardcastle, who had lost his Lancashire seat in the previous general election. 'The Press has become absolutely useless as an indication of opinion.'[2] It goes without saying that this mood of disenchantment was especially acute among those who were most adept at rigging editorial opinion. Yet the more the coinage of political journalism was debased, the better it circulated.

Accompanying his father on a visit to Hawarden in the autumn of 1881, Loulou Harcourt reported a consensus 'that at the present time the *Daily Telegraph* is about the worst paper published'. But Gladstone, looking back nostalgically,

> said that from '76 to '79 it was a real national power. During that time it regularly received news from Dizzy through Monty Corry and his was published the next morning in the form of a telegram from 'Our Vienna Correspondent'.

(Oddly, Gladstone forbore from mentioning his own earlier contacts with Thornton Hunt.) The younger Harcourt's disdain did not prevent him from attending 'a Soirée at the New Publishing Offices of the *Daily Telegraph* in Fleet Street' the following June, when 'we were shown all the papers being printed for tomorrow'. The quantity, if not the quality, was awesome. Nor did he refuse Lawson's gift of 'a ticket for the Royal Supper to which apparently only a select few were admitted. What an honour to be one of Levy's chosen ones,' he jested crudely in his diary. At the tender age of twenty, he could be more easily forgiven than some of his elders, who despised Lawson, yet grovelled to him.[3]

Loulou also enjoyed contacts with the *Morning Post*, though he abhorred its Toryism, through his 'Uncle Algy' Borthwick, who said 'that the whole political situation is due to one person and that is *Lady* Salisbury who has Ld. S. entirely under her thumb'. As private secretary to his father, he lunched at the House on 1 March 1882 with, among others, John Walter, whom he observed to be 'a very disaffected Liberal'. Walter counted appreciably less as one of the three members for Berkshire than as the owner of *The Times*. Since

[1] Austin to Churchill, 11 July 1884, Churchill Papers; National Union minutes, 23 July 1884; Salisbury, 24 August 1884, quoted in Cecil, *Salisbury*, III, 115; Churchill to J. T. Garrish, 5 January 1885 ('Not to go'), Churchill Papers.
[2] Salisbury to Hardcastle, 15 March 1883, Hardcastle Papers.
[3] L. V. Harcourt's diary, 3 November 1881 and 28 June 1882, Viscount Harcourt Papers.

Delane's day, his parliamentary and proprietary responsibilities impinged increasingly on each other, and *The Times* gave vent alternately to his disaffection and his contrition. 'I have no doubt the Radicals are sore about your vote' against closure proceedings in the raucous Irish debates of 1881, Chenery advised him. But *The Times*, he promised, would restore him to the party's good graces:

> With regard to the other rules we shall back up the Government; *ditto* with Irish business so that by the end of the Session we shall appear even to Reading and Newbury to have gone fairly straight with the Liberals.

Thus, in framing his editorial policies, Chenery was obliged to consider Walter's constituency requirements along with other factors. Not least, the paper was determined to fight on the winning side. On 9 December 1882, the upset victory of the Liberal candidate in a by-election at Liverpool (where 'for the first time since 1865 the ascendancy of the Conservative party ... has been broken') gave 'indisputable' proof that 'the Government has largely recovered its popularity of late', and that a reaction had set in against a Tory opposition that 'exhibited no trace of a fruitful political inspiration'. The assertion that Salisbury's policy of 'mere negation' was one 'that turns Conservatives into Liberals' set the stage for a Cabinet reshuffle in which Lord Derby took the colonial secretaryship. 'Surely the articles in *The Times* & today in the *Daily News* are officially inspired,' Chamberlain wrote to Sir William Harcourt. 'I assumed that Mr G. told them himself – as he required absolute secrecy from all of us.' (Chamberlain might have said of Gladstone, as Richard Crossman was to say of Harold Wilson, that he 'really and sincerely believes that as far as he is concerned he only briefs the press and never leaks'.[1]

Nevertheless, the popular impression was that Gladstone was above that sort of thing. 'I wish Mr Gladstone read newspapers,' Cooper lamented to Rosebery. 'I am sure if he did he would leave undone some of the things he does, and do some of the things he leaves undone.' And Churchill wondered aloud in Parliament: 'does the Prime Minister ever read *The Times*?' Like the Almighty, with whom he communicated more regularly, Gladstone moved in mysterious ways. To a few editors, whose discretion he trusted, he was willing to tip his hand, even to reveal some of the aces up his sleeve. On other occasions, he applied pressure to suppress information that imperilled his Irish legislation. The *Daily News* submitted under protest. 'Your request strikes almost at the very root of newspaper business, and personally I have no belief whatsoever in the policy of repression even in such cases as that about which you write,' responded Hill, who did 'not feel at liberty to disregard [the] very

[1] L. V. Harcourt's diary, 1 March 1882 and 19 October 1884, Viscount Harcourt Papers; Chenery to Walter, 'Monday' [1881], *Times* Archives; Chamberlain to Harcourt, 11 December 1882, Harcourt Papers; Crossman, *Diaries* (18 December 1967), II (London, 1976), 609.

strong representations' conveyed by Edward Hamilton, who had taken Godley's place as Gladstone's principal private secretary. Herbert de Reuter was less accommodating: 'I greatly regret that any publication of ours should have created difficulties for the Irish Executive,' he told Hamilton.

> but you will readily understand that we felt bound to keep the public informed of what was regarded as intelligence of great interest and would probably have been noticed by the newspapers even if ignored by ourselves.

A professional ethic, fortified by an awareness of intensified competition, limited the possibilities for old-style official control. Cooper subscribed to a self-denying ordinance:

> I remember I am a newspaper man, with the newspaper man's desire that his paper should have the first & best of everything; and at the same time I have an old fashioned notion that if I am corresponding with a Cabinet minister, I have no right to make use of what he says to me except with his full permission. But there is always the temptation. I have not yielded to it yet; but you see I am afraid of myself.

The dilemma could not have been put more poignantly.[1]

The newspaper that Gladstone followed most attentively was the *Pall Mall Gazette*. Any qualms he may have felt at the appointment to its editorship of Morley, a doctrinaire Radical who dallied with Chamberlain and Dilke, were allayed by the news that Stead, his ally in the Bulgarian agitation, was to become assistant editor. As soon as Stead had 'definitely determined to pitch my tent in the midst of heathendom', he acquainted Gladstone with his plans. 'May I send him "satisfaction & good wishes" from you?' Gladstone was asked by a secretary. 'Warmly,' he replied. 'He has been one of the most steady men in the worst times. I hope to see him in London.' In better times, Stead was to prove less steady.[2]

Morley departed on 25 August 1883. 'If the *Standard* mentions the fact that I leave this paper,' he wrote three days earlier to Escott, 'it would be a great favour if it cd. be stated that I leave not only "editorial control" (as the *D. News* said), but that I don't contribute to it henceforth or have, in fact, anything to do with it.' Stead, elevated to the editorship, chose as his deputy Alfred Milner, who had joined the staff the previous year. From the start, Milner was candid about his ambitions. 'As you know, I don't want to give

---

[1] Cooper to Rosebery, 16 July 1882, Rosebery Papers, Vol. 10,010, fol. 122; Winston S. Churchill, *Lord Randolph Churchill* (London, 1906; I, 388) reports this aside, as does Robert Rhodes James, *Lord Randolph Churchill* (London, 1959; p. 168), which is not to be found in *Parliamentary Debates*, 3rd ser., ccxcviii, col. 244 (11 May 1885); Hill to Hamilton, 10 August 1883, and de Reuter to Hamilton, 11 August 1883, Gladstone Papers, Add. MSS. 44,483, fols. 15–17; Cooper to Rosebery, 5 March 1885, Rosebery Papers, Vol. 10,011, fol. 69.

[2] Stead to Gladstone, 14 September 1880 (with comments), Gladstone Papers, Add. MSS. 44,303, fol. 335.

myself up to journalism, but it would be helpful to me to give some time to it,' he calculated to Stead. 'What papers do you advise me to take in besides *The Times*? I thought the *Standard, Morning Post & Daily News*. The foreign papers, you know, I see at my Club.' A Balliol man, Milner recruited the services of E. T. Cook, a graduate of New College. ('No mention of this matter has yet been made to Thompson, so you see how tentative it all is,' he cautioned Cook.) In 1879, as president of the Oxford Palmerston Club, Cook had recounted to Gladstone his efforts 'to consolidate the Liberal party in the university'. The atmosphere in Northumberland Street was quite different. 'Alas! Nothing could be less Oxonian in style & temper than the *Pall Mall Gazette*!' Milner exclaimed to G. J. Goschen.[1]

In 1884, Milner became private secretary to Goschen, who shared his German antecedents, his Oxford background, and his penchant for coalitionism. 'Of course, if I gave up the *Pall Mall*, there would be no difficulty about time,' he reasoned. 'But I still hesitate about such a step as that.' Although 'it was such fun to work with' Stead, whom he called 'a compound of Don Quixote and Phineas T. Barnum', Milner found it 'certainly rather compromising to get the credit of what one so largely disapproves'. Cook experienced the same stimulation and discomfort. 'The *P.M.G.* is rather a different thing from what it was in Morley's time, and a strange mixture of good and bad,' he confided to a friend.

> Whatever else you may say, I really don't think there's any other paper with such lots of interesting stuff in it as the *P.M.G.* And then what a storehouse of surprises it is! You never know whether you will hear the voice of culture (that's me, you know, and Milner), or the blatantest vulgarity.

Stead's storehouse was filled with surprises for Gladstone, too.[2]

In December 1883, the *Pall Mall Gazette* prepared and distributed a 'Circular of Enquiry'. Liberal members of Parliament were instructed rather imperiously to stipulate their legislative priorities. (The results were published on 3 January 1884.) Should a recipient fail to comply, it was 'taken for granted that he is prepared to support whatever measures the Government may bring forward, and that he will be classed by the *Pall Mall Gazette* accordingly'. Like the party whips, whom Stead preempted, the *World* condemned this outrageous interference: 'Never were Liberal MPs more unmercifully "heckled"' (19 December). But Stead continued to flex his editorial muscles.

---

[1] Morley to Escott, 22 August 1883, Escott Papers; Milner to Stead, 2 April and 11 September 1882, Stead Papers; Milner to Cook, 14 August 1883, quoted in Mills, *Cook*, pp. 41–42; Cook to Gladstone, 29 November 1879, Gladstone Papers, Add. MSS. 44,461, fol. 189; Milner to Goschen, 31 May 1884, Milner Papers.

[2] Milner to Goschen, 31 May and 18 August 1884, Milner Papers; Harold Herd, *March of Journalism* (London, 1952), p. 229; Cook to a friend, 21 April 1884, quoted in Mills, *Cook*, pp. 59–60.

He chastised the administration for ignoring the plight of the London poor, and pressed for the dispatch of General Charles Gordon (the subject of one of his celebrated interviews) to conquer the Nile valley. Told by Andrew Carnegie of Gladstone's displeasure, Stead remonstrated with the Prime Minister:

> . . . I should be false to every principle which moved me in my old fight in the North, if I faltered for a moment in proclaiming agst. Jingoes of all shades that in Egypt as in Bulgaria the policy of England ought to be dictated not by her apparent interests but by her national duty.

Disputing Stead's logic and doubting his prudence, Gladstone must have bristled at the suggestion that he was among the Jingoes. His son Herbert tried to bring Stead to reason, but to no avail. In a febrile attempt at self-exculpation, Stead asked 'why, if I was doing so much mischief, why in the name of common sense did you or Mr Hamilton or somebody not drop me a line & say so[?]' The blame, he insisted, rested with Gladstone: 'As soon as I became supreme' at the *Pall Mall Gazette*,

> I sought an interview & begged of him as a personal favour that he would communicate with me – especially about foreign affairs. Because, I said, I could not help seeing that I might do endless harm unless I was kept right. Mr Gladstone was good enough to recognize this & promised me that his secretaries would keep me informed. . . . But from them & from Downing St. I have never got to know anything as to what is going on in the Cabinet. Naturally enough you may say. 'You are not in the Cabinet.' But you forget that a newspaper must know what is going on or otherwise it is out of it. What is the use of knowing a week late when you want to influence a pending decision?

Stead's naïvety and presumption were alike staggering. However real his grievance, it did not excuse his belligerence. To accede to him was impossible. To argue with him was hopeless.[1]

In desperation, Herbert Gladstone turned to Reginald Brett, then private secretary to Hartington, who saw 'some reason for believing that Stead might be induced to alter the tone which he has hitherto adopted' towards the government and its foreign policy. The Prime Minister, 'not very sanguine of its success', gave his 'sanction and approval' to Brett's design. As instructed, Brett took Hartington into his confidence:

> You said to me some time ago that the Press had been badly managed by the Government.

[1] Stead to Gladstone, 26 May 1884, Gladstone Papers, Add. MSS. 44,303, fols. 341–42; Stead to Herbert Gladstone, 12 June 1884, Viscount Gladstone Papers, Add. MSS. 46,050, fol. 234.

It is perfectly true, and the fault lies – of course – with the people in Downing St. It transpired however a few days ago that something might perhaps . . . be done to soften the acrimony of the *Pall Mall Gazette*. . . . I think something can be done, though perhaps not all at once, to get rid of this regular evening assault upon the Government.

Through Yates Thompson nothing can be done, because he is aware that any pressure from him would drive Stead away, and the value of his paper has increased so much since Stead assumed the Editorship that he would not willingly part with him. But I have come to hear of a means which will, I have some expectation, be effectual and as it commits neither Mr Gladstone, nor you, nor the Government, I think it is worth trying. . . . It is however most desirable that no one should say that Stead has been 'squared', for if any statement of the kind were to come to his ears all attempts at conciliation would be perfectly futile.

Later that day, Brett 'saw Stead, and urged upon him the following points': Britain's 'agreement with France' to evacuate Egypt was an 'accomplished fact', which could 'only be upset by Bismarck, or by [a] hostile vote in the House of Commons'; whereas 'the *P.M.G.* could not influence Bismarck one way or the other', it might 'possibly bring about a hostile vote' in Parliament that 'would inevitably destroy the Government'; in that case, Stead would have to 'decide whether he wishes to eject the Government from office . . . and whether in a general election he would give his support to the Tories'; and, finally, Stead was asked to 'grant an armistice for some days and carefully consider these points'. Before Brett left him on the 18th, Stead had 'with some reluctance agreed'. The next afternoon, the *Pall Mall Gazette* made 'a conciliatory overture' to Gladstone, from whom Brett obtained 'two concessions': in the event of a parliamentary storm over the Anglo-French agreement, the Prime Minister 'should not indirectly . . . attack the *P.M.G.*'; and, as Brett unctuously phrased it, 'he should consent to throw the spell of his personality over Stead, by giving him an interview on some early day'. These conditions were vital. 'I must ask you again to remember that Stead must be let down easy,' Brett implored Herbert Gladstone at the end of a long day's work, 'and must be given some latitude in point of time to withdraw from the unpleasant position . . . into which he has got. . . . Absolute silence' was also essential, 'as Stead is not the sort of man who would allow it to be said of him that he had been "squared".'[1]

Having played the part of honest broker, Brett established himself as an *éminence grise* behind Stead's editorial throne. His relations with Milner were particularly close. 'We made a blunder yesterday in guessing Sir Charles Dilke, & not Northbrook, as the man to go to India' as governor-general,

[1] Brett's journal, 18 June 1884, and Brett to Hartington, 18 June 1884 (copy), Esher Papers; Brett to Herbert Gladstone, 18 June 1884, Viscount Gladstone Papers, Add. MSS. 46,050, fol. 248.

Milner confessed to Stead on 6 August 1884. 'Had I seen Brett..., the mistake might have been avoided', along with Yates Thompson's annoyance. Loulou Harcourt, invited to lunch at Brett's house in November, found Stead with him. He suspected that his host had 'had something to do with ... articles in that paper' advocating naval rearmament, 'if he has not actually written them'. Impossible to square, Stead was a personality whose rough edges continually rubbed against the official Liberal grain. Cooper thanked Rosebery for supplying the *Scotsman* with information about Egypt, and could not resist pointing out 'that it does not exactly tally with that of your wild ally the *Pall Mall Gazette*'. In January 1885, when a British expeditionary force arrived at Khartoum too late to rescue General Gordon, Stead's anger raged beyond control. 'Mr Gladstone refused to see that Gordon was in danger, and even to this hour he talks of his inability to remove him from Khartoum,' the *Pall Mall* scolded as late as 24 February. 'His inability to see the simplest facts, or rather the unexampled ability of explaining them away, was never more strongly demonstrated' than in his 'apology' to the Commons the night before.[1]

Gordon's fate and the popular cry for revenge rocked the government, which barely survived a vote of censure in the House. Gladstone, his prestige at its nadir, showed signs of physical strain. There was speculation that he would step down, leaving Hartington to form a broad-based war ministry. For wholly different and incompatible reasons, the scheme was promoted by Chamberlain within the Cabinet and by Goschen outside. Milner, whom Goschen employed to keep watch over the press, sent him a cutting from the *St James's Gazette* (20 January) which, 'together with a perfectly trashy paragraph in the *Globe* & our note in the *Pall Mall*', echoed Goschen's clarion call on the 19th for a coalition. *The Times* was predictably sympathetic, and 'the provincials ... – with the exception of the *Birmingham Post* wh. is unfriendly & the *Manchester Courier* wh. is silent – [were] appreciative ... in a greater degree than' Milner had dared to expect. The *Daily News* and the *Spectator* pondered the significance of Goschen's withdrawal from the Reform Club. On 29 January, Milner was pleased to forward to his chief 'a *Pall Mall* in wh. Stead in a clever, but as it seems to me, extravagant article attacks Chamberlain very much on your lines'. Morley wasted his time trying to temper Stead's hostility towards Chamberlain, who was driven to accept the existing ministerial arrangements as preferable to any reconstruction. As Cooper recognized, the drive for 'a middle party' was geared to isolate 'the Birmingham Beelzebub on the one hand and the Woodstock demon on the other'. In early February, the news that Khartoum had fallen solidified ministerial ranks. 'I do not think the Government will be turned out,' Lord Halifax observed on the 13th to Childers (whom Chamberlain had described as being

[1] Milner to Stead, 6 August 1884, Stead Papers; L. V. Harcourt's diary, 14 November 1884, Viscount Harcourt Papers; Cooper to Rosebery, 2 December 1884, Rosebery Papers, Vol. 10,011, fol. 50.

'much taken with my idea of a "Patriotic Ministry" '), 'but there is an ominous-looking article in last night's *Pall Mall* as to the cold fit coming over the Radicals and possibly over Chamberlain.' Goschen's campaign fizzled out. 'Even that astonishing extravaganza, the *Pall Mall Gazette*, is beginning to abandon him,' Philip Stanhope remarked to Escott.[1]

In the press, as in higher parliamentary echelons, the movement for a centre party – variously designated as 'national' or 'patriotic' – subsided, if only temporarily. 'This is not a time when Mr Gladstone and his colleagues can think of themselves and their own convenience,' stated the *Daily News* on 2 March. 'They are bound in honour not to shrink from office so long as the House of Commons does not formally withdraw from them its confidence.' The same day, the *Morning Post* advised its readers that 'we ought not to be surprised if the "disparaged" Government will continue in office for a few weeks longer'; and the *Standard* professed 'the belief that . . . it is . . . necessary for the Conservatives . . . to prepare themselves for coming responsibilities', which they would assume independently. A fortnight later, the substitution of Sir Michael Hicks Beach (Churchill's confederate) for Northcote as the Tory leader in the Commons signalled the resumption of traditional inter-party warfare and the repudiation of what Cooper dismissed as 'political Hermaphroditism'.

'Great excitement throughout the country and clamour for a forward policy, the Press almost unanimously pushing the Government deeper into the Sudan,' Kate Courtney, Leonard's wife, wrote in her journal in February. The *Pall Mall Gazette* was an exception: 'We decline to plunge blindly on to Khartoum as we plunged blindly on to Cairo' (13 February). The following month, a Russian advance on Afghanistan threatened further embroilments. Here, however, the government acted decisively to avert a confrontation, and Stead was the very soul of moderation. As the *Pall Mall* wrote on 30 March:

> Nearly every newspaper in the country, including not a few of those provincials who usually keep their heads, have been bellowing like a veritable Bull of Bashan morning and evening for war. . . . The *Daily News* of course says that this is a question which cannot be referred to arbitration – which is a good sign, for the *Daily News* is almost always wrong – and never so utterly wrong as when it masquerades as a demented Jingo.

Cooper, whose newspaper was among those Stead accused of warmongering,

---

[1] Milner to Goschen, 20 and 29 January 1885, and undated latters, Milner Papers; Garvin, *Chamberlain*, I, 561; Cooper to Rosebery, 19 January 1885, Rosebery Papers, Vol. 10,011, fol. 58; Halifax to Childers, 13 February 1885, quoted in Spencer Childers, *Life and Correspondence of Hugh C. E. Childers* (London, 1901), II, 191; Stanhope to Escott, 13 February 1885, Escott Papers; *also see* A. B. Cooke and John Vincent, *The Governing Passion* (Brighton, Sussex, 1974), pp. 30–33, 84n, 103. Stanhope and Milner ('a clever fellow, by repute') were, along with Gladstone, among Rosebery's guests at Mentmore on 24 January 1885. *The Diary of Sir Edward Walter Hamilton* (ed. D. W. R. Bahlman; Oxford, 1972), II, 779.

could 'see . . . almost no positive step advocated by *The Times* & the *Pall Mall Gazette* that has not been most mischievous to the extent to which it has been adopted'. Still, the dispute with Russia was settled by firm diplomacy. 'The chances of peace are now very great,' Childers revealed on 9 May, 'although we are not quite out of the wood, thanks to the extravagance of certain leading Tories, and the reckless mischief-making of the *Pall Mall Gazette*.'[1]

Of all his crusades, none better illustrated Stead's moral courage – or his breathless audacity – than his 'secret commission' to awaken the nation's conscience to the rampant evil of child prostitution. As evidence for his case, which he presented on 6 July, he ventured into 'Modern Babylon' to procure a 'Maiden Tribute'. Having technically committed the offence of abduction, he was sentenced to three months' imprisonment. The publicity accelerated the enactment of appropriate criminal legislation, and, in the first instance, boosted the sale of the *Pall Mall*. 'We cannot print papers fast enough,' a member of the staff told Robert Donald, who had recently become 'Stead's amanuensis'. But, as Greenwood gloated, Stead's latest escapade had done

> the paper a world of harm amongst decent folk, who will not take that sort of thing into their homes. This we find in the circulation of the *St James's* wh. has gone up many thousands: our new subscribers, of course, being the best of theirs.

To Greenwood's jaundiced eyes, it was especially 'pretty to see how the railway readers of the *P.M.G.* try to hide what they are reading: how queerly ashamed they look'. Such people were more Victorian than the Queen herself, who was described by one of her ladies-in-waiting as someone who 'read the *Pall Mall* every night & sympathized very keenly with . . . the "Maiden Tribute" & Co.'.[2]

It was from Holloway Gaol that Stead wrote to Gladstone on 17 December to pledge his support for 'the scheme of Home Rule which you are said to favour', and to express 'the sincere pleasure it gives me to be able once more to offer you whatever journalistic service the *P.M.G.* can render'. Gladstone, then between his second and third ministries, responded guardedly: 'If convenience and conviction shall bring the *P.M. Gazette* and myself upon the same lines at a critical moment, I am very glad.' Earlier that year, Edmund Yates of the *World* had also served time in Holloway as the result of his conviction for criminal libel. 'He is now constantly supplied with pâté de foie gras and other delicacies, and has his room full of flowers,' reported Loulou

---

[1] Kate Courtney's journal, February 1885, quoted in Gooch, *Courtney*, p. 222; Cooper to Rosebery, 25 March 1885, Rosebery Papers, Vol. 10,011, fols. 81–82; Childers to Sir John Adye, 9 May 1885, quoted in Childers, *Childers*, II, 192.

[2] H. A. Taylor, *Robert Donald* (London, 1934?), pp. 35–36; Greenwood to Blackwood, 16 July [1885], Blackwood Papers; Stead's diary, 15 March 1886, Stead Papers.

Harcourt, who could only 'wish he and all the other Editors of society papers were imprisoned with hard labour'. If the exasperated politicians had had their way in 1885, Fleet Street would have been empty and Holloway full.[1]

---

[1] Stead to Gladstone, 17 December 1885, Gladstone Papers, Add. MSS. 44,303 fol. 361; Gladstone to Stead, 18 December 1885 (copy), Gladstone Papers, Add. MSS. 44,493, fol. 238; L. V. Harcourt's diary, 23 January 1885, Viscount Harcourt Papers.

Seven

CONFLICTS OF PRINCIPLE

From the spring of 1885, when Lord Salisbury formed his first administration, until the summer of 1886, when he returned to Downing Street with a longer lease, the mosaic of High Victorian party politics crumbled, gradually to be reassembled in new patterns. Newspapers were among the jagged pieces.

If, as A. B. Cooke and John Vincent have trenchantly argued, 'politics in 1885–86 was beginning to be, as it has remained, something of a permanent campaign', it logically followed that the press should have been invested with greater value and responsibility; if, as they have further stated, 'the main problem confronting' politicians was 'that of presenting themselves and the world of parliamentary activity generally in a sufficiently attractive, necessary and interesting way to maintain a general consent to their hegemony', the press was all the more essential to their purpose.[1] Within 'the parliamentary community', to which journalists belonged either as elected or *ex officio* members, there occurred various shifts of alignment, all more or less predicated on the perpetuation of the existing system. Arguably, to a more significant extent than Cooke and Vincent have allowed, ideological concerns figured in the process. In any case, the intensity of political infighting was considerably heightened by the daily outpourings of the press, which generated excitement among ordinary readers, and, between the lines, conveyed hints of strategy to party professionals. Participants in the general turmoil, newspapers were inevitably affected by it. Their machinations, like those of the front-rank politicians with whom they collaborated in public campaigns and private intrigues, encouraged certain designs at the expense of others.

In Fleet Street as at Westminster, there was a rapid turnover of personnel, sometimes owing to natural causes, but more usually politically induced. In February 1884, Chenery died. No sooner was 'the breath ... out of his body' than the *World* speculated on the question of his successor: 'The death of the editor of *The Times* is an era in the existence of that great newspaper,' which may have been 'little more than the phantom of its former self', yet retained 'an authority in political affairs which its contemporaries can only upon excep-

[1] Cooke and Vincent, *Governing Passion*, pp. 5, 15.

tional occasions assume' (20 February). Walter's choice was G. E. Buckle, an Oxford prize scholar (and a fellow of All Souls) who had gone on to read law at Lincoln's Inn, and who was still shy of his thirtieth birthday at the time of his appointment. With diffidence, Buckle accepted an invitation to 'a fête in my honour. . . . I feel so inadequate to the duties of the post to which I have succeeded,' he told James Thursfield, one of his leader-writers, 'that my desire is to be as unnoticed, unregarded and anonymous as is compatible with the recognition of facts.'[1] His aspiration – if not his trepidation – was worthy of Delane. In spite of the *World*'s observation that Printing House Square had been transformed into 'a glass house' since Delane's day, its windows were sufficiently opaque for Buckle's presence in the editorial chair to remain undetected by the *World* as late as 12 March.

For once, the politicians were better informed. 'I have not yet made acquaintance with the new editor – Buckle – who is quite young and said to be an able fellow,' Edward Hamilton, Gladstone's private secretary, wrote in his diary on 5 March;

> but as yet there is certainly no sign of any improvement in the conduct of the paper. Its perpetual object is to run atilt against Mr G., towards whom it is always believed Walter entertains the strongest personal feelings of animosity.

Hamilton had his opportunity on 28 May, when he dined in 'curiously mixed company' at Chamberlain's. Among the assorted guests were Buckle '(. . . a seemingly pleasant man)', Carnegie '(the Scotch American millionaire who has lately bought up all the *Echoes* in this country)', and Churchill. A month later, noting that '*The Times* has somewhat improved in tone towards the Government about Egypt', Hamilton recorded that 'Mr G. proposes to have a talk with Buckle, the new editor'. That interview presumably took place before 22 July, when Buckle dined (along with Hamilton, Brett, and others) in Downing Street. 'Mr G. was much pleased with Buckle,' Hamilton wrote afterwards. 'Under his editorship *The Times* articles on the Franchise crisis have certainly been valuable.' Hamilton himself played host to Buckle in October, and found him 'a nice taking fellow – very quiet and reserved'.[2]

The politicians were grateful to have 'a nice taking fellow' at the helm of *The Times*, even one who took his inspiration, like his dinners, from diverse sources. Following in the footsteps of its proprietor, who 'impressed the whole staff with his personal authority . . . by appointing in Chenery's place a young scholar of his own choice', *The Times* came to stand 'on the Right Centre rather than on the Left Centre' of the political spectrum. But the transition was so smooth as to be almost imperceptible. At the start of his twenty-eight-

[1] Buckle to Thursfield, 20 February 1884, *Times* Archives.
[2] Hamilton, *Diary*, II, 571, 626, 645, 657, 701 (5 March, 28 May, 27 June, 22 July, and 7 October 1884).

year editorship, Buckle mingled with younger men who were attracted to
cross-party concepts. His closest parliamentary contact was probably Rosebery, who shared his misgivings about the government's Egyptian policy as
well as his resistance to the growing agitation for Irish Home Rule. Nevertheless, it seemed to Loulou Harcourt that 'John Morley and Buckle of *The Times*
are Chamberlain's confidants on all questions', and the bonds between Buckle
and Chamberlain were indeed stronger than one might have expected. So, up
to a point, were those between Buckle and Churchill, another potential coalitionist. Yet Buckle's code was stricter than his dining companions might infer
from his erudite conversation and self-effacing manner. He was 'glad to give'
Churchill 'space in *The Times* ... to reply to Lord Granville', who had
accused him of misrepresentation over the conduct of the Anglo-Russian
dispute. 'You will, I am sure,' he told Churchill, 'not be surprised to find,
along with your letter, a criticism of it.' In June 1885, when Salisbury took
office, Buckle

> asked for and obtained an interview with the new Prime Minister, and was
> received with a cordiality which rather surprised him. Its origin was soon
> made clear. 'You are the first person who has not come to see me in the last
> few days who is not wanting something at my hands – place, or decoration,
> or peerage. *You* only want information!'

Once again, Buckle was being 'a nice taking fellow'. He demonstrated soon
enough, however, that he was no cipher.[1]

While Buckle was establishing himself at *The Times*, Hill was nearing the
end of his tenure at the *Daily News*. For years, Labouchere had been eager to
replace him with a more full-blooded Radical. Sustained on the basis of divisions within the paper's directorate, Hill ultimately fell victim to the discords
within the Liberal hierarchy. As the editor of London's leading Liberal paper,
he was expected to promote ministerial interests. But the directives he
received were sporadic and seldom clear. 'Hill produced this morning ... a
good article, faithfully reproducing some ideas on the Egyptian difficulty
which I could not help embodying in a letter to him on Saturday evening,'
Hamilton wrote on 28 April 1884. Horace Seymour, another member of the
Gladstone secretariat, grumbled that 'Hill did not treat me as well'. Seymour
recalled having tried 'to keep him informed on the Egyptian mess, and Lord
Richard Grosvenor, not knowing the source of the article, said to me, "What
dreadful rubbish Hill has got into the *Daily News*"'. The fault was more probably Seymour's than Hill's, but the latter took the blame. Unable to satisfy two
of Gladstone's secretaries, Hill had little hope of satisfying Gladstone's front-
bench colleagues. Dilke, an old friend, angrily protested when the paper

---

[1] *History of The Times*, III, 5, 13; L. V. Harcourt's diary, 19 November 1884, Viscount Harcourt Papers; Buckle to Churchill [12?] May 1885, Churchill Papers; *The Times*, 14 May 1885;
Buckle's recollection, quoted in Cecil, *Salisbury*, III, 142.

published a letter (11 November 1884) that expressed 'disgust and alarm' in party ranks at the 'questionable dodges' allegedly employed by Chamberlain as a private businessman. 'A newspaper is not responsible for the good taste or opinions of writers who sign their own names,' retorted Hill, who explained that it would have been wrong to refuse the letter and still more wrong to dignify its contents with a refutation. In a jocular vein, Dilke complained when Hill criticized his blueprint for the redistribution of parliamentary seats: 'I hate you ... as every over worked man hates another who gives him more work to do. My Metropolitan scheme has been excellently well received by the Press except the *D.N.*', which upheld the principle of equal electoral districts. On financial matters, including the controversial naval and military estimates, Hill again stood alone, but on the government's side. 'You will have read a strong article in *The Times*, saying that our proposals are altogether inadequate,' Childers wrote to Gladstone. 'This appears to be the general sentiment of the Liberal Press, both town and country, except perhaps the *Daily News*.'[1]

Nothing would have better suited Hill's purpose, secured his position, and salved his conscience, than to co-operate with Liberal officials. But he could not reciprocate what he did not receive. As Gladstone's second ministry tottered to a fall, Hill addressed the Prime Minister

> personally on a matter which very seriously concerns the influence and position of the *Daily News*, not only as a newspaper, but in regard to the value of the support which it may be able to give the Government.

Not for the first time, it was 'quite clear that the *Standard* through some channel or other is habitually informed of communications ... with respect to the Afghan question, and also in regard to most others'. The *Daily News* was afforded no such consideration; on the contrary, its editor's queries were invariably ignored.

> Of course the effect of this advantage which the *Standard* has somehow gained and which it has had ever since the present Ministry came into power has been greatly to augment its influence and circulation and to transfer to it even Liberal readers who would otherwise support the *Daily News*.

The paper suffered from a loss of prestige, the government from the fact that its 'views and actions are now almost always first known through a hostile medium and with unfriendly colouring'. To counteract this mischief, Hill proposed the installation of some line of 'personal communication' between Bouverie Street and Downing Street.[2] By then, it was too late. Gladstone re-

[1] Hamilton, *Diary*, II, 604 (28 April 1884) and Seymour's comment, 604n; Dilke to Hill, 17 November 1884, and Hill to Dilke, 17 and 19 November 1884, Dilke Papers, Add. MSS. 43,898, fols. 82 ff.; Dilke to Hill, 8 January 1885, Dilke Papers, Add. MSS. 43,898, fol. 115; Childers to Gladstone, 18 December 1884, quoted in Childers, *Childers*, II, 170.
[2] Hill to Gladstone, 1 May 1885, Gladstone Papers, Add. MSS. 44,490, fols. 177–78.

signed on 9 June, after the Tories – with Irish votes and Liberal abstentions – carried an amendment to the budget. Within six months, Hill was also displaced.

Rosebery was an accessary to the plot. Always an enigmatic figure, he had entered the Gladstone Cabinet in its twilight hours and thereafter became all the more the repository of Gladstone's confidences. From Labouchere, who gave him 'all the benefits of intrigue without any of its inconvenience', Rosebery collected 'gossip about subterranean Irish manoeuvres' and other information which he did not necessarily transmit to his chief. With Escott put out of commission by a nervous breakdown, Labouchere proposed to make H. W. Lucy editor of the *Daily News*. But Lucy, the *Observer*'s 'Cross Bench' columnist as well as *Punch*'s 'Toby, MP', required persuasion. Rosebery graciously extended an invitation to Dalmeny. There, as Lucy recounted to his wife on 22 November, Rosebery 'entirely removed from my mind the obstacle which from the first has prevented me from even considering the matter – namely the thought that I should be the instrument of dispossessing Hill', to whom he owed a debt of loyalty. Rosebery impressed upon him that Hill 'will go whether or not. That has been certain for some time. Lord R. strongly urged me to accept the post, and intimated that the appointment would be very agreeable to the principal members of the late (and future) Government.' On the 23rd, Lucy sent a bread-and-butter letter to Rosebery, telling him that 'whereas this morning I was disposed to see L[abouchere] and decline the offer I shall now see him with a disposition to accept it', provided 'that I shall be permitted to retain my connection with *Punch*'. Labouchere gladly assented; but, as a part owner, he lacked the authority that Walter wielded at *The Times*. Lucy described him on 17 December as chasing 'wildly but vainly in search of Sam Morley who has mysteriously disappeared', and whose presence was required 'to complete the quorum of proprietors when final action is taken'. Consequently, it was not until 9 January 1886 that Lucy was able to announce to Churchill that

> Mr Hill has retired from the editorship of the *Daily News*, and the proprietors have invited me to take his place.... Of course there will remain the great gulf fixed between us on political matters; but I rejoice in an opening that will give me opportunity from time to time to express from a higher pulpit those feelings of esteem, admiration and personal regard which I have always had for your lordship, and have hitherto never failed to declare.

His employers would hardly have approved of such sentiments.[1]

Hill must have known what was afoot. The same cannot be said for certain

[1] Cooke and Vincent, *Governing Passion*, p. 132; Lucy to his wife, 22 November 1885 (copy), Rosebery Papers, Vol. 10,203, fol. 24; Lucy to Rosebery [23 November 1885], 27 November 1885, 17 December 1885, Rosebery Papers, Vol. 10,084, fols. 189, 199, 253; Lucy to Rosebery, 7 January 1886, Rosebery Papers, Vol. 10,085, fol. 12; Lucy to Churchill, 9 January 1886, Churchill Papers.

about Gladstone, with whom he exchanged letters in mid-December on the Irish situation and specifically on the divergencies within the Conservative Cabinet over secret negotiations with Parnell. It was in Gladstone's interest – and Ireland's – that Salisbury's alliance with the Irish nationalists, confirmed in the November elections, should bear fruit. Chamberlain, however, had other thoughts. 'I am sick of the vague generalities of John Morley and the *Daily News*,' he exclaimed to Labouchere on 26 December, 'and I am not going to swallow separation with my eyes shut.' Morley was already a fervent Home Ruler, putting his friendship with Chamberlain to severe strain. It did not help matters when, with Gladstone's approval, he undertook to write a series of leading articles for the *Daily News* after Lucy had taken charge. He 'was in the middle of the fourth' of these pieces when he received a summons from Gladstone, who offered him the Irish secretaryship in the next Liberal administration. After consulting Chamberlain, who was decidedly unenthusiastic, Morley accepted, and then 'finished the leader – such is my devotion to editorial commands'.[1]

Unlike Hill's leading articles, which 'were deemed to be rather too coldly critical', Lucy's were too flatulent. More dangerously, he threatened to alienate Nonconformist readers by befriending Dilke, whose career was irretrievably ruined by his involvement in a divorce scandal. Labouchere, appealing to Rosebery for further assistance 'in an incidental sort of way', apprised him of 'what is going on': Lucy, whose 'genius . . . does not seem to be in editing', unfortunately 'likes money, so he writes the political art[icle]s himself, but he knows nothing about politics, and his style is . . . that of a washer-woman'. In reporting the formation of Gladstone's third ministry, Lucy's incapacity was especially evident. 'What could be more ridiculous', Labouchere asked Rosebery on 13 February, than the *Daily News*'s suggestion that day 'that you and Ld. Granville were warming pans, appointed merely to enable Dilke – when white-washed – to become Secretary of State?'[2]

'Within six months', Lucy 'was back in his little box in the Reporters' Gallery of the House of Commons,' recalled Sir John Robinson, who assumed general control in his capacity as business manager. The *Pall Mall Gazette*, commenting on the transition, branded Lucy 'an even lighter weight' than Hill, his predecessor (7 June 1887). There now existed a cumbersome arrangement whereby P. W. Clayden, without pretence to editorial stature, headed the team of leader-writers. A former Unitarian minister with unimpeachable Nonconformist credentials, Clayden had stood unsuccessfully in three general elections before deciding 'to abjure the House of Commons for his desk in Bouverie Street'. Yet electoral failure had not cooled his Radical ardour.

[1] Hill to Gladstone, 14 December 1885, and Gladstone to Hill, 15 December 1885, Gladstone Papers, Add. MSS. 44,493, fols. 220, 231; Chamberlain to Labouchere, 26 December 1885, quoted in Thorold, *Labouchere*, p. 272; Mills, *Cook*, pp. 49–50.

[2] Robinson, *Fifty Years*, p. 374; Labouchere to Rosebery, 13 February [1886], Rosebery Papers, Vol. 10,041, fol. 54.

Robinson could be 'discussing with him the paper of the following day, and a quarter of an hour later he is haranguing a crowded audience at Islington on the iniquities of Her Majesty's Conservative Opposition'. A member of the executive committee of the National Liberal Federation, Clayden felt 'greatly the responsibility of having the political direction of the *Daily News*', for which he had been 'the writer of most of the leaders' during the Bulgarian crisis. Yet his resources were unequal to his instincts, and perhaps his opportunities to his talent.[1]

Clayden was not unusual in oscillating between a parliamentary and a journalistic career. The dislocations of 1885–86 invited many newspapermen to try their luck at the polls. C. P. Scott of the *Manchester Guardian* had made three attempts to capture a seat at Manchester before he eventually won at Leigh. Edward Russell of the *Liverpool Daily Post* sat for the Bridgeton division of Glasgow in the Parliaments of 1885 and 1886. James Annand was adopted to stand in the Tyneside division of Newcastle, but withdrew in June 1885, when he was offered the editorship of the *Newcastle Daily Leader*; he was 'assured by many of my political friends that I should be of more service to the Liberal Party in my capacity as a journalist than in the House of Commons', which he was ultimately to enter in 1906. Hugh Gilzean Reid sat for Aston Manor in the short-lived Parliament of 1885. The founder of the *North Eastern Daily Gazette*, he had more recently managed the Midland News Association on behalf of the Carnegie-Storey syndicate, and boasted to Chamberlain how he had transformed Conservative properties into Liberal ones that 'would bring large political influence and a good revenue'. Subsequently, with T. P. Ritzema, he established a provincial chain that included the *Northern Daily Telegraph* and the *Birmingham Daily Argus*. But the transition was not always so easy. S. Bennett was obliged to resign from the *Glasgow Herald* in 1885 so as to pursue his parliamentary ambitions, for his 'employers . . ., while personally friendly, do not care for one of their staff to be the expounder of socialistic views. Consequently,' he told Helen Taylor, from whom he requested financial assistance for his abortive candidacy, 'I will have to give up work for them before I make another public appearance.'[2]

Chamberlain, whose 'unauthorised programme' of Radical reforms was implicitly as much a blueprint for political as for social reconstruction, encouraged this reciprocity between parliamentarians and publicists. Carnegie was keen to lend a hand. Although his newspaper enterprise at Birmingham, like that at Wolverhampton, proved 'flat penny beer', he instructed Storey not to

---

[1] Robinson's speech at a Reform Club banquet, 1893, quoted in Robinson, *Fifty Years*, p. 332; Massingham, *London Daily Press*, p. 57; Clayden to Gladstone, 26 September 1888, and 30 November 1897, Gladstone Papers, Add. MSS. 44,504, fol. 278, and 44,526, fol. 225.

[2] G. B. Hodgson, *From Smithy to Senate: The Life Story of James Annand* (London, 1908?), pp. 90–91; Russell to Gladstone, 3 July 1885, Gladstone Papers, Add. MSS. 44,491, fol. 257; Reid to Chamberlain, 23 February 1884, Chamberlain Papers; Bennett to Helen Taylor, 18 October 1885, Mill-Taylor Collection, XVIII/1–2.

'give up'. Gilzean Reid, admitting that he was 'sometimes puzzled how – wisely – to make use of your valuable hints', expressed to Chamberlain the 'hope we have been rendering some service to the advanced cause'. Chamberlain was also on intimate terms with Russell, whom he thanked 'for the assistance you continue to give me in your paper'. Not everyone, however, was as willing to oblige. 'Stead does not like Chamberlain and is distrustful of Dilke,' Hamilton noted after a conversation. And Wemyss Reid saw in Chamberlain's speeches 'the amplest justification for the prejudice I have entertained regarding him since he entered upon public life by attacking Mr Gladstone'.[1]

Even before their rift over the issue of Irish Home Rule, Chamberlain was suspected of designs to shunt Gladstone to the sidelines and to seize the leadership for himself. Accusing fingers were pointed at him when the *Observer*, on 22 January 1885, accurately recounted Liberal disagreements over Egyptian policy. In May, Gladstone came close to blaming Chamberlain for the recurrent leaks that exposed the Liberal Cabinet to ridicule. 'I am at a loss to conceive how anything of this kind can have oozed,' he wrote after ministerial quarrels were detailed in the *Birmingham Daily Post*. 'But on account of the local origin I refer it to you.' The article in question had been written by Lucy as 'Toby, MP', but Chamberlain, protesting his innocence, replied that 'similar statements appeared in the Tory papers – the *Yorkshire Post* and *Manchester Courier* – yesterday morning, but I did not see them and have no conception how they got there'. Morley rebuked Stead for asserting in the *Pall Mall Gazette* that Chamberlain systematically betrayed Cabinet confidences and Gladstone's trust: 'The talk of wounding poor Mr G. is beautiful from *you* who have been stabbing and hacking at him with all your might for many months past – without much damage to his vitality, I admit.' Milner, too, faulted Stead for persecuting Chamberlain: 'The *Birmingham Post* is right in saying that it is not fair to saddle him with all the absurdities that are floating about in the shape of land reform schemes. He has sins enough of his own to answer for without that.' By then, Chamberlain and his feuding colleagues had surrendered office to a minority Conservative administration. 'I hope that the *P. M. G.* has done for itself,' Chamberlain wrote on 8 July to Escott, who proclaimed in that day's number of the *World* 'that the Radicals, for the moment, need have, and can have, no wish to upset the Tory coach'. When Escott fell 'seriously, though not ... dangerously ill' in the autumn, Edmund Yates sent Chamberlain assurances that 'the tone of the paper will, of course, be kept the same'. Chamberlain and Churchill took up a subscription for Escott's family.[2]

[1] Carnegie to Storey, 5 November 1884 (copy), Carnegie Papers; Gilzean Reid to Chamberlain, 5 March 1884, and Chamberlain to Russell, 10 March 1884 (copy?), Chamberlain Papers; Hamilton, *Diary*, II, 485 (22 September 1883); Reid to H. Gladstone, 18 January 1885, Viscount Gladstone Papers, Add. MSS. 46,041, fol. 59.
[2] Cooke and Vincent, *Governing Passion*, pp. 186–88; Gladstone to Chamberlain, 22 May 1885, and Chamberlain to Gladstone, 22 May 1885, quoted in Garvin, *Chamberlain*, I, 612–13; Morley to Stead, 23 May 1885, Stead Papers; Milner to Goschen, 15 September 1885, Milner

The Parliament of 1880 survived on borrowed time. Newspapers began to electioneer in anticipation of a dissolution, which could not be long deferred. The *Morning Post*, on the eve of a by-election in West Gloucestershire in March 1885, urged the electors not to be 'misled by the misapplication of a name into confounding the vagaries of to-day's Radicalism with the steady-going policy of Palmerston', which that paper professed to have 'advocated for thirty years'. The spirit of 'legitimate liberalism', as Palmerston and even Russell had embodied it, now resided among the Tories, while nominal Liberals had purportedly 'degenerated into a frantic struggle to keep their heads above water' (9 March and 2 April 1885). The Tories won the seat in West Gloucestershire, and went on to increase their share of the English and Welsh borough vote in the November elections. With backing from a solid phalanx of 86 Parnellite MPs, they continued to govern.

Lord Salisbury and his strategists had expected better results from the rural constituencies, where Chamberlain's agrarian schemes met with an unusually warm response. In Scotland, the Tory machine expended over £5,000 on the election, much of it wasted on the *Scottish People*, which was published in tandem with the heavily subsidized *Glasgow Evening News*. Reginald MacLeod, Northcote's son-in-law and an unsuccessful contender at Inverness, was identified as 'the manager of the Conservative press in Scotland' by Cooper, who asked Rosebery not to 'think me unduly egotistical if I say that the Edinburgh elections were a great victory for the *Scotsman*'. South of the Tweed, Conservatives relied on the news agencies to break the Liberal mono-poly. Captain R. W. E. Middleton, who created and supervised a network of professional constituency agents, confessed to misgivings about the Constitu-tional Press Agency, which was set up in 1884 to counteract the Liberal bias of the Central News Agency. He discouraged Salisbury from subscribing to the company, 'started as a private speculation', despite its avowed objective 'to tinge . . . with constitutional principles' the dispatches that it supplied to Con-servative and Liberal customers alike. 'The assistance rendered to the Party by this Association has I fancy been hitherto very small,' Middleton shrewdly calculated, 'and for the articles to obtain such ready admission to the columns of the Radical press, as claimed by the authors, the tinge of blue must have been very faint.' Lord Randolph Churchill, meanwhile, was operating as a free agent. His congratulatory telegram helped to launch the Conservative News Agency and to ensure 'that everyone connected with the enterprise will now be doubly careful to render it in every way worthy of your name, and to make it of political service in carrying out your views'.[1]

In the period that led up to the 1885 elections, Salisbury and Churchill were

---

Papers; Chamberlain to Escott, 8 July 1885, Escott Papers; Yates to Chamberlain, 17 October 1885, Chamberlain Papers.

[1] Hanham, *Elections and Party Management*, pp. 159–60; Cooper to Rosebery, 14 August and 27 November 1885, Rosebery Papers, Vol. 10,011, fols. 104–105, 131; Middleton to Salisbury, 14

concerned to muster press support as much against each other as against the common foe. The differences between them were substantive, not merely personal, reflecting deeply rooted tensions within Conservative ranks with regard to the extent and purpose of social reform. Salisbury, ever the traditionalist, sought to slow down and, if possible, to overturn the Churchillian bandwagon. At his behest, Alfred Austin wrote on 20 July 1884 to Mudford, suggesting that the *Standard* 'would do well' to give maximum publicity to Salisbury's imminent address to the National Union at Sheffield. Among other things, Austin made sure to 'point out . . . that the credit of the paper is now involved in the success or failure of the struggle' between the Salisbury and Churchill factions.[1] The *Standard* complied on the 23rd with a two-column transcript of Salisbury's speech, punctuated by references to 'prolonged cheering' by the assembled delegates. An accompanying leader supported Salisbury's stand – as opposed to Churchill's – on the franchise question: 'The country is distinctly appealed to to choose between the mixed form of government which we have inherited from our forefathers, and naked Democracy in its most oppressive and unbridled form.'

In 1884, and again the following year, the National Union considered recommendations for expanding and improving the Conservative press. A special committee was appointed, but a single meeting was sufficient for its members to conclude that they had no practical remedies to offer. One representative from Bristol unabashedly proposed 'nobbling', and drew up a list of ninety Tory papers worthy of direct subsidies from party coffers. Churchill might have been tempted, but Salisbury was dismissive of the idea: 'The difficulty & danger of attempting to buy particular newspapers is that you have no sort of security for the delivery of the goods you buy,' he cautioned Churchill. 'In my experience I have been taken in more than once,' he added revealingly.[2]

It suited Salisbury's temperament, no less than his predicament, to play a waiting game. In June 1885, he formed a caretaker government in which Churchill served as Secretary of State for India. Chamberlain, in a speech at West Islington on the 17th, provocatively asserted that Lord Randolph had planted 'his foot on Lord Salisbury's neck', but it would have been more apposite to say that Churchill was now under Salisbury's thumb. Before old wounds could heal, salt was poured into them by the *Standard*, which warned Salisbury on 31 July to beware of Churchill, 'at heart a greater Radical than Mr Chamberlain himself', who had 'done the Conservative Party almost irreparable harm' in the few weeks since taking office. Not unreasonably, Churchill assumed this

---

May 1884, Salisbury Papers (Christ Church); W. Allison to Churchill, 30 June 1885, Churchill Papers.

[1] Austin to Salisbury, 20 July 1884, Salisbury Papers.
[2] National Union minutes, 6 October 1885; Salisbury to Churchill, 8 October 1885, Churchill Papers.

vicious attack to have been instigated by the Prime Minister or by Lady Salisbury. Austin, however, promptly disclaimed responsibility. 'Have you read the first article in the *Standard* to-day?' he enquired of Salisbury. 'I need scarcely say I neither wrote nor inspired it, & I fail to see its opportuneness.' In any case, Churchill's honeymoon with Salisbury was over.[1]

Salisbury, through his lieutenants, lined up support from other newspapers as well. Borthwick, handed a safe seat at South Kensington, proffered the loyalty of the *Morning Post*, which Churchill had been heard in palmier days to call 'my paper'. Middleton was in touch with Madge of the *Globe*, whom he consulted about Conservative candidacies and kept abreast of electoral developments: 'It is a difficult matter to keep a list perfectly correct, of course, but if you wish our information you can always have it.' *The Times*, recovering from its campaign to promote a Goschen ministry, required little tutelage. John Walter did not stand in 1885, but retired to Bear Wood, where he waited to 'see how the cat jumps. I am only too thankful to be out of it,' he wrote to Stebbing, whose leaders showed a partiality for Salisbury. Churchill, by contrast, was effectively isolated. His only offer of fresh journalistic support came from Greenwood, whose own desperation emboldened him to advance a proposition. Anticipating, logically enough, that the Tories would be cast 'out of office before very long', Greenwood wondered: 'how would it do for you to have the original anti-Radical journal, the *St James's*, at your disposal – your own "organ"? . . . This would be a new thing for a man in your station,' he acknowledged, 'but many new things are becoming familiar & I *do not* suppose you would see anything alarming in that.' Rather disingenuously, Greenwood emphasized the commercial as well as the political benefits that would doubtless accrue. Drummond Wolff recommended the purchase. But Churchill, despite his ravenous appetite for publicity, did not bite.[2]

The general election of 1885 was a free-for-all that unleashed passions without resolving issues. Parnell had set the stage by declaring in a speech at Dublin on 24 August that his aim was nothing less than 'national independence' for Ireland. The following day, the English press bellowed in unison against the idea, which *The Times* flatly rejected as 'impossible', which the *Leeds Mercury* did not consider 'worth discussing', and which the *Standard* implored statesmen of both parties to oppose. Although the *Daily News* took the view that the Liberals were better equipped to deal resolutely with Irish disaffection, Gladstone hoped in vain for a settlement under Tory auspices in order to ensure the acquiescence of the House of Lords. Parnell, following the same logic, instructed Irishmen in British constituencies to back the Tories.

The electoral verdict was far too indecisive for either side to claim a victory,

[1] Austin to Salisbury, 31 July 1885, Salisbury Papers; Cooke and Vincent, *Governing Passion*, pp. 279–80.

[2] Lucas, *Glenesk*, pp. 309–14; Middleton to Madge, 3 September 1885, Chilston Papers; Walter to Stebbing, 14 November 1885, *Times* Collection (Texas); Greenwood to Churchill, 12 December 1885, Churchill Papers.

although their respective newspaper allies put up a brave front. 'The roll of the New Parliament, as made up to Saturday night, is of anything but a disappointing character,' the *Globe* insisted on Monday, 30 November, as the borough results began to trickle in. Dismissing Gladstone as 'the representative of a lost cause', the paper applauded the Tory performance in London, 'the return of a certain number of Liberals being readily explicable for local reasons'. At the Oxford and Cambridge Club, a tussle ensued when that day's issue of the *Globe* was placed on the file in the lobby. Frederick Moncrieff, aged sixty-four and 'a Member of the Club for exactly 40 years', described how 'as is perfectly usual I approached the paper with the intention of looking at the Election returns'. Another member, whom he did not know by name,

> immediately interposed himself between me and the paper: he gathered it up with both his hands and closed it, so as to prevent me seeing it. He then let it fall back to the board and it fell open at pages 4 & 5. The Election returns were at page 5, and while I was looking at them without in the least incommoding him, he deliberately raised up the second folio containing pages 3 & 4 and placed it over page 5 which he saw I was reading.

In a complaint to the general committee, Moncrieff said that his assailant had addressed him 'with abusive language', administered 'a push with some force, and placed his arm across the paper so as to prevent me reading it'. Finally, he 'gathered together' the *Globe* 'with both his hands, tore it from the file, . . . and went off with the pieces of the paper up the stairs.'[1] Whether or not newspapers were able to sway votes, it was obvious that they could inflame tempers.

Among the Liberal journals, only the *Pall Mall Gazette* inspired comparable feelings of loyalty and indignation. To Stead, whose ego required no massaging, Brett instanced the ways in which that paper had proved 'undoubtedly influential'. The *Daily News*, by his estimation, influenced no one. Its weakness was due partly to its managerial structure and partly to Gladstone's 'Delphic ambiguity' – as R. C. K. Ensor has called it – which it was at a loss to interpret. 'If you exercise any control over the *Daily News*, it ought to keep your party straight by purging it of the rancour of defeat,' Tim Healy, the Irish nationalist MP, wrote to Labouchere. 'Swear at us in private as much as you like, but avoid flinging bricks of the boomerang make,' he advised. Healy took particular offence at the *Daily News*'s designation of the Anglo-Irish electors as 'clots of turbid intrigue', and reckoned that this slur 'must have cost you a trifle at the polls'.[2]

---

[1] Moncrieff to the general committee, 30 November and 3 December 1885, and minutes of the general committee, 4 December 1885, Oxford and Cambridge University Club.
[2] Brett to Stead, 6 December 1885, Stead Papers; Ensor, *England 1870–1914*, p. 94; Healy to Labouchere, 10 December 1885, quoted in Thorold, *Labouchere*, pp. 249–50.

Unlike his agitated associates in Parliament and the press, Gladstone studiously declined to condemn the electoral opportunism of the Parnellites, who held the balance of power in the newly elected House of Commons. His reticence gave rise to suspicions that he was prepared to outbid Salisbury for Irish support, thus restoring him to the premiership under mutually discreditable conditions. 'I hope Mr Gladstone will not do what persistent rumour credits him with – viz. consent to purchase the Irish vote on Parnell's terms,' Buckle told Rosebery on 13 December. 'He would end his career, so long and so splendid, in a deplorable manner, if he did,' the editor of *The Times* predicted.

What is more, I think he would break up his party finally, & ensure Lord Salisbury a majority at a dissolution on the question next year. I am not sure that I should be sorry for either of these two consequences; but I should be greatly grieved if Mr Gladstone should lower himself so completely.[1]

Within forty-eight hours, Buckle had his answer. Although he underestimated ideological factors, which weighed heavily on Gladstone, he shrewdly intuited the subsequent drift of events.

*　　　　*　　　　*

Increasingly sympathetic towards Irish nationalist aspirations, Gladstone came slowly to the conclusion that the Conservative government possessed neither the power nor the genuine inclination to satisfy them. As in 1880, it became obvious that his moral leadership was required. Again, however, there were rumblings of opposition within his own party. On 13 December, the same day that Buckle wrote to Rosebery, Wemyss Reid sent Herbert Gladstone a 'very confidential and serious communication' in which he reported 'on very high authority' the existence of a Radical cabal 'to prevent the formation of a Govt. by your father' and specifically to undermine any Liberal concordat with Parnell. Reid, whose network of political contacts extended far beyond Leeds, identified the malcontents as Chamberlain, Dilke, and Morley. (He was surely mistaken in the case of Morley, who verified that 'much dirty intriguing is going on', but proclaimed that he would not 'be a party to snubbing the Old Man'.) The *Liverpool Daily Post* and the *Daily News* (11 and 12 December) engaged in speculation, as did the *Pall Mall Gazette* (14 December). Already Reid had taken the precaution of conveying a warning to Scott of the *Manchester Guardian* '& one or two other leading journalists whom I believe to be in sympathy with my desire to support your father as the one leader of our party'.[2]

---

[1] Buckle to Rosebery, 13 December 1885, Rosebery Papers, Vol. 10,084, fol. 241.
[2] Reid to H. Gladstone, 13 December 1885, Viscount Gladstone Papers, Add. MSS. 46,041, fols. 65 ff.; Morley to R. Spence Watson, 15 December 1885, quoted in Hirst, *Morley*, II, 272; J. L. Hammond, *Gladstone and the Irish Nation* (London, 1938), p. 439.

Herbert Gladstone, himself a zealous convert to the Home Rule cause, was more unsettled by Reid's indiscretion than by his revelation, which he knew to be incorrect in detail. That, however, did not prevent him from committing greater indiscretions of his own. He immediately replied to clarify his father's position, as he understood it, and to arrange 'to talk over the question with friends'. On the 15th, he journeyed to London, where he met Labouchere at the National Liberal Club and Reid at the Reform. At the same time that the elder Gladstone was informally assuring Balfour, whom he met at the Duke of Westminster's house, that the Tories could rely on bipartisan support for limited Irish concessions, the younger Gladstone was indicating the contrary. According to Herbert's intimations, Gladstone's categorical support for Home Rule was assured. 'Never was there a moment,' Morley later reflected, 'when every consideration of political prudence more imperatively counselled silence.' Yet never was there a moment when there was more contradictory babble.[1]

Under the impression that he was working to avert a Liberal split, Herbert Gladstone secured Reid's promise 'to influence all the provincial papers to which he has got access in the right direction'. He counted it 'a triumph' to have won over the *Leeds Mercury*, which he expected to 'give us valuable help'. Unrepentant, even after his father had disavowed his statement as mere speculation, Herbert was confident that his confabulation with Reid had

> brought about certain definite results.... The Liberal press took the cue, and not only in London. Leading papers, like the *Manchester Guardian* and the *Leeds Mercury*, came out definitely for Mr Gladstone and Home Rule. Even the *Scotsman* and *Western Morning News* – later to become Unionist – were not unfavourable to the new departure.

Here was an example – perhaps the most famous one in nineteenth-century history – of an attempt, perhaps bungled, to use the press to mobilize party opinion. It may be taken, at face value, as an exploratory technique. Or it may be seen to represent what Sir Denis Hamilton has described as 'the trick of establishing a notion in the reader's mind by plucking it out of the blue to deny it'. Either way, its effect was profound.[2]

Floated by Herbert Gladstone, the 'Hawarden Kite' – as it was known – entangled him in its tail. On the 17th, as arranged, the *Leeds Mercury* disclosed that Gladstone was considering a measure 'for the establishment of a Parliament in Dublin for dealing with purely Irish affairs'. Unexpectedly, the same report appeared simultaneously in the Tory *Standard*. How had it got there? Labouchere, who obtained his information from Robinson at the *Daily*

[1] H. Gladstone to Reid, 14 December 1885, Viscount Gladstone Papers, Add. MSS. 46,041, fols. 69 ff.; Morley, *Gladstone*, III, 266.

[2] Viscount Gladstone, *After Thirty Years* (London, 1928), pp. 308–33 (including extracts from diary entries, 14 and 15 December 1885); Sir Denis Hamilton, *Who Is To Own the British Press?* (London, 1976), p. 3.

News, informed both Rosebery and Chamberlain that Reid, after his interview with Herbert, had carried the story to Mudford. 'Could this have been stupidity,' wondered Labouchere, 'or was it intentional by order of Papa?' Confronted by these imputations, Reid vigorously denied collusion with the *Standard*. 'I must tell you at once that however the news reached that paper it came neither directly nor indirectly from me,' he protested to Herbert Gladstone. 'I own I am surprised & mortified to find that what you might suppose to have been a breach of good faith on my part has taken place.' Perhaps, he suggested, Mudford – on whom 'I have not set eyes ... since last April' – had received advance notification through 'the Liberal Press Agency, or some such body'; or perhaps Herbert's conversation at the National Liberal Club ('not the place to have any confidential interviews') had been overheard. Admittedly, Reid had visited the *Standard* office on the evening of the 16th, but not 'till I heard that they had ... a written scheme drawn up by your father', which of course did not exist.[1]

Reid's innocence was not easily credited by those familiar with the machinations of the political press. 'I am not a bit afraid of the row about Ireland; but I think it would be a good thing if somebody would jump upon Herbert Gladstone,' declared Cooper, in whose mind there was not the slightest doubt that Reid, provided with 'the sketch of what Mr G. intended', passed it along to Mudford, as 'the paragraph in the *Standard* was almost a verbal reproduction of it'. Furthermore, Cooper told Rosebery, 'Reid also showed it to the correspondents of the *Glasgow Herald* & the *Dundee Advertiser*'. The *Scotsman* might have scooped the *Standard*, but for the fact that its editor prided himself on being 'most unfashionably scrupulous'. Indeed, Cooper reminded Rosebery that, under the extraordinary circumstances, he might have 'made use of your conversation with me'; but he preferred 'that I should be without first things rather than that I should make use of communications which are not expressly given for publication'. There were not many journalists who exhibited such forbearance, and Cooper himself may not have always practised what he preached. In a later volume of reminiscences, he was alleged to have 'exceeded his legitimate rights' by quoting extensively from a correspondence with Childers 'which depended for its openness of utterance ... upon an understanding of private confidence and friendship'.[2]

While journalists debated questions of propriety, politicians pondered the implications of Herbert Gladstone's statement. It might have been unauthorized, but was it unsubstantiated? Neither Gladstone's telegraphed disclaimer

[1] Labouchere to Rosebery [19 December 1885], Rosebery Papers, Vol. 10,041, fol. 42; Labouchere to Chamberlain [20] December 1885, quoted in Thorold, *Labouchere*, pp. 253–54; Reid to H. Gladstone, 17 and 20 December 1885, Viscount Gladstone Papers, Add MSS. 46,041, fols. 75ff.

[2] Cooper to Rosebery, 22 December 1885, Rosebery Papers, Vol. 10,011, fols. 140–41; Childers, *Childers*, II, 299–301.

on the 17th nor Morley's speech at Newcastle on the 21st ('I say that such talk, whether it is in Liberal organs or in Tory organs, is as untrue as it is poor and contemptible') set minds to rest. Liberal dissidents, including Chamberlain and Hartington, remained convinced that there was some method to the madness. Tory ministers, including Cranbrook and Churchill, were ready to allow Gladstone to rush in foolishly where they themselves angelically feared to tread. Labouchere, commenting that 'the ways of Mr Gladstone are rather more mysterious than those of the Heathen Chinee', believed that the. 'Hawarden Kite' had been flown deliberately, and likewise that a pro-Home Rule article in the *Pall Mall Gazette* on 19 December 'was directly inspired from Hawarden'. In fact, Gladstone had denied any encouragement to Stead. 'Except what I have publicly spoken and written, all ideas ascribed to me are in truth other people's opinions: as the colors of the rainbow are in us, not in it,' he replied philosophically to a request for editorial guidance. Nevertheless, neither Stead nor other editors took him at his word. So far as Labouchere could infer from his cronies at the Reform Club, 'the outcry against Mr G. is only in the newspapers'. Bright took the same view. 'I have heard nothing from those who are called our Leaders,' he wrote to a friend on Christmas Day,

& I know nothing but what I see in the papers, & the bulk of that, I cannot doubt, is but the work of active imagination on the part of men who live by writing & by efforts to create sensation.[1]

To Gladstone's discomfort, the press fanned the flames of the Irish controversy and thereby deprived him of political options. The *Globe* regarded it as 'not a little ominous' that the *Leeds Mercury*, 'which has acquired such an authoritative character lately as an exponent of Gladstonian purposes', should advocate Home Rule, 'this monstrous scheme of national disintegration, as the only panacea for the country'. Even before the new Parliament had assembled, it was clear that 'another General Election is inevitable, unless the Moderate Liberals come in force to the aid of the Government', as the *Globe* beseeched them to do (28 and 30 December 1885). But the so-called 'Moderate Liberals' were a diverse lot, some of whom were more responsive than others to the prospect of inter-party collaboration. By the same token, not all of them were equally acceptable to the Conservative leaders, who differed in their objectives. That became evident on 27 January 1886, when the Salisbury ministry, defeated on an amendment to the Queen's speech, tendered its resignation. Neither Hartington nor Goschen, who refused a royal invitation, was

---

[1] Labouchere to Chamberlain [20] December 1885, quoted in Thorold, *Labouchere*, pp. 253–54; Gladstone to Stead, 18 December 1885 (copy), Gladstone Papers, Add. MSS. 44,493, fol. 238; Labouchere to Rosebery [19 December 1885], Rosebery Papers, Vol. 10,041, fol. 42; Bright to Thorold Rogers, 25 December 1885, Rogers Papers.

prepared to form a coalition, and the Queen reluctantly sent for Gladstone.

'It is impossible to conceal the fact that Mr Gladstone is more completely master of the country and of his Cabinet than he has ever yet been,' Brett told Chamberlain with apprehension. Hartington, whom Brett served as private secretary, declined office, as did Goschen and Sir Henry James. But Harcourt and Rosebery accepted major posts, and Chamberlain put aside his qualms to join as president of the Board of Trade. The most portentous appointment was that of Morley to the Irish Office. 'It would be impossible to over-estimate the political significance of this selection,' wrote *The Times*. 'This removes all doubt as to Mr Gladstone's course in dealing with Irish affairs, for it implies that he is in perfect harmony with Mr Morley's views' which were emphatically in favour of Home Rule (3 February). Like Chamberlain, *The Times* hoped against hope that Gladstone, who promised full Cabinet consultation, would not persevere in the direction of legislative separatism. All the same, Buckle declined to dispatch a reporter to a Conservative banquet at the Hotel Metropole where, 'owing to want of room', the press was excluded from dinner. 'This is an indignity to which *The Times* is not accustomed, & which I am sure you will understand we cannot put up with,' he protested to Salisbury.[1]

Other newspapermen did not stand on ceremony. Instructed 'definitely'· by Yates 'that I wish the tone of our political articles' in the *World* 'to be not merely "moderate Liberal", but with a decided Conservative bias', Escott expressed to Salisbury the conviction 'that neither the liberal party nor the country will stand another Gladstonian regime'. So as to guarantee victory at the next elections, which could come at any time, Conservative proprietors appealed to their party chiefs for assistance. Lord Folkestone (a Tory MP from 1892 until 1900, when he succeeded to the earldom of Radnor) invited Hicks Beach to address 'a meeting . . . to help the *Evening News*', which was reportedly losing £40,000 a year, much of it from Folkestone's own pocket. Hicks Beach, recognizing a solicitation, was unwilling to accept. 'I cannot myself put anything into the concern,' he explained to Akers-Douglas, soon to become the Tory chief whip, 'and I have so often subscribed in a small way to things of this kind, which have done no good, that I should feel very reluctant to prod others, who can afford it, to do so.' Cranbrook was similarly importuned, and in turn importuned Akers-Douglas, on behalf of the *Banner* which was 'doing very good work'. Latimer Neville, the master of Magdalene College, Cambridge, had 'started a halfpenny paper in Cambridgeshire which derives much from the *Banner*'; he seemed 'much interested', and Cranbrook had already 'helped him as far as I can'. And Balfour was called upon to help sustain the *Haddingtonshire Advertiser*. 'Some time ago', against his better judgment, he 'gave it considerable pecuniary assistance', which he was not prepared to renew. The *Advertiser* soon folded, leaving Balfour 'by far the largest loser,

<hr />

[1] Brett to Chamberlain, 9 February 1886, Esher Papers; Buckle to Salisbury, 13 February 1886, Salisbury Papers.

for I lose not only my original subscription, but a Loan of £500 secured upon the Plant'.[1]

As foreshadowed by Yates's directive to Escott, the Conservative press was to receive a boost from the schism in Liberal ranks. Yet, even before the Home Rule split was a *fait accompli*, the debility of Liberal journalism was painfully obvious. That is not to deny the spirit and indeed the courage of particular Liberal papers, pre-eminently the *Manchester Guardian*. 'Unless we are going to give pretty much what the Irish want,' it reasoned on 19 March, 'there is no sense in giving anything.' The general tone of Liberal papers, however, was one of flaccidity. The *Daily News* was a case in point. As late as 17 March, it continued to wait and see: 'When Mr Gladstone comes to make in the House of Commons full exposition of his plan we shall be in a better position to judge of its merits.' Reid, hoping to collect on the services he had rendered the previous December, badgered Herbert Gladstone to help him secure the editorship. He would not have aspired to the position 'if it had not been for the fact that the *D. N.* has ... displayed such an extraordinary amount of feebleness as to make it, from the journalistic point of view, impossible that the present arrangement can last'. A Nonconformist ('though not, I trust, a bigot'), he was confident that he had all the necessary qualifications to revitalize the paper. Labouchere, he feared, was 'inclined to regard me as being too much of a "moderate" and too independent for the post'. But, while he affirmed his independence, Reid amusingly confided that 'my moderation is not quite what it seems to be'. To no avail, Herbert Gladstone proposed Reid to Labouchere and Arnold Morley. Still, Reid did not despair of his chances. 'Sooner or later Lucy *must* go, & then I hope I may have a chance of following him,' Reid wrote that summer to Stead, whom he informed that

> the outcry against the *D.N.* is universal among Liberals, and a week or two back a strong effort was made by some members of the Govt. to get a change made. They not only wanted to have Lucy put out of the way, but to have me appointed in his place.

Reid could not escape from Leeds, nor the *Daily News* from its doldrums.[2]

Because Cabinet meetings were held infrequently, and the formulation of Irish policy was entrusted to a small committee, most ministers were compelled to rely on the press for random hints of Gladstone's intentions. On 13 March, when a draft formula was laid before them, Chamberlain and G. O. Trevelyan threatened to resign. They were prevailed upon to reconsider on the grounds that these proposals were tentative and that objections would be

[1] Yates to Escott, 27 January [1886], Escott Papers; Escott to Salisbury, 20 February 1886, Salisbury Papers; Beach to Akers-Douglas, 7 February 1886, and Cranbrook to Akers-Douglas, 9 February 1886, Chilston Papers; Balfour to C. Smith [March] 1886, and Balfour to Houston, 10 May 1886 (letterbook copies), Balfour Papers.
[2] Reid to H. Gladstone, 26 February, 1 and 17 March, and 2 April 1886, Viscount Gladstone Papers, Add. MSS. 46,041, fols. 81 ff., 85, 87, 91–92; Reid to Stead, 28 July 1886, Stead Papers.

entertained. On the 25th, the day before the Cabinet next met, Chamberlain was furious to see in the *Leeds Mercury* and elsewhere 'statements attributed to H. Gladstone' that justified his worst apprehensions. 'If he has made them or anything like them,' he told Harcourt, 'it is an unpardonable indiscretion.' The following afternoon, the Cabinet received the Home Rule Bill and, with it, the formal resignations of Chamberlain and Trevelyan. The public announcement was delayed until the 29th, and Chamberlain dined privately with Churchill that evening. Exchanging his seat on the ministerial front bench for one below the gangway, he invited speculation on how far he meant to carry his opposition. Nevertheless, it irritated him to have his motives impugned. 'Please deny on authority the ridiculous rumours published as to the negotiations between the leaders of the Conservative party and the Ministers who have resigned,' he wrote on 6 April to Bunce of the *Birmingham Daily Post*, who branded as

> absolutely false ... stories, ... wonderful in their audacity, ... that Mr Chamberlain is prepared to divide the Liberal party, or for the time to desert it, in order that, in alliance with the Tory leaders, he may inflict defeat and discredit upon the Prime Minister. [7 April]

Bunce was 'very glad' to hear that Chamberlain approved of his work. 'The [e]xplanation of your position is in every paper to-day with one exception – the *Leeds Mercury*,' he reported back. 'I took care that it went specially to *The Times*, & also had it sent to the Press Association, which did the rest.'[1]

On 8 April, Gladstone introduced his Home Rule Bill in the Commons. The presentation took three and a half hours. Chamberlain, who had previously indicated his intention to follow in debate, held his peace for the time being. Perhaps he calculated that a groundswell of Liberal opposition would induce Gladstone to withdraw the measure or, at least, to offer concessions. Possibly he expected the Whigs and Tories to do the job for him. Already dissension within the parliamentary Liberal Party had begun to reverberate in the press. Cooper pleaded with Rosebery on 4 April to dissociate himself from Home Rule for the sake of his own career, and instanced strong resistance on the part of the *Scotsman*'s readers:

> Since we published a week ago some of the heads of Mr Gladstone's Bill as it then was, there has been positive consternation in Scotland.... Since Monday I have talked with many men, and I have not met with one – No, not one – who did not declare that such a scheme as the one attributed to Mr G. was downright folly.... Many of Mr G's most ardent supporters in Mid Lothian have told me they would not vote for him in support of such a scheme.

---

[1] Chamberlain to Harcourt, 25 March 1886, Harcourt Papers; Chamberlain to Bunce, 6 April 1886, quoted in Garvin, *Chamberlain*, II, 209; Bunce to Chamberlain, 7 April 1886, Chamberlain Papers.

On the day after Gladstone unveiled the Bill, the *Scotsman* proclaimed categorically: 'This will never do!' From a 'prominent statesman', probably Childers, Cooper received a stern warning that his paper 'would lose influence, and I should be ostracised so far as the Liberal party was concerned'. He replied, as he recalled, 'that if the *Scotsman* was to lose influence by being honest, the sooner the influence went the better'. As for himself, 'if I was to be ostracised for acting conscientiously, ostracised I would be'.[1]

The *Scotsman*, hitherto a promulgator of Gladstonian opinion, was among the first and most fiery of the journalistic defectors. Manifesting a notable lack of enthusiasm, other papers waited for a lead from Chamberlain or, in some cases, from Hartington. The two rebels flirted with each other, but continued to stand apart. Their differences, articulated in speeches as well as letters to the press, inspired Gladstone with the hope that the Bill would pass its second reading. With Labouchere and Arnold Morley (both connected with the proprietorship of the *Daily News*) as intermediaries, attempts were made to bring Gladstone and Chamberlain together. But Chamberlain's diatribe in *The Times* on 8 May convinced Gladstone that it was 'hopeless to frame a measure of conciliation for him'. Thereafter, Chamberlain grew more militant and more responsive to Hartington's overtures. For a fleeting moment, it seemed even to Gladstone that Hartington, with Chamberlainite and moderate Tory support, might form a government. Accompanied by three trusty colleagues, Gladstone spent the weekend of 15–16 May as the guest of Algernon West at Coombe. There, 'in one of his frivolous, provoking moods', he amused the company by drawing up a hypothetical list of Hartington's Cabinet appointments. On Monday, the 17th, that list 'appeared, as he had written it, in the *Pall Mall Gazette*, and' – West recorded – 'we could not imagine how it got there'. While Gladstone was relaxing at Coombe, *The Times* played exactly the same game, projecting a Hartington ministry that would contain Chamberlain, Goschen, and Derby. The *Birmingham Daily Post* rebuked it for having stated 'without the faintest shade of authority' that Chamberlain was either willing to be 'entangled in such an alliance ... or working for any such project as the scheme which *The Times* imagines that he may be brought to support' (17 May).[2]

There were numerous stumbling blocks, Goschen not the least among them. And yet, Chamberlain was not averse to co-operation with Hartington for limited purposes. J. Powell Williams, MP for Birmingham South and a fellow dissident, was 'so anxious myself that your approach to Ld. Hartington shd. not be misunderstood in the country, as it is evidently misunderstood in the London press', that he took it upon himself 'to keep our own folks straight'.

[1] Cooper to Rosebery, 4 April 1886, Rosebery Papers, Vol. 10,011, fols. 156–58; Cooper, *An Editor's Retrospect*, p. 408; *Newspaper World*, 22 April 1916 (obituary of Cooper).
[2] West, *Recollections*, II, 277; *also see* Cooke and Vincent, *Governing Passion*, pp. 409–22.

His intervention took the form of an analysis of 'The Political Situation', signed 'by a Liberal Member' and published in the *Birmingham Daily Post* on the 17th. Taking seriously, as many did, the prevalent rumours that Gladstone was 'anxious to find a way out of the difficulty in which he is placed', Williams suggested that 'the withdrawal of the bill in favour of a general resolution declaring the principle of Home Rule for Ireland would probably meet the case'. Such a move would not only restore the unity of the Liberal Party, but also stave off a dissolution, a prospect especially dreaded by impecunious labour representatives. Should Gladstone reject this route of 'honourable escape', the consensus among 'the best-informed "Parliamentary hands"' was that the Queen would give 'a chance of forming a Government' to Hartington, who had recently 'advanced far in the direction of Mr Chamberlain's views'. To contemplate this eventuality, however, was 'quite premature', as there was every reason to believe that Gladstone would yet contrive to appease his Liberal critics, whose 'respect for and ... gratitude to him remain unchanged'. There can be no doubt that Williams's article faithfully reflected the momentary sentiments of Chamberlain, who confided that day to his brother that he and Gladstone 'might come together again'.[1]

This wistful mood quickly evaporated. Gladstone, far from scrapping the Bill, affirmed his intention to proceed to a second reading. His token concession was an assurance that a favourable vote would be taken to imply approval of the principle and not necessarily of the details, which would be subject to emendation in the autumn. On this score, the *Pall Mall Gazette* was propitiated: having strongly objected to the proposed exclusion of Irish members from the Imperial Parliament, it ultimately pronounced it 'the duty of every member who accepts the principle of Home Rule' to achieve passage of the Bill, 'and then direct his energies ... to render it impossible for the Ministry to propose again the wrong kind of Home Rule' (7 June). Others were not so easily pacified. The Hartingtonians, constituted as the Liberal Unionist Committee, were fortified in their determination to oppose outright. The Chamberlainites, a smaller group of Radical Unionists, were said to be divided between those who wished to abstain and those who were prepared to vote with the government on the understanding that their hollow gesture would be recognized as such.

Cooper gave no ground. An emissary, whom he knew to be 'on most intimate terms of friendship with Lord Rosebery', asked whether specific 'modifications' would induce the *Scotsman* to mute its attacks. He responded that his aversion was to the concept of Irish Home Rule, which he found unacceptable in any form. (As Morley subsequently observed to Bryce, Cooper – 'oddly enough' – was receptive to a measure of Home Rule for Scotland.) His repugnance against Gladstone's Irish policy was so great as to overcome his antipa-

---

[1] Williams to Chamberlain, 16 May 1886, and Chamberlain to Arthur Chamberlain, 17 May 1886, Chamberlain Papers.

thy to Chamberlain, whose position was pivotal. 'You and I have not always agreed in the recent past,' Cooper wrote with classic understatement on 21 May; 'but I think we are very closely together in this Irish business. It swallows up all else and will for some time to come.' Favouring Chamberlain with the advice he had formerly lavished on Rosebery, Cooper weighed the alternatives. 'The best of all solutions,' he supposed,

> would be a new Liberal ministry in which a scheme of safe Irish policy would be developed. Under it Mr G. would disappear, and the unity of the Liberal party would be restored. If that be not possible the election will have to be fought with vigour.

Four days later, Cooper's attitude – like everyone else's – had hardened, and he was prognosticating the imminent outbreak of civil warfare within the party:

> As sure as we are living, if a dissolution comes, Mr G. will be beaten. I have taken care that the opportunity was given to him to know all this. Approaches have been made to me ... from 10, Downing Street, and I have spoken out very freely.

He may have exaggerated his influence, but it could not be discounted.[1]

Others were not nearly so confident that Chamberlain, in the event, would cast his decisive vote against Home Rule. Buckle, although closer than Cooper to the parliamentary scene, feared a capitulation at the eleventh hour. Conceding that 'I have no right or business to remonstrate with you on the matter, except that I feel deeply about it', he told Chamberlain on the 27th that he would 'be bitterly disappointed if you do not oppose, & thereby defeat, the second reading of this pernicious bill'. He breathed more easily after the 31st, when Chamberlain, brandishing a letter from Bright, counselled his followers against abstention. Yet, even then, *The Times* did not slacken. Denouncing the 'Irish Separation Bill' as a sell-out to treacherous Parnellites, themselves the pawns of American 'Extremists', it raised the spectre of a 'reign of terror' against the loyal Protestant minority (5 and 7 June), whom the *Pall Mall Gazette* (31 May) reported to be arming in self-defence. It was later asserted that James Thursfield, 'being a convinced Home Ruler, asked to be excused from writing on the subject' in the paper. According to Thursfield's own vague recollection, however, the question had never come up, as Buckle had at his command the talents of other leader-writers, whose 'ceaseless bombardment of the Gladstonian position did more to defeat Home Rule than the speeches of any statesmen, except Chamberlain and Bright'.[2]

---

[1] Cooper, *An Editor's Retrospect*, p. 408; Cooper to Chamberlain, 21 and 25 May 1886, Chamberlain Papers; on Cooper's support for Scottish Home Rule, see Morley to Bryce, 25 November 1886, Bryce Papers, and the *Scotsman*, 11 October 1886.
[2] Buckle to Chamberlain [27 May 1886], Chamberlain Papers; '*The Times*: Delane to North-

Buckle need not have worried. Early on the morning of 8 June, the House divided 343 to 313, with Chamberlain contributing to the margin of victory over Home Rule. Without delay, Gladstone announced a dissolution and carried his cause to the country. The ensuing campaign, stiffly fought, failed to produce a clear-cut result. Contrary to *The Times*'s predictions, the Parnellites retained their full strength in Ireland. Belying Cooper's gleeful prophecies of doom, the Gladstonians held firm in Scotland: Trevelyan, narrowly defeated at Hawick, was elected at Bridgeton in 1887 only after he had returned to the Gladstonian fold; and Goschen, soundly rejected at East Edinburgh, eventually found sanctuary in the Tory citadel of St George's, Hanover Square. In Wales, too, the orthodox Liberals preserved their hegemony, and the dissident Liberals registered no impact. In south-western England and the Midlands, the Liberal Unionists fared better, arguably at the expense of their Conservative allies. Of the 394 Unionists in the new House, 78 carried a 'Liberal' prefix. Salisbury, resisting a plea for coalition from the Queen and other sources, formed an unalloyed Conservative administration, which he relied upon the Liberal Unionists to buttress from outside. It was not simply that he required their votes for an overall majority. The Liberal Unionists, now united behind Hartington, compensated in administrative experience and oratorical power for what they lacked in numbers. Conspicuous among their assets, which Salisbury hoped to draw upon, was a reservoir of press support.

*   *   *

The effect of the Home Rule crisis on the structure of the political press – and, by extension, on general patterns of electoral organization – has been variously gauged. On the one hand, it has been taken to clarify, and thus to confirm, implicit predilections: 'an indicator of pre-existent political affiliations and attitudes, rather than . . . an originator of them', according to Alan J. Lee. On the other, it has been depicted more dramatically as the impetus for major shifts of allegiance: 'No political question which ever agitated the country brought more changes in the Press World than the controversy . . . in regard to Home Rule for Ireland,' declaimed *Sell's Dictionary of the World's Press*. The truth, as usual, lay somewhere between the two extremes, but, on balance, closer to the second view.[1]

Sell's went too far, counting *The Times* and the *Daily Telegraph* among the papers that supported Gladstone in 1885 and deserted him in 1886. Nevertheless, its point was essentially valid. The weight of newspaper opinion had indeed abruptly shifted. As a writer in the *Outlook* (possibly Garvin) was to argue, the Liberal Party maintained a journalistic dominance until 'the

cliffe,' *Quarterly Review*, ccxxxix (1923), 95–96; Thursfield to Dawson, 22 January 1923, *Times* Archives.
[1] Lee, *Origins*, p. 161; *Sell's Dictionary* (London, 1893).

position was entirely reversed in 1886'. To contemporary observers, this transformation was beyond dispute. The National Union, where the inferiority of the Conservative press had provoked annual lamentation, heard in 1887 that 'the majority of daily newspapers', if not yet of the weeklies, 'are now Unionist'. And Unionism, in the press as in Parliament, proved a stopping-place on the road to Conservatism. In 1896, the *Constitutional Year Book*, an official Tory text, noted that, with four possible exceptions, the thirteen London Unionist dailies might be safely classified as Conservative.[1]

There is reason to suspect that several of the newspapers in question were responding more to popular taste than to conviction. Especially in the provinces, local and religious factors came into play; while in the Home Counties, the accelerating migration to the suburbs affected electoral preferences. But, in the main, the conversions were inspired by deliberate efforts on the part of Unionist politicians, whose mutual distrust made press support seem indispensable.

Over the next half a dozen years, as Salisbury consolidated his position, his techniques of newspaper management came to prevail. Unlike Churchill, among others, he was not eager to appropriate party funds for the creation of new journals or even for the maintenance of foundering properties. He did not object, of course, to such expenditure on the part of his Liberal Unionist allies, from whose prodigality he stood to benefit. Salisbury's own method, skilfully implemented by Middleton and Akers-Douglas, was to encourage defections from the Liberal camp. His earlier experience in journalism, besides affording him contacts, had taught him that the most economical way was usually also the best way to cultivate editorial friendships. *The Times*, for example, after its impulsive bid for a Hartington premiership in 1886, gradually warmed to Salisbury as 'the Prime Minister most accessible to the Press. He is not prone to give information: but when he does, he gives it freely, & his information can always be relied on.'[2] Salisbury's mastery was all the more redoubtable for the restraint with which it was exercised.

In other contexts, a policy of *laissez-faire* would not have worked half so well. But the Liberal disruption allowed Salisbury to sit back and collect the pieces. The Carnegie-Storey syndicate disintegrated, leaving Passmore Edwards to regain control of the *Echo* 'just in time to determine its attitude on the Home Rule Question', and to repudiate its Gladstonianism and his own. Midway through the 1886 elections, the appointment of Massingham as assistant editor of the *Daily Chronicle* prompted the *Pall Mall Gazette* to infer that this halfpenny paper, 'which has seemed for some time to be halting between two opinions, has now decided to wheel into line under the "Grand Old Flag"' (13 July); but the *Chronicle* pursued a mildly Unionist line until

---

[1] 'English Journalism,' *Outlook*, lxix (1901), 186; National Union minutes, 22–23 November 1887; *Constitutional Year Book* (London, 1896), p. 332.
[2] Sir Edward Hamilton's diary, 5 February 1887.

1890, when R. W. Boyle retired as editor, and the paper veered far to the left. Among the metropolitan evening journals, the Gladstonians were reduced to rely on the *Pall Mall Gazette*, increasingly erratic in its support, at least until the appearance of the *Star* in 1888. On morning news-stands, they had only the *Daily News*, which was chronically weak. No doubt, it was reflecting the division and confusion among its traditional readers. 'What we want is an energetic and fighting newspaper,' Morley wrote to Bryce on the eve of Salisbury's return to office. 'If only the *D. News* could be got hold of. Could we not all (you & me & F. Harrison) write a series of letters there?' And Reid, not without a vested interest, complained that 'the *D. N.* continues to serve us every possible bad turn, . . . & the whole purpose of the editor seems to be to keep in touch with Churchill & Chamberlain'.[1]

Among the various categories of weekly journals, the picture was no less bleak. The *Spectator* espoused the Unionist creed, leaving the Gladstonians bereft of a sixpenny 'quality' organ until 1889, when the *Speaker* was launched by members of the *Star* proprietorship. Of the society prints, Labouchere's *Truth* stayed loyal, in its impudent way, but the *World* fulminated against Home Rule, and many of its articles were said to have been written by Frank Hill, an apostate from Gladstonianism. The Nonconformist press, so vital to Liberal interests, was divided: the *Christian World* opposed official Liberal policy at the cost of 'some thousands of readers'; and the *Methodist Times*, conducted by the Rev Hugh Price Hughes, gave tepid support until Home Rule became synonymous not only with 'Rome Rule', but also with Parnell's adultery. The *Observer*, under Edward Dicey's editorship, became fervently Unionist. The mass-circulation *Lloyd's Weekly News* turned with a vengeance against Liberalism, as did the *Weekly Dispatch*, much to the embarrassment of its owner, Ashton Dilke. Morley was asked to nominate a new editor to replace Fox Bourne, 'who had to go on account of his anti-Home Rule writing', and Dr W. A. Hunter, the MP for Aberdeen Central, was chosen. Although Morley 'rejoiced much' at the substitution, Stead regarded this 'great secret' as 'small news when compared with what followed', namely Morley's disclosure that Sir Charles Dilke, ejected from his seat at Chelsea, 'was coming back to London to found an evening newspaper; that in order to prepare himself for the duties . . . he desires six months' run of the *P. M. G.* office'. Because Dilke was *persona non grata* to Stead and Yates Thompson, and politically inadmissible at the *St James's Gazette* and the *Globe*, Morley had to beg the indulgence of Edwards at the *Echo*. In the event, however, the scheme fell through.[2]

In Scotland, the Gladstonians suffered disproportionately heavy newspaper

[1] *Sell's* (1893); Lee, *Origins*, p. 160; Morley to Bryce, 23 July 1886, Bryce Papers; Reid to H. Gladstone, 5 August 1886, Viscount Gladstone Papers, Add. MSS. 40,041, fol. 102.
[2] *Sell's* (1893); Arthur Porritt, *More and More of Memories* (London, 1947), p. 76; Stead's diary, 9–10 September 1886, Stead Papers.

losses. Along with the *Scotsman*, the *Glasgow Herald* and the *Aberdeen Free Press* turned Unionist. With the single exception of the *Dundee Advertiser*, none of the surviving pillars of Gladstonian journalism was solidly based. Consequently, the *Scottish Leader* was hurriedly established to fill the gap. Yet it did not follow that the collapse of Gladstonianism in the press would lead to its eclipse at the polls. Aberdeen, for example, remained indomitably Gladstonian, although it lacked a Gladstonian paper until the *Northern Daily News* began publication in 1891. The effect on party morale, admittedly more difficult to quantify, was more pronounced.

With regard to English provincial journalism, the pattern was distinctly chequered. The *Birmingham Daily Post* followed predictably at Chamberlain's heels, and the *Western Morning News* at Hartington's. In those counties where Whig territorial influence ran strong, the complexion of the local press changed accordingly: in Cheshire, the Duke of Westminster secured control of the *Chester Courant* and carried it to the Unionist side. The defection to Unionism of the *York Herald*, whose editor found convenient accommodation on the *Plymouth Daily Mercury*, was partly offset by the commencement of the *Yorkshire Chronicle*. At Newcastle, the *Daily Chronicle* gave vent to the growing disaffection of its proprietor, Joseph Cowen, who withdrew from Parliament in 1886. The *Tyneside Echo*, a lesser Liberal property in the vicinity, fell victim to the Home Rule split. James Joicey, the wealthy member for Chester-le-Street, came to the rescue of Newcastle Gladstonianism by acquiring the *Northern Weekly Leader* (replete with the editorial services of James Annand), which he refurbished as a daily. At Liverpool, Sheffield, and Leeds, where Gladstonian journals flourished, Liberal Unionist competition was threatened, but failed to materialize. It was not until 1892 that the Unionist *Argus* rose to challenge the Gladstonian *Observer* at Bradford.

Less haphazard than it may appear at first glance, this paroxysm of journalistic activity conformed to certain basic rules, which approximated to those laid down in Salisbury's makeshift pact with Chamberlain and Hartington. Just as the Conservatives and the Liberal Unionists, while jealously maintaining their separateness, resolved to avoid mutual confrontation in the constituencies, they agreed to respect each other's claims in the press. Thus, in areas where Tory newspapers either predominated (as in greater London) or were at least competing effectively – and solvently – against Home Rule organs (as in Liverpool), any Liberal Unionist incursions were discouraged. In return, the Conservatives pledged not to intervene–or, at any rate, not to expand their holdings, in Liberal Unionist strongholds (such as Birmingham) or where the Liberal Unionists were pitted in direct combat with the Gladstonians (as in Newcastle). These arrangements did not always work smoothly, and incurred resentment on the part of the Conservative rank and file. Meeting at Bradford in October 1886, the National Union heard Sir Albert Rollit, a renegade Liberal with newspaper connections in the north-east, ascribe Tory reverses in the recent elections to 'the inadequate expression of Conservative views through the Press'.[1] But the Conservative leaders knew better than their restless followers the value of the newspaper dowry which the Liberal Unionists had brought to their marriage of convenience. They also appreciated the further services that the Liberal Unionists might perform.

Events in Manchester soon proved that Salisbury had not miscalculated, especially in his premiss that it was more advantageous to effect a take-over than to start an enterprise from scratch. As a full-blooded champion of Home Rule, the *Manchester Guardian* had forged far ahead of the *Manchester Examiner*, whose wavering had cost it readers and credibility. Symbolic of the *Examiner*'s 'laxity', as discerned by Hartley Aspden, was the inviolable practice of its editor, Dr Henry Dunckley, 'of catching his train home at eleven o'clock', when the latest stories were still breaking. J. E. Taylor, the *Guardian*'s proprietor, likewise considered the venerable Dunckley 'rather an indolent man'. Towards the close of 1888, a group of local Liberal Unionists, headed by Sir Joseph Lee, purchased the *Examiner*, along with its more robust stable-mate, the *Manchester Weekly Times*. Dunckley, relieved of his editorial duties, henceforth contributed his 'Letters of Verax' – the *Examiner*'s most popular feature – to the *Guardian*, and went home by a still earlier train.

Lee and his associates were said to have paid £18,000 for the property and a further £70,000 for its renovation. By May 1890, having exhausted their funds, they appealed to Lord Wolmer (later 2nd Earl of Selborne), the Liberal Unionist whip (and incidentally, Salisbury's son-in-law), 'to get Lord Derby or some other rich man to take up another £25,000 worth of shares, which would not necessarily be all called up'. Wolmer was sympathetic. 'A paper like the *Examiner* is bound to pay in the long run; . . . it takes a great expenditure of capital at first,' he reasoned to Hartington. 'I need not say that if the *Examiner* failed entirely it would be a great blow to us in the North. I think that *at all hazards* it must be kept going until after the next General Election.' Hartington, with typical Whig lethargy, neglected to approach Derby until Lee renewed his plea in the autumn. Then, enclosing 'a short statement as to the position of the paper' from Lee, he requested Derby's 'consideration'. As Hartington aptly put it, Derby responded 'very coldly': in Derby's own words, he could 'not be very sanguine of the success of a paper that needs to be held up by subsidies, especially when as in this case, it is not a new enterprise, but a journal of old standing in new hands'. Without committing himself, he promised to probe further. Sir John Ramsden, a former Liberal Unionist MP, 'unluckily' had 'no ready money whatever'. And the Duke of Westminster, having just given £3,000 towards 'buying up another inefficient Conservative paper which we are trying to convert into an efficient "Unionist" journal', offered only a pledge of '£1,000 next year if of any use'. (That, Hartington re-

[1] National Union minutes, 26 October 1886.

alized, 'won't help much'.) Not even W. H. Smith's expert opinion that the *Examiner* could be restored to commercial viability was able to attract investors. On 19 January 1891, informed by Lee that the moment of crisis had arrived, Hartington implored Derby to reconsider. With or without Derby's assistance, the Liberal Unionist Association assumed direct control at a cost of £8,900. Various expedients were tried to halt the downhill slide. The *Manchester Evening Times*, established to realize a profit (as the *Manchester Evening News* did for the *Guardian*), instead compounded the deficit and had to be abandoned after its forty-ninth issue. In mounting desperation, the new owners slashed the price of the *Examiner* to a halfpenny. Finally, on 14 November 1891, it was announced that the property had been sold to yet another syndicate in which the controlling interest was held by Colonel Thomas Sowler, the chief proprietor of the Tory *Manchester Courier*. More accurately, the property had been unloaded, for Wolmer confirmed that the 'net sum recovered' was a mere £390. The two companies were formally amalgamated on 15 March 1892, but Sowler – true to his promise to keep the Liberal Unionist flag flying in Manchester through the next elections – continued to publish the *Examiner* in reduced size from the *Courier* office until 10 March 1894, when it proclaimed as its epitaph 'that Liberal-Unionism has never been appreciated, never thoroughly understood'. In the span of three years, the paper had changed hands four times: the Gladstonians had lost one of their two morning journals in Manchester; the Liberal Unionists had squandered huge amounts of money; and the Conservatives had reaped the rewards. The formula could not have displeased Salisbury, who may even have regarded it as a portent.[1]

Compelled to fight on two fronts, the Gladstonians had to maintain their defences against the Conservatives and, at the same time, to compensate for Unionist usurpations. Much of their effort, particularly in Scotland, was retaliative. At Birmingham, they were without a voice until November 1891, when Gilzean Reid helped to start the evening *Argus*. More expeditiously, he joined with T. P. Ritzema to launch the *Northern Daily Telegraph*, 'the only Daily printed and published in Blackburn', with an influence that fanned out over the manufacturing districts of the North-West. To a greater extent than other Gladstonian ventures, including the *Lancashire Evening Post* which George Toulmin established at Preston in 1886 with 'the cordial support of the Liberal Party', the halfpenny *Telegraph* managed to rekindle the evangelical spark which had been flickering since Stead's departure from the *Northern Echo*. As

[1] Aspden, *Fifty Years a Journalist* (London, 1930), pp. 47–48; Ayerst, *Guardian*, pp. 231–32; Hartington to Wolmer, 11 and 23 October 1890, Selborne Papers; Wolmer to Hartington, 2 May 1890 and 5 September 1892, Westminster to Hartington, 21 October 1890, Derby to Hartington, 14 October 1890 and 18 January 1891, Ramsden to Hartington, 14 October 1890, Lee to Hartington, 16 November 1890, and Smith to Hartington, 29 October 1890, Devonshire Papers; Hartington to Derby, 13 October 1890 and 17 January 1891, Derby Papers; *Sells* (1892, 1893, 1895, and 1900).

stated without 'concealment or apology' in its inaugural issue (26 October 1886), the politics of the paper were to be 'distinctly and thoroughly Liberal'.[1] Making implicit reference to Lord Randolph Churchill's pronouncements on Tory democracy at Bradford, it gave assurances that these were not 'mere Randolphian promises'. Like the Gladstonian press as a whole, the *Northern Daily Telegraph* concentrated its fire on Tory spokesmen, and, for the time being, repressed its outrage against the Liberal Unionists, who might yet see the error of their ways.

In spite of a proliferation of new Liberal journals, the Unionist alliance was as invincible in the press as in Parliament. In Fleet Street, the lights of Liberalism were virtually extinguished. Gladstone, who had earlier declared a preference for provincial journalism, no longer had any choice. The minutes of the library committee of the Reform Club, a bastion of Gladstonianism, reflect his predicament. As late as 12 February 1884, the librarian was directed to inform a member, who had suggested that the *Western Daily Mail* might be a worthwhile acquisition, 'that . . . Country Papers are not subscribed for'. So little did the club esteem provincial press opinion that this respected penny daily, published in the Liberal interest at Plymouth since 1860, was unavailable until its proprietors presented a complimentary subscription. The Home Rule crisis forced the club to break with tradition. On 16 March 1886, the committee acceded to a request from Joseph Dodds, MP for Stockton, that the *Newcastle Daily Leader* and Gilzean Reid's *North Eastern Daily Gazette* should be ordered; the latter was also recommended by three other MPs, including Isaac Wilson, who sat for Middlesbrough, where it was published. On 15 June, a week after the Irish Bill was rejected, the committee unanimously approved arrangements for the delivery of provincial papers to the club, and the librarian reported that two additional stands had been placed in the morning room for their display. Thereafter, additions were regularly made to the list of provincial journals that the Reform took in. Yet, as ascertained by John Robinson on 3 December 1889, the club's 'supply' was 'actually less by 111 than that of the National Liberal Club'.

The decline in the circulation of the *Daily News* was accepted as fit retribution by Liberals, who denounced its pusillanimity. The *Echo*, being a lesser property, was a lesser disappointment: J. A. Spender, aged twenty-four, began his illustrious career as a leader-writer on its staff, but resigned to edit the *Eastern Morning News* at Hull after Edwards had 'definitely taken sides against Gladstone and Home Rule, and I was absolutely determined not to write to his order on that'. But the *Pall Mall Gazette* gave the greatest conster-

---

[1] By 17 December 1887, the *Northern Daily Telegraph* could boast that its sale was three times greater than that of the *Preston Evening Post* 'and at least six times that of the local Tory evening sheet'. Its main rivalry was with the Toulmin brothers, whose 'milk-and-water . . . Liberalism' had deprived Lancashire of a successful Radical organ, and whom the *Telegraph* left 'consumed with envy'. Endorsement of this view is to be found in the *Manchester Guardian Weekly*, 8 March 1946.

nation and provocation. Morley, who nursed tender feelings for Stead as a sort of protégé ('You sometimes make me blaspheme a little, but that does not go below the skin – and I hope that our friendship is stable'), tried to chasten him by recalling 'that Mr Gladstone declared that the *P. M. G.* was his opponent'. Stead was unmoved, especially when Morley added Gladstone's comment 'that the only man who knew how to support a Minister in the London press was Lawson of the *Daily Telegraph*'. As Stead wrote in his diary without too much exaggeration:

> Gladstone's admiration for the *Telegraph* dates from the time when Lawson used to begin & close every leading article by crying 'Hosanna to the People's William!' That kind of support Mr Gladstone always appreciates. When I did the same in the Bulgarian time, he thought there was no person like me, and said so. Contradiction is a thing which Mr Gladstone does not brook.

Undeniably, Gladstone found it easier to deal with the likes of Edward Russell, who humbly requested 'some statement of your ideas of the present phase of affairs' in order to ensure it due prominence in the *Liverpool Daily Post*. But Stead was not the friendly critic he made himself out to be. He lost no time in making contact with W. H. Smith, whom he addressed as 'the only member of the new Cabinet who has any clearly defined idea of what should be done in Ireland', and he trailed Balfour in the hope of picking up 'tips'.[1]

For better or worse, Stead's power at the *Pall Mall Gazette* was on the wane, and his editorship – never formally conferred – was not to survive the decade. Upon his release from gaol in 1886, he apologized to Yates Thompson for having jeopardized the paper's sale and advertising revenues, and promised that 'we are not going Maiden Tributing any more'. Instead he found other hobby-horses to ride. His frequent excursions abroad included a prolonged visit to Russia, where he dedicated himself to the pursuit of Anglo-Russian friendship. 'I am having a great time,' he wrote from St Petersburg to E. T. Cook, whom he had left in charge and whom he subsequently accused of publishing his 'Special Commissioner's Reports' in 'snippety instalments'. His glowing admiration for the Tsar contrasted with his sentiments on 22 June 1887, when the nation was celebrating Victoria's Jubilee: 'How much longer will it all last, we wonder? . . . As long as the Queen lasts, yes; but after the Queen? Who knows?' J. R. Bulwer, QC, a former Conservative MP, was so incensed by these 'anti-monarchial' views that he demanded that the United University Club should cancel all copies of the *Pall Mall Gazette*. Respectable opinion was further offended when Stead, taking up the cause of the con-

---

[1] Spender, *Life, Journalism and Politics* (London, 1927), I, 32–33; Morley to Stead, 24 December 1886, and Stead's diary, 28 July 1886, Stead Papers; Russell to Gladstone, 12 December 1886, Gladstone Papers, Add. MSS. 44,499, fol. 239; Stead to Smith, 26 July 1886, Hambleden Papers; Balfour to Stead, 24 December 1886 (letterbook copy), Balfour Papers.

demned Chicago anarchists, featured an interview with Eleanor Marx. 'The published version was all Stead and precious little of what I really said,' she complained. 'However, it is so important to get things into so immensely read a paper as the *Pall Mall* that one can't quarrel with its queer editor.'[1]

Milner was no longer on hand to exercise a stabilizing influence. A self-designated 'Radical' (though not of the 'narrow' type), he was the Liberal candidate at Harrow in 1885, but soon afterwards had 'no hesitation in saying that I am, for all practical purposes, a Tory'. For reasons of strategy, however, he saw 'the wisdom, nay the absolute necessity, of keeping up the Liberal Unionist party, for the time being at least, as a separate organisation'. With this motive, he wrote a series of thirteen leading articles for *The Times* during the summer of 1886. Wishing success to 'the Unionist Liberals . . . in their bold effort to reconvert the bulk of their party to its old principles' (6 August), he urged Conservative statesmen to undertake a programme, 'at once progressive and moderate', that 'would enable them to keep in touch with the main body of the Unionist Liberals' (14 August).[2]

The Times, determined to perpetuate both the Liberal rupture and the Unionist concordat, was the natural vehicle for Milner and, through him, for Goschen. During the 1886 campaign, and while Salisbury was constructing his administration, it publicized the activities of the Unionist Liberals (an intentional inversion) at the expense of the Home Rule Liberals and even the Conservatives. 'There has been no caprice & no hostility, but simply want of space,' Buckle explained to Churchill, whose platform appearances had got short shrift. 'I hope when you next speak there will not be half a dozen other prominent men on the stump the same night, & you will find *The Times* give you as much space as ever.' Meanwhile, he wished Churchill 'a thumping majority' at the polls.[3]

Churchill's return at Paddington came as no surprise. But his elevation to the Exchequer, coupled with the leadership of the House, astounded his friends and enemies alike. Buckle proffered congratulations. 'By the way,' he added, 'you might have dropped me a hint of your coming promotion' instead of allowing the first announcement to appear in 'the *Daily News* of all papers in the world'. Out of favour with *The Times*, which disapproved of the tactics he employed, Churchill saw no reason to accord it preferential treatment. The higher he rose, the more prickly he became. Previously, he had 'seemed to enjoy rather than resent . . . criticism', testified Lucy, who had written about him in *Punch*, the *Observer*, and other journals 'with freedom untrammelled by private relationship'. But, in 1886, Churchill was stung by a piece in the

[1] Stead to Yates Thompson, 13 January [1886], quoted in Robertson Scott, *Life and Death of a Newspaper*, pp. 143–45; Stead to Cook [1888], quoted in Mills, *Cook*, p. 100; general committee minutes, United University Club, 30 June and 7 July 1887; E. Marx to [?], 16 November 1887, quoted in Y. Kapp, *Eleanor Marx*, II (London, 1976), 218.

[2] Milner to Goschen, 17 October 1886, Milner Papers; index to leader-writers, *Times* Archives.

[3] Buckle to Churchill, 1 July 1886, Churchill Papers.

Daily News, which Lucy (who was not the author) 'chanced at the time' to be editing. He 'deliberately cut' Lucy, who painfully recalled that 'for four years we were strangers'. Escott, who contrived to keep on better terms, acknowledged his hero's increasingly thin skin:

> No politician of the century since the days of Mr Milner Gibson studied newspapers, whether published in London or the country, with the same catholicity and care as Churchill. Out of Fleet Street he seldom failed to receive usually justice, sometimes appreciation.

The London press, according to Escott, showed him 'coolness' at best.[1]

That was not absolutely true. Churchill's meddling in foreign affairs, while resented by Lord Iddesleigh (as Northcote had become) and other colleagues, won plaudits from the Russophobic *Morning Post*. 'However little reason I may have for feeling cordially towards Lord S[alisbury],' Borthwick told him, 'I may truthfully subscribe myself one of your earlier Friends and one of the firmest believers in your Future.' Borthwick's disaffection, more acute than his perception, was easily understood. Although 'deeply sensible of the services which in more than one capacity he has rendered to the Party', Salisbury had declined to recommend him for further honours in 1885. Prodded by his wife, whose snobbery exceeded his own, Borthwick now informed the dispensers of government patronage that there was 'a limit to what a man will stand and if I am treated with the same want of faith I think they will regret it'. In the Jubilee honours list, Salisbury gave him 'reason . . . for feeling cordially' by raising him from a knighthood to a baronetcy. Lady Borthwick probably set her sights on something higher, but Borthwick was, 'indeed, gratified at learning that the Queen has been pleased to confer a fresh distinction upon me'. Among his well-wishers was a voice from the distant past. 'As the Conductor, & Proprietor of the *Morning Post*, from 1831 to 1850, I feel *personally gratified*,' wrote C. Eastland Michele, who expressed gratitude to Borthwick 'for having so ably, & consistently, maintained the political principles it is my pride to have advocated during the period that journal was under my control'. With greater present-mindedness, the *Pall Mall Gazette* snorted that 'the omissions from this shabby list are even more striking than its contents. Where is the Jubilee baronetcy which was to have immortalised the proprietor and sealed the Unionism of the *Daily Telegraph*?' it asked impertinently. Like Borthwick, William Leng 'of that clever organ of Jingoism, the *Sheffield Daily Telegraph*', had been bedecked. 'But . . . where, oh where, is that Jubilee peerage which, in the patient person of Mr Walter, was to have shed the white halo of Royal favour over the blood-thumbed pages of "Parnellism and Crime"?' (22 June 1887).[2]

---

[1] Buckle to Churchill, 29 July 1886, Churchill Papers; Lucy, *Memories of Eight Parliaments*, pp. 270–71; Escott, *Randolph Spencer-Churchill* (London, 1895), pp. 293–94.
[2] Borthwick to Churchill, 24 September 1886, Churchill Papers; Salisbury to Iddesleigh, 23

The *Pall Mall* aimed its punches low, but not – as it proved – so low as *The Times*, whose proprietor it held up to derision. *The Times*'s sensational exposé of a link between 'Parnellism and Crime' was the climax, or possibly the dénouement, of a longer melodrama, and it must be seen in that context.

Settled in office, Salisbury earned and requited Buckle's respect. In November 1886, when Churchill divulged the news of Balfour's impending promotion to Cabinet rank, *The Times* complied with Salisbury's 'urgent request' to defer publication until royal approval had been secured. 'I think you ought to indemnify Buckle on some future occasion by giving him some good piece of exclusive information,' suggested Churchill, who had been cut down to size. Estranged from his colleagues, who rejected his budget proposals, he soon acted on his own advice. On the evening of 22 December, after attending a performance of *The School for Scandal*, he paid an unexpected call at Printing House Square. Exhibiting copies of his correspondence with the Prime Minister, he revealed – and authorized *The Times* to announce – his resignation from the Cabinet. His wife learned of his decision from *The Times* the next morning. 'Quite a surprise for you,' he greeted her at breakfast. Salisbury, however, had known what to expect. 'Send for *The Times*,' he told his wife when he awoke, after a good night's sleep, on the 23rd. 'Randolph resigned in the middle of the night and, if I know my man, it will be in *The Times* this morning.'[1]

Whether Churchill had solicited Buckle's editorial support, as was widely assumed, none was forthcoming. The crisis which he had hoped to precipitate was skilfully averted. Resisting external pressure for a broad-based Unionist ministry, Salisbury went no further in that direction than to replace Churchill with Goschen. The Hartingtonians were disappointed, and the Chamberlain-ites began to explore the possibility of Liberal reunification. That the *St James's Gazette* should have dismissed the idea of coalition as 'undesirable & unnecessary' was annoying to Goschen, yet entirely predictable. 'Nobody seems to befriend Churchill,' James Stuart, the Gladstonian MP for the Hoxton division of Shoreditch, observed to Herbert Gladstone. '*The Times* is wroth with him, and the *Standard* is wild at the possible Gladstone Chamberlain rapprochement.' (In fact, the *Standard* was more sceptical than 'wild' at the thought that Gladstone might 'overcome Mr Chamberlain's obstinacy', as it put it on 5 January.) Most infuriating to the Liberal Unionists was *The Times*'s insistence that day that Salisbury was 'the only possible Prime Minister'. Brett, who shuttled between the various leaders, complained to Chamberlain that 'Buckle is very obstinate, and not so discriminating as he should

---

December 1885 (copy?), Bathurst Papers; Borthwick to Andrew Montagu, 11 June 1887, and Borthwick to Salisbury, 21 June 1887, Salisbury Papers; Michele to Borthwick, 23 June 1887, Bathurst Papers.

[1] Buckle to Churchill, 28 November 1886, and Churchill to Salisbury [n.d.], quoted in James, *Churchill*, p. 278; *ibid.*, p. 298; Cecil, *Salisbury*, III, 334.

be'. In the belief that the antagonism of Chamberlain was too high a price to pay for the ostracism of Churchill, Brett tried to convince Buckle of the advantages to be obtained from 'detaching as many liberals as possible from the extreme party'. While Buckle was personally sympathetic, Brett was not optimistic:

> Heaven knows whether this lecture will have any effect. I think he is in the hands of his leader writers. And they are men very ignorant of all the essentials for firing accurate political judgments.

No sooner had *The Times* achieved its immediate purpose, which Brett perhaps mistook, than it thoroughly justified his doubts as to its ability to sight political targets.[1]

Beginning on 7 March, when Balfour's Irish Crimes Bill was before Parliament, *The Times* flaunted its ministerial colours by running the first in a series of articles on 'Parnellism and Crime'. The evidence on which the paper based these reports consisted of ten letters, five of them ostensibly bearing the signature of Parnell, which were purchased for the sum of £1,780. Here, or so it seemed, was conclusive proof that the Irish nationalist leader, now Gladstone's partner, had not only condoned, but also had actually helped to plot, the Phoenix Park murders in 1882. On the morning of 18 April, when the stringent measure was awaiting a second reading, one of the Parnell letters was published in facsimile. The putative author, who did 'not take in or even read *The Times* usually', appeared at first to be 'perfectly unconcerned'. That evening, however, he rose in the Commons to disclaim the document as 'a villainous and barefaced forgery'. *The Times* dared him to seek vindication in a court of law (20 April); but Parnell, knowing that English opinion was dead set against him, was reluctant to take proceedings. Instead F. H. O'Donnell, a former parliamentary follower, took up the legal challenge. He lost his case, but obliged *The Times* to release other incriminating materials.

Parnell, as well as taking a libel action in a Scottish court, then appealed to the House of Commons for a select committee to ascertain the authenticity of the evidence against him. The government refused, and instead set up a judicial commission to 'inquire into the charges and allegations'. With Churchill chiming in, Gladstonian and Irish members protested against this unusual procedure and, still more, against the appointment of three confirmed Unionists as commissioners. The appearance of Sir Richard Webster (later Lord Alverstone), the Attorney-General, as counsel for *The Times*, smacked all the more of collusion. Parnell was represented by Sir Charles Russell (later Lord Russell of Killowen), who had served as Attorney-General under Gladstone, with assistance from H. H. Asquith, the newly elected member for East Fife.

---

[1] Goschen to Milner, 29 December [1886], Milner Papers; Stuart to H. Gladstone, 6 January 1887, Viscount Gladstone Papers, Add. MSS. 46,052, fol. 215; Brett to Chamberlain, 6 January 1887 (copy), Esher Papers.

The proceedings dragged on for six months before Richard Pigott, the purvey-or of the spurious letters, was called to the witness-box. After two days of remorseless cross-examination, he fled to the Continent, where he avoided arrest by committing suicide. He left behind a confession that confirmed Parnell's innocence and his own guilt.

'In the immediate political excitements of Pigottism', as E. T. Cook discerned, 'a great blow' was struck 'to journalistic credit' in general and 'to anonymous journalism' in particular. Where did co-operation leave off and conspiracy begin? That was precisely the question posed by Sir William Har-court, a former employee at Printing House Square, who castigated the government for having set up the Parnell Commission in league with *The Times*. Challenged by Harcourt, Smith acknowledged that he had had 'com-munication' with Walter, who had 'called upon me, as it has been his practice to do, as an old friend, but we have made no arrangement whatever of any kind'. Such assurances failed to satisfy Harcourt, who took to public platforms to denounce the anti-Irish bias and partisan contrivances of *The Times*. His temper flared when Buckle refused to publish his letter refuting insinuations that Gladstone had intrigued against Forster in 1882. 'If you take the most rabid Nationalist paper, whether in Ireland or America, you will find nothing in it so disgraceful as the conduct of *The Times* newspaper,' Harcourt insisted. Chamberlain, estranged from him politically, but still a personal friend, was deeply vexed. 'People in England are greatly interested in *The Times* against Parnell & Co.,' he wrote to his American fiancée. 'Such a journal as *The Times* has a great reputation to keep up and would never bring accusations lightly.' To Hartington, nearer at hand, Chamberlain confessed his irritation with the Harcourtian allegations of the *Daily News* and the fact that he was 'very anxious to turn the flanks of the Opposition & to enlist public opinion definitely in favour of the proposed Commission'. His vexation was all the greater when the Commission ultimately vindicated Parnell and showed *The Times* to have been duped.[1]

It was not only 'the Pigott *débâcle*', as the official historians of *The Times* have called it; it was *The Times*'s, too. The forgery exposed, there remained the awkward question of how a newspaper of such repute could have been hoodwinked by so loathsome a creature: 'A ghastly, bloody, rotten, foetus,' as Churchill spat out, 'Pigott! Pigott!! Pigott!!!' Stead had been offered the letters for the *Pall Mall Gazette* and, to his credit, had refused to touch them. Walter and his general manager, J. C. MacDonald, had shown less probity. MacDonald, who bore the brunt in court, recounted the details of the transaction. His testimony, Asquith later recalled, was an 'amazing tale . . .

---

[1] Cook's diary, 4 March 1889, Cook Papers; *Parliamentary Debates*, 3rd ser., cccxxix, cols. 1012–15 (31 July 1888); Gardiner, *Harcourt*, II, 70–71; Chamberlain to Miss Endicott, 7 July 1888, quoted in Garvin, *Chamberlain*, II, 386; Chamberlain to Hartington, 23 July 1888, Devonshire Papers.

which remains almost unique in the annals of infantine simplicity and malevolent credulity'. Both MacDonald and Buckle offered their resignations; but Walter, who was as much to blame as anyone, did not accept them. *The Times* was discredited: 'Something of the awe of holy writ, which from the days of Barnes had clung about its columns, now faded away.' Gladstone wondered whether it 'would ever recover its former hold'. Including a payment of £5,000 to Parnell for libel damages, the total costs to the paper exceeded £200,000. Under these circumstances, for Salisbury to confer a peerage on Walter was unthinkable.[1]

Last, but not least, it was also the government's *débâcle*. 'I hear you are to be in Town this afternoon, & I shd. much like to have a talk with you in reference to this horrid scandal,' Buckle wrote to W. H. Smith on 10 December 1889. 'I saw Lord Salisbury yesterday, & at the close of our conversation he suggested that I shd. see you.' Although the verdict was anticipated, *The Times* that day persisted in saying that the Gladstonians would excuse 'any villainy perpetrated in the sacred cause of Parnellism'. Walter was adamant that he alone should bear the financial burden of the trial, but the paper would have been grateful for some gesture of moral support. Instead, on 11 February 1890, when Gladstone rejected *The Times*'s apology to Parnell as inadequate, Smith underscored 'our detestation of the act which has been committed and our measure of satisfaction that the hon. gentleman has been relieved absolutely and completely from the imputation under which for a time he laboured'. That was too much for Buckle, who invited Smith to lunch at the Athenaeum (where they might 'avoid the notice of the Parnellite paragraphist' who patrolled the Reform, where Buckle also belonged) on Valentine's Day. Before they met, Buckle thought it

> only honest to tell you that in this office we feel very sore about the language used by the Leader of the House on Tuesday night in answer to Mr Parnell. It was neither fair nor just to speak with equal 'detestation' of the act of Pigott & the act of *The Times*.

Over lunch, Smith was persuaded to offer an apology to Walter: 'I am told that some observations which fell from me on Tuesday evening *as they are reported* have given you pain.' Walter, far from mollified, preferred 'to reserve my opinion on the subject'. It was, therefore, hardly surprising that *The Times* soon began to criticize fundamental aspects of the government's Irish policy. Smith had his turn to protest when *The Times* misquoted him on 5 July. 'I fear we have done you – most unwittingly – an injustice in the leader of Saturday,' Buckle replied two days later. 'Much assertion on the part of the enemy had

[1] *History of The Times*, III, ch. 3; S. Koss, *Asquith* (London, 1976), pp. 27–28; James, *Churchill*, p. 345; Robinson's diary, 15 July 1890, quoted in Robinson, *Fifty Years*, pp. 110–11. Curiously, Austin asked in 1888 whether, 'in the event of your deciding to recommend the elevation of Mr Walter to the peerage', the *Standard* might have prior notification. Austin to Salisbury, 2 [February?] 1888, Salisbury Papers.

led us to believe that you *did* say what, now that you challenge it, I confess I cannot find anywhere reported.' Two could play the game.[1]

Fortunately for his own sake, Salisbury did not rely exclusively on *The Times* for support in the metropolitan press. The Countess of Limerick correctly surmised that Akers-Douglas, Salisbury's loyal lieutenant, had 'influence with the *Daily Telegraph*', where she hoped 'to get a paragraph inserted' extolling her husband's administrative talents. Spender, 'an impassioned Home Ruler', knew that his chances for a job on the *Telegraph* were slim, his letter of introduction to LeSage notwithstanding. Akers-Douglas, as MP for the St Augustine division of Kent and one of the 'Kentish gang', consulted on constituency affairs with Frederic Mudford, who edited the *Kentish Observer* and whose brother William (W. H.) edited the *Standard*. But Salisbury had other, less circuitous routes to the *Standard*. Its political leader-writer was Alfred Austin, a devoted admirer. Frequently, Austin submitted his copy for Salisbury's vetting, and incorporated changes that Salisbury jotted in the margins; frequently, too, these changes got struck out by the editor. The arrangement exactly suited Salisbury's requirements, despite – even, paradoxically, because of – these complications. Austin's special relationship allowed him to advance ministerial policy, as Salisbury's daughter had delicately phrased it, 'by calling attention to aspects of it upon which Lord Salisbury could not himself dwell publicly'. Yet, when the need arose, Salisbury could disclaim responsibility in good conscience. Expressing regret 'that the Sultan takes his views of English policy from the columns of the *Standard*', he informed the Queen:

> We have no influence with the paper by which we could keep it from any line of writing or tone of policy that we disapproved. Occasionally it will put in what it is asked to put in: but that is very rare. The paper is quite independent: but we have to bear the blame of its proceedings.

That Austin's 'assistance was certainly welcomed' goes without saying. That it was not 'directly invited' is open to question. Like her father, Lady Gwendolen Cecil knew the value of studied ambiguity.[2]

Austin, the servant of two masters, often found himself in an uncomfortable position. On the afternoon of 14 July 1886, he received a telegram from Mudford, who enjoined him to write a leader 'strong' against the notion of a

---

[1] Buckle to Smith, 10 December 1889, 14 February and 7 July 1890, and Smith to Walter, 17 February 1890 (copy), Hambleden Papers; *also see* Chilston, *W. H. Smith* (London, 1965), pp. 317–18.

[2] Lady Limerick to Akers-Douglas, 5 May 1886, quoted in Chilston, *Chief Whip*, p. 76; Spender, *Life, Journalism and Politics*, I, 30; F. Mudford to Akers-Douglas [1887], Chilston Papers; Salisbury to the Queen, 23 March 1887, Royal Archives A65/61. For the close relationship between the Mudford brothers, see F. Mudford to *Blackwood's Magazine* ('Gentlemen'), 18 June 1868, Blackwood Papers. For the Salisbury-Austin-Mudford relationship, see Cecil, *Salisbury*, IV (London, 1932), pp. 55 ff., and the more sophisticated analysis in Peter Marsh, *Discipline of Popular Government* (Hassocks, Sussex, 1978), p. 202.

Hartington premiership and scornful of Liberal Unionist claims for preferment. 'I fancy Mudford's wish ... arose simply from the fact that *The Times*
has been indicating Hartington as the Prime Minister,' Austin wrote to Salisbury. As fervently as he himself wished for Salisbury's restoration, Austin
sensed the danger of pushing the dissident Liberals into the open arms of the
Gladstonians, and he therefore stiffly protested to Mudford 'how mischievous
a dogmatic leader such as he asked for wd. be', especially in a paper that Salisbury was presumed to influence. Nevertheless, Mudford prevailed, and
Austin wrote as directed. The next day's *Standard* professed certainty that
'Her Majesty will naturally send for Lord Salisbury', and that the Liberal
Unionists would accept that their modest electoral gains had been made poss-
ible by Tory 'self-abnegation'. To soften the blow, Austin also wrote a letter,
signed 'A', at the foot of the leader page: 'It is to Lord Hartington, ... and
Lord Hartington only, not to Lord Salisbury or the Conservatives, that the
exhortation to form a National Party should be addressed.' The ordinary
reader might have taken this letter to imply disloyalty to Salisbury. But
Austin, like Salisbury, knew that more could be accomplished by conciliating
Hartington than by humiliating him.[1]

Mudford sought to exploit Austin's connection without compromising
himself in the process. When *The Times* announced the date that Parliament
was to convene before the information had reached the *Standard*, he took
Austin to task. 'You see how touchy he is; and I am anxious only to keep him
straight,' Austin told Salisbury; 'he not unnaturally thinks the fact could have
been notified to him with so much ease through me, as I happened to be at
your side at the time.' The Prime Minister took the view that *The Times*'s
advantage was 'purely accidental': 'I am considerably surprised at the
importance which seems to be attached to these very petty pieces of
information.' But Austin shared his editor's suspicions that 'Randolph
Churchill ... deliberately & systematically communicates important matters
to *The Times*, in the expectation of receiving an equivalent'. Seething with
distrust of Churchill, Austin did not 'conceal' from Salisbury

> that I am constantly beset by the fear that, in due course, he should, by a
> bold management of popular sentiment & a judicious manipulation of the
> more powerful organs of public opinion, dislodge you from that position of
> authority which is the country's only safeguard against evils as menacing as
> those from which Gladstone's impetuosity has saved us.

Churchill's resignation had come as a deliverance. Austin 'was glad to be
asked, when I got down to the *Standard*' on 28 January 1887 to deal with the
subject of Churchill's 'lame and inconclusive ... defence' to the Commons
the previous afternoon. 'I strove to write with measure,' he assured Salisbury.

---

[1] Austin to Salisbury, 15 July 1886, Salisbury Papers.

But I feel convinced that though his late colleagues may be bound to speak of him with reserve, it is necessary to convey to the public that, whatever his merits or demerits, a Conservative he is not.

Like Mudford, Salisbury was happy to give him *carte blanche*.[1]

That was not always the case. As the result of Churchill's departure, Salisbury had been forced to reshuffle his Cabinet. Among other changes, W. H. Smith was made First Lord of the Treasury and leader of the House, and, to propitiate Goschen, the aged Iddesleigh was removed from the Foreign Office, which became an annexe of Downing Street. Salisbury spoke to Austin 'in preparatory confidence' of his intentions, giving permission to alert Mudford, but forbidding any disclosure. When word seeped out through the Press Association, Mudford no longer felt bound by his oath of secrecy. Thus, on 4 January 1887, Iddesleigh learned of his fate from the *Standard*. Austin was no less aghast than his mentor. 'Really, Mudford is impossible,' he wrote in self-exculpation upon receipt of a rebuke that he had 'fully expected'. As instructed, he had prohibited Mudford 'in the most absolute manner to do what he has done'. Moreover, Austin had explicitly warned that

if you state that Smith is to be First Lord of the Treasury or that Lord Salisbury is to return to the Foreign Office, you will cause me to forfeit the confidence of those who at present extend it to me.

Under the circumstances, Austin was tempted to inform Mudford that 'I can trust him no more, & cannot again be the medium of communication between the Government & the paper'. But Salisbury apparently saw no point in that.[2]

The complexities of this triangular relationship were further elucidated when Mudford wrote Austin 'another letter, enclosing a cheque for £52.10 which he begged me to accept'. Apart from his disinclination to profit from Salisbury's embarrassment, Austin was upset to discover that Mudford 'misses the point – viz that I am not in the service of the State, & that I cannot . . . dissever my aid to it – such as it is – from my assistance to the paper'. The point had also eluded Salisbury, who 'rather surprised' Austin by his inability to 'see why I would not accept any material remuneration from the *Standard*'. On the grounds that 'I was using the paper (properly using it, I trust) not the paper me', Austin made it known that he had never accepted payment from Mudford 'for any information he has received in consequence of the confidence you repose in me; & I never shall'. Nevertheless, being 'perfectly businesslike', he always 'charged the paper £4.4 (four guineas) for work that I considered equivalent to writing a leader, & two guineas for expenses

[1] Austin to Salisbury, 28 and 29 November 1886, and 28 January 1887, Salisbury Papers; Salisbury to Austin, 29 November 1886, Austin Papers.
[2] Austin to Salisbury, 4 January 1887, Salisbury Papers; Cecil, *Salisbury*, III, 342.

incidental to it'. The price of a journalist's self-respect was never easy to reckon.[1]

Mudford was getting a bargain. But, then, so was Salisbury. 'I hope the leader in the *Standard* this morning is what you wanted,' Austin wrote to him on 8 March. 'I could not get it inserted earlier, & a little tact was necessary.' It would be useful, he pointed out, if Salisbury could see his way to 'send me a line, . . . saying you had read the article with pleasure (supposing this is so) & recognizing the assistance the *Standard* can be in influencing foreign opinion – or something of that kind'. The Prime Minister complied. 'I have read the article in the *Standard* this morning, on the condition of Europe, with great satisfaction,' he told Austin, who was sure to pass along the message to Mudford. 'It is a very good article and will do a great deal of good. It expresses the facts exactly as I believe they are'. Such exchanges were frequent. Salisbury was an old hand at the game of writing to editorial specifications.[2]

At the same time, he did not ignore other journals. Discreetly, he provided Cook of the *Pall Mall Gazette* with an official account of Churchill's resignation: 'Nothing that I have said here is confidential, but do not say or let it be seen that I have been in communication with you.' Churchill, again out-manoeuvred, was appalled to hear that the *Pall Mall* was 'in possession of Lord Salisbury's version' of the incident. 'Lord Salisbury has rigorously prohibited me from giving any explanation to the public, stipulating that any such explanations must be reserved for Parliament when it meets,' he told Cook. 'That being so, I feel sure that he would not violate for his own advantage a rule he has imposed on a former colleague.' Churchill was now as completely quarantined in the press as in Parliament. On 3 June 1887, he 'spoke at Wolverhampton at very great length, dealing chiefly with the question of economy' which had forced his resignation. 'On some points,' *The Times* editorialized the next day, 'his statements are little better than a travesty of the facts.' L. J. Jennings, one of his few remaining allies in the Commons, agreed that '*The Times* behaves as meanly as it can towards you', and urged him to publish past correspondence over naval estimates. 'The London papers will not admit that they were wrong in their assaults upon you until pressure from outside compels them,' reasoned Jennings, who had already 'primed the *Yorkshire Post* with some facts' and promised to 'write an article myself for the *Manchester Courier*, which now is once more amenable to reason'. On Jennings's advice, Churchill sent *The Times* a detailed letter on the 'miraculous inefficiency' of naval administration. 'The Editor has omitted and declines to publish one passage, which is in the nature of a personal attack, & has nothing to do with the argument,' Buckle curtly replied. 'The Editor would also suggest whether Lord Randolph Churchill will not, on reflection, modify some

[1] Austin to Salisbury, 4, 5 and 6 January 1887, Salisbury Papers.

[2] Austin to Salisbury, 8 March 1887, Salisbury Papers; Salisbury to Austin, 8 March 1887, quoted in Cecil, *Salisbury*, IV, 24.

of the injurious expressions he uses towards the journal whose space he desires to occupy.' Churchill's letter appeared on 18 June, along with a condemnation of its 'violent and injurious imputations'.[1]

By his 'Pigott' outburst, Churchill was to repay *The Times* in kind. To Balfour, whose Crimes Act failed to clamp the lid on Irish disorders, Buckle wrote consolingly from Printing House Square: 'You know that you have the warmest sympathy & support of many, I would fain to think, *most* of us here.' That was hardly enough, but it would have to do. Captain Middleton advised Lord Dartmouth, who wanted to expand Tory newspaper operations in the Midlands, that the Conservative Central Office had 'no fund from which I could obtain a loan or a gift'. If, however, Dartmouth compiled a list of potential investors, Middleton would 'be only too happy to do anything in my power' to induce them to subscribe. In this instance, perhaps Middleton and his chief were eager to avoid any semblance of a challenge to Chamberlain in his own territory. Yet in the Radcliffe-cum-Farnworth division of Lancashire, where the Gladstonians held sway, there was 'no Conservative Press'. A delegate to the National Union conference, meeting at Oxford in November 1887, asked plaintively: 'Can we get any assistance from anybody? I have appealed to London and I am told that they cannot help us in any way.'[2]

The unavoidable fact, which St Loe Strachey saw clearly in retrospect, was that the public was growing 'suspicious of papers started or bought for the purpose of backing up particular views', and preferred 'a newspaper to be a newspaper and not a daily political tract, designed to do them good'. Strachey had learned the lesson the hard way. On 30 March 1887, the first number of the monthly *Liberal Unionist* appeared under his editorship. It carried signed contributions from Chamberlain and Hartington, who redundantly welcomed this 'special organ of the Liberal Unionist party'. Implying 'no want of recognition of the services which have been rendered to our cause by the powerful and able journals of the Metropolis and the Provinces', Hartington went on to say that

> experience has shown how necessary it is to the success of a political cause that assistance should be rendered to it by an organ in the Press directed exclusively to collecting information and expressing views favourable to the cause it is sought to support or defend.

The *Liberal Unionist* had a respectable circulation, yet it could 'literally get no advertisements at all, not even £10 worth a month', and folded five years later. The printers explained to Strachey 'that the name and the fact that it was the organ of the Liberal Unionist Party was absolutely fatal to it with advertisers',

---

[1] Salisbury to Cook, 24 December 1886, and Churchill to Cook, 27 December 1886, quoted in Mills, *Cook*, pp. 97–98; Jennings to Churchill, 18 June 1887, and Buckle to Churchill, 19 June 1887 [presumably misdated], Churchill Papers.

[2] Buckle to Balfour, 18 October 1887, Balfour Papers; Middleton to Dartmouth, 16 February 1887, Chilston Papers; National Union minutes, 23 November 1887.

some of whom may well have belonged to the same political persuasion. As a rule, journalists were slower than printers to grasp this essential point. And politicians, guided by 'experience' like Hartington, were slowest of all.[1]

Prudence, no less than economy, therefore demanded that the political press should wear its party labels more discreetly. That, of course, did not mean that newspapers repudiated their partisan allegiances or that political leaders and their agents ceased to involve themselves in the workings of the press. Collaboration continued, but it gradually came to follow new lines and to take new forms. Even where traditional loyalties persisted, they neither inspired nor inhibited to the same extent. Ahead of its time, the *Economist* acknowledged on 11 January 1879 that it lately had been its 'misfortune to take a different view of the duty of the English Government . . . from that taken by the Liberal party as expounded by its Parliamentary leaders'. That had been a 'misfortune', the journal explained, because 'some deference to party combinations is indispensable', and divergences 'ought neither to be sought for, nor to be lightly taken hold of'. This interpretation continued to hold, but less rigidly. In 1887, Alice Cornwall (the legendary 'Princess Midas') purchased the *Sunday Times* as a gift for her fiancé, Phil Robinson, the war correspondent. Interviewed in Victoria, Australia, Miss Cornwall confirmed that she had become a London newspaper controller. 'Yes,' she said, 'I bought out the *Sunday Times*, a Conservative paper. It would be called Liberal out here, for mostly what is called Conservative at home is Liberal in Victoria, and so vice versa.'[2] All things considered, her criterion was as valid as any, and more than most.

[1] Strachey to Chamberlain, 20 March 1887, Chamberlain Papers; Hartington to Strachey, 28 March 1887 ('for publication'), and Strachey to Huth Jackson, 1 March 1909, Strachey Papers.
[2] Quoted in H. Hobson *et al.*, *The Pearl of Days* (London, 1972), p. 50.

Eight

NEW WINE IN OLD BOTTLES

Although no one could have predicted it at the time, Lord Salisbury's return to office in the summer of 1886 marked the beginning of twenty years of Unionist dominance, interrupted – but not seriously disturbed – by the lack-lustre Liberal governments of 1892–95. By 1888, the failure of the Round Table negotiations with Chamberlain had set the seal of permanence on the Unionist alliance. Not even a string of by-election victories could lift the Gladstonians from their gloom.

Their vulnerability was felt most acutely in the area of the press. Whether the diminution of journalistic support was the cause or effect of their predicament, it deeply rankled. Liberal newspapers were not only conspicuously fewer, but less politically reliable. 'The question of the press is one of the serious questions ahead for the Liberal party,' Sir Edward Hamilton wrote in his diary on 18 January 1888. 'London is without a single good newspaper; the *Daily News* is not what it ought to be, and the patronage of the *Pall Mall Gazette* is calculated to do more harm than good to any party.' Elsewhere, the prospects were no better. 'Several of the best Provincial papers have gone over wholly or in part; and others are at their wits' ends for want of funds.' All too easily, Hamilton ascribed the difficulty to 'the desertion of the bulk of the wealthy classes from the advanced Liberal camp'.[1]

Leaving aside the question of which brand of Liberalism was the more 'advanced', a distinction hotly disputed, there was a degree of validity to Hamilton's claim that such Whig grandees as Hartington and the Duke of Westminster, along with wealthy manufacturers like Chamberlain, now subsidized Unionist rather than Liberal newspaper enterprises. Nevertheless, there remained a sufficient number of rich Liberal loyalists on whose beneficence the party could draw. Captains of commerce and industry, they were usually Nonconformists who assumed proprietorial responsibilites as a concomitant of their philanthropic pursuits. Being men of business, they were accustomed to spending money, but not to burning it. They naturally hoped to hold their losses to a minimum, partly because wastefulness was an affront to

[1] Sir Edward Hamilton's diary, 18 January 1888.

their ethic of self-reliance, and partly because they craved some token reassurance that their cause was gaining ground. But few of them entertained any expectation of material profit, which they derived from other sources; and fewer still were pleasantly surprised to the contrary. Samuel Morley, typical of those who shared his social background and religious values, was 'almost disappointed' when his newspaper investment yielded a healthy dividend: 'I went into the *Daily News* not to make money, but to advocate principles.' George Cadbury summed up their credo by expressing his own

> profound conviction that money spent on charities was of infinitely less value than money spent in trying to arouse my fellow countrymen to the necessity of measures to ameliorate the condition of the poor, forsaken and downtrodden masses which can be done most effectively by a newspaper.

Accordingly, many of the journals which these men helped to found and to sustain conceived of Liberalism primarily as a moral dynamic to which they were prepared to subordinate, if necessary, electoral exigencies.[1]

While Hamilton was recording his melancholy thoughts, important changes were already taking place. The previous day, the first issue of the *Star* appeared, and sold 142,600 copies. Within two years, its circulation had almost doubled. A halfpenny evening paper, it was zestfully edited by T. P. O'Connor, who held his seat in the Commons far longer than his editorial chair. His staff included Massingham as assistant editor, George Bernard Shaw as assistant leader-writer, 'Captain Coe' as the sporting tipster, and such future Fleet Street luminaries as Robert Donald, Ernest Parke, Thomas Marlowe, James Douglas, and R. A. Bennett. Bold in its design, and sprightly in its contents, the *Star* limited its articles to the length of half a column. Its politics were pugnaciously Radical. Declaring 'war on all privilege', it stated at the outset its intention to evaluate any proposal, even an avowedly 'socialistic' one, by the extent to which 'it influences for good or evil the lot of the masses of the people'. Fortuitously, the *Star* arrived in time to report – and deplore – the imprisonment of John Burns and R. B. Cunninghame Graham, the quixotic MP for North-West Lanarkshire, for their participation in the Trafalgar Square riots on 'Bloody Sunday', the previous November.

Promulgating demands for housing reform, land redistribution, progressive taxation, free educational and library facilities, an overhaul of the poor law system, and 'work for the workers' (22 March 1889), the *Star* attempted to unite the divergent strands of late-Victorian progressivism. It provided a forum for Fabians, Marxists (Friedrich Engels availed himself of its correspondence columns for his epistolary 'bombardments'), and labour agitators, including Burns and H. H. Champion. Shaw's heady claim that the Fabians had 'collared the *Star* by a stage-army strategem' was wide of the mark. In fact,

[1] Hodder, *Samuel Morley*, p. 247; A. G. Gardiner, *Life of George Cadbury* (London, 1923), p. 236.

the paper required no collaring, and went out of its way to accommodate socialist ideas in order to stress their underlying affinity with the doctrines of advanced Liberalism. Its object, especially evident during the elections for the first London County Council, was that of assimilation.[1] 'Thanks to our efforts,' the *Star* boasted on the occasion of its first anniversary, 'the stupid ostracism of socialists has come to an end', with the result that 'Socialist organisations have abandoned much of the wild talk, the "viewy" aims, the impracticable methods which they had inherited from German sources'.

The groundwork for the *Star* was laid in the summer of 1887, when Labouchere, careful to avoid further competition for the *Daily News*, took it upon himself to persuade some wealthy Liberals that it was imperative to remedy their party's deficiency in the metropolitan evening press. That need would not have arisen if the *Echo* had not defected to the Unionists. Among the plutocrats whom Labouchere approached was John T. Brunner, MP for Northwich, who had accompanied him to Mitchelstown in County Cork, where their public meeting, stormed by the Irish constabulary, ended in bloodshed. ('Remember Mitchelstown!' Gladstone told the National Liberal Federation, no longer Chamberlain's 'caucus', in 1887.) The co-founder of Brunner Mond and Company, a parent firm of Imperial Chemical Industries, Brunner was dubbed the 'chemical Croesus' by *The Times*. He was an enlightened employer, who saw 'a strong case . . . for legislative control' over working conditions, which he anticipated by his own experiments with pension schemes, paid holidays, sick benefits, and the eight-hour day.

Labouchere put O'Connor in touch with Brunner and with another 'of the richest members of the Liberal Party', James Williamson (then MP for Lancaster and later Lord Ashton). To O'Connor, who brought them together,

> they seemed . . . to look at each other like two goats preparing for a fight, when one expressed his readiness to subscribe £10,000, the other answered immediately that he would contribute the same. . . . One of them entirely changed his mind and never subscribed a penny; the other, after long negotiation, agreed to subscribe £5,000 – half the amount he had originally promised.

This account, written long after O'Connor was worn out by having 'to watch over the indiscretions of Mr Massingham and Mr Shaw' and then summarily displaced, was not wholly accurate. Tim Healy heard from John Barry, another Irish MP, that Williamson had been willing 'to give £10,000', but only 'on condition that the directors had full power of dismissal, and that T. P.'s salary should be £800 a year, and that he should surrender all other work'. It was estimated that £100,000 was necessary to launch a new property, and the *Echo* might have been bought from Edwards for that amount. In the event,

[1] Paul Thompson, *Socialists, Liberals and Labour: The Struggle for London, 1885–1914* (London, 1967), pp. 97–100.

although they registered the company with nominal capital of £100,000, the proprietors of the *Star* proceeded with pledges of £40,000, a mere £6,000 of it in hand. Wilfrid Scawen Blunt, O'Connor's literary friend, was reportedly among the backers. More important, however, were Isaac Holden, a Bradford woollens manufacturer who sat for the Keighley division of Yorkshire, and J. J. Colman, the mustard manufacturer who sat for Norwich and had substantial newspaper holdings in East Anglia. The bulk of the investment came from Brunner, whose bearded countenance identified him as the second of O'Connor's 'two goats'. It was he who, on behalf of the directorate, conveyed the terms of O'Connor's appointment: £1,200 a year with a quarter of the profits after a five per cent dividend was distributed among the preference shareholders. And Brunner's private papers leave no doubt that he gave generously to the *Star* and, on numerous occasions, privately to its editor.[1]

That Hamilton should have failed to note the rising of the *Star* was itself a portent of its failure to satisfy the traditional criteria of political journalism. Devoted to Gladstone and his Home Rule policy, the paper was conducted with a mind to lead official Liberal opinion, not to follow it. This ambition led to conflict within the staff, within the proprietorship, and between the two. The problem was not, as Francis Williams has deduced, that the 'backers were politicians, not business men',[2] but rather that they were business men-politicians with different susceptibilities. Some responded more enthusiastically than others to O'Connor's campaigns for social reform and to his vision of a Lib-Lab alliance. The *Star*'s daily support for the 1889 dockers' strike, like its endorsement of Labour candidates for the London County Council, gave disquiet in some quarters. The writing was on the wall when it was decided that the editor could be removed by a vote of two-thirds of the shareholders, instead of a three-fourths majority as originally stipulated.

Although Brunner once replied brusquely to O'Connor that he 'had not time or energy to spare for all this worry', O'Connor's biographer was wrong to infer that Brunner 'gave him no help' in the struggle. With periodic advances of £500, O'Connor was able to increase his shares and thereby to strengthen his position. Yet he fell in the summer of 1890, when he was induced to sell his interest for £15,000: 'a tempting sum', he recalled, 'to a man who had not a penny when he started the paper'. Massingham stepped into the breach until December when, finding himself 'in the grips of Whig wirepulling', he resolved to 'assert my independence'. For Cook's 'private ear', he disclosed that 'the question at issue is one of policy, involving, in my opinion, the abandonment of the labour policy of the *Star*' which he had

---

[1] T. P. O'Connor, *Memoirs of an Old Parliamentarian*, II, 254 ff.; Wilson Pope *et al.*, *The Story of the Star, 1888–1938* (London, 1938), p. 11; S. Koss, *Sir John Brunner, Radical Plutocrat* (Cambridge, 1970), pp. 157–58; Healy to his brother, 27 August 1887, quoted in Healy, *Letters and Leaders of My Day* (New York, 1929), I, 276; Hamilton Fyfe, *T. P. O'Connor* (London, 1934), p. 145; Lee, *Origins*, p. 83; obituary of Holden, *The Times*, 14 August 1897.

[2] Williams, *Dangerous Estate*, pp. 133–34.

striven to uphold. Parke followed, and met the same frustration. Colman now emerged as the principal proprietor, with the chairmanship of the company vested in James Stuart, who had exchanged a professorial chair at Cambridge for a seat on the Liberal back benches. Stuart, Colman's son-in-law and subsequently a director of his mustard company, was an orthodox Gladstonian, who frequently wrote leading articles in that vein for the *Star*. They lacked the piquancy of Colman's more famous product. Ironically, the paper had no sooner modulated its Radical zeal than the party adopted the Newcastle Programme for more advanced social legislation.[1]

There is no evidence that 'the *Star*-spangled Brunner', as Cunninghame Graham called him, continued his affiliation after O'Connor's departure. Instead he entered into 'a financial partnership' with Wemyss Reid to found the *Speaker*, which Reid described to Gladstone as 'a first-class weekly journal' that would 'emulate the *Saturday Review* in its literary criticism whilst advocating strongly the cause of Liberalism as represented by you, including of course Home Rule for Ireland'. It appeared on 4 January 1890, just in time to send greetings to Gladstone on the occasion of his eightieth birthday. The Grand Old Man himself penned an article for its third issue, and other early contributors included Morley, Bryce, Dilke, Harrison, Oscar Wilde, J. M. Barrie, Sidney Webb, John Dillon, and R. B. Haldane. Bryce, who had been instrumental in getting the *Speaker* started, disapproved of the 'middles', which were Reid's 'stupid attempts' at levity. 'Nor am I wholly satisfied with the politics,' he confessed to E. A. Freeman. 'They are too partisan, too *Daily News*ish altogether.' Brunner thoroughly approved of the idea that 'we must take from Socialism what is good and reject what is bad or doubtful' (10 May 1890), but must have had misgivings when the *Speaker* went on to declare that Labour ought to be 'fought instead of courted' (20 July 1895). Resigned to a financial loss, he made periodic payments as high as £1,000 to meet payroll and printing expenses. But he was disappointed by the *Speaker*'s failure to dent the circulation of the anti-Home Rule *Spectator*: its sale reached a modest 4,000 at the end of the first year, then levelled off. In 1899, he handed over the property to a band of younger Liberals, among them J. L. Hammond, his private secretary, who became editor. Financial problems continued to beset the journal, which was rechristened the *Nation* – with Massingham as its editor – in 1907, and was ultimately incorporated with the *New Statesman*.[2]

Stuart was not the only one to forsake academic cloisters to serve as an intermediary between politics and journalism. After submitting two specimens of his writing, the first an account of 'the present state of politics in England' and

[1] Fyfe, *O'Connor*, p. 154; O'Connor, *Memoirs*, II, 270; Simonis, *Street of Ink*, pp. 9–10; O'Connor to Brunner, 6 February 1889, and 7 August 1890, Brunner Papers; Massingham to Stead, 9 December 1890, Stead Papers; Massingham to Cook, 13 January 1891, Cook Papers.

[2] Koss, *Brunner*, pp. 159–60; Reid to Gladstone, 3 January 1890, Gladstone Papers, Add. MSS. 44,509, fol. 10; Bryce to Freeman, 19 April and 9 August [1890], 14 September 1891, Bryce Papers; F. W. Hirst, *In The Golden Days* (London, 1947), pp. 202–203.

the second on 'tulips and tulip shows', W. L. Courtney left Oxford in 1889 to
take up work on the *Daily Telegraph*. 'It wasn't only the fact, it was the paper!'
recalled his widow. 'In Oxford we scarcely knew the *Telegraph*. We read only
The Times, unless we were so advanced as to want the *Daily News*, or so high-
brow as to swear by the *Manchester Guardian*.' E. B. Iwan-Müller, another
migrant from New College, Oxford, must have envied Courtney's destination.
Long interested in 'the rationale of Conservatism', he enlisted Balfour's assistance to secure him a berth on the *Manchester Courier*. 'I like my work immensely & everything goes smoothly as oil – and I hope to make such changes
in the paper as will give it the position it ought to occupy,' he wrote to Balfour
soon after his arrival in 1884. Anxious to obtain and disseminate 'the views entertained by the responsible leaders of the party', Iwan-Müller kept close
touch with his benefactor, who sat for a Manchester constituency. It was his
further ambition to make the *Courier* a sort of clearing house for Conservative
journalism in the North-West; but Henry Manners, Salisbury's principal
private secretary, thought that, 'taking all considerations together', the
scheme was not'wholly desirable to adopt, at any rate for the present'. Iwan-
Müller received greater encouragement from Milner, who called him 'my
best friend on the Press & the Govt's. chief journalistic supporter outside
London'. Outlining Goschen's plans for 'a big *coup* ... with regard to the
National Debt', Milner declared that whether these proposals 'will be appreciated as they ought to be, will depend largely upon the degree of cordiality &
understanding, which is shown *at the very outset*, by the Press'. Confident that
Iwan-Müller was 'disposed to back us in any case', he gave personal 'assurance' that 'you have in this instance a real good thing to back'. At the same
time, he held 'a shrewd suspicion that friend Randolph will be nasty about it, if
he dare'.[1]

Goschen had entered the Salisbury administration on the implied
understanding that, in due course, he would supersede W. H. Smith as leader
of the House of Commons. But Smith ('Old Morality') proved more successful
and therefore more durable than anyone had imagined. Besides, Goschen
commanded little support, even among his fellow Liberal Unionists. If there
was any rival to Smith, it was Balfour, who ultimately succeeded when Smith
died in 1891. When Balfour's name was first mooted in 1888, Milner told
Buckle that Goschen 'hardly could serve under Balfour'. At least 'at that
time', Milner later informed Goschen, the editor of *The Times* 'was entirely of
opinion that you had the stronger claim & would certainly have backed you
had the question arisen'. Of course, it was anyone's guess where Buckle might
have stood on questions that did not arise. 'I hope that valiant Scotsman,

[1] Mrs W. L. Courtney, *The Making of an Editor*, pp. 38–40; Iwan-Müller to W. Blackwood, 11
December 1881, Blackwood Papers; Iwan-Müller to Balfour, 30 May 1884, Balfour Papers;
Manners to Iwan-Müller, 14 February 1888 (draft copy), Salisbury Papers; Milner to Iwan-
Müller, 6 March 1888, Milner Papers.

Arthur Balfour, is heartening up all Scotch Unionists, of both parties,' he wrote to William Blackwood in October 1888. In any case, how much would *The Times*'s backing have been worth?[1]

That the paper enjoyed a special relationship with the Unionist ministers was well known along Fleet Street, where it was as much resented by Mudford of the *Standard* or Greenwood of the *St James's Gazette* as by any of their Liberal counterparts. On 2 March 1888, Buckle wrote to the Prime Minister 'with warmth' to protest that Foreign Office intelligence had been distributed through the Central News Agency and the Press Association, 'mere parasites who prey upon us, & who have sprung from the necessities of the country press, who wish to get London news cheap'. He considered it 'an indignity to *The Times* that an association of the kind should be used as a channel of communication between the F.O. & the leading journal'. Salisbury placated him with a 'promise to let *The Times* have advance copies of important papers at the same time as they are forwarded to the Houses of Parliament. That will exactly meet my difficulty,' Buckle replied gratefully, 'and in the best possible way.' Whether this extraordinary procedure met Salisbury's difficulty was quite another matter. The following year, *The Times* embarrassed the Foreign Office 'with tales of outrages' from its special correspondents in Athens, and Salisbury admitted 'I can never get Buckle to listen to me against his Specials'.[2]

Like every other major London daily, *The Times* – especially in the aftermath of the Pigott affair – came to be regarded as a dubious political asset. When Austin likened Mudford to 'a weather-vane' that required 'no external current to make him shift about', he might have been describing Buckle or Greenwood, O'Connor or Stead, all of whom were equally unstable from a party point of view. Consequently, the politicians briefly turned away from the metropolis and towards the provinces, where there were better prospects for imposing discipline.[3]

One of the ways in which the Unionists, especially, attempted to fertilize this journalistic back-garden was by distributing honours. Hitherto, these rewards had been given stintingly to representatives of the London press, including Borthwick and Hardman of the *Morning Post*. In 1887, Salisbury broke new ground by conferring a knighthood on William Leng, the proprietor of the *Sheffield Daily Telegraph*. Churchill, revealing a disquieting interest in Birmingham politics, nominated John Jaffray for a baronetcy. 'He has a predominant voice in the management of the *Birmingham Daily Post* with a circulation in the Midlands of 50,000, and of the *Evening Mail* with a circulation of 70,000,' Churchill explained to Smith, whom he urged to 'bring this

---

[1] Milner to Goschen, 14 January 1892, Milner Papers; Buckle to Blackwood, 15 October 1888, Blackwood Papers.

[2] Buckle to Salisbury, 2 and 4 March 1888, Salisbury Papers; Salisbury to Smith, 3 October 1889, Hambleden Papers.

[3] Austin to Salisbury, 17 February 1888, Salisbury Papers.

matter before Lord Salisbury'. As Jaffray had reportedly declined the offer of a knighthood from Gladstone, something better was required. 'The *Post* has at length after much sitting on the rail definitely thrown in its lot with the Unionists. The *Mail* has supported them all along.' But Churchill was less concerned with past performance than with future contingencies. 'Just between ourselves,' he told Smith,

> there is no love lost between Jaffray and Joe C., and it might possibly be vital to us in the event of the latter ever leaving us to have Jaffray firmly attached to us. The knowledge moreover that Jaffray had taken a baronetcy from us and would not go against us in his papers, would always act as a powerful restraint on Joe C. if he contemplated any change of attitude.

While not oblivious to Jaffray's claims, Salisbury was in no mood to oblige Jaffray's sponsor, who was eyeing Bright's seat at Birmingham Central. By 1892, Jaffray had grown impatient. J. Powell Williams recounted to Chamberlain a conversation with Bunce, the editor of the *Post*, who said 'that he honestly fears the effect upon the policy of the paper if Jaffray is not recommended for what he wants'. Williams was willing to 'admit, of course, that our victories here, and round here, are mainly owing to you. . . . But,' he pointed out, 'the *Post* has certainly helped to hold the fort; and when *you* have been concerned, its course has always been without blame.' Through a mishap, Chamberlain did not respond quickly enough to an inquiry from Wolmer, the Liberal Unionist whip, who therefore did not include Jaffray's name on the list he drew up for Hartington to transmit to Salisbury, and thence to the Queen. Gladstone courteously rectified the error, and it was technically to him that Jaffray owed his baronetcy.[1]

At Manchester, the case was similar, but less protracted. Iwan-Müller pressed hard for some gesture of public recognition for Thomas Sowler. Balfour, the recipient of his appeals, responded with assurances 'that I feel very strongly the claim . . . and that the Prime Minister feels the more so'. Nevertheless, probably with Jaffray in mind, Balfour cited 'very great difficulties connected with honours to the Press at this moment the precise nature of which I will fully explain to you when we meet'. Before that was possible, Iwan-Müller related that Manchester buzzed with rumours that Colonel Sowler was about to become Sir Thomas. The story was credible enough: Leng had been 'made a member of the Carlton, and then a Jubilee knight', while no attention had been paid to Sowler, who 'is not only the proprietor of *the* Tory paper of Lancashire', but also an active fund-raiser who had contested Manchester South in 1886. Balfour, whose hand had been forced, wrote promptly to Akers-Douglas:

---

[1] Churchill to Smith, 14 April 1888 (copy), and Smith to Salisbury, 14 April 1888 (copy), Churchill Papers; Williams to Chamberlain, 19 July 1892, and Wolmer to Chamberlain, 25 July 1892, Chamberlain Papers.

I have been trying to keep matters smooth with regard to Colonel Sowler, the owner of the *Manchester Courier*. Sowler is a most excellent, loyal, and generous fellow; but, unfortunately, they have been spreading abroad through Manchester the report that he is to be knighted; and the fact that Leng has received this honour, and has, moreover, been selected for the Carlton, with claims which, in Sowler's opinion are inferior to his own, of course does not mend matters. Do you think it would be possible to get him selected for the Carlton at an early date? He really has done more for the party than almost anybody in Lancashire.

Sowler collected his reward in increments. Eighteen months after his admission to the Carlton Club was railroaded through, Balfour wrote to say that 'it has been a very great satisfaction to me that the Prime Minister has been able to recommend your name to the Queen for a knighthood'; and, he added, 'if I have been able in any way to contribute to your getting it, it is only a just return for the many kindnesses which you have done me in Manchester'.[1]

Jaffray and Sowler, each in his way, had held the politicians to ransom. In both cases, it had paid off. Why did Chamberlain, Balfour, and the others capitulate to them? The explanation is to be found in the suspicions that persisted between Liberal Unionists and Conservatives, as well as those between personalities within the respective camps.

Chamberlain required the *Birmingham Daily Post* to help defend his fief, especially when Bright's death created a vacuum which Churchill aspired to fill. Williams was relieved to learn that the paper would resist any Randolphian incursion and, better still, that 'Jaffray and Bunce are agreed that there is no *local* Tory whom the *Daily Post* can support for any vacancy at any time'. Relations between the Unionist allies in Birmingham were badly strained, with the threat of parliamentary repercussions. 'The Tories here ... are as bad as bad can be,' Chamberlain told Hartington, instancing a 'most studiously offensive & violent article' in the *Birmingham Gazette*. That Captain Middleton was the chairman of the syndicate which controlled this Tory organ made all the more insidious its advice that Conservatives should vote for the Gladstonian candidate for the Town Council instead of Chamberlain's son Austen, 'whom I have allowed to stand as the only person capable of serving the seat'. This article was 'one of a series, each more offensive & insulting than the last'. Balfour, in turn, took Chamberlain to task for anti-Conservative and even pro-Home Rule sentiments that crept into the *Birmingham Daily Post*. On the same day that he remonstrated with Bunce, Chamberlain wrote to Balfour to disclaim responsibility:

Please note that the *Daily Post* is not my organ & that it is not under my

---

[1] Iwan-Müller to Balfour, 16 May 1888, Balfour Papers; Balfour to Iwan-Müller, 15 May 1888, Balfour to Akers-Douglas, 18 May 1888, and Balfour to Sowler, 31 December 1889 (letterbook copies), Balfour Papers.

influence in any general sense. I can get things inserted & have sometimes made it the channel for the publication of my views but it is really entirely independent & often differs from me on both national & local policy.

Who was fooling whom?[1]

'Do you think anything can be done about the *Birmingham Gazette*?' Hartington asked Wolmer. 'I don't suppose that Middleton has anything to do with the attacks of which Chamberlain complains.' Before Wolmer could obtain assurances from Middleton 'that the article complained of in no way came under my notice before its publication and that I had expressed my disapproval of the tone adopted', Chamberlain lodged a stiff protest with Smith. Persistently misspelling Middleton's name as 'Myddlton', and seemingly unaware of his intimate connection with Salisbury, Chamberlain assumed him to be the instrument of 'the Randolph section of the Conservatives'. Smith sorted out the facts, which he deputed Hartington to communicate to Chamberlain at Birmingham. 'I am afraid the split is very far from healed there,' Hartington observed ruefully. According to Cooper, the same tensions existed 'in some parts of Scotland'.[2]

So long as Chamberlain clung to his territorial rights, which he considered the basis of Liberal Unionist autonomy, the split could never heal. As late as the spring of 1895, weeks before he took office in Salisbury's third ministry, Chamberlain's demands again threatened to disrupt the Unionist alliance. A vacancy occurred in Warwick and Leamington when A. W. Peel retired as Speaker, and Chamberlain lost no time in claiming the constituency for the Liberal Unionists. In the *New Review*, George Curzon protested bitterly, but anonymously, against this display of 'back-parlour' tactics, and the *Standard* (3 April 1895) issued a particularly vitriolic attack which Austin was presumed to have written at Salisbury's instigation. Plunged into 'an awful mess', Wolmer confided to the Duke of Devonshire (as Hartington had become in 1891), that it was 'not too much to say that the *Standard* & *New Review* have fairly upset Mr Chamberlain', who

has talked separately to Balfour & Douglas & myself in a way that fairly brought lumps into our throats. He said he was prepared to stand anything from the Gladstonians, but 'to be stabbed in the back by his friends' was more than he could stand.

[1] Williams to Chamberlain, 31 March 1889, and Chamberlain to Bunce, 26 September 1889 (copy), Chamberlain Papers; Chamberlain to Hartington, 3 September and 14 October 1889, Devonshire Papers; Chamberlain to Balfour, 26 September 1889, Balfour Papers. Writing to Salisbury's private secretary, Middleton stressed 'that our *Birmingham Gazette*' should get 'first tip' before 'Chamberlain's paper, the *Post*'. Middleton to McDonnell, 7 August 1890, Salisbury Papers (Christ Church).
[2] Hartington to Wolmer, 15 October 1889, and Cooper to Wolmer, 7 October 1890, Selborne Papers; Middleton to Salisbury, 28 October 1889, Salisbury Papers (Christ Church); Chamberlain to Smith, 25 October 1889 (copy), Chamberlain Papers; Middleton to Smith, 28 October 1889 (letterbook copy), Chilston Papers; Hartington to Smith, 3 November 1889, Hambleden Papers.

Devonshire, seeking to end the recriminations, cautioned Chamberlain against 'taking any step in consequence of these annoyances unless you have reason to believe that any of the responsible leaders of the Conservative party have anything to do with them'. He reported a conversation with Salisbury, who 'bewailed the indiscretions of the *Standard*'. Wolmer and Balfour, too, tried to apply balm to Chamberlain's wounds. But Salisbury, despite his remarks to Devonshire, left them to fester. 'I hope Chamberlain's feelings are subsiding,' he wrote to Wolmer.

I never came across so sensitive a public man before. I have known one distinguished statesman who went half-mad whenever he was caricatured in
Punch: and another who wished to resign his office, because he was never
caricatured in *Punch* – which he looked upon as a slight on his public importance. But I never met any one before who was disturbed by articles in the
Standard.

Salisbury's cynicism was fully warranted, and exceeded only by his appointment of Austin to the Poet Laureateship the following year.[1]

*   *   *

Although they did not compete directly with the *Star*, the two *Gazettes* – the *St James's* and the *Pall Mall* – experienced much the same difficulty without the compensation of financial success. In both cases, editorial propensities ran counter to proprietorial injunctions, with the result that political service was impaired. Weakened by changes in management, the *St James's* stagnated, while the *Pall Mall* struggled to assert a new identity.

Predictably, the *St James's* was the first to succumb. Greenwood's judgment had grown increasingly wayward, and the circulation had continued to drop. It had enraged Healy to discover that 'the fellow who writes as "an old Fenian" in the *St James's Gazette*' had been none other than the disreputable Pigott, 'whom the boys would not touch with the tongs'. Fortunately, Greenwood had not published any of Pigott's forgeries, though he would have been tempted at the chance. His hard-line Conservatism soured him against Salisbury, who seemed 'so much occupied with foreign affairs, & so used up in transacting them, that he has no time to look after his team & not much nerve in driving it'. Too much authority devolved upon Goschen who, if he had his way, would bring Hartington into the Cabinet. 'Party newspapers,' Greenwood was soon to reflect in the pages of the *Nineteenth Century*, 'are often in the dilemma of

---

[1] 'Two Demagogues: A Parallel and a Moral,' *New Review*, xii (1895), 363–72; Wolmer to Devonshire, 16 April 1895, and Devonshire to Chamberlain, 17 April 1895 (draft copy), Devonshire Papers; Salisbury to Wolmer, 20 April 1895, Selborne Papers; *also see* Marsh, *Discipline of Popular Government*, pp. 237–41.

having to choose between party principles – or even something more important – and the party chiefs.' As his tenure at the *St James's* neared its end, Greenwood personified that dilemma and made clear where his choice lay.[1]

By the start of 1888, Henry Hucks Gibbs, the owner of the *St James's*, had had enough of a bad thing. The paper did nothing to further the parliamentary ambitions he nursed for himself and his son. Greenwood, informed of Gibbs's impending divestiture, scurried to find a new proprietor. The man he recruited was Edward Steinkopff, who was variously described to Robertson Scott as 'a Pomeranian Jew from Glasgow, a very rich man who left a million and a half', and, less flatteringly, 'a vulgar, loud-speaking German'. According to Sidney Low, Steinkopff 'was understood to have something to do with the manufacture of that peculiar, gaseous English product mysteriously known as mineral waters'. W. H. Smith, on holiday in the south of France, learned of the changes at the *St James's* from a 'very circumstantial story' in *Figaro*. 'Who is Mr Steinkopff and where does his money come from?' he wrote to Akers-Douglas. Within eight months, Steinkopff had applied to Smith, inviting him to nominate an editor to succeed Greenwood, who had resigned. Smith, keeping his distance, replied through Middleton that he knew 'nobody suitable for your purposes. Probably amongst the staff of the other London Daily papers would be the most likely place to find the man you require.' In fact, Steinkopff had to look no further than to Low, Greenwood's second-in-command, who edited the *St James's* through the ensuing decade. Greenwood, twice wounded, now retreated from the battlefield of daily journalism. In February 1891, he brought out a weekly 'under the somewhat dangerous & ambitious title of the *Anti-Jacobin*'; it was a somewhat anachronistic title as well, but wholly apposite. The price was initially fixed at twopence, Greenwood told William Blackwood, 'so that a smart strongly written journal shall not be beyond any poor Gentleman's pocket'. But the operating expense was beyond his own pocket, and the *Anti-Jacobin* was forced to treble its price before its demise in January 1892.[2]

The *Pall Mall Gazette*, stepfather to the *St James's*, experienced comparable difficulties. Relatively more prosperous, it neither paid its own way nor satisfied political expectations. Stead, increasingly the captive of his passions and prejudices, was beyond human control. 'You might as well suspect me of inspiring the north-east wind,' Morley replied to Chamberlain, who had accused him of inciting Stead's attacks in the *Newcastle Daily Leader*.[3] In his

[1] Healy to Labouchere, 7 January 1886, quoted in Thorold, *Labouchere*, p. 282; Greenwood to Blackwood, 26 July 1887, Blackwood Papers; Greenwood, 'The Press and Government,' *Nineteenth Century*, xxviii (1890), 109.

[2] Robertson Scott, *Pall Mall Gazette*, pp. 269–70; Chapman-Huston, *Lost Historian*, pp. 59–60; Smith to Akers-Douglas, 23 January [1888], and Middleton to Steinkopff, 13 August 1888, Chilston Papers; Greenwood to Blackwood, 17 January [1891], Blackwood Papers; *Sell's* (1893).

[3] Morley to Chamberlain, 7 March 1887, quoted in Garvin, *Chamberlain*, II, 291.

own paper, Stead's tirades and transgressions were even more provocative. Often credited with the birth of the so-called New Journalism, Stead represented the Old Journalism in its death throes.

It is possible to argue, as did the official historians of *The Times*, that 'the root cause of the . . . *Pall Mall*'s troubles lay less in its politics and in its editors than in its trade position': admittedly, it was a 'hard journalistic fact' that the *Pall Mall*, 'designed as a "class paper"', catered to 'an audience that was narrow or at least small'.[1] That, however, is to adopt a modern perspective, which contemporaries would have dismissed as a tautology. It was precisely as 'a class paper' that the *Pall Mall* was supposed to influence political opinion, and it was precisely on these grounds that its failure was most egregious. That the paper held to an outdated definition of political opinion was, by far, the lesser of two problems.More importantly, it could not reconcile its policies to the wider conflicts within Liberalism. To be sure, Stead did not help matters. Yet, in many ways, he was more the symptom than the cause of the paper's distress.

Arthur G. Symonds, the secretary of the National Reform Union, waited until Stead was gone to put the case to Cook, the new editor. 'Years ago – when Mr Yates Thompson first took up the *Pall Mall* – I had a long talk with him about making it *the* organ of the Liberal Party, especially in the Provinces', and, for that purpose, Symonds had distributed 'some thousands of circulars on the subject to Liberal Associations, Clubs, & individuals all over the country'. Since that time, he had remained a 'constant reader' of the paper and its weekly edition, the *Budget*. While continuing to 'hold the same views as to the functions which the *Pall Mall* could & should fulfil in the party', he had lost confidence. Furthermore, although he did not spell it out, his concept of party had changed. 'I need not tell you,' he nevertheless proceeded to tell Cook,

> that the line taken by the *Pall Mall* on the Egyptian question did not recommend itself to the party as a whole, nor were [we] at all satisfied with the attitude it took on the Home Rule question at first. However, these points do not matter much, as now the paper undoubtedly recommends itself to the great bulk of the *Radical* party, & I believe wd. be readily accepted as their organ.

Shifting his emphasis from Liberalism to Radicalism, Symonds felt compelled to bring 'two points' to Cook's attention: the paper had 'almost ceased' to concern itself with the provinces, where the centres of moral and electoral strength were to be found; and it had repaid 'the material help' of the National Reform Union with a cold indifference. 'The Radical party', he argued,

> is no longer content to be merely official, & to 'toe the line' to orders from

[1] *History of The Times*, III, 95.

Parliament St. or from the front Opposition bench. . . . London – so hostile to Liberalism – has taken the place of Birmingham with its dictation & masterful system. From this danger & mischief I once hoped the *Pall Mall* wd. save the party, for it was nothing if not independent – even to the point of opposition. But I have been disappointed.[1]

Either way, then, the *Pall Mall* could not win. When it dissented from official party views, it was deemed treacherous; when it defended them, provided it could make them out, its Radical credentials were impugned. Like O'Connor at the *Star*. Stead could navigate more easily between the cross-currents of the old and the new journalism, which – with his help – have been vastly exaggerated, than between those of the old and the new liberalism.

'Crisis at *P.M.G.* begins,' Cook signalled in his diary on 25 June 1888, when Stead returned from his Russian adventures to face an irate proprietor. It did not abate until 14 December 1889. when Stead tendered his resignation. In the interim, he clashed incessantly with Yates Thompson who, at one point, docked £200 of his salary. His friends in public life fended him off. 'I fear that we must for the present content ourselves with being on good terms privately,' explained Balfour; 'politically, I do not see any immediate prospect of such a consummation.' Those who already regarded him with distrust, if not incredulity, became still more censorious. Gladstone, after reading 'with the utmost surprise' an article in the *Pall Mall* (4 September 1889) 'purporting to give a statement of my views on the Irish University question', remarked that he was not aware that Stead had 'asked for an interview for any such purpose', and thereupon delivered a lecture on journalistic good manners. In April 1889, Stead muttered mystically about leaving Northumberland Street on 30 June to start the *New Times*, with money from Cecil Rhodes and premises in Waterloo House; but nothing further was heard of the project. Nevertheless, his position was obviously untenable. In November, Yates Thompson instituted changes which were calculated to assert his authority and to intensify Stead's discomfort. 'The new form of the *P.M.G.* is loathsome to work upon, & I sincerely commiserate [with] you there anent,' Milner wrote to him. On 14 December, Stead nonchalantly disclosed that he had agreed to edit a new *Sixpenny Monthly* for George Newnes, whose weekly *Tit-Bits* had been a runaway success since 1881. 'Balfour & some twenty other big people' had given him encouragement. As Yates Thompson had 'no intention of going halves in my editor with Mr Newnes', Stead gave a fortnight's notice. The *Sixpenny Monthly* evolved into the weekly *Review of Reviews*, and made its début within weeks.[2]

[1] Symonds to Cook, 18 August 1890, Cook Papers.
[2] Cook's diary, 25 June and 4 November 1888, 4 April and 14 December 1889, Cook Papers; Balfour to Stead, 10 January 1889 (letterbook copy), Balfour Papers; Gladstone to Stead, 5 September 1889 (copy), Gladstone Papers, Add. MSS. 44, 303,fols. 409–10; Milner to Stead, 1 November 1889, Stead Papers.

'I suppose we may all congratulate you now on being the new editor of the *P.M.G.*,' J. A. Spender wrote to Cook on 18 December 1889. 'Henceforth I shall regard you with very great awe as being – you yourselves have said it – more than a Cabinet minister.' Cook did not yet, if ever, see himself in that light. His early days were clouded by 'Thompson's change of mind and Stead's desire to come back' in the capacity of 'political director'. Eager to put 'an end to the bother', Cook acceded to these awkward terms, which Stead violated by an intemperate outburst in the *Star*. Cook was now free of him. A steadfast Home Ruler – not that it had prevented Milner from trying to lure him into Parliament – he was a conscientious editor, who won praise from Massingham for making the *Pall Mall* into 'essentially a young man's paper'. The leading members of its staff, all under the age of forty, included the Spender brothers, Harold and J. A., and Harold Cox, a Fabian. 'The *Pall Mall* to-day performs the useful function of an organ of independent Liberalism, critical on some points of the party programme, but careful to march in the main with the general movement,' Massingham concluded in 1892. 'On social questions, and in relation to what may be called the new Collectivism, it is more advanced than the *Daily News*, and occupies a mid position between that paper and the *Daily Chronicle*.'[1]

No sooner uttered, these words ceased to apply. Cook's editorship lasted barely twenty-one months, and ended, as we shall see, with the reversion of the *Pall Mall* to its original Tory affiliation. During this relatively brief interlude, the paper exercised a self-restraint of which Stead would have been incapable. This was never more evident than in November 1890, when the Home Rule cause was besmirched by revelations of Parnell's adultery. Absolved of his complicity in the Phoenix Park murders, Parnell fell victim to a divorce scandal and, this time, offered no defence. Irish Catholic and English Nonconformist opinion turned savagely against him, and his parliamentary followers were divided. To the delight of his opponents, Gladstone was forced to dissociate himself and his Irish policy from Parnell, who stubbornly refused to step aside. Few Unionist newspapers were as charitable as the *Daily Telegraph*, which professed itself 'in no mood to exult' in the misfortune of 'a political adversary, ... overthrown by irrelevant accident, wholly unconnected with the struggle in which we are engaged' (17 November). To many of them, including *The Times*, Parnell's sinfulness was the very essence of the political struggle. For that matter, few Liberal newspapers showed such worldliness. Edward Russell recalled that his *Liverpool Daily Post* had gratified Gladstone by insisting 'that it would be wise to let Mr Parnell down gently and to do all that could be done to prevent the Liberal-Irish cause from being ruined'. On 24 November, after the National Liberal Federation had de-

---

[1] Spender to Cook, 18 December [1889], and Cook's diary, 9 January 1890, Cook Papers; Milner to Cook, June [n.d.] 1886, quoted in Mills, *Cook*, p. 61; Massingham, *London Daily Press*, pp. 157–59.

livered its verdict at Sheffield, Gladstone composed a letter to Morley, who was entrusted to convey its contents privately to Parnell. The following afternoon, when Morley reported that Parnell remained 'obdurate', Gladstone authorized its immediate publication. ''Tis too late now,' said Morley, with his knowledge of Fleet Street deadlines. 'Oh, no,' retorted Gladstone, 'the *Pall Mall* will bring it out in a special edition.' The letter was not released until eight o'clock that evening; 'just too late for the *Pall Mall Gazette*, it was given for publication to the morning papers'.[1]

That Gladstone could take for granted the *Pall Mall*'s compliance was a sign of the change that had occurred since Stead's day. On 29 November, Cook was summoned to Gladstone's residence in Carlton House Gardens, where the Liberal chiefs were assembled. He received compliments for his paper's deportment, and he and James Stuart of the *Star* obtained a briefing on Gladstone's proposed reply to Parnell's forthcoming manifesto. Morley, who had sat in Cook's chair, undertook to keep him informed of Irish developments. From John Dillon, who was consulting Irish nationalist supporters in America, Morley received 'a cable ... to the effect that the bitter tone of some of the London Liberal papers is "increasing their difficulties"'. Without delay, Morley communicated Dillon's message to Cook: 'It is, no doubt, difficult from your point of view not to strike Mr Parnell,' he acknowledged, 'but I suppose that what Dillon would like would be less denunciation of Mr P. and a strongly sympathetic spirit for Ireland's confusion.'[2]

One might suppose that Yates Thompson would have been flattered by these attentions. To the contrary, having got rid of Morley in 1883, he was not disposed to welcome him at the back door. When Yates Thompson told Stead that 'Cook is the best editor I have ever had', it was surely more a gibe at Stead than a tribute to Cook. In May 1892, Yates Thompson mentioned being 'tempted' by an offer of £50,000 for the paper. It was tendered by lawyers, whom Cook believed to represent Henry Lowenfeld, 'the Polish Jew who is Kops Ale', a suitably non-alcoholic beverage. The would-be purchaser was as obscure in his motives as in his background. After dropping this bombshell, and ascertaining that Cook 'had no desire to leave the *Pall Mall Gazette*', Yates Thompson appeared to have withstood temptation.

With the return of a modest Liberal majority in the July elections, Cook set off on a holiday in Italy. There, on 22 September, he received a letter which brought him back to London in two days' time. His disconsolate colleagues could only confirm that the *Pall Mall* had been sold out from under them. Like 'a youth on a visit', Cook went to see Yates Thompson at his country house in Berkhamsted, where (as he recorded in his diary) he found his employer

[1] Russell, *That Reminds Me*, pp. 318 ff.; Morley's 'note.' of 25 November and Gladstone's memorandum of 28 November 1890, quoted in Morley, *Gladstone*, III, 441, 445.
[2] Cook's diary, 29 November 1890, and Morley to Cook, 14 December 1890, Cook Papers.

in his most infelicitous & unsympathetic mood – very much engrossed with his own excellent bargain, and wanting my opinion thereon. He had put £20,000 into it. Now [he] had [the] chance of selling [for] £50,000, besides profit he had recently drawn out, and avoiding heavy capital expend[iture] shortly necessary for new machines, enlargement of premises, &c.

(As Stead was to put it, Yates Thompson's 'only desire ... was to be able to look his father-in-law in [the] face & say he had got all both had put in & lots more besides'.) With regard to the possible effect on the Liberal Party, Yates Thompson felt

no compunctions at all. They have never done anything for me, tho' I did a real service to them in 1880 by turning the paper round. They despise the press. Mr G. might easily have kept the *Chronicle* & probably the *Telegraph* also if he had bought Lloyd & Lawson; & if they had ever done anything for me, I don't suppose I shd. be selling now.

It was not simply that the Liberals had denied him a baronetcy. Yates Thompson urged Cook to

think of Harcourt's insolent remark to [a] meeting of new MPs after the election: 'Maj[ority] of 40 is a great thing to have won in spite of the opposition of *The Times* and the support of the *Daily News*'.

The Pall Mall Gazette, for all its dutiful effort, had not even qualified for Harcourt's sarcasm.

Cook, who recognized a lost cause when he saw one, 'pressed him as to [the] identity of [the] real purchaser'. The transfer was to be made to T. Dove Keighley, known simply as a member of the National Liberal Club. Obviously, he was 'only the man of straw', the stalking-horse for someone more significant. Some assumed that Keighley was the agent of Steinkopff, who probably intended to amalgamate the two *Gazettes*. Others, with more vivid imaginations, detected the hidden hand of Lord Randolph Churchill or the tentacles of the German Emperor. Yates Thompson, 'pledged to secrecy', divulged nothing more than that his customer was 'a rich man of business, much in the same position as Steinkopff when he bought [the] *St James's*'. It was his hunch that the man of mystery 'merely wanted a paper "as a man might want a pony"', and without political objectives. On this score, he had Keighley's word, which 'of course ... was not binding, that the purchaser was a Liberal & intended to carry on [the] paper as at present'. On the afternoon of 30 September, when the contracts were signed, Yates Thompson, 'hardly keeping up and big tears on his cheeks', made the 'serious announcement personally' to the assembled staff: 'This is a painful separation to me in some ways, and I flatter myself none of you will rejoice at it. I do not think that lightly.' Knowing what he must have known, he could rest assured that he was not mistaken.[1]

The next day, Cook 'lunched at home', where T. P. O'Connor came to interview him for the new halfpenny evening *Sun*. Under the lucrative terms of his settlement with the proprietors of the *Star*, O'Connor had been barred from London journalism for a three-year period, which had finally come to an end. The *Sun* was his 'return blow'; but, begun with 'insufficient capital', it quickly became an 'agony' from which he was happy to be extricated three years later. Cook could profit from his experience, and also from Stead's. The *Review of Reviews* had realized an excellent sale, but Stead's 'libellous' articles had driven Newnes to fear that the journal might 'land you back in Holloway, with me in the adjoining cell'. In March 1890, Stead had negotiated a 'fair and reasonable price' – reportedly £10,000 – whereby he was able (with a friend's assistance) to buy out Newnes and assume 'my own responsibility'. Thereafter, he was ever more the gadfly. Balfour, disinclined to include newspapers among the reading matter supplied to workhouses, jested that 'an exception might be made in favour of the *Review of Reviews*', a specimen of 'current literature' from which he 'received much entertainment'. But Chamberlain, equally true to form, was so much annoyed by Stead's 'persistent and apparently personal hostility' that he declined to grant him an interview 'until I have some evidence of your good intentions'.[2]

Stead, generous with his advice, thought that Cook should stay on as long as possible at the *Pall Mall*, as much for his own sake as the paper's. That option was put to Cook by Keighley, who spoke in a vague and 'absurd' way of creating a system of dual control, not unlike the one that Cook had grudgingly accepted at the commencement of his editorship. Clayden of the *Daily News*, who was 'very friendly and sympathetic', gave the same counsel: after all, he himself 'was really political editor', with 'Robinson only arranging for other articles'. Unwittingly, however, Clayden weakened his case by describing the challenges to his partial authority from Liberal politicians on the one hand and from Labouchere on the other. Cook's position would be still more anomalous, as the ownership of the paper had to be considered among the imponderables.[3]

'Where is the *Pall Mall* going to?' A. J. Mundella asked Stead on 12 October. 'I should be sorry to see it in reactionary hands.' Cook had a better sense of the answer on the 13th, when he was paid a 'surprise visit' by F. A.

[1] Mills, *Cook*, pp. 113, 116–17; Robertson Scott, *Life and Death of a Newspaper*, pp. 271–72; Cook's diary [24?] September and 3 October 1892, Cook Papers. The records of the National Liberal Club confirm Keighley's membership from 1884–94, but reveal nothing about him save his move from a Soho to a Kensington address.

[2] Cook's diary, 1 October 1892, Cook Papers; O'Connor, *Memoirs*, II,270; Newnes to Stead, 10 January and 28 February 1890, and Stead to Newnes, 7 March 1890 (copy?), Stead Papers; Balfour to Stead, 18 April 1890 (letterbook copy), Balfour Papers; Chamberlain to Stead, 11 April 1891 (copy), Chamberlain Papers.

[3] Cook's diary, 1, 3, and 8 October 1892, Cook Papers.

Maxse, a convert to Unionism. Whereas Keighley had maintained the fiction that the anonymous purchaser was inclined towards Liberalism, going so far as to hint that Massingham might serve if Cook would not, Maxse dispelled any lingering doubts. The new owner, yet to be named, was not only a Tory, but also one who 'was making heavy pecuniary sacrifices for his political convictions'. For that reason, it was impossible to guarantee Cook 'unfettered control for a year', as he had requested; 'but the curve was to be gradual; there wd. be no idea of course of asking me to write a word of which I disapproved; but why,' Maxse entreated, 'should I not write on more or less neutral subjects?' If nothing else, the conversation yielded a metaphor that Cook elaborated upon in his farewell speech: 'He did not object to being a humble penny-a-liner if the line was straight, but he would not consent to be a mercenary curvilineator.'[1]

Unwilling to act as 'a stop-gap', Cook notified Rosebery on the 15th that 'after today I shall cease to be connected with the *Pall Mall*'. He repeated Maxse's phrase that 'the curve will be very gradual', but predicted that 'by the time Parliament meets, the *Pall Mall* will, I fear, be in opposition – at any rate so far as Home Rule is concerned'. Although Rosebery mourned 'the loss of the *Pall Mall*' as the result of its 'disestablishment', he himself had no immediate cause for complaint. Its leading article on the 17th, celebrating the virtue of 'Permanence of Policy', hailed him as 'the fittest man' for the foreign secretaryship. J. A. Spender, however, could not 'restrain a chortle..., though the occasion might also be one for tears', at the sight of 'the Poor *P.M.G.*' wrapping Rosebery in Salisbury's mantle. Like Cook, he and various others had withdrawn from the paper. The arrival of Kinloch Cooke, seconded from the *Observer*, went largely unnoticed. Those who tried to call attention to the change were understandably bewildered. On 17 October, for example, the *Manchester Guardian* presumed that Lowenfeld was responsible, and that 'the capture was planned in the Liberal Unionist camp'; and the *Daily Chronicle*, with fewer details, saw 'Tory democracy' as the *Pall Mall*'s 'new line'.[2]

Cook had time to spare to correct these misapprehensions, though not all the facts were yet available. As the 'London Correspondent' for the *Manchester Guardian*, he wrote a breathless article on the 18th, for which he received gratitude and a gratuity from C. P. Scott. 'One of the diversions of the moment is to suggest plausible reasons for what has evidently been a deliberate effort to secure control of one or more of the existing London papers,' he declared.

> With respect to the changes in Northumberland-street, I can say on the best authority that the sale of the *Pall Mall Gazette* has been contemplated and a

[1] Mundella to Stead, 12 October 1892, Stead Papers; Cook's diary, 13 October 1892, Cook Papers; Robertson Scott, *Life and Death of a Newspaper*, p. 173; Mills, *Cook*, p. 125.
[2] Cook to Rosebery, 15 October 1892, Rosebery Papers, Vol. 10,090, fol. 202; Rosebery to Cook, 21 and 22 October 1892, and Spender to Cook, 17 October 1892, Cook Papers.

matter of negotiation for two or three months past – in fact from the morrow of the general election. There is all the more significance in this statement because some Liberals are contending that a paper strongly committed to a certain line in politics ought not to be disposed of without at least giving the option of purchase to men of the same political colour, and it is sufficient to say that in ordinary circumstances the outgoing proprietor of the *Pall Mall Gazette* might have willingly given effect to this general proposition.

Capable of being read as either a stern indictment or a lame defence of Yates Thompson (what did Cook mean by 'ordinary circumstances'?), this argument recalled Greenwood's complaint when the *Pall Mall* had changed hands in 1880. More generally, it raised a fundamental question which was to be the *leitmotiv* of newspaper history in the twentieth century, when a steadily shrinking market left political parties without representation in the national press.

It was not until 26 November that the *Pall Mall* flew Tory colours from its mast: henceforth it made a practice of speaking of 'we . . . who are Unionist' (13 December). By then, it was common knowledge that its owner was W. Waldorf Astor, whose antecedents were American, not Polish. 'Why William Waldorf decided to enter journalism no one knows,' Lord Beaverbrook later minuted.[1] His motives are not at all difficult to deduce. Eager to cut a figure in his adopted homeland, he turned instinctively to newspaper ownership. A barony awaited him in 1916, and a viscountcy the next year. His eldest son, who succeeded first to his press holdings and then to his peerage, stood for Parliament as a Unionist in the general election of January 1910, but entered as a Conservative in December of that year. Kinloch Cooke quickly and quietly gave way to Henry Cust, a full-fledged Conservative, who sat for the Stamford division of Lincolnshire. As late as 5 November, Yates Thompson mistook Cust for the proprietor. Iwan-Müller became Cust's chief assistant, doubtless on Balfour's recommendation.

While the paper was turning the 'curve', Cook was collecting offers of pecuniary support from various Liberal stalwarts, all outraged by what had happened. With their assistance, added to the year's salary he received as severance pay (and, if necessary, a mortgage on his home), he might have made a bid for the *St James's* or perhaps begun a new weekly. Instead, with backing from Newnes, whom one might have thought to have had his fill of former *Pall Mall* editors, he proceeded to launch a third *Gazette*, the *Westminster*. The core of his old staff migrated with him. Printed on green-tinted stock to ease the eyesight of 'persons going home in badly-lighted railway carriages, omnibuses, &c.', it was nicknamed 'the pea-green incorruptible' by *Punch*. The innovation did not command universal approval. 'Green is an unlucky colour, as Mr Parnell always said,' warned H. M. Hyndman; and Gladstone,

---

[1] Beaverbrook Papers C/15.

feeling his age, remarked that 'what he suffers from in reading is want of light, and the violent contrast between black and white suits him best'. Indeed 'a speedy re-incarnation', the newest *Gazette* appeared on 30 January 1893. Discounting Brett's opinion that the contents would hardly matter, as 'everybody will buy it from sheer curiosity', the paper went out of its way to praise 'the sincere and courageous line' taken up by Gladstone's government, which it deemed 'the bounden duty of every Liberal journalist to give the most cordial support'. That its own support 'will at the same time be independent goes without saying; for no other kind of support is possible to an honest man, or acceptable to a wise one'.[1]

As a concept, support was more easily invoked than defined. Politicians as well as journalists found it convenient to equivocate as to the mutual obligations it entailed. Morley, who regarded the reconversion of the *Pall Mall* to Toryism 'as a most disagreeable and damaging blow', did not 'doubt ... that a new paper on the lines of the *P.M.G.* would certainly receive all the support that is practicable from the Liberal party and its chief men'. Rosebery was, at once, no less encouraging and no less circumspect, 'propounding ... the value of independent support'. What did either of them mean in actual terms? By the same token, what did Cook take them to mean? He demurred when Bryce contended that 'it is only human nature to say anybody can support us when right: we want somebody to do so when wrong'. Yet Bryce had a point, and Cook had only a platitude.[2]

How far could a newspaper assert its independence without losing its cordiality, denying its support, or exacerbating intra-party tensions? Cook, who had recently scorned Maxse's suggestion that he might continue to write for the *Pall Mall* on 'neutral subjects', would have been hard pressed to answer. Greenwood, writing in the *Westminster* on 1 February, repeated his well-rehearsed argument that the journalist's proper 'place is on a stage apart, between the official leaders of his party and the mass of those whose appointed generals they are'. In his case, which was hardly inspirational, this was definitely more an afterthought than a principle. In Cook's, it was idealism carried to the point of wishful thinking. When O'Connor, who was nobody's cat's-paw, heard such rhetoric, he had 'to reply that ... I have found that independence was a euphemism for personal vanity, personal interest, or mere crankiness of temper and opinion', whether it was an editor or a politician 'who assumes to himself the ... adjective'. F. Carruthers Gould, the brilliant cartoonist who accompanied Cook from the *Pall Mall* to the *Westminster*, was more realistic. 'I have never, since I devoted my pencil and pen to the service of the party, thought it any part of my duty to attack my own side,' he stated.

[1] Hyndman to Cook, 6 February 1893, and Brett to Cook, 12 January 1893, Cook Papers; West to Cook, 31 January 1893, quoted in Mills, *Cook*, p. 134.
[2] Morley to Cook, 26 October 1892, and Cook's diary, 25 October 1892, and 16 January 1893, Cook Papers.

'When my Conservative friends have asked me, "Why don't you sometimes caricature your own people?" I have replied "That's *your* work, not mine!"'[1]

To emphasize his 'absolute discretion' over the *Westminster*, Cook extracted the assurance that, in some unforeseen circumstance, he 'could turn it into a Tory organ'. Yet despite his determination that the paper was not 'to be a "mere *D[aily] N[ews]*"' (which he disdained as a party mouthpiece, but which he nevertheless left the *Westminster* to edit in 1895), he accepted Newnes's judgment that 'our success will depend on getting a good "send-off" from some of the party leaders', and accordingly solicited Rosebery's endorsement. Nor did his scruples deter him from hastening to choose a name for the new journal in time for the government whip to inscribe it on the list for official advertisements 'instead of [the] *Pall Mall*'. Quite simply, Cook wanted to have his cake and to eat it, too. He had in mind a model that, at least in the context of that day, was nearly as fanciful as the one constructed by Maxse, who

> wish[ed] the experiment could be tried of having a journal half Radical & half Unionist. I would give the right hand column to the one party under its own editor and the left hand column to the other for controversy, & correspondence under another one. Literature & news would be superintended by a third neutral editor.

An independent Liberal paper, like an independent Unionist one, was a contradiction in terms, which future generations would attempt to resolve.[2]

* * *

Had there been the remotest possibility that Cook's independence might lead him and the *Westminster Gazette* into the Tory camp, Newnes would not have dared to equip him with such sweeping guarantees. A lifelong Liberal, whose parliamentary career spanned a quarter century, Newnes was rewarded in 1895 with the baronetcy that Yates Thompson had coveted. His was one of the many honours dispensed to persons connected in various capacities with the press, although 'political services' was the usual euphemism. Salisbury had already baroneted Borthwick, whom Disraeli had previously knighted; in 1895, he raised him to the peerage as Baron Glenesk for having 'rendered such long and valuable services to the Conservative party'. Unable to bring himself to make specific reference to the *Morning Post*, not his favourite paper, Salisbury confessed to Devonshire that he was 'only constitutionally responsible' for this ennoblement: Borthwick 'has great merits but his most efficient merit for this purpose is that the Queen is very fond of him. She pressed me hard in 1892, but there was not room.' That year, Salisbury had conferred a baronetcy

---

[1] Greenwood to Cook, 'Tuesday' [January 1893], Cook Papers; O'Connor, 'The New Journalism,' *New Review*, i (1889), 433; F. C. Gould, draft autobiography.

[2] Mills, *Cook*, p. 127; Cook to Rosebery, 31 October 1892, Rosebery Papers, Vol. 10,090, f. 230; Newnes to Cook, 27 December 1892, and Maxse to Cook, 25 October 1892, Cook Papers.

on George Armstrong of the *Globe* and a barony on Hucks Gibbs, who had kept the *St James's Gazette* afloat. The previous year, however, there had been an empty slot on Salisbury's honours list. Coleridge Kennard of the *Evening News* died on Christmas Day, a week before his 'excellent claims' could be met.[1]

Gladstone, in turn, was 'constitutionally responsible' for obtaining a baronetcy for Edward Lawson, whom Balfour made Baron Burnham in 1903. Among the members of the *Star* directorate, Isaac Holden became a baronet in 1893, and Colman reportedly refused a comparable distinction. Wemyss Reid, the recipient of a knighthood in 1894, urged Herbert Gladstone to consider Brunner for a baronetcy: 'He has done much – very much – as you are probably aware for ... Liberalism in the Press, and has I imagine sunk quite £20,000 in this way without the slightest thought of reward.' Brunner, who declined for fear that 'people would imagine he had been bought', accepted a baronetcy from Rosebery three years later, in company with Newnes. Rosebery was also responsible for knighting William Howard Russell in belated recognition of his dispatches from the Crimea. Gladstone, seemingly making up for lost time, recommended knighthoods in 1893 for Edward Russell of the *Liverpool Daily Post*, John Leng of the *Dundee Advertiser* (whose Tory brother had been made a Jubilee knight), and Hugh Gilzean Reid of the *Northern Daily Telegraph* and assorted other properties. Like Holden, Brunner, and Newnes (or Borthwick, Gibbs, Armstrong, and Kennard on the other side), each of these men was serving – or had served, however briefly – in Parliament, thus making it difficult to say that his 'political services' were strictly journalistic. But John Robinson, knighted in the same batch, was undoubtedly honoured for his newspaper work; and, unlike Wemyss Reid and William Howard Russell, he did not have to wait until he retired to garner his laurels. Working journalists, who were neither MPs nor men of letters in the more dignified sense, remained exceptions to the rule. With due diffidence, Bunce declined the knighthood which Chamberlain sought to obtain for him in 1896. And Cooper, grateful for the 'honour which Lord Salisbury and the Duke of Devonshire propose to advise the Crown to bestow upon me' in the same year, told Lord Selborne (as Wolmer had become) that he entertained 'a great objection to those honours being accepted by men whose sole claim to them is that they are connected with more or less influential newspapers. That is my case.'[2]

The honours traffic added to the complications of politicians' dealings with the press. Editors and proprietors, perpetually jealous of one another, began

[1] Newnes to Rosebery, 28 December 1894, Rosebery Papers, Vol. 10,158, fol. 41; Lucas, *Glenesk*, p. 351; Salisbury to Devonshire, 4 October 1895, Devonshire Papers; Austin to Salisbury, 20 December 1890, and 2 January 1891, Salisbury Papers.

[2] Reid to H. Gladstone, 2 November 1892, Rosebery Papers, Vol. 10,157, fols. 147–48; Koss, *Brunner*, pp. 176–77; Bunce to Chamberlain, 12 April 1896, Chamberlain Papers; Cooper to Selborne, 13 February 1896, Selborne Papers; *History of The Times*, III, 782.

to importune for new and greater dignities. Veterans like Escott, Sala, and Greenwood pleaded pathetically for civil list pensions. And, as always, newspapers competed for special concessions, including financial aid which they seldom received. Political leaders were themselves largely to blame. Notoriously incapable of abiding by their self-denying ordinances, they invited solicitations. Unwilling to run the risk of alienating potential support, much less of forfeiting existing support, they dangled incentives which journalists grasped out of hope or frustration.

In 1888, four years after he had founded the first students' representative council at the University of Edinburgh, Robert Fitzroy Bell invited Balfour to assist a new magazine for young Conservatives. 'I am very little qualified to give an opinion upon Press undertakings,' replied Balfour, who admitted 'that my own experience of such has been uniformly unfortunate as I have lost more money than I care to think of without I fear doing much good'. As a gesture, however, he was 'glad to become a contributor to the extent of six copies a week'. Bell was more easily satisfied than Austin, to whom Balfour soon afterwards sent a cheque for an undisclosed amount 'on account of the *N[ational [R]eview]*'. That was more than he was prepared to do for the *Union*, which he did not consider 'of the slightest use'; its absorption by Ashmead Bartlett's *England*, which followed, seemed to him 'to be an excellent solution of the difficulty'. That Middleton had misunderstood Balfour to advise that the *Union* 'should be financed' was a tacit acknowledgment of the availability of party funds for this purpose. It was Middleton's policy to deny that any such funds existed. Forwarding to Salisbury the prospectus for the *Crewe and Nantwich Advertiser*, designed to advance 'Constitutional principles' throughout Cheshire, Middleton commented: 'The proposed newspaper will be of great advantage to our Party, but it is of course a private speculation. Your refusal might be couched in gentle terms.' More to Middleton's liking was the notification he received from Kennard's solicitor in May 1890 that, for the first time, the *Evening News* 'is going to pay interest on the preference shares at the end of the year!' That, in itself, warranted a baronetcy for Kennard, who had carried on the paper with 'energy & zeal' and 'without getting a single shilling from the party'.[1]

The Liberal Unionists, here as elsewhere, took their cue from the Conservatives. In 1888, their total expenditure on publications, including newspaper subsidies, was 'between 8 & 9 thousand', a sum that Wolmer thought 'might be profitably increased to 10'. Even so, the executive committee of the Liberal Unionist Association had to turn down a request from the *Lynn News* owing to 'serious liabilities on account of the provincial Press'. In 1890–91, the *Man-*

---

[1] Balfour to Bell, 28 June 1888, Balfour to Austin, 4 February 1889, and Balfour to Akers-Douglas, 20 January 1890 (letterbook copies), Balfour Papers; W. Hargreaves to Salisbury, 25 February 1890 (with Middleton's comments) and Bernard Parker to Middleton, 16 May 1890, Salisbury Papers (Christ Church).

chester Examiner stretched their resources to the utmost. Walter Morrison, the Liberal Unionist standard-bearer in the Skipton division of Yorkshire, heard from Frank Hill in 1893 that the *Leeds Mercury* was on the market. The asking price of £80,000 did not 'seem excessive', as its income was estimated 'to be some £40,000 a year, which seems very high indeed for a Provincial newspaper'. But, on closer inspection, the paper was seen 'to be going downhill' and its price 'exorbitant'. The Manchester mistake was not repeated at Leeds.[1]

Unionism, in either of its varieties, appeared to have lost its momentum in the press. 'It requires great skill & educated power to bring home to the masses why they should vote for our people,' Montagu Burrows, a local Tory activist, wrote to W.H. Smith after the Conservatives had suffered 'a municipal defeat' at Oxford in 1889. 'Yet the skill & educated power seem to be on the Radical side,' he noted. 'The vulgar must be got at in their own way. How few Conservatives understand that way.' J.R. Oswald preached the same sermon when the National Union met at Liverpool a year later: 'It is not because the working classes are disposed to look askance at Conservatism that they are not all with you,' he told his fellow delegates; 'it is because of the neglect of the duty of going amongst them in order to toast your toes and read your *Daily Telegraph* or *Standard*.' With greater weight, if less cogency, Churchill levelled the same accusations at a Garrick Club dinner on 1 March 1890. To an audience that included Robinson and Lawson, he prophesied that the Liberals would 'sweep the country' at the next elections as a consequence of having nurtured the local press. 'With mischief in my mind', Robinson 'asked him if he knew what had become of a certain Paddington paper which had been started to represent Tory democracy'. (Robinson 'knew it had been carried on with his money'.) Churchill said, 'after looking at me and laughing, that it was dead'.[2]

An outcast from his party, but still a force to be reckoned with, Churchill continued to intrigue with and through the press. Before his departure for Africa on a tour subsidized by the *Daily Graphic* to the tune of £2,200 for twenty articles, he offered the *Morning Post* the text of the memorandum he had written against the Parnell commission in 1888. 'I shall write a short letter to the *M.P.* explaining that I publish it as an answer to the accusation of disloyalty to the party and of stabbing the Govt. in the back,' he promised Borthwick, who seized the opportunity. In every way, Churchill's collaboration with the *Daily Graphic* proved more profitable. 'Randolph's philippic has fallen flatter than the proverbial pancake,' Iwan-Müller informed Balfour. Churchill could not be controlled, but perhaps something

[1] Wolmer to Hartington, 6 December 1888, and Morrison to Devonshire, 11 May and 6 November 1893, Devonshire Papers; Hartington to Wolmer, 1 December 1889, Selborne Papers.
[2] Burrows to Smith, 16 November 1889, Hambleden Papers; National Union minutes, 18 November 1890; Robinson's diary, quoted in Robinson, *Fifty Years*, pp. 122–23.

could be done to restrain his newspaper accomplices. The following September, Sir William Hardman died, having edited the *Morning Post* for eighteen years. 'His services to the Constitutional Party ... only terminated with his life,' wrote his obituarist on the 13th. Balfour schemed to install Iwan-Müller. 'So far as I am personally concerned,' he wrote to Borthwick, 'I should be very sorry to see him go to London. At the same time, I think he is far too good a man to be wasted in the Provinces.' (For his part, Iwan-Müller declared '*viva voce*' that he was 'not too anxious to remain in Manchester'.) Borthwick, already convinced that he was being 'damnably used' by the party chiefs, saw through this Trojan-horse strategy. Instead he chose A. K. Moore, a member of his staff since 1881; and, when Moore died in 1895, W. Algernon Locker was brought from the *Globe* to succeed him.[1]

The *Morning Post*, never securely fastened, was not the only London paper to slip from the official Tory net. Captain Armstrong of the *Globe* was stricken by a 'long illness'. His wife wrote to tell W. H. Smith that 'our eldest boy (the one who married last June)' had taken 'his father's place at the *Globe* in everything except the Editorial work, and is doing extremely well'. But the paper was losing circulation and authority. The *Standard*, which Mudford continued to edit until his retirement at the turn of the century, was increasingly conducted by Byron Curtis, a survivor from Johnstone's régime, whom Austin found distressingly weak. On 11 October 1891, Austin wrote – as directed – 'an article strongly urging that Arthur Balfour should be made Leader of the House of Commons', but Curtis 'telegraphed that Mudford is away, & that he dared not' print it without consultation. Lawson and Buckle badgered Schomberg McDonnell, Salisbury's new principal private secretary, on the same question. McDonnell was 'rather afraid' that Buckle 'may begin to discuss the alternatives in *The Times*. If he does, mischief will follow', and he therefore proposed 'asking him & Mr Lawson to abstain from inordinate conjecture for the next few days'. Iwan-Müller, always more considerate, withheld his congratulations until the official announcement, meanwhile making certain that the *Manchester Courier* 'has *not* advocated your appointment. I am sure you will appreciate the reason,' he told Balfour; 'so many know now that I have the honour of your friendship that I am very jealous of any suspicion that you "require" me in your interests – jealous of course not for my sake but for yours.' In reply, Balfour could 'only wish to repeat the thanks which I have before conveyed to you for your kind estimate of my efforts for our common Party'.[2]

The Times gave particular cause for anxiety. Parnell's melodramatic death

[1] Churchill to Borthwick, 14 March 1890, quoted in Lucas, *Glenesk*, p. 329; Iwan-Müller to Balfour, 10 April 1890, and undated letter ['ansd. 1.1.91'], Balfour to Borthwick, 22 September 1890 (letterbook copy), Balfour Papers; Borthwick to Churchill, 15 August [1892?], Churchill Papers.
[2] Mrs Alice Armstrong to Smith, 18 January [1891?], and Austin to Smith, 11 July 1888, Hambleden Papers; Austin to Salisbury, 12 October 1891, and McDonnell to Salisbury, 7 October

in 1891 relieved the Liberals of an embarrassment and perhaps removed other obstacles. Rosebery, a rising star on the Liberal horizon, was already a favourite in Printing House Square. 'Even though you belabour *The Times* & the Unionists, I shall warmly welcome your reappearance,' Buckle wrote to him, after Lady Rosebery's death. With his Foreign Office experience, Rosebery helped Buckle to select correspondents to send to Vienna and Berlin. In the autumn of 1891, it was difficult to gauge the strength, and sometimes the direction, of *The Times*'s commitment. On 21 October, Buckle called on Salisbury to share the findings of 'his Commissioner, who is preparing a series of articles on the political organisation of London & the Provinces'. The next day, C. F. Moberly Bell, who had succeeded MacDonald as general manager, wrote to Rosebery: 'You have proved so good a friend to the paper that I am going to tell you something which I think will please you', namely the appointment of Sir Donald Mackenzie Wallace as foreign assistant editor, 'a sort of Secretary of State for Foreign Affairs to Buckle'. Bell was confident that Rosebery could approve of this change in what he curiously described as 'an old Conservative institution (though *Liberal paper*!!) like *The Times*'. Whatever he meant, Wallace's professional expertise made it unnecessary for the paper to double-check its foreign correspondents' reports with Whitehall, as LeSage of the *Telegraph* habitually did.[1]

The Liberals, by contrast, seemed to be recovering a degree of their former vitality. By the early '90s, they had established newspapers to repair much of the provincial and Scottish damage they sustained in 1886. D. H. Saunders earned praise from Herbert Gladstone for the Dundee *People's Journal*, and undeservedly from Sir Henry Campbell-Bannerman for the *Democrat*, 'one of the clearest & straightest hitters I know'. In fact, D. H. Saunders, whose son George was successively Berlin correspondent for the *Morning Post* and *The Times*, bore no responsibility for the *Democrat*. That weekly, variously associated with the Irish Land League and Henry George's 'single-tax' movement, was supported by William Saunders, uncle to the Spender brothers, who had founded the *Western Morning News* at Plymouth, the *Eastern Morning News* at Hull, and the Central Press Agency. Campbell-Bannerman's confusion was understandable, but nonetheless revealing. H. J. Wilson helped to save the *Sheffield Independent* from extinction; and the *Leeds Mercury*, weakened by Reid's departure in 1889, limped along. In 1890, with the advent of A. E. Fletcher to its editorship, the *Daily Chronicle* returned to the Gladstonian fold. Two years later, the halfpenny *Morning Leader* was begun as a companion to the evening *Star*. F. W. Wilson, Colman's partner at Norwich, was managing director, and Ernest Parke was editor until

1891, Salisbury Papers; Iwan-Müller to Balfour, 11 October 1891, and Balfour to Iwan-Müller, 17 October 1891 (letterbook copy), Balfour Papers.

[1] Buckle to Rosebery, 7 May 1891, and Bell to Rosebery, 22 October 1891, Rosebery Papers, Vol. 10,089, fols. 29, 82–83; memorandum by McDonnell, 21 October 1891, Salisbury Papers.

the paper's amalgamation with the *Daily News* in 1912. Just as the *Star* was most popular for its racing tips, the *Morning Leader* specialized in cricket news. Yet it proved more politically useful and certainly more durable than its new halfpenny Unionist rival, the *Morning*, which is remembered (if at all) for having brought Kennedy Jones to Fleet Street. Within six months, Chester Ives, its Anglo-American proprietor, had lost £30,000, and the property then became a shuttlecock between syndicates of Liberals and Conservatives, who changed its name to the *London Morning* (1898) and the *Morning Herald.* (1899), before merging it in 1900 with the *Daily Express*.[1]

By the start of 1892, Salisbury's second government stood on its last legs, its parliamentary majority nearly halved through by-election defeats and defections. Fearful of Churchill, who had returned bold and bearded from Africa, Salisbury was reduced to deputing McDonnell to sound out Borthwick. Under these uneasy conditions, newspapermen functioned as political monitors. Chamberlain felt compelled to refute publicly suggestions in the *Standard* and *The Times* that he might accept 'a position of great reponsibility' in order to prop up the beleaguered administration. Balfour received Stead at a series of late-morning breakfasts, and made a special effort to cultivate Cooper. The question that confronted the ministerialists was not whether to resign, but when. 'I think your summary of the pros and cons quite sound so far as it goes, and not far from complete,' Balfour wrote to Iwan-Müller on 2 May. Its logic would not have persuaded Churchill, who primed the *Morning Post* with arguments in favour of delay. On 13 June, that paper railed against the dissolution as a sell-out to 'Mr Labouchere and his friends [who] are eager for the Election not because they are strong to-day, but because they will be weaker to-morrow'. Its only consolation was Churchill's unopposed return at Paddington: 'Friends of the Union may be excused for regarding the bloodless victory of so distinguished a member of the Conservative Party as auguring well for the future' (2 July).[2]

But the early result at Paddington was no augury at all. Gladstone emerged from the fray with a working majority of forty. 'Not enough' by his own standards, it would have inspired envy on the part of some of his twentieth-century successors. He must have been pleased by the smooth performance of the Liberal press. It was probably during the campaign, or in its aftermath, that he spent a Sunday afternoon with Henry Norman of the *Pall Mall Gazette*.

[1] H. Gladstone to Saunders, 30 July 1889, and Campbell-Bannerman to Saunders, 8 February 1889, Saunders Papers; *History of The Times*, III, 100–101, 119; C. A. Barker, *Henry George* (London, 1955), p. 410; obituary of D. H. Saunders, *Dundee Advertiser*, 25 Feb. 1904; obituary of William Saunders, *The Times*, 2 May 1895.

[2] Memorandum by McDonnell, 23 January 1892, Salisbury Papers; memorandum by Chamberlain for a Liberal Unionist meeting on 8 February 1892, quoted in Garvin, *Chamberlain*, II, 58; Balfour to Stead, 8 March and 26 April 1892, Balfour to Iwan-Müller, 2 May 1892, Balfour to Cooper, 16 May 1892, and Balfour to McDonnell, 16 May 1892 (letterbook copies), Balfour Papers; Borthwick to Churchill [June 1892], Churchill Papers (with reference to an article entitled 'Why Resign?' which Borthwick accepted for publication).

'Mr Gladstone received me with very great kindness,' Norman told Herbert Gladstone, who had fixed the interview,

> & said to me much that is of the highest interest & importance at the present moment, & that will have the widest circulation. Every provincial Liberal paper will copy it from the *P.M.G.* tomorrow.
>
> Mr Gladstone understood distinctly that I asked for his views for publication, & specifically indicated certain things he told me as being . . . made privately & not to be included in anything I might write.

During its few remaining months under Liberal auspices, the *Pall Mall* gave resolute service. On 13 August, Cook called Gladstone's attention to a report in that morning's *Daily Telegraph* to the effect that Rosebery had refused office in the new administration. He requested 'any information for my private guidance' from Gladstone, who could only 'say . . . that the *D.T.* appears to know what I do not'. That was enough for the *Pall Mall* to be able to scoff at the conjecture. Buckle, who took the rumour more seriously, implored Rosebery not to retire from public life: 'It seems to me that if ever a man had a career marked plainly upon him by duty, you have.' Dreading the prospect of a return to the isolationist policies of the early '80s, he informed Rosebery

> as a fact . . . that Stead (& he stands for many others) would have been very lukewarm in this election did he not feel sure that you were to return to the F.O. He voted, & many others did, for a continuous foreign policy, *and* Home Rule.

Buckle's revelations about Stead were as nothing compared with his own confession.[1]

Among the losers, there were the usual recriminations. 'Lord S. does not understand the value of the H. of C. nor the feelings of the constituencies,' grumbled Borthwick. 'These people cannot possibly stay in,' Lawson assured Salisbury rather prematurely on 19 August. 'Already there are ominous growls. . . . Half the ministry is jealous of the other half: nobody is satisfied with the distribution of places.' According to Lawson, 'Professor Stuart is beginning hostilities in the *Star*, because he is in the cold'. Yet it is doubtful that Stuart, an archetypal backbencher, either seriously expected a ministerial post or had the capacity to inflict harm. One could not say the same of Labouchere, who had given an explosive interview to J. H. Dalziel, the proprietor of *Reynolds's News* and a Liberal MP since March. For Salisbury's amusement, Lawson enclosed a transcript 'which, of course, I cannot use: but which is very informing'. Vetoed by the Queen as a revenge for his attacks on the royal

---

[1] Norman to H. Gladstone, 'Sunday afternoon' [1892], Viscount Gladstone papers, Add MSS. 46,042, fol. 104; Cook to Gladstone, 13 August 1892, Gladstone Papers, Add MSS. 44,515, fols. 139–40 (with Gladstone's note); Buckle to Rosebery, 14 August 1892, Rosebery Papers, Vol. 10,090, fols. 123 ff.

family in *Truth*, 'Labby' was excluded from office. As if to salt his wounds, Arnold Morley, another proprietor of the *Daily News*, was named Postmaster-General. Wemyss Reid confirmed that Labouchere was 'bitterly incensed' and intent on stirring up trouble. 'But I have ascertained that he wants one thing (a big thing) and that if he could get it he would give up *Truth*, his seat in Parliament and his political career.' That prize, the ambassadorship in Washington, was also denied him. It was at this point, and not (as he afterwards maintained) later in the decade, that Labouchere ended his connection with the *Daily News*.[1]

After the elections, various journals changed hands or were abandoned. Sowler was now free to snuff out the *Manchester Examiner*, and Yates Thompson could sell the *Pall Mall Gazette* with a relatively clear conscience. In most cases, party leaders had anticipated these changes as matters of course. Middleton, for example, had considered it 'quite unnecessary' for Salisbury to subscribe out of pocket or party funds to the *St Stephen's Review*: 'The paper ... will certainly run to the election', and that was his primary concern. On the same grounds, Balfour had denied his commendation to *England*. Many of the casualties were newcomers, which lost their *raison d'être* after the campaign. The *Cambridge Daily Independent Press*, an evening paper started in January 1892, published its last number on 21 July. 'Experience has shown,' the editor explained,

> that apart from the excitement of an election, there is not sufficient scope in this district for such a paper as we aimed at supplying. When politics are quiet, sporting news is the thing chiefly in demand, and that is not a line in which we have any great ambition to excel.

Sell's Dictionary quoted his statement in a lengthy catalogue of closures and amalgamations.[2]

Before the year was out, there were rumblings that Passmore Edwards was again contemplating the sale of the *Echo*, which might then 'go back to its original politics'. Edward Marjoribanks (later Lord Tweedmouth), the Liberal whip, encouraged Loulou Harcourt to explore this possibility, possibly with assistance from Dalziel ('who has considerable knowledge of the press world & who can be trusted'), instead of attempting to 'start a new enterprise, especially with Newnes's venture & the probability that T. P. will break out himself in another evening paper when he is free to do so'. Furthermore, Marjoribanks wished to 'be very cautious about giving official encouragement to a

---

[1] Borthwick to Akers-Douglas, 15 August 1892, quoted in Chilston, *Chief Whip*, p. 173; Lawson to Salisbury, 19 August 1892, Salisbury Papers; Reid to Morley, 23 September 1892 (copy), Rosebery Papers, Vol. 10,041, fol. 58; Robinson, *Fifty Years*, p. 377; *also see* P. Guedalla, *The Queen and Mr Gladstone* (London, 1933), II, 437–40.

[2] M. P. Shorrock to Salisbury, 11 June 1892 (with Middleton's comments), Salisbury Papers (Christ Church); Balfour to A. Bosenthal, 30 December 1891 (letterbook copy), Balfour Papers; *Sells* (1893).

new rival to the *Star*. Colman and Stuart are already sufficiently ill disposed & this would be the last straw.' In the event, Harcourt and his friends did nothing, and Edwards kept control of the *Echo* for five more years. He could not bear to part with the paper, which had become his persona, though for 'many years he . . . devoted the whole of the profits he derived from it, and more, too, to erecting drinking fountains, or building hospitals, or public libraries, or founding convalescent homes', or endowing other charitable works. 'In establishing and sustaining the *Echo*,' Edwards told an audience in the summer of 1893, 'he was realising a long-cherished dream': it 'consisted of producing a paper devoted to the public good, . . . not for individual gain or sectional advantage, but for the benefit of the people'. This humanitarian spirit, once expressed through party affiliations, now seemed to him incompatible with them.[1]

T. P. O'Connor's 'break-out', the *Sun*, could be better described as his strait-jacket. Liberal hopes rested with the *Westminster Gazette* and, to a lesser extent, with *London*, a weekly journal of civic affairs begun in February 1893 by Robert Donald, with backing from the London Reform Union and infusions of capital from Frank Lloyd. Like Newnes and Dalziel, Lloyd made his fortune from the mass circulation 'popular' press, but craved the influence and respectability that, as yet, stood in inverse ratio to sales figures. Relatively speaking, the *Westminster* was no more successful than *London* as a commercial venture. Nevertheless, as a political organ it was peerless. Newnes's initial outlay was approximately £100,000, including the construction and equipment of premises for production. 'During the fifteen years that he was proprietor he was out of pocket in sums varying from £5,000 to £10,000 per annum,' wrote J. A. Spender, who replaced Cook as editor in 1895. With a circulation that seldom exceeded 25,000 copies, the paper 'in all probability . . . had about 100,000 readers per night'. But quality mattered more than quantity, as much in terms of readership as in contents. Like the other *Gazettes*, the *Westminster* was 'appealing to a select audience of politically instructed readers, who in those days were the makers of opinion, and from whom an immense influence radiates outwards to the multitude'. This was all quite different for Newnes. While *Tit-Bits*, the cornerstone of his press empire, ran treasure hunts, the *Westminster* awarded prizes for Greek and Latin verse. Newnes gave advice on type-faces and page layout, but, to Spender's recollection, 'never at any time asked himself how a particular line of policy would affect the business prospects of his paper'. Cook may have recalled otherwise from the early days, when Newnes, dismayed by the 'bad prospects' of the *Westminster*, criticized the monotony of the correpondence columns, and described 'how he had invented letters for *Tit-Bits*'.[2]

---

[1] Marjoribanks to L. Harcourt, 9 and 14 December 1892, Viscount Harcourt Papers; speech by Edwards, quoted in the *Journalist* (July 1893).
[2] Taylor, *Robert Donald*, p. 44–45; Spender, *Life, Journalism and Politics*, II, 135–38; Hulda

The Liberal leaders found the *Westminster* scintillating enough, and their approval was Newnes's reward. Inevitably, they compared it with the *Pall Mall*. Gladstone, early in his fourth administration, met Cook at a dinner party given by G. W. E. Russell, the newly elected MP for Bedfordshire North: 'I have not troubled much,' he said, 'to look at the *P.M.G.* lately.' Shaw-Lefevre, a member of Gladstone's Cabinet, congratulated Cook on the appearance of the *Westminster*. 'The *P.M.G.* has already sunk to a dullness which makes the reading of it almost impossible,' he added. With a new editor and a largely untried staff, the *Pall Mall* faltered for a time. Cust, unlike Cook, was contractually 'bound by *any instructions* and *directions* which may be given him by the proprietor, whose rights of *controlling the policy*' were underscored in his own hand. Before taking up his duties, Cust 'felt it only right to consult with Lord Salisbury and Mr Balfour', who 'both entirely agreed' that he 'could not be a mere Party hack but that, while adhering to the main principles of Conservatism, I should seek to retain the right of independent criticism and speak freely my mind even when adverse to themselves as regards the conduct of affairs'. Balfour, whom Cust knew as a fellow member of the Souls, reportedly welcomed this declaration of independence with the injudicious remark that 'such papers as the *St James's Gazette* or the *Standard* are . . . of no earthly value to the party in the way of making opinion, as their criticisms are a foregone conclusion'. The parlance of the day required no less, and Balfour presumably knew how little it meant. As Cust was humbly to assure Astor: 'In all my conversations with the Party leaders I have always represented myself as your editor.' His dilemma warrants investigation.[1]

Dividing his working hours between Northumberland Street and Westminster, which Cook thought beyond the capacity of any man, 'Harry' Cust also led a strenuous social life. Very much the man about town, he populated some of the most illustrious nurseries with his illegitimate offspring, who immortalized his 'dashing' profile. These nocturnal adventures met with strong disapproval from Astor, who did not mind if his MP-editor burnt his candle at both ends, but disliked the sparks in between. On 16 December 1893, he took up Cust's 'good suggestion that I should call "any morning at 7.30 at the *Gazette* office, & see the busy morning's work commenced at that early hour"'. Predictably, Cust was not on hand to greet him, and he waited until 7.55 before leaving a note. 'You always get the better of me on so many points,' he twitted Cust, who could not have claimed the excuse of a late-night

Friedrichs, *Life of George Newnes* (London, 1911), p. 161; Cook's diary, 12 January and [n.d.] October 1894, Cook Papers. In the second entry, Cook reported that an accountant had told him that Newnes had thus far invested £45,000, of which £35,000 'was gone'.

[1] Cook's diary, n.d., quoted in Mills, *Cook*, p. 131; Shaw-Lefevre to Cook, 3 February 1893, Cook Papers; agreement of 12 November 1892 between Astor and Cust, and Cust's memorandum, n.d., quoted in Robertson Scott, *Life and Death of a Newspaper*, pp. 376–77.

sitting at the House, 'that it makes me merry to be able to score now & then.' It would have been less of a strain on Cust had 'that notorious criminal Sir Charles Dilke', as Wilfrid Scawen Blunt wrongly suspected, become the owner of the *Pall Mall*. President of the Crabbet Club, 'a little company of notable figures in the world of English politics and letters who came to Crabbet to play lawn-tennis and to talk', Blunt had looked to Cust to fulfil 'C.C.' principles by breaking with the 'dull respectability' of his predecessors, all 'marked offenders against the wholesome law of frivolity'. The strait-laced Astor saw to it that Cust did nothing of the sort.[1]

Astor's purse was seemingly bottomless, but his patience quickly wore thin. As early as February 1893, Stead, itching to return to daily journalism, proposed a debenture scheme to bid for the *Pall Mall* or, failing that, to start his *Penny Paper*, which eventually ran for five months in 1904. Brett discouraged him from seeking a partnership with Carnegie – 'Through *him* no good will come' – and urged him to 'write to Astor *straight* or else *see* him'. Stead and Astor would have made an even more incongruous pair. At least Cust had the right political views and, for better or worse, country-house manners. Despite his reputation as 'one of the prominent young men of the Tory party', he candidly admitted that 'inside the House I am of but little use, having no special knowledge & less power of speech. But,' he told Salisbury, 'my connection with the Press gives me facilities which I think might be turned to good account both for the party & the Country'. Professing himself 'very anxious to be of all the service I can in fighting the Home Rule Bill', which Gladstone had resuscitated, he proposed a series of articles which would appear 'first in the *Pall Mall Gazette*', then in the weekly *Pall Mall Budget*, and finally in 'a single convenient pamphlet of which I would, in addition to offering it for universal sale, distribute (say) 50,000 copies to clubs, institutes, associations, & wherever else it might be thought desirable, free of charge'. The idea commended itself to the party chiefs. Salisbury complied with a 'Home Rule Article' and later with a cheque for £105 to help offset the costs of the pamphlet. 'I wish & hope the other contributors to the *Pall Mall* articles on Home Rule will do likewise,' Middleton advised him. It was not, incidentally, unusual for the *Gazettes* to undertake pamphleteering: the *Westminster* reproduced its articles on 'The Peers versus the People', and one Liberal MP spoke to Newnes 'about taking some thousand copies'.[2]

Relations between the *Pall Mall* and the Conservatives were not always so harmonious. Although Iwan-Müller was hired as Cust's editorial assistant, Balfour had hesitated to approach Astor, whom he did not expect to be 'very

[1] Astor to Cust, 16 December 1893, and Blunt to Cust, 25 November 1892, Cust Papers; *DNB* (entry on Blunt); Max Egremont, *Balfour* (London, 1980), p. 113.

[2] Brett to Stead, 25 February and 18 June 1893, Stead Papers; L. Springfield, *Some Piquant People* (London, 1924), pp. 78–79; Cust to Salisbury, 20 February 1893, Salisbury Papers; Middleton to Salisbury, 5 June and 28 September 1893, Salisbury Papers (Christ Church); Newnes to Cook, 15 February 1894, Cook Papers.

amenable to such arguments that I can put before him'. On behalf of the Liberal Unionists, Balfour asked Cust's permission for 'a certain illustration which appeared in the *P.M.G.* to be issued by them (to the number I believe about a million) without any acknowledgement of the source from which it was taken'. He chaffed Cust, as he would never have dared to chaff Astor, that the Liberal Unionists apparently conceived of the *Pall Mall* as 'a journal so discredited in public estimation that on the rare occasion when it produces anything good its value would be destroyed in the eyes of the discriminating public if any suspicion of its origin were permitted to get abroad'. The contents of the paper were sacrosanct to Astor, who fancied himself something of a literary man and submitted vacuous paragraphs that Cust either disregarded or returned. Reprimanding his editor for indulging in 'attacks ... without my consent' on various mercantile and civic projects, Astor wrote from Cliveden on 18 March 1894:

> In future, I shall expect that anything I send to be printed – provided it be not obscene, or inciting to a breach of the peace – be immediately published, in either the *Gazette* or the *Budget*, as I may indicate, & without the slightest alteration.

Nor would he allow Cust to come between him and the staff:

> From my point of view, every one employed in the *Pall Mall* building is engaged for me, & paid by me to do my work. I therefore consider myself at liberty to talk with entire freedom to any one so employed about his occupation.

Before we condemn Astor for crude Yankee methods, we may reflect that Lawson and Borthwick behaved in much the same way, as had Labouchere and Yates Thompson, among others. Not every Fleet Street magnate was as self-effacing as Newnes, who was said to have kept his distance from the *Westminster* office lest anyone suspect that he was trying to interfere.[1]

Nevertheless, one must sympathize with Cust. Henry Leslie, who stayed on as manager after the Liberal exodus, paid tribute to him as 'the most brilliant editor in his time'. And the compositors esteemed him as ' a thorough English gentleman' (unlike Astor), who was 'in touch with us in a way that no other editor had been'. If Cust did not make his mark in journalism, it was at least in part because Astor did not permit him the latitude to do so. In February 1894, he was adopted to stand at the next election for North Manchester, having explained to his Lincolnshire constituents, who were dispersed over 156 villages, that he was finding it difficult to combine editorial and political work. When the election came in July 1895, he did not stand in either place, and was out of Parliament until 1900, when he won a seat at Bermondsey that was

[1] Balfour to Iwan-Müller, 8 August 1893, and Balfour to Cust, 9 September 1893 (letterbook copies), Balfour Papers; Astor to Cust, 18 March 1894, Cust Papers; Mills, *Cook*, p. 153.

swept away in the Liberal landslide of 1906. He was no more successful in other spheres. The heir to the Brownlow barony, which came with a seventeenth-century house attributed to Wren, he died – 'childless' – before he could inherit.[1]

For a time, Astor seemed to have mellowed, and Cust may have thought of giving up politics for journalism. On 31 January 1894, the *Pall Mall* broke the news that Gladstone, who was on holiday at Biarritz, had 'finally decided to resign office almost immediately'. Denied at first, this report was confirmed on 3 March, giving the *Pall Mall* the distinction of having made (in Garvin's words) 'one of the celebrated announcements of newspaper history'. Newnes was 'very sorry at [the] *P.M.G.*'s score', and complained to Cook that 'they might have tipped us'. After all, the *Westminster* was 'toiling and slaving' (and 'spending', too) 'for the party, & then [the] *P.M.G.* is able to look as if it knew better than we what is really going on'. Sir Algernon West told Cook that the *Pall Mall*'s source was probably 'some servant', but admitted that advance notice had been offered to *The Times*. Astor basked in the afterglow of this *coup*, and was further heartened by the paper's advertising receipts. Returning to London on a Saturday afternoon in August, he 'had the gratification of buying the last remaining copy of the *Budget*' at Paddington Station, and his 'pleasure . . . was greatly enhanced when I came to examine its pages'. Able to 'find no fault whatever', he gave credit to Cust for 'the vast improvement'. Promising 'to cooperate with you very vigorously through my supervision of the Managerial department', he anticipated that 'the year 1895 should open very auspiciously for us, & that we may come within sight of the greatest journalistic success ever accomplished in this country'.[2]

To the contrary, 1895 brought mounting tensions between editor and proprietor. Yates Thompson, who had been waiting for Newnes to tire of the *Westminster*, heard from George Smith in January that the '*P.M.G.* was now in the market': more modestly, he bought *London* for £500, retaining Donald's editorial services for £350. On 9 February, Astor instructed Cust that the *Pall Mall* was to come out 'distinctly & unequivocally on the side of the Moderates' in the London County Council elections, and with 'such antagonism to the Progressives as will show beyond peradventure where we stand'. Cust acceded to his wishes, but with less fervency than Astor would have liked. Nor did he oppose the death duties and estate taxes imposed by Harcourt's 1894 budget with sufficient truculence. Worst of all, Cust treated the United States with a flippancy which offended Astor's transatlantic loyalties. A leading article, 'Drink to me Olney with Thine Eyes', was intended as a pun on the name of the American Secretary of State; to Astor, a temperance advo-

---

[1] Leslie's recollection, quoted in Simonis, *Street of Ink*, p. 107; illuminated address from the 'chapel', *Pall Mall Gazette*, 8 February 1896, Cust Papers.
[2] Garvin, *Chamberlain*, II, 591; Cook's diary, 5 and 8 March 1894, Cook Papers; Astor to Cust, 28 August 1894, 9 February 1895, and 3 February 1896 (copy), Cust Papers.

cate, it carried still another, equally objectionable connotation. Early in 1896, 'confronted by a dangerous controversy between England and the United States in which I am deeply interested', he refused 'any longer [to] be responsible for the utterances of a paper over which I exercise only a nominal control'.[1]

The end came with lightning speed. On Saturday, 1 February, Cust 'went by appointment to see Astor at his office' on the Victoria Embankment. During the preceding week, the *Pall Mall* had religiously applauded Salisbury, Chamberlain, and Balfour, while it castigated Gladstone, Morley, Irish nationalists, and 'Kruger the Crude' of the Transvaal. 'Astor was most kind and affable,' Cust's wife set forth in a memorandum, 'discussing the latest improvements to the building..., and then going into the question of whether Harry was in person to represent the *P.M.G.* at the Tsar's coronation.' The conversation shifted to 'the American Crisis', whereupon Astor was provoked to announce

without any warning ... that he wished to make a change in the Editorial arrangements, and requested Harry and Iwan-Müller to resign immediately and leave on that day week. On being pressed, he admitted that not only had he from the very outset been consulted by Harry as to the line he wished taken, but that the conduct of the paper had throughout been faultless. When pressed for further reasons, he fell back on the Harcourt death duties, but again had to admit that his instructions had been fully carried out....

Harry now left on the understanding that he was to think it over and give his answer on Monday, when they were to meet again. Not having been able to see Arthur Balfour, as he wished, he wrote to ask for a day's delay before settling such a serious matter. But he received a letter in reply clinching it: recapitulating all the points that had already been disproved and asking for immediate resignations. After consultation with A. J. B. and others, Harry and Müller wrote refusing to resign on such flimsy pretexts, and received next day the formal notice to quit. On the very same day, the solicitor was sent at the luncheon hour – when it has always been an understood thing that the whole of the editorial staff was out – and told all the people in the Office; – so that it became of course irrevocable and known all over journalistic London. The whole of the Office resigned at once! though of course Harry made them retract for the sake of their daily bread.

On Monday, the 3rd, the *Pall Mall* gave no sign to its readers of these internal disturbances. 'Really some one will have to muzzle Mr Gladstone,' it stated. But it was Cust who was being muzzled. On the 8th, he inserted a notice that he would 'not be responsible for any opinions that may appear ... after today', and that 'private letters' should be addressed to him at the Carlton Club.

[1] Cook's diary, 9 September 1893 and 26 January 1895, Cook Papers; Astor to Cust, 9 February 1895, and 3 February 1896 (copy), Cust Papers.

Sir Douglas Straight, a former MP and pensioned jurist, returned to journalism to take his place.[1]

The *habitués* of Clubland took these editorial dislocations in their stride. In response to members' enquiries, the general committee of the New University Club stated on 2 May 1893 that subscriptions to the *Pall Mall* and *St James's* 'have not been withdrawn in favour of the *Westminster Gazette*, but that paper is delivered earlier than the others'; on 14 April 1896 and again on 4 August 1896, the club secretary was obliged 'to express regret & explain' that delivery of the *St James's* was unpardonably late. At the Reform Club, where one might have expected a more partisan reaction, it was resolved on 6 March 1894 that one copy each of the *Pall Mall*, the *St James's*, and the first edition of the *Globe* should be discontinued; but, far from betokening a purge of Tory journals, the library committee ordered 'that 3 copies of the 6th edition of the *Globe* be taken in place thereof' for its racing results. It was further decided to replace the defunct *Manchester Examiner* with the Conservative *Manchester Courier*, and the *Birmingham Daily Argus* with the *Liverpool Courier*, owned by J. A. Willox, the Tory MP for Everton. If only in its newspaper patronage, the Reform was becoming less partisan.

To those outside this 'select audience of politically instructed readers', as J. A. Spender called it, the competition among the three *Gazettes* was remote and inconsequential. Changes in the conduct of the *Star* or the *Echo* or the *Daily Chronicle* would have registered a wider impact; and changes in *Lloyd's Weekly News* or *Reynolds's News* would have touched the lives of far more people, without necessarily affecting their political behaviour. In a speech at Brussels in 1891, Eleanor Marx contrasted the structure of the British press with that of Continental societies. That there were no British 'organs belonging to a definitely constituted working class party' was only to be expected, as such a party had yet to be constituted. 'Such papers as we have are either private property, run more or less as a speculation, ...or...newspapers, giving very valuable information, no doubt, but absolutely no theoretical teaching.' By her exacting standards, even *Justice*, published by Hyndman's Social Democratic Federation, was merely the organ of a sect, and did 'not reach the mass of the workers'.[2] She may have misconstrued the reasons, but few would quibble with her essential observation. Like Marxist critics of later generations, whether they have condemned the iniquities of the press in particular or the media in general, she was inclined to confuse cause and effect. By the time she delivered her report, British journal-

[1] N[ina] C[ust] to V.W. (undated copy), Cust Papers. These details are corroborated by Astor's two letters to Cust, 3 February 1896, and Cust's replies of 3 February (which repeats the description of the *Pall Mall*'s conduct on American affairs as 'faultless') and 7 February 1896, Cust Papers. The only discrepancy is that Iwan-Müller stayed on briefly, though 'the caprices of Astor give me pause'. Iwan-Müller to Balfour, 15 February 1896 (from the *Pall Mall Gazette* office), Balfour Papers.
[2] Quoted in Kapp, *Eleanor Marx*, II, 487.

ism was moving away from the concept of 'theoretical teaching', which belonged to the age of Cobden and Bright. The working classes, literate and largely enfranchised, were themselves basically responsible. Information, not didacticism, was what they wanted. In common with other political traditionalists, among whom she would have been loath to classify herself, Eleanor Marx postulated an outmoded definition of the political press.

*   *   *

Coined as an epithet in the 1880s, the New Journalism became a label to be worn with pride in the following decade. Affixed indiscriminately, it covered a multitude of sins, mostly of omission rather than commission. To recognize it as a trend was to promote a self-fulfilling prophecy. For the phenomenon existed by calling attention to itself. What was new about it was the extent to which it evoked comment, invited speculation, and engendered passions.

In the May 1887 number of the *Nineteenth Century*, Matthew Arnold dignified the New Journalism by the very act of deploring it. 'It has much to recommend it,' he conceded;

> it is full of ability, novelty, variety, sensation, sympathy, generous instincts; its one great fault is that it is *feather-brained*. It throws out assertions at a venture because it wishes them true; does not correct either them or itself, if they are false; and to get at the state of things as they truly are seems to feel no concern whatever.

Critics of the press had been saying as much for decades, if not for centuries. But changes in society, more profound than those in journalistic techniques, invested Arnold's critique with a sense of urgency. Needless to say, not everyone saw the development in such stark terms. Some did not see it at all. Arthur Otway, writing in the same number of the *Nineteenth Century*, contended that 'no proper comparison ... between the English and French press' was possible: 'The English press deals mostly with facts, and is eminently practical, whilst the French press is emotional, influencing the feelings rather than the reason of its readers.' Obviously, both Arnold and Otway could not have been correct. Yet neither was demonstrably wrong. Then, and long afterwards, the new and old journalisms existed side by side. What men saw depended upon where they looked.[1]

Stead, alternately revered and reviled as the progenitor of the New Journalism, gave currency to the appellation in a self-justifying essay, 'Government by Journalism', which he fittingly wrote for the *Contemporary Review* during his incarceration in Holloway. In this and other articles, published as a collection – *A Journalist on Journalism* – in 1891, Stead preached what he attempted

[1] Arnold, 'Up to Easter,' and Otway, 'Fallacies of the French Press,' *Nineteenth Century*, xxi (1887), 638, 725.

to practise. The vigour of his prose was nearly as remarkable as the audacity of his pretensions, which grew over the years. To put him into context is automatically to cut him down to size. More a popularizer than an innovator, he was known for a dramatic style of reporting, infused with social consciousness. Yet his missionary zeal was a carry-over from the *Northern Echo* in the 1870s, and his hubristic claims to political power were a throw-back to Henry Reeve in the 1850s. His use of the interview, thought to be a 'distinctly shocking American practice', can be traced to Henry Mayhew and William Howard Russell. Nor was his aversion to anonymous journalism the least original. Typographical experiments, including the insertion of maps and cross-heads, anticipated Stead, and subsequently realized their potential in other hands. In summary, his achievement was impressive, but its significance was more limited than he himself liked to think. Because a sense of proportion was never among his abundant gifts, his pronouncements cannot be taken at face value. Moberly Bell of *The Times* put the case very well. 'If Stead told me that he had eaten an apple, I should firmly believe that *he* firmly believed he had,' he told Strachey of the *Spectator*. 'I don't for a moment think Stead is a liar but his positive assertion of a *fact* would not bring me any nearer to believing it, still less of an opinion.'[1]

O'Connor, another of the founding fathers of the New Journalism, waited until 1889 to proclaim that 'beyond doubt we are on the eve of a new departure' in the profession. Rejecting the political inferences that Stead had drawn, he saw 'the main point of difference' reflected in 'the more personal tone of the more modern methods'. That was altogether more reasonable. By then, the New Journalism was becoming a byword and, ironically, Stead was on the point of departure from the daily press. 'I presume the "New Journalism" will continue,' J. A. Spender wrote to Cook, Stead's successor at the *Pall Mall*. It was an uncharacteristic thought to have occurred to Spender, who perpetuated the sober traditions of the old journalism throughout his long career. But the designation had come to acquire an elasticity that stretched in every convenient direction. To some, it applied primarily – if not exclusively – to the visual aspects of a paper. 'Perhaps you would like to enlarge your type in some parts, spread out your headlines more, & break up the articles into subheads,' Newnes tentatively suggested to Cook, relocated to the *Westminster*. 'You need not be afraid of giving too little. There is a general feeling in the House of Commons that you are now giving too much.'[2]

Without proposing to remake the *Westminster* in the image of *Tit-Bits*, Newnes was reacting against a tendency, which persisted from the days when

---

[1] Kenton Bird, 'Who Conducted the First Interview?' *Journalism Studies Review*, iv (1979), 8–11; Moberly Bell to Strachey, 22 February 1896, Strachey Papers.

[2] O'Connor, 'The New Journalism,' *New Review*, i (1889), 423; Spender to Cook, 18 December [1889], and Newnes to Cook, 14 February 1893, Cook Papers.

papers were stamped and newsprint was expensive, to cram as much as possible on to each and every page. When R. D. Blumenfeld, the future editor of the *Daily Express*, came from New York to London in 1887, he was struck by the solemn appearance of the morning papers, all 'great heavy-sided blanket sheets full of dull advertisements and duller news announcements. They all looked alike and were equally heavy.' Within the next few years, the *Star*, the *Morning Leader*, and *Morning* ventured to break with convention. Robinson of the *Daily News* 'didn't at all like the look' of these halfpenny interlopers, and declared to Cook that he 'had no intention of introducing illustrations', though he 'might be forced to some day'. Nor did he approve of interviewing, and the *Daily News* sneered when the *Globe* adopted this 'fresher, less conventional way of addressing the public' (4 February 1892). A. P. Wadsworth may have had the *Daily News* in mind when he remarked that 'the penny papers were strangely insensitive... [to] what was happening in the field of the cheap periodicals.... They had even retrogressed in attractiveness and were sometimes duller than they had been forty years before.'[1]

At the same time, many of the 'quality' dailies borrowed according to their needs from the New Journalism. To younger men, including Spender and Massingham, it was distinguished not by its wrappings, but by its social concerns. As little as Robinson or Buckle, they did not regard it as a justification for lowering literary standards or striving for cheap effects. Nevertheless, it became synonymous with these developments. E. M. Phillipps saw the New Journalism as conveying 'that easy personal style, that trick of bright colloquial language, that wealth of intimate and picturesque detail, and that determination to arrest, amuse, or startle, which had transformed our Press' since 1880. Phillipps possibly exaggerated and surely predated the phenomenon; but by 1895, when he was writing, it was real enough. The evening and weekly journals 'best exemplified' this determination to provide entertainment. The morning papers did not lag far behind, however: 'Even *The Times* does not "dare to be dull" so boldly as of old, and the most are ever in deadly fear of offering anything that shall be beyond the calibre of the "man in the street".' Beneath its staid surface, the *Daily Telegraph* titillated its massive readership with lurid crime reports. Lord Burnham, its 'honest biographer', was compelled to admit that the paper 'thrived on crime' and 'sometimes overdid it'. The only thing that could be 'said in defence' of the *Telegraph*'s performance was that the Oscar Wilde trial was covered more extensively in 'that supposed pillar of respectability, *The Times*'. Like the *Evening News* and the *Star*, the *Globe* made the most of the Whitechapel murders. And *The Times*'s reports on the Parnell scandal were worthy of Zola or Flaubert. Sensationalism was undeniably an integral part of the New Journalism. But it was common long

---

[1] Blumenfeld, *The Press in My Time* (London, 1933), p. 32; Cook's diary, 20 June 1892, Cook Papers; Wadsworth, *Newspaper Circulations*, p. 24.

before Stead's 'Maiden Tribute', probably as long as there had been news-papers.

> And guilt hath wed legality;
> And useful through the nation,
> Is prurience to publicity
> And sin to circulation.

So wrote W. M. Praed in the *Morning Chronicle* on 12 August 1823, more than a quarter of a century before Stead's birth.[1]

Contempories debated whether the New Journalism was a force for good or evil: did newspapers sacrifice their moral authority by pandering to popular tastes or did they derive new authority, secondhand, from the customers whose demands they satisfied? In either case, the effect was to shift the focus of public attention away from parliamentary politics. Perhaps, in its diverse forms, the New Journalism was merely acknowledging public indifference. Cook, preparing to launch the *Westminster*, called on Lord Rothschild, who 'said he didn't care what [the] politics of [the] new paper were – his interest was to get a good newspaper, with reliable news, not too outrageous headings, and [the] same things always in [the] same place'. Not surprisingly, Rothschild also recommended full coverage of financial affairs. By 1890, Sala had come to realize 'that the general public are interested in a multitude of other things besides politics'. Consequently, his leading articles in the *Daily Telegraph* shied away from political topics, and the paper went in for magazine-style features. Its rivals served up serialized fiction, personality sketches, sport, fashion, and illustrations. Without forsaking their party allegiances, newspapers lavished proportionately less space on them. Politicians' speeches, formerly published verbatim in the first person, were presented in abridged form – epitomes – or paraphrased. Looking back, A. G. Gardiner

> remembered one particular speech, made by Disraeli in 1873, which occupied three and a half hours. The next morning, the *Manchester Guardian* had two solid pages of it under the single headline,'Mr Disraeli at the Free Trade Hall.' There was no paragraphing, leading, or cross-heads. That was typical of reporting in the 'seventies and 'eighties.

The *Pall Mall* (3 November 1885) specified the Central Press Agency's criteria for reporting speeches: Chamberlain, Churchill, Gladstone, and Salisbury were rated 'Class I' and entitled to verbatim coverage; Hartington and Spencer (in the light of the Irish question) were each worth a full column; Hicks Beach, Harcourt, Cross, Childers, and Trevelyan were ordinarily half-a-column men; and the humdrum Northcote was buried in the heap. In the

[1] E. M. Phillipps, 'The New Journalism,' *New Review*, xiii (1895), 182; Burnham, *Peterborough Court*, p. 81; Massingham, *London Daily Press*, p. 174; Praed, 'Chancery Morals,' reprinted in *Political and Occasional Poems of W. M. Praed* (ed. Sir G. Young; London, 1888), p. 8.

1890s, mass burial became the general practice, with a vast saving in column inches and expense. Gladstone, who was even more prolix than Disraeli, was said to have cost the Press Association, which distributed his speeches, no less than £400 a year. By cutting down on speeches, newspapers had more room for non-political matter, including advertisements. For the purposes of the present study, this was the single most striking development in late-Victorian journalism.[1]

The politicians, as one might imagine, took strong exception to this practice. 'It is true no doubt that a great many more people will read your Electoral Programme than will read my speeches,' Balfour told Stead. 'Still on the whole I am disposed to think that it is best to adhere to the general rule that it is through speeches that . . . a politician's opinions are communicated to those who take any interest in them.' He was begging the issue, as the number of 'those who take any interest' was apparently dwindling. To be fair, Balfour was not simply craving the maximum publicity for his own disquisitions. He himself relied on the press to acquaint him with his opponents' views and, for this purpose, Iwan-Müller enlisted someone to 'do the work of searching Radical speeches for you' in the *Daily News*, the *Dundee Advertiser*, the *Newcastle Chronicle*, and the *Western Morning News*, which continued to provide 'verbatim reports on all the important speeches on the Radical side'. Significantly, only one London paper was on Iwan-Müller's list, and it was not *The Times*.[2]

With Churchill, who was struggling to make a comeback in the face of rapid physical decline, the motive was more personal. 'We thoroughly appreciate the good work you are doing for the Unionist cause, and have given unabridged reports of many of your speeches,' Buckle wrote to him somewhat patronizingly on 18 May 1893. 'But occasionally considerations of space make it impossible for us to avoid abridgement.' Two months later, Churchill had further cause for complaint when 'it was hopelessly impossible' for *The Times* 'to get in the report of your speech at Birmingham' on either of two successive days. Buckle, who found the text 'particularly interesting', could only 'regret much that this *contretemps* should have happened'. And, on 6 November, he informed Churchill that it had been necessary again to 'greatly abridge the report of your speech'. As Churchill was increasingly prone to ramble incoherently, this neglect may have been an act of editorial kindness. Yet it was logically defended on other grounds. 'We had three men to report you last night, but the best and the biggest speeches are subject to the inexorable laws of space,' Moberly Bell explained to Churchill on 18 October 1893. 'Statesmen little know that the length of their reports depend upon the quantity of

---

[1] Cook's diary, 11 January 1893, Cook Papers; Blumenfeld, *Press*, p. 126; Gardiner, speech at the Institute of Journalists, 10 October 1928, the *Institute Journal* (November 1928), 224; Lee, *Origins*, p. 247.

[2] Balfour to Stead, 10 June 1892, Stead Papers; Iwan-Müller to Balfour, 28 October [1892], Balfour Papers.

advertisements,' he continued. 'If we have enough to justify a big paper we shall be able to give you twice as much room as if we have few and are thereby restricted to a half paper.' In the age of the New Journalism, the advertising manager paid the piper and called the tune.[1]

Top-ranking parliamentarians, who had been used to receiving in the press the equivalent of the columns they filled in *Hansard*, were fortunate to secure abbreviated reports of their speeches. They were more fortunate still if their phrases were not wrenched from context and their messages garbled. 'This is not a letter of protest,' insisted Rosebery, who went on to protest to Moberly Bell about the way *The Times* had misquoted him at Rochdale. As 'scarcely anyone reads speeches', the incident 'would seem prima facie not to matter'; but there were 'the few who do read them in order to pick holes, & here is a hole ready made'. Nevertheless, it would have been more wounding to be ignored. 'Morley's meeting at Leeds (which was got up for him by Joshua Rowntree) had passed off almost unnoticed,' Wemyss Reid wrote, as if to congratulate Rosebery. '*The Times* reported him verbatim, but it was significant that neither the *Chronicle* nor the *Daily News* did so.' Most politicians would have been content to be 'almost unnoticed' to this extent. Rosebery's detachment was hardly typical, even in 1913, when he asked the members of the Press Club:

> Did any reader of the last twenty years ever read the speeches that were reported? I have no doubt that those whose duty it is to criticize, laud them, or rebuke them in the public Press felt it their painful duty to read the speeches. But did anybody else? Did any important reader of the newspapers, the man who bought a paper on his way to the city in the morning and an evening paper in the evening – did he ever read the speeches? I can conscientiously say, having been a speaker myself, that I never could find anybody who read my speeches.

The journalists in his audience must have known that he was right. R. A. Scott-James, who considered Rosebery's remarks 'exaggerated perhaps, but in the main true', acknowledged that the substitution of interpretative reporting for the 'almost mechanical function' of verbatim reproduction imposed 'a harder, more delicate task on the journalist. His triumph may be greater, but there are more chances of failure, more opportunities of abusing his power.' That, too, was a byproduct of the New Journalism.[2]

No longer treated as oracles, whose every utterance demanded transcription, politicians lost a good deal of their mystique. Arguably, what Scott-James

---

[1] Buckle to Churchill, 18 May, 1 July, and 6 November 1893, and Moberly Bell to Churchill, 18 October 1893, Churchill Papers.

[2] Rosebery to Moberly Bell, 30 April 1896, *Times* Archives; Reid to Rosebery, 7 June 1896, Rosebery Papers, Vol. 10,056, fols. 39–40; speech by Rosebery at the Press Club, April 1913, quoted in R. A. Scott-James, *The Influence of the Press* (London, 1914?), p. 276.

called 'the superstition which gathered round politicians as politicians' was already broken by the 1890s, and the contents of newspapers merely reflected a growing awareness that party politics did not 'embrace the whole public life of the country'. Party managers were relieved when the press trained its spotlight elsewhere. Robert Hudson, the secretary of the National Liberal Federation, prevailed upon the *Westminster Gazette* to cease its annual tabulation of the coverage allocated to individual politicians, as it was intensifying the rivalries between them. Akers-Douglas appealed to the *St James's Gazette* and *The Times*, among other papers, to desist from the practice of publishing 'black lists' of Tory MPs who were absent from the division lobbies, 'as I am sure the policy is a bad one'. However important to the Liberal politicians who hoped to see their names on the *Westminster*'s roster, or conversely to Conservative politicians who hoped not to see their names on the *St James's* 'black list', these exercises were meaningless to the general public. Newspapers, including the 'high-brow' ones which did not pretend to appeal directly to the masses, could not remain oblivious to popular sentiment; nor could they help reflecting it in some factitious or attenuated form. Political leaders were compensated for their losses by being afforded wider contacts and new insights. Continuing as mentors of the press, they became its students as well. If the new democracy was to be mastered, it had to be understood. Chamberlain, who made the mistake of taking Balfour at his word, wondered 'may not this disregard of the Press be carried too far? After all,' he remonstrated in December 1894,

> there is no other way of finding out the heart of public opinion & [this] knowledge ... is always necessary to a politician. It is very well to know what is right – but it is also well to know what is possible – & where, among many roads to choose from, the line of least resistance is to be found.

The New Journalism, which travelled along the path – some would have said the gutter – of least resistance, was not, then, without its uses as a handle on the new democracy.[1]

*   *   *

Months before Chamberlain put his rhetorical question to Balfour, Alfred Harmsworth (later Lord Northcliffe, by courtesy of Balfour) arrived in Fleet Street as the proprietor of the *Evening News*. He was to bulk large in the history of the political press, and could claim not only to have personified the New Journalism, but also to have consummated it. But he carried with him

---

[1] Scott-James, *Influence*, pp. 278–79; J. A. Spender, *Sir Robert Donald* (London, 1930), pp. 43–44; Akers-Douglas to Salisbury, 31 May 1893, quoted in Chilston, *Chief Whip*, pp. 246–47; Chamberlain to Balfour, 8 December 1894, Balfour Papers.

and built upon old traditions. For the time being, those were the traits with which he was identified and which he himself played up. For that reason, it is necessary to delineate the political milieu into which he intruded.

Its Home Rule legislation torpedoed by the House of Lords, the Liberal government seemed on the verge of a split in February 1894, ostensibly over the question of naval estimates. Cooper, who kept a weather eye on the situation, considered it 'worthy of note that the *Scottish Leader*, which certainly has had tips from Marjoribanks, has . . . spoken of dissolution being near'. In March, as foretold by the *Pall Mall Gazette*, the long imminence of Gladstone's retirement came to an end. The ministry regrouped around Rosebery, who was supported more ardently at Court and in the press than in the parliamentary party, where Harcourt was the preferred candidate. On the whole, the Liberal newspapers backed Rosebery as the more attractive of the rival claimants, who might overcome divisions and appeal more successfully to the electorate in due course. According to Cook, Massingham, assistant editor to Fletcher on the *Daily Chronicle*, 'had been judiciously dined', with the result that that paper 'ultimately ran Rosebery', whom Massingham celebrated in his 'House and Lobby' column (27 February) 'as a man of character, of personal force, even of a certain magnetism'. Cook could not afford to throw stones at other editorial glass houses: his frequent attendance at Rosebery's London address won him the nickname 'Cook of Berkeley Square'. The Unionist papers, more impressed by Rosebery's management of foreign affairs than by his record as a municipal reformer, regarded him as the lesser of two evils, and looked to him to temper Liberal wrath against the House of Lords, to awaken his colleagues to the glories of empire, and to shelve – if not jettison – the commitment to Home Rule.[1]

By accepting an expiring lease on Downing Street, Rosebery disregarded Buckle's '(unasked) advice' to 'avoid the chief place for these few months, if you may with honour' so as to gain time 'to develop your own policy and shake off the trammels with which your present administration must be encumbered'. In Rosebery's better interest, Buckle thereupon vowed to work for the dislodgment of the new government. Only in opposition, he reasoned, could Rosebery 'modify the domestic policy' of the Liberals in order 'that the gulf which now exists between them & the Unionists may be bridged over, & all parties may, as in the past, work for the same ends, though differing as to time & manner'. Having imbibed the Palmerstonian air of Printing House Square, Buckle hoped to recapture what had never existed quite as he imagined. Rosebery may have encouraged his expectations, but he failed to satisfy them. By keeping Morley as Irish secretary and making Harcourt leader of the Commons, he signalled his bondage to Gladstonian tenets. When

---

[1] Cooper to Wolmer, 17 February 1894, Selborne Papers; Cook's diary, 7 March 1894, Cook Papers; *also see* A. F. Havighurst, *Radical Journalist: H. W. Massingham* (Cambridge, 1974), pp. 70–72.

he persevered with Welsh disestablishment and other shibboleths enumerated in the Newcastle Programme, *The Times* turned against him with a vengeance. 'I am not surprised, tho' I am sorry, to hear what you say about Rosebery's feelings,' Buckle wrote to Brett in June 1894.

His irritation is very natural, though not, I hope, justified. It is of course impossible to criticise severely a policy with which you do not agree, carried on by tactics of which you do not approve, without giving occasional pain to the statesman responsible for that policy & those tactics. But I have always meant my fighting to be fair, however hard the knocks may be. . . . I told Rosebery when he took office that I should do my best to overthrow his Government. It would be a little unreasonable of him to object to my being as good as my word. He ought really to be pleased, for in spite of all attacks he has lasted longer than most people, myself included, expected.

In November, when the Rosebery government was still (in Harcourt's pungent phrase) 'hanging on by the eyelids', Moberly Bell offered the same explanation to Cook. *The Times*, he reminded the editor of the *Westminster*, which he recognized 'as the ablest amongst our political opponents', had

supported Lord Rosebery as Foreign Secretary and as Premier even against some of his own party – and if it went against him openly on one point it did so after full warning given beforehand that on that one point it could not follow him, after placing before him every argument which had weight with us & after receiving his written admission that our action was not dictated by party motives.

Cook confessed privately to similar misgivings. Rosebery's speeches seemed to him to 'have suffered from the same cause that made many of Mr G's very uninteresting – namely that interminable Newcastle programme'. It saddened him to see 'a Liberal Prime Minister oppressed nowadays by the bothersome necessity of giving formal recognition in each speech to every item in that long catechism'. Haldane and the Webbs, who had persuaded Massingham to assist the 'successful Rosebery intrigue', were soon imploring him 'to keep the *Chronicle* an independent force'.[1]

A disappointment to everyone, not least himself, Rosebery retained office for sixteen months, during which time he was plagued by insomnia and by quarrels with and among his Cabinet associates. In May 1894, there was a one-day truce for Asquith's second wedding, where Rosebery – who signed the register with Gladstone and Balfour – confided to Cook that his complimen-

[1] Buckle to Rosebery, 2 and 4 March 1894, Rosebery Papers, Vol. 10,092, fols. 23, 37–39; Buckle to Brett, 13 June 1894, enclosed in Brett to Rosebery, 15 June 1894, and Cook to Brett, 18 May 1894, enclosed in Brett to Rosebery, 21 May [1894], Rosebery Papers, Vol. 10,007, fols. 31 ff., 39 ff.; Moberly Bell to Cook, 5 November 1894, Cook Papers; Beatrice Webb, *Our Partnership* (eds. B. Drake and M. Cole; London, 1948), pp. 115–16 (diary entry of 12 March 1894).

tary references to 'Labour people' were 'mostly on [the] advice of Scott of the *Manchester Guardian*'. Morley, for one, found the *Guardian* less inspiring, particularly when it assessed 'The Position in Ireland' (16 November) and threw back at him the 'wise warnings' he had issued to Forster in 1881–82. 'When I consider the way in which Mr Balfour was defended by his friends, and contrast it with the poor cavils, carpings, and lies ... you admit into your paper ..., it is rather sickening,' Morley protested to Scott from Dublin Castle on 1 December.

> If you think I am on the wrong tack, you are well entitled to say so, just as I used to say it of Mr Forster. If you don't think so, why allow irresponsible men – without showing any better tack – to teach the Lancashire electors that the Home Rule Minister is a dreamer who does not know what he is about? That isn't the way to popularize Home Rule.

Four days later, Morley was already 'sorry ... that I had written'. Nevertheless, his outburst showed how badly frayed ministerial nerves had become. 'I always fancy that the Country Correspondents of our Liberal London papers must be Tories,' G. W. E. Russell chided Cook; 'for they invariably send up attacks upon Liberals, and suppress replies.' The *Daily News*, with two of its leader-writers (Justin McCarthy and Herbert Paul) in Parliament and one of its proprietors (Arnold Morley) in the Cabinet, was generally misprized.[1]

But it was doubtless the *Daily Chronicle* that gave the greatest irritation. In March 1894, Fletcher quit, ostensibly after a dispute with Frank Lloyd over the publication of racing news. To Cook, who had 'greatly helped me to secure the position', he revealed his intention to 'relinquish' it 'for reasons wh. most journalists will regard as Utopian'. Massingham, who replaced him with as little fanfare as possible, insisted that Fletcher's 'resignation has no relation whatever to political matters. He will probably go into parliament, and will continue to do some work for the paper.' Although Fletcher did stand at the next election, and again unsuccessfully in 1900, there is evidence that matters were not nearly so straightforward. According to William Clarke, a leader-writer for the *Chronicle*, efforts had begun the previous autumn 'to oust Fletcher by intrigue'. The alleged culprit was Henry Norman, who had 'succeeded in hypnotising (I can use no other word) the proprietors; & he and Massingham were responsible for the idiotic way in which the paper went into raptures over Rosebery. They are in short, Rosebery's newspaper tools.' With Massingham's elevation to the editorship, Norman became second in command. By then, Massingham's enthusiasm for Rosebery had begun to pale: 'There is no great man at the head of affairs from whom we can expect initiative,' he wrote sadly to Haldane, whom he saw as a potential Prime Mini-

---

[1] Cook's diary, 10 May 1894, Cook Papers; Morley to Scott, 1 and 5 December 1894, *Guardian* Archives; Russell to Cook, 24 February 1895, Cook Papers; Robinson, *Fifty Years*, p. 235.

ster. But the anti-Roseberian wing of the party, pilloried as 'the old gang', bore the brunt of his despair. Margot Asquith had 'a good talk *à trois*' with Harcourt and Morley, who visited her sickbed. 'Knowing ... that both of them were highly sensitive to the Press', she encouraged them to speak their minds. Morley could 'only say' that, like Chamberlain, he 'would rather have the newspapers ... for me than against me'. Harcourt contradicted him: 'My dear chap, you would surely not rather have the *Daily Chronicle* on your side. Why, bless my soul, our party has had more harm done it through the *Daily Chronicle* than anything else.' The conversation was a tonic to Margot, who countered that the *Chronicle*'s 'screams, though pitched a little high, are effective!' Morley could appreciate her soft spot for Massingham, 'because your husband is one of his heroes'. But Harcourt was unmoved: 'Well, all I can say is he always abuses me and I am glad of it.'[1]

'What a dreary waste is politics at present both at home and abroad!' W. J. Courthope exclaimed in the spring of 1894 to Austin, his erstwhile collaborator on the *National Review*. 'You must be feeling this personally when writing for the *Standard*,' he supposed. Indeed, Austin was acutely depressed. 'Newspapers are like Corporations. They have no soul to save,' he lamented to Salisbury, from whom he had wheedled an article on the House of Lords question for the December number of the *National Review*. Wishing to call attention to Salisbury's views and the journal that contained them, Austin wrote a leader for the *Standard* which was ruined by 'the interpolation of a cantankerous editor'. For the same purpose, he had written 'for the first, &, I should say, for the last time', in the *Saturday Review*, where another editor tacked on a conclusion that gave 'a wonderful display of ignorance of everything you have ever said on the subject'. (In truth, neither the *Standard*'s preface nor the *Saturday Review*'s epilogue seriously detracted from Austin's remarks which, published simultaneously on 1 December, were otherwise virtually identical in both journals.) Declining to follow his uncle's example, Balfour refused to grace the pages of the *New Review*. In December 1894, three months after that journal had been used by Escott 'to create a predisposition' in favour of Rosebery, it got 'a fresh start' under the 'imprimatur' of W. E. Henley, who promised to keep its 'politics ... independent, as of yore, but ... sound – *i.e.* Imperialist – all through'. Balfour reckoned that were he 'to give any production of mine to the *New Review* before I gave it to the *National* or to *Blackwood* – to mention no others – I should be torn to pieces'. He was 'delighted, however, to put £50 into the concern, provided the shares are not in my name', he told Iwan-Müller, who acted as his agent in the transaction. As he was 'violating my self-imposed

[1] Fletcher to Cook, 21 March 1895, and Massingham to Cook, 20 March 1895, Cook Papers; Massingham to Haldane, 14 January 1895, Haldane Papers, Vol. 5904, fols. 24–25; Clarke to William Demarest Lloyd, 12 and 22 October, and 21 November 1894, quoted in Havighurst, *Radical Journalist*, p. 74; Margot Asquith, *Autobiography* (London, 1920), II, 288–90.

pledges by this modest contribution, I must at all events try & keep my failings a secret from the world'.[1]

The longer the elections were delayed, the greater the journalistic passions that built up. Strachey, impatient to see Chamberlain prominently situated in a strong Unionist government, was prepared to defer that pleasure to see the Liberals 'drink to the dregs the cup of humiliation they have been so sedulously filling up'. However adamantly newspapers may have asserted their independence, few of them stood 'outside the trammels of party' with the *Sunday Times*, which could 'watch the struggles of party politicians as an entomologist observes the contest of rival tribes of ants' (30 June 1895). Most had never ceased campaigning since the previous elections in 1892. Their partisanship extended even to their literary pages, or so contended Arnold White, whose book – five years in the writing – was cruelly 'slain' in the *Westminster Gazette*. Cook rejected his imputations as absurd, but White claimed to 'have made a serious and prolonged study of the matter', and concluded that '*all* political Editors' were equally biased. A writer for the *Observer*, White was girding himself to stand for a third time as a Liberal Unionist candidate. In that capacity, he was deputed to respond to the 'hateful slander' of Chamberlain which had appeared in the *Standard* and the *New Review* (in which Balfour was a silent shareholder!) in April, when the Unionist alliance threatened to crack.[2]

Solidarity was restored none too soon. On 21 June, the Liberals were defeated in the Commons on a snap vote, and gratefully seized the opportunity to surrender office. Rosebery and Harcourt, who could agree on little else, decided that resignation was preferable to dissolution. Accordingly, it was Salisbury's task to form a ministry and to call a general election in July. Sidney Low of the *St James's* resisted an entreaty to stand in the Conservative interest at Bethnal Green, but Fletcher and White were among a score of Fleet Street notables who took to the field. C. P. Scott, making his fourth try, was at last returned. At Portsmouth, the Tory challenger was Alfred Harmsworth, whose press properties (with their sales figures as quoted by his brother Harold on 12 June 1895) included *Answers* (442,400), *Comic Cuts* (391,000), *Home Chat* (185,800), *Marvel* (164,000), *Boys' Friend* (145,750), *Chips* (265,000), *Forget-Me-Not* (145,000), and, since the previous August, the *Evening News*. It was, as one of his biographers has reflected, 'his one unhappy adventure into labelled politics'. Arriving to set up headquarters in

---

[1] Courthope to Austin, 24 May 1894, Bodleian MS Eng. lett, e. 1, fol. 110; Austin to Salisbury, 1 December 1894, Salisbury Papers; Escott to Rosebery, 27 August 1894, Rosebery Papers, Vol. 10,097, fol. 133; Henley to David Hannay, 9 December 1894, Hannay Papers; Iwan-Müller to Balfour [28?] November 1894, and 15 February 1895, and Balfour to Iwan-Müller, 8 December 1894 (letterbook copy), Balfour Papers.

[2] Strachey to Chamberlain, 29 December 1894, Chamberlain Papers; White to Cook, 15 July 1894, Cook Papers; Powell Williams to Chamberlain, 11 April 1895, Chamberlain Papers.

the constituency, he bought out the local *Evening Mail*, which he retitled the *Southern Daily Mail* and used to boom his candidacy. Neither a short-term political success nor a long-term financial asset, the paper was 'voluntarily liquidated' a dozen years later. By then, Harmsworth was Northcliffe, and Portsmouth was far behind him.[1]

[1] Tom Clarke, *Northcliffe in History* (London, 1950?), p. 13; R. Pound and G. Harmsworth, *Northcliffe* (London, 1959), pp. 180–81, 187.

Nine

FIN DE SIÈCLE

To a public that hungered insatiably after novelty, no less than to biographers who have chased after heroic figures, Alfred Harmsworth has continually exerted a strong appeal. Whether or not he embodied the spirit of his age, he certainly packaged it for popular consumption. According to legends, many of his own fabrication, he burst upon Fleet Street with unprecedented energy and acumen, with a flamboyance that staggered even the imagination of W. T. Stead, and with a healthy contempt for conventions, including the political subservience of the press. In time, his vaulting ambition, coupled with the mammoth scale of his operations, lent verisimilitude to the Harmsworth myth. Yet his initial aspirations were relatively modest, and his early practices were not especially unusual. If indeed he 'led ... a newspaper revolution' – as claimed by Cecil King, his nephew and disciple – he did so from behind.[1] The effect may have been Napoleonic, but the strategy was that of the Duke of ·Plaza-Toro.

The eldest of seven brothers, whom he helped his widowed mother to raise, Harmsworth was twenty-eight years old when he entered the field of daily journalism by adding the *Evening News* to a chain of more profitable and less dignified periodicals, of which *Answers* (founded in 1888) was the first and strongest link. As before, he was following in the footsteps of George Newnes, who had branched out from *Tit-Bits* to launch such diverse properties as the *Strand Magazine*, the *Million*, and the *Review of Reviews*, before establishing the *Westminster Gazette*. Frank Lloyd, C. A. Pearson, and J. H. Dalziel were among other travellers along the same well-marked route.

Always on the look-out for an opportunity, Kennedy Jones had spotted from his window at the *Sun*, where he was working – evidently not too arduously – as sub-editor, the arrival of 'a smart carriage' in Tudor Street. From it alighted Harmsworth and his 'atrractive and particularly well-dressed' young wife. In July 1894, Jones – 'K.J.' to his friends – crossed the street to offer Harmsworth, whom he 'only knew by sight', a business proposition. The *Evening News* was up for sale. Since Kennard's death, the paper had been

[1] Cecil King, *The Future of The Press* (London, 1967), p. 51.

managed at an increasing loss by H. H. Marks, the principal proprietor of the *Financial News*, who was soon to be elected Tory MP for the St George's division of Tower Hamlets. Too busy to provide further editorial supervision, Marks nevertheless tendered a bid on behalf of himself and the executors of the Kennard estate. There were also murmurs of interest from a Liberal syndicate, headed by Thomas Graham, the co-founder of the *Wolverhampton Evening Star* and formerly chairman of the Carnegie-Storey Midlands News Association. Harmsworth consulted with his brother Harold (later the 1st Viscount Rothermere), who kept the family accounts and thought that 'it would be worth our while . . . if we could pick the paper up for a song'. Alfred, always more adventurous, was ready to sing at a higher pitch. On 27 August, he was 'in great doubt all day whether we would get the *Evening News* or not, there being other competitors and matters difficult to arrange'. The next day, he signed the sale contract, paying £25,000 for the 'gold brick', as Harold sardonically referred to the purchase.[1]

'Good God, man, you're not going to turn [it] into an evening *Answers*, are you?' asked Jones, when Harmsworth unfolded his plans for the paper. His own intention was more grandiose: as soon as the *Evening News* was 'put . . . on its legs', it would become the pivot of 'a circle of morning papers, centring on London and looking to London for their news and opinions'. The understanding that its politics were to remain Conservative gave no disquiet to Jones, whose previous employment had been on the Liberal *Sun*, but surprisingly distressed Harold Harmsworth. 'I have no wish to identify myself with the Conservative Party and it would certainly not suit your purpose to do so either,' he told his brother. Alfred, who was to stand as a Tory candidate the following year, felt no such qualms, which in Harold's case were presumably more mercantile than ideological. Two other Harmsworth brothers, Cecil and Leicester, pursued parliamentary careers as Liberals. Cecil 'often wondered what Alfred's politics really are', and he was not alone. 'It would be speaking too strongly to say that the Harmsworth of these days was unscrupulous, or even that he was without scruples,' one of his employees later wrote. 'But it may fairly be suggested that he was not a bigoted holder of such scruples as he possessed.'[2]

On 31 August, the readers of the *Evening News* were apprised of the fact that, 'yesterday afternoon at four o'clock', the paper 'formally passed into the hands of a new proprietary', of which Harmsworth ('well known to the public as the founder of *Answers* and several other successful periodicals') was chairman. A statutory leader made reasonably clear where the paper stood:

[1] Pound and Harmsworth, *Northcliffe*, pp. 170–73; Jones, *Fleet Street and Downing Street*, p. 118.
[2] Francis Williams, *The Right to Know* (London, 1969), p. 72; Jones, *Fleet Street and Downing Street*, p. 133; Pound and Harmsworth, *Northcliffe*, pp. 171, 181; Springfield, *Some Piquant People*, p. 223.

Free from fad and prejudice, the *Evening News* will preach the gospel of
loyalty to the Empire and faith in the combined efforts of the peoples united
under the British flag. While strongly and unfalteringly Conservative and
Unionist in Imperial politics, the *Evening News* will occupy an advanced
democratic platform on all social matters, . . . non-sectarian in all questions
affecting the religious belief of the community, sympathetic towards labour
and friendly to every phase of communal advancement.

The formula was wholly traditional, and there is no reason to suspect that the
motives of the new proprietor were otherwise. Harmsworth may have been an
upstart, but he was no insurgent. He responded warmly to the embrace of
Tory leaders, who proffered congratulations, invitations, and an opportunity
to join them in Parliament. With Harold to attend to the balance sheets (which
soon reflected a dramatic improvement), and Jones to invigorate the features
of the paper, Alfred was free to contemplate other ventures. That is not to say
that he ignored the changes that were occurring at the office in Whitefriars
Street, where he frequently descended. On one occasion, he ordered Jones to
cut back on the racing news, possibly at the risk of losing readers. Profit was
paramount, but Harmsworth also had his respectability to consider.

The purchaser of the *Evening News* was younger and more impressionable
than the founder of the *Daily Mail* in 1896. In the interim, he had experienced
electoral defeat at Portsmouth, conceivably a greater blow to his vanity than
he later cared to admit. The self-styled tribune of the 'ordinary man' finished
in third place, behind two Gladstonian Liberals, at a time when the forces of
Gladstonianism were elsewhere in retreat. After the declaration of the poll, he
jauntily called on Cook, and 'said he had been with Salisbury who was in tremendous spirits and had promised him a very early seat'. That would cast
doubt on the story that his immediate reaction was to shrug and say that
'anyway my real place is in the House of Lords'. Nor is it likely that Salisbury
made any such promise. Never again a candidate, Harmsworth henceforth
offered himself to the public only through his papers. He came to recognize
that he was not cut out for parliamentary service, and rarely attended the
House of Lords when he eventually got there. The press was his vocation and,
in a way, his sublimation. Even the halfpenny *Daily Mail*, a less hidebound
animal than the *Evening News*, began with an obligation to 'worship the political idol which Victorian journalism had set up'. Jones, who made this admission, went on to stress that 'politics never obsessed us', and he credited the *Mail*
with having done 'more . . . than anything else to reduce parliamentary proceedings and the speeches of politicians to their right proportions in the daily
prints'. Had he looked around, he might have noticed that this tendency was
widespread. Would the *Mail* have carried it so far, one wonders, had Harmsworth been elected the previous year? In terms of circulation, the *Mail* was
incontrovertibly a breakthrough, largely at the expense of the *Daily Tele-*

graph. Here, as Wickham Steed recognized, 'Alfred Harmsworth started a newspaper revolution'. Yet its political ramifications remained slight. The nineteenth-century Harmsworth, as distinct from the twentieth-century Northcliffe, was an entrepreneur who played the old game. Only later, and then gradually, did he amend the rules.[1]

Harmsworth not among them, the Conservatives numbered 341 in the new Parliament. With 70 Liberal Unionist allies, they had a still more commanding majority. The Liberals, who went into the fray disunited, came out devastated. Harcourt and Morley were among the casualties, and temporarily out of play. The *Daily Chronicle* bade them good riddance, exulting that 'it is upon the older, stagnant, hopeless form of the Liberal creed that the heaviest blows have fallen' (16 July). Newnes took his defeat at Newmarket 'in very good humour'; according to J. A. Spender, who conveyed 'this gossip with all necessary reserve'; by October Newnes 'already had the chance of a "safe seat" immediately but says he doesn't want to go into Parliament again just yet'. During the campaign, the *Westminster Gazette* put on a brave face: 'The Liberal cause,' it maintained on 15 July, 'was sadly down on its luck', with the result that 'the capture of seats was out of all proportion to the voting strength of the victors'. The *Standard*, from a different vantage point, saw the outcome as a 'revolt of the National Conscience against the late Government' and particularly its 'Gospel of Plunder' (13 July), which the collectivists at the *Daily Chronicle* had failed to detect. The *Pall Mall Gazette*, having celebrated with the Liberals in 1892, now celebrated more boisterously with the Unionists. For what it was worth, the *Daily News* had stayed loyal. Like the Liberals themselves, its message was confused and its personnel were in disarray. 'I greatly admire the political leaders on the front page of the *Westminster Gazette*,' Robinson, its manager, wrote to Cook with a tinge of embarrassment. 'At the present moment, so far as the *Daily News* is concerned, I am unfortunately circumscribed, as two of my best writers are away electioneering,' he disclosed. 'Can the writer of your articles come here each night until the Elections are over and give me the same sort of assistance as you are receiving?' What may have been taken as a compliment was more a commentary on the impoverishment of Liberal journalism.[2]

At *The Times*, Buckle had to contend not only with a new political situation, which he welcomed, but also with a new chief proprietor. Arthur Fraser Walter, the fourth of his line, succeeded his father in 1894 and professed his determination to continue 'on the old lines'. It was not clear where, or how far, these would run. Not without managerial experience, A. F. Walter lacked his father's intimate acquaintance with political affairs. His primary concern was to restore the financial vigour of an enterprise with a falling circulation and

[1] Cook's diary, 18 July 1895, Cook Papers; Williams, *Right to Know*, p. 74; Jones, *Fleet Street and Downing Street*, pp. 139–40; Wickham Steed, *The Press* (London, 1935), p. 141.

[2] Spender to Cook, 15 October 1895, and Robinson to Cook, 15 July 1895, Cook Papers.

shrinking dividends. Buckle, self-conscious about the paper's continued decline during his editorship, tried to allay anxieties. 'If, as seems fairly certain, the Home Rule bogey is laid, at any rate for some time, the tension will be relaxed, and we shall no longer have the strenuous fighting of the last few years,' he told Walter on 21 July, as the elections were winding up. 'This is a very welcome prospect to all of us, and I have already spoken to the principal leader writers of the desirability of adopting a less militant tone. You have probably noticed this,' he assumed, 'in the leaders first on Harcourt's & then on Morley's, defeat.' Mentioning his own cordial relations with Rosebery and 'most of the other Opposition leaders', Buckle aimed to extend *The Times*'s appeal laterally, across party lines. It was too much to expect that he should also have aimed to extend it vertically, across class barriers. 'In quiet times, such as we trust we are entering on now,' he reasoned,

> the 'critical' or 'umpire' attitude of the Paper, to use your very apt expressions, is certainly the right one. When a great national question comes up, the Paper has to take a strong line, &, if possible, make its view prevail. That is what we have done with regard to Home Rule – with success. No doubt, looking back upon the struggle, I can remember incidents open to your charge of Party bias, though bias in favour of a Party which is made up of the best men of all parties & has, as is now proved & as we always believed, the nation at its back, is not an unworthy bias even for the Paper.

For his own part, Buckle insisted: 'If I have any bias, beyond a bias in favour of great principles to which the Paper is committed, you may be sure I shall do my best to shake it off.'[1] Without going so far as to equate Walter with Harmsworth, one may perceive a mutual acceptance of the maxim that partisanship was a brake on profitability.

Needless to say, with the election of a Conservative majority of such magnitude, Tory journals could well afford to mute their stridency. When the party in power was the party that a paper naturally supported, and all the more when the opposition was weak and divided, a non-political stance could be comfortably adopted. Non-political was not to imply anti-political, for the tendency was to curtail partiamentary reporting, not to banish it. In a vast majority of cases, non-political journals were instinctively conservative in their social attitudes and Conservative in their conditioned reflexes to public policy. To say that a newspaperman was 'a partisan of non-partyism', as the official historians of *The Times* tagged Harmsworth and Pearson, was to hide behind a false syllogism. More affirmatively, various publications – including Henley's *New Review* – labelled themselves 'Imperialist', which was tantamount to the same thing. There was nothing to prevent a paper which postured at being above or outside party from promoting party causes, participating in party wrangles, or serving political ambitions. Buckle, who

[1] Buckle to Walter, 21 July 1895, *Times* Archives.

had promised only to temper his bias, not to abjure his allegiance, depended upon Salisbury's administration to see to it that 'no great national question comes up' to knock *The Times* from its pedestal. Before long, however, he was 'unhappy about the details' of St John Brodrick's 'War Office scheme', and he appealed to Balfour 'to help to prevent what may be a serious miscarriage'. So long as he could iron out these differences behind the scenes, which he could not do when the Liberals were in office, Buckle satisfied his proprietor on the one hand and his conscience on the other.[1]

Liberal journalists did not have this option. For them to become non-political or even less politically orthodox was, in effect, to capitulate to the Unionist ascendancy. Yet Liberal newspapers were often profoundly dissatisfied with their party's programme, and sought to distance themselves from it. Some, like 'the Girton girls who edit the *Daily Chronicle*' (as James Annand mocked them), blamed the shattering defeat on a failure to meet the just demands of organized labour; others complained of a deviation from time-honoured principles. Newnes, flattered by the offer of a swift and safe passage back to Westminster, was approached by Rosebery, who asked him 'to examine and consider . . . whether it would not be a good speculation to bring out an evening paper in Edinburgh', where the local *Evening News* 'under the guise of Liberalism unceasingly attacks modern Liberalism and its professors'. Rosebery was careful to 'say a "good speculation", because I am steadily hostile to all newspaper enterprise which is not on a commercial basis'. Quoting Alexander Russel, Cooper's predecessor on the *Scotsman*, he described a 'kept newspaper' as one that 'starts with the mark of death upon it, and unless refreshed with constant subsidies from well-meaning philanthropists, soon vanishes amid the exultation of its opponents & the dismay of its friends'. Newnes, who could not have expressed it better, promised to 'see if anything can be done', notwithstanding his 'fear that the city is not big enough to support what must be a costly undertaking'. His inquiries confirmed his judgement.[2]

It was logical for Rosebery to have turned to Newnes, whose *Westminster Gazette* commanded his respect and admiration. Cook 'went up to see R. at Berkeley Square' on 1 November, and found him 'very complimentary about [the] *W.G.*'. Rosebery had 'just left' Campbell-Bannerman, 'who said it was the one solace abroad – it was a paper with wh. he agreed with every word it said. And,' Rosebery added, 'I think I can say almost as much.' Not everyone shared his high opinion of Newnes. Charles Morley, who had shifted from the *Pall Mall Budget* to the *Westminster Budget*, took 'a consistently melancholy view of the Proprietor's character & intentions', and had to be reminded by

---

[1] *History of The Times*, III, 120; Buckle to Balfour [2 September 1895], Sandars Papers.

[2] Annand, 'The Demoralisation of Liberalism,' *New Review*, xiii (1895), 253; Rosebery to Newnes, 16 October 1895 (copy), and Newnes to Rosebery, 19 October 1895, Rosebery Papers, Vol. 10, 131, fol. 26, and Vol. 10,106, fols. 71–72.

Spender 'what Proprietors can be & usually are in other offices'. Cook himself did not place Newnes above suspicion, and was dismayed when, without consultation, Newnes joined with Frank Hill to buy the *Weekly Dispatch*. Nevertheless, it was he who deserted Newnes, and not vice versa.[1]

The issues that confronted the Unionist government in its infancy revolved almost exclusively around foreign and colonial affairs, the respective departments of Salisbury and Chamberlain: recurrent Turkish atrocities in Armenia, the Venezuelan boundary dispute with the United States, and the crisis in South Africa aggravated by Jameson's raid on the Transvaal. Each of these controversies rallied public support to the ministry and, to varying extents, provoked further discord among the Liberals. Recalling the momentous outcry against the Bulgarian horrors, Balfour employed his private secretary, J. S. Sandars, to scan the *Daily News* and the *Daily Chronicle* for responses to the Turkish question. Rosebery could well have used Sandars's services. He deputed T. E. Ellis, the Liberal chief whip, to urge the *Daily News* 'to call attention to Turkish misrule in Armenia', and was icily informed 'that the editor had hardly been doing anything else for months and months, until he feared he must have seriously taxed the patience of his readers'. The *Daily News*, the single 'quality' Liberal morning paper, was a source of mounting uneasiness. By early December, as Sir Wemyss Reid observed to Rosebery, it had 'assumed a distinctly unfriendly tone with regard to your leadership. This is entirely the doing of Robinson, who I gather is offended because you asked Ellis to write to him on your behalf instead of writing direct!' But Robinson was not so childish, nor the problem so simple.[2]

At the time of Labouchere's divestiture, his shares in the *Daily News* were divided between Lord Ashton (formerly James Williamson) and Lord (formerly Sir Thomas) Brassey, with the residue going into common stock. Arnold Morley and Henry Oppenheim continued as senior proprietors. Editorial responsibilities were similarly divided between Robinson, who was nominally general manager, and Clayden, who was anomalously known as political director. On 17 December 1895, Arnold Morley invited Cook to become editor, a possibility that John Morley 'had vaguely raised . . . months before'. Despite his disparagement of the *Daily News* – perhaps, oddly enough, because of it – Cook was irresistibly tempted. Before he accepted, certain conditions had to be met. Arnold Morley assured him on the 28th that 'there was no idea whatever of interference', and that the editor would reign supreme; the proprietors 'only met once a quarter', and Cook was to let him know if any individual proprietor 'endeavoured to influence, esp[ecially] in City matters', as Oppenheim had been wont to do.[3]

[1] Cook's diary, 1 November 1895, Spender to Cook, 15 October 1895, and Cook to Newnes, 20 November 1895 ('not sent'), Cook Papers.
[2] Sandars to Balfour, 11, 13, and 19 December 1895, Balfour Papers; Robinson, *Fifty Years*, p. 235; Reid to Rosebery, 3 December 1895, Rosebery Papers, Vol. 10,056, fols. 23 ff.
[3] Robinson, *Fifty Years*, p. 377; Cook's diary, 17 and 28 December 1895, Cook Papers.

In late December, Rosebery returned from a holiday in Spain and learned of the impending changes at the *Daily News*: 'that Robinson was to restrict himself to the managership, and that Cook had been offered the Editorship'. Contrary to the prevalent belief that Rosebery had engineered the *coup* to install his protégé in Bouverie Street, he had mixed feelings. To Herbert Paul, who had recently lost his seat at South Edinburgh and returned full-time as political leader-writer, Rosebery promptly wrote to 'express my deep regret that for the second time in a few months you should have met with a great discouragement in your career'. Paul had requested Rosebery to recommend him to Oppenheim, but Rosebery had hesitated to ask a favour of a man 'whom I do not know intimately, and from whom I should have disliked to receive a not unmerited injunction to mind my own business'. Rosebery's misgivings were real enough. Chances were that the *Westminster* would be lost and that the *Daily News* was beyond redemption. When Cook saw him on 2 January 1896, Rosebery 'seemed to have in his mind that [the] *D.N.* didn't matter', and offered complaints rather than congratulations. 'One can't take it up without nausea,' he told the editor-designate. 'One always knows what it's going to say and that one won't like it. For years it lived on saying ditto to W.E.G. and now it ekes out a precarious existence by saying ditto to what it thinks he wd. think.'[1]

J. A. Spender, who later said that Cook had apprised him of his plans 'early in December', wrote to him from the *Westminster* office on the 21st after hearing a flurry of rumours and seeing a cryptic paragraph in the *Observer*. 'I may say sincerely that I desire nothing so much at present as that we may go on here as we have hitherto gone on,' he told Cook. 'But if it must be changed, I don't want to fall between two stools. . . . I should not like to find myself suddenly face to face with a new editor', possibly a migrant from one of Newnes's other properties or, worse, a Liberal Unionist nominated by J. B. Boyle, the manager. Rosebery 'hoped very much' that Newnes would select Spender, who had 'greatly impressed' him. Ellis urged him to write in support of Spender, but Rosebery 'thought this might offend Newnes and also Paul'. Instead, on 7 January, he took pen in hand and, at the risk of being thought 'impertinently intrusive', confessed to Newnes his 'ardent hope that under its new editor, whoever he may be, the *Westminster* may continue on its present lines of pre-eminent usefulness to the Liberal Party'. Paying generous tribute to the paper's past performance ('The *Westminster* appears to me to guide, stimulate, and instruct the Liberal Party throughout the country to an extraordinary degree'), he could not 'but feel anxiety as to what course you may be contemplating'. Two days later, Newnes replied, more eager to recount his grievances (for which he may have held Rosebery responsible) than to impart

---

[1] Rosebery to Paul, 29 December 1895, Rosebery Papers, Vol. 10,131, fol. 42; Cook's diary, 2 January 1896, Cook Papers.

information. The *Westminster*, he agreed, had reached

> an important moment in its brief history, because already the 'compact' which I made with the staff of the *Pall Mall Gazette* is broken by the decoying of Mr Cook to the *Daily News*. I do not complain, because I suppose the exigencies of great newspaper properties sometimes necessitate the effacement of sentiment, but I must say that I did not expect that the breaking up of the compact which I had made, under peculiar stress of circumstances, from a party point of view, would be shattered by the Maxim guns (not Moral-Maxim) of Mr Arnold Morley & the *Daily News*. But I bear no malice, only a little 'soreness'.

Looking ahead, Newnes was as eager as Rosebery to ensure 'that the influence of the paper should not be impaired'. But, in keeping with present trends, he wanted 'very much to make it more newsy & popular. That will increase its usefulness.' On the crucial issue of personnel, Newnes was not ready to tip his hand. 'Great pressure has been brought to bear upon me to appoint Mr Herbert Paul, who has written the leaders for the *Daily News* for a very long time (or many of them),' he revealed. 'Several members of your Administration have joined in the paean of praise to the Apostle Paul.' Yet, as 'the *Daily News* people have passed over the Apostle & have taken my ewe lamb', he did not propose to accept a reject. Rosebery was left on tenterhooks, as Newnes doubtless intended, and must have regretted having written.[1]

Newnes later jotted in an autobiographical fragment: 'It would astonish many people if I were to mention by name some of the number of men of high position in the intellectual world who applied for the post' vacated by Cook. 'I thought it only right to give the position to Mr Spender, who had been next in command.' Spender, who confirmed that 'several members of Parliament' were in the running, did not rate his own chances very highly. He 'waited in some trepidation, expecting any day to hear that the appointment had been made'. Newnes, after interviewing a stream of applicants, sent for Spender, whom he reminded 'quite genially' of his youth – 'I was not then quite thirty-three' – and to whom he offered the editorship. At Newnes's 'entirely welcome' suggestion, F. C. Gould became assistant editor. Spender chose Charles Geake, who directed the Liberal Publication Department in Parliament Street, as his assistant leader-writer. At the *Budget*, Hulda Friedrichs replaced Charles Morley, who left to edit the *Pall Mall Magazine*, an illustrated sixpenny weekly. Rosebery, hearing of Spender's appointment, called it the 'only good news for [the] Lib[eral] Party for a long time', and rejoiced with Cook that the *Daily News* and the *Westminster* were 'to be in pract[ically] the same hands'. Gould communicated these arrangements to Rosebery at Ment-

---

[1] Spender, *Life, Journalism and Politics*, I, 62; Spender to Cook, 21 December 1895, and Cook's diary, 2 January 1896, Cook Papers; Rosebery to Newnes, 7 January 1896 (copy), and Newnes to Rosebery, 9 January 1896, Rosebery Papers, Vol. 10,107, fols. 26–27, 36.

more, and carried back his host's approval. Only then did Newnes renew the correspondence. 'Gould is a man of many ideas,' he wrote to Rosebery, who required no persuasion, '& I hope now the compact is broken to take more personal part, & that we shall improve the paper.' Behind the promise, there lurked a threat.[1]

Spender formally took charge of the *Westminster* on 1 February, the same day that Cook commenced his tenure at the *Daily News*. Of the two, Cook had the more daunting task, as his presence and Roseberyite views were alike resented by key members of the staff. 'I wish you were at the *D.N.* now instead of going there in a month,' Moberly Bell wrote to him on 6 January. 'I envy you,' he declared facetiously, 'for you start with the certainty that nothing could make it worse. It's like succeeding Granville at the F.O.' A. J. Wilson of the *Standard*, who had 'nothing whatever to do with *Standard* politics', was equally pleased at the prospect of Cook's advent to the helm of 'what is still ... the premier Liberal newspaper of the United Kingdom. You have made the *Westminster* much the best evening paper we have & I doubt not the *Daily News* will soon in your hands plunge ahead.' John Morley, however, cautioned Cook to 'remember [that the] *D.N.* clientele [was] very diff[eren]t to the *W.G.*', and therefore it would be unwise to plunge too quickly or too far. 'Don't suppose I'm saying this to induce you to alter your line,' Morley hastened to add. Moberly Bell, who could not be suspected of an ulterior motive, tendered the same advice: 'If I may give a hint born of experience not perhaps very dissimilar to yours, I would say "go slowly – approve of everything & change it imperceptibly".'[2]

Cook did not underestimate the resistance he faced from entrenched interests. Ten days before his arrival in Bouverie Street, the *Daily News* commemorated its jubilee with a banquet. In the official account of the occasion, which was more a wake than a celebration, Sir John R. Robinson was designated 'Manager and Editor'. Upon learning of Cook's commission from the *Observer*, his impulse had been to resign, but 'friends dissuaded him from doing so'. Years later, he reflected that 'the greatest mistake of my life was remaining at the *Daily News* after Mr Cook was appointed Editor'. Herbert Paul, who stayed on as political leader-writer, was no less disgruntled. Spender's wife, who 'had a long talk with Mrs Paul' on 3 February, ascertained that 'Paul's grievance is first of all with Arnold Morley'. Spender was not surprised. 'A. M. has a reputation for doing pleasant things in a disagreeable manner,' he told Cook,

so one can imagine how he would have done a disagreeable thing. He

[1] Newnes's notes, quoted in H. Friedrichs, *Newnes*, p. 231; Spender, *Life, Journalism and Politics*, I, 62–63; Cook's diary, 15 January 1896, Cook Papers; Newnes to Rosebery, 14 January 1896, Rosebery Papers, Vol. 10,107, fol. 44.

[2] Moberly Bell to Cook, 6 January and 24 February 1896, A. J. Wilson to Cook, 16 January 1896, and Cook's diary, 16 January and 24 June 1896, Cook Papers.

appears first of all to have told Paul that there was no truth at all in the report of your appointment & to have assured him that if an editor was to be appointed, his claims would be considered first of all. . . . He took the same course in varying degrees with other members of the staff. That, at least, is what they report.

Paul and Robinson respected Cook's professional competence, but felt that he had been foisted upon them in order to wean the paper from its Gladstonian traditions. On imperial questions, which loomed ever larger, they regarded Cook as an apologist for the government's expansionist and militarist policies. Lord Ashton, representing their views among the proprietors, complained that Cook's leading articles were sometimes 'worse than the worst Toryism'. Rosebery, however, was entirely supportive. He invited Cook to spend Sunday, 16 March, at the Durdans, his house near Epsom, where he 'strongly approved' the *Daily News*'s line on the British advance into the Sudan, and urged him to 'keep it up till [the] Govt. showed its hand'. They 'talked a lot about the *D.N.*' and the way that divisions of opinion within the staff mirrored in microcosm those within the party. Rosebery 'said what a fraud Lucy was' as parliamentary correspondent, and advised Cook to 'arrange to see . . . frequently' William McArthur, the most Roseberian of the Liberal whips, 'else a danger of sitting at [the] office & getting out of touch with [the] party'.[1]

Political contacts were exploited, not always successfully, as a means of prising out inside information on foreign affairs, which were increasingly tense and complex. Middleton provided Kennedy Jones with a letter of introduction to McDonnell, Salisbury's principal private secretary: 'The bearer is the editor of the *Evening News*, Harmsworth's paper, and as they are real good friends to us I want if possible to do them a good turn.' The War Office had permitted a handful of journalists to accompany a military expedition against the Ashanti warriors in the interior of western Africa. Although Middleton thought 'it is very important we should help our friends if possible', McDonnell 'cd. not obtain any relaxation of War Office rules' so as to accommodate the *Evening News*. By contrast, *The Times* knew more than it could prudently reveal. Valentine Chirol, its correspondent in Berlin, was 'told . . . most confidentially' the contents of Queen Victoria's letter to her grandson, the German Emperor, who had provocatively telegraphed a message of solidarity to President Kruger of the Transvaal. But he allowed the *Daily Telegraph* to break the story. 'I don't suppose it anyhow matters very much,' he told Moberly Bell, '& one must sometimes pay the penalty for being behind the scenes by not appearing to know as much as one does know.' Lord Glenesk (as Borthwick had become) protested that the government fed exclusively to *The Times* items of intelligence which it denied to other papers and to the press agencies

[1] McCarthy and Robinson, *The 'Daily News' Jubilee*, p. 144; Robinson, *Fifty Years*, pp. 379–80; Spender to Cook, 4 February 1896, and Cook's diary, 15 March 1896, and 12 December 1899, Cook Papers.

generally. McDonnell acknowledged that there were grounds for such a complaint, and Salisbury agreed to instruct officials at the Foreign Office, the Colonial Office, and the Admiralty to make amends. To *The Times*, the question was not one of privilege, but one of accuracy. In April 1896, it brought a legal action against the Central News Agency, 'charging it with having palmed off upon us fabricated & untrustworthy telegrams' from Cairo which contradicted the 'confidential information' the paper had received from the Foreign Office. There was the disturbing possibility that, in the event of 'extreme pressure' from the judge, Salisbury might be called upon to testify in court 'as to the bona fide character' of *The Times*'s evidence.[1]

On the subject of Chamberlain's complicity in the Jameson Raid, which had elicited Kaiser Wilhelm II's 'Kruger telegram', there was considerable controversy, which a select committee of the Commons failed to lay to rest. Of the culpability of Cecil Rhodes, who was forced to resign the premiership of the Cape Colony, there was no doubt. Press opinion divided, not necessarily along conventional party lines, as to the extenuating factors. 'When you want a man to build you a house you don't enquire into his moral or ethical qualities,' reasoned Moberly Bell. 'Why should you when you want to build an Empire?' Strachey, who took a more censorious view in the *Spectator*, deduced that the manager of *The Times* was under the spell of Stead, an enthusiast for Rhodes and his vision of Anglo-Saxon destiny. 'I have *seen* Stead twice. I have spoken to him once – for about 5 minutes in the House of Commons smoking room,' Moberly Bell informed Strachey. 'About a fortnight afterwards,' he recounted,

> I was solemnly warned not to allow myself to be *too much* under Stead's influence. Asking an explanation, I was told that Stead had spoken of me in the highest terms, said that he had my complete confidence, & [that I] told him various things that I had intended to do on *The Times* at his (Stead's) suggestion. My informant concluded by warning me in the strongest terms against trusting him with a syllable. . . . Of that very man Stead had told me that he knew his innermost thoughts.

Apart from Stead, Rhodes's Liberal defenders included Cook, who was greatly influenced by Edmund Garrett, who had followed him from *Gazette* to *Gazette*, and was now editor of the *Cape Times*. 'For God's sake clear out of the *Daily News* before you completely ruin it,' a reader of sixteen years' standing wrote from West Hampstead. 'Everyone I meet is asking how much of Rhodes' money you have "netted".' Spender stood closer to Cook's position than to the *Manchester Guardian* in its condemnation of Rhodes's skulldug-

---

[1] Middleton to McDonnell, 19 December 1895 (with McDonnell's comments), Salisbury Papers (Christ Church); Chirol to Bell [January 1896], *Times* Archives; Glenesk to Salisbury, 14 January 1896 (with Salisbury's comments), Glenesk to McDonnell, 14 January 1896 (with McDonnell's comments), and Buckle to Salisbury, 5 April 1896, Salisbury Papers.

gery. The *Daily Chronicle*, which had branded the Jameson Raid 'a lawless expedition' (2 and 3 January 1896), was not particularly concerned with assigning guilt. Dining with the Webbs after the South African debate, Massingham was dazzled by Chamberlain's 'superb rope dancing', and 'bubbled over with the joy of the political dramatic critic', more impressed by the spectacle than the plot.[1]

While Rhodes's territorial designs were temporarily checked, the empire-builders of Fleet Street continued undeterred. Through the spring of 1896, Newnes and Harmsworth raced against each other to bring out a morning paper. From the *Westminster Gazette* office, Herbert Baxter wrote to Cook on 31 March that, the previous day, 'Sir George spoke to me' about his venture. Baxter could 'infer from what he said that he thinks that I ought to take it in hand for nothing. This I do not see my way to do.' Under Newnes's own editorship, the *Daily Courier* appeared on the morning of 23 April. Priced at a penny, it ceased publication on 15 August. By then, Harmsworth's halfpenny *Daily Mail*, begun with an investment of £15,000, was an established success. Looking back, its founder suggested that any of his rivals might have done the same: 'Their lack of initiative and their subservience to Party was a direct invitation to the assault administered by the *Daily Mail* on Monday, May 4, 1896.' Harmsworth was never more unreliable than when, out of character, he was being modest.[2]

'On Monday next Harmsworth is producing his new paper, the *Daily Mail*, a morning ½d. paper, and I think it ought to prove of very great value to our Party,' Middleton told McDonnell on 1 May. Salisbury was to receive a presentation copy of the first issue, and Middleton professed that 'I should be very glad if a suitable reply could be made so as to encourage the undertaking, as I am very anxious this should be run on the same valuable lines that Harmsworth is running the *Evening News*'. The Prime Minister complied with a telegram of good wishes. Balfour was a shade more reticent. He wrote to Harmsworth on the 7th:

> Though it is impossible for me, for obvious reasons, to appear among the list of those who publish congratulatory comments in the columns of the *Daily Mail*, perhaps you will allow me privately to express my high appreciation of your new undertaking. That, if it succeeds, it will greatly conduce to the wide dissemination of sound political principles, I feel assured. You have taken the lead in newspaper enterprise and both you and the Party are to be congratulated.

[1] Moberly Bell to Strachey, 13 and 26 February 1896, Strachey Papers; W. Simpson to Cook, 20 February 1896, Cook Papers; Beatrice Webb's diary, 30 July 1897, quoted in Webb, *Our Partnership*, p. 143; Cook, *Edmund Garrett* (London, 1909), ch. vii.

[2] Baxter to Cook, 31 March 1896, Cook Papers; *History of The Times*, III, 116–17; Pound and Harmsworth, *Northcliffe*, p. 205.

Gladstone, too, cabled a greeting, although he neither required nor expected any political recompense.[1]

There is no denying Harmsworth's unique flair for attracting readers and advertising clients, his resourceful use of capital, or his fertile imagination. Although it took until 15 June 1898 for the United University Club to accept 'the suggestion that the *Daily Mail* be taken in', an old news-vendor outside King's Cross Station described how the paper was bought by 'thousands of working men who never bought a morning paper before'. Harmsworth had tapped a new market. Salisbury, in an often-quoted remark, disparaged the *Mail* as 'a paper written by office boys for office boys'; but Harmsworth appreciated that office boys had halfpennies jingling in their pockets, aspirations ('Who is this Man-in-the-Street? He's tomorrow's £1,000-a-year man. So he hopes and thinks'), curiosity, and the vote. Harmsworth's commercial achievement has been well documented, and his impact on popular culture speaks for itself. Yet his political involvements have tended to be ignored, largely because he subsequently kicked over the traces. As their titles imply, *The Romance of the Daily Mail* (1903) and *The Mystery of the Daily Mail* (1921) made no serious effort to chart the paper's history; and neither Harmsworth's panegyrists nor his debunkers have taken the trouble to unravel his political entanglements. The *Daily Mail* was revolutionary in many respects, but perfectly ordinary in its partisan responses. 'Party politics are the last and most obstinate of the follies you have inherited from the Old Journalism,' Bernard Shaw told Harmsworth on the occasion of the *Mail*'s first anniversary. Harmsworth's estrangement from politics was gradual and never complete. Only after he had suffered a string of disappointments, real or imagined, did he adopt a non-party stand, which he then persuaded himself and posterity he had held from the start.[2]

By antecedents and arguably by instinct, Harmsworth was a sort of Liberal. That, in itself, was not remarkable in the late-Victorian period, when Liberalism admitted to diverse and contradictory definitions. Alfred 'believed far more in men than in politics', recalled his brother Cecil, who was elected Liberal MP for Droitwich in 1906. Cecil and Leicester brooked their eldest brother's 'amused contempt' for their 'chin-beard friends' on the Liberal back benches. Yet Alfred himself had 'almost as many personal friends among Liberals (and Irish Nationalists) as among Conservatives'. Probably the closest was Rosebery, his next-door neighbour in Berkeley Square from May 1897. Had Rosebery retained the Liberal leadership, and reconciled that party to the currents of imperialism, he might have counted Harmsworth among his devoted supporters. There was little practical difference, and a good deal of

[1] Middleton to McDonnell, 1 May 1896 (with McDonnell's comments), Salisbury Papers (Christ Church); Balfour to Harmsworth, 7 May 1896 ('private'), Northcliffe Papers, Dep. 4890/1; Pound and Harmsworth, *Northcliffe*, pp. 202–203.

[2] *Newspaper Owner and Manager*, quoted in Pound and Harmsworth, *Northcliffe*, p. 213; Shaw to Harmsworth, 4 May 1897, quoted in *ibid.*, p. 219; Clarke, *Northcliffe in History*, pp. 152–53.

common sentiment, between Rosebery's Liberal Imperialism and Harmsworth's Tory populism. But it was soon apparent, as the dowager Duchess of Devonshire put it to Harmsworth, that Rosebery, unlike his Derby-winning horses, was a non-starter. A pleasant companion for a motor-ride, he was not a driving force in politics. Heeding Rosebery's advice, Harmsworth cancelled the Sunday edition of the *Daily Mail* as a 'frank concession to the religious feeling of the public' (17 May 1899), but declined to follow him into the political wilderness. There, after all, was not where Harmsworth could collect the glittering prizes that he craved as much for mercantile as psychological reasons. Newnes's baronetcy, he noted enviously, was not simply an honour, but an 'enormous advantage to him . . . in the formation of his company'. In the process of forming and capitalizing Harmsworth Brothers, Ltd., he became aware of the utility of such distinctions. 'On our side,' he complained to Lord Onslow, 'owners of newspapers of comparatively slight influence are rewarded, and my predecessor in the *Evening News* received recognition, though the journal was a failure'; but 'the Party leaders are no doubt quite ignorant of the revolution which the *Daily Mail* . . . is making in London journalism'. His facts were wrong, but his indignation was real enough. For Harmsworth, 'our side' was the side that dispensed patronage. He had to wait until 1903 for his baronetcy, but a barony followed in 1905 and a viscountcy in 1917. There were allegations that they were purchased by contributions to party funds. If so, it was a shrewd investment, as Sir Alfred Harmsworth stood a better chance of attracting capital, and Lord Northcliffe stood the best chance of all.[1]

The Times, so warm in its support for the government during the winter that it invited charges of having abetted the Jameson Raid, cooled during the summer months. 'Too much time has already been lost,' it said on 16 July 1896, 'in making believe that matters of vital controversy are non-contentious.' Lord Rothschild met Moberly Bell at a dinner on the 20th, and 'gathered from him the reason of *The Times*'s hostility . . . was due (a) to the abandonment of the Education Bill, which he felt was a feeble surrender by a powerful Govt. to a weak Opposition'; and '(b) to the promotion of the Irish Land Bill by the Government'. The *Daily Telegraph* had also grown tepid. Iwan-Müller, who had joined its leader-writing staff, found it 'a somewhat curiously managed journal', and 'a rudderless ship'. He appealed to Salisbury for some '"lead" as to the general line to be followed with regard to international relations at the present time. . . . What I desire is to keep a paper which has so much influence of its kind *straight on the subject of foreign politics*'. In response, Salisbury sent an 'intensely interesting and valuable letter'. The South African question was relatively easier to sort out than the perennial Turkish imbroglio in its latest manifestation. To make certain that

---

[1] Clarke, *Northcliffe in History*, pp. 186, 192; Harmsworth to Onslow, 18 October 1897, quoted in Pound and Harmsworth, *Northcliffe*, pp. 233–34; Herd, *March of Journalism*, p. 242.

even the office boys were kept informed, the *Daily Mail* sent Robert Dennis, one of its reporters, to obtain 'some "tip" about Turkey'. Middleton referred him to McDonnell: 'As Harmsworth is such a loyal supporter of ours, I feel sure you will do anything you *can* in the way he wishes.'[1]

The government's reaction to Turkish massacres of the Armenian Christian community was to call in vain for concerted action by the European powers. Rosebery stayed silent. No doubt he marvelled how some of his followers, fresh from denouncing Rhodes for having taken unilateral action against the Transvaal, were clamouring to launch an independent crusade against the Porte. After the butchery of 6,000 Armenians in Constantinople in late August, the *Daily Chronicle* demanded 'to know what, in Lord Rosebery's opinion, ought to be done' (5 September). Although Asquith broke ranks with Rosebery to tell the *Chronicle* that he was 'in entire accord with the conviction that the time has come when Great Britain should refuse to hold further terms with a Government which has become a mere instrument for executing the purposes of a will either criminal or insane' (12 September), Rosebery declared in *The Times* that this was a 'national question' on which any separate Liberal 'impulse' would be 'a mistake' (14 September). Forsaking Rosebery, 'the Veiled Prophet', the *Chronicle* stated on the 17th that 'it is to Lord Salisbury that we turn with much sympathy'. Rosebery's antagonists in the party watched gleefully. 'I suppose you see the *Daily Chronicle*,' Harcourt wrote to his son. 'Their rage with Rosebery is amusing.' Rosebery's friends were similarly inclined to make light of the matter. 'The *Daily Chronicle* is doing you real good by its scandalous & transparent malice,' Reid assured 'the Veiled Prophet' on the 18th. 'Massingham behaves like a baby who shrieks as though the universe were out of joint whenever he has a pain in his stomach.'[2]

If Rosebery was not prepared to play the part of Gladstone, the prototype was ready to hand. Massingham had privately beseeched the Grand Old Man, aged eighty-six, 'for any word of counsel . . . more especially in the unhappy circumstances in which the Liberal Party is placed'. On 24 September, Gladstone journeyed to Liverpool, where he delivered his last speech, a rousing call for British intervention in the interests of humanity. Rosebery was mortified. While he could 'see the humorous side of the attacks of the *D.C.*', it struck him that 'Mr G. is doing his best, unintentionally I have no doubt, to render my position intolerable'. That Gladstone's attitude towards Rosebery, if not towards the Sultan ('the Great Assassin'), was scrupulously polite did not lead the *Chronicle* to temper its criticisms. At the National Liberal Club on 2 October, Cook 'met Harold Spender . . . who pointed out to me [a] note in that day's *D.C.* violently attacking Rosebery'. Yet neither the *Daily Chronicle*

[1] Sandars to Balfour, 21 July 1896, Balfour Papers; Iwan-Müller to Salisbury, 24 August and 2 September 1896, Salisbury Papers; Middleton to McDonnell, 18 September 1896, Salisbury Papers (Christ Church).
[2] Harcourt to L. V. Harcourt [September 1896], quoted in Gardiner, *Harcourt*, II, 414; Reid to Rosebery, 8 September 1896, Rosebery Papers, Vol. 10,056, fol. 53.

nor Gladstone, even in tandem, posed any serious threat to Rosebery's leadership. Only Harcourt was placed to mount a challenge, if he so wished. To
Massingham, who primed him with arguments, he had 'many things I should
like to say ... on the situation which I cannot well write'. Did they meet
instead? Charles Geake claimed to have 'conclusive' proof 'that Massingham
was at Malwood', Harcourt's country house, 'on Sunday October 4th though I
am told he denies it'. This detail was important, especially to Rosebery, in
interpreting Harcourt's speech to his constituents at Ebbw Vale on Monday,
the 5th. Superficially, Harcourt seemed to minimize his differences with Rosebery. But the *Chronicle* fastened upon them, and praised Harcourt for having
spoken 'with authority, with weight, with wisdom' (6 October). It was all too
much for Rosebery, who that day announced his resignation of the Liberal
leadership. 'The *Chronicle* has irritated R. but he did not give any importance
to its action alone,' explained R. C. Munro Ferguson (later Lord Novar), his
parliamentary secretary. 'Our press, however, what there is of it, was v. lukewarm.' Although Rosebery publicly emphasized his 'conflict of opinion with
Mr Gladstone', and privately described Gladstone's re-emergence as 'the last
straw on my back', it is clear that Harcourt's betrayal, real or imagined,
weighed heaviest upon him. 'Rosebery's decision to resign came shortly after
he had read the *Daily Chronicle* on Harcourt,' Massingham's biographer has
written. 'This perhaps was the precipitating cause.' If, as Rosebery had reason
to suspect, Harcourt had coached Massingham, the *Chronicle*'s leader of 6
October was truly decisive.[1]

Cook was dumbfounded by the announcement. 'It was and is still a "stag-
gerer",' he wrote to Rosebery with a mixture of regret and resentment.
'Journalistically, it is a great blow for those of us who have had the privilege of
agreeing with you, for we are thrown over.' Rosebery's complaint that he had
received support 'scarcely from any quarter' was hardly a compliment to the
Daily News. Nevertheless, that paper felt 'no little sympathy for a man whose
personal and honourable pride is superior to any pride of place, and who finds
the position of leader without the entire loyalty of his followers one not easily
to be borne' (8 October). Cook immediately telegraphed to Gladstone, soliciting a response to Rosebery's action, and advising him that the *Daily News*
'proposes his reinstatement unless you step into the breach'. Gladstone,
having had a second innings two decades earlier, was too old to try a third.
Throughout the ensuing weeks, the *Daily News* refused to accept Rosebery's
resignation as irrevocable, and looked to his return on a vote of confidence.

---

[1] Massingham to Gladstone, various letters and telegrams, 10–17 September 1896, Gladstone
Papers, Add. MSS. 44,523, fols. 253–92 *passim*; Morley, *Gladstone*, III, 521–22; Rosebery to
Reid, 28 September 1896 (copy), and Geake to Rosebery, 14 October 1896, Rosebery Papers,
Vol. 10,131, fols. 102–103, and Vol. 10,109, fol. 95; Cook's diary, 2 October 1896, Cook Papers;
Munro Ferguson to Campbell-Bannerman, 12 October 1896, Campbell-Bannerman Papers, Add.
MSS. 41,221, fols. 264–65; Havighurst, *Radical Journalist*, p. 91; *also see* Peter Stansky, *Ambitions
and Strategies* (Oxford, 1964), pp. 209–12.

Arnold Morley called at the office on the afternoon of the 12th, and thoroughly approved of Cook's 'Rosebery line'. The *Chronicle*, no longer bellicose, recognized more accurately that there was to be no restoration. It was more than satisfied with the *de facto* arrangement whereby Lord Kimberley led the opposition in the upper house, and Harcourt in the lower one.[1]

'There is much in journalism, as in almost all other things, that I do not love,' Rosebery told Cook on the 13th, when the dust had begun to settle, 'but you and Spender have made me conscious of a chivalry and charm in it.' Spender, more circumspect than Cook, who had 'engaged in a slanging-match' (as one historian has aptly called it) with Massingham, gave further evidence of these qualities in a letter to Rosebery the next day. 'If I charge myself with anything on looking back,' he confessed, 'it is that such little support as I was able to give was not sufficiently explicit & personal. Unfortunately when it is too explicit, newspaper help is often more harm than help to a public man.' To be sure, Cook and Spender were not alone is offering condolences. On 8 October, Harmsworth made a pilgrimage to Dalmeny and was invited to stay to lunch. 'I thought the *Daily Mail* came from the other camp,' remarked Rosebery, who did not mean the Harcourtians. 'The *Daily Mail* is independent and Imperial,' Harmsworth reportedly retorted. That, for Rosebery, was good enough.[2]

* * *

As the century drew to a close, it becomes fashionable for publicists to identify themselves by sentiment rather than by policy, by attachment to personality rather than to programme. Chamberlain, anchored in the Unionist administration, was, at least for the time being, no longer a free floater; but Rosebery, emancipated from the constraints of party leadership, took his place. His own intentions were altogether less important than what he was taken to represent. Might he follow Chamberlain's path by subordinating his Liberalism to his imperialism? Might he detach Chamberlain from the Unionist coalition to form a patriotic alliance of the centre? The popular passions generated by imperial issues initially promised – or threatened – to efface the traditional political divisions, which they ultimately came to reinforce. With the Liberals split into warring factions, and the Unionists at odds over education and other domestic questions, parties seemed to have lost their legitimacy along with their cohesion. The old system was regarded as moribund, and it remained to be seen what would rise in its place.

For Harmsworth, who gloried in the vulgarity of the new imperialism, a rea-

[1] Cook to Rosebery, 7 October 1896, Rosebery Papers, Vol. 10,108, fol. 99; Cook to Gladstone, 8 October 1896 (telegram), Gladstone Papers, Add. MSS. 44,524, fol. 57; Cook's diary, 12 October 1896, Cook Papers.

[2] Rosebery to Cook, 13 October 1896, Cook Papers; Spender to Rosebery, 14 October 1896, Rosebery Papers, Vol. 10,109, fol. 97; H. C. G. Matthew, *The Liberal Imperialists* (Oxford, 1973), p. 25; Pound and Harmsworth, *Northcliffe*, p. 220.

lignment of parties could come none too soon. 'With more confidence than insight', his official biographers have admitted, he told a meeting of share-holders in 1897 that he personally conducted 'the political aspect of our papers' with as little reverence for old-fashioned Conservatism as for Manchester-style Radicalism. 'We are Unionist and Imperialist. We have no sympathy whatever with the politicians of the 'sixties, the 'seventies or the 'eighties,' he declaimed. This sense of rootlessness was shared and articulated more eloquently by intellectuals with whom he otherwise had nothing in common. Taking its name from the tavern in Fleet Street where it held its monthly meetings, the Rainbow Circle was formed late in 1894, and began to publish the *Progressive Review* in 1896. Like Harmsworth, the members of the Circle recognized 'the ethical deficiencies of the old radicalism', and were vari-ously attracted to theories of national efficiency. The editorial committee for the *Review*, constituted on 6 January 1896, included William Clarke (formerly of the *Daily Chronicle*), J. A. Hobson (soon to take up a connection with the *Manchester Guardian*), Sidney Webb, Herbert Samuel, and J. Ramsay Mac-Donald. Among the political journalists who soon joined the group were W. M. Crook, G. H. Perris, J. M. Robertson and A. G. Gardiner. In its inaugural number, the *Progressive Review* maintained the 'urgent need for a re-formation and re-statement of the principles of Progress' as a prelude to 'a clear rational application of those principles in a progressive policy and a pro-gressive party'. Harmsworth, of course, pursued neither rationalism nor pro-gress in the same sense. Yet, in his crude and clumsy way, he likewise sought to put politics on a new footing. His goal, vaguely defined, was to promote a fusion of imperialist forces, whereas the Rainbow Circle was primarily dedica-ted to trans-party concepts of social reform. Both movements foundered in turn on the rock of political nomenclature. Liberal Imperialists could not combine with their Unionist counterparts, any more than 'the definitely Social-ist members' of the Rainbow Circle could agree with 'the definitely Liberal members' on the attributes, let alone 'the relative merits', of Liberalism and Socialism.[1]

Before the primacy of party re-asserted itself, newspapers struggled to attune themselves to these changes of circumstance. Some managed so well that party officials were never fully to recover their jurisdiction. The Liberal press had the harder time of it. Unable to divert attention from the issues that tore their party asunder, Liberal journals quickly succumbed to them. Thus, they assisted in the process of disintegration. Associated with one or another of the party's sections or 'schools', they automatically implicated those with whom they sided in party quarrels. 'I must be as careful as possible not to give anybody the least excuse for representing me as committing *you* to anything,' Reid told Rosebery. 'I have always tried hard to avoid this; & have even gone

---

[1] Pound and Harmsworth, *Northcliffe*, p. 231; Rainbow Circle, minutes of 7 November 1894, 6 March 1895, 6 January 1896, and 1 April 1908; *Progressive Review*, i (1896), 3.

out of my way to keep references to you out of the *Speaker* in order that nobody might pretend to suppose that I was acting as your spokesman.' Nevertheless, 'men like Morley insist upon connecting the most innocent expressions of opinion with the "intrigue" which they have conjured up'. Reid scarcely exaggerated, except perhaps with respect to his own forbearance. Just as Rosebery had gauged Harcourt's loyalty through the editorial columns of the *Daily Chronicle*, his rivals interpreted his intentions through the utterances of the *Speaker*, the *Westminster*, and especially the *Daily News*. Rosebery, languid by nature, might have preferred to remain 'the Veiled Prophet'; but he was denied that luxury as much by enthusiasts who extolled him as by critics who sniped at him. Imperial developments, culminating in the declaration of war in South Africa, steadily widened the rift between Liberal statesmen. Journalists, who could not help commenting on these controversies, showed up party unity for the fiction it was. Doubtless they were more provocative than the politicians thought necessary, but they had their own consciences and constituencies to satisfy. 'Don't you wish you could open a paper,' John Morley asked Campbell-Bannerman, 'without reading that you and I and Asquith are all ready to cut one another's throats – all for the sweet privilege of *leading* the Liberal Party?' That, too, was more than either of them could reasonably expect.[1]

Tensions ran high between the various Liberal journals and, in most cases, within them. At the *Daily Chronicle*, Massingham had diverged sharply from Henry Norman, who had declared to Rosebery as early as 1 July 1895 his determination 'to promote the birth, by and by, of that Party, "unnamed as yet", at whose head we want to see you'. The *Chronicle*, as the *Outlook* later tartly commented, 'called Lord Rosebery to assume the cloak of Mr Gladstone and presently tore that garment from Lord Rosebery's back' (2 December 1899). Norman offered his resignation as assistant editor, but Massingham persuaded him to undertake a series of foreign missions. In February 1897, he was in Greece, remitting emotive pleas for British intervention in Crete. The *Westminster* and the *Daily News* dismissed the idea as impractical, if not irresponsible, although Henry Oppenheim called on Cook and 'sang the praises of [the] *D.C.* at the expense of [the] *D. N.* – re Norman at Atticus'. With Massingham and Norman in mind, the *Daily News* warned that 'those who without the most searching consideration are shouting to Athens to defy Europe and to declare war are incurring the most grievous responsibility' (27 February). Reid, who reported the Greek crisis in the *Speaker* with similar restraint, understood Cook's dilemma only too well. 'I know something of the cost at which a journalist takes such a line as this,' he empathized, '& I know too that a great journal never so fully justifies its position & the influence which it wields, as

[1] Reid to Rosebery, 12 June 1897, Rosebery Papers, Vol. 10,056, fols. 108–109; Morley to Campbell-Bannerman, 16 October 1897, Campbell-Bannerman Papers, Add. MSS. 41,223, fol. 56.

when it is daring to oppose itself to a strong popular current.' Reid had freer
rein and, as the editor of a weekly, a more relaxed schedule, yet he felt a compunction to take into account the Gladstonian sentiments of his proprietor, Sir
John Brunner, who was fervently anti-Turk.[1]

Cook was the servant of a divided proprietorship, and it told on him.
Whereas Arnold Morley was firm in his allegiance to Rosebery, Lord Ashton
inclined towards the 'Little England' camp, and eventually surfaced among
the 'pro-Boers'. Oppenheim, whose politics were nebulous, would drop by the
office, where he 'bored' Cook 'with his views on the Transvaal'. On domestic
issues, there existed considerable agreement between the *Daily News* and the
Daily Chronicle, both susceptible to the influence of the Webbs. On 11
December 1897, for example, Cook published and commended a statement on
'the legitimate action of Trade Unions' in the engineering dispute, 'drawn up
by Webb' and signed by various Fabians and Positivists. But imperial issues
overshadowed all else. Massingham, who would live to repent of his words,
called upon Lloyd George to 'take in hand the resurrecting of the Liberal Party
& do what Lord Randolph Churchill did for the Tory Party'. Meanwhile, he
hit at the *Daily News* as a way of hitting indirectly at Rosebery. Labouchere,
the moving force behind the Radical Committee, followed the same procedure
in *Truth* and, Cook heard on good authority, planted falsehoods in the *Pall
Mall Gazette*. Reputed to be the keeper of Rosebery's conscience, Cook was
attacked from left and right. Charles Geake furnished arguments to meet the
aspersions of the *St James's Gazette*: 'Please do not consider this letter an
interference, or as a hint ... that the *D.N.* cannot conduct its own case.'
Andrew Carnegie urged him to ignore the brickbats in the *Review of Reviews*:
'Really I do not think that Mr Stead's screeds deserve reply – he sometimes
gets "off the hooks" and for the time being is a crank.' Carnegie complimented Cook for having made the *Daily News* 'very much more sprightly than it
was', and added that 'the man you left in charge of the *Westminster* is keeping
up the reputation for it'. Spender, who stood in Cook's shadow, won praise in
his own right from Frederick Greenwood, who 'declared the *W.G.* to be the
best edited paper in London – infinitely superior to the *P.M.G.*'. Still more
unexpectedly, Cook found an ally in Moberly Bell of *The Times*, who vowed
that he would not 'abuse' the *Daily News*, 'for I want to *make* it a rival'.[2]

The Times was afflicted by its own internal disorders. Throughout 1897 and
beyond, Buckle continued to solicit and receive confidential advice from the
Foreign Office on Anglo-American and Anglo-French excitements. But the

[1] Norman to Rosebery, 1 July 1895, Rosebery Papers, Vol. 10,105, fol. 149; Reid to Cook, 5
March 1897, and Cook's diary, 19 February 1897, Cook Papers; Koss, *Brunner*, p. 180.

[2] Cook's diary, 19 February and 11 December 1897, Geake to Cook, 16 December 1897, Car-
negie to Cook, 18 December 1897, Moberly Bell to Cook, 8 January 1898, Cook Papers; Lloyd
George to his wife, 9 September 1897, quoted in *Lloyd George Family Letters* (ed. K. O. Morgan;
Cardiff and London, 1973), p. 112; A. Spurgeon (of the National Press Agency) to Spender, 28
May 1897, Spender Papers, Add. MSS. 46,391, fol. 16.

support it gave the government was equivocal. Brett, who considered that the paper 'has been behaving like a beast', heard

> that Buckle is in a very precarious position. His line is not at all the line which *The Times* has been taking. He objected last week to putting in some effusions of Moberly Bell's, but the latter appealed to Walter who insisted that they should be inserted.

Meeting Cook at Rosebery's house, McDonnell remarked that 'Buckle had behaved very badly', and was instrumental in wrecking the chances of a loan for China. It struck him as 'funny' to see the *Daily News* and *Westminster* 'supporting Sally', as he affectionately referred to Salisbury, against the *Globe* and the *Standard*.[1]

In February 1898, Austin ended 'thirty-two years of association' with the *Standard*, which acquired the leader-writing services of Sidney Low, on the rebound from the *St James's*. The previous July, Low had received a letter from Steinkopff, 'suggesting further expenditure on the *St James's* and proposing a new arrangement for myself'. Low rejected the scheme, but accepted a roving commission with an understanding that, upon his return, Steinkopff would subscribe £5,000 to 'finance a weekly journal and give him control'. On 29 October 1897, he confirmed to Cook 'that I am giving up the editorship of the *Gazette* in the course of the next few weeks', but that he was 'not entirely severing my connection with the paper & shall probably be taking a trip abroad somewhere for them before long'. His attachment to the *Standard* gave Steinkopff the excuse to default on both promises. Low refused the editorship of the *Johannesburg Star*, and also that of the *Morning Post*, which was offered 'on conditions that would have kept him in leading strings'. Instead, he stayed with the *Standard* until 1904, when it was sold to C. A. Pearson, who had bought the *St James's* the previous year. Hugh Chisholm, who replaced Low on the *St James's* (and who was himself replaced by S. H. Jeyes in 1899), refuted allegations that the paper was conducted in the interest, and possibly in the pay, of Berlin. 'My proprietor, Mr Steinkopff, is, of course, German by birth,' he told W. M. Crook of the *Echo*; 'but he is for that reason (as is the case with so many Germans resident in Great Britain) more hostile to Germany & German policy than a good many Britons.' As for the *Echo*'s insinuation that the *St James's* was, like Salisbury, a believer in the 'Concert of Europe', a Bismarckian fallacy, Chisholm maintained 'that we have attacked the "Concert" quite as bitterly in the last six months or more as *The Times* or *Standard* – or *Daily News*'. His disclaimer did not prevent the official history of *The Times* from repeating the canard that the *St James's* 'was assisted during this period by a close connection with the German Embassy ... [that] seems to have continued for some years'.[2]

[1] Brett to Stead [1897], Stead Papers; Cook's diary, 26 February 1898, Cook Papers.
[2] Austin to Salisbury, 5 February 1898, Salisbury Papers; Low to Cook, 29 October 1897, Cook

With questions of foreign and colonial policy providing the major impetus, these proprietorial and editorial changes assumed epidemic proportions. In January 1898, the *Morning* was acquired by a Liberal syndicate, directed by Joseph Cooke, owner of the *Sheffield Independent* and other provincial properties (and among the rescuers of the *Leeds Mercury*), and J. E. Mac-Manus, formerly connected with the *Daily Mail*. The following year, with Cooke as managing director, the paper was briefly linked to the *Echo* under the administration of Consolidated Newspapers, Ltd., which was registered with capital of £150,000 subscribed by Gilzean Reid, and a number of MPs, including J. Batty Langley, D. F. Goddard, and Thomas Lough. On 24 April 1899, the *Morning* was transformed into the *Morning Herald*, which aimed to be 'perfectly candid' with its readers. 'The editorial view of public questions is Progressive and Liberal', without 'slavish allegiance to any faction'. Yet, aware that 'we are living in a new age', the *Morning Herald* would 'neither live for politics nor by politics', and would endeavour 'to give the public a really good substantial half-pennyworth of reading on six days of the week, and six days only'. To Kennedy Jones, who had got his start in London journalism on the old *Morning*, 'the new note ... sounded clearly': 'Politics were out of fashion; the people wanted news, not views.' Unfortunately, the people did not want either from the *Morning Herald*, which Pearson acquired in April 1900 and converted in September into the *Daily Express and Morning Herald*, with news articles and headlines splashed across the front page. About the same time, Mudford retired from the *Standard*, leaving Byron Curtis in command. Only for the *Morning Post*, the greybeard of London dailies, did time stand still. In 1897, J. Nicoll Dunn, who had been trained under Cust at the *Pall Mall*, succeeded Algernon Locker as editor. The tone remained much the same as in Disraeli's novel, *Lothair* (1870), where, after breakfast at Vauxe, 'the ladies had retired, stealing off with the *Morning Post*, the gentlemen gradually disappearing for the solace of their cigars'. Lord Randolph Churchill was gone, of course, but Glenesk had found a worthy successor. 'Contrary to my habit, I asked for a *Morning Post* today,' Haldane wrote on 15 July 1898 to Lady Randolph, whose son Winston had delivered his second public speech, duly reported.[1]

The *Echo*, struggling with difficulties of its own, could not bear the extra burden of the *Morning Herald*. On 15 November 1897, Sir Wemyss Reid learned from Rosebery 'of the sale of the *Echo*' by Passmore Edwards: 'I hope it may have fallen into good hands.' The new editor was W. M. Crook, who had assisted the Rev Hugh Price Hughes on the *Methodist Times*, a weekly

---

Papers; Chapman-Huston, *Lost Historian*, pp. 94–100; Chisholm to Crook, 9 February [1898], Crook Papers; *History of The Times*, III, 121.

[1] *Sell's* (1899); Jones, *Fleet Street and Downing Street*, pp. 157–58; *History of The Times*, III, 119; Haldane to Lady Randolph Churchill, 15 July 1898, quoted in Randolph S. Churchill, *Winston S. Churchill*, I (London, 1966), 396.

'journal of religious and social movement' which called itself 'the most widely-quoted religious newspaper in the English-speaking world' (6 January 1898). Hughes, like many Wesleyan clerical and lay leaders, was a staunch imperialist. Rosebery, assuming Crook to be the same, 'heartily' wished him success. But Crook stood against the denominational tide. With better justification, Sir Robert Reid (later Lord Loreburn), rejoiced in Crook's appointment as a victory for the anti-Roseberians. 'I am indeed glad you are to edit the *Echo*,' he wrote. 'I revere that paper for its constant & quiet support & humanitarian vision.... Do continue it.' P. W. Clayden, a lost soul on the *Daily News*, could not 'imagine a more satisfactory appointment, and one more full of happy augury for the Liberal Party in London.... You will make the *Echo* a power,' he predicted. 'Henceforth it will be the evening organ of the party, and will be looked up to as an authority as it has never yet been.' From personal experience and from an acquaintance with 'the men you have to do with', Clayden ominously expressed the 'hope they will leave you as free as I was left at the *D.N.*' in bygone days.[1]

The proprietors of the *Echo* were Thomas Lough, Liberal MP for West Islington, and John Barker, who stood twice at Maidstone before his election there in 1900. They entrusted the management of the concern to Gilzean Reid. The arrangement, like so many others in Fleet Street, caused a degree of confusion. 'I am rather in a fix about assigning the Editorship of the *Echo* in our Newspaper table in *Who's Who*,' Douglas Sladen confessed to Crook. In response to a questionnaire, Gilzean Reid had specified himself and Lough as joint editors. Lough, who had helped to found the *Star* and who proffered support to Cook when the *Pall Mall* changed hands, recognized Crook as the responsible party. That did not mean, however, that he took a back seat. On 2 January 1898, he wrote to Crook from Bishop's Stortford, where he was spending the holiday weekend with Barker: 'We both like Friday & Saturday's papers, and Mr B. thinks well of the changes you have introduced so far, and hopes soon to see them tell on the prosperity of the co[mpan]y.' Opposed to the scramble for territory along the China coast, he promised to call at the office 'to give you some tips re our attack on Salisbury over this matter, as I think it would be popular and that the time has come for it.... The *Echo* must wake the country up.' The paper had to rouse itself, however, before it could rouse the country.[2]

The transfer of the *Echo* to a band of earnest Nonconformists served to remind the *Daily News* of its sacred obligation. Cook, whose considerations were strictly non-theological, told Arnold Morley and Oppenheim that 'it wd. be serious if we estranged Noncons.' by supporting the endowment of a

---

[1] Reid to Rosebery, 15 November 1897, Rosebery Papers, Vol. 10,056, fols. 139–40; Reid to Crook, 17 January [1898; misdated 1897], Clayden to Crook, 27 December 1897, and Rosebery to Crook, 10 January 1898, Crook Papers.

[2] Sladen to Crook, 10 January 1898, and Lough to Crook, 2 January 1898, Crook Papers.

Roman Catholic university in Ireland. Soon thereafter, he was addressed by
William Thomas, a Baptist minister in South Hackney, who had attended the
meetings of the National Council of Evangelical Free Churches at Bristol,
where he

> heard the *Daily Chronicle* severely attacked and the accusation made 'that
> Nonconformity has no leading Daily in full sympathy with its principles and
> position'. I remember when the *Daily News* occupied that position, but
> during the Editorship of Mr Fletcher – chiefly I think through religious arti-
> cles and extensive reviews of religious books – the *Daily Chronicle* came
> into the front, but its position in relation to Nonconformity has greatly
> changed and the need for a sympathetic daily is keenly felt among Noncon-
> formists.

Cook was urged to restore the *Daily News* to 'its former position', an idea attractive to him for several reasons. Not only might he thereby increase the circulation of the paper, but he might also assist Sir Robert Perks and other
activists in recruiting Nonconformist support for Rosebery. The trick would be
to evangelize the Evangelicals to imperialism, without falling captive to their
insularity. Later that year, Cook 'lightly touched upon' the subject in a conversation with Arnold Morley, who pondered 'the possibility of strengthening our
position with the great body of political Nonconformists in the country'.
Admittedly, 'of late years the *D.N.* has lost ground in that direction, & it is certainly worth trying to regain it', especially as Morley noted presciently, when
'we are entering upon a period when ecclesiastical and Educational questions
will occupy a prominent position'. Yet Morley, whose own Congregationalist
roots ran deep, was inclined to be cautious. 'I doubt if you quite realize the
lengths to which one would have to go to satisfy the extreme sections,' he told
Cook.

> The *Daily News* has lost many readers to the *Chronicle*. But why? Cer-
> tainly not because the *Chronicle* is sectarian. In my opinion because the
> *Chronicle* got the start of the *Daily News* by some years in enlarging its size
> and scope – and also no doubt by spending large sums of money on its devel-
> opment generally. So with the *Telegraph* and the *Mail*. Their secret is their
> width, not their narrowness of range.

Speaking as a former whip, who lost his seat in the *débâcle* of 1895, Morley
saw the Liberals as 'a composite party – largely Nonconformist of course, but
certainly not exclusively so. . . . But please,' he begged Cook, 'do not think
that I am not alive to the importance in questions of practical politics of taking
what one may rightly call the Liberal-Nonconformist line.' Cook, having
adopted interviews as a concession to the new journalism, portrayed a gallery

of prominent Free Churchmen as a sop to the old Nonconformity.[1]

On the whole, it was easier to satisfy the secular demands of Liberalism. T. E. Ellis, the chief whip, credited the *Daily News* for having induced G. W. Palmer, defeated at Reading in the last elections, to contest a by-election at Wokingham, 'one of the most *gallant* bits of service to the Party that I know within my experience'. According to Ellis, 'one of the considerations' which influenced Palmer 'was a sentence' in the *Daily News*'s leading article on 17 March, 'saying the Home Counties should not be allowed to become the monopoly and preserve of Toryism'. Palmer lost the fight at Wokingham on 30 March, but regained his seat at Reading in July, after the death of his Tory successor. In May, Gladstone died, and the *Daily News*, on the day of his funeral, appealed somewhat tastelessly for Rosebery's return. The movement gathered support through the summer and autumn of 1898, with the buildup to the Fashoda crisis and the threat of an armed clash between French and British troops along the upper Nile. 'You observe,' wrote John Morley to Harcourt on 9 October, 'the violent jingoism of the *Daily News, Westmr. Gazette, Speaker*, and *Chronicle*.' The *Daily News* was, by far, the most truculent of the lot. 'The chief element of danger', it stated on 27 September, 'is to be found in the widespread belief prevailing on the Continent that Lord Salisbury's squeezability is unlimited.' Harcourt shared Morley's despondency:

> I have long known that the chosen people of the Liberal Press and Party have addicted themselves to strange gods and that we shall see at least as powerful a contingent of Liberal Jingoism as of Liberal Unionism. Khartoum and Fashoda will rally the popular sentiment as much as Trafalgar and Salamanca. . . . We shall either see the submission of France which will be popular or a war with France which will be more popular still.

In the event, it was Harcourt who submitted.[2]

On 12 October, Rosebery lifted his veil in a speech at Epsom. Even the *Daily Chronicle* considered his words 'proper and necessary' (13 October). He followed with other platform appearances, including one that stole the limelight from Harcourt at the Mansion House dinner on 4 November. Whether or not he had launched a co-ordinated campaign, he gave all the appearances of making a bid for a come-back. The *Daily News* was jubilant at the prospect. On 6 November, Cook 'lunched with R. at Brooks's. We drank stout & champ[agne], Dizzy's drink, wh. he said was [the] best pick me up he knew'. Rosebery 'asked as usual about my post bag & said [that the] *D.N.* [was] much improved – now a very good newspaper!' He might have said the same of the *Daily Chronicle* which, on 6 December, ran a leading article sharply critical of

[1] Cook's diary, 25 February 1898, Thomas to Cook, 14 March 1898, A. Morley to Cook, 21 November 1898, Cook Papers.

[2] Ellis to Cook, 18 March 1898, Cook Papers; Morley to Harcourt, 9 October 1898, and Morley to Harcourt, 10 October 1898, Harcourt Papers; *also see* Matthew, *Liberal Imperialists*, pp. 29–30.

Harcourt's desultory leadership. The same morning, the *Daily Mail* opened a competition, offering £100 to any 'Liberal or Radical whose reply is most in accord with the replies of the majority' of respondents on three questions:

(1) What is your choice of Leader?

(2) Name five points of the programme on which you think the party could rally, in the order of their importance.

(3) Are you in favour of again bringing up the Home Rule Bill? State definitely 'Yes' or 'No'.

Entries were to be submitted on postcards, with the editor of the *Mail* reserving 'to himself the right to print any reply'. It was further stipulated that 'anonymous replies will not be printed, and Conservative readers are barred'. Thus, Harmsworth's post-bag was also open to Rosebery, and it did not escape Sir Edward Hamilton's attention that the two men had recently been in contact. Perhaps they, too, had drunk stout and champagne.[1]

On 8 December, in a public exchange of letters with John Morley, Harcourt bowed out as leader of the Liberal opposition. Morley, in a speech to his constituents on 17 January 1899, likewise vacated his seat on the front bench. As Harcourt had drafted his letter of resignation after the *Mail* had announced its competition, Harmsworth's official biographers were able to conclude that their hero's 'audacity . . . had shaken if not convulsed a great English political party'. In any case, Harmsworth stirred the cauldron, intensifying the party's distress in the weeks that followed. The *Daily Chronicle* was 'compelled' on Saturday, 10 December,

> to hold over for want of space a great mass of correspondence which has reached us during the last two or three posts on Liberal policy, and also our own remarks on the subject. We shall deal with this matter on Monday.

The *Mail*, 'not in the secrets of the Liberal wire-pullers', suspected that the *Chronicle* had been 'effectively muzzled', and waited 'to see whether the *Daily News* will dare to open its lips or not'. Meanwhile, it published 'a trio of votes' in its own straw-poll, all answering 'No' to the question of Home Rule, and nominating Chamberlain, Harcourt, and Rosebery for the party leadership (12 December). The *Echo* was infuriated by such presumption. 'All the papers – especially the Tory ones – are busy discussing the Liberal programme, as if the programme of the Liberal Party was ever, or is now going to be, made by a few newspaper editors,' it scolded on the 12th:

> We can understand strong Tory papers like the *Daily Mail* being under that delusion, for their party is accustomed to having not only the policy of the party, but the policy of their press, dictated to them. . . . Evidently the

---

[1] Cook's diary, 6 November 1898, Cook Papers; Havighurst, *Radical Journalist*, p. 102; Stansky, *Ambitions and Strategies*, p. 298; Sir Edward Hamilton's diary, 17 December 1898.

Daily Mail thinks that the Liberal Party is conducted on similar principles; but it isn't.

On one point, however, the *Echo* and the *Daily Mail* were agreed. Both, for different reasons, regarded Asquith as the logical choice to lead the Liberals in the Commons. Lough took Crook to task for rating Asquith as 'first favourite': 'I think running Asquith as Leader was a breach of your contract with me,' he notified his editor on the 13th. 'Neither do I like giving up *Harcourt* so easily. He is *my first favourite*, Morley *second*.' Crook, by then editor for nearly a year, stiffly protested that the *Echo* was no less entitled than Lough to state a preference. 'You took my letter too seriously,' Lough then assured him. 'I have no *great* fault to find with your leaders – perhaps a little more reticence and criticism would be better than so much readiness to gulp.' As for the leadership sweepstakes, Lough's 'chief objection to Rosebery & Asquith is their unsatisfactory position re Ireland'. He professed to be keeping an open mind, and urged Crook to do the same: 'I don't want any of them to have the *Echo cheap* although its price is but ½d.'[1]

Strongly pressed by his imperialist friends, Asquith gave serious thought to the proposition of declaring his candidacy. But he could not afford to lose the income from his part-time legal practice. Possibly, too, he did not wish to be stamped as a *locum tenens* for Rosebery. Harcourt, who had left the door ajar, waited in vain to be summoned back. Having taken 'a stand against a Jingo invasion of the Liberal Party', he regarded as 'very significant' a leading article in the *Daily Chronicle* on 20 December that drew the distinction between unbridled expansionism and 'a right kind of imperialism which is essential to a just conception of the duty of an English Government'. From these tempered phrases, Harcourt deduced that 'Friend Massingham has discovered that ... the opinion of the Provinces is not for, but against, imperialism'. Stead, taking time off from his latest peace crusade, also noted 'a slight slump in Imperialism' at this time. Judging that the moment was not ripe, Rosebery drew back.[2]

For the sake of the party as well as their professional reputations, Liberal journalists tried to assist in working out a compromise. Sir Wemyss Reid received 'a call from an entire stranger', L. T. Hobhouse of the *Manchester Guardian*, 'who had written the communications on the crisis that have appeared in that paper'. Hobhouse, Reid told Rosebery on 16 December, 'has been closeted several times this week with J. M[orley]. He was brought to me yesterday by a friend, who said that he came in the interests of peace.' The purpose of the visit was to ascertain Rosebery's intentions and policies, which Reid was unwilling – and probably unable – to comment upon. Cook, in the

[1] Pound and Harmsworth, *Northcliffe*, p. 250; Lough to Crook, 13 and 15 December 1898, Crook Papers.
[2] Koss, *Asquith* (London, 1976), pp. 43–45; Harcourt to Morley, 21 December 1898, quoted in Gardiner, *Harcourt*, II, 477; Sir Edward Hamilton's diary, 15 January 1899.

Daily News, was as hostile to the Little Englanders in the party as to the French at Fashoda. But Crook, in the *Echo*, was a pacifist on both counts: in his comprehensive survey of 'Possible Liberal Leaders', he was polite – and even generous – to Asquith and Grey. Morley, on the other hand, was smartly rebuked for having followed Harcourt into splendid isolation. 'While we agree with very much of what Mr John Morley said last night,' the *Echo* wrote on 18 January 1899, 'we cannot but regret the manner of his saying it, and the method of action he has taken to emphasize his thoughts.' Morley's peevishness was contrasted with the statesmanlike speeches of Rosebery, Grey, and Asquith, 'of whom we feel that there can be no doubt whatsoever of their individual loyalty to the great principles of progress'. The *Chronicle*, too, chastised Morley for 'standing aloof from the party' in time of need (18 January). Neither Massingham nor Crook was turning Jingo: the former, in fact, was becoming increasingly critical of imperialist exploits. Both, however, were eager to put an end to party wrangles. Campbell-Bannerman, to whom Asquith had pledged his support on 19 December, was emerging as the man of the middle, satisfactory – or, at any rate, unobjectionable – to both sides. By 17 January, Massingham could confidently tell him that there was 'a quite unanimous feeling of approval' in his favour. Gathered at the Reform Club on 6 February, the parliamentary Liberal Party bore out this appraisal.[1]

War, averted in the Sudan in February 1899, broke out in South Africa seven months later. Combining agility with doggedness, Campbell-Bannerman contrived to keep a semblance of unity between the Liberal Imperialists on one flank and the Gladstonian fundamentalists on the other. The Liberal press was already a battlefield of another kind. Herbert Gladstone, appointed chief whip in April, was congratulated by his father's old private secretary, Horace Seymour, who remarked: 'There is not a single Liberal daily now worth the name. The *Daily News* is beneath contempt and the *Chronicle* only a shade better.' Inspired by Garrett of the *Cape Times*, Cook championed the rights of the English-speaking Uitlander minority in the Transvaal, and became an apologist for the heavy-handed diplomacy of Milner, now High Commissioner. As such, he supported Chamberlain's colonial policy to the point of helping to draft a Cabinet dispatch. Massingham gravitated in the opposite direction, allegedly under the influence of Harold Spender, his parliamentary correspondent. It was significant that Norman quit the *Chronicle* in May, and that Spender and H. W. Nevinson thereafter supplanted him. For a time, Massingham tried to deflect, if not to dampen, their passions; but, during his illness that summer, Frederic Harrison heard that 'the *Daily Chronicle* is forming a committee to protest against war', which seemed inevitable. Massingham was back in the office on 4 September, when

[1] Reid to Rosebery, 17 December 1898, Rosebery Papers, Vol. 10,056, fols. 169 ff.; Massingham to Campbell-Bannerman, 17 January 1899, Campbell-Bannerman Papers, Add. MSS. 41,234, fol. 67b.

Nevinson celebrated in his diary that he 'at last takes my position on the whole war'. Five days later, when Nevinson embarked for South Africa, the *Chronicle* gave him the best possible send-off: 'We shall go to war on an issue which has been deliberately changed during the course of negotiations and we shall earn for ourselves in South Africa a heritage of hatred.'[1]

On 21 November, the imperial views of the *Chronicle* changed overnight with the replacement of Massingham by W. J. Fisher. 'I only resigned when I was peremptorily required to maintain absolute silence on the policy of the Government in South Africa until after the conclusion of the war,' Massingham explained to Bryce. 'That was impossible.' This statement was true enough, but only part of the story. Cook, who sent a message of commiseration – 'I wrote to him & he answered,' he recorded with a hint of disbelief – knew that there had 'been friction for some time': Frank Lloyd, the proprietor, was distressed to see the 'circ[ulation] falling off & Mrs F. Lloyd [was] said to have resented attacks on Hugh Price Hughes'. Harold Spender and Vaughan Nash, who wrote on labour affairs, departed with Massingham. Nevinson learned of the upheaval some weeks later at Ladysmith, where he was under siege with the British forces; it was 'an overwhelming blow for me – all my hopes & position & power gone at once'. Henceforth, 'Scrutator' of *Truth* would 'merely glance over' the *Chronicle* 'to bring home to myself to what base uses a so-called Liberal journal can be put, under the censorship of a jingo paper manufacturer who owns it' (30 November). The *Daily Mail*, which purchased 600 tons of paper each week from 'the Messrs Lloyd, the largest paper manufacturers in the world', noted that 'Mr Frank Lloyd gave £2,000 to the British War Fund, while the *Daily Chronicle* . . . merely condoled with the sufferings of the Boers' (27 November). More soberly, the *Speaker*, which itself had recently changed hands and perspective, lamented that the London daily press 'is now virtually unanimous on the side of Mr Rhodes' (9 December). Rosebery saw a certain grim humour in the situation. 'The *Chronicle* sheds its chiefs almost as often as the Liberal Party,' he told J. A. Spender.[2]

'It will be the death of the *D.C.*,' J. L. Hammond prophesied to Hobhouse. 'Everyone who used to take it in now takes the *M.G.*' Massingham, Nash, and Harold Spender – whom Hobhouse described as 'the men who have constituted the character of the paper' – soon found a refuge on the *Manchester Guardian*, where their 'pro-Boer' attitudes were the norm. Hammond, who had been 'anxious to obtain an appointment on the editorial staff of a Liberal paper' at least since February 1898, when he applied to Cook, became editor

[1] Seymour to H. Gladstone, 16 April 1899, Viscount Gladstone Papers, Add. MSS. 46,057, fol. 149; Cook's diary, 21 September 1899, Cook Papers; Harold Spender, *The Fire of Life* (London, 1926?), p. 97; Harrison to Morley, 1 August [1899], Harrison Papers; Nevinson's diary, 4 September 1899 *et seq.*

[2] Massingham to Bryce, 5 December 1899, Bryce Papers; Cook's diary, 1 December 1899, Cook Papers; Spender, *Fire of Life*, pp. 99–100; Nevinson's diary, 17 January 1900; Rosebery to Spender, 25 November 1899, quoted in Wilson Harris, *J. A. Spender* (London, 1946), p. 45.

of the *Speaker* in early October. That position was in the gift of Sir John Brunner, whom he had served as private secretary, and who recoiled from Reid's strenuous imperialism. Brunner and Reid parted on cordial terms: 'I was, & am, quite willing to go on for another ten years as I have done since 1890,' Reid wrote to Rosebery after he had received six months' notice; 'but of course I cannot compel Brunner (who has behaved exceedingly well during all my connection with him) to continue to make a pecuniary sacrifice if his own inclination does not lead him to do so.' Although Hammond could count on Brunner, who was '*quite sound* on this business, to ... sink something', he was obliged to cast about for other funds. R. C. ('Rudie') Lehmann, three times a Liberal candidate before his return at South Leicestershire in 1906, was chairman of the directorate from October 1899 to August 1906.[1]

*   *   *

After the forcible conversion of the *Chronicle*, the *Speaker* counted only the *Morning Leader*, the *Star*, and the *Westminster Gazette* as capable of maintaining 'any debate' against 'the solid phalanx of the entire morning penny press' (9 December). The *Morning Leader* and the *Star*, both under the same management, carried relatively little political weight. The *Westminster* was in a different league, possibly in a league by itself. Sir Robert Edgcumbe, a Liberal stalwart, offered J. A. Spender a 'reminiscence' of a memorable train journey:

> I was travelling to London on a Thursday afternoon, 9th November 1899, and was alone in my compartment. At Hatfield Lord Salisbury got into the same carriage and as the train moved off, he was handed three evening papers. Shortly after we started he took them up, opened first the *Globe* and immediately threw it on the floor of the carriage, then he opened the *Evening Standard* and treated it in a similar manner, lastly he opened the *Westminster Gazette* and proceeded to read it diligently until we arrived at King's Cross Station. He was on his way to London to speak that night at the Lord Mayor's banquet.

Thus, despite a narrow circulation, the *Westminster* had a wide political appeal. 'It is not easy to get the *Westm. Gazette* in our region,' Bryce reported. 'I tried all round Oxford Circus tonight in vain and at last succeeded only in the Langham Hotel – so you see demand exceeds supply.' What sort of a paper could have attracted both Salisbury and Bryce? Taking care neither 'to exclude left-wing letters and articles' nor (as he interrupted his holiday in

[1] Hammond to Hobhouse, 5 December 1899, Hammond Papers; Hobhouse to Scott, 26 November 1899, *Guardian* Archives; Reid to Rosebery, 24 May 1899, Rosebery Papers, Vol. 10,056, fols. 209–10; Hammond to Cook, 16 February 1898, Cook Papers; Lehmann to Hammond, 12 July 1912, Hammond Papers.

Venice to instruct Gould) to have 'too much *Manchester Guardian* quoted in the *W.G.*', J. A. Spender avoided extremes. Aware that he 'seemed to be steering the unheroic course of the "smoother" who was oiling his own waters', he later acknowledged 'the trouble I was in during most of the time'. Although an editorial fascination with Rosebery sometimes bled through, the *Westminster* dutifully upheld Campbell-Bannerman, and thereby defied classification as either a defender or an opponent of the South African war.[1]

The *Echo* was conspicuously absent from the *Speaker*'s inventory. Early in 1899, there had been a ' "bust-up" on the Board', which led to the temporary withdrawal of Lough and Barker and the eventual dethronement of Crook. Like Lloyd at the *Chronicle*, the proprietors of the *Echo* had reason to believe that opposition to the war effort was a check on circulation and a drain on advertising revenues. Crook's resignation, announced in early December 1899, took effect on 9 January 1900. Ramsay MacDonald was 'exceeding sorry to hear the news', but applauded Crook's fidelity to principle: 'Times have come to a terrible pass & goodness knows what is to be the issue. It is very very sad that those of us who do *believe* are so split up.' Crook left for America, carrying a letter of introduction to Paul Dana of the *New York Sun* from John Redmond, who commended him as 'a friend of mine, a most accomplished journalist & cultured Irishman ... who until recently was Editor of the London *Echo*, but who because of his Anti War sentiments has been forced to relinquish the position'. Under Crook, the *Echo* had taken the view that the war in South Africa was unjust and unnecessary, and 'that the dispute ... on the question of the franchise in the Transvaal was not a case to be settled by an appeal to the sword at all, but by recourse to diplomacy, conciliatory, not provocative diplomacy' such as Milner had practised (12 December 1899). After Crook's departure, the paper paid fulsome tributes to British military commanders, Lords Kitchener and Roberts ('"Bobs" Africanus'), and put a premium on imperial solidarity. As hostilities dragged on, the *Echo* grew more Chamberlainite than Chamberlain himself. 'The Government must be aroused to sharp action,' it demanded on 12 January 1901. 'What they are to do they must do quickly. The country will not tolerate another year of helpless inactivity and hopeless bungling.'[2]

On his return to London in the spring of 1900, Crook brought a suit against Consolidated Newspapers, Ltd., the holding company of the *Echo*, for a commission on the paper's profits during the period of his editorship. J. Bamford Slack (later Liberal MP for Mid-Hertfordshire), acting as his solicitor, cast light on the paper's finances in the process of evaluating Crook's claim:

---

[1] Edgcumbe to Spender [August 1903], and Spender to Gould, 16 September 1899, Spender Papers, Add. MSS. 46,391, fols. 120, 42; Bryce to Cook, 4 February [1899?], Cook Papers; Spender, *Life, Journalism and Politics*, I, 102–103.

[2] Lough to Crook, 5 January 1899, MacDonald to Crook, 3 December 1899, Redmond to Dana, 12 February 1900, Crook Papers.

From the accounts you will see that the *Echo* made a profit for the year ending 30th Sept. 1898 of £3420.18.1, so that you would under your agreement be entitled if you had been there for the whole of that year to about £34 – being one per cent of such profits. As a matter of fact however you were only there about nine months as you really commenced your duties in January 1898. Moreover from the auditor's note . . . it appears that the only profits earned after Mr Lough came into the saddle was a sum of £300 and that the actual working of the *Echo* from January to September 1898 showed a profit of only about £50. The Balance Sheet for the following period, namely that up to the 31st December 1899, shows a very heavy loss during these fifteen months, namely – £1249 the *Echo* and £5682 the *Morning Herald*. Of course if we employed an accountant to go through the Books & check these accounts and insist upon proper deductions being made because of the manner in which the *Echo* was depleted & impoverished by the *Morning Herald*, we might possibly make out a claim, but it seems to me that even then we should have considerable difficulty and great expense would be involved.

Undeterred, Crook proceeded with his action, and hired as his counsel Rufus Isaacs (later Liberal MP for Reading and still later the 1st Marquess of Reading), whose fee Bamford Slack considered 'somewhat excessive'. Lough regretted Crook's perseverance, which 'places me in a great difficulty as *at this moment* we are trying very hard to settle all outstanding differences' between members of the proprietary. On 10 July 1900, he was able to report 'that the first step towards our getting into power at the Consolidated has been accomplished': Joseph Cooke and several others 'have retired from the Board, which Mr Barker & I again have joined'. Best of all, the *Morning Herald* had been sold off to Pearson. Under the circumstances, Crook agreed to submit to arbitration. In September 1901, F. W. Pethick Lawrence, soon to gain fame and notoriety as a patron of the women suffragists, took control of the *Echo*. Ramsay MacDonald was named chief leader-writer, and Crook accepted an invitation from Lough, who hung on as a director, 'to undertake the provision of Political Notes daily in the paper'. As editor, 'Pathetic' Lawrence showed good intentions, but limited powers of application. Even with injections of capital from H. J. Wilson, the veteran Liberal MP, the *Echo* went from bad to worse until 1905, when it expired.[1]

Just as the *Echo* trudged in the footsteps of the *Daily Chronicle*, with Crook suffering the same fate as Massingham, the *Daily News* was to follow in the wake of the *Echo*, only with better long-term results. That change did not occur, however, until the beginning of 1901, and meanwhile the Liberal press

[1] Slack to Crook, 28 May and 19 July 1900, and Lough to Crook, 30 June and 10 July 1900, and 21 November 1901, Crook Papers; *Sell's* (1901); F. W. Pethick Lawrence, *Fate Has Been Kind* (London, 1942), pp. 57 ff.; Springfield, *Some Piquant People*, p. 22.

was in as sorry a state as the Liberal Party. Earlier attempts to redress the balance had failed. Dislodged from the *Chronicle*, Massingham initially hoped to retaliate by establishing a new daily. In a prospectus, which J. A. Hobson helped him to draft, he called for a minimum investment of £200,000. To Harcourt, he mentioned 'the figure' of £250,000, which seemed 'absolutely out of reach'. Stead, a fellow exile from daily journalism, quickly insinuated himself into the picture. While Massingham sounded out like-minded politicians (including Morley, Bryce, and Dilke), he discussed the project with Brett, who recommended an approach to Carnegie:

> He must be a first rate businessman, to have made all those millions. He has wealth – like Monte Carlo. He wants power. Why don't you suggest to him quite straight (1) that he should put down £500,000 (which is a trifle to him) in a big *Liberal* paper. (2) Vest 1/5th share in you, and another 1/5th in me, keeping 3/5ths for himself. (3) Massingham (or any one else) for Editor. (4) The management to be distinct from the Editorship. (5) Mr Carnegie to be able to redeem the 2/5ths at any time upon terms to be settled beforehand. (6) The paper to be run on Anglo-American Liberal lines.

By Brett's calculation: 'This is the psychological moment. No delay is possible. For the thing is sure to be done.' He was confident that 'we could make this the biggest thing in newspapers ever seen in about 3 years, or less: and knock Harmsworth clean out. . . . It would amuse me!' Stead promptly wrote to Carnegie, more or less as Brett had dictated:

> The disaster which I foreshadowed to you some time ago has just taken place. Mr Massingham with his two assistants, Mr Harold Spender (brother of the Spender of the *Westminster Gazette*), and Mr Naish [*sic*], have been compelled to leave the *Daily Chronicle*, which is henceforth going to support the Government in its South African crime. Not only so, but the directors of your old *Echo* have decided to adopt the same policy, and Mr Crook, who has steadily maintained a noble battle against Jingoism on the *Echo*, is now also turned out. We have now, therefore, four of the ablest journalists in London practically gagged, and there is no longer any morning paper, with the exception of the halfpenny *Leader*, that has a word to say against the war in the Transvaal.

More specifically on his own account than Massingham's, Stead offered Carnegie a plan for 'an endowed newspaper, although in my opinion a really first-class newspaper, adequately supported, would be its own endowment'. Tampering with Brett's figures, Stead reckoned that it could be launched with £250,000, although it would be better to begin with £500,000 and 'a reserve fund of the same amount, to be drawn upon in case of need'. Letting his imagination run wild, he spoke in terms of 'a series of newspapers as . . . the best possible answer to those who are bent upon silencing the voice of the Liberal party', and concluded that 'the mere fact that such papers had a million at their back would save an immense sum in advertising, and would be the best possible means of warning the enemies of mankind that the children of light mean business'. Not surprisingly, Carnegie responded in the negative. Whether he might have been tempted by Brett's more concrete proposals is a moot point. E. H. Stout, who was business manager at the *Review of Reviews*, was less optimistic than Brett. 'I believe it is the worst possible time you could have struck to raise the money,' he told Stead. 'I do not know what schemes you may be thinking of in your note to Massingham where you seem to indicate that something was "on foot"; but knowing nothing else, my present opinion is that any such scheme is hopeless.' In Stout's opinion, nothing could be done without the assistance of some '"smart financial man" who can run the show'. Rebuffed by Carnegie, the counter-revolutionaries turned to a smart financial woman. 'I hear that the Little Englander paper which is to be started by Lady Carlisle for Massingham has collected some £70,000 – Carnegie being the principal subscriber,' Cook wrote to Rosebery on 31 December 1899. He had been unreliably informed. As late as February, Stead claimed to have collected pledges only to the sum of £40,000, and the idea was abandoned when Massingham went to the *Manchester Guardian* in March.[1]

'Have you been noticing the correspondence in the *D.N.* under the heading "The Country & the War"?' Cook asked Rosebery at the close of 1899. 'It is significant, I think.' Readers' responses seemed to back the view that Cook was keeping 'the party from becoming a "Kruger clique"'. Henry Norman, for one, saw him in that radiant light. 'The fight you are making for patriotism and common sense in the *Daily News* is beyond praise,' he wrote in March 1900, reporting that

> a very prominent Liberal the other day said to me, talking of this subject: 'I cut out a leader in the *Daily News* which I think is the best I ever saw in my life'. He took out his pocket-book and showed it to me – the one about those asses and the 'Gladstone League'. *I* took out *my* pocket-book and showed him the same thing.

Cook's efforts notwithstanding, public opinion doubted the Liberals' capacity for patriotism, especially after Chamberlain's crude campaign gibe that 'a seat lost to the Government is a seat gained (or sold) to the Boers'. At the general election that autumn, the party struggled desperately to hold its eroded ground. Over a dozen 'pro-Boer' spokesmen, as they were labelled, lost their seats; others, like Lloyd George, scraped through with hairbreadth majorities.

---

[1] Harcourt to Morley, 3 December 1899, quoted in Gardiner, *Harcourt*, II, 513; Brett to Stead, 1 December 1899, and Stout to Stead, 7 December 1899, Stead Papers; Stead to Carnegie, 2 December 1899, Carnegie Papers; Cook to Rosebery, 31 December 1899, Rosebery Papers, Vol. 10,112, fols. 260–61; Havighurst, *Radical Journalist*, pp. 111–12.

According to *The Times*'s tabulation, 'more than 80' of the 184 Liberals in the new House – as opposed to 63 in the last – could 'be expected to support the Government on questions affecting the war' (17 October). The *Daily News*, most alarmed by 'the enormous Tory vote in the English boroughs' (13 October), reasoned that Liberal Imperialism was the only means by which the party might recapture 'its former appeal to the national imagination' (19 October). Even so, Cook declined to affiliate with the breakaway Liberal Imperialist Council, arguing that 'permeation is better than proscription', and observing from the grammar of its manifesto that 'they are determined on splitting – even their infinitives' (20 October). Lord Brassey, a major shareholder in the *Daily News*, was the titular president of the Council, and J. Saxon Mills, Cook's colleague and future biographer, was among its officials. Subsequently, when the body was reconstituted first as the Liberal Imperialist League and then as the Liberal League, Cook was less reticent. By then, however, he was no longer editor of the *Daily News* and was writing leaders for Fisher on the *Chronicle*.[1]

The year 1900 saw Liberalism at its nadir at the polls and in print. 'I find from small indications among our friends that public opinion is more deeply demoralised than I had known,' C. P. Scott, editor of the *Manchester Guardian* and MP for Leigh (which he held in October by a margin of 120 votes), wrote to Hobhouse in January. Rather prematurely, he discerned cause for optimism:

> ... Rabid & reckless Imperialism has received a rude & salutary check & there is a distinct reaction towards moderation & sound policy. Our regular sales are I think practically unaffected & we have even gained a large number of additional postal subscribers – many of them old readers of the *Chronicle*. But we lose a good bit of the casual sales which wd. naturally come to us at a time of great public excitement & the *Daily Mail*, partly because of its war policy, but very much more because of its general flashiness and of its price – the ½d. make a lot of difference to small clerks and the like who think twice & thrice before they spend a penny a day on their newspaper. On the whole I feel not the smallest reason for discouragement. We are weathering the storm & shall weather it with ease, success, and lasting credit.

Still unshaken, Scott soon received larger indications of the popular mood. The 'City of Refuge', as Nevinson called the *Guardian* office, was besieged by irate Mancunians. H. O. Rouse, then an apprentice compositor, recalled vividly how the police, who stood guard round the building in Cross Street, routinely searched his lunch-box for bombs. Hired by the Tory *Manchester Courier*, a brass band blared the funeral march from *Saul*. In May, when news

---

[1] Cook to Rosebery, 31 December 1899, Rosebery Papers, Vol. 10,112, fols. 260–61; Mills, *Cook*, pp. 182, 189–90; Matthew, *Liberal Imperialists*, pp. 86–87.

came of the relief of Mafeking, a Union Jack was hurriedly hoisted from the roof to avert violence from the crowd below. Trains steamed into Manchester 'full of men who expressed their attitude by crumpling the paper into a ball and throwing it away ostentatiously, when they had read the telegrams from New York, Galveston, and New Orleans'. By the end of the war, the paper was estimated to have lost one-seventh of its readership: its daily sale of nearly 42,000 copies topped that of _The Times_, but the penny _Guardian_ sold at a third the price.[1]

E. C. Bentley, who eventually gave his middle name – Clerihew – to a form of double-couplet verse, was then a young lawyer and a contributor to _Punch_ and the _Speaker_. 'The state of the nation worries me more and more daily,' he confessed in his diary on 1 February 1900. 'The entire powerful portion of the press is not only upon the other side, but is marked by a total absence of conscience that reveals an appalling state of things.' Contemplating a change of profession, Bentley 'hadn't an idea until this war came that journalists were so morally lax'. The _Daily News_, which he was to join the following year, was as bad as any and worse than most. Slanting its content and comment in Rosebery's favour, it consistently undermined Campbell-Bannerman's leadership. Rosebery's rectorial address at Glasgow on 16 November was extravagantly praised, while Campbell-Bannerman's speech at Dundee, where he referred – perhaps not accidentally – to the Liberal Imperialist Council as the Liberal Unionist Council, was deplored. 'Your statement as regards Lord R. was perfectly reasonable and candid,' J. Emmott Barlow, Liberal MP for Frome, assured Campbell-Bannerman. 'What is to be done with the _Daily News_! We cannot go on with such a paper as our official organ. It does a great deal more harm than good.' Fortunately, relief was on the way.[2]

Before it arrived, and indeed for some time afterwards, Campbell-Bannerman was in dire straits. Better equipped than either Rosebery or Harcourt to withstand journalistic pinpricks, he admitted to J. A. Spender that 'the tone of _The Times_ and other papers' grated upon him: 'I am not very thin-skinned, & I confess it is rather contempt than resentment that their silly facetiousness excites in me.' Leicester Harmsworth, the newly elected member for Caithness, called on 22 November 1900 and bluntly requested him to step aside for Rosebery. Harmsworth described how, when he had urged his eldest brother 'to join the Liberal Party & carry his paper (1,400,000 circulation) with him', Alfred had asked 'how could he, to a disunited party?' Leicester inflated the sale of the _Daily Mail_, which Wadsworth put at 989,000; possibly he added in the _Evening News_, the _Weekly Dispatch_ (bought from

[1] Scott to Hobhouse, 4 January 1900, _Guardian_ Archives; Ayerst, _Guardian_, p. 280; R. H. Gretton, _A Modern History of the English People 1880–1922_ (New York, 1930), p. 526.

[2] Bentley's diary, 1 February 1900, Bentley Papers, Bodleian MS. Eng. Misc. e. 829; E. C. Bentley, _Those Days_ (London, 1940), p. 216; Barlow to Campbell-Bannerman, 18 November 1900, Campbell-Bannerman Papers, Add. MSS. 41,236, fol. 24.

Newnes for £25,000), and other family properties. Brother Cecil, defeated at Droitwich in the October elections and again in a rancorous by-election at North-East Lanark in September 1901, was a Liberal Leaguer like Leicester: in the summer of 1900, he decided 'to expend his spare cash and spare time in starting a monthly review', the *New Liberal Review*, which Alfred understood 'to be . . . the organ of the Imperial Liberal Council, but which he hopes to make something more than a mere political barrel organ'. Brother Harold, defeated as a Liberal at Gravesend in 1900 and as a Liberal Unionist at Mid-Shropshire in 1906, was an interim Roseberian, who offered to support the Liberal League through papers at Leeds, Glasgow, and Edinburgh.[1]

The Harmsworth brethren, a congregation unto themselves, were not alone in worshipping at Rosebery's altar. Since the outbreak of war, Harcourt had been waiting for 'the Rosebery rocket . . . to fizzle out', confident that '*The Times* will get tired of puffing him, and his hold on our people is limited.' Nevertheless, the critics of Liberalism continued to regard Rosebery as a Liberal saviour. On 4 October 1899, Lawson commissioned J. L. Garvin to write for the *Daily Telegraph* ' a second letter from a Liberal, with as much force, vigour and directness as you can put into it'. The purpose was 'to show that the obvious duty of Lord Rosebery and Sir Edward Grey ought, in the opinion of a great bulk of their party, to be no longer shirked'. To say the least, it was absurd for either Lawson or Garvin to ventriloquize as Liberals; but that did not restrict them. For inspiration, Garvin was advised to 'read carefully the first-leader in the *Daily News* to-day', where 'you will see developed the ample ground upon which true Liberalism is bound to oppose Kruger'. Garvin did the job so well that, on 24 January 1900, Lawson bade him 'to sit down and write another leader, in plain, vigorous, telling words, basing your article on the pith and spirit' of Rosebery's latest speech at Chatham. 'In doing this evade any expression that would look like a desire to put Lord Rosebery into Lord Salisbury's place,' he instructed, 'or anything that might tend to make people believe that we thought of side or politics, but go in as strongly as you please for the tone and moral of the speech.' The *Daily News* and other Liberal advocates of imperialism espoused Rosebery out of admiration. The *Telegraph* and other ministerial journals, while genuinely attracted to his doctrines of national efficiency, utilized him as a wedge.[2]

That instrument, as Lawson was aware, was potentially double-edged. Designed to widen divisions in Liberal ranks, it threatened to expose divergences among the Unionists. There was persistent talk, much of it idle chatter, that Rosebery might form an administration with the participation of

[1] Campbell-Bannerman to Spender, 16 May 1901, Spender Papers, Add. MSS. 46,388, fol. 6; memorandum by Campbell-Bannerman, 22 November 1900, Campbell-Bannerman Papers, 2nd ser.; Harmsworth to Strachey, 7 July 1900, Strachey Papers; H. Harmsworth to Rosebery, 22 February 1902, Rosebery Papers, Vol. 10,168, fols. 34–35.
[2] Harcourt to L. V. Harcourt, 1 November 1899, quoted in Gardiner, *Harcourt*, II, 512; Lawson to Garvin, 4 October 1899 (copy), and 24 January 1900, Garvin Papers.

Milner and Chamberlain, and the benediction of the Fabians. Old, and grieving over his wife's death, Salisbury could not continue for long. In the months preceding the declaration of war, he was outwardly more cautious than Chamberlain; thereafter, he was less intransigent on the question of war aims, and appeared to lack resolution. Buckle complained to Leo Amery, who had joined the foreign – or, as it symbolically became, the foreign and imperial – department of *The Times*, that, 'though the spirit of the country is admirable, the Government (except perhaps Joe) seems nerveless & flaccid; & the Prime Minister especially always says the wrong thing'. Moberly Bell was convinced that Rosebery had a 'splendid chance' if only he would take it. 'You have more time, more power, to think out these questions' of national policy 'than the Ministers have – more experience than some – more intelligence than others,' he wrote beseechingly to Rosebery on 19 November 1900. 'Give us – give them – the lead – if they follow the credit is yours, if they do not the best part of the opposition & perhaps of the other side too will follow you.' Rosebery, unable to see why 'any private citizen [should] be summoned from retirement, to fill the sour and ungrateful task of critic, or perhaps foil', pointedly reminded him 'that many of those who call out for a strong Opposition have done their best at the recent Election, and with great success, to exterminate it'.[1]

As early as 10 June 1899, the *Telegraph* was demanding 'an ultimatum, supported by such a military demonstration as the burghers of the Transvaal would either see to be irresistible or would only face with the certainty of defeat and disaster'. Two days later, Lawson told McDonnell 'secretly that the somewhat violent article ... was the result of direct inspiration by Mr Chamberlain'. He was 'most anxious' to obtain an interview with Salisbury, 'and from what he tells me' McDonnell thought 'it most desirable he should do so'. Salisbury fitted him into a crowded agenda at 4.45 on the afternoon of the 13th. 'Buckle comes at six,' he reminded his private secretary; 'they should not meet.' At the Colonial Office, Chamberlain received his own visitors from Fleet Street. S. H. Jeyes, the new editor of the *Standard*, came on 21 August, 'very anxious to know what line to take with regard to the Transvaal crisis'. A subordinate, who attended to him, minuted that 'Mr Jeyes seemed in great doubt as to whether he should preach peace or war, but I hope that after what I said he will not commit the *Standard* to any definite verdict just yet.' Chamberlain, though not Salisbury, might have preferred otherwise.[2]

On matters of electoral tactics and constitutional procedure, differences of emphasis cloaked conflicts of interest. The burgeoning Harmsworth press was courted by the Conservatives, the Liberal Unionists, and the Liberal Imperial-

---

[1] Buckle to Amery, 23 February 1900, Amery Papers; E. Moberly Bell, *Life and Letters of C. F. Moberly Bell* (London, 1927), pp. 223–24; Moberly Bell to Rosebery, 19 November 1900, Rosebery Papers, Vol. 10,113, fol. 301; Rosebery to Moberly Bell, 23 November 1900, *Times* Archives.

[2] McDonnell to Salisbury, 12 June 1899 (with Salisbury's comments), Salisbury Papers; memorandum to Chamberlain by A[mpthill?], 21 August 1899, Chamberlain Papers.

ists, each with their own objectives. Balfour sent Alfred Harmsworth 'a single word' (in fact, a long screed) 'of hearty thanks for the admirable service done to the Party by the *Daily Mail*' during the by-election campaign at St Pancras in July 1899. In reply, he received a tirade on the party's neglect of its newspaper assets. 'I will certainly speak to Middleton on the subject of the Press – the great importance of which I recognise – and at the same time my own incompetence to advise upon it,' he promised Harmsworth. Andrew Bonar Law, adopted to stand for a Glasgow constituency in the 1900 elections, was eager to obtain better publicity from the local Harmsworth organ:

> The [*Glasgow*] *Herald* is a party newspaper, aiming at strengthening its party in Glasgow & since I am one of the Unionist candidates it seems to me that the fact that I am unknown should be reason why a Unionist paper should try to bring my name forward as prominently as possible in the interest of the Unionist Party in the constituency which I am to fight.

As Bonar Law was to learn the hard way, the Harmsworths' support could never be taken for granted. In the 1901 by-election at North-East Lanark, for example, the *Glasgow Herald* and the *Daily Mail* strongly backed Cecil Harmsworth, a Liberal Imperialist, against his Unionist rival; and Harold Harmsworth volunteered to put the *Glasgow Herald* at Rosebery's disposal. The only newspapers on which Unionist politicians could depend absolutely were the few in which they actually held shares. Harold Spender, to whom Lloyd George later assigned the task of compiling a list of company directorships 'held by the principal Ministers in the last two Tory Administrations', identified St John Brodrick, the Secretary of State for War, as a director of the *Globe*. To be sure, there were others, including Balfour, who were involved less formally in newspaper management.[1]

The jingo press took no pains to distinguish between opponents of government policy: all were indiscriminately and often unjustifiably pilloried as 'pro-Boers'. Similarly, the critics of imperialism saw no practical distinctions among their antagonists: to John Morley's palate, Liberal Imperialism was only 'Chamberlain wine with a Rosebery label'. In the war of words, stereotypes were a potent weapon, and neither side had a monopoly on them. To impugn the patriotism of the dissidents – men of the calibre of Morley, Scott, Lloyd George, and Courtney – was as reprehensible as to assert that Milner and Chamberlain were perpetrating a capitalist plot on behalf of Rhodes. It ought not to detract from the moral courage of the *Manchester Guardian* to recall that J. A. Hobson's dispatches from South Africa were tinged with a virulent anti-Semitism. Nor is it to condone the invective of the *Daily Mail* and the *Morning Post*, to name but two of the offenders, to ac-

[1] Balfour to Harmsworth, 18 and 25 July 1899, Northcliffe Papers, Dep. 4890/1; Bonar Law to James Kennedy, 14 October 1899, Bonar Law Papers 12/1/79; memorandum by Harold Spender, 4 April 1913, Lloyd George Papers C/9/4/24.

knowledge that their victims were sometimes misguided in their zeal. Quite simply, one man's fact was another's fiction. The high mortality rates and in-sanitary conditions of the concentration camps, into which Boer civilians were herded, were graphically described in the *Manchester Guardian*, but eluded the gaze of Amery, who 'was tremendously impressed by the arrangements made for the health and happiness of the people there'.[1]

Confronted by an overwhelming hostility, Liberal journalists who con-demned the origins and the conduct of the war were at an obvious dis-advantage. Stead, for one, gloried in his martyrdom. 'Although I may stand absolutely alone today', he declared to J. W. Robertson Scott, who was shortly to leave the *Chronicle* with Massingham, 'there will rally around me all that is best in the nation before long.' To the malcontents 'below the gangway', it was painful enough to be consigned to the wilderness without having papers like the *Daily Telegraph* lecturing them on the responsibilities of 'true Liberal-ism' from a text in the *Daily News*. 'The papers of the Unionist Party, of course, rain down blessings on Lord Rosebery's head,' Labouchere wrote in *Truth* on 2 November 1899.

So does the *Daily News*. I suppose that this journal may now be taken as the exponent of the Liberal Imperialism which is to come into existence in ten years. In the meantime, it supports Mr Chamberlain, and it exults at the defeat of Mr [Harold] Spender at Bow and Bromley, where the electors 'declined to vote for a Liberal candidate recommended to them by Mr Morley'.... Were it not that some London Editors are apt to regard them-selves as omniscient, it is not clear what special sources of knowledge in regard to Liberal opinion outside Fleet-street and a few London clubs, the Editor of the *Daily News* enjoys. Under the rule of Sir John Robinson and his predecessors, the *Daily News* used to be one of the soundest of Radical organs. What is it now? It is neither Tory fish nor Liberal fowl, whilst the faintest suspicion of good Radical red herring has disappeared.

Labouchere might have paused to reflect that he had only himself to blame. Had he kept his one-quarter shareholding, the problem need never have arisen. On 12 December 1899, Arnold Morley and Oppenheim visited the office in Bouverie Street, and discussed that morning's leading article, in which Cook had separated the Roseberian sheep from the Little Englander goats. Oppenheim 'said he thought it very good'. Morley 'laughed & said he wasn't sure which head he came under'. Brassey's appreciation went without saying. But Ashton, definitely a goat, 'charged' Morley 'to say how strongly he disapproved'. Morley related that 'Ashton wanted to resign publicly his pro-prietorship. That, said A. M., would have been inconvenient, and after $\frac{3}{4}$ hr. talk I made it all right & he withdraws his intention. I explained how difficult it

---

[1] Ayerst, *Guardian*, pp. 283–86; Amery to his mother, 24 May 1902 (from Pretoria), Amery Papers.

wd. have been for the proprietors . . . to interfere.' Yet Ashton was far from persuaded. That day, he gave notice that the paper was 'losing money and he wanted to be quit of the whole thing'.[1]

It was less 'inconvenient' to act upon commercial rather than ideological grounds. The directors of Consolidated Newspapers had done so with regard to Crook, and Frank Lloyd had maintained that financial considerations alone dictated his ultimatum to Massingham. Brunner had pleaded the same excuse in extricating himself from the *Speaker*. The pretext was never without substance. G. B. Dibblee, the young and energetic manager of the *Manchester Guardian*, modernized production and built circulation with the result that record profits were realized in 1895 and 1896. His achievement undone by an editorial policy with which he felt no sympathy, he submitted his resignation in 1899, but was induced to stay on until 1903. Beyond any doubt, opposition to the war did not pay. On the other hand, Liberal support for the war scarcely paid better. If Liberal readers wanted imperialism at their breakfast tables, they could satisfy their appetites with the threepenny *Times*, any of the Tory penny papers, or, most economically, with the halfpenny *Mail*, which began a northern edition at Manchester in February 1900. In spite of Cook's appointment, the circulation of the *Daily News* continued to drop through the '90s, and sank below 56,000 in 1899. The next year, the trend was modestly reversed with a sale of 61,000; but there was no dramatic rise until 1904, when that paper – like the *Chronicle* – reduced its price to a halfpenny to become more competitive with the *Mail* and Pearson's *Daily Express*. By then, of course, the war was over, and a reaction against imperialism had set in.

After the 'khaki' election in the autumn of 1900, further attempts were made to collect capital to establish a new Liberal paper or to buy out an existing one. Massingham, a fifth wheel on the *Manchester Guardian*, joined forces with Crook, a more dependable ally than Stead. R. R. Cherry, who had just stood unsuccessfully for one Liverpool seat and was to be elected for another in 1906, received a prospectus from Crook: 'I entirely approve of the plan – & I will undertake to subscribe £100 & possibly more. . . . If Massingham is editor I am sure he will make the paper a success.' Men of means were not lacking. The difficulty was that they could not agree in their requirements. J. Corrie Grant, who stood in a by-election at Harrow in April 1899, encountered still greater frustration in his efforts to reconcile the competing demands of potential subscribers who, save for their distaste for the war, held contrary views on Home Rule, temperance, and labour questions. It took political initiative to accomplish what journalists themselves could not arrange.[2]

Lloyd George, who had dabbled in journalism as the contributor of Welsh

[1] Stead to Robertson Scott, 16 October 1899, Stead Papers; Cook's diary, 12 December 1899, Cook Papers.

[2] Cherry to Crook, 3 November 1900, Crook Papers; Koss, *Fleet Street Radical: A. G. Gardiner and the 'Daily News'* (London, 1973), pp. 38–41, which provides the basis for the following narrative.

lobby notes to the *Manchester Guardian*, had a lifelong obsession with the press. Hearing that the proprietors of the *Daily News* were in conflict with each other, and in Arnold Morley's case with members of their families, he composed 'two very careful letters'. He read them to Harold Spender over dinner at Gatti's, before sending them to George Cadbury and Franklin Thomasson, two wealthy Liberal businessmen. Each agreed to put up £20,000. A further £35,000 was provided by other proprietors, including R. C. Lehmann. John Morley was among the purchasers of debentures, which raised £40,000. Capital in hand, Lloyd George opened negotiations. By the end of the year, the deal was clinched, and there remained only the legal formalities to complete. 'Yesterday we met at the office of the *D.N.* solicitor and agreed with the other side on a price for the goodwill of the *D.N.*,' Lehmann told his wife on 8 January 1901. 'They asked £50,000; we offered £40,000 – and eventually the difference was split at £45,000, a very good bargain for us I am sure.'[1]

Before the contracts were signed, Lloyd George proclaimed that, in the future, the *Daily News* would 'take a neutral line on the war'. Cook, who had left the *Pall Mall Gazette* in 1892 rather than pledge himself to neutrality, could not remain. Arnold Morley confirmed to him that the new owners were 'men with whom you will not be able to work', and Robinson added that they were 'extreme men' who would retain Herbert Paul and bring in a new editor. On 2 January, Massingham informed Scott from London that he was leaving the *Manchester Guardian* for the *Daily News*, 'which represents an attempt to put Liberalism here on the basis which the *Guardian* has so firmly established in Manchester'. There was no suggestion of any 'neutral line'. Harold Spender, eager to escape from Manchester, wrote to Scott that 'Lloyd George, to whose efforts the new paper is almost entirely due, has put before me so strongly the necessity of my supporting him, that it really, I think, becomes my duty to do so'. Scott, 'obliged to make some rearrangement of our staff in consequence of the loss of Massingham & Spender', who were followed by Nash, extended an invitation to R. C. K. Ensor.[2]

According to Stead, it was originally proposed that John Morley should edit the *Daily News*, with Massingham as 'acting editor'. But Morley used his influence in securing the appointment of Lehmann, previously on the staff of *Punch*, who thereupon resigned the seat on the board to which his investment of £10,000 entitled him. Robinson 'did not consider himself justified in accepting' an offer to serve as 'a sort of consulting director'. Aged seventy-two, he took the opportunity to retire. P. W. Clayden, a year his senior, presided during a brief interregnum that capped his long career in Fleet Street. 'I have often said – and it is the result of many years of observation &

[1] Cadbury to Scott, 1 January 1902, *Guardian* Archives; Lehmann to his wife, 8 January 1901, Lehmann Papers.
[2] Cook's diary, 12 December 1900 *et seq.*, Cook Papers; Massingham to Scott, 2 January 1901, Spender to Scott, 3 January 1901, and Scott to Ensor, 5 January 1901 (copy), *Guardian* Archives.

experience – that there is no such training for all a man's faculties as the editorship of a daily paper,' he wrote to Crook. 'It brings all the world before one and calls for prompt, decisive & accurate judgment on men and things, every day & many times a day.'[1]

Cook went down with all flags flying. Determined that he 'could not on any account do [the] trimming' for men of Lloyd George's stamp, not that they had asked him, he declared in his farewell leader that his 'object' had been 'to keep steadily in view the larger interests and duties of the country as an Imperial power, and to sink, in some measure, mere party considerations in the face of national emergencies' (10 January). The Liberal Imperialist chiefs showered him with messages of mutual commiseration, and Rosebery admitted to Perks that 'the cause has received a great blow. . . . We shall now have a Liberalism preached from the old Liberal pulpit which will alienate every sane man in the country.' More curiously, strolling with Cook at Mentmore soon afterwards, Rosebery remarked that 'it was a great pity Harmsworth was away' at the time of the transaction: 'He did not believe it would have happened if he had been at home.' J. Saxon Mills, who was biding his time, was required to expunge from an article on King's College, London, any reference to Milner, perhaps its most celebrated living graduate. In early February, he left for South Africa. 'The *D.N.* catastrophe was of course a great trial to me, as I was very happy & comfortable there,' he confessed to Crook. 'My sorrow is not mitigated by the contemplation of the paper under its present leadership. But we both belong to the noble army of martyrs & you know my feelings without my telling you.' Mills embarked, hoping 'to cooperate over there with the forces (if such there be!) that are making for peace & reconciliation – founded of course upon the pre-ordained and inevitable basis of British supremacy'. From Cape Town, he implored Crook to 'reconsider this pro-Boer nonsense . . . and come down honestly on the side of nation or force or destiny or God Almighty – as you like best to put it'. In a letter to *The Times* (6 July 1901), he claimed to know that General Botha, the Boer commander, was an avid reader of the *Daily News* and much encouraged by its line.[2]

In fact, the paper was hardly as pacifist as its critics alleged. It quietly turned from divisive imperial themes to social concerns, dear to the heart of Cadbury, who chaired the board of directors, of which Lloyd George was a member. A cocoa manufacturer and a devout Quaker, Cadbury proscribed advertisements for alcoholic beverages and, to the detriment of sales, all racing and betting features. Any profit he made was to be spent on 'better housing for the people', which he personally provided for his workers at Bournville, outside Birmingham. But, with a fall in circulation to 39,000, there

[1] *Review of Reviews*, xxiii (1901), 153; Robinson, *Fifty Years*, p. 381; Clayden to Crook, 2 January 1901, Crook Papers.
[2] Rosebery to Perks, 6 January 1901 (letterbook copy), Rosebery Papers, Vol. 10,131, fols. 261–62; Cook's diary, 12 January 1901, Cook Papers; Mills to Crook, 8 February and 6 November 1901, Crook Papers.

was no profit. To Harold Spender, he disclosed that the early months of his chairmanship had cost him £10,000. When Spender consoled him with the thought that his expenditure had probably 'saved ten thousand lives' by revealing the conditions in the South African concentration camps, 'his face brightened with a beautiful smile. "Ah! in that case," he said, "I will willingly bear the loss."'[1]

The armed struggle in South Africa degenerated into a guerrilla war, and the contest for the Liberal leadership into a 'war to the knife – and fork', as *Punch*'s 'Toby, MP' called it. At a series of banquet meetings, the feuding leaders hit at each other. On 14 June 1901, in a speech to the National Reform Union at the Holborn Restaurant, Campbell-Bannerman sharpened his cutlery and reviewed the tactics to which British commandoes had resorted in their desperate efforts to quash Boer resistance. 'A phrase often used is that "war is war",' he began, alluding to a callous statement by Brodrick. 'When is war not a war?' he asked rhetorically. 'When it is carried on by methods of barbarism in South Africa.' There was enthusiastic applause from those present, including John Morley and Harcourt, and from the *Daily News* and the *Manchester Guardian*. The Unionist press railed that Campbell-Bannerman had cast an unpardonable slur on British soldiery, and at last stood revealed as a 'pro-Boer'. The *Westminster Gazette* regretted that he had gone so far. J. A. Spender, who shared a Balliol background with Asquith, Grey, and Milner, stepped up his campaign for an accommodation between Campbell-Bannerman and Rosebery. Morley wrote him off as 'a thorough Roseberyite', but he was strongly backed by Asquith, who concurred 'that it is time for those of us who are not willing that the official and propagandist machinery should be captured by Lloyd George and his friends, to bestir themselves', and also by Herbert Gladstone, the chief whip. Lehmann, after attending the National Liberal Federation sessions at Derby, assured Campbell-Bannerman of 'overwhelming confidence in you and profound distrust of the Liberal hamperers'. Crook, among others, supplied him with 'news about the Camps' to substantiate the 'methods of barbarism' accusation. 'It is most significant and important,' replied Campbell-Bannerman, who obviously wished to disengage himself from the extremists. 'I was speaking last night, but I did not enter into details.'[2]

Lehmann's main purpose in writing to Campbell-Bannerman was to invoke his assistance in carrying on the *Speaker*:

We have lately been appealing for funds . . . and have met with a cordial

[1] Spender, *Fire of Life*, pp. 107–13.

[2] Hirst's diary, 15 July 1901, quoted in Hirst, *In the Golden Days*, p. 226; Asquith to Perks, 19 June 1901, Perks Papers; Spender to H. Gladstone, 17 December 1901, Viscount Gladstone Papers, Add. MSS. 46,042, fols. 1–2; Lehmann to Campbell-Bannerman, 7 December 1901, Campbell-Bannerman Papers, Add. MSS. 41,236, fols. 223–25; Campbell-Bannerman to Crook, 11 December 1901, Crook Papers.

response from Lord Ripon, J. P. Thomasson, L. V. Harcourt, Thomas Shaw and others. Could you suggest any men who might be willing to help us? . . . I do not ask *you* for any contribution, for your position, I think, precludes that – but any suggestions or advice from you would be warmly welcomed.

Lord Ripon donated £200: 'I wish I could give more, but I cannot.' Herbert Gladstone was 'glad to put £100 into the *Speaker*', presumably out of personal, not party funds. Loulou Harcourt 'kindly agreed to assist the work of the *Speaker* by taking 100 shares' at one pound each. Lord Farrer promised 'a few hundreds more if absolutely necessary'. In the summer of 1902, there were abortive plans for Hammond to be replaced by the peripatetic Massingham, backed by 'a publisher who was ready to invest money & give personal help'. In 1906, the journal was taken over by the Rowntree Trust – established by Joseph Rowntree, another cocoa Quaker, who already owned the *Northern Echo* at Darlington – and in March 1907 it was refashioned as the *Nation* with Massingham in the chair.[1]

Lehmann had more pressing problems at hand. On 18 July 1901, only seven months after his appointment, he resigned the editorship of the *Daily News*. He had effected notable improvements, chiefly with regard to personnel: Harold Spender complemented Paul as a political leader-writer; Massingham superseded Lucy, whose parliamentary reports were only 'the rinsings of his blotting pad'; and P. W. Wilson, E. C. Bentley, Hilaire Belloc, and G. K. Chesterton were recruited. Lehmann could not, however, get on with David Edwards, whom Lloyd George had installed as manager, and his fellow proprietors failed to take his part. Paul, who agreed that Lehmann had 'been abominably treated', begged him to reconsider for the sake of the paper, which 'cannot stand these constant changes. It will smash, and the chief organ of Liberalism in England will be extinguished'. But Morley, for whom the act of resignation was not so much a habit as an ethic, told Lehmann that the directors 'made your position one that you could not hold with a shred of self-respect'. Edwards, one of Lloyd George's cronies from Caernarvon, took over. It was Stead's 'impression . . . that Edwards has some hold on Lloyd George who . . . has behaved almost as badly as Edwards in this affair'.[2]

As the *Daily News* completed its first year under 'pro-Boer' management, other disputes surfaced. J. P. Thomasson, Franklin's father and the custodian of the family purse, was moved to tell Cadbury 'frankly that I don't feel disposed to put more money' into a paper with a dwindling circulation and a more

---

[1] Lehmann to Campbell-Bannerman, 7 December 1901, Campbell-Bannerman Papers, Add. MSS. 41,236, fols. 223–25; Ripon to Hammond, 1 October 1901, H. Gladstone to Farrer, 1 October 1901, Farrer to Hammond, 25 October 1901, and Hammond to Hobhouse, 19 and 28 August 1902, Hammond Papers; J. E. Allen to L. V. Harcourt, 12 November 1901 (with prospectus), Viscount Harcourt Papers.

[2] Paul to Lehmann, 19 July 1901, and Morley to Lehmann, 22 July 1901, Lehmann Papers; 'Willie' Stead to Cook, 30 December 1901, Cook Papers.

'socialistic' policy than he could swallow: 'I don't for instance think the State has anything to do with Old Age Pensions or Housing the people.... Politicians nowadays seem to think the State should be *generous* whereas I think its business is simply to be just.' Thus spoke the old Liberalism to the new. As befitted a Bolton textile manufacturer, Thomasson was rooted in the Manchester school of political economy. Having 'always avoided mixing myself up with newspapers till the offer of the *D.N.* was made us a year ago, & then there was not much time to consider the question', he now shuddered to think 'what the *D.N.* may go in for' after the war. 'I think it wd. be better to accept any suitable offer made by a Liberal or Liberals, say at or towards the end of the opening session of Parliament, rather than postpone it till all our money is gone and we should not obtain as good terms.' Cadbury, a Liberal of quite another persuasion, was 'very strongly for Old Age Pensions, & the taxing of land values & increasing the amount of the liquor license to pay for them'. So he described himself to Scott, to whom he sent a confidential copy of Thomasson's letter, and whom he asked: 'Is it possible, however harmoniously we may desire to work together, that there can be consecutive policy, or that the responsible parties can take any very definite line, or feel the confidence in the Board which they ought to do?'[1]

Rosebery's speech at Chesterfield on 16 December brought matters to a head. He stressed the need for a 'clean slate', implying a repudiation of Home Rule, and policies that would identify Liberalism with 'the new sentiment of Empire which occupies the nation'. Critical of the 'methods of barbarism' phrase, he nevertheless endorsed the National Liberal Federation's protest about the camps, and rejected Milner's call for unconditional surrender in favour of the granting of amnesty. According to Asquith's eldest son, Rosebery had been 'forced into it rather cleverly by the Lib. Imp. press wh. made such a fuss about the speech for months before-hand' that he could no longer sit on the fence. Cadbury was 'delighted' with Rosebery's performance 'as he went much further than I should have expected him to go, and even though I entirely differ with him on many points'. Edwards, however, condemned the heresy of the 'clean slate' and noted the thorns on Rosebery's olive branch. Cadbury fired off an angry letter to Lloyd George, who had just risked life and limb by carrying the anti-war banner to Birmingham Town Hall in the heart of Chamberlain country. 'I think the *Daily News* is making a great mistake in not accepting the conciliatory lines laid down by Lord Rosebery,' he complained. 'If you see Spender or Edwards, you might say that I am very much disappointed with their attitude towards Rosebery, & I think that Edwards will have a bad time of it when the Directors meet unless they change their attitude.' In the event, three of the five directors supported Edwards against Cadbury, who was left to 'believe the only chance for the *Daily News*

---

[1] Thomasson to Cadbury, 19 December 1901 (copy), and Cadbury to Scott, 20 December 1901, *Guardian* Archives.

would be for one individual practically to have unlimited control'. He might have said the same about the Liberal Party.[1]

'Of course,' Cadbury admitted to Scott, 'my personal comfort would be served by selling out my shares and getting out of the concern for which as far as I can see as a man of business there is little or no chance of success.' But he was no ordinary man of business. In preparation for a showdown on 9 January 1902, he sought advice from T. P. Ritzema, owner-manager of the *Northern Daily Telegraph*, who had helped to establish the *Daily Argus* at Birmingham, and who provisionally agreed to supervise the business affairs of the *Daily News* if Cadbury obtained an exclusive proprietorship. Together with Ritzema, he arranged a conference with Scott at Manchester on 2 January. By then, he had accepted as his 'duty' the 'tremendous responsibility' of running the *Daily News* as a 'power for peace'. It was not personal influence that he craved. 'My sole desire in taking up so great a responsibility,' he averred to Scott,

> would be that whoever was in command might feel that I should always support him in helping forward any movement that would promote the welfare of the masses of this country, and to carry on a paper that every true Christian patriot of every denomination and of none could take up with a certainty that it would plead for righteousness.

Nor was it financial gain. J. E. Taylor, the patriarch of the *Manchester Guardian*, heard that, 'in private conclave, . . . when some of the proprietors' of the *Daily News* 'expressed the fear of not getting any dividends, . . . Mr Cadbury said that he for one should be well satisfied to go without profit in such an enterprise'.[2]

Nothing short of a reconstruction of the board could rid the *Daily News* of Edwards, who – as Cadbury explained to Scott – was, under the terms of 'the agreement first made, . . . upon our backs for five years like the old man of the sea'. Cadbury was keen on having Hobhouse, whose presence in Bouverie Street would ratify what Taylor had once envisaged as 'a friendly alliance' between the *Manchester Guardian* and 'the regenerated *Daily News*'. Scott, dismissing the idea that he himself might exercise remote control from Manchester, tactfully promoted Hobhouse's candidacy: 'I would gladly advise with your Editor on any question of policy on which he cared to consult me and if he were a friend of mine that would be easy.' On the understanding that Scott had been a party to the selection, Cadbury was convinced that 'men like Messrs Massingham, Paul, etc.', none of whom he considered suitable, 'would be

---

[1] Raymond Asquith to John Buchan, 19 December 1901, quoted in John Jolliffe, *Raymond Asquith* (London 1980), p. 85; Cadbury to Scott, 20 December 1901, *Guardian* Archives; Cadbury to H. Gladstone, 19 December 1901, and Cadbury to Lloyd George, 19 December 1901 (copy), Viscount Gladstone Papers, Add. MSS. 46,059, fols. 102–103.

[2] Cadbury to Scott, 20 and 28 December 1901, and Taylor to Scott, 31 December 1901, *Guardian* Archives.

willing for their services to be retained while kept in hand by the Editor'. Meanwhile, Ritzema nominated as business manager H. C. Derwent of the *Bradford Daily Telegraph*, who had worked with him at Blackburn, and who commended himself to Cadbury as 'a devoted Christian worker, superinten- dent of a Sunday School, etc., a combination rather difficult to meet with in a first-class man of business'.[1]

At its meeting on 9 January, the *Daily News* board decided 'to wind up the Company and make it into a private concern'. Franklin Thomasson and Lehmann voted with Cadbury; Lloyd George and H. S. Leon, the former MP for Buckingham, against. It was not yet clear who would buy out whom, and nearly a month went by before J. P. Thomasson, who was on holiday in the south of France, informed Cadbury of his unwillingness to take 'the burden off my shoulders'. Cadbury 'fully agreed', calculating that 'if a change had not been made a few years would have seen the end of the existence of the *Daily News* or, worse, its passage' – like the *Birmingham Daily Gazette* – 'into the hands of Harmsworth, probably for a very small sum'. On Ritzema's advice, he thought 'it would be unwise at first to make many changes in the staff', with the exception of a substitute for Edwards, who was sent packing with a gen- erous indemnity. Ritzema's nominee was A. G. Gardiner, 'a man of his own training', who began on the morning of 3 March. Cadbury expressed to Scott the hope that 'in time we shall make use of your suggestion to obtain some help from Mr Hobhouse', who soon left the leader-writing staff of the *Manchester Guardian* to resume his academic pursuits. Possibly, out of consideration for Scott, Cadbury exaggerated his lack of enthusiasm and the transitory nature of Gardiner's appointment. But, then, he had only Ritzema's word that his new editor and future biographer was equal to the challenge. Taylor was sorry that the *Daily News* had not chosen someone of greater stature: 'I am afraid Cadbury is not going the right way to make the *D.N.* a success. He needs a very able and experienced Pressman to guide him.' On the contrary, Cadbury soon came to see the advantage of having an editor who was not compromised by association with any faction or indeed by reputation. As he boasted to Herbert Gladstone, 'our chief Editor, Mr Gardiner, is fortunately for the paper a very retiring man who does not go into Society and who will therefore I think be able to retain his independence'. A report of the Press Association re- vealed that Cadbury had spent a further £135,000 in bringing about these changes. He had brought the *Daily News* out of the nineteenth century and into the twentieth, and his achievement will be examined in that context.[2]

While these disruptions were occurring at the *Daily News*, other Liberal papers were in turmoil. H. J. Palmer, the president of the Institute of Journal-

---

[1] Cadbury to Scott, 20 December 1901, Taylor to Scott, 7 January 1901, Scott to Cadbury, 12 January 1902 (copy), Cadbury to Scott, 3 and 12 January 1902, *Guardian* Archives.

[2] Cadbury to Scott, 15 February 1902, and Taylor to Scott, 27 February 1902, *Guardian* Archives; Cadbury to H. Gladstone, 9 June 1902, Viscount Gladstone Papers, Add. MSS. 46,059, fol. 218.

ists, surveyed 'the Outlook for Liberal Journalism from a Conservative Point of View' and found, to his satisfaction, a 'marked ascendancy of the Conservative and Unionist Press', especially 'so far as the morning journals are concerned'. Although he was not inclined to believe that these conditions were 'materially influenced by the political reaction' against Liberalism, but rather by the relative attractiveness of Tory competitors, it would be hard to deny that the impotence of the Liberal Party contributed significantly to 'the dry rot of the Liberal monopoly' in the daily press. In February 1901, Lough engaged. Hammond, at a fee of four guineas a week, to supervise the leaders and editorial notes of the *Echo*, and to draw up comparisons between that paper and the *Evening News* and the *Star*. On 15 October, J. A. Hobson put the case in the *Echo* for a new progressive alliance of Radicals and Labour men: 'the Liberal Party is broken as never before, educated Socialists are despairing of Utopian politics, and the working classes are confronted with dangers to the efficacy of trade organisation which must drive them ever deeper into politics.' The *Echo* endorsed this front-page appeal to the extent of sponsoring a conference to promote a realignment of the political left. 'The events of the last two years, and more particularly of the last few months,' it stated in an accompanying leader,

> have forced many of us to reconsider our attitudes towards the grouping of English parties. A political party may be defined as a body of men agreeing in their general outlook on public affairs and on the main tenets of a coherent body of ideas. When these conditions are no longer satisfied, the party as a thing virtually ceases to exist, though as a name it may live on.

Ramsay MacDonald, in his capacity as secretary of the Labour Representation Committee, was sympathetic, but preferred to wait on events. J. A. Murray Macdonald, defeated at Bow and Bromley in 1895 and returned at Falkirk in 1906, was more responsive. The scheme went ahead under the aegis of Crook and Percy Alden, briefly editor of the *Echo* and MP for Tottenham after 1906. All of them were members of the Rainbow Circle. W. S. Caine, who had returned to the Liberal fold after a flirtation with Chamberlain, was in accord with the programme Crook had sent to him, but did not think it opportune: 'It only emphasizes the lamentable differences which prevail in the Liberal Party.... At present I don't want to say anything in public until I despair of seeing some reunion of the Liberal Party on advanced & progressive lines.'[1]

Palmer took the view that the Liberal press had previously thrived because 'the responsible chiefs of the Liberal Party saw that the first requisite of a newspaper was news; therefore they took their journalists into their confi-

---

[1] *Sell's* (1902); Lough to Hammond, 12 February 1901, Hammond Papers; Caine to Crook, 16 October 1901, and Murray Macdonald to Alden, 19 October 1901, Crook Papers.

dence.' What he ignored was that, at the turn of the century, the Liberal chiefs
lacked responsibility and, consequently, their journalists were either denied
tutelage or else received contradictory advice, which was equally counter-
productive. The *Echo* represented this plight at one end of the spectrum, the
Daily Chronicle at the other. In its coverage of an August by-election at
Andover, the *Chronicle* was inspired by William Allard, the secretary of the
Home Counties Liberal Federation and an organizer for the Liberal League.
George Judd, the Liberal contender, was extolled as 'a splendid type of an
English yeoman', who stood 'over six feet in his stockings, . . . is a fine shot
and good rider', and was 'as sound as can be . . . on all the leading questions of
the day': in Judd's opinion, 'we ought to press on the campaign [in South
Africa] as vigorously as possible until the Boers have surrendered. My com-
plaint against the Government is that they have not done this as they ought to
have done' (24 August). Philip Stanhope (later Lord Weardale), whose 'pro-
Boer' notoriety had cost him his seat at Burnley in the general election, was
furious. 'The *Daily Chronicle* of course can write what it likes and call itself
Liberal being Tory, or Tory if in the future it again becomes Liberal', he told
Loulou Harcourt, but 'the action of Allard in the matter' was insupportable.
Herbert Samuel, another Rainbow Circler, shared their disgust with Fisher
and Cook's jingoism, and subsequently obtained Allard's assurances that he
was 'in no way responsible for the astounding comments of the *Daily Chronicle*'. As a member of the executive committee of the Home Counties Liberal
Federation, Samuel had 'thought of writing . . . to the *Chronicle* in answer to
their articles, but on consideration decided that it was better not to keep the
controversy alive by a correspondence of that kind'. Had Allard maintained
his influence, the *Chronicle* would not have deleted from its report of Rosebery's Chesterfield speech the disavowal of Campbell-Bannerman's 'methods
of barbarism' remark. 'Is the enclosed from today's *D.C.* supposed to represent Rosebery's attitude?' Henry Norman demanded of Herbert Gladstone,
to whom he sent a cutting of the expurgated text. 'I ask, because if it does not,
would it not be well for me to write privately to Lloyd pointing out how mischievous it is? And, if so, may I say that this is the official view?' Norman wondered how Cook, of all people, could have been made 'to play the part of
wrecker'.[1]

One may infer that Gladstone declined to sanction Norman's proposed
intervention. There was simply no 'official view' to be put. J. A. Spender,
striving to steer a middle course in the *Westminster Gazette*, soon discovered
as much. In his 'zeal for unity', he too had 'passed lightly over certain passages
about the domestic affairs of the party and concentrated instead on the South
African parts' of Rosebery's Chesterfield speech, only to incur Sir William

[1] *Sell's* (1902); Stanhope to L. V. Harcourt, 24 August 1901, and Samuel to L. V. Harcourt, 10
November 1901, Viscount Harcourt Papers; Norman to H. Gladstone, 30 December 1901,
Viscount Gladstone Papers, Add. MSS. 46,042, fol. 117.

Harcourt's reprobation. Resolved to show Harcourt wrong in his view that
Rosebery had meant 'mischief', Spender prevailed on Campbell-Bannerman
to see Rosebery at Berkeley Square, where he 'got what he considered to be a
severe snub for his pains. Whereupon Harcourt said in his audible way, "I told
you so".' For his own pains, Spender was regarded with distrust. J. E. Taylor
was quite sure that 'Spender is somewhat under the Rosebery influence. His
father-in-law has told me that he has gone for weekends occasionally to the
Durdans.' To play the part of peacemaker was to invite suspicion.[1]

'What do you think of the amenities of Rosebery and C. B.?' J. H. Morgan,
a young Liberal journalist, asked Ensor in March 1902, when the rift seemed
to be mending. To Morgan's relief, 'the *Chronicle* has kept its temper unexpectedly well & shown (I think) a certain measure of tact.' By contrast, the
Daily News no longer seemed quite so promising. 'It looks very much subedi-
ted, and I wonder whether any room is left for Belloc, Chesterton, & the other
people. It has the air of being entirely the production of compositors.' The
Speaker continued to dangle on a shoestring. Hammond, apologizing to Hobhouse for the derisory fees paid to contributors, was 'by no means without
hope that [it] may last long enough to feel the benefits of a reaction. . . . For
the present the facts are stern & cheerless enough & we have to bear with
them.' Hobhouse, perhaps mistaking Cadbury's intentions, wanted to 'know
what is being planned as to a peace paper in London to replace the *Chronicle*'.
If such a project existed, it was stillborn. Liberalism, deprived of its cohesion
and electoral impetus, had lost its momentum in the press. The new properties
that were founded, like Pearson's *Daily Express*, were aggressively imperialist, if only idiosyncratically Tory.[2]

On 13 October 1901, the Sunday *People* 'attained its twentieth year'.
Marking the occasion, the editor reflected on his predecessors' 'belief . . . that
there was room enough and to spare for a great Conservative popular paper.
And events have proved the belief to be correct.' Was it coincidental that the
People, begun precariously in the year of Disraeli's death, fulfilled its promise
in the period of Salisbury's ascendancy? H. J. Palmer discerned 'reasons for
doubting the belief widely entertained that the prosperity of newspapers rises
and falls with and by reason of political mutations'. Yet the fact remains that
such a belief was indeed widely entertained when he wrote in 1902. That his
arguments were more applicable to provincial than to metropolitan journalism
was to be expected, for Palmer preceded his tenure at the *Yorkshire Post* with
experience on the *Sheffield Daily Telegraph*. Gardiner, Iwan-Müller, Garvin,
Massingham, or the two Spenders, who had inhabited both worlds, would
have disputed his assertions. 'By a certain law equivalent to the survival of the

[1] Spender, *Life, Journalism and Politics*, I, 106; Taylor to Scott, 31 December 1901, *Guardian*
Archives.
[2] Morgan to Ensor, 11–12 March 1902, Ensor Papers; Hammond to Hobhouse, 19 November
1901, and Hobhouse to Hammond, 2 December 1901, Hammond Papers.

fittest,' Edward Dicey postulated in 1905 that 'the ablest individual journalists somehow drift up to London.'[1]

Political mutations (especially as interpreted 'from a Conservative point of view') had already come to matter less than commercial requirements in the operations of the provincial press. In time, they would come to matter proportionately less in Fleet Street as well. For the time being, however, they remained the crucial factor in the conduct of national papers. Newcomers like Harmsworth and Pearson might negotiate around them, but were usually content to exploit them. The link between party organization and the political press may have been weakened and even twisted to some degree. But, as the Liberals showed in their adversity no less conclusively than the Unionists in their hegemony, the link had not yet been broken.

---

[1] Dicey, 'Journalism New and Old,' *Fortnightly Review*, lxxxiii (1905), 915.

Ten

RETROSPECT AND PROSPECT

On 22 January 1901, Queen Victoria died, having seen in the new century. In July 1902, Lord Salisbury retired from the premiership, having seen in a new monarch and the conclusion of peace in South Africa. The following year, Alfred Harmsworth obtained his long-coveted baronetcy, having seen in changes in journalism for which he did not hesitate to take responsibility; he was soon to exchange it for a barony, a still more emphatic proof of his arrival.

Any of these events might conveniently serve as a halting-place for the present narrative. None, of course, was itself a watershed in the history of the political press, but each was heavily laden with symbolic value. Their cumulative effect, enhanced by concurrent developments – the succession of Balfour, the Liberal revival after the Education Act of 1902, Chamberlain's detachment from the Unionist ministry and his Tariff Reform campaign, the rise of an independent Labour Party – was to create a distinctly new atmosphere. Newspapers variously recorded and reflected the transition from old to new, thus reinforcing the popular impression. Their rôle, as always, was ambiguous: on the one hand, they daily bore witness to change; on the other, they represented elements of continuity, the *Daily Mail* no less than the *Daily News* or *The Times*. The nineteenth-century press had anticipated certain attitudes and trends which became more pronounced in the twentieth century. Likewise, the twentieth-century press inherited and maintained certain traditions from the past.

Particularly with regard to an organic institution, no line of historical demarcation can avoid being somewhat artificial. But such lines are always necessary for purposes of exposition, and need not imply superficiality. All things considered, the turn of the century qualifies as the appropriate point to interrupt – though not to terminate – this study. In those years, the leaders of public opinion were engaged in an intensive reappraisal of national values and institutions, domestic conditions and international priorities. It is therefore logical to pause at this juncture to take stock of the political press, its accomplishment, its attributes, and its potential. How had it evolved over the previous fifty years, since its emancipation from official controls? How was it likely to evolve over the next fifty years in response to the further advance of democracy, the emergence of class politics, and mounting economic pressures? To answer these questions, one must look at the patterns of newspaper management, the shifting attitudes of politicians and journalists towards each other, and the operative assumptions that they continued to share.

*   *   *

After the abolition of the stamp duty in 1855, the Victorian political press arose on the intellectual and technological foundations of the preceding generation. The initial result was a ramshackle edifice, propped up by parliamentary factions which often enveloped the techniques of the younger Pitt with the moral philosophy of Bentham and John Stuart Mill. The ends may have been different, but the means were essentially the same. Newspapers were vastly more plentiful in number and supply, but had altered neither their appearance nor their self-perceptions. The subsequent removal of other legislative and legal restraints facilitated commercial expansion without disrupting customary procedures. Like the Reform Act of 1832, the repeal of the 'taxes on knowledge' may be seen to have preserved far more than it destroyed. Its effects would not be fully felt until the last decade of the century, when 'knowledge' – taking a more popular form than had been anticipated – was generally extended. Meanwhile, the arena was enlarged to incorporate new interests, whose challenges were easily contained.

No longer annexed to the administration of the day, journals became the affiliates – and sometimes the clients – of competing political groups. As these groups crystallized into mass party organizations, arrangements required renegotiation. When fissures appeared within parties, the press acquired still greater leverage, which it did not scruple to employ to its own benefit. The system gradually changed, partly because newspaper proprietors sought to take advantage of new opportunities for financial profit, partly because editors and leader-writers came to aspire to a more direct influence, and partly because politicians and journalists alike were increasingly obliged to take account of social and electoral developments. One may also detect a heightening of mutual disillusionment, more pronounced among Liberal idealists than among Tory pragmatists. As observed from Fleet Street, parliamentary proceedings had lost their lustre along with their centrality by the end of the century. As observed from Westminster, newspapers had lost their sense of purpose along with their partisan dependability.

The point to be emphasized is that these changes were slow to occur and far from complete. There was no sudden break, no point of departure, no revolution, but instead a perpetual see-saw motion that wore down confidence. The young Harmsworth claimed to have defied tradition, and indeed to have destroyed it single-handedly in the process. Yet the old order was sufficiently flexible to accommodate even him; and, at least for a time, he seemed to presage a revival. This is not to deny that he abetted the transformation, possibly in ways he did not intend. Without him, the consequences would have been less colourful, but not substantially different. The political press was already tottering when he bought the *Evening News* in 1894. When he died in 1922 it was still tottering, having withstood the mighty blows he had inflicted. The forms survived the functions for which they were originally devised. Their uses grew more restricted, perhaps, too, more counter-productive. Nevertheless, they were not discarded so long as political leaders and their confederates imputed them with varying degrees of value.

The longevity of public careers ensured that nineteenth-century practices would carry over well into the twentieth century. Trained in the old school, editors like Gardiner, Spender, Scott, Garvin, H. A. Gwynne, and Geoffrey Robinson (later Dawson) remained bound by its precepts. Politicians were no less durable and instrumental. As they marched ahead, they tended to look backwards. Like generals, who are said always to map their strategies on the battlefields of the previous war, political combatants have habitually responded to circumstance by invoking precedent. Even the most innovative among them defined the political press by the experience of their elders. This time-lag was evident at every stage. A generation after the Reform Act of 1832, Palmerston perfected the Pittite arts of newspaper manipulation. Russell, Derby, and, most successfully, Disraeli strove to overtake him. Gladstone and Salisbury saw the late-Victorian press through mid-Victorian lenses, comporting themselves in the Home Rule crisis of 1886–87 as they had done in the franchise controversy of 1866–67, a landmark for each of them. In turn, they were the models against whom Chamberlain, Lord Randolph Churchill, and Rosebery reacted: repudiation was second only to imitation as the sincerest form of flattery. Balfour and Asquith, Lloyd George and MacDonald, with Winston Churchill bringing up the rear, sustained the old methods in the new century. That they tried was altogether less surprising than that they largely succeeded.

There was no escaping the fact that, over the course of decades, the structure of the press had changed as markedly as the composition of political society. Yet, in both adjacent worlds, basic patterns remained undisturbed. The political press was never conceived as a comprehensive phenomenon: early in Victoria's reign, it had systematically excluded the illegal unstamped publications and the Chartist prints; later on, it had bypassed the popular dailies and the bulk of provincial properties; at the turn of the century, it had yet to encompass the new, mass-circulation dailies. The market for 'quality' newspapers had sharply diminished, leaving most of them to struggle for survival. Fewer and more vulnerable, they came to devote proportionately less space to parliamentary affairs. Their pretensions, however, stayed intact. Paradoxically, as the political press became more isolated, it grew in esteem.

Obviously, club opinion could no longer pass for national opinion. All the same, popularity did not in itself confer authority. More exclusively designated than ever before or since, the political press held to its prerogatives as tenaciously as the Crown, the Church, or the House of Lords. Its dominance, inexplicable in either social or commercial terms, was nonetheless absolute, accepted even by contemporaries who stoutly opposed privilege in other spheres. Newspaper owners (among whom we must consider William Waldorf Astor and George Cadbury as well as Harmsworth and Pearson) recognized and respected the boundaries of the political press. Journalists tailored their careers to its specifications. Politicians abided by its conventions. Each of these interlocking categories deserves investigation.

Of the three, the response of party politicians was the most significant, the most complex, and the most curious. Often they were men with literary credentials (or aspirations), who held (or had held) shares in newspapers. One might expect that, instinctively, they would have rapidly abandoned the old-fashioned press for the newer journals so as to enjoy closer contact with the expanded electorate. On the contrary, they and their satellites proved to be inveterate traditionalists. Thus, within parliamentary circles, the reasoned discourses of the *Westminster Gazette* had far greater resonance than the clatter of the *Daily Mail* or the *Daily Express*. Despite its decreased sales and meagre dividends, *The Times* retained its aura. And papers like the *Daily News*, the *Daily Telegraph*, the *Standard*, and the *Morning Post* basked in the afterglow of their earlier reputations.

It goes without saying that quality should have mattered more than quantity to men of breeding and refinement. Yet Lloyd George, infamous as a rabble-rouser, shared their sensibility. Preparing to launch his land campaign in 1913, he deemed it 'of first-class importance that when we come to strike we should have the support of a paper like the *Manchester Guardian*, which appeals so much to the "intellectuals" of our Party'. For this purpose, it made no difference that the circulation of the *Manchester Guardian* dipped to a low of 30,000 that year. 'It is not enough to carry "the crowd" with you in a great campaign like this,' he wrote to Scott; 'you must convince the thoughtful men in the Party. No Paper carries such weight with this class as yours.' To be sure, the *Daily Mail* reached more widely, but could only create a nuisance. The *Manchester Guardian*, with a mere fraction of the *Mail*'s circulation, cut more deeply and was assumed to create opinion. For a newspaper to boast a healthy circulation was almost to imply that it had betrayed its heritage. There were limits, however. John Morley had protested that Hammond did not 'think sufficiently of the *S[peaker]* as a journal endeavouring to *attract* a public', without which it sacrificed prestige.[1]

What politicians gave the press can be inferred from the preceding chapters: varying amounts of encouragement; confidential information and guidelines;

[1] Lloyd George to Scott, 4 September 1913, *Guardian* Archives; Morley to Hammond, 15 December 1900, Hammond Papers.

social inducements; professional rewards, including honours; and transfusions of capital from private and party funds, which were nominally separate. As late as November 1900, E. T. Cook accepted as 'well understood that news of appointments and other early "tips", as they are called, are the natural perquisites of the papers supporting the Government of the day'.[1] What politicians received from the press is somewhat more problematic, and therefore a subject of debate. In theory, newspapers were equipped to render an assortment of useful services: they, too, had intelligence to impart and favours to bestow; they could rally the faithful and, if necessary, harry the feckless. In practice, however, newspapermen were too impatient and otherwise too unpredictable to satisfy politicians' requirements. Nevertheless, that kept neither them from trying nor their mentors from hoping.

Ideally, the relationship between politicians and the press was a reciprocal one. In the interests of a higher cause, each side was to profit with the assistance of the other. Politicians, consonant with their legislative duties, were expected to initiate. Journalists, with the elaborate mechanisms at their disposal, were expected to publicize. As we have seen, this principle was honoured more in the breach than in the observance. In addition, the political press was invested with a quasi-constitutional function. It was supposed to serve as a two-way mirror, projecting policy in one direction and popular attitudes in the other. The apparatus was so complicated as to confound the most skilful engineers. Politicians were content only when they gazed into the mirror and saw their own images. Journalists who did not accommodate them were accused of distortion.

*   *   *

In a provocative analysis of 'the current of opinion' during the 1830s, William Thomas has emphasized the interpretative properties of the press. 'It is true that newspapers often make public opinion,' he has argued, 'but there is also an important sense in which they reflect it, more faithfully than election results,' which quickly go stale:

A newspaper editor has in his sales a daily or weekly index of the public reaction to a particular editorial 'line'. If he supports an unpopular set of opinions, he notices it in a reduced circulation. If he happens to tap some hidden reservoir of public feeling, as Barnes did for *The Times* when he attacked the new Poor Law, he very soon finds whether or not it has taken with his readers.... In this sense any swing of newspaper comment in favour of one political party has to be taken seriously as evidence of public opinion.[2]

[1] Cook to Balfour, 13 November 1900 (copy), Cook Papers.
[2] Thomas, *Philosophic Radicals*, pp. 305–306.

To take seriously such evidence is not, of course, to eliminate other variables such as principle and personality. Rather it is to posit a correlation between editorial predilections and general shifts of partisan allegiance, between the viability of newspaper enterprises and the acceptability of their public views. Moreover, it is to presuppose that readers were alert to these inflexions and immediately responsive to them, and that editors were adept at testing public reactions.

Bearing in mind that 'any swing of newspaper comment' might be artificially stimulated for ulterior motives, and also that circulation was not invariably the first priority, Thomas's axiom holds well enough for the period he has ex-amined and better still for the second half of the nineteenth century. The decline of Whiggism, the resurgence of Toryism, the fluctuations of Liberal Unionism and Liberal Imperialism can all be measured by successive swings of the editorial pendulum. The extension of literacy and the suffrage, attended by a growing commercialization of the press, strengthened the tendency for newspapers to reflect the vicissitudes of political preference. It must be clearly understood that, both in the 1830s and subsequently, this attribute was limited to a cluster of influential journals which could justly claim to speak for edu-cated opinion. Thomas's observation was based on *The Times*, the *Morning Chronicle*, and especially on the *Examiner* (under Fonblanque's editorship 'one of the most respected weekly newspapers of its time'), not on the Chartist *Northern Star* or Hetherington's *Twopenny Dispatch* (specializing 'in Murders, Rapes, Suicides, Burnings, Maimings, Theatricals, Races, Pugilism, and . . . every sort of devilment that will make it sell').[1] By the same token, the newspapers of political consequence in the early years of the twentieth century were a select few, self-consciously concerned with public issues, and – as Lloyd George perceived – addressed to 'thoughtful men' rather than to 'the crowd'.

It is essential to establish the boundaries of the political press in order to understand its lingering pretensions, and the deference accorded to it. In December 1901, writing in the *Nineteenth Century* (soon to change its name, *faute de mieux*, to the *Nineteenth Century and After*), G. M. Trevelyan con-demned 'the white peril' of cheap journalism. Ruskin's celebration of the printing press as 'an instrument by which the inner life of man can be en-nobled' was rejected as hopelessly romantic. 'Fifty years ago the majority of those who could read were in some real sense educated,' declared Trevelyan, a young historian stamped by his Whig upbringing.

> Therefore the press, following the law of supply and demand, was so used as to appeal to an educated public. . . . Now these conditions have been reversed. The number of people who can read is enormous; the proportion

---

[1] Thomas, *Philosophic Radicals*, p. 312; *Destructive*, 7 June 1834, quoted in Hollis, *Pauper Press*, p. 122.

of those who are educated is small. The printing-press, following the law of supply and demand, now appeals to the uneducated mass of all classes.

(According to Raymond Williams, however, 'throughout the nineteenth century the numbers of people who either bought or read newspapers were far below the lowest possible estimates of the numbers of people who were able to read'.) Had Trevelyan seriously believed his gloomy proposition, he would not have joined with his brother Charles (then Liberal MP for the Elland division of Yorkshire and later a Labour minister) to plan 'a new Radical journal' in 1903. The 'white peril' at home, like the 'yellow peril' overseas, was a threat born of hysteria. There remained a press within the press, read by a nation within the nation. At this time, when the total registered electorate approached seven million – 58 per cent of the adult male population – G. K. Chesterton described 'the people of which the politician has to think' as being 'some million absolutely distinct individuals each sitting in his own breakfast room reading his own morning paper'. Edward Dicey, without claims to being a social historian, discerned two types of newspapers for two types of readers: the penny dailies, which 'still represent the small trading classes, the shop keepers, the clerks, as distinguished from the working men proper'; and the halfpenny papers, representing 'the elector who earns his day's work and lodging for himself and his family by the labour of his own hands'. In a separate category was *The Times*, for which Rosebery 'spent threepence a day out of my small pocket money'.[1]

The political press was under siege, but not to the extent that Trevelyan suggested. The complexities of the franchise, including a system of plural voting, perpetuated the existence and characteristics of quality journals. So, too, did the two-party system in operation both at Westminster and in the constituencies. Moberly Bell was inclined to 'suppose that in every 200 who vote there are 95 who vote Liberal and 95 who vote Conservative from habit – the remaining 10 vote according to what they call their intelligence and practically decide the Election. They are the people,' he calculated, 'that have to be convinced one way or another', the ones whom *The Times* and other politically dedicated journals attempted to sway. 'They are I expect people very much like myself,' he postulated;

> they do not take an overwhelming interest in politics – they have mostly their occupations which absorb the greater part of their time . . . – but they have the rudiments of conscience, common sense & intelligence. They honestly want to use their vote in the right way but they do not aspire to lead. They want to be led by someone in whom they have confidence and to such a

[1] Trevelyan, 'The White Peril,' *Nineteenth Century*, 1 (1901), 1047; Williams, 'The press and popular culture,' in Boyce, *et al.*, eds., *Newspaper History*, p. 42; K. R. Swan to Ensor, 3 July 1903, Ensor Papers; Chesterton, *Robert Browning* (London, 1903), pp. 28–29; Rosebery to Moberly Bell, 1 January 1901, *Times* Archives; Dicey, 'Journalism Old and New,' *Fortnightly Review*, lxxxiii (1905), 915–16.

man they would willingly give a very free hand. Their motto is 'men not measures'.[1]

In other words, they were Lloyd George's 'thoughtful men', each possessing a vote (or maybe two), a relatively open mind, and a breakfast room.

Specifically to men of this class, newspapers spoke – often eloquently – on political themes. Who paid them heed? Alas, it is impossible to say who read what newspapers for which particular features. The audience that each paper intended to reach is more easily intuited than that which it actually succeeded in reaching: one is constantly surprised – and reassured – to find exceptions to every rule. While readers of the *Westminster Gazette* presumably enjoyed Gould's cartoons as a bonus, they may have been more attracted by the book reviews than by Spender's incisive commentaries. Readers of the *Star* and the *Globe* probably devoured the racing news at the expense of the political articles, which were most likely skimmed, if that. What was absorbed by osmosis can only be guessed. As mentioned previously, railway commuters into Manchester bought the *Manchester Guardian* for its transatlantic commercial reports, not for its 'pro-Boer' disquisitions. Tastes were becoming more fickle. 'One of the strongest Liberals I ever knew,' wrote Wilson Harris, who began on the *Daily News* and wound up as editor of the *Spectator* from 1932 to 1953, 'was found buying the *Daily Mail* for weeks because he had rashly dipped into the serial in a copy he had picked up in the train.'[2]

Along with the bottom rungs of the working class, lunatics, and convicts, women were unenfranchised and therefore technically beyond the pale of the political press. (Though peers too were ineligible to vote, they were an integral part of the political community.) Women received the vote in 1919, when the electorate trebled, and the major newspapers afterwards took greater account of their public interests. There were women's papers before that time, including *Woman*, a penny illustrated weekly that Arnold Bennett joined in 1894 and edited from 1896 to 1900. As he recalled, it 'was supposed to be, and was, an "advanced" paper', which 'did mysteriously acquire a reputation for being in the van of progressive movements'. But, in keeping with the times, 'politics were excluded from its pages. A woman's politics were those of her husband, if she had one; and those of her male relatives if she was unmarried.' There was, of course, nothing to stop a woman from perusing the paper that her husband or father left behind on the breakfast table or carried home at night. Nevertheless, the political press *per se* was distinctly a gentleman's press, as much in terms of sex as class. In 1903, Harmsworth tried the experiment of a daily halfpenny paper written by and for women. His *Daily Mirror*, quickly converted into a picture paper with a male staff and a male outlook,

[1] Moberly Bell to Rosebery, 27 November 1900, Rosebery Papers, Vol. 10,113, fols. 320 ff.
[2] Harris, *Daily Press*, p. 19.

taught him two lessons: 'Women can't write and don't want to read.'[1]

There is no reason to believe that practising politicians, themselves exclusively male and preponderantly upper class, were any more receptive than the ordinary reader to heterodox arguments. Gladstone, disapproving of a position taken up by R. H. Hutton in the *Spectator*, reportedly wrote to Wemyss Reid: 'I have so great a respect for Mr Hutton, and am so anxious to maintain it unimpaired, that I have absolutely ceased to read the *Spectator*.' Although Sir Edward Grey claimed to have been converted to the Home Rule cause by Morley's philippics in the *Pall Mall Gazette*, it is doubtful whether newspaper criticisms affected his own later policies at the Foreign Office. Chamberlain may have lectured Balfour on the inestimable value of the press as a 'way of finding out the heart of public opinion', if only to perceive 'where the line of least resistance is to be found'; yet his Tariff Reform crusade, which lies beyond the purview of the present volume, showed how he himself treated newspapers primarily as sounding-boards. That politicians were attentive students of the press does not mean that they accepted instruction from it. Like Gladstone over the Bulgarian question of 1876, they might sometimes be galvanized by a newspaper agitation. But they were rarely led against their wills, and usually contrived to do the leading.[2]

According to W. T. Stead, the newspapers of the 1880s conducted 'an exhaustive interrogation of public opinion', from which editors were able to gauge popular sentiment and, in moments of crisis, lay before Parliament 'an unmistakable demonstration of what the opinion of the people really is'. Looking back on the events of that decade, Sidney Low was sceptical. 'Public opinion is a shifting abstraction,' he stated, and neither editors nor statesmen could keep pace with it. He cited the example of Lord Granville, foreign secretary in 1882, when Britain intervened in Egypt. 'How could he possibly be aware what public opinion wanted or what it really thought?' asked Low.

> How can any Minister know? He reads (if he is industrious) half a dozen newspapers daily. He gains from them the views of half a dozen or a dozen men, perhaps penetrating and judicious, perhaps not, who have small opportunity of ascertaining the views of more than a very limited number of their fellow-countrymen. A newspaper editor, a busy man absorbed in the details of an extensive business enterprise, can do no more than form a hasty and incomplete estimate of the emotions which at any time possess the minds of the eight or ten millions of persons who constitute the electorate.

Stead, true to form, was wildly optimistic in his evaluation. Low was a shade too pessimistic, though he over-estimated the size of the electorate and prob-

[1] Bennett, 'Editing a Woman's Paper' (1927), reprinted in *Sketches for Autobiography* (ed. J. Hepburn; London, 1980), pp. 31–34; Williams, *Right to Know*, p. 93.
[2] Reid to Rosebery, 6 January 1896, Rosebery Papers, Vol. 10,056, fol. 27; G. M. Trevelyan, *Grey of Fallodon* (London, 1937), p. 33; Chamberlain to Balfour, 8 December 1894, Balfour Papers.

ably the number of papers that the most industrious statesman had the time
and patience to read. On balance, Low was closer to the truth. The Bulgarian
agitation was Stead's moment of glory, and he never recaptured or recovered
from it. Even so, newspapers were a better index to public opinion than anything else then available. Their contents, properly sifted, were certainly more
indicative than parliamentary division lists, by-election results, or general
election returns. But the job of sifting was a challenge too important to be left
to newspapermen themselves.[1]

'Of course it is still true, and will most likely always remain true, that, like
the Athenian Sophist, great newspapers will teach the conventional prejudices
of those who pay for it.' So Morley observed in 1882, upon the conclusion of
his tenure at the *Fortnightly Review*. Still, he detected 'infinitely less of this
than there used to be. The press is more and more taking the tone of a man
speaking to a man'. His confidence was soon to be shaken by the New Journalism, which spoke to office-boys in the tones of office-boys. Before 1855, 'great
newspapers' (to borrow Morley's designation) had been the clients of the
Treasury. Thereafter, they gradually became the clients of commercial
interests. By stages, the press went from being 'a sort of co-operative society'
between officials and publicists into one, as described by Wickham Steed, 'in
which the public is a partner'. That had its advantages, but also its manifest
drawbacks. 'The Press is always tempted to give the public "what the public
wants"; and journalists who can guess what the public really "wants" are
worth their weight in gold,' wrote Steed. The difficulty, as he saw it retrospec-
tively, was that some journalists, 'together with the owners of the papers they
serve, may think the average of public taste so low that the lower their appeal
to it the more successful they will be. . . . Their method is to "play down" to
the public.' At the other extreme, there were 'editors and owners who think it
their duty to enlighten and to educate their readers'; entertaining 'too lofty an
idea of what the public wants', they were inclined to engage in 'schoolmastering'. In between, there was 'a third class of newspaper proprietors and journalists [which] thinks that the right method is to humour the public to a certain
extent by trying to give what is good for it in so attractive a form that it will like
what it gets'. Steed, who had joined the staff of *The Times* in 1895 and was
editor from 1919 to 1922, considered this middle group 'the wisest'. In due
course, we shall see how well he followed his own advice.[2]

The Times, on which Steed was employed as Rome correspondent at the
turn of the century, fitted his definition of a schoolmaster. It was straining,
however, to adapt itself. Leo Amery, whose dispatches from South Africa put
the urgent case for War Office reform, was made aware of the problem by his

[1] Stead, 'The Future of Journalism,' *Contemporary Review*, 1 (1886), 663–79; Low, 'Lord
Cromer on Gordon and the Gladstone Cabinet,' *Nineteenth Century*, lxiii (1908), 681–82.
[2] Morley, 'Valedictory,' *Fortnightly Review*, n.s. xxxii (1882), 515–16; Steed, *The Press*,
pp. 16–17.

superiors. Moberly Bell reminded him on 13 May 1900 that 'whatever your Harmsworths and Pearsons don't know they do know the public'. Unlike them, *The Times* could not 'descend to chatter about Mrs Plantagenet-Jones of Peckham but it could do a great deal more than it does by making the public understand the *men* it is writing about instead of only trying to interest them in abstract theories'. Three days later, Valentine Chirol, head of the foreign department at Printing House Square, wrote to Amery in the same vein:

> You cannot get the Man in the Street to fight concrete stupidity with abstract ideas, & my belief is we shall achieve nothing unless we can set up concrete intelligence against concrete stupidity & then call upon the M. in the S. to back his fancy. For instance you won't reform the W.O. by leading articles & elaborate schemes from the most highly specialised pens. What you have to do is to fix upon two or three men to whom you can pin your faith & then run them for all you are worth. If *The Times* will do that, I think it will carry a large body of opinion with it.

These letters to Amery, whom Moberly Bell and Buckle were grooming to succeed to the editorship (but who opted for a career in Parliament), are revealing on several counts. They go far to explain the tendency of newspapers to focus on personalities in the political conflicts of the Edwardian age. Secondly, they imply a grudging appreciation for the methods – though not the extravagances – of Harmsworth, whose clandestine take-over of *The Times* in 1908 was materially assisted by Moberly Bell. And, most significantly, they testify that the management of *The Times* was more anxious to marshal opinion than to sell papers for the mere sake of selling papers.[1]

Encased in tradition, *The Times* was scarcely insulated from the harsh realities of newspaper finance. In 1895, E. M. Phillipps mischievously foresaw the adoption of 'all sorts of methods, including some that have hitherto been confined to cheap shops, so that, ere long, we shall not be surprised to find even *The Times* giving away the equivalent for a screw of tea or tobacco with every copy sold'. More tastefully, *The Times* branched out into the field of 'sundry publications', including a weekly edition, law reports, an atlas, and a connection with the *Encyclopaedia Britannica* (available on '*The Times* System of Easy Payments'). In 1904, a discount subscription scheme was introduced; and, the following year, *The Times* Book Club was established with handsome premises in New Bond Street. Arthur Walter, the chief proprietor, thereby hoped to appease certain dividend-hungry minority shareholders, one of whom successfully took legal action in 1900 to inspect the company accounts. Instead, he was reproached for having resorted to 'alien' (*i.e.* American) methods of merchandising. His 'annoyance at these criticisms', the official historians of the paper have written, 'was not decreased by the reflec-

[1] Moberly Bell to Amery, 13 May 1900, and Chirol to Amery, 16 May 1900, Amery Papers; *History of The Times*, IV, part 1 (London, 1952), 4.

tion that they had some justification'. What were the alternatives? Short of suspending publication, as his solicitor threatened at one point, Walter might 'make an arrangement with a political party . . . in return for a subsidy direct from the party chest or indirectly from a party member himself to be rewarded by party honours'. Family tradition, no less than 'the dictates of conscience', allegedly militated against so drastic a step, which would have 'turned *The Times* into a Conservative Party paper after the model of the *Standard* or the *Pall Mall Gazette*; or a Liberal paper like the *Daily News* or the *Westminster Gazette*'. If solvency was Walter's objective, none of those models could have attracted him.[1]

At the start of the twentieth century, the larger vessels of the political press were becalmed, and the smaller ones were sinking. 'Journalism had become like most other such things in England, . . . somewhat sleepy and much diminished in importance,' Chesterton remarked in his novel, *The Napoleon of Notting Hill* (1904). 'This was partly due,' he explained, 'to the disappearance of party government and public speaking, partly to the compromise or dead-lock which had made foreign wars impossible, but mostly, of course, to the temper of the whole nation, which was that of a people in a kind of back-water.' By the time that these words – which came to have an unintended irony – appeared in print, the situation had been altered by Chamberlain's dramatic break with fiscal orthodoxy. His espousal of protectionism in May 1903, followed by his resignation from the Unionist government in September, will be the point of departure for the second volume of this study: among its extensive ramifications, it revivified the older organs of political journalism and, at the same time, drew newcomers into the orbit.

Pearson, whose political awakening came in 1903, helped to sweep away some of the debris. On 24 April 1900, he launched the *Daily Express*, which he proclaimed over his initials to 'be the organ of no political party nor the instrument of any social clique'. The same month, he bought the *Morning Herald*, which he merged with the *Daily Express* five months later. S. K. Ratcliffe, thrown out of work by 'the stoppage of the *Morning Herald* . . . or rather, the "amalgamation" with the *Express*', went to the *Echo* as joint-editor ('I apparently haven't any real power') with H. K. Newton, one of the directors of Consolidated Newspapers. 'The prospect is not cheerful,' he accurately told W. M. Crook. 'The *Echo* is doomed – there can't be two opinions about it. Newton confessed to me this morning that he knew nothing about newspaper management.'[2] Nor was Newton steadfast in his Liberalism: in 1906, he stood as a Conservative in North-East Essex, where he was elected as a Unionist in 1910. Pearson, whose consuming interest was his Fresh Air

---

[1] E. M. Phillipps, 'The New Journalism,' *New Review*, xiii (1895), 182; *History of The Times*, III, ch. xiv.
[2] Ratcliffe to Crook, 3 September 1900, Crook Papers.

Fund, was similarly ignorant and malleable, but vastly more adventurous. On the foundations of the weekly magazine that bore his name (his version of Newnes's *Tit-Bits* and Harmsworth's *Answers*), he built an empire that included papers in Birmingham, Newcastle, and Leicester. In 1903, he acquired the *St James's Gazette* as an evening escort for the *Daily Express*. In November 1904, he bought the *Standard* and the *Evening Standard* from the Johnstone family, to whom he was related; not needing two penny evening papers, he soon merged the *St James's* with the *Evening Standard*. While he reserved for himself the titular editorship of the *Express*, he appointed William Woodward as editor of the *Evening Standard* and H. A. Gwynne, the foreign director of Reuters, as editor of the *Standard*.

Few proprietors showed such resilience. Cadbury carried on the *Daily News* at a loss, compounded by a compositors' strike which John Burns was called upon to mediate. Stead's son 'Willie' heard 'upon the best authority', which would have ruled out his father, that the paper lost £11,000 in the eleven months after Cook's departure. 'I give the *D.N.* two years to go to pieces in,' he told Cook. 'My prediction I believe will be well within the mark.' Liberal Imperialists, from whose custody the *Daily News* had been wrenched, took grim satisfaction from its distress. 'The *Daily News* prints only 28,000 a day, & is losing £400 a week,' Perks informed Rosebery in April 1903. By September, however, the paper at last seemed to Morley to have 'a look of life about it such as it has not worn for a long time'. The next year, its price was reduced to a halfpenny, as was that of the *Daily Chronicle*, restored to prosperity under the direction of Robert Donald. The *Pall Mall Gazette* continued to gnaw at the Astor family fortune, the *Westminster Gazette* was a burden cheerfully borne ᴊy Newnes, and the *Morning Post* was one of the infirmities of Glenesᴋ's old age. The proprietorship of a political journal was a luxury for those who could afford it. With a bank overdraft, which he did not pay off until 1910, Scott purchased the copyright of the *Manchester Guardian* for the 'clearly extortionate' sum of £80,000, thus ensuring his editorial sovereignty.[1]

Apart from Scott, the owners of politically orientated newspapers were men who derived their incomes from other investments, including non-political publications. Under the circumstances, why should tycoons like Pearson and Harmsworth have wished to dissipate their money and energies on the political press? Initially neither did; or, at least, neither said he did. Yet Pearson's *Daily Express* suffered heavy losses until 1903, when it was politicized under the spell of Chamberlain. And Harmsworth's *Daily Mail*, never as apolitical as he made out, became more shrilly partisan, while his *Daily Mirror* and *Daily Citizen* avoided politics to their own detriment. Once ensconced in a Fleet Street office, where politicians or their emissaries came to call, it was difficult

---

[1] W. Stead to Cook, 7 and 17 February 1901, Cook Papers; Perks to Rosebery, 4 April 1903, Rosebery Papers, Vol. 10,051, fol. 73; Morley to Gardiner, 30 September 1903, Gardiner Papers; Ayerst, *Guardian*, pp. 315–18.

for any proprietor to resist playing the part. Northcliffe (as Harmsworth became in 1905) has been portrayed by Francis Williams as someone who

> liked to believe, and was supported in this belief by many sycophants and much uninformed opinion, that his financial and circulation success was balanced by an equal power to influence public and political opinion. There is little evidence that this is true. He voiced, and not infrequently exaggerated, the political prejudices of the readers of his popular papers. He played on their fears and hopes and sometimes stampeded them into hysteria.

Not unusually, Northcliffe saw himself as an active, not a passive force. 'I am not the least afraid of public opinion,' he later boasted to Geoffrey Robinson. 'I stood up against it . . . in the Dreyfus case. I took my life in my hands prior to the Boer War, . . . when a pamphlet was placed in every seat in the House of Commons, accusing me of being paid by Mr Rhodes.'[1]

The differences between formulating and exaggerating opinion, between guiding and stampeding the public, were ones of degree. It is not surprising that Harmsworth should have failed to comprehend these subtleties. One man's 'political prejudices' were another's political commitment. One man's 'hysteria' was another's patriotism. During the period of the Boer War, the process surged out of control, if only because it could not be contained within normal channels. As in the 1850s, restraints had ceased to apply. For decades, the use of newspaper propaganda for purposes of political education had been debated by intellectuals, many of them party publicists. They had had little idea of the passions that an undisciplined press could ignite among undisciplined readers. Although Harmsworth recalled having been victimized for supporting the war, his antagonists had greater cause for complaint. Anti-war demonstrations were broken up by mobs, incited by newspaper rhetoric. Stead, whom the New Journalism had left behind, recommended that 'the editor of the *Sun* and of the *Globe* and Alfred Harmsworth should all be tucked away in Holloway for a week' so that 'we should have a chance of rescuing one of the fundamental English liberties from the ruin which threatens it'.[2] Modern Babylon was a more brutal place than he had dared to imagine.

The popular press did not ennoble the inner life of man, though it did ennoble the outer husk of Harmsworth. Among the more high-brow political journals, staid in their appearance and muted in their enthusiasms, the same debilitating influences were at work. Transfers of ownership and replacements of editors occurred with unsettling frequency. Yet the distinction was preserved, partly by those who aspired to surmount it. Pearson entered the field of political journalism first by buying the *St James's Gazette* and the two *Standards*, then by hitching the *Daily Express* to Chamberlain. Harmsworth,

---

[1] Williams, *Dangerous Estate*, p. 158; Northcliffe to Robinson, 7 May 1913, quoted in *History of The Times*, IV, part 1, 131.
[2] Stead to Bryce, 3 March 1900, Stead Papers.

who had a toe-hold through the *Evening News* (which, unlike the *Daily Mail*, was officially 'Unionist'), made a bid for *The Times*. 'It will be a great coup if you can get it,' he told R. D. Blumenfeld, whom he deputed to approach Walter. 'Never mind. We'll get it sooner or later,' he remarked when Blumenfeld returned empty-handed.[1] That plum was not to fall to him until 1908. In the meantime, he demonstrated his respectability by his management of the *Observer*, which he bought from the Beer family in 1905 for the pittance of £4,000.

More plainly than ever before, the experience of the Boer War revealed to politicians and newspapermen alike the contradictions implicit in the conduct of the political press. In a classic work, *Democracy and the Organisation of Political Parties* (1902), M. Ostrogorski viewed partisanship as inimical to the 'real duty' of a newspaper, 'which is to enlighten the reader':

> As for improving the political judgment of their readers, the great majority of the newspapers utterly fail to do so. No doubt, if the standpoint of the Organisation is adopted, for whom the *education* of the voters consists in crying up the doings of the party in question to them, and in inspiring hatred and disgust for the opposite party, it must be admitted that, with a certain number of exceptions, the Press performs its task very creditably.

A political scientist, not a journalist, Ostrogorski could console himself that

> the public no longer has its old belief in the leading article, and the number of people who systematically abstain from reading it, knowing beforehand that it is outrageously biassed, is rapidly increasing. People read the paper for its non-political views, and often vote with its opponents. I have frequently had occasion to note that in a locality where the Press of the party is prosperous, ... the party is beaten at the elections, sometimes badly beaten.[2]

The conditions that Ostrogorski described were, in fact, hardly new. But, by the time he pursued his research, they had become more pronounced. One may logically infer that the 'certain number of exceptions' to which he made passing reference were precisely those organs of the political press which Lloyd George assumed to weigh on the consciences of 'thoughtful men', and which Moberly Bell believed capable of influencing the ten men among every two hundred who held the balance of power in every election.

Had Ostrogorski written a decade earlier, or had he waited for wartime acrimonies to abate, he might have tempered some of his assertions. Nevertheless, he articulated the unease that many felt at the time. What he prized as 'education' or 'enlightenment' was what Wickham Steed derided as 'schoolmastering'. Ostrogorski may also be faulted for deceiving himself that 'the

---

[1] Diary entry of 16 October 1900, Blumenfeld, *R.D.B.'s Diary* (London, 1930), p. 95–96.
[2] Ostrogorski, *Democracy and the Organisation of Political Parties* (London, 1902), I, 409–10.

standpoint of the Organisation' had ever been less than crucial, and for discounting the rôle that 'hatred and disgust' had always played in determining electoral preference.

Moreover, he confused journalistic prosperity (itself a nebulous concept) in a particular locality with journalistic strength in the nation at large. With a few notable exceptions, as this study has attempted to demonstrate, the provincial press had little light apart from that which it reflected prismatically from the centre. By the turn of the century, it was politically eclipsed by the London dailies. Arnold Bennett, who had got his start in journalism as an unpaid contributor to the *Staffordshire Knot*, described in his novel, *The Card* (1911), how the 'ridiculous public' of the Five Towns 'did not seem to care which paper was put into its hands in exchange for its halfpenny, so long as the sporting news was put there'. Lest it be thought that he exaggerated for comic effect, it should be noted that such complaints were commonplace. The corpses of party-affiliated provincial dailies and weeklies littered the ground, and surviving provincial papers were increasingly the property of commercial conglomerates, resolved not to offend anyone by taking a party stand. Typical was the plight of the *Eastbourne Standard*, which folded on 20 December 1901 after a quarter-century of publication: *Sell's* gave 'lack of practical sympathy from members of the Conservative party' as the reason. Political society took its inspiration from Fleet Street and, to a lesser extent, from regional newspapers managed from Fleet Street. Politicians recognized this fact and acted accordingly. Lord Salisbury declined an invitation from H. J. Palmer, editor of the *Yorkshire Post*, to attend a banquet of the Newspaper Society. 'The country press,' his private secretary minuted, 'is a very useful stick with which to beat the Metropolitan papers when they go wrong.' That was much the best that could be said for it.[1]

*   *   *

The task of politicians was to keep the political press from going wrong. That of proprietors was to keep it from going bust. Newspapers could not be run indefinitely out of the generosity of their owners, augmented by supplementary funds funnelled through party agencies. Eventually, they had to be made to pay their way, however modestly. Prolonged commercial failure denoted an inability to get across their ideas, and ultimately cast doubt on the efficacy of those ideas. To Harmsworth, who was far from unique in this respect, it also meant 'a lack of professional progress, and this he could not bear'.[2]

Neither politicians nor proprietors could succeed without the patronage of

---

[1] *Sell's* (1903); Palmer to McDonnell, 28 December 1900, and McDonnell's note of 5 January 1901, Salisbury Papers (Christ Church).
[2] A. M. Gollin, *The Observer and J. L. Garvin* (London, 1960), p. 26.

the public, which had a dual personality: to the politician, the average citizen (Chirol's 'Man in the Street') was first and foremost an elector, who relied on the press for information; to the newspaper-owner, he was familiarly known as a reader, who intermittently had the opportunity to go to the polls. For either the politician or the proprietor to succeed in his respective vocation, a favourable response was required. Politicians could bear the hardships of opposition so long as they saw the prospect for eventual vindication. Likewise, most proprietors were willing to accept a short-term loss, provided that they could foresee long-term profits.

The public, then, was a third component, which declared its preferences as much by the pennies and halfpennies it spent each day as by the ballots it cast at irregular intervals. There was also a fourth, no less volatile than the others. It consisted of the salaried men – and women – who filled the columns of the press. Without them, the proprietors would have nothing to sell and the public nothing to buy. Cynics might suggest that they wrote simply for pay, or even for their private amusement. Perhaps, in later years, many did. Through the nineteenth century and until the First World War, however, journalists' personal commitments were as important as their literary talents in advancing the causes they served.

In the mid-Victorian decades, it was considered unthinkable – or, at any rate, disreputable – for a self-respecting journalist to take employment on a newspaper with an editorial policy contrary to his own convictions. It was better not to write than to write on behalf of the wrong side. In 1860, when 'Radical poison [was] daily and weekly administered in excess', with scarcely any 'Conservative antidote', there existed little 'inducement . . . for the young man who is about to commence a literary career to take to Conservatism'. Times changed, with the result that G. G. Armstrong sadly confessed that 'no Liberal journalist of my generation and the generation succeeding mine would dream of advising a young man of sincere Liberal outlook to take the risk now of becoming a journalist'. Armstrong's own career was a case in point. The son of a Unitarian minister, he left the *Liverpool Daily Post* late in 1892 to seek fame and fortune in London. Without success, he applied at the Fleet Street office of the *Manchester Guardian*, at the *Speaker*, and at the *Daily Chronicle*, where Massingham was too busy to see him. ('I could never forgive him.') Graham Wallas had given Armstrong a letter of introduction to a sub-editor on the *Observer*, and had sensibly advised that he 'would be much more likely to get a situation on the old *Pall Mall*', its staff depleted by Cook's exodus, than on the new *Westminster Gazette*. Armstrong nursed misgivings, however, even after A. J. Mundella's nephew had assured him 'that it is all right to go on a moderately Tory paper like the *P.M.G.* or the *Observer* if you only do such subordinate work as is unaffected by politics'. Rather than risk contamination, he returned to the provinces, where he successively held jobs on Liberal organs in Nottingham, Middlesbrough, Sheffield, Bradford, and Bolton.

After a brief stint in London on the *Morning Leader*, he became editor of the Rowntrees' *Northern Echo* at Darlington, 'the only Liberal morning paper between Bradford and the Tweed . . . and . . . a vehicle for the promulgation of Liberal ideas throughout these northern counties' (19 April 1904). Finally, he concluded his travels on the *Daily News*.[1]

Others were not quite so mobile. J. W. Robertson Scott, as a young man in Birmingham, 'belonged to the Liberal "Four Hundred" – what the enemy called the Caucus – and at a Bingley Hall meeting saw Gladstone's notes slither down among the reporters'. Eager to join in the scramble, he accepted a job on the Tory *Birmingham Daily Gazette*, but 'virtuously stipulated that, as a Liberal, I should write nothing in support of the inimical cause'. Later, when he was better placed to dictate terms, he worked for six years on the *Pall Mall Gazette*, which he left for the *Westminster* when Yates Thompson sold out to Astor. Ultimately, before he quit 'daily journalism and went to live in the country', he served under Massingham on the *Daily Chronicle*. 'I resigned from the *Chronicle*,' he stated categorically, 'for the reason that I retired from the *Pall Mall Gazette*, because it changed its politics.'[2]

There are countless examples of journalists who sacrificed promotion or, more painfully, London appointments for the sake of their principles. J. A. Spender went to Hull rather than bow to the Unionist demands of Edwards's *Echo*. His brother Harold went to Manchester rather than work on a jingo *Chronicle*. More than a family trait, their attitude was based on nineteenth-century orthodoxy. However quixotic their actions may now appear, they would have seemed wholly logical – and morally imperative – to professionals like Arthur Arnold, J. D. Cook, J. Mortimer Granville, Thomas Hamber, Frederick Greenwood and E. T. Cook.

Younger men, especially those who stood on the political left, were as unbending in the 1900s as their predecessors had been in the 1860s and '70s. Pondering his prospects for a career in metropolitan journalism, J. H. Morgan had 'seriously to consider whether I can with a good conscience accept a place on the *D. Chron.* staff, for its politics I detest. I sometimes think of the *Daily News* upon which I might bring several influences to bear,' he wrote on New Year's Day 1902 to Ensor, one Balliol man to another. Without much choice, Morgan went to the *Chronicle*, where he stayed until 1904, when he followed Ensor at the *Manchester Guardian*. Ensor was subsequently a leader-writer on the *Daily News* from 1909 to 1911, and on the *Daily Chronicle* from 1912 to 1930. H. N. Brailsford, another of his Oxford contemporaries, had a conscience still more difficult to appease. In 1900, he was hired as a leader-writer for the *Morning Leader*, which he knew to be 'cheap, popular & sometimes

---

[1] 'Conservative Journalism,' *New Quarterly Review*, ix (1860), 393–96; G. G. Armstrong, *Memories* (London, 1944), pp. 47–48, 113.
[2] Robertson Scott, *The Day Before Yesterday* (London, 1951), pp. 259, 262, and *Faith and Works in Fleet Street* (London, 1947), p. xv.

vulgar, but it is staunch & loyal, has a good circulation & is preparing to reform itself into as good a paper as one can expect for ½d.' Besides, he told Gilbert Murray: 'As there is no other London paper but the *Westminster* for which I could write just now, I am very glad to be on the *Leader*'s staff.' (Significantly, he laid equal stress on ideology and location.) A lapsed Fabian, Brailsford had 'always been a Socialist', who was finding it increasingly difficult to reconcile his private beliefs with his professional connections. 'I should be greatly obliged if you would give me some information about the I.L.P.,' he wrote in 1907 to Ensor, a recent convert.

> Above all, is it tolerant enough to allow me to earn my living on Liberal papers? I write chiefly on foreign affairs & on literary subjects, & when I turn to domestic themes, I avoid any on which the views of the paper for which I write would conflict with my own. In short, I have never, I think, written a line that was inconsistent with a sane Socialism. . . . Would this be good enough for the I.L.P.? Or would they insist on my taking no Liberal gold?

Considering that Ramsay MacDonald applied in 1905 to replace Vaughan Nash as labour correspondent for the *Daily News*, Brailsford need not have fretted. Yet, in 1908, he confessed to H. W. Nevinson that he regarded his employment on the *Daily News* as incompatible with his socialist ideals.[1]

L. T. Hobhouse, an apostle of the New Liberalism, could appreciate Brailsford's moral dilemma, which he put in a wider context. After a decade's hiatus, he returned to the *Manchester Guardian* as a special contributor of leading articles and a director of the company. 'It is not illiberal for an editor to decline the services of a member of the opposite party as a leader-writer, or even as a political reviewer in any capacity in which his opinions would affect his work,' he insisted in his treatise, *Liberalism* (1911). 'It is illiberal to reject him as a compositor or as a clerk, or in any capacity in which his opinions would not affect his work for the paper.' Hobhouse was thinking specifically of Liberals and Tories, and would not have debarred Brailsford, an erstwhile correspondent for the *Manchester Guardian* and a consultant to Scott on Balkan topics and the women's suffrage question. Brailsford's qualms about accepting 'Liberal gold' were not reciprocated by Hobhouse, whose ecumenical view of Liberalism led him to embrace moderate (as opposed to 'mechanical') socialism as an invigorating force.[2]

It is possible to satirize this obsession with journalistic ethics, as C. E. Montague did in his novel, *A Hind Let Loose* (1910). Nevertheless, its implications must be taken seriously. To some extent Hobhouse obscured the

[1] Morgan to Ensor [1 January 1902], Ensor Papers, Brailsford to Murray, 11 January 1900, Murray Papers; Brailsford to Ensor, 24 August [1907], Ensor Papers; Nevinson's diary, 20 September 1908.

[2] L. T. Hobhouse, *Liberalism* (London, 1911), p. 119; for Hobhouse as a 'moral reformist', see Peter Clarke, *Liberals and Social Democrats* (Cambridge, 1979), pp. 62–74.

vital issue. No newspaper ever demanded an oath of party allegiance from its compositors and clerks. Nor was it required that other functionaries should subscribe to the editorial tenets of the journals from which they drew their salaries. Only in the higher ranks was discrimination practised. For a dedicated Tory to write political features for the *Daily News* or the *Manchester Guardian*, or a dedicated Liberal to assume comparable responsibilities at the *Standard* or the *Morning Post*, would have been sheer masochism. At the lower levels, things were different, and always had been. In the 1880s, Hartley Aspden had moved with 'chameleon dexterity' from a Liberal paper to the *Birmingham Daily Gazette*, 'a paper of exactly opposite political faith'. But, as he himself conceded, he was merely a cog in the wheel. 'The reporter has nothing to do with the political side of his newspaper,' Aspden observed from experience. 'Every reporter has political views of his own, but he does not air them in his newspaper as that is the prerogative attached to the editorial side of the journal he represents.' Political loyalty was expected – indeed extracted – only from those who were in a position to exercise that prerogative: editors, leader-writers, and certain 'political reviewers', as Hobhouse called them. Thus, it implied no contradiction for Robert Donald to tell a prospective employee of the *Daily Chronicle*: 'We're a Liberal paper, but most of the staff seem to be Tories or Socialists.'[1]

From all indications, those who sat in editorial chairs were less compromising than the general public and less likely to be compromised than the newspaper owners who employed them. E. T. Cook, too prominent to behave with 'chameleon dexterity', received a visit from an American journalist, who was at a loss to understand Massingham's displacement from the *Daily Chronicle* in 1899. In America, declared the caller, journalists 'had no private opinions any more than a counsel'. To illustrate the point, he told Cook

> a story of a political boss who, noticing silver articles in a Chicago paper, said 'Introduce me to that man: I should like to see him President of the U.S.' Afterwards in New York, struck by gold articles in a New Y[ork] paper, [he] said 'Introduce me to that man: I should like to see him shot.' It was the same man.

British journalists were not nearly so flexible, least of all on matters of economic doctrine, but they were beginning to move in that direction. American notions about political responsibility followed in the wake of American publicity techniques and typographical innovations. Their initial impact was restricted to the newer journals at the periphery of the political press. By a sort of Cox and Box arrangement, the *Daily Mail* was edited by Thomas Marlowe, a recruit from the Liberal *Star*, and S. J. Pryor, who interrupted his service to become managing editor of the short-lived Liberal *Tribune*. Generally, however, editors were bound by party commitments, which they sometimes

[1] Aspden, *Fifty Years a Journalist*, p. 19; Taylor, *Donald*, p. 256.

resisted proprietorial pressure to maintain. Leader-writers, too, were expected to toe the party line. Even if, as Sidney Low pseudonymously suggested after his release from the *St James's Gazette*, 'commenting on party politics . . . is for the most part terribly hack work', it was dangerous to leave it to the hacks. Harold Spender 'once possessed a friend, a hard-bitten Scotch journalist, who . . . [wrote] a Liberal London letter before dinner, and a Tory leading article after dinner'. He explained to Spender 'that he found this order more suitable to the nature of the views expressed. He felt more Conservative after a bottle of good wine than before.' Under various intoxicating influences, leader-writers could adapt to circumstance. But the metropolitan political press demanded sobriety.[1]

At the higher echelons of newspaper management, this code remained inviolate. In the lower ranks, it eventually broke down after the First World War, when the Liberal press collapsed and the Labour press failed to expand to fill the vacuum. If journalists were to ply their craft, they could no longer afford to be choosy. 'The writing of a story from a Conservative angle by a Liberal, or from a Liberal angle by a Socialist, is not necessarily a task that will give them sleepless nights,' the *Journal* of the Institute of Journalists stated in April 1930. 'Nor should a sub-editor who is asked to "splash" a political story with which he is in entire disagreement hand in his resignation forthwith.' By then, there was considerably less room for manoeuvre. To uphold tradition would be to 'preclude a Socialist from working on the staff of any paper but the *Daily Herald* [founded in 1912] and it would limit the Liberal's choice to the *Daily Chronicle* and the *Daily News* [which had absorbed the *Westminster Gazette* in 1928], as far as Fleet Street is concerned'. Two months later, the amalgamation of the *Daily Chronicle* and the *Daily News* into the *News Chronicle* reduced by half the options available to a conscientious Liberal journalist in London. 'Editors must stand in a class apart,' this article nonetheless insisted. 'The honest editor finds no alternative to resignation if the policy of the paper he conducts is changed in such a manner that he cannot support it.'[2]

The political press, as always, was a barometer of political change. The pressure of events combined with the pressures of newspaper economics to destroy the vestiges of the old system. More than any other single factor, the decline of the Liberal Party undermined what had been a Liberal orthodoxy. In the nineteenth century, it was always easier for a qualified Liberal to shift to a Tory paper than for his Tory counterpart to storm the citadel of Liberal journalism. After 1918, the Tory press was enriched by an influx of Liberal talent. Ernest Parke, editor of the *Morning Leader* until its merger with the

[1] Cook's diary, 8 December 1899, Cook Papers; Clarke, *Northcliffe in History*, p. 99; Arthur Shadwell [Sidney Low], 'Journalism as a Profession,' *National Review*, xxi (1898), 853; Spender, *Fire of Life*, p. 29.

[2] Institute of Journalists, *Journal*, xviii (1930), 70.

Daily News in 1912, became editor of Beaverbrook's *Sunday Express* in 1920. Colin Coote, Liberal MP for Ely from 1917 to 1922, was thereafter a foreign correspondent and leader-writer for *The Times*, which he left in 1942 for the *Daily Telegraph*. 'During his 14 years as editor,' according to his obituarist in *The Times* (23 November 1979), 'Coote guided the political policy of the *Daily Telegraph* with skill and shrewdness; indeed his traditional Liberalism was a cogent influence in enabling that avowedly Conservative newspaper to maintain its vigorously independent judgment.' It is not to disparage Coote's accomplishment to say that this tribute would have been meaningless to his Victorian forbears, who would have wondered how traditional Liberalism could have assisted the vigorously independent judgment of an avowedly Conservative newspaper. But a new rhetoric dictated its own logic.

'Liberalism', once a formal designation, became an instinct. 'Independence' came to be used with even greater elasticity. During the Spanish Civil War, for example, the London district of the Institute of Journalists 'declared itself free of political issues', and claimed thereby to have 'struck a blow for the political independence of journalists, as journalists'. As one of the members baldly put it: 'We are employed by newspapers and we take the sides of those newspapers.'[1] Nineteenth-century political journalists, regardless of party, would have rejected such independence as the worst type of servitude.

More recently, independence has acquired an atomistic quality. Joan Lestor, Labour MP for Sheffield, Brightside, defended parliamentary colleagues who had contributed articles to the *Morning Star* and other Communist publications. 'The fact that you write for a newspaper does not mean you necessarily agree with all its editorial comment,' *The Times* quoted her as saying in September 1977. 'This is a bit of guilt-by-association tactics.' Her argument, eminently logical in its context, helps to chart the distance between the conventions of the 1870s and those of the 1970s. Gladstone, in making common cause with Hill and Stead, or Disraeli, in collaborating with Delane and Borthwick, accepted the consequences of guilt by association. They, and other public figures who worked with and through the press, expected to be judged by the company they kept. Except for occasional letters to the editor, usually demanding an apology or a retraction, their prose did not appear in the papers with which they disagreed. Perhaps they were more scrupulous, which is not to say that they had more scruples. Above all else, they had more choice. In the twentieth century, politicians became more flexible as newspapers became more self-serving, fewer, and less politically distinct. In Fleet Street, as in Doris Lessing's *Four-Gated City* (1969): 'The newspapers that remained might call themselves right, left or liberal, but the people who wrote them were interchangeable, for these people wrote for them all at the same time, or in rapid succession.'

[1] Institute of Journalists, *Journal*, xxiv (1936), 207.

*　　　*　　　*

Half a century after the birth of the mass circulation press, no longer taxed and officially controlled, newspapers had changed profoundly, though not beyond recognition. More fundamental changes were to occur during the next half-century, when competition intensified, economic and social pressures became more acute, and newer media usurped many of the functions traditionally associated with written journalism.

The remarkable thing about the British press, as it entered the twentieth century, was its resemblance – more real than apparent – to the press of mid-Victorian times, in some respects to that of pre-Victorian times. The problems, like the phenomenon itself, had grown tremendously in scale; but they were fundamentally the same. 'The commercialism of the press was the subject of much critical comment from the 1820s,' when advertising receipts were already the crucial element, predicated both on circulation figures and on the 'unity and popularity' of the political combination with which a paper was identified. So Ivon Asquith has observed of the *Morning Chronicle* under James Perry; he might well have been describing the *Standard* under Hamber and Mudford, *The Times* under Chenery and Buckle, or the *Daily News* under Hill, Cook, and Gardiner.[1] The trend towards sensationalism was also instanced and deplored in every generation. The formation of newspaper chains was not unprecedented, though the process accelerated after 1855 and was to be carried to new limits after 1900.

There had always been newspapers which had paid proportionately less attention than others to affairs at Westminster. To varying extents, they had specialized instead in lighter features, characterized as entertainment or trivia. In addition, there were journals which, for trade or other purposes, totally eschewed politics. None of these had ever qualified for membership in the political press. The essential difference between a full-fledged political journal in 1900 and its equivalent, say, in 1865, was the relative decrease in the amount of explicitly political matter it contained. Typographical flourishes were merely external signs of this adjustment, and arguably incidental to it: a paper might conceivably adopt sub-heads, display advertising, and front-page headlines without altering its perspective. More significantly, the balance of coverage shifted. Foreign news, more extensively reported, crowded parliamentary proceedings from the pages of the more dignified dailies. Items of cultural interest and social concern were more conspicuously featured. The percentage of space allocated to party topics was reduced, sometimes sharply. Yet, at least for the time being, the difference was basically one of proportions rather than emphasis.

[1] Ivon Asquith, 'The structure, ownership and control of the press, 1780–1855,' in Boyce, *et al.*, eds., *Newspaper History*, p. 108, and 'Advertising and the Press,' *Historical Journal*, xviii (1975), 723.

Statesmen, no longer able to command verbatim transcriptions of their speeches, nevertheless continued to depend on the political press to encapsulate their views and to endorse them. While it was useless to pretend that newspapers could shape party policy, they retained a responsibility for helping to expound it. They could not make political careers, as Delane had done.

> We had intended you to be
> The next Prime Minister but three,

Belloc informed an eminent Edwardian in 1908.

> The stocks were sold; the Press was squared;
> The Middle Class was quite prepared.
> But as it is! . . . My language fails!
> Go out and govern New South Wales!

Even so, they might sometimes unmake careers. Certainly their importance in building party morale had not yet diminished. Willed into existence by parliamentary leaders, who had sought weapons for themselves and forums for their ideas, the political press was kept alive by those who deployed its diminishing assets.

Not all politicians sat in Parliament. Many hovered in the background, attending to the requisites of party organization. 'In the front rank' of partisan instruments, Ostrogorski put 'the Press, *i.e.* the organs of the parties, which the latter themselves consider as their most valuable auxiliaries'. Editors, who occasionally doubled as MPs, were seen – and saw themselves – as party agents. Their professional competence was partly measured by their capacity to rouse party spirits. E. T. Cook, for all his vague talk about newspaper independence in the early 1890s, declined an offer to return to the *Pall Mall Gazette* 'as editor on independent lines' in 1903. 'Apart from my opinions,' he wrote in his diary, 'it seems to me that an independent journal which leaned to (a very different thing from adhering rigidly to) neither side and to no organized group or party would not be a very influential organ.' Sidney Low was no less emphatic on this score: 'A paper that has no mind of its own has no influence, however large its circulation.' Independence from party, as opposed to independence from party dictation, was inimical to the concept of a political press. When it eventually developed, the concept was destroyed.[1]

Influence, then, was the paramount objective. It was defined more narrowly, and perhaps more realistically, in 1900 than before. But it was still to be used for public purposes rather than for personal gratification or commercial aggrandizement. Newspapers, properly lubricated, were the gears which kept the party machinery in motion. Major political figures relied on them to advance their ambitions and their programmes. Lesser politicians habitually

---

[1] Ostrogorski, *Democracy*, I, 409; Cook's diary, 4 March 1903, Cook Papers; Shadwell [Low], 'Journalism as a Profession,' *National Review*, xxi (1898), 853.

proved their devotion to the party cause by maintaining the political press. Instead of contributing directly (and anonymously) to party campaign funds, which many of them did as well, wealthy backbenchers undertook to salvage derelict newspaper properties so as to save them from the enemy or from the predatory Harmsworth, who seemed to J. E. Taylor willing to 'carry on any paper, Liberal, Tory, Liberal Unionist, it does not matter at all!'[1]

In the autumn of 1900, the situation at the *Leeds Mercury* was 'rather desperate'. According to Sir Wemyss Reid, its former editor, 'the heavy expenses of the War & the rise in the price of paper have for the moment put the finances into a bad state & *the resources of the B[aines] family are practically exhausted*'. George Whiteley, Liberal MP for the Pudsey division of Yorkshire (and later Lord Marchamley), was eager to help out. 'Please tell me how I can best serve the party interests?' he asked Herbert Gladstone, the Liberal chief whip, who supervised the rescue operation from afar. Whiteley joined with Sir James Kitson, Liberal MP for Colne Valley (and later Lord Airedale), each offering £10,000 contingent on the other. The plan was aborted, Reid confidentially told Gladstone, because 'our friends . . . looked too much at the purely financial & too little at the political side of the question'. Through Perks, Reid thereupon made contact with Harmsworth, who reportedly 'gave £30,000' to transfer the *Leeds Mercury* to the control of his brothers, who made it into a halfpenny illustrated paper. A year later, Harmsworth purchased 'the wreck' of the *Manchester Courier*, which the younger Thomas Sowler (who died in 1899) had managed in succession to his father (who died in 1890). 'The late Tom Sowler (junior) sold to the public for £300,000 what to my knowledge was not worth more than £75,000 et voilà l'histoire,' Iwan-Müller wrote to Balfour. J. E. Taylor heard that Harmsworth had paid '£80,000, a tidy sum for a non-paying concern'. The misfortunes of provincial newspaper families like the Baineses and the Sowlers were exploited by the press magnates, against whom party syndicates were powerless to compete.[2]

'Now that the project for buying the *Mercury* has definitely collapsed', Whiteley was ready to 'subscribe £5,000 if another £20,000 is forthcoming' towards the purchase of the evening *Leeds Daily News*. And Kitson agreed to provide 'about £1,200 p.a.' to assist in arrangements for provincial newspapers to publish articles supplied by Liberal headquarters. These were men who could not have made their mark – or, for that matter, obtained their peerages – by other forms of party service. Thomas Lough, whose reward was an under-

[1] Taylor to Scott, 11 January 1902, *Guardian* Archives.
[2] Reid to H. Gladstone, 4 June, 4 July, 9 and 23 October, and 5 November 1901, Viscount Gladstone Papers, Add. MSS. 46,041, fols. 143–57; Whiteley to H. Gladstone, 16 January 1901, Viscount Gladstone Papers, Add. MSS. 46,058, fol. 190; Kitson to H. Gladstone, 18 December 1900, Viscount Gladstone Papers, Add. MSS. 46,028, fol. 106; Cook's diary, 10–12 August 1901, Cook Papers; Iwan-Müller to Balfour, 2 January 1901, Balfour Papers; Taylor to Scott, 11 January 1902, *Guardian* Archives.

secretaryship in the next Liberal administration and a privy councillorship thereafter, had helped to launch the *Star* and to keep the *Echo* afloat. 'It is gratifying to me to find that one may be of use *as I wish to be* for my life is too far past me to be willing to fool around even in parliament doing nothing,' he awkwardly confessed to Campbell-Bannerman. On the Conservative side, too, there were individuals who assisted party organs as a means of obtaining preferment or simply of making themselves better known and more useful. Without incurring 'responsibility pecuniary or editorial', George Wyndham 'worked like a nigger' through the winter of 1897–98 to launch the weekly *Outlook* 'as a raft out of the wreckage of the *New Review*'; before severing his connection with the journal and setting foot on ministerial slopes, he told his wife that '*Outlook* has done me no harm but rather the reverse'. C. S. Goldman, who succeeded to the proprietorship, admitted to Cook that he had become 'predominant partner' of the *Outlook* in order 'to exercise influence thru' the press. He had lost £9,000 . . . & got no influence', but became Unionist member for Penryn and Falmouth in 1910.[1]

Fifty years after its emancipation, the political press was less than the whole of British journalism, yet distinctly more than the sum of its parts. The age of corporate and concentrated ownership had dawned, with the result that proprietors (even would-be proprietors like Whiteley and Kitson) were increasingly determined to realize an adequate return on their capital investment. On the other hand, this period was also regarded as the golden age of editors, when men of exceptional literary ability and political insight occupied the major chairs in Fleet Street. The press was steadily becoming more commercialized: it was *always* becoming more commercialized. All the same, it remained highly politicized. Like Parliament, the focus of their attention, political newspapers modified their procedures to accommodate new interests and to absorb new talents, but continued to operate within an established framework.

On 18 August 1913, in his presidential address to the Institute of Journalists, Robert Donald surveyed the changes that had occurred in the newspaper world during the past twenty years. He noted 'a check in the increase of newspapers', a 'concentration of ownership' in fewer hands, a further 'incursion of the London Press into the provinces', and a general improvement in the standards and professional status of the 'working journalist'. For better or worse, these changes would definitely continue over the next twenty years:

---

[1] Whiteley to H. Gladstone, 23 June 1901, Viscount Gladstone Papers, Add. MSS. 46,058, fol. 294; Kitson to H. Gladstone, 14 and 31 May 1901, Viscount Gladstone Papers, Add. MSS. 46,028, fols. 108–109, 121; Lough to Campbell-Bannerman, 7 August 1903, Campbell-Bannerman Papers, Add. MSS. 41,222, fol. 223; Wyndham to 'Ettie' Grenfell, 26 December 1897. Desborough Papers; Wyndham to his wife, 2 and 24 February 1898, Wyndham Papers; J. W. Mackail and G. Wyndham, *Life and Letters of George Wyndham* (London, 1925), I, 319–20; Cook's diary, 29 April 1903, Cook Papers.

I would say with some confidence that daily newspapers will be fewer, the tendency towards combinations will increase, and colossal circulations will continue to grow. A paper which has not at least a half-million readers will not be considered as an organ of the people. The weak newspapers which cannot spend huge sums on news, on features, and on circulation, will, of course, be squeezed out, and the paper run as a luxury or for a mission, and not as a business enterprise, will be too expensive except for millionaire idealists.

Although he was wonderfully prescient ('The chief competition to the national newspapers of the future will not be from other newspapers, but from other methods of disseminating news'), he did not predict the demise of the political press: 'Clearly every public body must have its own organ.' Such newspapers would be necessary 'to act as watchdogs and critics ..., and as a check to bureaucracy'. As advocates of progress, they might work to ensure that 'the millions now wasted on wars and armaments' would instead be 'devoted to the promotion of science, the endowment of research, the spread of education, and the increase of social amenities'.[1]

Within a year, the outbreak of war belied Donald's sanguine expectations and ultimately doomed his editorship at the *Daily Chronicle*. Political journalists, especially those imbued with Liberal optimism, were better qualified to serve as commentators than as prophets. Appreciating this fact, newspapermen (including the few among them who strayed into Parliament) usually avoided public platforms and confined themselves to the columns of their papers, where they addressed the topics of the day. Their articles, written hurriedly and rushed into print, lose a degree of pungency and often intelligibility with the passing of time. There is nothing colder than the ashes of yesterday's burning issue. Journalism, at its very best, is the most ephemeral species of literature.

A modern student of the nineteenth-century political press, leafing through its faded and disintegrating pages (earlier copies, printed on better quality stock, crack rather than crumble), cannot hope to comprehend every allusion or to discern the complex interplay of forces behind the scenes. Nevertheless, those pages afford an invaluable record of political history as it unfolded, and testify to the pervasive influence of the press in that process. There was always more to the contents of a newspaper than met the eye of its casual reader. The object of this book has been to reveal, by selective illustration, the power relationships through which party politics moulded the press and, conversely, the press affected the conduct and concerns of party politics.

[1] Speech to the conference of the Institute of Journalists at York, 18 August 1913, *The Times*, 19 August 1913.

MANUSCRIPT SOURCES

In addition to serial publications (usually identified in the text) and other published sources (cited in the footnotes), this book rests on manuscript collections, as enumerated below. Some of these archives will figure more prominently in the sequel to this study, but contain items which were used for purposes of contrast and comparison. Other collections, from which direct quotation was not made, are not included.

Aberdeen (4th Earl of Aberdeen) Papers, British Library.
Leo Amery Papers, courtesy of Mr Julian Amery, MP.
H. H. Asquith (Earl of Oxford and Asquith) Papers, Bodleian Library, Oxford.
Astor Papers, The Library, University of Reading.
Alfred Austin Papers, The Library, University of Bristol.
A. J. Balfour (Earl of Balfour) Papers, British Library.
R. M. Barrington-Ward Papers, courtesy of Mr Mark Barrington-Ward.
Bathurst Papers (including Glenesk correspondence), courtesy of the Earl Bathurst.
Beaverbrook (Max Aitken, Baron Beaverbrook) Papers, House of Lords Record Office.
Jeremy Bentham Papers, University College, London.
E. C. Bentley's diary, MS.Eng. Misc.e. 829, Bodleian Library, Oxford.
Blackwood Papers, National Library of Scotland, Edinburgh.
Robert Blatchford Papers, Central Library, Manchester.
R. D. Blumenfeld Papers, House of Lords Record Office.
Andrew Bonar Law Papers, House of Lords Record Office.
John Bright Papers, British Library.
Sir John Brunner Papers, Sydney Jones Library, University of Liverpool.
James (Viscount) Bryce Papers, Bodleian Library, Oxford.
George Cadbury Papers, The Library, University of Birmingham.
Sir Henry Campbell-Bannerman Papers, British Library.
Andrew Carnegie Papers, Library of Congress, Washington, D.C.
Joseph Chamberlain Papers, The Library, University of Birmingham.
Chilston (Aretas Akers-Douglas, 1st Viscount Chilston) Papers, Kent Archives Office.
Lord Randolph Churchill Papers, Churchill College, Cambridge.
Clarendon (4th Earl of Clarendon) Papers, Clar. dep.c. 103, Bodleian Library, Oxford.
Richard Cobden Papers, British Library.
Conservative Party Archives, Conservative Research Department (since transferred to Conservative Central Office and to the Bodleian Library, Oxford).
Sir Edward Cook Papers, courtesy of Mr Robin Duff and Professor J. E. Mennell.
Courtney (Leonard Courtney, Baron Courtney of Penwith) Papers, British Library of Political and Economic Science, London.
W. M. Crook Papers, Bodleian Library, Oxford.
Cross (R. A. Cross, 1st Viscount Cross) Papers, British Library.
Henry Cust Papers, The Library, Columbia University.
Derby (14th Earl of Derby) Papers, courtesy of Lord Blake.
Derby (15th Earl of Derby) Papers, Liverpool Record Office.

Desborough Papers, Hertford County Record Office.
Devonshire (Lord Hartington, 8th Duke of Devonshire) Papers, Chatsworth.
Sir Charles Dilke Papers, British Library.
Robert Donald Papers, House of Lords Record Office.
Sir John Easthope Papers, William R. Perkins Library, Duke University.
Elibank (Alexander Murray, 1st Baron Murray of Elibank) Papers, National Library of Scotland, Edinburgh.
Edward Ellice Papers, National Library of Scotland, Edinburgh.
T. E. Ellis Papers, National Library of Wales, Aberystwyth.
R. C. K. Ensor Papers, Corpus Christi College, Oxford.
T. H. S. Escott Papers, British Library.
Esher (Reginald Brett, 2nd Viscount Esher) Papers, Churchill College, Cambridge.
A. G. Gardiner Papers, British Library of Political and Economic Science, London.
J. L. Garvin Papers, University of Texas at Austin.
Viscount Gladstone (Herbert Gladstone) Papers, British Library.
W. E. Gladstone Papers, British Library.
F. C. Gould, draft autobiography, House of Lords Record Office.
Granville (2nd Earl of Granville) Papers, Public Record Office.
Charles Greville–Henry Reeve Correspondence, British Library.
Guardian Archives, John Rylands University Library, Manchester.
H. A. Gwynne Papers, Bodleian Library, Oxford.
R. B. Haldane (Viscount Haldane of Cloan) Papers, National Library of Scotland, Edinburgh.
Hambleden (W. H. Smith) Papers, W. H. Smith & Son Ltd.
Sir Edward Hamilton's diary, British Library.
J. L. Hammond Papers, Bodleian Library, Oxford.
David Hannay Papers, University College, London.
Viscount Harcourt (L. V. Harcourt) Papers, Bodleian Library, Oxford.
Sir William Harcourt Papers, Bodleian Library Oxford.
Edward Hardcastle Papers, William R. Perkins Library, Duke University.
Frederic Harrison Papers, British Library of Political and Economic Science, London.
Hughenden (Benjamin Disraeli, Earl of Beaconsfield) Papers, Hughenden Manor (since transferred to the Bodleian Library, Oxford).
Thornton Hunt Papers, MS.Eng.Lett.d.88, Bodleian Library, Oxford.
T. H. Huxley Papers, Imperial College, London.
Iddesleigh (Sir Stafford Northcote, 1st Earl of Iddesleigh) Papers, British Library.
Labour Party Archives, Transport House.
R. C. Lehmann Papers, courtesy of Mr John Lehmann.
David Lloyd George (Earl Lloyd-George of Dwyfor) Papers, House of Lords Record Office.
Arthur Mann Papers, courtesy of Mr E. Peter Wright.
L. J. Maxse Papers, West Sussex Record Office.
John Stuart Mill–Harriet Taylor Collection, British Library of Political and Economic Science, London.
Alfred (Viscount) Milner Papers, Bodleian Library, Oxford
Sir William Molesworth Papers, William R. Perkins Library, Duke University.
C. E. Montague-Francis Dodd Correspondence, British Library.
Benjamin Moran's diary, Library of Congress, Washington, D. C.
A. J. Mundella Papers, The Library, University of Sheffield.
Gilbert Murray Papers, Bodleian Library, Oxford.
National Liberal Club records, National Liberal Club, London.
National Union of Conservative and Constitutional Associations minutes and reports, Conservative Central Office.
H. W. Nevinson's diary, Bodleian Library, Oxford.
New University Club records, United Oxford and Cambridge University Club, London.
Northcliffe (Alfred Harmsworth, Viscount Northcliffe) Papers, British Library.
Oxford and Cambridge University Club records, United Oxford and Cambridge University Club.
Palmerston (3rd Viscount Palmerston) Papers, British Library; and Broadlands Papers, National Register of Archives.

Joseph Parkes Papers, University College, London.
Passfield (Beatrice and Sidney Webb) Papers, British Library of Political and Economic Science, London.
Sir Robert Peel Papers, British Library.
R. W. Perks Papers, courtesy of Sir Malcolm Perks.
Rainbow Circle minute-books, courtesy of Mr Stephen Wilson.
William Rathbone Papers, Sydney Jones Library, University of Liverpool.
Reform Club records, Reform Club.
Henry Richard Papers, National Library of Wales, Aberystwyth.
Thorold Rogers Papers, Magdalen College, Oxford.
Rosebery (5th Earl of Rosebery) Papers, National Library of Scotland, Edinburgh.
Rowntree Trust records, courtesy of Mr A. P. Duncum.
Royal Archives, Windsor.
Sir Edward Russell Papers, Sydney Jones Library, University of Liverpool.
Lord John Russell (Earl Russell) Papers, Public Record Office.
Salisbury (3rd Marquess of Salisbury) Papers, Hatfield House and Christ Church, Oxford.
Herbert (Viscount) Samuel Papers, House of Lords Record Office.
J. S. Sandars Papers, Bodleian Library, Oxford.
D. H. and George Saunders Papers, Churchill College, Cambridge.
C. P. Scott Papers, British Library.
Selborne (Viscount Wolmer, 2nd Earl of Selborne) Papers, Bodleian Library, Oxford.
Bernard Shaw Papers, British Library.
J. A. Spender Papers, British Library.
Edward Stanhope Papers, County Archives, Lincoln.
W. T. Stead Papers, courtesy of Professor Joseph O. Baylen.
J. St Loe Strachey Papers, House of Lords Record Office.
Joseph Sturge Papers, British Library.
Frank Swinnerton Papers, University of Arkansas.
Times Archives, New Printing House Square, London.
Times Collection, University of Texas at Austin.
United University Club records, United Oxford and Cambridge University Club.
Sir Edward Watkin Papers, Central Library, Manchester.
George Wilson Papers, Central Library, Manchester.
George Wyndham Papers, Grosvenor Estate Office, London.

INDEX

Aberdeen, 4th Earl of: communicates with *Times*, 62, 63, 82–83, 103; as premier, 68, 85–86, 104–105, 106; assailed by press, 80, 105; and Crimean War, 101, 125

Aberdeen Free Press, 289

Acton, 1st Baron, 214, 233, 244

Addington, Henry (1st Viscount Sidmouth), 39, 40

Addison, Joseph, 31

Adullamites, 169–71, 179

Advertisement supplements, 66–67

Advertisement tax, 1, 32, 49–50, 54, 61, 65, 66, 67–68

Advertiser (King's Lynn), 207

Afghanistan, 221, 261

Aitken, Max: *see* Beaverbrook, Baron

Akers-Douglas, Aretas (1st Viscount Chilston), 280, 287, 300, 313, 315, 317, 349

Alabama claims, 195

Albert, Prince, 72, 78, 103, 129, 138

Alden, Percy, 405

Allard, William, 406

Allcard, William, 115, 119

Althorp, Viscount (3rd Earl Spencer), 75

Amery, L. S., 394, 396, 418–19

Andrews, Alexander, 73

Annand, James, 270, 289, 361

Answers, 354, 356, 357, 421

Anti-Corn Law Association, 61

Anti-Corn Law Circular, 61

Anti-Corn Law League, 61–62, 95; *also see* Free Trade

Anti-Jacobin: 18th century, 44; Greenwood's, 317

Argus, 45

Argyll, 8th Duke of, 112, 203

Armstrong, G. G., 425–26

Armstrong, Captain George, 181, 182, 205, 245, 248, 328, 331

Arnold, Arthur, 188, 189, 200, 216, 426

Arnold, Edwin, 97, 200

Arnold, Matthew, 343

Arnold, W. T., 242

Ashburton Treaty, 76

Ashley, (Anthony) Evelyn, 94

Ashmead Bartlett, Ellis: *see* Bartlett, Ellis Ashmead

Ashton, 1st Baron: *see* Williamson, James

Aspden, Hartley, 228, 290, 428

Aspinall, Arthur, 20, 32–33, 36, 37, 43–44, 48, 51

Asquith, H. H. (Earl of Oxford and Asquith), 12, 297, 298–99, 353, 371, 375, 383, 384, 400, 402, 411

Asquith, Ivon, 431

Asquith, Margot (Countess of Oxford and Asquith), 353

Asquith, Raymond, 402

Association for Promoting the Repeal of the Taxes on Knowledge, 65

Astor, David, 16, 19

Astor, Lady (Nancy Astor), 16

Astor, Waldorf (2nd Viscount Astor), 325

Astor, William Waldorf (1st Viscount Astor), 16, 325, 337–41, 412, 426

Astor family, 421

Athenaeum, 45

Athenaeum, 158, 299

Attlee, Clement (Earl Attlee), 16

Aurora, 47

Austin, Alfred: as Salisbury's agent, 12, 238, 245, 249–50, 273–74, 300–303, 315–16; as leader-writer, 13, 216–17, 312, 331; starts *National Review*, 249, 329, 353; leaves *Standard*, 377

Australia, political labels in, 305

Bagehot, Walter, 89, 138

Baines, Edward, 61, 160, 225

Baines, Frederick, 242

Baines family, 61, 122, 433; *also see Leeds Mercury*

Baldwin, Charles, 46, 135

Baldwin, Stanley (Earl Baldwin of Bewdley), 12

Balfour, A. J. (1st Earl of Balfour): press involvement, 12, 249, 280, 239, 333, 335, 352, 395; as premier, 13, 400, 409; reassured by Gladstone, 277; banters with Stead, 293, 319, 323, 333; as Irish Secretary, 296, 297, 352; uses Iwan-Müller, 311, 325, 330, 331, 347, 353–54, 433; and *Times*, 311–12, 360–61; dispenses honours, 313–14, 328; relations with Chamberlain, 314–15, 417; becomes leader of the House, 331; advises Cust, 337,

338–39, 341; and political speeches, 347, 362; relations with Harmsworth, 349, 368, 395

Banner, 249, 280
Barker, John, 379, 387, 388
Barlow, J. Emmott, 392
Barnes, Thomas, 40, 59, 75, 299, 413
Barrie, J. M., 233, 310
Barrington, Lord, 249
Barrington-Ward, Robin, 16
Barry, John, 308
Bartlett, Ellis Ashmead, 245, 246, 329
Bass, Michael, 178
Bate, Rev H.: *see* Dudley, Rev H. Bate
Bathurst, Lady (Lilias Borthwick), 199
Baxter, Herbert, 368
Bayne, Peter 127
Beach, Sir Michael Hicks (1st Viscount St Aldwyn): *see* Hicks Beach, Sir Michael
Beaconsfield, 1st Earl of: *see* Disraeli, Benjamin
Beaconsfield Club, 158
Beaverbrook, Baron (Max Aitken), 18–19, 325, 430
Bedford, 7th Duke of, 113, 116
Bee-Hive, 192, 205
Beefsteak Club, 203
Beer family, 423
Behan, Mr, 157
Bell, C. F. Moberly: *see* Moberly Bell, C. F.
Bell, John, 41, 107
Bell, Robert Fitzroy, 329
Bellamy, John, 38
Belloc, Hilaire, 401, 407, 432
Bell's Life in London, 51, 159
Bell's Weekly Messenger, 51, 92–93, 177, 206
Beloff, (Sir) Max, 27
Benjafield, John, 41
Bennett, Arnold, 200, 416, 424
Bennett, R. A., 307
Bennett, S., 270
Bentham, Jeremy, 33–36, 37, 45, 55, 74, 410
Bentinck, Lord George, 78
Bentinck, Lord Henry, 78
Bentley, E. C., 392, 401
Beresford, Major William, 81
Beresford Hope, A. J.: *see* Hope, A. J. Beresford
Berry family, 97
Berthold's Pocket Handkerchief, 56
Bevan, Aneurin, 16
Birch, James, 92, 154–55
Birmingham 'Caucus', 426
Birmingham Daily Argus, 270, 291, 342, 403
Birmingham Daily Gazette, 314, 315, 404, 426, 428
Birmingham Daily Post, 185, 219–20, 240, 260, 271, 282, 283, 289, 312–14
Birmingham Evening Mail, 312–13
Bismarck, Prince Otto von, 259
Black, John, 75
Blackburn Times, 228
Blackwood, John, 131, 134, 165
Blackwood, William, 28, 174, 183, 233, 312, 317

Blackwood's Magazine, 233, 353
Blake, Robert (Baron Blake), 26, 47, 85, 223
Blanchard, Samuel Laman, 58
'Bloody Sunday', 307
Blumenfeld, R. D., 345, 423
Blunt, Wilfrid Scawen, 309, 338
Bonaparte, Napoleon, 36, 44; *also see* France
Bonar Law, Andrew, 395
Booth, Albert, 122
Borthwick, Algernon (Baron Glenesk): inherits *Morning Post*, 81; solicited by Tories, 85; flies *Owl*, 94; allegedly in France's pay, 135, 138n; relations with Disraeli, 199–200, 430; honoured, 200, 228, 295, 312, 327, 328; as a politician, 216, 225, 274; allegiance to Churchill, 250–51, 295, 330, 333, 378; opposes Salisbury, 250, 334; as 'Uncle Algy', 254; as proprietor, 331, 339, 366–67, 421
Borthwick, Lady, 295
Borthwick, Lilias: *see* Bathurst, Lady
Borthwick, Oliver, 199
Borthwick, Peter, 65, 78–80, 81–82, 199, 225
Botha, Louis, 399
Bourne, H. R. Fox, 45, 87–88, 160, 190, 191, 199, 288
Bourne, W. H., 43
Bourne family, 43
Bowles, Thomas Gibson, 216
Boyle, J. B., 363
Boyle, R. W., 288
Boys' Friend, 354
Bradbury, William, 95
Bradbury and Evans, 95
Bradford, Lady, 208
Bradford Argus, 289
Bradford Daily Telegraph, 404
Bradford Observer, 289
Bradlaugh, Charles, 216
Brailsford, H. N., 426–27
Brand, H. W. B., 176
Brassey, Sir Thomas (1st Earl Brassey), 362, 391, 396
Brett, Reginald (2nd Viscount Esher), 244, 259–60, 265, 280, 297, 338, 351, 377, 389, 390
Briggs, Asa (Baron Briggs), 70, 141
Bright, John: posits power of the press, 11, 99, 102–103, 104–105, 114; newspaper involvement, 61–62, 107–109, 120, 123, 124–25, 126–27, 204; scorns *Manchester Guardian*, 61, 122; writes for papers, 62, 105, 110–11; as a Free Trader, 66, 67, 68; as a franchise reformer, 92, 140, 169, 171; relations with *Times*, 113, 116, 128, 129, 130, 131, 140, 167, 168, 169, 195; as a minister, 128, 187; admired by *Standard*, 136; assailed by *Morning Herald*, 142; praises *Daily News*, 157; in 1865 elections, 164–65: detests *Pall Mall Gazette*, 229; and Hawarden Kite, 279; mentioned, 117, 139, 313, 314, 343
Bristol, Dean of: *see* Elliot, Gilbert
British Lion, 184, 185
British Press, 45
British Statesman, 47

British War Fund, 385
Briton, 33
Brodrick, George, 10
Brodrick, St John (1st Earl of Midleton), 13, 361, 395, 400
Brooks's Club, 158, 381
Brougham, Henry (1st Baron Brougham and Vaux), 45, 58, 75, 113
Brunner, Sir John, 308, 309, 310, 328, 376, 386, 397
Bryce, James (Viscount Bryce), 175, 284, 288, 310, 326, 386, 389
Buccleuch, 5th Duke of, 207
Buckle, G. E.: as archivist, 28; becomes editor of *Times*, 265–66; relations with Chamberlain, 266, 285, 394; relations with Churchill, 266, 294, 296–97, 303–304, 347; Irish views, 276, 285–86; relations with Salisbury, 280, 296, 331, 332, 394; commits Pigottism, 296–99; relations with Balfour, 311–12; relations with Rosebery, 332, 351; editorial policy and position, 345, 359–60, 376–77; mentioned, 419, 431
Bulgarian agitation, 14, 98, 202, 209–11, 212, 213n, 229, 256, 270, 293, 362, 417
Bulgarian Horrors and the Questions of the East, The, 210
Bulwer, J. R., 293
Bulwer-Lytton, Edward (1st Baron Lytton), 49, 55, 89
Bunce, J. C., 219, 240, 241, 244, 282, 313, 314, 328
Burdett-Coutts, Baroness, 245
Burdett-Coutts, William (William Ashmead Bartlett), 245
Burke, Edmund, 36
Burnham, 1st Baron: *see* Lawson, Edward Levy
Burnham, 4th Baron, 345
Burns, John, 307, 421
Burrows, Montagu, 330
Byles, W. P., 68n

Cadbury, George, 307, 398, 399–400, 401–404, 407, 412, 421
Caine, W. S., 405
Cairnes, J. E., 191, 194
Cairns, Lord, 175
Cambridge, 2nd Duke of, 97
Cambridge Daily Independent Press, 335
Campbell-Bannerman, Sir Henry: confused, 332; as Liberal leader, 375, 384, 392; supported by Spender, 387, 406–407; decries 'methods of barbarism', 400; mentioned, 434
Canning, George, 40, 44
Cape Times, 367, 384
Cardwell, Edward, 87, 168, 188
Carlile, Richard, 56
Carlingford, Baron, 199
Carlisle, 7th Earl of, 156
Carlisle, Lady, 390
Carlton Club, 81, 158, 180, 186, 313, 314, 341
Carlyle, Thomas, 39
Carnarvon, 4th Earl of, 212, 236, 249, 252

Carnegie, Andrew, 189, 235, 258, 265, 270, 287, 338, 357, 376, 389–90
Caroline, Queen, 40
Cassell, Petter, and Galpin, 188
Cave of Adullam: *see* Adullamites
Cavendish, Lord Frederick, 241
Cavour, Camillo, Conte de, 141
Caxton, William, 1
Cecil, Lady Gwendolen, 28, 300
Cecil, Lord Robert: *see* Salisbury, 3rd Marquess of
Cecil Club, 249
Central Conservative Association, 252
Central News Agency, 367
Central Press Agency, 149, 206, 272, 312, 332, 346
Chamberlain, Arthur, 284
Chamberlain, (Sir) Austen, 314
Chamberlain, Joseph: manipulates press, 4, 12, 204, 219–21, 235–36, 240, 289, 313, 394, 411; relations with Morley, 10, 219, 230–31, 232, 256; criticized by press, 198, 267, 288, 313–16, 354; accused of 'leaks', 239–40, 243–44, 271; relations with Churchill, 250, 271, 273, 282, 288; relations with Gladstone, 255, 296, 306; relations with Stead, 260, 317, 323; as a coalitionist, 260–61, 266, 394; dealings with Cooper, 260, 284–85; dealings with Buckle, 265, 266, 285–86, 296–97; presents 'unauthorised programme', 270–271; opposes Home Rule, 276–86; stimulates Unionist journalism, 288, 289, 304, 306, 373; defends Parnell Commission, 298; recommends honours, 313, 328; boosted by press, 333, 341, 346, 353, 396, 422; reproves Balfour, 349, 417; South African policy, 362, 367, 384, 395; in 'khaki' election, 390; advocates Tariff Reform, 409, 417, 420; mentioned, 382, 405
Champion, H. H. 307
Chartism, 60, 62, 127, 411, 414
Chenery, Thomas, 208, 213–14, 233, 227, 236n, 251, 255, 264, 265, 431
Cherry, R. R., 397
Chester Courant, 289
Chesterton, G. K., 401, 407, 415, 420
Childers, H. C. E., 245, 260, 267, 278, 283, 346
Chilston, 1st Viscount: *see* Akers-Douglas, Aretas
Chips, 354
Chirol, (Sir) Valentine, 366, 419, 425
Chisholm, Hugh, 377
Christian World, 288
Chronicle, 176, 177, 184
Churchill, Lady Randolph, 378
Churchill, Lord Randolph: manipulates press, 4, 12, 250–51, 272–73, 274, 330–31, 411; patronizes Escott, 236, 250, 253, 271, 295; attacks 'old gang', 250–54, 260; on Gladstone's reading habits, 255; relations with Chamberlain, 250, 271, 273, 282, 288; relations with Buckle and *Times*, 266, 294, 301, 303–304; commands Lucy's devotion, 268, 294–95; on Irish issues, 279, 297, 298, 304;

resigns office, 296–97, 301–302; recommends honours, 312–13; ambitions in Birmingham, 312, 313, 314; arouses suspicion, 311, 315, 322; supported by *Morning Post*, 250–51, 295, 330, 333, 378; rated 'Class I', 346; attempts comeback, 347, mentioned, 265, 292, 376

Churchill, (Sir) Winston, 12, 378, 411

City Carlton Club, 158

City Conservative Club, 158

City Constitutional Club, 158

City Liberal Club, 158

Clarendon, 4th Earl of: newspaper tastes, 59; as a press favourite, 80, 86, 188; relations with Delane and *Times*, 72, 102, 104, 111–12, 113, 131n, 133, 140, 168, 172, 173, 176, 195; mentioned, 101, 170

Clarendon, Lady, 82

Clarke, W. W., 115–20, 133, 147

Clarke, William, 352, 374

Clayden, P. W., 269–70, 323, 362, 379, 398–99

Clement, William Innell, 51

Clerkenwell News, 203

Clubland, 13, 21, 25, 93, 112, 113, 131, 158–59, 181, 184, 203, 221, 234, 292, 293, 342, 396, 411

Cobbett, William, 36, 46, 55

Cobden, Richard: attacks 'taxes on knowledge', 2, 20, 53, 67; as Free Trader, 61–62, 65, 160; visits Midhurst, 92–93; criticizes *Daily News*, 99–100, 104; castigates *Times*, 103, 105, 106, 128–29, 130–31, 187; newspaper involvement, 11, 99, 106–10, 120, 123–25; mentioned, 42, 117, 157, 343

Collet, C. D., 93

Coleridge, Samuel Taylor, 42

Colman, J. J., 217, 309, 310, 328, 332, 336

Comic Cuts, 354

Communist Party, 17, 430

Congress of Berlin, 212

Conservative, 182, 206

Conservative Central Office, 206, 249, 304

Conservative Club, 158

Conservative Magazine, 151

Conservative News Agency, 272

Conservative Newspaper Union, 207

Consolidated Newspapers, Ltd., 378, 387–88, 397, 420

Constitutional, 47, 58

Constitutional Club, 158

Constitutional Press Agency, 272

Constitutional Year Book, 287

Contemporary Review, 343

Cook, (Sir) Edward T.: relations with Harmsworth, 6, 358; hired at *Pall Mall*, 13, 257; edits *Pall Mall*, 293, 319–21, 334; evicted from *Pall Mall*, 321–25, 379, 425, 426; devoted to Rosebery, 324, 326, 327, 350, 351, 363, 364–65, 367–68, 372–73, 376, 377, 381, 390; preaches 'independence', 325–27, 432; edits *Westminster*, 337, 344, 345, 346, 352, 354; disdains *Daily News*, 327; edits *Daily News*, 336, 362–64, 379–80, 431; imperial views, 366, 367, 381, 384, 390, 391,

406; evicted from *Daily News*, 398–99, 421; professional principles, 413, 428; mentioned, 63, 298, 303, 309, 352, 371

Cook, J. D., 66, 67, 87, 88, 98, 103–104, 185, 426

Cooke, A. B., 264

Cooke, C. Kinloch, 324, 325

Cooke, Joseph, 378, 388

Cooper, Charles: on provincial journalism, 21–22, 223–24, 239; writes for *Morning Star*, 124; patronized by Rosebery, 186, 239, 260; anti-Dilke, 220; explains his principles, 256, 278, 328; favours 'middle party', 260; accused of war-mongering, 261; claims electoral victory, 272; opposes Home Rule, 282–83, 284–85; on Unionist tensions, 315; cultivated by Balfour, 333, anticipates Liberal split, 350; mentioned, 361

Cooper, Robert J., 157–58

Coote, Sir Colin, 5, 430

Cornhill Magazine, 160, 229

Corn Laws, 54, 62–64, 99; *also see* Anti-Corn Law League *and* Free Trade

Cornish, K. H., 150

Cornwall, Alice ('Princess Midas'), 305

Corry, Montagu (1st Baron Rowton), 176, 178, 179, 180, 199, 200, 201, 202, 204, 207, 212, 214, 223, 254

Coulson, Walter, 45

Coulton, David T., 91, 178

Courier, 44, 46, 48

Court Circular, 177

Courthope, W. J., 249, 353

Courtney, Kate (Lady Courtney), 261

Courtney, Leonard (1st Baron Courtney of Penwith), 175, 185–86, 195, 213, 216, 220–21, 261, 395

Courtney, W. L., 97–98, 311

Cowen, Joseph, 216, 289

Cowper, 7th Earl, 241

Cox, Harold, 320

Cox, Rev J. E., 177

Crabbet Club, 338

Cranborne, Viscount: *see* Salisbury, 3rd Marquess of

Cranbrook, 1st Earl of, 234, 279, 280

Crete, 375

Crewe and Nantwich Advertiser, 329

Crimean War, 90, 101–103, 328

Croker, John Wilson, 47

Crompton, T. B., 78, 79, 80

Crook, W. M., 374, 378–79, 383, 384, 387–88, 389, 397, 399, 400, 405, 420

Cross, R. A. (1st Viscount Cross), 249, 346

Crossman, R. H. S., 5–6, 255

Crowe, Eyre Evans, 75, 94, 95, 100

Cruikshank, R. J., 8

Cubitt, George, 178, 180, 182, 245

Cunninghame Graham, R. B., 307, 310

Curran, James, 30n

Curtis, Byron, 331, 378

Curzon, George (1st Marquess Curzon of Kedleston), 315

Cust, Henry, 325, 337–41, 378

Daily Chronicle: price and circulation, 93, 397, 421; acquired by Lloyd, 203, 204; Irish views, 287; its Liberalism, 332, 426, 428; reports speeches, 348, 362; pro-Rosebery, 350, 351, 352; challenges Rosebery, 371–73; 'sheds its chiefs', 352, 385, 388, 396; in Liberal leadership struggles, 352–53, 359, 361, 371–73, 381, 382, 383; eclipses *Daily News*, 380; imperialism, 381, 383, 384, 406, 407, 425; edited by Donald, 435; mentioned, 12, 219, 235n, 240, 320, 322, 324, 342, 373, 425

Daily Citizen, 421

Daily Courier, 368

Daily Express, 17, 18, 200, 333, 345, 378, 397, 412, 420, 421, 422

Daily Graphic, 24, 330

Daily Herald, 6, 429

Daily Mail: grants an interview, 13; partisanship, 17, 24, 395, 421, 423; founded, 358, 368–69; cancels Sunday edition, 370; requests 'some tip', 371; 'Independent and Imperial', 373–74, 395; popularity, 380, 391, 397, 416; runs competition, 382–83; as agent of continuity, 409; has nuisance value, 412; mentioned, 18, 378, 385, 428

Daily Mirror, 17, 416, 421

Daily News: compared to *Genesis*, 13; started, 53; and newspaper taxes, 67; assails *Times*, 71; and Free Trade, 85; supports Aberdeen, 86; early policy, 93, 95–96, 97, 99; its Gladstonianism, 99, 165, 172, 175, 188, 208, 209, 224, 226, 238, 255, 260, 281, 363; disappoints Radicals, 100–101, 103, 106, 108, 109, 113, 126, 203; Russell's interest in, 116–18, 119, 147, 155; absorbs *Morning Star*, 127–28; praises Disraeli, 141; anticipates Liberal unity, 145–46, 147; and US Civil War, 157; in 1865 elections, 163; revitalized, 192–93; and Chamberlain, 198; and Labouchere, 203, 216, 308, 323, 335, 339, 396; opposes Bulgarian Horrors, 209–210, 211, 212, 213; and Dilke, 220, 266–67; editorial dislocations, 230, 267–70, 281, 323; and the Irish question, 275 ff., 298; Liberals rely on, 288, 292, 306, 322, 352, 359; and Churchill, 294–95; read at Oxford, 311; seen as subservient, 327; keeps its old ways, 345, 347, 348; edited by Cook, 362–66, 367; celebrates jubilee, 365; in Liberal leadership struggles, 372–73, 375, 376, 381, 383–84; supports 'Sally', 377; committed to Nonconformity, 380–81; espouses imperialism, 381, 390, 391, 392, 393, 396; drop in sales, 397; under 'pro-Boer' control, 397–400, 401–404, 407; absorbs *Morning Leader*, 333; reputation, 409, 412, 420; financial distress, 421; mentioned, 110, 123, 159, 184, 196, 218, 222, 238, 240, 243, 257, 261, 307, 320, 379, 416, 426, 427, 428, 429, 431

Daily Politician, 47

Daily Telegraph: partisanship, 17; circulation, 93, 97, 137, 371; early years, 97–99, 126, 154; taken over by Levy, 109; applauds Palmerston, 155, 156, 161–62; relations with Russell, 161, 168; refutes *Times*, 170–71; venerates Gladstone, 171–72, 175–76, 254, 293, 322, 334; in 1874 elections, 196, 197; shifts to Tory-Imperialism, 200–203, 204, 218–19; sits out Bulgarian agitation, 211, 229; committed to Tories, 212, 226, 254, 322, 401; in 1880 elections, 223, 225; pro-Hartington, 226–27; rivalry with *Standard*, 249; on Irish issues, 286, 320; influenced by Salisbury, 300; unknown at Oxford, 311; popular qualities, 215, 345, 346; rivalry with *Mail*, 358–59; favours Rosebery, 393; inspired by Chamberlain, 394; preaches to Liberals, 396; mentioned, 19, 88, 130, 159, 169, 173, 188, 205, 207, 221, 233, 240, 332, 366, 430

Dalziel, J. H. (Baron Dalziel of Kirkcaldy), 334, 335, 336, 356

Dana, Paul, 387

Dartmouth, 5th Earl of, 304

Dasent, G. W., 71, 168, 176, 185, 195

Davis, Jefferson, 169

Davitt, Michael, 192

Dawson, Geoffrey: *see* Robinson, Geoffrey

Day, 47, 169, 179–80, 184, 188

Dean of Bristol: *see* Elliot, Gilbert

Delane, Captain George, 131n

Delane, John Thaddeus: his self-perception, 9, 19; appointed editor of *Times*, 63; relations with Disraeli, 64, 84, 85, 133–34, 175, 176, 196, 197, 207–208, 430; relations with Gladstone, 65, 171, 172, 173, 175, 195, 197, 208–209; sets forth policy, 71, 72; fealty to Palmerston, 82, 101–102, 129–30, 131, 139, 155–56, 165–66; supports Aberdeen, 82, 101–102, 103; as a coalitionist, 85; relations with Clarendon, 102, 112, 133, 172, 173, 176; antipathy to Russell, 111–12, 113, 132, 133, 155, 167, 169–70; relies on Lowe, 112, 165; sees after his friends, 128–29; 155, 156, 432; in 1865 elections, 164; cultivated by Derby, ·173–74; in 1868 elections, 185; tries to co-operate with Liberals, 195–96, 197; participates in Bulgarian agitation, 209, 210–11; retires, 213; mentioned, 72, 159, 191, 198, 205, 221, 255, 265

Delane, W. F. A., 87

Democrat, 192, 332

Dennis, Robert, 371

Derby, 14th Earl of: nobbles press, 11, 74, 82, 89, 133, 135, 173–74; upholds duties, 65; relations with *Times*, 72, 73, 139–40, 172, 173–74; and the *Press*, 89–90, 91; as premier, 134, 136, 140, 144, 146, 148, 155, 173, 175; portrayed in *Punch*, 154; leaps into dark, 174; mentioned, 80, 81, 98, 166, 178, 180

Derby, 15th Earl of (Lord Stanley), 89, 114, 134, 137–38, 150, 170, 172, 211, 212, 255, 283, 290, 291, 411

Derwent, H. C., 404

Destructive, 56

Devonshire, dowager Duchess of, 370

Devonshire, 8th Duke of: *see* Hartington, Lord

Devonshire Club, 158
Dial, 127
Dibblee, G. B., 397
Dicey, Edward, 97, 186, 216, 288, 408, 415
Dickens, Charles, 53, 95
Dickens, John, 95, 96
Dictionary of National Biography, 97, 160
Dilke, Ashton, 216, 288
Dilke, Charles Wentworth, 96
Dilke, Sir Charles Wentworth, 96, 194, 220, 239, 240, 241, 256, 259, 266–67, 269, 271, 276, 288, 310, 338, 389
Dillon, John, 310, 321
Disraeli, Benjamin (1st Earl of Beaconsfield): manipulates press, 11, 74, 115, 120, 137–38, 149, 150, 151–53, 177, 204, 206, 228, 229, 411, 430; as 'Runnymede', 45; starts *Representative*, 46–47; as novelist, 47, 60, 89, 378; as Young Englander, 64; as protectionist, 64–65, 84, 85; relations with Delane and *Times*, 64, 84, 85, 133–34, 136, 185, 196, 207–208; backed by *Morning Post*, 78, 80, 199–200, 430; eulogizes Wellington, 84; other press affiliations, 85, 142, 151–53, 154, 179–82, 183, 226, 254; launches the *Press*, 89–92, 111, 123, 134; opposes Palmerston, 132; relations with Salisbury, 136–37, 205; scores 'great success', 141; in 1865 elections, 161, 163, 164, 165; as a reformer, 174; as premier, 175, 198; declines office, 196; gains press support, 199–200, 201–203; advised by Queen, 207; discounts Turkish atrocities, 209, 211; attends Berlin Congress, 212; as imperialist, 212, 215, 222; in 1880 elections, 215, 223, 225, 237; 'dead or dying', 213, 250, 407; mentioned, 114, 116, 158, 243, 327, 346, 381
Disraeli, Mary Anne, 91, 141
Dodds, Joseph, 292
Donald, (Sir) Robert, 7, 262, 307, 336, 340, 421, 428, 434–35
Douglas, James, 307
Doyle, Andrew, 75
Dreyfus affair, 422
Drew, Mary Gladstone: *see* Gladstone, Mary
Dublin Express, 159
Dublin World, 92n
Dudley, Rev Henry Bate, 41, 42
Duncan, James, 75
Dunckley, Dr Henry, 290
Dundee Advertiser, 239, 278, 289, 328, 347
Dunn, J. Nicoll, 378
Durham, 1st Earl of, 75
Dyke, Sir William Hart, 180

Eastbourne Standard, 424
Eastern Morning News (Hull), 292, 332
Easthope, Sir John, 38, 58, 74–76, 86–87
Ecclesiastical Titles Bill (1851), 82
Echo, 93, 185, 188–89, 199, 216, 219, 235, 239, 287, 292, 308, 335, 342, 378–80, 382–83, 384, 387–88, 389, 406, 420, 426, 433–34
Economist, 62, 99, 131, 305
Edgcumbe, Sir Robert, 386

Edinburgh Evening Courant, 178, 207
Edinburgh Evening News, 361
Edinburgh Review, 71, 73, 216, 223
Editor's Handysheet, 207, 243
Education Acts: (1870), 1, 121, 194, 225; (1902), 409
Edwards, David, 401, 402–403, 404
Edwards, J. Passmore, 189, 216, 287, 288, 292, 335–36, 378, 426
Egypt, British occupation of, 190, 251, 258, 259, 260, 261, 266, 271, 318, 417
Elcho, Lord, 169, 179
Eliot, George (Mary Ann Evans), 151
Ellice, Edward, 114, 116, 117, 118, 133, 148–49
Elliot, Gilbert (Dean of Bristol), 115, 116, 117, 118, 120, 132
Elliot, Henry, 155
Ellis, T. E., 362, 363, 381
Elton, Sir Arthur, 88, 109
Empire, 114
Empire Free Trade, 4, 18
Encyclopaedia Britannica, 419
Enfield, Lord, 113
Engels, Friedrich, 192, 307
England, 246, 248, 329, 335
Ensor, (Sir) Robert, 199, 275, 398, 407, 426
Escott, T. H. S., 9–10, 28, 81, 154, 182–83, 198, 201, 208, 219, 221, 233, 235–40, 244–45, 249, 250, 252–53, 256, 261, 271, 280, 281, 295, 329, 353
Evans, D. M., 183
Evans, Howard, 189
Evening Chronicle, 45
Evening Herald, 135
Evening News, 246, 248, 280, 328, 329, 345, 349, 354, 356–58, 366, 368, 370, 392, 405, 411, 423
Evening Standard, 24, 127, 135, 159, 386, 421, 422
Evening Star, 127
Ewart, William, 65
Examiner, 58, 94, 99, 101, 115, 126, 190–91, 197, 209, 217n, 414
Exeter Gazette, 178
Express, 127–28, 159

Fabian Society, 307, 320, 376, 394, 427
Farmer and Mark Lane Express, 249
Farmer's Newspaper, 185
Farrer, 1st Baron, 401
Fashoda crisis, 381, 384
Fawcett, Henry, 221
Fawcett, (Dame) Millicent, 190
Fergusson, R. C. Munro (Viscount Novar), 372
Figaro, 245, 317
Financial News, 357
Financial Times, 24
First World War, 16, 425, 429, 435
Fisher, W. J., 385, 391, 406
Fitzroy, E. A., 177
Fletcher, A. E., 332, 350, 352, 354, 380
Folkestone, Lord (Earl of Radnor), 280
Fonblanque, Albany, 99, 190, 414

Forbes, Archibald, 192
Forget-Me-Not, 354
Forster, John, 94, 96
Forster, W. E., 188, 194, 198, 209, 231, 240–41, 242, 243, 352
Fortescue, 3rd Earl, 112
Fortnightly Review, 187, 198, 216, 217, 221, 236, 250, 253, 418
Fourth Party, 250, 251
Fowler, Frank, 150
Fox, Charles James, 42
Fox, William Johnson, 95
Fox Bourne, H. R.: *see* Bourne, H. R. Fox
France: journalism in, 35, 70, 216, 217, 342; revolution in, 37, 40, 42, 44, 55; *Times* criticizes, 72; commercial treaty with, 129; assists Italians, 141; imperial rivalry with, 381, 384
Franchise Reform Bill (1859), 140, 141
Franco-Prussian War, 192, 195
Freeman, E. A., 203–204, 210, 310
Free Trade, 78, 79, 81, 201; *also see* Anti-Corn Law League
Fremantle, Sir Thomas, 78
Fresh Air Fund, 420–21
Friedrichs, Hulda, 364
Froude, J. A., 229

Gallenga, Antonio, 236n
Gardiner, A. G., 7, 14, 346, 374, 404, 407, 411, 431
Garnett, Jeremiah, 48
Garrett, Edmund, 367, 384
Garrick Club, 330
Garvin, J. L., 8, 15, 19, 21, 29, 219, 237, 286, 340, 393, 407, 411
Geake, Charles, 364, 372, 376
General Elections: (1837), 59, 61; (1841), 164; (1857), 119, 122; (1859), 141; (1865), 160, 161–65, 167; (1868), 179, 180, 185–86; (1874), 198, 201; (1880), 149, 193, 216, 217–18, 223 ff., 237, 243; (1885), 270, 274–75; (1886), 270, 275, 286, 288, 294; (1892), 290, 321, 333, 334–35; (1895), 339, 354–55, 359, 360, 380; (1900), 339, 390–91, 397, 406; (1906), 149, 217, 340; (1945), 16, 21, 74, 149; (1966), 5
Gentleman's Magazine, 30
George III, King, 39
George IV, King (Prince of Wales and Prince Regent), 39, 40, 41, 46
George, Henry, 332
Gibbs, H. Hucks (1st Baron Aldenham), 233, 317, 328
Gibson, Thomas Milner: *see* Milner-Gibson, Thomas
Giffard, Stanley Lees, 46
Gladstone, Herbert (Viscount Gladstone), 225, 238–39, 242–43, 259, 277–79, 281–82, 296, 328, 332, 334, 384, 400, 401, 404, 406, 433
Gladstone, Mary, 214
Gladstone, W. E.: 'awareness' of press, 11–12, 255–56; derides Clubland journalism, 21, 93; as fiscal reformer, 65, 66, 67–68, 69, 85, 98,
107, 109, 129; newspaper involvement, 74, 87, 96, 114–15, 120, 176–77, 411, 430; declines Stanley's bid, 83; relations with *Telegraph* (Cook and Hunt), 88, 98–99, 156, 161, 172–73, 175–76; inspires *Morning Chronicle*, 103–104; relations with *Times* and its editors, 106, 165, 170, 172, 173, 176, 195, 265; as possible coalitionist, 116, 139; praised by *Morning Star*, 123; declines office, 134; and Italian question, 141, 173; upholds Derby, 144; joins Palmerston, 147; as franchise reformer, 157, 169, 170, 171; gains press support, 160, 172, 221; ousted at Oxford, 160, 161, 163, 165; praised by *Daily News*, 165, 193–94, 210, 212, 214, 222, 239, 266, 267, 281, 363; as premier, 176, 187, 197; and *Echo*, 189; and *Morning Advertiser*, 199; loses backing of *Telegraph*, 200–201, 254; prefers provincial press, 204, 224, 291–92; resigns leadership, 208–209; decries Bulgarian Horrors, 209, 210, 256, 417; wages Midlothian campaign, 210, 212–13, 214, 215; resents press, 211; relations with Chamberlain, 219–20, 271, 296; resumes leadership 226–27; relations with *Pall Mall*, 228, 230, 333–34, 337, 341; relations with Morley, 230, 231; opposed by *St James's*, 234; compliments *Standard*, 237; converts to Home Rule, 241, 243, 262, 274 ff., 282 ff., 338, 350; resents leaks, 244; retirement rumoured, 250; feuds with Stead, 257–59, 262, 279, 293, 319; forms third ministry, 269, 280; his 'impetuosity', 301; writes for *Speaker*, 310; distributes honours, 313, 322, 328; disowns Parnell, 320–21; greets *Westminster Gazette*, 325–26; retires, 340, 350; rated 'Class I', 356; greets *Daily Mail*, 369; re-emerges, 371–72; reads *Spectator*, 417; mentioned, 14, 99, 113, 117, 122, 208, 250–51, 297, 308, 351, 381, 426
Gladstone, William Henry, 225
Gladstone League, 390
Glasgow Evening News, 272
Glasgow Herald, 207, 239, 270, 278, 289, 395
Glasgow News, 207, 227
Glenesk, Baron: *see* Borthwick, Algernon
Globe, 45–46, 85, 86, 90, 93, 114, 116, 119, 132, 139, 142, 143, 145, 148, 149, 159, 163, 164, 173, 178–82, 199, 201, 207, 212, 218, 220, 225, 244, 245, 246, 249, 260, 274, 275, 279, 288, 331, 342, 345, 377, 386, 395, 416, 422
Glover, William, 88, 109
Glyn, G. G., 175, 176
Goddard, D. F., 378
Goderich, Viscount (1st Earl of Ripon), 113
Godley, A. D., 13
Godley (John) Arthur (1st Baron Kilbracken), 244, 256
Goldman, C. S., 434
Goodman, Baron, 19
Gordon, General Charles, 258, 260
Gorst, (Sir) John, 154, 184, 206, 241, 243, 246, 253
Goschen, G. J., (1st Viscount Goschen), 135, 257, 260, 261, 274, 279, 283, 286, 294, 296,

302, 311, 316
Gould, F. C., 326–27, 364–65, 387, 416
Graham, Sir James, 64, 103, 104
Graham, Thomas, 357
Grant, 'Baron' Albert, 189
Grant, J. Corrie, 397
Grant, James, 43, 69, 81, 96, 103, 189
Granville, 2nd Earl, 66, 67, 72, 82, 142, 172, 173, 176, 188, 195, 209, 213, 214, 227, 266, 269, 365, 417
Granville, Dr J. Mortimer, 180, 182, 426
Green, J. R., 13
Greenwood, Frederick, 14, 160, 211, 222, 228–29, 230–31, 232–33, 233–34, 235, 246–47, 262, 274, 312, 316–17, 325, 326, 329, 426
Greville, Charles, 44, 64, 72, 82, 87, 92–93, 103, 106, 113–14, 118, 133
Greville, Thomas, 44
Grey, 2nd Earl, 45, 48, 117
Grey, Sir Edward (Viscount Grey of Fallodon), 384, 393, 400, 417
Grosvenor, 2nd Earl: *see* Westminster, 1st Duke of
Grosvenor, Captain R. W., (2nd Baron Ebury), 162, 163
Grosvenor, Lord Richard, 266
Guardian: see Manchester Guardian
Guardian (1817), 48
Gwynne, H. A., 19, 411, 421

Haddingtonshire Advertiser, 280
Haldane, R. B. (Viscount Haldane of Cloan), 310, 351, 352
Halifax, 1st Viscount (Sir Charles Wood), 66, 260
Hallam, Henry, 31
Halsey, A. H., 24
Haly, W. T., 110, 115
Hamber, Captain Thomas, 135, 136, 152–54, 183, 204–205, 426, 431
Hamilton, Sir Denis, 277
Hamilton, (Sir) Edward, 256, 258, 265, 266, 271, 306, 307, 309, 382
Hamilton, John, 111, 114, 125
Hammond, J. L., 310, 386, 401, 405, 407, 412
Hannay, David, 233
Hannay, James, 233
Hansard, 348
Harcourt, L. V. (1st Viscount Harcourt), 254–55, 260, 262–63, 335–36, 371, 401, 406
Harcourt, Sir William, 87, 88, 102, 195, 200, 208, 216, 226, 241, 252–53, 255, 280, 298, 322, 340, 341, 346, 350–51, 353, 354, 359, 360, 371, 372, 373, 375, 381, 382, 383, 392, 400, 406–407
Hardcastle, Edward, 254
Hardcastle, J. A., 216, 219
Hardinge, 1st Viscount, 84
Hardman, (Sir) William, 199, 223, 312, 331
Hargreaves, William, 131
Harley, Robert (1st Earl of Oxford), 250
Harmsworth, Alfred (Viscount Northcliffe): craves influence, 6–7, 421–22; starts *Daily Mail*, 11, 358, 368–69; professional pride, 13;
buys *Evening News*, 246, 349–50, 356–58; stands at Portsmouth, 354–55, 359; partisanship, 358–59, 360, 369–70, 371, 392–93, 394–95; relations with Balfour, 368, 395; relations with Rosebery, 369–70, 373, 399; covets honours, 370, 409, 422; 'Unionist and Imperialist', 373–74; opens his postbag, 382–83; arouses fears, 404, 433; as a 'revolutionary', 410–11; aims at women readers, 416–17; exerts appeal, 419, 421; Stead denounces, 422; bids for *Times*, 423; fears failure, 424; mentioned, 19, 34, 121, 125, 408, 412
Harmsworth, Cecil, 357, 369, 393, 395
Harmsworth, Harold (1st Viscount Rothermere), 19, 354, 357, 358, 393, 395
Harmsworth, Leicester, 357, 369, 392, 393
Harnay, George Julian, 60
Harris, William, 219
Harris, Wilson, 416
Harrison, Frederic, 191, 288, 310, 384
Harrison, Stanley, 4n
Hartington, Lord (8th Duke of Devonshire), 208–209, 213, 221, 223, 225, 226, 244, 258, 260, 277, 279, 283, 284, 287, 289, 290–91, 298, 300–301, 304–305, 306, 313–16, 328, 346
Hastings, Warren, 41
Hatton, Joseph, 248
'Hawarden Kite', 276–79
Hayward, Abraham, 25, 87, 102, 122, 144, 167, 169, 197, 211, 214, 227
Hazlitt, William, 2n, 39, 42–43, 46
Healy, T. M., 275, 308, 316
Henley, W. E., 233, 353, 360
Herbert, Sidney (1st Baron Herbert of Lea), 79, 87, 88, 113, 132, 147
Hetherington, Henry, 56, 414
Hicks Beach, Sir Michael (1st Viscount St Aldwyn), 261, 280, 346
Higgins, M. J., 176
Hill, Frank Harrison, 186, 192, 198, 208, 209, 212, 220, 222, 226, 235, 239, 244, 267–68, 269, 288, 330, 362, 430, 431
Hindle, Wilfrid, 81
History of The Times, quoted, 53, 130, 230, 298, 318, 360, 377
Hitchman, Francis, 27, 218, 219, 223, 224
Hobhouse, L. T., 383, 385, 391, 404, 407, 427, 428
Hobson, J. A., 374, 389, 395, 405
Hogarth, George, 95
Holden, (Sir) Isaac, 309, 328
Holland, Stuart, 4n
Hollis, Patricia, 55, 56
Home Chat, 354
Home Counties Liberal Federation, 406
Home News, 236
Home Rule, 4, 242, 243, 271, 276 ff., 282 ff., 286 ff., 318, 320–21, 334, 338, 350, 351–52, 382, 397, 417
Hooper, George, 139
Hope, Alexander Beresford, 89, 181, 185
Houghton, 1st Baron: *see* Milnes, Richard Monckton

Hour, 183
Howard, Anthony, 8
Hudson, Sir James, 155
Hudson, (Sir) Robert, 349
Hughes, Rev Hugh Price, 288, 378–79, 385
Hughes, Thomas, 162
Hume, Joseph, 59
Hunt, Frederick Knight, 70–71, 72, 73, 95, 96
Hunt, George Ward, 175
Hunt, J. H. Leigh, 97
Hunt, Thornton, 58, 97, 98, 156–57, 161, 172–73, 200, 254
Hunter, Dr W. A., 288
Hutton, R. H., 89, 180, 417
Huxley, T. H., 217
Hyndman, H. M., 325, 342

Iddesleigh, 1st Earl of: *see* Northcote, Sir Stafford
Illustrated London News, 129, 151
Illustrated Weekly News, 101
Independent Labour Party, 409, 427
Indian Mutiny, 126
Institute of Journalists, 7, 404–405, 429, 434
Irish Crimes Act (1887), 297
Irish Land League, 332
Irish University question, 194, 195, 196, 319
Isaacs, Rufus (1st Marquess of Reading), 388
Ismail, Khedive of Egypt, 222, 251
Italy, unification of, 141, 144, 155, 173
Ives, Chester, 333
Iwan-Müller, E. B., 311, 313, 325, 330, 331, 333, 338–39, 341, 342n, 347, 353, 360, 407, 433

Jack the Ripper, 248
Jackson, Sir William, 97
Jaffray, John, 185, 312–13, 314
Jamaica, uprising in, 154, 169
James, Sir Henry (Baron James of Hereford), 280
Jameson Raid, 362, 368, 370
Jennings, L. J., 303
Jerrold, Douglas, 58
Jeyes, S. H., 377, 394
Johannesburg Star, 377
John Bull, 48, 150, 177, 207
Johnson, Dr Samuel, 30–31, 35
Johnstone, James, 126, 135, 136, 138, 154, 331
Johnstone family, 421
Joicey, James, 289
Jones, Andrew, 27n
Jones, Ernest, 127
Jones, Kennedy, 10, 11, 15, 219, 333, 356, 357, 358, 366, 378
Judd, George, 406
Junior Carlton Club, 158, 250
Justice, 342

Kebbel, T. E., 160, 179n, 180, 233, 237
Keighley, T. Dove, 322, 323
Keith-Falconer, Sir Charles, 205, 206
Kemplay, Christopher, 177
Kennard, Coleridge, 150, 246, 248, 250, 328,

329, 356, 357, 370
Kentish Mercury, 227
Kentish Observer, 300
Khartoum, fall of, 260
Khedive of Egypt: *see* Ismail
Kimberley, 1st Earl of, 373
King, Cecil Harmsworth, 356
King, H. S., 229
Kitchener, H. H. (1st Earl Kitchener of Khartoum), 387
Kitson, James (1st Baron Airedale), 242, 433, 434
Knox, Alexander, 119, 132
Knox, Robert, 80, 83–84, 134
Kruger, Stephanus Johannes Paulus, 341, 366, 367, 390, 393

Labouchere, Henry: and *Daily News*, 193, 266, 268, 269, 281, 283, 323, 362, 396; feud with Lawson, 203; as Radical MP, 216, 217, 333, 376; relations with Chamberlain, 235; and 'Hawarden Kite', 277–78, 279; and *Truth*, 288; helps to start *Star*, 308; excluded from office, 335
Labour Representation Committee, 405
Lancashire Evening Post, 228, 291
Langley, J. Batty, 378
Lawson, Edward Levy (1st Baron Burnham), 97, 157, 162, 200, 201, 202, 203, 229, 254, 293, 322, 328, 330, 331, 334, 339, 393, 394
Lawson, W. R., 207
Leader, 151
Lee, Alan J., 92, 137n, 206, 286
Lee, Sir Joseph, 290, 291
Lee, Richard, 177
Leeds Daily News, 433
Leeds Intelligencer, 177
Leeds Mercury, 61, 62, 106, 109, 125, 177, 186, 198, 224, 225, 243, 274, 277–79, 282, 330, 332, 378, 433
Lehmann, R. C., 386, 398, 400, 401
Leng, (Sir) John, 328
Leng, (Sir) William Christopher, 219, 295, 312, 313, 328
Leon, H. S., 404
Leopold I, King of the Belgians, 59
LeSage, J. M., 97, 300, 332
Leslie, Henry, 339
Lessing, Doris, 430
Lestor, Joan, 430
Levy, J. M., 88, 98, 200
Levy-Lawson, Edward: *see* Lawson, Edward Levy
Lewes, George Henry, 151
Lewis, Sir George Cornewall, 68
Liberal Imperialist Council, 391, 392, 393
Liberal (Imperialist) League, 391, 393, 406
Liberal Press Agency, 278
Liberal Publication Department, 364
Liberal Unionist, 304–305
Liberal Unionist Association, 291, 329
Liberal Unionist Committee, 284
Liberal Unionist Council, 392
Licensing Act (1872), 199

Licensed Victuallers' Association, 96, 199
Limerick, Countess of, 300
Lincoln, Abraham, 129
Lincoln, Earl of: *see* Newcastle, 5th Duke of
Literature, 233
Liverpool, 2nd Earl of, 37, 40
Liverpool Courier, 342
Liverpool Daily Post, 97, 239, 270, 276, 320, 328, 425
Lloyd, Edward, 203, 204, 235n, 322
Lloyd, Frank, 352, 356, 385, 387, 397, 406
Lloyd, Mrs Frank, 385
Lloyd, Richard, 215
Lloyd, Trevor, 223, 224
Lloyd George, David (Earl Lloyd-George), 4, 12, 14, 26, 215, 376, 390, 395, 397–98, 399, 401, 402, 404, 411, 412, 414, 416, 423
Lloyd's Weekly London Newspaper, 52, 184, 204, 235n, 248, 288, 342
Lobby Correspondents, 238–39
Locker, W. Algernon, 331, 378
Lockhart, John, 12, 47
London, 336
London Committee for Obtaining Repeal of the Taxes on Knowledge, 65
London County Council, 188, 308, 309, 340
London Gazette, 96, 192, 213n
London Morning, 333
London Reform Union, 336
London Review, 151
Lonsdale, 3rd Earl of, 81
Lough, Thomas, 378, 379, 383, 387, 388, 405, 433–34
Low, (Sir) Sidney, 233, 317, 354, 377, 417, 429, 432
Lowe, Robert (1st Viscount Sherbrooke), 10, 73, 112–13, 133n, 139, 156, 165, 167–68, 169, 170, 173, 175, 176, 187, 194, 195, 216
Lowenfeld, Henry, 321, 324
Lucas, Samuel (of the *Morning Star*), 111, 126, 127
Lucas, Samuel (of the *Press*), 90–91
Lucy, (Sir) H. W., 198, 238, 268, 269, 271, 281, 294–95, 366, 400, 401
Lushington, Godfrey, 185
Lyndhurst, 1st Baron, 58
Lynn News, 329
Lytton, 1st Earl of, 150–51, 187, 249

Maberly, John, 75
McArthur, William, 366
McCarthy, Justin, 111, 127, 169, 216, 352
Macaulay, T. B. (1st Baron Macaulay), 2n
Macclesfield Chronicle, 228
McCullagh, William Torrens: *see* Torrens, William McCullagh
MacDonald, J. C., 214, 298–99, 332
MacDonald, J. Ramsay, 374, 387, 388, 405, 411, 427
Macdonell, James, 162, 210–11
McDonnell, (Sir) Schomberg, 331, 366, 368, 371, 377, 394
Macgillivray, Simon, 75
Mackay, Charles, 75, 95, 151

Mackie, Alexander, 206
Mackintosh, Sir James, 42
MacLeod, Reginald, 272
McManus, J. E., 378
Macmillan, Harold, 15, 18, 19, 21
Madge, W. T., 182, 248, 274
'Maiden Tribute', 234, 262, 346
Maine, Sir Henry, 89, 229, 233
Malmesbury, 3rd Earl of, 79–81, 82, 83, 84, 91, 117, 134, 135, 137, 140, 142, 144, 178
Manchester Courier, 218, 260, 271, 291, 303, 311, 314, 331, 342, 391, 433
Manchester Evening News, 291
Manchester Evening Times, 291
Manchester Examiner, 99, 107, 108, 123, 290–91, 329–30, 335, 342
Manchester Guardian: archives of, 28; founded, 48; early character, 61; antagonizes Bright, 61–62, 122; goes daily, 97; and Crimean War, 102, 106; circulation, 108, 311; and Bulgarian agitation, 209; in 1880 elections, 224; takes up Irish question, 240, 242, 276, 277, 281, 290, 351; Cook writes for, 324; reports Disraeli's speech, 346; opposes South African policy, 368, 374, 387, 390, 391–92, 395, 396, 397, 400, 416; 'friendly alliance' with *Daily News*, 398, 403–404; speaks to 'thoughtful men', 412; Scott buys, 421; mentioned, 230, 270, 291, 383, 426, 427
Manchester Times, 61, 99
Manchester Weekly Times, 290
Mann, Arthur, 7
Manners, Henry (Marquis of Granby), 311
Manners, Lord John (7th Duke of Rutland), 79
Manning, Henry Edward, Cardinal Archbishop, 195
Marjoribanks, Edward (2nd Baron Tweedmouth), 335, 350
Marks, H. H., 357
Marlow Chronicle and Wycombe Times, 206
Marlowe, Thomas, 19, 307, 428
Martin, Kingsley, 8
Martineau, Harriet, 96
Marvel, 354
Marx, Eleanor, 294, 342–43
Massingham, H. W.: quoted, 25–26, 98, 135, 154, 189, 234, 320; works on *Daily News*, 96, 398, 403; works on *Daily Chronicle*, 287, 350, 352–53, 368, 371–73, 375, 383, 385, 396, 397; works on *Star*, 307, 308, 309–10; plans new daily, 389–90, 397; joins *Manchester Guardian*, 390; edits *Nation*, 401; mentioned, 324, 345, 407, 425, 426
Maxse, Admiral F. A., 191, 323–24, 326
Mayhew, Henry, 344
Melbourne, 2nd Viscount, 44, 45, 48, 57, 59, 76
Meredith, George, 217
Merle, Gibbon, 139
Methodist Times, 288, 378–79
'Methods of Barbarism', 400, 402, 406
Meynell, Wilfred, 216, 219
Miall, Edward, 62
Michele, C. Eastland, 77–80, 295
Middleton, Captain R. W. E., 272, 274, 287,

304, 314, 315, 329, 335, 338, 366, 368, 371, 395
Midland News Association, 270, 357
Midleton, 1st Earl of: *see* Brodrick, St John
Midlothian Campaign, 213, 214, 215
Mill, John Stuart, 111, 162–63, 186, 189, 190, 191, 240, 410
Million, 356
Mills, J. Saxon, 230, 232, 391, 399
Milner, Alfred (Viscount Milner), 256–57, 260, 294, 311, 319, 384, 387, 394, 395, 400, 402
Milner-Gibson, Thomas, 65, 66, 68, 71, 134, 147, 295
Milnes, Richard Monckton (1st Baron Houghton), 64, 229
Minto, 2nd Earl of, 116
Moberly Bell, C. F., 193, 332, 344, 347, 348, 351, 365, 367, 370, 376, 394, 415, 419, 423
Molesworth, Sir William, 59, 86, 104, 105, 112, 116
Monck, 1st Baron, 156
Moncrieff, Frederick, 275
Moniteur, 36
Montague, C. E., 427
Moore, A. K., 331
Moran, Benjamin, 155–56
Morgan, J. H., 407, 426
Morison, Stanley, 52, 219
Morley, 1st Earl of, 58
Morley, Arnold, 192, 217, 281, 283, 335, 352, 362, 365–66, 373, 376, 380, 396, 398
Morley, Charles, 361, 364
Morley, John (Viscount Morley of Blackburn), quits journalism for politics, 9, 217; edits *Pall Mall Gazette*, 13–14, 216, 223, 230, 231, 235, 256–57; as Cobden's biographer, 62, 130; as *Saturday Reviewer*, 89; edits *Morning Star*, 111, 128; writes for *Leader*, 151; as a Millite, 186; edits *Fortnightly*, 187, 221; other press connections, 191, 192, 310, 398, 401, 412; publishes 'Valedictory', 216, 418; ties with Chamberlain, 219, 240, 244, 269; relations with Stead, 232, 271, 288, 293, 317; attacks Forster, 240–41; alleged conspirator, 277; and Irish affairs, 277, 280, 320, 321, 350, 351, 417; complains about press, 288, 326, 353; loses seat, 359, 360; in Liberal leadership squabbles, 375, 382, 384, 395; as anti-imperialist, 381, 396, 400; mentioned, 250, 341, 348, 365, 389
Morley, Samuel, 192, 212, 217, 268, 307
Morning, 333, 345, 378
Morning Advertiser, 23, 57, 67, 96, 103, 109, 114, 116, 160, 162–63, 164, 183, 199
Morning Chronicle, 37, 38, 42, 49, 51, 58, 61, 66, 67–68, 74–75, 75–76, 80, 85, 86–87, 88, 94, 102, 103, 109, 111, 115, 117, 119, 122, 346, 414, 431
Morning Herald, 42–43, 49, 59, 62–63, 67–68, 82, 83, 85, 87, 103, 110, 111, 114, 134, 135, 137, 142, 143, 145, 151–52, 163, 164, 169, 178, 183, 333
Morning Herald (1899–1900), 378, 388, 420
Morning Journal, 46

Morning Leader, 332–33, 345, 386, 389, 426, 427, 429–30
Morning Post: founded, 38, 41–43; character of, 42, 94; 'brawls', 59; on press taxes, 67–68; rejects Peel, 77–78; embraces Palmerston, 81, 85, 103, 105, 132, 138, 146, 148, 156, 161, 199–200, 208, 272; irritates Russell, 116; allegedly in France's pay, 135, 138n; in 1865 elections, 163, 164, 165; relations with Gladstone, 175, 188, 212; relations with Disraeli, 196, 199–200, 208; pro-Turk, 211; its Toryism, 218, 223, 225, 254, 261, 331, 428; as Churchill's paper, 250–51, 274, 330, 333, 378; Salisbury dislikes, 327; editorial changes, 377, 378; mentioned, 19, 24, 65, 122, 169, 207, 216, 240, 257, 395, 411, 421
Morning Star. (1856–69), 21, 47, 93, 110–11, 114, 115, 123–30, 136, 143, 145, 147, 157, 159, 160, 169, 172, 174, 186, 204
Morning Star (1966 –), 18, 430
Morris, Mowbray, 192
Morrison, Walter, 330
Mudford, Frederic, 300
Mudford, W. H.: his professional pride, 13, 186, 237; starts out, 44; edits *Standard*, 154, 183, 252, 253, 273, 300; chides Escott, 236; dealings with politicians, 245, 301; divulges information, 278, 302; resents *Times*, 312; retires, 331, 378; mentioned, 431
Mundella, A. J., 323, 425
Murray, Alexander, Master of Elibank (1st Baron Murray of Elibank), 13
Murray, Gilbert, 427
Murray, John, 46–47
Murray MacDonald, J. A., 405
Mystery of the Daily Mail, 369

Napier, Sir Charles, 104
Napier, Sir Joseph, 155
Napier of Magdala, 1st Baron, 138
Napoleon, Louis (Napoleon III), 88, 135, 138n, 139
Nash, Vaughan, 385, 389, 427
Nation, 310, 401
Nation (New York), 121–22, 224
National Council of Evangelical Free Churches, 380
National Education League, 219
National Front, 3
National Liberal Club, 277, 278, 292, 322, 371
National Liberal Federation, 242, 250, 308, 320–21, 349, 402
National Reform Association, 95
National Reforn Union, 318, 400
National Reformer, 216
National Review, 249, 329, 353
National Union of Conservative and Constitutional Associations, 184, 206, 207, 248, 250, 252, 273, 287, 289, 304, 330
Nelson, Sir Horatio (1st Viscount Nelson), 51
Neville, Latimer, 246, 280
Nevinson, H. W., 15, 384–85, 427
New Liberal Review, 393
New Quarterly Review, 137, 149

New Review, 315, 353, 354, 360, 434
New Social Movement, 205
New Statesman, 310
New Times: Stoddart's, 42, 46; Stead's, 319
New University Club, 159, 342
New York Herald, 125
New York Sun, 387
New York Tribune, 125
Newcastle, 5th Duke of (Earl of Lincoln), 87, 105, 106, 132
Newcastle Chronicle, 216, 240, 289, 347
Newcastle Daily Leader, 270, 292, 317
Newcastle Programme, 350
Newdegate, Charles N., 150
Newnes, Sir George, 319, 323, 325, 327, 328, 335, 336, 337, 339, 340, 344, 356, 359, 361–62, 363–64, 365, 368, 392–93
News Chronicle, 8, 429
News of the World, 52
Newspaper Press Directory, 92
Newspaper Society, 424
Newspaper Stamp Abolition Committee, 65
Newton, H. K., 420
Nineteenth Century, 316, 343, 414
Nonconformist, 62
Norfolk, 11th Duke of, 38
Norman, (Sir) Henry, 333–34, 352, 375, 384, 390, 406
North, Lord (2nd Earl of Guilford), 32
North British Mail, 48
North Briton, 33
North Eastern Daily Gazette, 270, 292
Northbrook, 1st Earl of, 259
Northcliffe, Viscount: *see* Harmsworth, Alfred
Northcote, Sir Stafford (1st Earl of Iddesleigh), 178, 204, 205, 206, 221–22, 246, 250, 252, 261, 272, 295, 302, 346
Northern Daily News, 289
Northern Daily Telegraph, 162, 270, 291, 328, 403
Northern Echo, 203, 209, 210, 211, 213, 215, 231, 291, 344, 401, 426
Northern Star, 60, 414
Northern Weekly Leader, 289
Northumberland, 4th Duke of, 89

Observer, 15, 16, 19, 43, 48, 51–52, 144, 157, 159, 233, 271, 288, 324, 354, 363, 365, 423, 425
O'Connell, Daniel, 53
O'Connor, Feargus, 60
O'Connor, T. P., 96, 216, 226, 308–309, 312, 319, 323, 326, 336, 344
O'Donnell, F. H., 297
'Oldcastle, John': *see* Meynell, Wilfred
Olney, Richard, 340
Onslow, 4th Earl of, 370
Oppenheim, Henry, 192, 222, 362, 375, 379, 396
Oracle, 42
Osborne, Ralph Bernal, 140
Ostrogorski, M., 423, 432
Oswald, J. R., 330
Otway, Arthur, 343

Outlook, 286, 375, 434
Owenism, 56
Owl, 94
Oxford and Cambridge Club, 93, 158, 185, 275, 334
Oxford Palmerston Club, 257

Pall Mall Budget, 318, 338, 339, 340, 361, 364
Pall Mall Gazette: its successive editorships, 16, 25, 217, 256–57, 319–20, 337–41, 364; started, 127; Clubland readership, 159, 160, 184, 342; tries morning publication, 182; relations with Gladstone, 187, 196, 211, 256, 257–58, 279, 333–34; in 1873 crisis, 196, 197; wounds Villiers, 198; denounces Derby 212; its Toryism, 219, 222; 'tells lies', 220; sold by Smith, 229; turns Liberal, 229–93, 325; rivalled by *St James's* 234, 235; attacks Forster, 240–41, 242; scorns Lucy, 269; piques Chamberlain, 271; imputed influence, 275; on Irish questions, 276, 284, 285, 318–19, 417; discloses secrets, 283, 376; out-of-bounds to Dilke, 288; provokes and offends, 293, 294, 295, 306; refuses Pigott letters, 298; briefed by Salisbury, 303; faces financial difficulties, 316, 317–18, 421; reverts to Toryism, 321–22, 325, 335, 379, 420, 426; reports speeches, 346–47; foretells Gladstone's retirement, 349; in 1895 elections, 359; mentioned, 235, 287, 367, 378, 425, 432
Pall Mall Magazine, 364
Palmer, G. W., 381
Palmer, H. J., 404, 405, 407, 424
Palmerston, 3rd Viscount: deploys press skills, 4, 11, 74, 77, 92, 115, 120, 132, 134, 138, 148, 155, 411; commands *Globe*, 45, 82, 86, 111, 114, 132, 139, 142, 143, 145–46, 148, 153, 163, 178; relations with *Times* and Delane, 72, 77, 86, 106, 112, 130, 131, 132, 133, 139, 155, 156, 166, 208; revered by *Morning Post*, 77, 79, 81, 85, 103, 132, 138, 148, 156, 161, 163, 165, 272; relations with other papers, 75–76, 81–83, 86–87, 100, 132, 143, 148, 154, 156, 157; rivalry with Russell, 84, 117, 145–49; and Crimean War, 101–102; becomes premier, 106; and Italian question, 141–42, 144; dealings with Tories, 143–44, 152; unifies Liberals, 147; in 1865 elections, 160, 161; decline and death, 166–68; leaves vacuum, 170; mentioned, 68, 69, 157, 162
Palmerston, Lady, 11, 101
Panmure, 2nd Baron, 116
Paper duty, repeal of (1861), 1, 54, 60, 65, 69, 92, 98, 129, 156
Parke, Ernest, 307, 310, 332, 429–30
Parkes, Joseph, 74, 75, 115, 117, 118, 130, 133
Parnell, Charles Stewart, 241, 242, 248, 269, 274, 276, 288, 297–99, 320–21, 325, 331–32, 345
Parnell Commission, 297–98, 330
'Parnellism and Crime', 296–300
Paul, Herbert, 352, 363, 364, 365–66, 398, 401, 403
Paxton, Sir Joseph, 95

Peace Society, 100
Pearson, (Sir) C. Arthur, 356, 360, 378, 407, 412, 419, 420–21, 422
Peel, A. W., 315
Peel, Sir Robert (2nd Baronet), 26, 62–63, 65, 75, 77, 78, 160
Peel, Sir Robert (3rd Baronet), 156
Peel, Lady, 156
Penny Paper, 338
People, 248, 407
People's Banner, 186
People's Charter, 127
People's Charter Union, 65
People's Journal (Dundee), 332
Percy, Earl, 245, 248
Perks, Sir Robert, 380, 399, 421, 433
Perris, G. H., 374
Perry, James, 38, 51, 431
Pethick Lawrence, F. W. (1st Baron Pethick-Lawrence), 388
Philipps, Mr., 82
Phillipps, E. M., 345, 419
Phinn, Thomas, 112
Phoenix Park murders, 241, 297, 320
Pigott, Richard, 298, 304, 312, 316
Pitt, William (the Younger), 32, 36, 38, 39, 41, 42, 43, 44, 410, 411
Place, Francis, 58, 59, 75
Plaza-Toro, Duke of, 356
Plymouth Daily Mercury, 289
Poor Law Amendment Act (1834), 59, 413
Poor Man's Guardian, 56
Porcupine, 36, 47
Portland, 4th Duke of, 78
Portsmouth Evening Mail: see Southern Daily Mail
Potter, George, 192
Powles, J. D., 83
Praed, William, 346
Press, 89–90, 111, 115, 122, 123, 134, 137, 149–50, 151, 178, 180
Press Association, 282, 302, 312, 347, 404
Press Club, 348
Press Council, 3, 17
Preston Guardian, 228
Primrose Chronicle, 246
Primrose League, 246, 252n
Prince Regent: *see* George IV
Progressive Review, 374
Protectionism: *see* Tariff Reform *and* Free Trade
Prowett, C. G., 150
Pryor, S. J., 428
Puck, 159
Punch, 42, 135, 154, 216, 238, 268, 316, 325, 392, 398, 400

Quarterly Review, 27, 46, 47, 218

Radical Committee, 376
Raikes, Henry Cecil, 178, 249
Rainbow Circle, 374, 405, 406
Ralph, John, 248
Ramsden, Sir John, 290

Randall, Michael, 5–6
Ratcliffe, S. K., 420
Rawson, Henry, 97, 123, 124, 127, 193
Redmond, John, 387
Reeve, Henry, 63, 71–72, 73, 82, 106, 113, 223, 344
Reform Acts: (1832), 54, 55, 57, 58, 410, 411; (1867), 26, 54, 121, 158, 169, 174; (1884), 26, 158
Reform Bills: (1859), 140–41; (1866), 170, 171
Reform Club, 104, 116, 131, 140, 151, 158, 159, 162, 184, 186, 239, 260, 277, 279, 292, 299, 342, 384
Reform League, 169, 173
Regency crisis (1788), 39
Reid, (Sir) Hugh Gilzean, 162, 270, 271, 291, 328, 378, 379
Reid, Sir Robert (1st Earl of Loreburn), 379
Reid, (Sir) Wemyss, 186, 198, 219, 223, 225, 231–32, 238–43, 271, 277–79, 281, 288, 310, 328, 332, 335, 348, 362, 371, 375–76, 378, 383, 386, 417, 433
Representative, 47, 83
Republican, 56
Reuter, Herbert de, 256
Reuters Agency, 238, 421
Review of Reviews, 319, 323, 356, 376, 390
Reynolds, G. W. M., 89
Reynolds's Newspaper, 89, 184, 204, 334, 342
Rhodes, Cecil, 319, 367, 371, 385, 395, 422
Richard, Rev Henry, 100, 106, 109, 110, 123, 125, 126, 128
Richards, A. B., 199
Richmond, 3rd Duke of, 41
Rideout, W. J., 81
Ripon, 1st Marquess of, 401
Ritzema, T. P., 270, 291, 403, 404
Roberts, 1st Earl, 387
Robertson, E. J., 19
Robertson, J. M., 374
Robertson Scott, J. M.: *see* Scott, J. M. Robertson
Robinson, Geoffrey (Geoffrey Dawson), 12, 411, 422
Robinson, Henry Crabb, 40
Robinson, (Sir) John, 96, 192, 269–70, 277, 292, 323, 328, 330, 345, 359, 363, 365–66, 396, 398
Robinson, Phil, 305
Rochdale Observer, 130
Roebuck, J. A., 106
Rogers, Thorold, 128, 169, 204
Rollit, Sir Albert, 289
Romance of the Daily Mail, 369
Rose, Sir Philip, 178
Rosebery, 5th Earl of: manages press, 12, 191, 269, 361, 411; collaborates with Cooper and *Scotsman*, 186, 224, 239, 260, 272, 282, 284–85; relations with Buckle and *Times*, 266, 276, 332, 334, 348, 360; serves under Gladstone, 280; uses 'Cook of Berkeley Square', 324, 326, 327, 363, 364–65, 367–68, 372–73, 376, 377, 381, 390; in Liberal leadership struggles, 350, 352; hangs on 'by the eyelids',

351; resigns premiership, 351; offends Robinson, 362; relations with Harmsworth, 369–70, 373, 390; resigns leadership, 371–73; as press favourite, 373, 375, 379, 381–82, 383–84, 385, 387, 392, 393, 395, 396; speaks at Chesterfield, 402, 406; spends threepence, 415; mentioned, 231, 278, 421
Rosebery, Lady, 332
Rothermere, 1st Viscount: *see* Harmsworth, Harold
Rothschild, 1st Baron, 346, 370
Round Table negotiations, 306
Rouse, H. O., 391
Rowntree, Joseph, 401
Rowntree, Joshua, 348
Rowntree, Trust, 401, 426
Royal Commission on the Press (1947–48), 21
Ruskin, John, 233, 414
Russel, Alexander, 119, 361
Russell, 1st Earl: *see* Russell, Lord John
Russell, Sir Charles (1st Baron Russell of Killowen), 297
Russell, Sir Edward, 111, 239, 271, 293, 320, 328
Russell, G. W. E., 337, 352
Russell, Lord John (1st Earl Russell): tries to deal with press, 11, 74, 115–20, 411; and *Globe*, 45, 77, 139, 178; upholds stamp duty, 65; troubles with *Times*, 72, 86, 104, 111–12, 113, 128, 132, 133, 155–56, 169, 170, 173; combats 'papal aggression', 82; toppled from office, 84; and Crimean War, 101, 103, 104; as Palmerston's rival, 133, 140, 144–46; as Palmerston's ally, 146, 147, 160, 165, 167–68; as franchise reformer, 169, 170, 171; mentioned, 106, 136, 142, 161, 272
Russell, Robert, 94
Russell, (Sir) William Howard, 94, 106, 113, 129, 185, 193n, 328, 344
Russo-Turkish War, 202
Rylands, Peter, 228

St Cyr, Marquis de, Marshall of France, 85
St James's Chronicle, 46, 150, 178
St James's Gazette, 233–34, 246–47, 253, 260, 262, 274, 288, 296, 312, 317, 328, 337, 342, 349, 376, 377, 378, 321, 422, 429
St John, Bayle, 97
St John, Horace, 97
St John, J. A., 97
Saint Paul's, 186
St Stephen's Club, 158
St Stephen's Review, 335
Sala, G. A., 97, 98, 151, 329, 346
Salisbury, 2nd Marquess of, 137
Salisbury, 3rd Marquess of (Lord Robert Cecil, Viscount Cranborne): as a journalist, 9–10, 89, 136, 185, 216; collaborates with Austin, 12, 13, 245, 300–301, 315–16, 353; manipulates press, 183, 204, 205, 237, 246, 248, 249, 250, 272–73, 274, 287, 290, 329, 335, 360, 394, 411, 424; under press fire, 212, 253, 379; relations with Borthwick, 252, 295; defines press freedom, 254; as Tory leader, 255; as

premier, 264, 289; backed by Irish, 269, 276; in 1886 elections, 279, 286; relations with Buckle and *Times*, 280, 296, 299, 300, 312, 331, 361, 366–67; distributes honours, 313–15, 316, 327–28; fears Churchill, 333; in 1892 elections, 334–35; consulted by Cust, 337, 338; praised by press, 341, 346, 371; writes for *National Review*, 353; calls 1895 elections, 354; relations with Harmsworth, 358, 366, 368–69; reading habits, 386; threatened by Rosebery, 393–94; retires, 408; mentioned, 288, 311, 362, 407
Salisbury, Lady, 254, 274, 394
Samuel, Herbert (1st Viscount Samuel), 406
Sandars, J. S., 363
Saturday Analyst, 151
Saturday Review, 89, 110, 115, 122, 133, 151, 159, 185, 216, 229, 310, 353
Saunders, D. H., 332
Saunders, George, 332
Saunders, William, 332
Scotsman, 22, 97, 109n, 119, 124, 186, 207, 213, 219, 220, 224, 239, 240, 242, 260, 272, 277, 278, 282–83, 284, 289, 361
Scott, C. P., 28, 209, 230, 270, 276, 324, 351, 354, 391, 395, 402, 403, 404, 411, 421
Scott, J. M. Robertson, 317, 393, 426
Scott, Sir Walter, 12, 47
Scottish Leader, 289, 350
Scottish People, 272
Scott-James, R. A., 348
Searle, E. W., 141
Second World War, 16, 19; 21
Selborne, 2nd Earl of: *see* Wolmer, Viscount
Sell's Dictionary of the World's Press, 286, 335
Senior, Nassau, 75
Seymour, Horace, 266
Seymour-Ure, Colin, 74, 238
Shannon, R. T., 209
Shaw, George Bernard, 307, 308, 369
Shaw, Thomas (1st Baron Craigmyle), 241, 401
Shaw-Lefevre, Sir John George (1st Baron Eversley), 241, 337
Sheffield Daily Telegraph, 219, 295, 312, 407
Sheffield Independent, 61, 332, 378
Sixpenny Monthly, 319
Slack, J. Bamford, 387–88
Sladen, Douglas, 379
Slap at the Church, 56
Sleigh, Colonel A. B., 97, 109, 123
Slide, Quintus, 186
Smith, George, 159, 229, 231, 322, 340
Smith, Goldwin, 88, 128, 157, 195, 202–203, 229
Smith, John Abel, 115–16
Smith, John Benjamin, 115–16, 119
Smith, W. H., 60, 162–63, 188, 203, 204, 205, 211, 235, 243–48, 291, 293, 298, 299–300, 302, 311, 317, 331
Smollett, Tobias, 31–32, 33
Smythe, George, 64, 78, 89
Social Democratic Federation, 342
Solly, Rev Henry, 192
Somerset, 12th Duke of, 169, 170, 173

South African War, 368, 374, 384–85, 387, 389 ff., 395–97, 400, 416, 422
South East London and Kentish Mercury, 3
Southern Daily Mail (Portsmouth), 355
Southwood, Viscount (J. S. Elias), 6
Sowler, Colonel Thomas, 291, 313–14, 335, 433
Sowler, Thomas, Jr., 433
Speaker, 288, 310, 375, 376, 381, 385–86, 392, 397, 400–401, 407, 412, 425
Spectator, 48, 58, 89, 90, 91n, 100, 101, 155, 188, 253, 260, 288, 310, 344, 367, 416, 417
Spectator, Mr, 31
Spencer, 3rd Earl: *see* Althrop, Viscount
Spencer, 5th Earl, 179, 188, 230, 241, 346
Spencer, Herbert, 151
Spender, Harold, 320, 332, 371, 385, 389, 395, 396, 398, 400, 401, 407, 426, 429
Spender, J. A.: starts out, 292, 300, 426; at *Pall Mall Gazette*, 320, 324; edits *Westminster*, 336, 363–65; views on journalism, 342, 344, 345; gossips, 359, 365–66; defends Newnes, 361–62; as an imperialist, 367–68; complimented, 373, 376; as 'a smoother', 386–87, 400, 406–407; mentioned, 332, 385, 389, 410, 416
Spofforth, Markham, 178, 179
Stamp duty: enacted, 31, 42, 49, 61; raised, 32, 33; reduced, 52–53, 54, 58, 60, 94; campaign for abolition, 53–54, 58, 65; repealed, 1, 54, 61, 69, 71, 94, 96, 105, 106, 107, 113, 121, 134, 151, 410
Standard: linked to Salisbury, 10, 12, 237, 273–74, 300–303; shows 'independence of spirit', 13–14; early years, 46, 62–63, 82, 85; reacts to Palmerston, 83, 145; its Toryism, 87, 111, 135–37, 153–54, 158, 211, 218, 223, 248, 252–53, 377, 420, 428; price and circulation, 93, 129, 151; changes of ownership, 126, 421, 422; tries morning publication, 135; relations with Gladstone, 173, 187–88, 213, 296; relieved of *Morning Herald*, 182; dealings with Disraeli, 196, 204–205; publishes Greenwood, 231; Escott writes for, 236, 250, 256; discloses secrets, 239, 243–45, 267, 277–78; rivalry with *Daily Telegraph*, 274; opposes Home Rule, 274; dealings with Chamberlain, 315–16, 333, 354, 394; editorial changes at, 331, 378, 421; Balfour discounts, 337; mentioned, 103, 159, 178, 186, 200, 207, 216, 218, 240, 243, 311, 330, 353, 359, 412, 431
Stanhope, 6th Earl, 236
Stanhope, Edward, 249, 252
Stanhope, Philip (1st Baron Weardale), 261, 406
Stanley, Lord: *see* Derby, 14th Earl of, *or* Derby, 15th Earl of
Stansfeld, Sir James, 231
Star, 288, 307–309, 319, 320, 321, 328, 333, 342, 345, 379, 386, 405, 416, 434
Statesman, 45
Stead, W. T.: on press power and influence, 14, 19, 25, 343–44, 346, 416, 422; relations with Gladstone, 14, 207, 256, 271, 279, 293, 319, 321, 430; edits *Northern Echo*, 203, 209,

291; leads Bulgarian agitation, 206, 210, 293; difficulties with Chamberlain, 219, 271, 323; hired at *Pall Mall*, 230–31, 235; goes 'Maiden Tributing', 234, 262–63, 293–94; edits *Pall Mall*, 256; his political instability, 257–63, 293–94, 312, 376, 397; relations with Balfour, 293, 319, 323, 333; refuses Pigott letters, 298; leaves *Pall Mall*, 318, 319–22, 323; starts *Review of Reviews*, 319, 323; pro-Rosebery, 334; proposes new papers, 338, 389–90; on imperial issues, 367, 383, 396; mentioned, 125, 288, 347, 356, 398, 421
Stead, William ('Willie'), 421
Stebbing, William, 175, 196, 209n, 210, 213, 274
Steed, Wickham, 359, 418, 423
Steinkopff, Edward, 317, 322, 377
Stephen, Sir James Fitzjames, 89, 233
Stephen, (Sir) Leslie, 13, 160, 186–87, 230, 233
Stoddart, Dr John, 40, 42–43, 46
Storey, Samuel, 189, 235, 270, 287, 357
Stout, E. H., 390
Strachey, J. St Loe, 304, 344, 354, 367
Straight, Sir Douglas, 342
Strand Magazine, 356
Street, T. G., 44
Stuart, Daniel, 42, 44
Stuart, James, 296
Stuart, Professor James, 310, 321, 334, 336
Stuart, Peter, 42
Stuart-Wortley, James, 94
Sturge, Charles, 126
Sturge, Joseph, 101, 107, 124, 125, 126
Suez Canal, purchase of, 201–202, 208, 221–22
Sun, 36, 37, 41, 62, 132, 147, 159, 184, 205, 206
Sun (1893–1906), 206, 323, 336, 422
Sunday Express, 430
Sunday Gazette, 159, 184
Sunday newspapers, early history, 50–51, 52, 61
Sunday Times, 24, 48, 52, 92, 97, 141, 206, 248, 305, 354
Swift, Jonathan, 31
Swinburne, Algernon Charles, 190
Symonds, Arthur G., 318–19

Talleyrand, Charles Maurice de, 44
Tariff Reform, 4, 408, 417, 420
Tattersall, Richard, 41
Taylor, Helen, 191, 192, 270
Taylor, J. E., 290, 403, 404, 407, 433
Taylor, John, 41
Taylor, P. A., 191
Thackeray, William Makepeace, 58, 160, 229
Thomas, Rev Dr David, 127
Thomas, Frederick Moy, 94
Thomas, William, 53, 413–14
Thomas, Rev William, 380
Thomasson, Franklin, 398, 401, 404
Thomasson, J. P., 401–402, 404
Thompson, George, 114
Thompson, Henry Yates, 230–31, 235, 257, 259, 260, 288, 293, 318, 319, 322–23, 325, 327, 339, 340, 426

Thomson of Fleet, 1st Baron, 6
Thursfield, James, 285
Times, The: its non-partisan partisanship, 5, 24, 46, 266, 359–60; builds its reputation, 9, 38–39, 40, 49, 413; inspires provincials, 22; archives of, 28, 29; meets competition, 42–43, 44, 47, 59, 60–61, 71, 86–87, 89, 96, 124, 129; Disraeli writes in, 45; and newspaper taxes, 52–53, 54, 66, 67–69; reflects Walter's views, 59; and Corn Laws, 62–64; reacts to Palmerston, 72, 132, 133, 140, 166; urges coalition, 85, 226, 227, 260, 276, 287, 301; anti-Russell, 86, 111–12, 113, 116, 132–33, 155–56, 167–68, 170–71; circulation and influence, 92, 114, 126, 187, 218, 412; hires W. H. Russell, 94–95; reports Crimean War, 101–103, 105–106; relations with Bright, 113, 116, 128–29, 130, 131, 140, 169, 171; at odds with Disraeli, 134, 136, 141, 153, 175; pro-Derby, 146, 173; in 1865 elections, 164; penalized, 168; and reform, 171, 172; in 1868 elections, 185; relations with Gladstone, 188, 194–95, 213–14, 215, 255; favours Disraeli, 196, 207–208; in 1874 elections, 197; and Bulgarian agitation, 209–11, 213; in 1880 elections, 222, 223; foreign coverage, 238; Irish policies, 240, 242, 274, 276, 280, 282–83, 285, 286; relations with Churchill, 251, 294, 296, 301, 303, 304, 347–48; Buckle named editor, 265; warms to Salisbury, 287, 296, 301, 312, 366, 367; Milner writes for, 294; investigates 'Parnellism and Crime', 297–300; backs Balfour, 311–12; condemns Parnell, 320; in 1892 elections, 322; favours Rosebery 331–32, 348, 350–51, 393; keeps black list, 349; hostile to government, 370; its councils divided, 376–77; in 1900 elections, 391; grates on Campbell-Bannerman, 392; its readership, 415; as 'schoolmaster', 418; branches out, 419–20; Harmsworth bids for, 422–23; mentioned, 6, 10, 12, 75, 91, 100, 119, 159, 160, 192–93, 204, 216, 220, 239, 257, 276, 308, 333, 344, 397, 399, 409, 430, 431
Times Book Club, 419
Tit-Bits, 319, 336, 344, 356, 421
'Toby, MP': *see* Lucy, (Sir) H. W.
Topham, Captain Edward, 43
Torrens, Colonel Robert, 45
Torrens, W. T. McCullagh, 139, 190
Torrington, 7th Viscount, 156, 168
Toulmin, George, 228, 285
Toulmin, John, 228
Town and Country Newspaper, 206
Townsend, George H., 89, 137–38
Traill, H. D., 233
Traveller, 45
Travellers' Club, 158
Trent dispute, 155–56
Trevelyan, (Sir) C. P., 404
Trevelyan, G. M., 413–14
Trevelyan, Sir G. O., 281, 286, 346
Tribune, 428
Trollope, Anthony, 186, 198, 236

True Briton, 36, 37, 45, 47
Truth, 193, 221, 288, 335, 376, 385
Tucker, Marwood, 180, 181, 182, 212
Twopenny Dispatch, 414
Tyneside Echo, 289

Union, 329
United Service Club, 158
United States: journalism in, 23, 70, 74, 125, 244, 419, 428; fights war for independence, 33; British relations with, 76, 133, 155–56, 195, 362; fights Civil War, 154, 157, 169; Irish in, 321; Astor's loyalty to, 340–41
United University Club, 93, 158, 221, 234, 293, 369
Universalist, 35
Unstamped press, 23, 51, 56–59, 411

Vanity Fair, 216, 221, 250
Venezuela dispute, 362
Vicar's Lantern, 62
Victoria, Queen-Empress, 5, 7, 43, 59, 76, 79, 86, 103, 104, 113, 114, 142, 169, 173, 175, 196, 207, 211, 215, 223, 226, 262, 280, 284, 286, 293, 295, 300, 313, 314, 327, 334–35, 366, 409, 411
Villiers, Charles, 188, 198
Villiers, Edward, 59n
Villiers, George: *see* Clarendon, 4th Earl of
Vincent, John, 94, 96, 99, 264
Vizetelly, Henry, 233
Voules, Horace, 188

Wace, Dr Henry, 223
Wadsworth, A. P., 36, 47, 48, 52, 345
Walker, Thomas, 96, 147, 192, 213n
Wallace, Sir Donald Mackenzie, 332
Wallas, Graham, 425
Walmsley, Sir Joshua, 95, 119
Walpole, Spencer, 152
Walter, A. F., 359–60, 419–20
Walter, John (1739–1812), 38–39, 39–40
Walter, John (1776–1847), 39–40, 57, 59, 63–64
Walter, John (1818–94), 72–73, 105, 131, 150, 168, 170, 172, 185, 213, 214, 216, 254–55, 265, 268, 274, 295, 299
Walter, William, 39
Warrington and Mid-Cheshire Examiner, 228
Watkin, Edward, 129
Watson, Aaron, 190
Watson, George, 23
Webb, Beatrice (Lady Passfield), 351, 368, 376
Webb, Sidney (Baron Passfield), 310, 351, 368, 374, 376
Webster, George, 206–207
Webster, Sir Richard (Viscount Alverstone), 297
Weekly Chronicle, 52
Weekly Dispatch, 52, 57, 89, 101, 132, 206, 216, 217n, 288, 362, 392
Weekly Mail, 150
Weekly Times, 52
Weir, William, 95, 96, 119
Wellington, 1st Duke of, 45, 48, 84, 85

Wellington, 2nd Duke of, 129, 130
Weltje, Louis, 41
West, Sir Algernon, 241, 283, 340
West Kent Courier, 227
Westcombe, Charles, 178–79, 180
Western Daily Mail, 292
Western Daily Daily News, 216
Western Morning News, 277, 289, 332, 347
Westminster, 3rd Marquess and 1st Duke of (2nd Earl Grosvenor), 169, 179, 180, 277, 289, 290, 306
Westminster Budget, 361, 364
Westminster Conservative Association, 181
Westminster Gazette: its character, 24, 336–37, 386–87, 411, 416, 420; started, 325–27, 346, 356; 'toils and slaves' for party, 340, 359; read in clubs, 342; Newnes's plans for, 344; earns praise, 351, 361; in Liberal leadership struggles, 375, 400, 406–407; supports Salisbury, 377; mentioned 338, 349, 354, 363, 381, 389, 421, 426, 427, 429; *also see* Spender, J. A.
Wharncliffe, 1st Earl of, 94
White, Arnold, 354
Whiteley, George (1st Baron Marchamley), 433, 434
White's Club, 158
Who's Who, 379
Wicks, Frederick, 207, 227
Wilberforce, William, 40
Wilde, Oscar, 11, 310, 345
Wilhelm II, Kaiser, 322, 366, 367
Wilkes, John, 33
Williams, Francis (Baron Francis-Williams), 309, 422
Williams, J. Powell, 283–84, 313, 314
Williams, Raymond, 2n, 415
Williamson, James (1st Baron Ashton), 308, 362, 366, 376, 396–97

Willox, J. A., 342
Wills, W. H., 95
Wilson, A. J., 365
Wilson, F. W., 332
Wilson, George, 99, 100, 107, 108, 123, 125
Wilson, H. J., 332, 388
Wilson, (Sir) Harold, 17, 255
Wilson, Isaac, 292
Wilson, James ('Jemmy'), 131
Wilson, P. W., 401
Wilson, Trevor, 27
Winn, Rowland (1st Baron St Oswald), 186, 251
Wiseman, Nicholas, Cardinal Archbishop, 82
Witness, 56
Wolff, Sir Henry Drummond, 94, 151, 274
Wolmer, Viscount (2nd Earl of Selborne), 290, 313, 315, 316, 328, 329
Wolverhampton Evening Star, 357
Woman, 416
Wood, Sir Charles: *see* Halifax, 1st Viscount
Woodfall, William, 38
Woodham, H. A., 195
Woodward, William, 421
World, 28, 38, 43, 193, 207, 221, 236, 250, 257, 262, 264, 265, 271, 280, 288
Wyndham, George, 434

Yates, Edmund, 127, 207, 221, 262, 271, 280
Yates Thompson, Henry: *see* Thompson, Henry Yates
York Herald, 289
Yorkshire Chronicle, 289
Yorkshire Post, 7, 149, 177, 180, 248, 271, 303, 407, 424
Young England, 64, 78
Young, G. F., 83
Young, Sir John, 25, 80, 87, 88, 102